For Reference

Not to be taken from this room

D0207809

BOLLINGEN SERIES XX

THE COLLECTED WORKS

OF

C. G. JUNG

VOLUME 20

EDITORS

† SIR HERBERT READ

MICHAEL FORDHAM, F.R.C.PSYCH., HON. F.B.PS.S.

GERHARD ADLER, PH.D.

WILLIAM MC GUIRE, *executive editor*

GENERAL INDEX

to the

Collected Works of

C. G. Jung

COMPILED BY BARBARA FORRYAN

AND JANET M. GLOVER

BOLLINGEN SERIES XX

PRINCETON UNIVERSITY PRESS

THIS EDITION IS BEING PUBLISHED IN THE
UNITED STATES OF AMERICA FOR BOLLINGEN
FOUNDATION BY PRINCETON UNIVERSITY
PRESS AND IN ENGLAND BY ROUTLEDGE &
KEGAN PAUL, LTD. IN THE AMERICAN EDI-
TION, ALL THE VOLUMES COMPRISING THE
COLLECTED WORKS CONSTITUTE NUMBER XX
IN BOLLINGEN SERIES. THE PRESENT VOL-
UME IS NUMBER 20 OF THE COLLECTED
WORKS AND IS THE NINETEENTH TO APPEAR.

LIBRARY OF CONGRESS CATALOGUE CARD NUMBER: 75-156
ISBN 0-691-09867-0
MANUFACTURED IN THE U.S.A.

EDITORIAL NOTE

In preparing the General Index, the aim has been to follow the principles laid down for the original volume indexes by the late A.S.B. Glover (1896–1966), who compiled most of them.

While the contents of the volume indexes are the basis of the General Index, the extent of indexing has been amplified and the systems of cross-reference and grouping have been improved—or such was the intention. Each index citation has been verified in the text, resulting not only in the correction of errors but in the discovery of occasional items that were missed out. The General Index employs paragraph numbers rather than page numbers; an advantage is that the references apply to successive editions of the same volume in which the pagination was altered. In the absence of paragraph numbers, page numbers are used, preceded by *p.* Volume numbers are printed in bold type.

Certain subjects, because of their ramification, have been treated in separate sub-indexes, alphabetically placed in the General Index: Alchemical Collections, Alchemical Writers and Texts, Animals, Bible, Codices and Manuscripts, Colours, Freud, Jung, Numbers, and Trees. The sub-index for the Bible has been arranged by book, chapter, and verse, and an effort has been made to indicate the translation quoted.

Essay and chapter titles that contain the subject word are indexed at the beginning of a subject entry, before other subheadings. All the significant words in each title have been indexed in this way, so that a quick guide is provided to the location of major subjects treated in Jung's works.

Some major entries have been divided into separate groups, particularly if a word is extensively used with clearly different meanings—for example, *anima* and the *Mercury/Mercurius* group. The different meanings often overlap, however, especially in the entries for *spirit(s)* and *self*. It is hoped that the limited amount of codifying and classifying that has been done is not counter to the spirit of Jung's thinking.

On the whole, however, it was found best not to attempt too strict a methodizing of Jung's ideas in the index entries, but to index each statement as fully as possible, even at the risk of giving the index an excessively detailed character. Where the same idea is discussed in a number of passages using slightly different words, cross-references should enable the reader to find all the relevant passages in the text. In general, the words of the text have been used to form index entries, where reasonable, rather than paraphrasing.

*

Janet M. Glover began work on the project of the General Index after A.S.B. Glover's death and carried it well along until ill health obliged her to retire.* Barbara Forryan (who had made several of the volume indexes) continued and completed the work, in particular supervising the verification and amplification of the entries and giving the index its final form. Betty Stephenson supplied a most important continuity by typing the entire General Index and controlling style as she did so. Others who assisted were Joan Bethell, Phoebe Latham, Pat Layton, Sandra MacQuillan, Jean Shave, and Bruce Stevenson. All of the aforementioned are residents of England. On the American side, Pamela Long gave editorial assistance in the final copy preparation and William McGuire supervised the index on behalf of the editorial committee.

Grateful acknowledgment is made to Delight Ansley for professional help and advice.

* Mrs. Glover died 1 April 1977.

GENERAL INDEX
TO THE
COLLECTED WORKS OF
C. G. JUNG

A

Aalders, C., **18** (*p826n*)

Aarau conference, **11** 511

Aaron, **9ii** 168, 361; **13** 167

abaissement du niveau mental (concept
of Janet), **3** 12&*n*, 29, 59, 76,
505–6, 537, 569; **6** 199, 765; **8**
152, 841, 856, 912; **9i** 213, 244,
264; **9ii** 53; **10** 795; **15** 166*n*; **16**
361; **17** 204; **18** 139, 154, 162,
511, 794;
  automatism and, **3** 55, 300;
  as depression, **7** 344;
  as dissociation/dissolution of
  consciousness/loss of soul, etc.,
  3 55; **5** 671; **9i** 213–14, 244; **12**
  116, 437; **16** 372, 477;
  as lowering of attention/
  energy, **3** 24, 300, 544; **15** 123;
  neurosis and, **3** 506, 516–17,
  541;
  one-sidedness of, **3** 578;
  psychogenesis of, **3** 513;
  in schizophrenia, **3** 512, 546;
  11 848; **18** 829;
  sleep as, **3** 523; **9ii** 315;
  "word salad" and, **3** 157

abandonment, **9i** 285;
  and helpful powers, **11** 525

Abarbanel, Isaac, **9ii** 128;
  Mashmi'a Yeshu'ah, **9ii** 168;
  Ma'yene ha-Yeshu'ah, **9ii** 128*n*

Abarbanel/Abrabanel, Judah, *see*
Leone Ebreo

abasia, **2** 914; **4** 10

Abba, Rabbi, **9ii** 133

Abbas, prefect of Mesopotamia, **11**
365

abdomen, crab as representation of,
18 194

Abdul Baha, religion of Bahaism,
11 861

Abegg, Emil, **5** 214*n*; **6** 349*n*;
  *Der Messiasglaube in Indien und
  Iran*, **14** 595*n*

Abegg, Lily: *The Mind of East Asia*, **8**
924*n*;
  Ostasien denkt anders, J.'s
  foreword, **18** 1483–5

Abeghian, Manuk: *Der armenische
Volksglaube*, **5** 163*n*, 486*n*

Abel, **11** 327, 641, 643, 654, 669; **14**
555;
  as prefiguration: of Christ, **11**
  650; (with Cain), of Christ and
  Satan, **11** 254*n*, 618–19, 628,
  629

Abelard, Peter, **5** 14, 22; **6** 58; **8**
393; **14** 314;
  conceptualism, **6** 69–72, 74, 95,
  540; **7** 80; **14** 630*n*; **16** 559;
  nominalism and realism, **7**
  80;
  epitaph on, *see* Godfrey, Prior of
  St. Swithin's;
  and Heloise, **6** 68;
  and universals, **6** 68–79, 94–5;
  "relative realism" of, **8** 4*n*

Abercius inscription, **9i** 551*n*; **9ii**
127, 145*n*, 162, 178, 180

aberrations, mental, **13** 429

ability, mathematical, **17** 258

ablution (alchemical)/*ablutio*, *see*
opus, alchemical, stages in *s.v.*

ablution (ritual), **9i** 231; **9ii** 293

abnegation, self-, see *tapas*

abnormality: and disease, **17** 130;
  emotional, **1** 204, 223;
  psychic, **17** 256

abortion/abortifacients, **9i** 295; **13**
171*n*

Abot de Rabbi Nathan, tr. J. Goldin,
9ii 175*n*

aboulia, **2** 798; **3** 15, 30, 184

above and below, **13** 175, 457;
  growth from, **13** 333, 350;
  as pair of opposites, **10** 773,
  912; **13** 457; **15** 213;
  powers of, **13** 137*n*, 279, 280;
  water above and below
  heavens, **13** 188;
  see also displacement

Abrabanel, *see* Leone Ebreo

3

Achamoth, *see* Gnostic(s)-ism *s.v.* Sophia

Acheron, **12** 513

"Acherusian lake," **5** 572

achievement, lack of, **3** 184

Achomawi, *see* American Indians: NORTH *s.v.*

Achurayim, four, **9i** 535*n*, 576&*n*, 579, 588&*n*

acoustic control, *see* misreading *s.v.* distractibility

acquisitiveness, *see* West/Western *s.v.* man

Acta Archelai, see Hegemonius

Acta Joannis, see BIBLE: Apocrypha/ etc. *s.v.* John, Acts of

Acta Sanctorum, **6** 966; glossolalia in, **1** 143

Actaeon, **14** 188

acting/actor: in dream, **12** 254–5; and hysteria, **1** 465; and patient's fantasies, **1** 120, 304; *see also* simulation

action(s): automatic, **1** 119, 163; **5** (*p*448); and emotion, **1** 220; fear of, **3** 170; instinctive, **8** 265; and non-action, **13** 20*n*, 38; symptomatic, **1** 176; **3** 95, 102 104, 120, 184; **4** 338; **7** 323; **8** 154 (*see also* Freud *s.v.* symptomatic action); volitional, **8** 363

active and passive, **13** 105; **14** 1, 655

active imagination, **6** 722*n*; **7** 366*n*; **8** 166–75 (*term not used*), 403, 414, 599; **9i** 101, 110, 263*n*, 319, 398, 528, 581, 622, 623*n*, 698; **9ii** 382; **11** 137, 875; **12** 123, 357, 448; **13** 86*n*, 201*n*, 374; **14** 345, 706 (*term not used*), 736, 752–5; **16** 400; **18** 4, 390, 392, 395, 399, 400, 1253, 1787, 1789; and alchemical operation, **14** 446, 749; and anima/animus contents, **9ii** 39;

archetypal motifs in, **18** 1480; dangers of, **14** 755; and mandalas, **9i** 627; symbols in, **9i** 334; **14** 128, 146; and symbols of wholeness, **9ii** 351; and transformation process, **9i** 621; *see also* fantasy(-ies) *s.v.* active imagination

activity: and character, **6** 244–7; drive to, **8** 240, 245; feelings of, disturbances in, **3** 170; mental, **1** 189–91, 339*n*; motor, **1** 219; passivity and, **4** 634; pressure of, **1** 219; of unconscious: autonomous, **7** 204/445, 205/446; instinctive, **7** 253; mythological, **7** 160*n*

act of God, *see* uncontrollable natural forces

actor, *see* acting

Acts of Apostles, *see* BIBLE: N.T.

Acts of John, see BIBLE: Apocrypha/ etc. *s.v.* John

Acts of Peter, see BIBLE: Apocrypha/ etc. *s.v.* Peter

Acts of Thomas, see BIBLE: Apocrypha/ etc. *s.v.* Thomas, Acts of

actus purus, see God *s.v.*

Adad, storm-god, Babylonian, **11** 173, 175

Adah, wife of Esau, **5** 280

Adam, **1** 64; **6** 33; **9i** 56; **9ii** 295, 310; **11** 458*n*, 624, 631; **12** 347, 433, 453, 475, 529; **13** 107*n*, 110*n*, 148*n*, 168, 173&*n*, 182, 203; **14** 460, 493*n*; **16** 458*n*; TITLE: "Adam and Eve," **14** 544–653; and Adam Kadmon, *see* Adam Kadmon *s.v.* old/Second Adam; as adept/philosopher, first, **14** 570–84; androgyny/dual nature/hermaphroditism of, **9ii** 319; **11** 161&*n*, 356, 618, 625; **12** 192*n*;

Adam (*cont.*):

13 268; 14 8, 12, 276, 526, 545,
551, 580, 581, 585–7, 590, 631,
652;

and angel Harus, 14 587;

as Anthropos/Archanthropos/
original man/Protanthropos, 5
671; 9ii 307, 318, 340*n*; 11
576, 641; 12 150, 456–7, 476;
13 173, 209, 268; 14 276, 590,
592&*n*, 600, 606, 611, 616,
647–8; Naassene, 9ii 313, 326;
14 587, 652;

as *aqua permanens*, 14 545;

as arcane substance, 13 110*n*;
14 544–58, 570;

and arrow, motif of piercing/
wounding, 14 23, 144, 549,
550; 16 519;

ascent of, 12 456; 13 182;

back of, 14 587*n*;

in bath, 13 273*n*; 14 549; with
Venus, 13 273*n*; 14 416, 546–7;

body of Belial, 9i 576*n*;

children of, 11 618, 619, 628;
14 556; Seth/Sheth, 5 368&*n*;
11 576; 13 173*n*, 400; 14 570,
572 (*see also* Abel; Cain);

Christ/Jesus and, 9ii 71, 307,
367; 11 628; 12 456(7), 459; 14
570, 653*n*; and the Cross, 5
368, pl. xxxvii; as death and
resurrection, 18 527, 529;
Christ as first, second/Secundus
Adam, 5 396; 9ii 313; 14 526,
579, 631, 639; 18 638 (*see also
below* Second (Adam) as
Christ); in genealogy of, 8 559;
13 400;

colours in, 14 552&*n*, 555;

creation of, 12 185, 328*n*, *fig.*
71; 14 12*n*, 552, 555, 570, 586,
587, 588, 589, 631;

death and burial of, 14 555–6;

and tree of Paradise, 5 368;

derivation of name, 14 632;

and devil/Satan, 14 554, 589;

earthly, physical/heavenly, spiritual, 12 456(5), 458, 475; 13

209*n*; 14 552, 588, 592;

and Eve, *see sep. entry below;*

fall/sin of, 5 69, 368, 396, 398,
412, 415, 671; 13 400; 14 20,
585, 600, 609, 685; 16 468*n*,
472*n*; and Christ, 5 671;

first, 9i 596*n*;

first, and second, 9ii 70; 14
592, 596, 611;

and four elements, *see* elements, four, in alchemy *s.v.*;

gift of intelligence, 14 584;

in Gnosticism, *see* Gnostic(-ism)
s.v.;

grave of, 14 555–6;

hermaphroditism of, *see above*
androgyny;

higher, 9ii 307, 367, 378, 390;
and lapis, 9ii 375; Naassene, 9ii
334; and lower, 9ii 359, 369;
—, Naassene, 9ii 402;

as hook of Yod, 14 38*n*;

and lapis, 12 426*n*; 14 545,
569;

legends/traditions concerning,
14 571–2;

and Lilith, 5 369; 11 619, 624;
13 399; 14 589; as "mistress of
spirits," 14 589; as parallel to
Sophia, 11 619;

as macrocosm, 14 590;

and "man of light," 13 168;

and Mercurius, *see* Mercurius
s.v.;

as microcosm, 14 552;

"mountain" of, 5 288*n*;

numbers and, 14 553–5;

and number three, 11 104*n*; 14
554, 652;

and ogdoad, 14 553;

"old," 8 766; 13 106; 14 43,
550, 596–605, 611, 616, 618,
647, 648; and dark Eve, 14
616;

polarity of, 14 585–95;

as *prima materia*, 11 618; 12
426&*n*, *fig.* 131; 14 552, 569,
570, 590;

as prophet, 14 573&*n*, 583;

quaternity/quaternary nature of, *see* quaternity *s.v.*;

rebirth/renewal of, **14** 484, 546;

and Satan, *see above* devil;

Second, **14** 567, 648; in alchemy, **11** 161, 625; **12** 475, 476; as Christ, **9ii** 313, 319, 321, 375; **11** 94, 414, 713; **12** 476; **13** 106, 400; **14** 144, 484, 565, 631, 639 (*see also above* Christ as first, second Adam); as *homo philosophicus*, **9i** 238*n*; **11** 94; and Khidr, **9i** 247;

self symbolized by, **14** 558, 593;

and serpent, **9ii** 369, 385–6;

and Shulamite, **14** 592, 598, 600;

and Son of God, **12** 456, 457;

as statue, **14** 80*n*, 559–69, 627;

tail of, **14** 589, 602;

as tetrad, **14** 553;

as Thoth, *see* Thoth *s.v.*;

as totality/wholeness, **14** 558, 593, 629–53;

and tree, **12** 537; **13** 418–19; genealogical, from navel, **5** 324; **8** 559; of Paradise, **5** 368; **13** 173; phallus as, **5** 324; **12** *fig.* 131; **16** 519 (*see also* Adam and Eve *s.v.* genitals);

see also Adamas; Adam Kadmon

Adam and Eve, **9ii** 322; **10** 571; **12** 347, 426*n*; **13** 110*n*, 398, *figs.* B4, 32; **14** 104;

    TITLE: "Adam and Eve," **14** 544–653;

as anima and animus, **16** 519;

in Cabala, **14** 592, 652;

in Christianity, **14** 526, 581, 582;

first parents, **3** 421; **11** 579, 619, 628; **13** 316, 427;

genitals of, **13** 180; **16** 519;

as King and Queen, **14** 570;

as opposites, **14** 544;

and philosophical tree, **16** 519;

second, **11** 625;

as syzygy, **9ii** 400

adamah, see earth *s.v.*

"Adam and Eve, Life of," *see* BIBLE: Apocrypha etc. *s.v.*

Adamantius: *Der Dialog des Adamantius,* **9ii** 99*n*

Adamanus, "first man" (Arabic), **14** 587

Adamas, **13** 366*n*; **14** 566*n*, 627; androgynous, **14** 587; arch-man, **9ii** 326, 328; Original Man, and Korybas, **14** 589; perfect man, **13** 419; **14** 589*n*

adamas (steel), *see* steel

Adam Kadmon, **14** 591, 606, 611, 620; **18** 638; androgyny of, **14** 652; birth of, **14** 609, 646–7; and Christ, **11** 94; **14** 607, 648; cosmogonic, **14** 653; as *filius philosophorum,* **13** 168; as *homo maximus*/primeval/primordial man, **13** 268*n*; **14** 44, 548, 592, 600, 648; as "inner" primordial man, **14** 548, 606; and lapis, **14** 640; as mediator, **14** 592&*n*; as Mercurius, **13** 268; "old"/Second Adam, **11** 94; **14** 596, 600, 647, 648; as One and Many, **14** 594, 619; original man, **14** 44; as self, **14** 619; as son-lover, **14** 609; and transformative process, **14** 618, 619

Adam's Bridge, **10** 1002

Adam Scotus: *De tripartitio tabernaculo,* **9ii** 158&*n*

Adamski, G.: Ufo eye-witness, **10** 612;

    Flying Saucers Have Landed, **18** 1433*n*

Adam von Bodenstein, *see* Bodenstein

adaptation/adaptability, **3** 19*n*, 529;

adaptation (*cont.*):
4 312, 410, 419–26; 6 28, 262, 470, 626, 694; 7 80, 81, 236, 240n, 326–7, 337, 462n; 8 42, 63–7; 11 539; 17 107a, 289, 338; TITLE: "Adaptation, Individuation, Collectivity," 18 1084–1106;
abnormal, 4 570;
affects and, 9ii 15;
in analysis, 18 1091–4;
collective and individual, 6 161, 502; 7 82; 17 255;
to collective unconscious, 7 252;
by differentiated function, 6 171, 344, 556, 899, 947, 956;
diminished, 10 483;
and direction, 8 64;
educational aim of, 6 760;
energetics of, 18 1090;
external, 17 172;
of extravert, 6 564; and introvert, 7 80;
failure in, 4 574; 5 200, 341; 6 809;
faulty, 7 319;
as goal of treatment, 16 277;
harmonious, 8 75;
individual systems of, 6 932;
infantile, 4 312; resistance to, 4 572;
instinct and, 5 351;
by intuition, 6 240, 611;
lack of, 13 12;
loss of, 5 220;
in marriage, 17 331b;
maximum and minimum, 7 518(3);
need of continuous, 8 143;
and neurosis, 10 345; 16 5; 18 1087; as failure in adaptation, 5 220; 13 473;
new, 4 563; 5 450;
normal, 16 152, 161;
to own nature, 17 172;
to parents, 5 431, 465;
passive, 6 427;

phylogenetic attempts at, 6 512;
psychological, 4 623, 634; 5 192, 258; 18 1084–98; libido and, 8 60; projection and, 10 41;
psychotherapy and, 10 1043;
rapid, 6 464, 471;
to reality, 5 456; 6 93, 191, 344, 427, 744; 7 252, 462n, 521(2); 8 697; enhanced, 4 284; loss of, 4 71, 274; 8 597;
regression and, 5 351, 506;
religion as, 6 313;
social, 7 518(3); 16 24, 152, 167;
stages of, 8 60;
and transference, 4 448, 662;
see also mental defectives *s.v.*
adaptedness, 10 547; 13 24
Adar, month of, 9ii 181
"Addam et processum," *see* ALCHEMICAL WRITERS: *Theatr. chem. s.v.* Melchior Cibinensis
adder, *see* ANIMALS *s.v.* serpent/snake
Adebar, *see* ANIMALS *s.v.* stork
Adech, *see* Paracelsus *s.v.* ARCANA
Ademarus, 12 224n
adept(s), alchemical term, 13 162, 174, 187, 211&n, 212, 221, 278, 355, 393, 397, 398, 408, 435, 436, 445; 14 654, 694; 16 468;
Adam as first, 14 570–84;
individuation of, 13 435;
moon-plant of, 13 406;
mountain of, 12 *fig.* 93; 13 241n;
and *soror mystica,* 16 421–2, 437, 538n;
see also artifex
adhista, see *athista*
Adhvaryu (priest of Yajur-Vedá), 13 340
Ādi-Buddha, *see* Buddha *s.v.*
adiposity, 8 780
Ādityas (solar gods), 13 339
adjective(s), 2 48–51, 55, 64, 475,

god of, **9i** 702; (*see also* Shu);
lead of the, **12** 443;
as *prima materia*, **12** 409*n*, 410*n*,
425;
and soul, **8** 664; **12** 165*n*, 243;
aerial, **12** 336*n*;
and spirit(s), **13** 198, 201, 245,
261; **14** 161;
-world, in mandala, **13** *fig*. A4;
see also elements; water *s.v.* air
aerial life force, **13** 200
Aerial Phenomena Research Organization (APRO), **18** (*p*626*n*),
1446;
Bulletin, **18** 1446–8
aeroplane(s)/aircraft, **10** 603;
airman, **10** 648;
in dreams, **12** 147, 153; **13** 466,
472; motif/symbol, **8** 535; **11**
90
Aeschylus, **5** 471*n*;
Prometheus, tr. H. W. Smyth, **5**
671*n*
Aesculapius/Asklepios, **5** 457*n*, 577;
9i 553; **11** 160*n*; **12** 246; **14** 144*n*,
304*n*, 483*n*, 493*n*; **18** 257;
dog of, **5** 355;
incubation dreams and healing, **8** 549;
snake of, *see* ANIMALS *s.v.*
serpent/snake;
Telesphoros and, see Cabir;
see also Kerényi *s.v. Asklepios*
"aes Hermetis," **9ii** 241
Aesop's fable(s), **8** 449;
patient's reproduction of, **1**
395–6
aesthetic(s)/aestheticism, **3** 419; **6**
194&*n*, 230&*n*, 232–3; **7** 167; **13**
66; **15** (*p*85), 135; **16** 489; **17**
266; **18** 799;
TITLE: "The Type Problem in
Aesthetics," **6** 484–504;
attitude, see attitude(s) *s.v.*;
condition, **6** 187&*n*, 208;
and empathy, **6** 485–94; (*see
also* Worringer);
enjoyment, **6** 872;
mood, **6** 195–200, 206;

and morals, conflict, **6** 223; **9i**
60;
values, **10** 862;
see also instinct *s.v.*; interest *s.v.*
aestphara, **13** 170*n*
aether, **7** 151; **13** 215; **14** 218*n*, 270,
452;
and soul, **13** 412*n*;
spirit in, **13** 102, 198
aetiological: disturbances, **13** 464;
role of affect, *see* affect;
theories, **3** 466
aetiology, **3** 467; **13** 143;
of neuroses, *see* neurosis(-es)
s.v.;
of schizophrenia, **3** (*p*272)
Aetius: *De placitis philosophorum,* **9i**
573*n*
Aetna, **5** 626
Afanas'ev, E. N.: *Russian Fairy Tales,*
9i 435*n*
affect(s), **1** 41, 221, 245, 307, 354,
357; **3** 210; **5** 7, 19*n*, 644; **6** 455,
463, 681 (Def.), 808, 885–6,
889–92; **7** 272, 275, 307, 323–4;
9ii 15, 61; **11** 561–3, 642; **12** 182;
13 12, 17, 48–9, 60, 452, 466,
478; **16** 266–7, 270; **18** 42, 90;
abreacted/unabreacted, **1** 298;
4 31–3, 35, 208;
and accident, **1** 307;
aetiological role of, **1** 338, 349;
4 28–9;
and anima/animus relationship, **9ii** 31;
archetypes and, **8** 841;
association experiments and, **2**
166, 171–2, 331, 891;
and attitude, **8** 630–1;
autoerotic, **16** 476;
as autonomous complex, **8** 628;
autonomy of, **13** 58; **16** 267;
children's, intensity of, **4** 344;
in complexes, **2** 1352;
control of, **10** 680;
damming up/blocking of, **3**
433; **4** 31, 208; **18** 1147;
deliverance from, **6** 330;
differentiated, **6** 262–4;

East, **5** 536; **8** 802; **9i** 177; **10** 280, 324;
"going native" in, **18** 341;
J.'s journey to, *see* Jung: JOURNEYS
myths in, *see sep. entry below;*
South, rock-carvings in, *see* rock-drawings *s.v.* Rhodesian;
West, **5** pl. XVII;
white and black in, **10** 97;
witch-craft, and familiar, **5** 452*n*;
see also Egypt, Elgonyi; Ethiopia; Kavirondas; Kenya; Somali; Uganda; Yoruba
Africa, myths in: Basuto, **5** 291*n*, 579*n*; **13**133;
   Big Snake, **5** 620;
   birth of hero in stable, **5** 291*n*, 579*n*;
   creation, **5** 620; **6** 367;
   of death, **5** 538;
   hero-, **5** 362;
   of Namaqua, mother-myth, **5** 530*n*;
   Nigerian, **5** 392*n*;
   of S. Africa, **5** 367*n*, 452*n*;
   of Uganda, **5** 594;
   of West Africa, **6** 367;
   Zulu, **5** 298*n*
Africanus, **14** 353*n*
afterlife, belief in, **10** 623; *see also* reincarnation
afternoon of life, *see* life, stages of
Agadir, Morocco, **18** 1305&*n*
Agamemnon, **4** 347
agape/Agape, **9ii** 147
Agathias Scholasticus, Byzantine historian, **14** 91&*n*
Agatho, *see* Priscius
Agathodaimon, *see* ANIMALS: serpent(s)/snakes *s.v.*
Agdistis, **14** 27*n*
age/aging/old, **7** 88, 90; **8** 785, 789, 795, 808;
   in fairytales, **9i** 401–18, 420;
   "getting wooden in," **8** 800;
   law of, **5** 617;

of patient, as *indicium,* **16** 75;
physiological and psychological, **8** 248;
among primitives, **8** 86, 788, 802;
and tree symbol, **13** 350;
and youth, **7** 114, 117;
see also man *s.v.* old; woman *s.v.* old
ages, two, in pseudo-Clement, **9ii** 100
aggregation: gaseous, **13** 261;
   states of, **9ii** 393–4, 405
aggression/aggressiveness, **6** 651, 859; **12** 118;
   of patient, **1** 328, 386–7;
   and religion, **10** 652
"aghast," etymology of, **8** 627
aging, *see* age
agnata fides, **13** 207
Agni, god of fire, **5** 208, 210, 211&*n*, 214*n*, 239, 240, 271, 421, 515; **6** 338&*n*, 348, 349&*n*–50&*n*, 352–3&*nn*; **13** 340;
   on the ram, **5** pl. XIII*b*;
   and soma, **5** 246–7, 526
agnoia/ἀγνοία, **9i** 487; **9ii** 299; **13** 455
ἀγνωδία (agnosia), **9ii** 298&*n*, 299, 301*n*, **18** 1515–16, 1827, 1831;
   God's, **9ii** 303
agnosticism, **11** 735; **13** 82; **18** 1660
Agnostus, Irenaeus, pseud. F. Grick, *see* ALCHEMICAL WRITERS *s.v. Prodromus Rhodostauroticus*
agoraphobia, **7** 353; **18** 856
Agricola, Georg(ius): *De animantibus subterraneis,* **9i** 268*n*; **13** 124*n*
agriculture, and libido, **8** 85
Agrippa von Nettesheim, Heinrich (Henricus) Cornelius, **8** 393, 932; **13** 164, 167, 168, 229, 234; **15** 10; **18** 1757;
   on alchemy, **16** 414&*n*;
   WORKS:
      De incertitudine et vanitate omnium scientiarum et artium/The Vanity of Arts and Sciences, **12**

Agrippa (*cont.*):
313&*n*, 422*n*; **13** 152; **14**
27&*n*, 188*n*; **15** 9; **16** 414&*n*;
De occulta philosophia libri tres,
5 *fig.* 26; **8** 393*n*, 930–2; **13**
148&*nn*, 168*n*, 193*nn*, 224*n*,
234*n*
Ahamarama, *see* Miller, Miss F. *s.v.*
"Chiwantopel"
ahamkāra, **11** 955, 958
Ahasuerus, **5** (*p*460); **12** 160;
and Wandering/eternal Jew,
legend of, **5** 281, 282, 285, 293;
6 454; **10** 374
Ahijah, **12** 543
Ahlenstiel, H., *see* Bash, K. W.
Ahmed-ibn-Tulun, mosque of, **12**
155
Aholah, **5** 280
Aholibamah, **5** 169, 171–2, 280
Ahriman, *see* Persia/etc. *s.v.*
Ahura-Mazda, *see* Persia/etc. *s.v.*
Aidoneus, and Kore, **5** 572
Aigremont, Dr., pseud. (Siegmar
Baron von Schultze-Galléra):
*Fuss- und Schuh-symbolik und
-Erotik,* **5** 356*n*, 421*n*, 481*n*; **7**
128*n*; **14** 725*n*;
Volkserotik und Pflanzenwelt, **5**
208*n*, 392*n*
Ailly, Pierre d', **9ii** 136, 138&*n*,
153–4;
*Concordantia astronomie cum
theologia,* etc., **9ii** 128*n*, 130*nn*;
"De octava coniunctione max-
ima," **9ii** 156&*n*
aim(s):
TITLE: "The Aims of Psychotherapy," **16** 66–113;
of analysis/analytical psychology, etc., **6** 695;
autoerotic, in science, **16** 86;
and causes, **4** 677;
cultural, **7** 114;
final, **7** 501*n*;
natural, of man, **7** 114;
of psychotherapy, *see* psychotherapy *s.v.*;
social usefulness, **16** 110;

therapeutic, **16** 81, 113;
of treatment, *see* treatment *s.v.*;
see also goal(s)
Ain-Soph, **9i** 576*n*
aiolos, see soul *s.v.* definition of
Aion/*Deus Leontocephalus,* **5** 163*n*,
425; **14** 379;
Aion, **9ii**;
key god, **18** 266;
with signs of zodiac, **5** 423*n*, pl.
XLIV;
soul as image of (Pindar), **11**
373;
see also Aeon(s)/aeon(s)
Aipolos, **9ii** 338
air, *see* aër/air
aircraft/airplane, *see* aeroplane(s)
airman, as observer, **10** 648
aischrologia, **18** 264&*n*; *see also*
scurrility
Aitareya Upanishad, see Upanishads
s.v.
Aithiops, **14** 726; *see also* Ethiopian
ajña, **16** 560
Akathriel, **9ii** 110&*n*
Akbar the Great (India), **10** 983
Akhmim manuscript, *see* CODICES
s.v.
Aksakow, A. N.: *Animismus und
Spiritismus,* **18** 698*n*
Akori, **14** 352
alabaster, **13** 87; **14** 626
Alain/Alan of Lille/Alanus de In-
sulis: alchemists and, **11** 161*n*; **12**
480*n*;
Elucidatio in Cantica Canticorum,
13 389&*n*;
M. Baumgartner, *Die Philosophie
des Alanus de Insulis,* **9i** 572*n*;
11 229*n*
"Alanus," *see* ALCHEMICAL COLLEC-
TIONS: *Theatr. chem. s.v.* "Dicta
Alani"
Alaska, *see* Tlingit
Albaon, **14** 537, 632*n*
albedo, see COLOURS *s.v.*
Alberich, **10** 389
Albertus Magnus, **8** 393; **9ii** 130*n*,
133*n*, 404; **10** 864; **12** 465, 471*n*;

13 158*n*, 377, 444, 448; **14** 302, 626*n*, 722*n*, 738, 739; **16** 221, 533*n*; **18** 1530;
and alchemy, his knowledge of, **9ii** 143; **11** 161*n*; **12** 524; **14** 13;
WORKS:
"Ave Praeclara" (attrib.), **12** 481; **13** 448*n*;
"De mineralibus et rebus metallicis," in *Opera* ed. A. and E. Borgnet, **13** 173*n*;
De mirabilibus mundi, **8** 859–60; **18** 1222;
Philosophia naturalis, **12** *fig.* 117;
see also ALCHEMICAL COLLECTIONS: *Theatr. chem. s.v.*
Albigenses, **9ii** 235
al-Bukhari, **5** 282
Albumasar/Abu Ma'shar/Abu Mansor (Ja'far ibn Muhammad al-Balkhī, **9ii** 128, 131*n*, 133*n*, 153, 154;
De magnis coniunctionibus, **9ii** 130*nn*, 151*n*, 156;
Introductio maior, **9ii** 130*n*
albumen, **4** 764

ALCHEMICAL COLLECTIONS

This sub-index deals with the large Renaissance collections of alchemical texts. Under each title, the names of the texts and (when known) their authors are listed alphabetically. The sub-index ALCHEMICAL WRITERS AND TEXTS, which follows this one, contains all names in this category and gives references in sources other than the collections, in addition to cross-references to the collections where relevant.

Ars chemica (1566), **14** 3*n*
"Consilium coniugii"/"Studium Consilii coniugii de massa solis et lunae," **11** 154*n*, 354*n*, 361; **12** 99*n*, 209, 336*n*, 338*n*, 423*n*, 426, 471*n*, 531; **13** 109*n*, 110, 117, 125, 137*n*, 142*n*, 163*n*, 188&*n*, 267*n*, 409*n*, 423, 445; **14** 1*n*, 2*nn*, 7, 21, 23*nn*, 34*n*, 36*n*, 41&*n*, 75*n*, 80*n*, 110*nn*, 114, 134*n*, 135*n*, 142, 143&*nn*, 154*n*, 155*n*, 172*n*, 181*nn*, 291–2, 316&*n*, 354*n*, 404*n*, 423, 460, 496*n*, 658, 729*n*; **16** 353*n*, 402*n*, 454*n*, 495*n*; *without title of treatise,* **14** 140*n*
Hermes Trismegistus: "Tractatus aureus seu septem tractatus seu capitula aurei," **5** 465*n*; **9i** 238&*n*; **9ii** 292*n*; **11** 47*n*, 161*n*; **12** 140*n*, 155*n*, 192*n*, 358*n*, 385*n*, 454, 488*n*; **13** 173*n*, 184&*n*, 283*n*; **14** 37*n*, 117*n*, 118*n*, 245*n*, 361*n*, 460, 496, 727*n*; **16** 384*n*, 450&*n*, 494*n*; *without title or author,* **13** 112*n*
Hortulanus: "Commentariolum in Tabulam smaragdinam," **11** 160*n*, **13** 137*n*
Artis auriferae (1593), **12** 464; **18** 1704*n*
[Other editions: 1572, from which the "Visio Arislei" is sometimes quoted in **14**; "Allegoriae super librum Turbae" in **9i** 268*n*; "Ros. phil." in **14** 15*n*; and "Tractatus aureus" in **9i** 293*n*; and 1610 (3 vols.), from which "Rosinus ad Euthiciam" is quoted in **14**]
"Aenigmata philosophorum/sapientum/ex visione Arislei," *see below* "Visio Arislei"
"Allegoriae super librum Turbae," **9i** 268*n*; **9ii** 192*n*, 193, 194*n*, 195*n*; **11** 92*n*, 361; **12** 338*n*, 433*n*, 438*n*, 449*n*; **13** 101, 112*n*, 139*n*, 272, 273*n*, 401*n*, 406*n*, 441*n*; **14** 157, 180*n*
Arisleus, *see below* "Visio Arislei;" *see also below* "Ros. phil." *s.v.* "Visio Arislei"

Artis auriferae (cont.):

Aristotle, *see below* "Tractatulus Aristotelis"

Arnaldus de Villa Nova/Arnold of Villanova: "Flos florum," **13** 103; "Thesaurus thesaurorum et Rosarius," **14** 180, 181*nn*, 277*n*; *without title or author,* **14** 630*n*

"Aurora consurgens quae dicitur Aurea hora," **8** 388; **9i** 238*n*; **9ii** 241*n*, 376*n*, 377*n*, 380; **11** 93&*n*, 154*n*; **12** 336*n*, 338*nn*, 403*n*, 423*n*, 464, 511*n*; **13** 113, 158, 255*n*, 256*n*, 261*n*, 356*n*, 359*n*, 374*n*, 409; **14** 14*nn*, 58*n*, 75*n*, 80*n*, 135*n*, 143*n*, 155, 157*n*, 181*n*, 240*n*, 360*n*, 374*n*; **16** 384*n*, 472*n*; *without title of treatise,* **14** 243*n*

Avicenna, *see below* "Tractatulus Avicennae"

Calid, *see below* Kalid

"Clangor buccinae," **14** 2*n*, 240*n*, 244*n*, 630*n*

"De arte chymica/"Liber de arte chimica," **9i** 238*n*; **11** 47*n*; **12** 462*n*, 505&*nn*; **13** 137*n*, 269*n*; **14** 41*n*, 120, 142*n*, 235*n*, 295*n*, 630*n*, 729*n*; **16** 454*n*

"Dicta Belini," *see below* "Ros. phil." *s.v.*

"Exercitationes in Turbam," *see below* "In Turbam philosophorum exercitationes"

Hermes Trismegistus, *see below* "Ros. phil." *s.v.* "Tractatus aureus"

"Hortulanus super epistolam Hermetis," *see below* "Ros. phil." *s.v.*

"Interpretatio cuiusdam epistolae Alexandri Macedonum regis nomine," **9ii** 256*n*

"In Turbam philosophorum exercitationes," **9ii** 193; **12** 336&*n*, 338*n*; **13** 86*n*, 89*n*, 109*n*, 267*n*, 282*n*, 283*nn*; **14**

121, 172*n*, 499*n*, 655*n*, 657*n*, 659*n*; **16** 454*nn*, 455*n*

Kalid/Calid:

"Liber secretorum alchemiae," **9i** 238*n*; **13** 380*n*, 381*n*; **14** 174&*n*, 176–7, 179, 180*n*; **16** 353*n*, 458&*nn*

"Liber trium verborum," **12** 477&*n*; **14** 168*n*; **16** 461*n*; quoted in "Rosarium," **13** 103*n*

"Liber de arte chimica," *see above* "De arte chymica"

"Lilius," *see below* "Ros. phil." *s.v.*

"Ludus puerorum," **14** 65*n*

Maria Prophetissa: "Practica . . . in artem alchi(e)micam," **9ii** 378; **12** 209*n*, 338*n*, 422*n*, 484*nn*; **13** 113, 407; **14** 31*n*; **16** 403*n*, 459*n*

Merlinus: "Allegoria de arcano lapidis"/"Allegoria Merlini," **12** 439*n*, 475*n*; **14** 357, 365, 401, 405, 424, 669*n*; **16** 472*n*; "Aenigma Merlini," **16** 472

Morienus Romanus: "Sermo de transmutatione metallica/metallorum, vel Liber de compositione alchemiae," **8** 388*n*, 394*n*; **9ii** 256; **12** 386&*n*, 404*n*, 420*n*, 421*n*, 423*n*, 514*n*; **13** 414*n*; **14** 45&*nn*, 64*n*, 316*n*, 341*n*, 344*n*, 404*n*, 493*n*, 513*n*, 529; **16** 403*n*, 408*n*, 484*nn*, 529; **18** 1699*n*

"Opusculum authoris ignoti"/"Authoris ignoti, philosophici lapidis secreta metaphorice describentis" (attrib. Rhasis), **13** 125*n*; **14** 7*n*

Rachaidibus: "Fragmenta philosophorum Regis Persarum de materia lapidis" "Fragment from the Persian Philosophers," **9i** 238*n*; **14** 218&*n*

Rhasis, *see above* "Opusculum"

"Rosarium philosophorum," **9i**

De alchemia (1541)

Geber: "Summae perfectionis metallorum (sive perfecti magisterii)," **13** 254, 258*n*

Hermes Trismegistus: "Tabula smaragdina," **12** 214*n*; **13** 392*n*; **14** 12*n*, 217*n*, 303*n*, 304*n*, 701*n*

Hortulanus: "Commentarius in (super) Tabulam smaragdinam," **12** 220*on*, 433&*nn*; **13** 175*n*; **16** 498&*n*

"Rosarius minor," **12** 235*n*

De alchimia (1550), vol. II

"Rosarium philosophorum . . . cum figuris rei perfectionem ostendentibus," **9i** 238*n*; **11** 92*n*, 98*n*, 154*n*; **12** 475*n*, 501, *figs.* 25, 167, 169, 234, 235, 268; **13** 113, 161*n*, 180*n*, 183*n*, 190*n*, 261&*nn*, 387, *fig.* B2; cf. *fig.* B3; **14** 289, 352; **16** 401, (*p*203*n*), 451*n*, 520, 527, *figs.* 1–10; **18** 1780–9; "Tractatus aureus" in, **13** 161*n*

Musaeum hermeticum (1678); title page, **14** 188*n*

[Other edns.: 1625, *see* **12** *fig.* 240; ed. and tr. A. E. Waite, *The Hermetic Museum Restored and Enlarged* (1893), **9i** 705*n*, *fig.* 50; **9ii** 204*n*; **11** 92*n*; **14** 3*n*, 65*n*]

"Aquarium sapientum, seu Hydrolithus sophicus" [Siebmacher], **12** 356*n*, 381*n*, 398*n*, 431&*n*, 478; **13** 231, 255*n*, 256*nn*, 263*n*, 267*nn*, 270, 283*n*, 384&*n*, 385; **14** 45*n*, 77*n*, 329, 354*n*, 394, 419*n*, 460, 485, 492&*n*, 494&*n*, 570, 729; *cf.* **8** 962; *without title of treatise*, **14** 154*n*, 657*n*, 699*n*

[Barcius], *see below* "Gloria mundi"

Cremer, John: "Testamentum," **12** 404*n*

Flamel, Nicolas: "Tractatus brevis seu Summarium philo-

sophicum," **12** 459*n*; **13** 267*n*, 403*n*, 407*n*, 408*n*; **14** 140*n*, 404*n*, 408*n*

"Gloria mundi, alias Tabula paradysi" [Barcius (F. von Sternberg)], **9ii** 200&*n*; **12** 356*n*, 446*n*, 459*n*, 497*n*; **13** 122*n*, 255*n*, 257*n*, 268*n*, 273*n*, 374*n*, 404, 408*n*, 410; **14** 37*n*, 154*nn*, 167*n*, 219*n*, 241*n*, 244*n*, 254, 259*n*, 318, 321, 329, 337, 341, 389*n*, 404, 419*n*, 545, 570, 630*n*; **16** 496*n*; *without author or title*, **9ii** 143*n*; **13** 415*n*; **14** 235*n*, 319*n*

Helvetius, Johann Friedrich: "Vitulus aureus," **14** 642*n*; **18** 1528

Hermes Trismegistus: "Tractatus aureus de lapide philosophorum," **12** 356*n*, 427*n*; **13** 255*nn*, 256*n*, 261*n*, 262*n*, 264*n*, 267*n*, 282*n*, 374*n*; **14** 36*n*, 38, 110*n*, 134*nn*, 135&*n*, 136, 241*n*, 244*n*, 329, 415, 464*n*, 534, 536; **16** 472*n*, 475*n*; *without title or author*, **14** 493*n*, 655*nn*, 658*n*

"Hydrolithus sophicus," *see above* "Aquarium sapientum"

Jean de Meung/Joannes a Mehung: "Demonstratio naturae," **12** 381*n*; **14** 140*n*

Lambspringk/Lambspring: "De lapide philosophorum figurae et emblemata" ("Figurae"), **5** pl. LIX*a*; **9i** 705*n*, *fig.* 50; **9ii** 147*n*, 224, 234; **12** 441*n*, 446*n*, 459*n*, 518, *figs.* 168, 179, 240 [1625 edn.]; **13** 109*n*, *fig.* B6; **14** 3, 354*n*, 404*n*, 506*n*; **16** 459*n*, 494*n*; *without title or author*, **14** 669*n*

"Liber Alze," **14** 65*n*, 245; *without title or author*, **14** 727*n*

Madathanus, Henricus: "Aureum saeculum redivivum," **12** 356*n*; **14** 14*n*, 44*n*; *without title or author*, **14** 49*n*

*   *

ALCHEMICAL WRITERS AND TEXTS

This sub-index includes—besides straightforward names of writers and titles of tracts—the names of alchemists of whom no works are extant; fictitious names of alchemists; and modern authors who have edited, translated, or paraphrased alchemical texts. There are cross-references to ALCHEMICAL COLLECTIONS (previous sub-index). Other cross-references (unless otherwise stated) are to other entries within this sub-index.

The following authors and title in the main body of the General Index have subheadings for their associations with alchemy: Agrippa von Nettesheim; Alanus de Insulis; Albertus Magnus; Aldrovandus; *Corpus Hermeticum;* Goethe; Paracelsus; Reitzenstein; Waite.

Abraham le Juif/the Jew, forgeries/replacements of his lost work "Rindenbuch":
by Eleazar, *see* Eleazar *s.v. Uraltes Chymisches Werk;*
"Livre des figures hiéroglifiques," Paris BN MS. Fr. 14765, **12** *fig.* 217; **14** 18*n*, 634&*n*, 720, pl. 3
Abū Bakr Muhammad ibn-Zakarīyā, *see* Rhazes
Abu'l Qāsim Muhammad ibn Ahmad al-'Irāqī:
Kitāb al-'ilm al muktasab etc., ed. E. J. Holmyard, **11** 160*n*; **12** 473&*n*, 516&*n*, 537&*n*; **13** 173*n*, 273*n*, 402&*n*, 406, 408*n*, 409*n*; **14** 5&*n*, 6*n*, 12, 73*n*, 158*n*, 389&*n*, 415*n*, 660*n*, 727*n*; **16** 403*n*, 497*n*
Adolphus Senior, *see* Senior, Adolphus
Aegidius de Vadis, *see Theatr. chem. s.v.*
"Aenigma Merlini," *see Art. aurif.:* Merlinus *s.v.*
Agrippa von Nettesheim, *see main index*
Alanus de Insulis, *see main index s.v.* Alain/Alan of Lille
Albertus Magnus, *see main index*
Aldrovandus, *see main index*
Alfidius/Alphidius, **11** 161*n*; **12** 382, 450*n*, 462, 465; **13** 392&*n*, 429; **14** 2*n*; **16** 458, 484
Alfonso X, King of Castile: *Clavis sapientiae,* **18** 1788

"Allegoriae sapientum supra librum Turbae," containing "Dicta Belini," see *Bibl. chem. cur.* and *Theatr. chem. s.v.*
"Allegoriae super librum Turbae," see *Art. aurif.* and *Bibl. chem. cur. s.v.*
"Allegoria Merlini," see *Art. aurif. s.v.* Merlinus
Alphidius, *see* Alfidius
Altus: *Mutus liber* (1677), **9i** 53*n*; **14** 181*nn*, 436; **16** 505, 538*n*; see also *Bibl. chem. cur. s.v.* "Mutus liber"
Andreae, Johann Valentin, *see* Rosencreutz, Christian
Anthonius de Abbatia: *Epistolae duae,* **14** 31*n*
"Aphorismi Basiliani," see *Theatr. chem. s.v.* "Aphorismi" and *s.v.* Happelius
Apollonius of Tyana/*probably* Belinus, Bolinus, etc., **9ii** 193*n*; **11** 228, 861; **12** 336*n*; **14** 15*n*, 164&*n*, 165; **15** 91;
attrib. "Dicta Belini," see *Bibl. chem. cur. s.v.* "Allegoriae sapientum;" *Theatr. chem. s.v.* "Allegoriae sapientum"
"Aquarium sapientum," **8** 962; see also *Mus. herm. s.v.*
Aquinas, *see* Thomas Aquinas, pseudo-
Archelaos, **12** 435*n*; **13** 158*n*; **15** 19
Arisleus, **9ii** 220&*n*; see also *Art. aurif.:* "Rosarium philosophorum" *s.v.* "Visio Arislei," *and* "Visio Arislei"

Merlinus/Merculinus/Merqûlius/
Marqûlius, **16** 457, 472*n*; see also
Art. aurif. s.v. Merlinus
Meung, Jean de, see *Mus. herm. s.v.*
Jean de Meung
Michelspacher, Steffan: *Cabala,* **12**
fig. 93; **13** 241*n*
Micreris, see *Theatr. chem. s.v.* "Trac-
tatus Micreris"
Morienus Romanus/Marianus/
Morienes, **9ii** 258; **12** 462&*n*,
558; **13** 158*n*; **14** 135*n*, 247, 741;
15 19; **16** 440; **18** 1699&*n*; see
also *Art. aurif. s.v.; Bibl. chem. cur.
s.v.*
Muḥammad bin Umail, *see* Senior
Muḥammad Ibn Ishak al Nadīm,*see*
Nadīm
Mutus liber, see Altus; and *see*
Bibl. chem. cur. s.v. "Mutus
liber"
Mylius, Johann Daniel: *Philosophia
reformata,* **8** 388*n*; **9i** 246*n*, 268*n*,
580*n*; **9ii** 143*n*, 215&*n*, 241*nn*,
292*n*, 307*n*, 345&*n*, 373*n*, 376*n*,
377*n*; **11** 47*n*, 62*n*, 151&*n*, 152,
154*n*, 155&*n*, 354*n*, 355*n*, 356*n*;
12 99*n*, 140*n*, (*p*225), 338*n*, 427,
469*n*, 518,*figs.* 21, 34, 114, 125,
163, 188, 200, 218, 223; **13** 95*n*,
113–14, 161*n*, 163*n*, 173*n*, 188,
255*nn*, 256*n*, 261, 263, 267*nn*,
268, 270, 273*nn*, 274*nn*, 276*n*,
282*n*, 337*n*, 398*n*, 403*n*, 406,
407*n*, 422; **14** 4*n*, 5&*nn*, 11*n*,
14*nn*, 21*n*, 37*n*, 39*n*, 41&*n*, 45*n*,
49*n*, 58*n*, 80*n*, 110*n*, 117*nn*, 119*n*,
134*nn*, 135*nn*, 136, 138*n*, 142&*n*,
143, 157*n*, 164, 167*n*, 168*nn*,
181*n*, 235*n*, 241, 244, 245,
246&*n*, 284*n*, 295, 316*nn*, 320*n*,
338, 354*n*, 389&*n*, 401*n*, 404*n*,
405*n*, 416*n*, 419*n*, 451*n*, 460,
462*n*, 534*n*, 552*n*, 567, 570*n*, 623,
630*n*, 642*n*, 658*n*, 718*n*, 727*n*,
729*n*, 731; **15** 37*n*; **16** 376*n*,
389*n*, 454*n*, 460*n*, 525*n*; "Sym-
bolum Saturni" in, **13** 398*n*, 407*n*

Nadīm, Muḥammad Ibn Ishak al-:
Fihrist, **13** 287*n*, **14** 690*n*
Nazari, Giovanni Battista: *Della
tramutatione metallica sogni tre,* **12**
356&*n*; **13** 88*n*
Nikephorus Blemmides, **12** 441*n*
Norton, Samuel:
Catholicon physicorum, **12** *fig.*
221;
Mercurius redivivus, **12** *figs.* 122,
214
Norton, Thomas, **12** 404*n*;
"Ordinall of Alchimy," **12**
404*n*;
see also *Mus. herm. s.v.; Theatr.
chem. Brit. s.v.*
Olympiodorus: treatise in Berthelot, *Coll. alch. grecs,* **9ii** 377*n*,
420&*n*; **11** 154*n*, 344*n*; **12** 338*n*,
423*n*, 426, 456*n*; **13** 97&*n*, 109*n*,
139*n*, 164*n*, 173*n*, 251*n*, 372&*n*,
430&*n*; **14** 6*n*, 10*n*, 23&*n*, 64*n*,
110*n*, 117*n*, 183&*n*, 335*n*, 389*n*,
493&*n*, 726&*n*; **16** 408*n*; **18**
1700;
Petasios/Petesis quoted in, **13**
97, 139*n*, 251; **14** 493
Oporinus, Johannes/Oporin, **13**
154, 155, 169; **15** 8
Orandus, Eirenaeus, *see* Flamel *s.v.*
Exposition
Orthelius, see *Theatr. chem. s.v.*
Ostanes/Astanus, **9ii** 244*n*, 376*n*,
386*n*; **11** 151, 361; **12** 451; **13**
299*n*, 359*n*, 414*n*, 428, 436, 437;
14 5–6, 317&*n*;
and Cleopatra, **12** 483; **13** 131,
191–2;
Nile stone of, **11** 151, 355; **12**
405, 447; **13** 133, 265;
treatise in Berthelot, *Coll. alch.
grecs,* **12** 405*n*; **14** 317*n*;
"Book of Ostanes"/"Le Livre
d'Ostanès," in "Kitâb el Foçul,"
Berthelot, *Chimie au moyen âge,*
11 154*n*; **12** 356&*n*, 405*n*,
536&*n*; **13** 105*n*, 407&*n*,
424&*n*, 445&*n*

Zosimos (*cont.*):
  and omega/round element, **9ii**
  377; **10** 728; **11** 92*n*, 366;
  Rimas, **13** 287*n*;
  as "Rosinus," **9ii** 241*n*; **12**
  530&*n* (see also *Art. aurif. s.v.*
  "Rosinus");
  and Theosebeia/Euthicia, **9i**
  372; **12** 408; **13** 96*n*, 372; **14**
  181*n*, 245&*n*, 321*n*; **16** 505&*n*;
  18 1280 (see also *Art. aurif.*:
  "Rosinus ad Euthiciam");
  torture in, **11** 345; **14** 451*n*;
  visions of, **5** 200, 484, 553*n*; **9ii**
  283; **11** 297, 324*n*, 344–55,
  359, 374–5, 410–12, 420; **12**
  66, 80, 356, 392*n*; **13** 85–144,
  273, 359*n*, 370, 439; **14** 451*n*;
  WORKS:
  "Book of Sophe the Egyptian," in Berthelot, *Coll. alch.*
  grecs, **12** 413*n*; **14** 168*n*,
  353&*n*;
  "Concerning the Art"/"Sur
  l'art," and other treatises in
  Berthelot, *Coll. alch. grecs*, **5**
  200*n*, 512*n*, 671*n*; **9i** 537*n*;
  9ii 118*n*, 307*n*, 376*n*; **11** 92*n*,
  120*n*, 152*n*, 154*n*, 159*n*,
  161*n*, 344&*nn*, 348*n*, 355*n*,
  366*n*; **12** 66*n*, 80*n*, 336*n*,
  392*n*, 405&*n*, 408*n*, 456*n*,
  457*n*, 458*n*, 517*n*, 530*n*; **13**
  86&*nn*, 96*n*, 124*n*, 126*n*,
  127*n*, 139*n*, 168*n*, 265*n*,
  270&*n*, 359*n*, 370*n*, 371*n*,
  414*n*; **14** 2*n*, 6*n*, 27*n*, 113*n*,
  309*n*, 316*n*, 317*n*, 321*n*,
  555*n*, 591*n*, 626*n*, 663*n*,
  683*n*; **16** 353*nn*, 403*n*, 472*n*

*   *

alchemy/alchemist(s) **9i** 433*n*; **10**
628–31, 633, 727–8, 746; **11**
150–4, 344, 440, 707; **12** 342–3,
362, 376, 394, 404, 451–2, 558,
564; **13** 106, 121, 158, 219, 278,
393; **14** 654, 790–2; **16** (*p*165),
353–4; **17** 198; **18** 264, 380, 638,
674, 1281;
  TITLES: "The Alchemical Interpretation of the Fish," **9ii**
  239–66; *Alchemical Studies*, **13**;
  "Alchemy and Psychology," **18**
  1700–3; "Background to the
  Psychology of Christian Alchemical Symbolism," **9ii**
  267–86; "Faust and Alchemy,"
  18 1692–9; "The Fish in Alchemy," **9ii** 193–238; "Foreword to a Catalogue on Alchemy," **18** 1691; "Individual
  Dream Symbolism in Relation
  to Alchemy," **12** 44–331; "Introduction to the Religious and
  Psychological Problems of Alchemy," **12** 1–43; *Psychology and
  Alchemy*, **12**; "Religious Ideas in
  Alchemy," **12** 332–554;
  aberration of, **12** 395, 515; **13**
  252;
  and active imagination, **11** 793;
  afflictio animae in, **16** 408*n*;
  allegorical aspect of, **11** 344; **12**
  40; **13** 88;
  anima complex in, **9i** 516;
  Arab, *see* Arab(s);
  arcane: remedies, **13** 158; terminology of, **13** 157, 169, 231;
  art of, **12** 564; **13** 86, (*pp*61,
  64), 158, 171, 267, 383; **16**
  414*n*; black, **12** 85, 101; dangers of, **13** 139&*n*, 164, 302,
  429–35, 439; as divine gift, **14**
  443; forbidden, **13** 154; kabba-
  listic, **13** 148*n*; magic, **13** 156; of
  metals, **13** 86; nature its basis,
  16 411, 413; "requires the
  whole man," **18** 1414; royal, **13**
  252, 355; rules of, **13** 267; sacred, **13** 99; secret(s) of, **13**
  99*n*, 113; **16** 411, 498, *see also*
  below secret doctrine of *and see*
  secret(s) *s.v.* of opus/art;

alchemy (*cont.*):

116, 138, 194, 199, 396; **14** 354, 374, 720, 737; and Church, **13** 134;

Latin, **9ii** 143; **13** 87*n*, 124, 187*n*, 254, 374*n*; **18** 479, 533, 1530;

leitmotiv of, **13** 94;

lightning as symbol in, **9i** 533&*n*;

literature of, **13** 88, 109, 252;

loneliness of, *see below* solitary life of;

as *ludus puerorum*/child's play, **12** 302, *fig.* 95;

and Manicheism, **12** 469*n*;

Mater Alchimia, **9ii** 267, 368; **14** 14, 15, 80*n*, 360;

matter in, **9ii** 120; **13** 175; **14** 238, 319, 336, 509;

meanings in, many interconnected, **13** 90;

medieval, **7** 361; **9ii** 334; **13** (*p*4), 132, 163, 360; **16** 221;

meditation in, **11** 344;

and motif of hero's birth, **9i** 248*n*;

mystical aspect of, **13** 116, 139–40, 284; **16** 354, 479;

and mythology, **13** 252, 396; **14** 401, 486&*n*, 677, 735;

and natural science, **9ii** 266, 267, 274, 368; **12** 346; **13** 163;

nature philosophy of, **5** 113*n*; **11** 153; **13** 184, 198; **18** 1475;

Negroes as symbols in, **9ii** 329;

obscurity/mystification in, **12** 40, 93, 342–5, 401–3, 424, 502; **13** 138, 356; **16** 497&*n*;

"obscurum per obscurius," **12** 41, 332, 345;

pagan, **13** 393;

pagan elements in, **9ii** 274; **12** 31, 547;

parables of, **11** 344; **14** 189;

Paracelsan, **13** 166; **15** 19, 26–8; and German alchemists, **13** 162; *labor Sophiae* of, **13** 209,

210; spiritual trends in, **13** 180*n* (*see also* Paracelsus *s.v.* as alchemist);

paradoxes/ambiguities of, **14** 90, 110, 256, 274, 598–9, 633, 649; **16** 498;

personification in, **13** 122;

as philosophy/philosophical, **7** 360, 361; **8** 932; **9i** 142; **10** 727; **11** 470; **12** 26, 172, 332, 403, 502, 554; **13** 143, 145, 157, 158*n*, 162, 171*n*, 184, 198, 254*n*; **15** 28; **16** 498*n*; **18** 1684, 1830;

physical speculations of, **9ii** 392–5;

and pre-Christian rites, **18** 616;

procedures, three and four, **12** 31;

and prolongation of life, **9i** 241;

psychic factor in, **12** 403; **13** 173;

and psychic identity, **13** 122;

psychological content/significance of, **7** 360; **12** (*pp*v, x), 26, 332; **14** 335, 445–6, 523, 677, 686, 694–7, 711, 737, 772, 776–7, 779; **18** 1700–3;

psychological secrets of, **13** 90;

and psychology, modern, **4** 748;

psychology of, **12** 354; **13** 125; **18** 1531;

quest for the unattainable, **13** 143;

and revelation, **14** 344;

royal pair in, *see* Gabricus, Beya; king *s.v.* and queen;

sacrifice in, **11** 361–3;

and science: measurement in, **14** 147; modern, **9ii** 144 (*see also above* chemistry; energy; natural science);

secret doctrine of, **13** 157, 164 (*see also above* arcane *s.v.* secret of);

smells in, **14** 432;

solitary life of, **12** 41, 422;
and soul, concept of, **9i** 706;
and soul in chains, **10** 633;
spiritual discipline of, **7** 360; **18** 1590;
stages in their work, *see* opus, alchemical *s.v.* stages in
symbols/symbolism, *see* alchemy, symbols in, *below;*
terms used in, **11** 400;
and transmutation of the elements, **8** 90;
trinitarian and quaternarian standpoints, **18** 1133;
two parts of (practica, theoria), *see* opus *s.v.*;
Ufo-form and, **10** 631;
and unconscious, **9ii** 191, 219; **11** 105, 375, 440; **12** 448; **14** 457;
and uniting symbol, **9i** 523;
and washing of black corpse, **11** 423;
wholeness/totality in, **9ii** 265; **14** 22, 716;
Wilhelm and, **18** 1131–2;
at work, **12** *figs.* 2, 124, 133, 137, 143, 144;
the work, stages in, *see* opus, alchemical, stages in;
work-room of, **12** *fig.* 145; **16** 399;
and yoga, **16** 219;
see also adept; *aqua permanens;* arcane substance; artifex; athanor; *coniunctio; distractio; filius philosophorum;* hierosgamos; *krater; lapis philosophorum; meditatio;* Mercurius; *nuptiae chymicae;* opus, alchemical; *peregrinatio; prima materia; sal;* tetrameria; tincture; *vas;*
see also under anima (soul);
ANIMALS: birds, dragon, fish, lion, peacock, serpent, stork, uroboros; Anthropos; *aqua;* arsenic; astrology; baptism; birth; blood; Böhme; Cathari;

centre; colour(s); *corpus mysticum;* crown; devil; dogma; dreams; elements; elixir; familiar; fantasy; filth; fire; God; head; hermaphrodite; Holy Ghost; Increatum; king; light; mandala; Mass; melancholy; metals; microcosmos; mountain; oil; opposites, union of; pair; projection; quaternity; queen; quicksilver; redemption; rotundum; scintillae; self; self-knowledge; spirit; thinking; torment; torture; transformation; tree; triad; understanding; union; visions; water; woman

alchemy, symbols/symbolism in, **9ii** 265–6; **11** 276, 755; **12** 39–40, 516, 565, *figs.* 3, 4, 112; **13** 106, 117, 394–5; **14** 633, 654, 790; **16** 219, (*p*165), 503; **18** 1691, 1700;
TITLE: "Alchemical Symbolism in the History of Religion," **12** 516–54;
and Christian symbolism, **12** 40, 518, 526, 554; **13** 394; **14** 525; **16** 533;
and dream symbolism, **11** 105; **12** 39, 40, 448;
and ecclesiastical symbolism, **16** 471;
and Gnostic symbolism, **12** 40, 518, 554;
and individuation process, **12** 40, 555;
pictorial, **12** 503;
and psychology/structure of the unconscious, **12** 43; **13** 90;
reduction of, to chemical substances, **13** 396;
two categories of, **9ii** 246;
and wholeness, **9ii** 265
alchera/alcheringa/alcheringamijina, *see* Australian aborigines *s.v.*
"Alchymistisches MS," *see* CODICES AND MS *s.v.* Basel
Alciati, Andrea: *Emblemata,* **5** 261n;

Alciati (*cont.*):
9ii 243; **13** 350*n*, 412
Alcibiades, **14** 564
Alcmene, **5** 450*n*;
alcohol, **2** 133, 134; **9i** 387; **9ii** 353;
14 358*n*, 681;
mythological analogue of, **5**
200;
use of, **1** 6, 26, 33
alcoholic intoxication/alcoholism, **1**
154, 190, 212; **2** 116&*n*, 132, 133,
134, 388, 450*n*, 491, 882; **3** 328; **6**
573, 805;
in J.'s cases, **1** 193, 194, 197–
204;
"cured by Jesus," **18** 558, 621;
in family constellation, **2** 1006,
1008;
in galvanometer experiments,
2 1032, 1033, 1271–6, 1277–
81;
hysterical, **6** 565;
paranoia of, **3** 461;
of recruits, **2** 1315
Aldrich, C. R., **17** (*p*63); *The Primitive Mind and Modern Civilization*,
J.'s foreword, **18** 1296
Aldrovandus, Ulysses, **9i** 53*n*; **14**
56*n*, 71–4, 93, 98;
and alchemy, **14** 74;
Dendrologiae libri duo, **9i** 223*n*;
13 458*n*; **14** 71&*n*, 73*n*
alembic, **5** 245; **14** 81*n*;
three, significance of, **9ii** 380;
see also vas/vessel
aleph and tau, **13** 271
alertness, **8** 690; *see also* attention
"Alexander, Empress," *see* association-chains *s.v.*
Alexander the Great of Macedon, **5**
288; **9i** 253, 604; **10** 984; **12**
457&*n*; **13** 415, 428; **14** 65, 241*n*,
279*n*, 319; **18** 509;
as the "two-horned," **5** 283*n*,
pl. XX*a*;
see also Dhulqarnein; Khidr/El
Khidr
Alexander Jannaeus, **5** 594

Alexander Polyhistor, **12** 409*n*
Alexander, Romance of, **13** 403*n*,
459; **14** 157*n*
Alexander à Suchten, **13** 165
Alexandria, **6** 21; **9ii** 145, 164,
241*n*; **11** 178; **16** 505;
philosophy of, **11** 193
Alexandros, **18** 243
alexipharmakon, *see* Mercurius *s.v.*
alexipharmic, **12** 522*n*, 529, 538,
549; **13** 133, 170, 353*n*, 390
Alexis, **14** 96
Alexius Comnenus, **9ii** 229
"Alfabet des Ben-Sira," **14** 571*n*
Alfidius, *see* ALCHEMICAL WRITERS
s.v.
Alfonso X, King of Castile, **18**
1788
Alfred the Great, King, **18** 650
alga, gelatinous, **13** 190*n*
Algonquins, *see* American Indians:
NORTH *s.v.*
Ali, M. T., *see under* ALCHEMICAL
WRITERS: Senior
alicorn, *see* ANIMALS *s.v.*
alienation, **8** 590;
from the world, **7** 369
alienist(s), *see* psychiatrist(s)
Ali Illahija ("extinguishers of
light"), **5** 581*n*
"aliquis," **3** 117, 217*n*
Al Irāqī, *see* ALCHEMICAL WRITERS
s.v. Abu'l Qāsim
aljira, **11** 782
Alkia, **16** 483*n*
Allah, **10** 398, 622; **11** 454; as
monad, **18** 1611
all-being, non-existent, **10** 774
"Allegoria de arcano lapidis," *see*
ALCHEMICAL COLLECTIONS: *Art.
aurif. s.v.* Merlinus
allegoriae Christi, **12** 20; *see also*
Christ *s.v.*
"Allegoriae sapientum supra lib-
rum Turbae," see ALCHEMICAL
COLLECTIONS: *Bibl. chem.* and
Theatr. chem. s.v.
"Allegoriae super librum Turbae,"

see ALCHEMICAL COLLECTIONS: *Art. aurif.* and *Bibl. chem. s.v.*

"Allegoria Merlini," *see* ALCHEMICAL COLLECTIONS: *Art. aurif. s.v.* Merlinus

allegory, **3** 136, **13** 88; **15** 128;
in alchemy, **11** 344; **12** 40;
Christian, **11** 460;
of Christ and devil, **9ii** 127;
of Christ/piety, stork as, **13** 417 (*see also* Christ *s.v.*);
conscious, **13** 121;
ecclesiastical, **13** 321;
euhemeristic, **13** 395;
of Mary, the rose is, **13** 389;
patristic, **12** 20, 453;
of sheep and shepherd, **12** 72;
and symbol, distinguished, *see* symbol(s) *s.v.*

Allenby, A. I., **18** (*p*656*n*); *A Psychological Study of the Origins of Monotheism,* **9ii** 427*n*; J.'s foreword, **18** 1486–96

Allendorf, J.L.K., **5** 268

Allendy, R., **18** (*p*765*n*); *Le Symbolisme des nombres,* **12** 313&*n*

Allgemeine Ärtzliche Gesellschaft für Psychotherapie, *see* Psychotherapy, General Medical Society for

alliteration, as symptom, **3** 578

All-Merciful, the, Great Mother as, **7** 379

"All-oneness," **6** 52, 54

"all-or-none reaction," **8** 264, 266, 272, 278, 376, 384

Allport, G. W., **15** 44*n*

allurements, divine, gods as, **8** 930

"all will be well," **18** 1629, 1640, 1641

Alma Mater, university as, **13** 147

Almaricus/Almaric of Bene, and Holy Ghost Movement, **9ii** 138

alma Venus, *see* Venus *s.v.*

almond-tree, *see* TREES *s.v.*

almus, **5** 519*n*, pl. XIV*a*

aloofness, *see* isolation

alpha and omega, **13** 271, 363;

Christ as, **14** 423

Alphidius, *see* ALCHEMICAL WRITERS *s.v.* Alfidius

Alps/Alpine, **10** 238

"also-I," **8** 764

Also sprach Zarathustra, see Nietzsche *s.v.*

Alt, Konrad, **2** 205*n*

al-Tabari, *see* Tabari

altar, **7** 175; **9i** 380; **13** 86; 434; **18** 537;
bowl-shaped, **13** 86;
censing of, **11** 318–20;
in dream, **7** 175–82; **17** 275, 277;
high and low, **11** 911, 936;
number four, and, **11** 90

alter-ego, **16** 430; *see also* ego

alternation of day and night, **13** 38

altruism, **4** 654;
abnormal, **18** 1398;
conscious, of extravert, **6** 588, 972

Altus, see ALCHEMICAL WRITERS *s.v.*

alum/alumen, **12** 484*n*; **13** 375; **14** 712;
of Mercurius, **14** 712*n*

Alverdes, F.: "Die Wirksamkeit von Archetypen in den Instinkthandlungen der Tiere," **8** 282*n*

Alvernus, *see* William of Auvergne

Alypius, **5** 102

Alze, Liber, *see* ALCHEMICAL COLLECTIONS: *Mus. herm. s.v.* Liber Alze

amaritudo/bitterness, *see* sea *s.v.* bitterness

amazement, **3** 3

amber, **13** 215

ambergris, **12** 535; **13** 193*n*

ambiguity: conviction and, **11** 79;
of Mercurius, *see* Mercurius *s.v.* dual

ambitendency, **3** 425; **5** 253, 680*n*; **6** 684, 705; *see also* ambivalence

ambition(s): corruptive effect of, **5** 171;
inordinate, **8** 236;

ambition (*cont.*):
  love and, **17** 222;
  of mother, **17** 133, 221–3;
  parents', **17** 247;
  unfulfilled, **17** 288
ambivalence, **3** 425; **4** 26, 27; **5** 165,
  680*n*; **6** 684, 705*n*; **9ii** 24; **16**
  384; **18** 1077–9;
    TITLES: "The Ambivalence of
    the Fish Symbol," **9ii** 181–92;
    "The Concept of Ambiva-
    lence," **18** 1077–81;
    of anima, **9i** 357;
    in erotic jokes, **18** 1079;
    of father imago, **4** 742;
    of instincts, **4** 654;
    of maternal attributes, **9i** 158;
    of spirit, *see* spirit *s.v.*;
    see also ambitendency
Amboina, **8** 842*n*
ambra, see Paracelsus *s.v.* ARCANA
Ambrose, St., **5** 158; **6** 392; **12** 418,
  522; **13** 384*n*, 390*n*, 407*n*, 448;
  14 28, 148, 285*n*, 372, 474;
    and Apostles' Creed, **11** 211;
    on Christian water symbolism,
    9ii 143&*n*; **11** 313; **14** 372;
    on *kenosis*, see *kenosis s.v.*
    on *vas*/vessel symbolism, **6** 394;
    WORKS:
      *Commentarius in Cantica Can-
      ticorum,* **14** 372*n*;
      De excessu fratris, **14** 474*n*;
      De institutione Virginis, **6** 392*n*,
      394*n*;
      De interpellatione Job et David,
      13 407*n*;
      De Noe et arca, **16** 533*n*;
      *De XLII mansionibus filiorum
      Israel,* **13** 448*n*;
      Epistolae, **14** 372*n*;
      Explanationes in Psalmos, **9ii**
      143*n*, 373*n*; **14** 148*n*, 372*n*;
      *Explanatio symboli ad initian-
      dos,* **11** 211*n*;
      Hexameron, **14** 28*n*, 474*n*;
      Tractatus in Joannem, **11** 313*n*
Ambrose, St. (pseudo-): *Expositio*

*beati Ambrosii Episcopi super Apo-
calypsin,* **6** 392&*nn*
ambrosia, fount of, **13** 406*n*
Amen (Egypt), **9ii** 322
Amenophis IV (Egypt), **5** 147–8,*fig.*
  5; **8** 92; **14** 356*n*
Amente (Egypt), **14** 482
America(n)/United States of Amer-
  ica, **3** 124–5; **7** 494; **8** 788; **9i**
  48; **12** 86, 87, 178, 200; **18** 16,
  24, 209, 320;
    TITLES: "The Complications of
    American Psychology," **10**
    946–80; "Press Communiqué
    on Visiting the United States,"
    18 1300–4; "Report on Amer-
    ica," **18** 1284;
    areas of, **5** 400; **10** 937; North
    Germanic, **10** 94;
    commerce and industry in, **18**
    1327;
    communism and, **10** 523;
    conscious and unconscious in,
    10 103;
    cross symbol in, **4** 477;
    death of friend in, **8** 852;
    European immigrants in, **10**
    18, 94, 948–9; **18** 1118;
    and Europeans, differences, **10**
    949, 967;
    Indianization in, **10** 18, 94,
    948, 970, 978 (*see also* American
    Indians);
    initiation in, **10** 100, 977;
    J.'s case, of business man, **7** 75,
    111, 117;
    J.'s journey to, *see* Jung *s.v.*;
    lack of soul in, **10** 926;
    laughter and emotional ex-
    pression, **10** 95, 953–4, 964;
    as matriarchy, **10** 790;
    mother complexes of, **5** 272;
    Negro-complex of, **10** 961; **18**
    1284;
    Negroes in, *see* Negro(es) *s.v.*
    American;
    primitive layer in, **18** 94, 341;
    psychoanalysis in, **4** 203;

anahata, **16** 562
Anahita/Anaitis, *see* Ardvisura Ana-
hita/Anaitis
anal: birth theory, **5** 277–9;
complex, **18** 1055–6, 1058;
eroticism, **4** 53, 58, (*p*76);
fantasy, **18** 1062;
region, **5** 276;
see also anus
analgesia, **1** 262;
total, **1** 235;
see also hypalgesia
analogy(-ies), **3** 25, 218; **4** 553; **5**
146, 149, 192, 203; **7** 235/455; **8**
309; **13** 83; **16** 353;
and associations, **16** 96;
fantastic, **7** 348;
formation of, **9ii** 414;
lunar, **7** 250;
magic by, **8** 314;
objective, **7** 492;
primitive, **13** 44;
of sexual act, **5** 226;
solar, **7** 250;
and symbol, see symbol(s) *s.v.*;
telluric, **7** 250;
thinking in, **7** 221; **17** 44
analysis, **4** 575; **6** 910; **7** 129, 218,
225, 243/464, 461; **8** 529; **9i** 83;
10 888; **16** 275–6;
and active imagination, *see* active imagination;
adaptation in, **18** 1091–4;
aim/goal of, **6** 695; **7** 387 (*see
also* aims *s.v.* therapeutic);
of analyst, *see* analyst *s.v.* (*see
also below* training; *see also* doctor *s.v.* analysis of);
anamnestic, **17** 177–80, 184;
beginning of, **8** 497; and
dreams, *see* dream(s) *s.v.* beginning;
of children, **17** 142–3;
not a "cure," **8** 142, 143;
dangers of, **7** 192–3, 240/460,
468; **14** 755; for analyst, **18**
353;
demands of, on doctor, **17** 291;

and dementia praecox, **3** 152;
of doctor, *see* doctor *s.v.*;
dream-, *see* dreams, analysis/
etc.;
early days of, **12** 5;
effect of, **7** 223–4, 236, 499;
fantasy invention during, **4**
413;
first part of, **4** 436–8;
Freud's method, **3** 298 (*see also*
Freud; psychanalysis; psychoanalysis);
group, **14** 125*n*;
and hysteria, 35, 152;
as initiation process, **11** 842,
854;
and insight, **4** 647; **7** 224;
and liberation of animal instincts, **7** 439;
on objective level, *see* objective
s.v. level, interpretation/etc.;
objective psyche, **12** 48;
of persona, **7** 246/466;
personal, **7** 236; and archetypes, **9i** 97;
and production of conscious
ego, **11** 904;
projection in, **6** 402;
prolonged, **12** 5;
psychology and, **7** 502;
of pupil, **18** 575;
as quickened maturation, **8**
552; **18** 399;
reductive, *see* reductive *s.v.*;
of repressions, **7** 202/443;
and resistance, *see* resistance
s.v.;
and return to church, **18** 671;
second stage, **4** 443, 452;
self-, **4** 449; **8** 809;
on subjective level, *see* subjective *s.v.* interpretations
sublimation through, **7** 71,
439;
suggestion and, *see* suggestion
s.v. psychoanalysis/etc.;
symptom-, **16** 199; **17** 176;
and synthesis, **7** 122; **9ii** 410;

analysis (*cont.*):
  13 238;
  technique of, **7** 440;
  training, **10** 350; **16** 237, 238, 366; **18** 1160 (*see also* analyst *s.v.* analysis of; doctor *s.v.* analysis of);
  of transference, *see* transference *s.v.*;
  and type theory, **6** 92;
  of unconscious, *see* unconscious *s.v.*;
  unwillingness to terminate, **8** 140;
  see also psychanalysis; psychoanalysis
analyst: analysis of, **4** 447, 449, 450, 536, (*p*253), 586, 633; **8** 498; **16** 8, 165; **18** 323 (*see also* analysis *s.v.* training; doctor *s.v.* analysis of);
  challenges to, **18** 1170-1;
  complexes of, **16** 8;
  and dangers of unconscious, **14** 753;
  and dream-interpretation, **8** 498;
  fear of loss of, **4** 168;
  as hairdresser (in dreams), **13** 479;
  interference by, **4** 625, 634;
  lay, **11** 545;
  loss of balance by, **4** 536;
  love of, **4** 632, 639, 663 (*see also* transference);
  neurotic, **18** 345;
  not a superman, **18** 497;
  own psychic problems of, **18** 1172;
  and patient, relationship, **4** 435, 536, 661; **8** 145-6, 515; **10** 534; **17** 173; **18** 1172;
  patient's: projections onto, **18** 322; of moral defects onto, **4** 535; of parental imagos onto, **9i** 122; of personal imagos onto, **18** 369; resistance to, **18** 505; sexual fantasy about, **18** 333;

personality of, **4** 447, 450, 586, 632, 640; **10** 888; and transference, **18** 329;
possibility of deceiving, **4** 649, 650;
projection of analyst's psychology onto patient, **8** 498;
provocation by, **18** 350;
requirements for, **4** 455;
resistances of, **4** 421;
as saviour, *see* saviour *s.v.*;
sex of, and patients' reactions, **10** 889;
"snake's eyes" of, **18** 326;
and transference, **4** 428-9; **14** 751;
unconsciousness of, **10** 889;
winning independence of, **14** 754;
see also doctor; psychotherapist
analytical: method, **6** 923; **16** 140, 276; **17** 282; **18** 1391;
  process/procedure: **4** 626; end and goal of, **12** 3-4; first part of, **14** 181;
  psychology, *see below*;
  -reductive method, *see* reductive *s.v.*;
  treatment, **6** 812; **7** 119; **14** 180*n*; a dialectical process, *see* dialectic/etc. *s.v.* procedure
analytical psychology, **4** 523; **7** (*pp*v, 7), 191, 293*n*, 410, 431; **8** 279, 529; **10** 887; **12** 1, 9*n*, 411; **14** 602; **16** 118, 172; **18** 1239, 1299, 1391, 1808-9;
  TITLES: "Analytical Psychology and Education," **17** 199-229; "Analytical Psychology and Weltanschauung," **8** 689-741; "Basic Postulates of Analytical Psychology," **8** 649-88; "Good and Evil in Analytical Psychology," **10** 858-86; "On the Relation of Analytical Psychology to Poetry," **15** 97-132; Prefaces to *Collected Papers on Analytical Psychology*, **4** 670-92; *Two Essays*

on Analytical Psychology, **7**;
achievements of, **16** 121;
and active imagination, **11** 793;
aim of, *see* aims *s.v.* analysis;
clash of doctor and clergyman in, **11** 548;
dialectical method of, **18** 1391;
dream-images in, **5** 4;
dream interpretations in, *see* dreams, analysis/etc. of;
and education, *see* education *s.v.*;
and experimental psychology, **17** 170;
first use of term, **2** 1355 & *n*;
fundamental viewpoints, **17** 100–1;
and normal psychology, **17** 130;
phenomenological standpoint of, **18** 1233;
and Protestantism, **11** 544;
and psychoanalysis, differentiated, **16** 115; **17** 99;
self in, **11** 808; **13** 134;
sources of, **10** 22;
and teacher, **17** 108, 142;
and unconscious, **11** 779
and *Weltanschauung,* **8** 701, 730;
Zurich School of, *see* Zurich Society/School for Analytical Psychology;
see also depth psychology
anamnesis/anamnestic, **4** 221; **7** 182; **9i** 319; **9ii** 73, 279; **14** 306; **16** 34, 194, 198, 251, 303; **17** 281;
analysis, **17** 177–80, 184;
of fire-making, **5** 250;
in the Miller fantasies, **5** 47–55;
and psychoanalysis, **4** 525, 528, 622;
"ritual," **14** 603, 605;
in simulated insanity, **1** 330, 338
ānanda (bliss), **6** 190, 370, 422; **11** 913, 924

Ananke (Necessity), **5** 102*n*, 426*n*
anarchy/anarchism, **4** 655; **6** 322; **11** 144;
psychic, **11** 866
Anastasius I (Pope), **6** 23;
Anastasius Sinaita: *Anagogicae contemplationes,* **16** 553*n*
anātman, **11** 949; *see also* atman
Anatomical Institute, **18** 486
anatomy/anatomical/anatomist, **8** 688, 717; **11** 460; **13** 11; **15** 34;
comparative, **5** 26; **13** 353*n*;
dissection, **15** 22;
interior, **13** 173&*n*;
and psychiatry, **3** 466, 467;
and psychic disturbances, **3** 323–32
Anaxagoras, **5** 67, 76, (*p*453); **12** 410*n*, 433, 435*n*
Anaximander, **12** 428*n*
Anaximenes, **12** 410*n*, 428*n*
ancestor(-tress)/ancestral, **9i** 156, 316; **11** 339, 997; **13** 130 & *n*, 460;
children and, *see* child(ren) *s.v.*;
-columns, **4** 512;
cult, **7** 296; **8** 575;
identification with, **6** 231; **9i** 224, 226; **12** 171;
life of, **7** 118, 120; **12** 174;
psychic inheritance from, **7** 300, 336; **8** 673, 717; **11** 814; **17** 93;
soul of, **7** 233*n*; **9i** 224; **13** 128;
-spirits, **6** 531; **7** 293; **8** 335; **10** 140, 969; **12** 171; **14** 743; **17** 96;
symbolism, **12** 174;
see also animal (s) *s.v.* ancestry, man's; Australian aborigines/primitives
anchorite(s), **4** 276; **5** 119*n*; **10** 649; **11** 475
Ancient of Days/*Antiquus dierum,* **9i** 412; **11** 668, 708; **12** 313; **13** 362*n*; **14** 7*n*, 374, 377, 405, 436
ancient world/antiquity, **5** 17&*n*; **6** 540; **13** 69;

805, 806, 820;
  and Orpheus, **10** 809;
  The Secret of the Saucers, **10** 791
Angelus Silesius (Johann Scheffler),
  6 432; **7** 396; **9i** 19; **11** 282, 733,
  840, 892, 959; **13** 151; **14** 124,
  132, 199, 284, 429, 444&*n*, 447;
  15 10; **18** 1552, 1675;
  "Cherubinischer Wanders-
  mann"/"Cherubinic Wander-
  er," **6** 432*n*; **9ii** 321; **14** 123*n*,
  132*nn*, 137*n*, 284*n*, 429*n*, 443*n*,
  444*n*; **16** 482*n*, 504*n*;
  Selections from *The Cherubinic
  Wanderer,* ed. J.E.C. Flitch, **9ii**
  321*n*; **14** 123*n*;
  Sämtliche Poetische Werke, ed.
  H. L. Held, **14** 25*n*, 196*n*
Anger, Rudolph: "Der Stern der
  Weisen und das Geburtsjahr
  Christi," **9ii** 128*n*
anger, **3** 103; **8** 456; **14** 171; **18** 46;
  in patients' reactions, **1** 199,
  217;
  see also affect(s): rage(s)
Angkor Wat, **5** pl. XXV
angle of vision, in swoon state, **8** 955
Anglicus, Richardus, *see* ALCHEMI-
  CAL COLLECTIONS: *Theatr. chem.*
  s.v. Richardus
Anglo-Saxons, migrations of, **10**
  1001
Angola, **18** 81*n*
Angrâmainyu, **5** 421, 664
anhāta-chakra, **13** 334
ani, **8** 125
Ani, Papyrus of, **9ii** 129*n*; **11** 348*n*
Aniada/Aniadus/Aniadin, *see* Paracelsus *s.v.* ARCANA
anima (J.'s concept), **5** 528*n*; **6** 377,
  797–811 (Def.); **7** 295, 328–9,
  356, 384, 393, 507; **9i** 57–8, 62,
  114–15, 222, 294, 296, 355, 433,
  434, 444, 485, 512, 516, 564*n*,
  634, 706; **9ii** 56, 58–9; **10** 694,
  809; **11** 47, 49, 51, 71, 73, 128–9,
  741; **12** 68, 94, 321; **13** 126, 453,
  455, 458; **14** 75, 86, 129*n*, 616,

619, 674; **15** 210; **16** 521; **17** 338;
  18 150*n*, 429, 1262;
  TITLES: "Anima and Animus,"
  7 296–340; "Animus and
  Anima," **13** 57–63; "Concerning the Archetypes, with Spe-
  cial Reference to the Anima
  Concept," **9i** 111–47; "The
  Syzygy: Anima and Animus,"
  9ii 20–42;
  activation of, **14** 424;
  activity of, **7** 341, 370;
  ambivalence of, **9i** 357;
  and androgyne, **16** 529;
  and *anima,* alchemical, differentiation, **14** 736;
  and animals, **7** 374; **9i** 358;
  and animus, relationship, **9ii**
  29–31; **14** 612; **16** 469; affect
  in, **9ii** 31; compared, **7** 331;
  pair of opposites, **9ii** 425; **16**
  437; problem, **9ii** 58; syzygy,
  9ii 422; in transference, **16**
  422–3, 441, 469 (*see also*
  animosity);
  anything but ideal, **7** 310;
  as archetype, **5** 83*n*, 406*n*, 514,
  607, 611; **7** 185; **9i** 57–9, 80,
  86, 158, 175, 306, 309, 634; **9ii**
  13, 19, 26, 27, 40; **10** 71; **12**
  92*n*, 108, 192*n*; **13** 58, 218; **14**
  71, 159, 218, 313, 415*n*; **16** 504;
  18 829, 1158; of life, **5** 678; **9i**
  66; **14** 313, 646; of mother,
  divine, **18** 1652; mother as first
  incarnation of, **5** 508;
  assimilation, **7** 384; **13** 223*n*;
  autoerotic, **16** 504;
  autonomy/autonomous, **5** 563;
  7 370; **9i** 63; **9ii** 40; complex, **7**
  295, 339, 374, 387; factor, **9ii**
  422; personality, **7** 322, 370,
  374; **13** 61; **16** 504; valency of,
  7 378;
  bipolar, **9i** 356;
  as birds, **9i** 358, 365, 371, 376;
  black (Shulamite), **14** 646, 647;
  as Brünhilde, **5** 563, 607;

anima (*cont.*)
  as chaos, **14** 422;
  as Chinese *p'o* soul, **13** 57–8
  Christianization of, **12** 112;
  compensatory, **7** 304, 328, 507;
  complex, in alchemy, **9i** 516;
  and consciousness, coming into, **14** 498, 614; as effect of, **13** 62;
  conservative, **9i** 60;
  constellation of, **9i** 144;
  contains secret of precious stone, **13** 131;
  creative function, **12** 242;
  daemonic, **7** 374, 508; **9i** 77; **16** 529;
  dark, **7** 318 (*see also below* light and dark);
  definition, **7** 521; **9ii** 20*n*; **13** 58;
  dialectics with, **7** 323;
  as Diana, **14** 193;
  differentiation from, **7** 310, 317;
  dissociation from, **13** 454;
  dissolution of, **7** 391;
  as divine maiden, **14** 103;
  in dreams, **7** 338, 507; **9ii** 39; **11** 48; **12** 130, 246; **14** 424;
  education of, **7** 323;
  ego and, **7** 377, 380, 382, 389, 510; **9ii** 34; **12** 242*n*; **13** 223*n*; **14** 613; **16** 434; as non-ego, **12** 137; as opposites, **16** 434;
  emotionality of, **13** 457;
  empirical concept, **9i** 114; **9ii** 25;
  and Eros, **9ii** 29, 33, 41; **13** 60; **16** 361;
  erotic aspect, **16** 519;
  as Eve, **16** 519;
  evil/wicked, **9ii** 423; **12** 192, 273;
  experiences, significance of, **9i** 382;
  expressed by dogma, **16** 442;
  as factor, **9i** 57; **9ii** 40, 422;
  fateful quality of, **10** 714;

  fear of, **9ii** 62;
  feeling-quality, **9ii** 53;
  femininity of, **9i** 58, 142 (*see also below* man's *s.v.*);
  -figure, **10** 713, 714; **13** 131; autonomy of, **9ii** 53; compensating, **10** 693; as Helen, **16** 361&*n*; projection onto, **10** 714; **18** 1696; in schizophrenic's painting, **18** 412; tree as projection of, **13** 458; **14** 70; "white lady," **10** 713;
  first formulation, **7** (*p296n*);
  as function, **7** 339; **9ii** 40; inferior (fourth), **12** 145, 150, 192, 201, 295; of relationship to unconscious, **7** 374, 387, 510; **13** 62; **16** 504 (*see also below* relationship);
  and ghost, **13** 58;
  a Gnostic concept, **11** 460;
  as hermaphrodite, **16** 454, 529, 535;
  of hero, **9i** 440, 442;
  of Hiawatha, **5** 543;
  "hidden nature" and, **11** 152*n*;
  historical aspect, **7** 299; **9i** 60, 516;
  identity with, **5** 431*n*; **6** 807
  -image, **16** 433; beloved as carrier of, **12** 92*n*; and mother, **9i** 141; —, as first carrier of, **5** 431*n*, 484, 508, 605; **7** 314; **12** 92*n*; and mother-imago, **5** 608 (*see also below* mother); sister as carrier of, **12** 92;
  insight and, **11** 240;
  integration of, **7** 377–8; **9ii** 33, 40;
  jealous mistress, **7** 320;
  king and, **14** 80, 536;
  as Kore, **9i** 310, 356, 381–3;
  as liberty, **9ii** 56;
  as life, *see above* archetype;
  as *ligamentum corporis et spiritus*, **9i** 555;
  light and dark, **15** 210, 213 (*see also above* dark);

link with eternal images, **13**
457;
in literature, **9i** 53*n*, 145; **9ii**
26*n*, 424; **10** 775; **13** 58;
localization of, **9i** 518;
loss of, **9i** 147;
Luna as/lunar, **14** 20*n*, 218,
225;
magical attributes, **16** 433;
man's: and *anima mundi*, **11**
759; unconscious femininity, **5**
678; **7** 141*n*; **11** 48; **12** 192 (*see
also above* femininity);
and mana, **7** 376, 378;
marriage with, **16** 433;
and marriage quaternity, **16**
432–3, 437;
matrix of divine figures, **16**
504;
as mediatrix/mediator/medium
between conscious and unconscious, **10** 715; **12** 242*n*; **13**
223*n*; **14** 498*n*;
as Melusina, **12** *fig.* 132; **13**
180, *fig.* B5, 216–18;
as mermaid, **14** 75;
Messenger of the Grail, **7** 374;
as Miriam, **9ii** 329, 360;
moods, **7** 331; **11** 48;
and mother, **9i** 61, 146, 357; **12**
92; **14** 422; -complex, **9i** 162;
-imago, **5** 606; **7** 316; **9ii** 26;
-sister-wife-daughter, **5** 458,
607; **9i** 516; **14** 415*n*; **16** 438
(*see also above* -image *s.v.*
mother);
motif, **18** 1279–81;
mythological aspects of, **9i**
147*n*;
and neurosis, **9i** 115;
as nightmare, **14** 80;
nixie/elfin nature, **9i** 53, 55, 64;
16 538*n*;
as numen/numinous, **9i** 59; **9ii**
425; **16** 438;
objectivation of, **7** 321;
old man and, **9i** 417;
as old woman, **14** 92;

and persona, *see* persona *s.v.*;
as a personality, **7** 314, 321; **11**
48 (*see also above* autonomous;
below uni-personality);
and personification, **7** 332,
338–9, 370; **9ii** 26; **13** 61; of
(collective) unconscious, **5** 500,
678; **7** 510; **9i** 439; **9ii** 20*n*, 40;
10 714; **11** 48, 107; **12** 65, 112,
129, 145, 192, 242*n*; **13** 62; **14**
128, 181, 217, 321, 538, 646;
16 474, 504; **18** 187 (*see also
below* unconscious); of inferior
functions, **18** 187;
in plural form, **14** 128&*n*;
positive and negative, **9ii** 425;
11 48*n*; **14** 216, 539, 613;
possession, **9i** 223; **9ii** 29, 43;
10 78; **13** 223*n*; **14** 225, 231;
pregnant, **14** 217;
prima materia as, **16** 519;
problem, **7** 318; **9i** 485*n*;
projection of, **7** 309, 314, 508;
9i 61, 141, 168, 182, 311*n*, 383,
559; **9ii** 26, 35, 39, 57, 381; **12**
108; **13** 460; **14** 70, 231, 647;
16 421, 433, 438, 442, 454*n*,
504; **17** 338–41 (*see also above*
-figure *s.v.* projection);
as prostitute, **10** 76;
psychology, **7** 370;
as psychopomp, *see* psychopomp *s.v.*;
as queen in alchemy, **14** 736;
reactions, **7** 329;
recognition of, **9ii** 42, 424;
reconciles and unites, **16** 522;
regression to antiquity, **12** 112;
and relationship/relatedness, **9i**
485*n*, 487 (*see also above* function *s.v.*);
and religion, **11** 71;
religious tinge in, **9i** 356;
resisting the, **11** 128;
secret knowledge, **9i** 64;
as serpent, **5** 678; **9i** 59, 358,
376;
and shadow: contamination, **12**

anima mundi, **8** 931; **9i** 427; **9ii** 246; **11** 92, 152, 759; **12** *fig.* 91; **14** 93, 270, 321–3, 372, 374, 450, 704, 719, 748, 764, 766, 770, 779; **18** 1361;
  alchemical retort as, **13** 245;
  and Anthropos, *see* Anthropos *s.v.*;
  and arcane substance/*prima materia,* **11** 152, 160; **13** 173;
  as demiurge, **11** 160;
  devil as, **13** 163*n*;
  dragon as, **9i** 707;
  Holy Ghost as, **8** 393;
  imprisoned in matter/Physis, **11** 263; **13** 89, 404;
  light-seeds/scintilla of, **14** 68, 416*n*;
  man as, **14** 732;
  Mercurius as, *see* Mercurius *s.v.*;
  Platonic, in *Timaeus,* **11** 113, 190;
  as psychopomp, **12** *fig.* 18;
  redemption of, **12** 413;
  as soul, and world-wheel, **9ii** 212;
  as sphere, **11** 92; **12** 109*n*, 116, 433; **13** 102;
  as world-mother, **5** 550;
  as world-soul, **13** 263 (*see also* world-soul)
animae transitus, **14** 578
animal(s) (for separate species, *see* ANIMALS), **1** 67; **4** 470, 556; **11** 229; **13** 128, 137*n*, 188, 244, 392; **14** 277;
  ancestry, man's, **7** 159; **12** 171 (*see also below s.vv.* instinct/nature; soul);
  and anima, **7** 374; **9i** 358;
  as archetypal images of divine beings, **5** 264; **9i** 267, 419;
  and archetype(s), **7** 109, 158, 185; child-archetype, **9i** 270, 273*n*, 286; spirit, **9i** 398, 421;
  biting by, **12** 183, 186, 272, 273, *fig.* 118;

Christian attitude to, **10** 32; **18** 222 (*see also below* Jesus, sayings of);
cloacal, **18** 1055–6;
complexes in, **10** 842;
as conscience of Epimetheus, **6** 299*n*;
creation of, **11** 634–5; **13** 301;
differentiation among, **7** 198;
as "doctor," **5** 503; **7** 154*n*;
in dreams, **6** 671; **7** 132; **8** 535, 558; **9i** 396; **18** 525; as affects, **10** 680; battle of, as unconscious functions, **6** 671; and diagnosis of physical disorder, **5** 681; **16** 343–7; **18** 135&*n*, 231, 299, 300; killed by doctor, **5** 261; parents represented by, **5** 264; as sexual symbols, **5** 8; **7** 45; and sympathetic system, **18** 194, 203, 412; transformed into humans, **11** 56, 109; **12** 183–4;
emotional manifestations in, **18** 540;
in fairytales, **9i** 405, 420, 421;
fighting, **6** 671; **14** 506*n*, 669;
founding, **18** 536;
four: Chinese, **12** 548; **14** 573; in Daniel's vision, **13** 365; and evangelists, **18** 416; in Ezekiel's vision, *see* Ezekiel *s.v.*; in paintings, **13** *figs.* 24, 25; of Yahweh, **11** 600;
as function of knowing and intuition, **9i** 425;
"helpful," motif of, **5** 264, 538, 546; **8** 558; **9i** 156, 421, 435; **9ii** 291; **13** 241*n*; **16** 85;
herds of, as symbol of psychic disunity, **14** 388;
hypnotism among, **4** 591;
instinct in, *see* instinct *s.v.*;
-instinct/nature, in man, **5** 261, 398, 421, 460, 653; **6** 372, 456, 457; **7** 30, 32, 35–6, 133, 134,

animal (*cont.*):
214, 384, 428, 520; **10** 32; **11** 541; **12** 169, 171, 189; **13** 120, 244; **14** 581, 602; **17** 106; as beast in man, **6** 357; as divine power, **5** 524; liberated by analysis, **7** 439; in religion, **5** 411*n*, 415; repressed, **7** 28/439; sacrificed, **5** 659; subjugation of, **5** 104, 351, 396, 398; **7** 17/427 (*see also below* soul, in man);
and "intelligent" acts of compensation, **18** 1491;
and Jesus, sayings of, **9i** 74; **9ii** 224; **12** 433*n*;
killing of, as transgression against mother, **5** 503;
learning capacity of, **10** 556;
as libido symbols, **5** 261, 421, 659; **7** 133;
love for, as compensation, **6** 468;
magical, **5** 503; **9i** 435; **11** 230;
magnetism, **10** 21; **16** 4, 231; **17** 128; **18** 700, 702, 797;
and man, distinguished, **6** 458, 518;
in mandala(s), **9i** 660; **13** *figs.* 24, 25;
memory in, limitations, **4** 403;
and mother: belong to Great Mother, **5** 503; as foster-mother, **5** 494, pls. II, L*a*; symbolic representative of animal mother, **5** 503; terrifying animal as, **9i** 161;
nature, man's, *see above* instinct;
noises in mania, *see* mania *s.v.*;
and pagan conceptions of divinity, **5** 89; **7** 97; **11** 600; identity of god and his animal attri-

bute, **14** 601;
passions as, **14** 171;
poltergeist in form of, **9i** 457;
produced by Sol/Luna coniunctio, **14** 172;
psyche/psychic processes, **5** 258; **7** 40; **8** 387; **9i** 225; **12** 104, 118; **18** 540;
psychological parallelisms with, **13** 11;
as psychopomp, *see* psychopomp *s.v.*;
as redeemer, *see* redeemer *s.v.* symbolism;
sacred, **13** (*p*63*n*);
sacrifice/sacrificial, *see* sacrifice *s.v.*;
as saviour, **12** 494;
as self, symbols of, **9i** 315; **9ii** 356;
sense of smell in, **18** 780;
sensus naturae in, **8** 393; **13** 148;
skins of, **5** 399*n*;
social sense in, **4** 641;
soul, in man, **7** 35; **9ii** 370&*n*; **14** 279, 282, 287 (*see also above* ancestry; instinct);
soul of, **6** 299; **7** 172; **12** 494;
space/time orientation in, **8** 842;
symbols, **6** 456;
symbolism, and ancestor symbolism, **12** 174;
talking, **9i** 396, 421, 425;
three/triad of, **13** 176*n*, 228&*n*;
totem, **6** 231, 531;
training of, and adaptation, **4** 410;
as the unconscious, **5** 503; **12** 186; **14** 277, 279;
unconsciousness, in man, **5** 415; **7** 87;
variations of behaviour in, **7** 198

*   *

ANIMALS

This sub-index lists separate species, including mammals, birds, insects, reptiles, etc., and fabulous beasts.

alicorn, **12** 518, 529; *see also* unicorn
anser Hermetis, see goose
ant(s), **3** 193; **4** 729; **8** 902, 906;
    leaf-cutting, instinct in, **8** 398
anteaters, **10** 118
antelope, **12** 532
ape(s), **8** 654; **10** 556; **11** 56; **12** 169,
    173, 175, 191, 246; **13** 360;
        of God/*Simia dei*, devil as, **9i**
        456; **11** 120*n*, 252, 262, 263; **12**
        173, 181, 204, *fig.* 67;
        Hanuman, **5** 311;
        -man, **12** 117, 119, *fig.* 35;
        Thoth as, **12** 173;
        see also baboon; gibbon; monkey
ass/donkey, **10** 133; **13** 165, 228*n*;
    16 340;
        in Apuleius, **5** 102*n*; **13** 228*n*;
        14 406&*n*;
        of Balaam, **5** 421;
        of Buridan, **7** 487; **10** 709, 855;
        as Christ, **9i** 463;
        as *daemon triunus*, **12** 539;
        feast of, **9i** 461–3;
        jawbone of Samson's, **5** 638;
        mock crucifixion/worship of, **5**
        421, 622, pl. XLIII; **9i** 463; **9ii**
        129; **12** 539;
        one-horned, **12** 518, 526*n*, 535,
        547;
        patient's vision of, **9i** 352;
        she-, and foal, **5** 421*n*, 622;
        three-legged, **12** 535–9
avis Hermetis, see bird *s.v.* of Hermes
baboon, **12** 173;
        cynocephalus/dog-headed,   **8**
        411; **14** 277, 279; Mercurius as,
        13 359; Thoth as, **12** 175, *fig.*
        68
barbel, *see* fish
basilisk, **12** 173, 365, 460; **13** 180;
    14 87, 172; *see also* serpent
bat, wings of, **13** *fig.* B2

bear, **10** 132; **12** 117, *fig.* 90; **13**
    365; **14** 3*n*, 172;
        and Artemis, **5** 89*n*, 496*n*;
        and Artio, goddess, **5** pl. L*b*;
        chthonic, **12** 263;
        constellations of, *see* Bear *in
        main index;*
        in dreams, **9i** 340–3, 351; with
        four-coloured eyes, **11** 90, 128;
        12 262–3;
        helpful, in fairytale, **9i** 423,
        424;
        Kore as, **9i** 311;
        as mother-symbol, **5** 482–4,
        496;
        as *prima materia*, **12** 263, *fig.* 90;
        -skin, vision of man with, **11**
        487;
        as symbol of the self, **9i** 315; **9ii**
        356
beast(s): blond, *see* blond beast;
    Nietzsche *s.v.* blond;
        lady of the, **9ii** 178
beaver, **8** 81
bees, **8** 956; **9i** 352;
        and dead lion, riddle, **5** 526;
        and Mary, **9i** 312*n*;
        "Woman of the —," **9i** 312n
beetle/scarab, **5** 358; **8** 843, 845,
    847, 850, 855, 857, 982; **9i** 663;
    18 1203;
        Cetonia aurata, **8** 843, 982;
        in dream, **18** 202, 203;
        Mercurius and, **12** 530;
        one-horned, **12** 518, 530–1; **14**
        712*n*;
        sun-, **12** 530;
        as symbol of self, **9i** 315; **9ii**
        356
Behemoth, **5** 87–9; **6** 311, 318*n*,
    434; **9ii** 181, 185; **11** 635; **12** 547;
    14 338;
        as eucharistic food, **9ii** 178;
        and Leviathan, **6** 445*n*, 456–8;

57

Behemoth (*cont.*):
> 9ii 185, 188, 228; 11 681;
> 14 574; battle with, 9ii 133,
> 181

birds, 4 665, 728, 739; 8 559; 12
2 14, 3 19, 404, 433, 497*n*; 13 148,
3 18, 4 15–17; 14 3*n*, 5, 8 1*n*, 637;
16 494, 538*n*;
> in alchemy, 12 (*p*287), *fig.* 2 2;
> 13 3 2 1, 374, 4 15; 14 180&*nn*,
> 248; 16 459;
> angels as, 5 369*n*, 538;
> anima as, 9i 358, 365, 371, 376;
> black, 9ii 356; 11 1 1 1; 12 307;
> 14 248;
> and Christ, allegory of, 9ii 127;
> as death omen, 8 844–5,
> 850&*n*, 851, 857;
> in dreams/waking dreams, 9i
> 359, 365; 11 1 1 1; 12 307;
> earth-, 9i 586;
> as Epimethean symbol, 6 458;
> gold and silver, 12 *fig.* 142c;
> green, 13 374; 14 136;
> of Heaven, 13 4 14;
> helpful, 5 369*n*; in fairytales, 9i
> 405, 435; and hero, 5 538&*n*,
> 547;
> of Hermes/*avis Hermetis*, in al-
> chemy, 12 *fig.* 267; 13 250; 14
> 6, 248, 727; chick of Hermes,
> Mercurius as, 14 637; origin
> and meaning of, 14 250; point
> (chick) in egg-yolk as, 9ii 345;
> 13 188; 14 4 1;
>> INSTANCES: dove, 12 *fig.* 178;
>> goose, 9i 686; 12 457*n*, *fig.* 198;
>> 14 727*n*; ibis, 14 250; peacock,
>> 14 391; pelican, 12 457*n*; ra-
>> ven, 14 727; stork, 12 457*n*;
>> swan/*cygnus Hermetis*, 12 *fig.*
>> 198;
> as Holy Ghost, symbol of, 6 458
> (*see also* dove *s.v.*);
> as ideal, symbol of, 6 458;
> language of, 5 624*n*;
> in mandalas/pictures, 9i 3 2 1,
> 572, 597, 604, 660; 13 3 2 1,

338, 343, pl. A4, *figs.* 13, 16,
22, 25, 28, 30, 32;
> Mercurius as, *see* Mercurius
> *s.v.*;
> mythical, 13 471–2;
> and opposites, paired, 13 462;
> 14 3, 483*n*; 16 459;
> scarlet (*Chu-niao*), 14 248&*n*,
> 401*n*;
> as self, symbols of, 9ii 356;
> and snake, 14 483*n*;
> soul-/as soul-images, 5 3 15&*n*,
> 547; 8 586; in underworld, 5
> 3 15*n*, 369*n*;
> as spirits, 5 538; 9i 586; 13 3 2 1;
> 14 3;
> as spiritualization, 12 *fig.* 2 2;
> as sun's ascent, 5 538;
> tail of, 5 367*n*;
> as thought(s), symbol of, 6 458;
> 12 305; 13 3 2 1, 338;
> and tree, 13 4 14–15;
> on tree of contemplation, 13
> 4 14;
> two fighting, 14 3; 16 459;
> two, flying and plucked/winged
> and wingless, 14 3, 180&*nn*;
> white, 9ii 356;
> as wishful thinking, 5 367*n*;
> *see also* chicken; cock; cockatoo;
> crane; dove; eagle; falcon;
> fowl; golden plover; goose;
> griffin; hawk/sea hawk; hen;
> hoopoe; ibis; kingfisher; mag-
> pie; night-heron; owl; peacock/
> hen; phoenix; raven; stork;
> swallow; swan; vulture; weaver-
> bird; woodpecker

blindworm, 7 150

boa-constrictor, *see* serpent *s.v.*

boar, 12 526*n*

bull(s)/bullock(s), 6 350; 9i 323,
588*n*; 11 177; 12 183, 457*n*, 533;
13 193*n*, 341, 401;
> as anima, 5 662;
> Apis-, 5 148*n*, 351, 579*n*; 14
> 356*n*;
> Behemoth as, 9ii 185;

Christ as, **12** 520–1;
and cows, **6** 340; **12** 180;
-deities, **9i** 551;
and dragon, **5** 596;
in dreams, **7** 45; **10** 30; **16** 340;
in Egyptian ritual, **5** 148; **11**
348n; **14** 350n (see also above
Apis-);
as father, **5** 396;
as fertility symbol, **4** 497; **5**
671; **16** 340 (see also Mithras/
Mithraism s.v.);
in Gilgamesh epos, **18** 237,
238;
one-horned, **9ii** 311; **12** 528;
in Rig-Veda, **5** 322–3;
-sacrifice, **5** 658n, 663–5 (see also
Mithras/Mithraism s.v.);
as self, symbol of, **9ii** 356;
and snake, "father of," **5** 671;
18 1079;
as sun-symbol, **5** 163n, 283n;
Zagreus as, **5** 527;
see also calves; cattle; cow; ox;
and see zodiac, twelve signs of;
Taurus
butterfly, **4** 237, 263;
and caterpillars, **4** 237, 263,
269;
and psyche, **5** 372; **8** 663;
symbol of self, **9i** 315;
see also moth
calf, **14** 407n
calves, two-headed, **10** 608; see also
cattle
camel, **12** 535; **14** 407n
caput corvi, see raven/crow s.v.
cat(s), **7** 8/417; **9ii** 57; **12** 494; **13** fig.
32;
carrying of, **3** 207;
in dreams, **2** 825–7; **4** 181, 182,
189;
and earthquakes, **10** 636;
Egyptian sculpture of, **18** 325,
326;
as Kore-/mother-figure, **9i** 311;
tomcat, **11** 362;
Tum as, **5** 425

caterpillar(s), **4** 237, 263, 269; **10**
636
catfish, **18** 67n
cattle: bewitchment of, **8** 571;
goddess of, **5** 662;
of Laodonia, **5** 212;
origin of, **5** 664;
sickness of, and fire-making
rite, **5** 212;
see also bull; calves; cow; ox
cauda pavonis, see peacock
centaurs, **5** 422&n;
origin, **5** 460n
cervus/servus fugitivus, see deer/stag
chamaeleon, **14** 182, 183
chicken/chick, see hen
ch'i-lin, see unicorn s.v. China
chimera, **5** 265; **13** 176n
cock(s), **12** 494; **13** 148; **14** 24;
and Aion, **5** 425;
and Cautopates, **5** 299;
in dream, **8** 945;
and hen, **12** fig. 167; **13** 278; **16**
353&n;
as lust, in World Wheel, **9i** 644;
12 123;
and Peter, **5** 289;
and Phrygian god Men, **5** 299,
pl. XXIa;
plucked while living, **11** 361;
13 139n, 441;
as sun animal, **5** 299n;
as time symbol, **5** 425
cockatoo, anthropological symbol,
13 253
cockchafer, **12** 168
cockroach, **18** 1589
corvus, see raven/etc.
cow, **6** 351–2; **9i** 414; **14** 86;
burial in, for rebirth, **5** 682n; **9i**
231;
in dream, **18** 1291;
heavenly, **5** 351, 360, 408n,
423n, 454, pl. XXXb, fig. 25;
as mother, **5** 263, 358, 558, pl.
La; archetype, **9i** 156;
see also bull; calves; cattle
coyote, **7** 154n;

coyote (*cont.*):
    as trickster-figure, **9i** 473
crab, **9i** *fig.* 3;
    and Cancer, zodiacal sign, **9i**
    604–5;
    and crayfish, **9i** 604;
    in patient's dream, **5** 365; **7**
    123–40, 144; **18** 170, 180, 182,
    190, 192, 195, 196, 199, 201;
    represents abdomen, **18** 194;
    symbol: of contents of uncon-
    scious, **7** 158, 162–3; of self, **9i**
    315
cranes, **8** 850*n*
crayfish, **9i** 604
crocodile(s), **5** 147*n*; **6** 947; **8** 941;
    9i 270, 486*n*, 604*n*; **9ii** 385; **10**
    106, 115, 117, 129, 939; **11** 599;
    13 105*n*;
    as Kore/mother-figure, **9i** 311;
    as opposites, **13** 315, *fig.* 10
crow, *see* raven
cygnus Hermetis, see swan
cynocephalus, see baboon
deer/stag, **12** 544, 548, *fig.* 246; **13**
    248;
    antlers, **4** 665;
    as Christ, **8** 559&*n*;
    as lapis (*cervus fugitivus*), **14**
    188*n*;
    as Luna, **14** 24;
    as Mercurius, **8** 559*n*; **9ii** 234;
    (*cervus fugitivus*), **12** 84, 187,
    518; **13** 218, 259; **16** 478;
    as soul and spirit (with un-
    icorn), *see* unicorn *s.v.* stag
dog(s)/bitch/*canis*, **4** 235; **5** 217,
    354; **13** 90, 319; **14** 172, 506*n*; **16**
    496;
    TITLE: "The Dog," **14** 174–88;
    Armenian bitch, Luna as, **14** 24,
    172*n*, 174–5; **16** 458;
    begetting of, **13** 97*n*;
    black, and mandrake, **13** 410;
    canicula, **5** 355; **14** 181;
    Coetanean/*coetaneum*, **14** 174;
    16 353&*n*, 458;
    Corascene, **14** 27, 172*n*, 174,

182; **16** 353*n*, 458*n*;
Gabricus as, **13** 125;
in Gnosticism, as Logos, **14**
    174*n*;
and Hecate, attributes of, **5**
    355, 577; **14** 21*n*, 24;
Indian, **14** 174*n*;
in Khidr legend, **9i** 242*n*;
as lapis, **14** 177*n*;
-like woman, significance of, **13**
    278;
lion and, **14** 407;
as Logos, **13** 278*n*; **14** 174*n*,
    176;
Mephistopheles as, *see* Goethe:
    Faust: Characters *s.v.* Mephis-
    topheles
miraculous, in fairytale, **9i**
    404*n*;
in Mithraic sacrifice, **5** 354;
and moon, **14** 183;
moon as bitch, **14** 24, 174, 181
    (*see also above* Armenian bitch);
proverbial, **7** 324, 497;
psychic processes in, **8** 364;
puppy of celestial hue (*filius
    canis coelici coloris*), **13** 278*n*; **14**
    174–7;
rabid, **14** 154, 182–3;
-sacrifices, **5** 577;
-star, **5** 354;
talking, "Clever Hans," **8** 364*n*;
    18 893&*n*;
three/triad of conscious, in
    mandala, **9i** 693;
and underworld, **5** 577;
and wolf, fighting, **14** 3;
wolf-, Mercurius as, **9ii** 234
dolphin(s), **9i** 298, 327, 328; **13**
    334;
    and womb, **5** 369*n*
donkey, *see* ass
dove(s), **5** 367*n*; **7** 395; **9ii** 178*n*; **11**
    276, 431*n*; **13** 459; **14** 73*n*; **16**
    451&*n*, 454, *fig.* 3;
    as *avis Hermetis,* **12** *fig.* 178;
    Christ as, **14** 205&*n*;
    of Diana, **14** 73*n*, 182, 185&*n*,

187, 408&*n*, 410;
and Holy Ghost/Paraclete,
symbol of, **5** 150, 198, 492; **6**
458; **8** 319, 336; **9i** 108; **11**
486; **12** 500, *fig.* 166; **13** 119;
14 73*n*, 205, 352; **16** 410, 416,
455, *fig.* 4;
as Mary, **9i** 93; **14** 73*n*, 205&*n*;
as Mercurius, **12** 518&*n*, *fig.*
134; **16** 453;
Noah's, **14** 205*n*, 625; **16** 381,
410;
sacred to Church, **18** 222;
Sophia/Sapientia as, **8** 336; **9i**
93; **9ii** 307; **11** 646; **14** 205;
as symbol of female elements,
14 81;
white, **9ii** 215; **11** 150, 160*n*; **12**
443, 500; **13** 123*n*; **14** 81
dragon (s), **7** 129; **8** 558; **9i** 282; **12**
173, 336, 404, 454, 460, 547, *figs.*
46, 47, 73, 118, 187, 189, 196,
199; **14** 15, 85, 86, 147, 473, 506*n*,
546;
in Acts of Thomas, **9ii** 307;
in alchemical process, **9i** 686;
as anima, **9i** 362;
as *anima mundi*, **9i** 707;
in Apocalypse, **5** 314, *fig.* 22;
9ii 22, 163; **11** 710, 711, 713;
13 290; **14** 264, 416;
assault by, **5** *fig.* 35;
Babylonian, **14** 140, 408, 420;
blood of, **14** 415;
bull and, **5** 596;
burning, **13** 444;
castle, **13** 33;
and cave, legends of, **5** 567*n*,
572–4; **18** 258, 263, 270;
Chinese, **9ii** 385; **10** 939; **11**
931; and P'an Ku, **14** 573; and
"River Map" in *I Ching*, **9i** 642;
of Tao, **9i** 40;
as Christ and Antichrist, **5** 576;
13 416; **14** 141, 483;
chthonic, **9i** 270, 707; **9ii** 385;
13 417;
constellation of, **8** 394; **14** 176;

crowned, **14** 472;
as devil, **11** 713; **14** 235, 238;
dismemberment of, **11** 357,
403; **13** 87; **14** 15, 155, 238,
404, 493;
as divine water, **13** 109*n*;
in dreams, **9i** 349, 351, 362;
earth-, **14** 241, 244;
egg synonym for, **13** 109;
in fairytales, **9i** 417;
as *filius macrocosmi*, **14** 141;
fire-spitting, **13** 398, 426; **14**
30, 632;
four-headed, **12** *fig.* 142C.;
in Gnosticism, **14** 627;
green/*draco viridis*, **13** 319;
as guardians (of treasure), **5**
395; **7** 261/477; **9i** 267; **13** 314;
14 85;
head/*caput dragonis* and tail of,
9ii 158; **13** 105*n*, 381*n*, 416; **14**
140–2, 408, 493*n*;
and hero myth/conflict, **4** 494,
738; **5** 569, 575, pl. XVIII; **6**
445&*n*, 448, 790; **8** 415, 555,
718; **12** 437; **13** 118, 319, *fig.*
14; **14** 301, 756; **18** 195, 233,
234, 249, 530, 548; identity of
hero and dragon, **5** 580; **18**
195; as psychologem, **5** 580;
of Hesperides, **5** 577;
and incest taboo, **5** 395; **14**
188;
killing of, **11** 351; **13** 109*n*,
426; **14** 168–9, 188;
and lion, **14** 404;
and maiden, **5** 671;
many-eyed, Pantophthalmus,
13 114, 267;
mercurial fire in belly of, **13**
257;
Mercurius as, **9i** 553&*n*, 556,
689; **11** 420; **12** 84, 209, 404,
427, 518, 530, 548, *figs.* 38, 54;
13 168*n*, 267;
mother-, *see* mother *s.v.*;
motif, **14** 264; **18** 80, 191, 195,
196;

dragon (*cont.*):

of neurosis, **7** 48;

"night sea journey" in, **8** 68–9, 326 (*see also* whale/whale-dragon);

nigredo as, **14** 733;

old, **13** 267; **14** 548;

one-horned, **12** 518;

poisonous, **13** 267, 426; **14** 172;

positive significance of, **9ii** 385; **10** 939;

as *prima materia,* **9ii** 240; **12** 26, 425, 427, 530, *figs.* 142 C&F, 267; sacrifice of, in alchemy, **5** 646n; **11** 349, 403;

salt as, **14** 244, 338;

of the sea, **14** 301;

as self/symbol of self, **9i** 315; **14** 296;

self-consuming/devouring/tail-eating, **5** pl. LIX*a*; **11** 351, 420; **12** *figs.* 46, 47, 142Q; **13** 105, 115, 168n, 322; **14** 143, 241, 244 (*see also* uroboros);

self-creating and self-destroying, **12** 26, 460; **13** 115; **14** 143;

as snake, synonym/link, **9ii** 369n, 385; **18** 258, 533;

Sol as, **14** 168–9;

and springs/waters, **5** 503n; **8** 335;

stone of, **9ii** 213, 214;

sulphur as, **14** 135&n;

and sun, fight, **5** 425;

teeth, sowing of, **14** 85–6;

Tiamat, Babylonian mother-dragon, *see* Tiamat;

and tree, **13** 314, 417, 461;

two, **9ii** 181n; **13** 267, 314, 315; **14** 307;

as the unconscious, **5** 580; **13** 118, 314, *fig.* 9; **14** 277;

whale-, *see* whale-dragon;

winged/wingless, **9i** 556; **9ii** 185; **13** 267; **14** 3, 140, 296; **16** 353, 459, 494;

and woman, **5** 315&n, 574n;

—, buried together, **14** 15, 65, 293, 657n, 669; *coniugium*/ embrace, **14** 30, 168, 293, 669

eagle(s), **9i** 588n; **12** 173, 336, 518, *figs.* 97, 142G,K, 200, 229; **13** 228, 361, 398, 418, 459; **14** 147, 172, 182, 404, 453n;

in alchemical symbolism, **5** 235n;

as allegory of Christ, **9ii** 127; **14** 147;

arrow-shooting, nine, **14** 23n, 416;

black, **11** 111n; **12** 304;

brazen, **13** 124; **14** 317n;

double, **12** *figs.* 20, 98, 266;

and dragon, in alchemical process, **9i** 686;

in dreams/visual impressions, **12** 304–6; **13** 466–75, 479;

Elijah as, **10** 622n;

in II Esdras vision, **9ii** 185; **12** 57n;

in Ezekiel's vision, **13** 361;

Mercurius as, **12** 84, 518; **13** 246; **14** 637;

self-devouring, **14** 172n;

silver, **12** *fig.* 142 G, b;

soul as, **9ii** 118&n; **12** 306;

as spirit, **14** 453n;

as sun, **5** 235n, 633; **14** 175;

in tetramorph, **14** 573n;

and toad, as opposites, **14** 2, 172;

and vulture/crow, **12** 220n, 305;

white, **12** *fig.* 142b;

of Zarathustra, **14** 483n

eel, **18** 1228

elephant, **4** 337; **12** 117, 526n, 536; in Buddha myth, **5** 490n, 492; as symbol of self, **9i** 315; **9ii** 356; white, **16** 551, 560

elk, and trickster figure, **9i** 473

falcon: Indra as, **5** 659; Ra as, **9i** 661

fish(es), **7** 129, **9i** 254; **9ii** 385; **12** 171, 433; **13** 90, *fig.* 32; **14** 147;

fish (*cont.*):
-king, Mishe-Nahma, **5** 537;
in Lambspringk, **9ii** 224, 234;
14 3;
and Leviathan, **9ii** 183–5;
loss of, in Koran/Khidr legend,
5 282, 291; **9i** 244–7; **9ii** 173;
as love, sacred and profane, **9ii**
198–9;
magnetism of, **9ii** 239;
of Manu, **5** 290*n*; **9ii** 127, 176;
12 533;
Matsya (Hindu), **9ii** 272;
meals, pagan, **9ii** 186; **13** *fig.*
B1; of "Thracian riders," **9ii**
127 (*see also above* Christ *s.v.*
meals);
Messianic significance of, **9ii**
178, 224;
monk as, **9ii** 175;
as mother: evil symbol of, **9i**
157; Terrible Mother, **5** 369;
Nun as, **5** 290*n*; **9i** 244; **9ii** 173,
186;
and Oannes, *see* Oannes;
and opposites, in God, **9ii**
183–5;
oxyrhynchus, **9ii** 187&*n*;
in patients' mandalas, **9i** 669–
73; **13** 334;
Platonic month of, **9ii** (*p*ix),
231;
pot-fish, **13** 193*n*;
pregnancy by swallowing, **17**
44;
and psychopompos, symbol of,
9ii 225;
pulmo marinus, **9ii** 197;
ray, **10** 713;
as redeemer-figure, **9ii** 291; **16**
254;
as renewal and rebirth, symbol
of, **5** 290;
"round," **9i** 246; **9ii** 195–9,
213–14, 217–19, 223; **11** 92&*n*;
12 433*n*; **13** 101&*n*;
as ruling power, **9ii** 229, 231;
as saviour, symbol of, **9i** 38;

as self, symbol of, **9ii** 122, 225,
286, 296, 356;
as sepulchral symbol, **9ii** 178;
and serpent/snake, **9i** 671; **9ii**
291;
seven, on earthenware lamp,
12 *fig.* 202;
as Son, symbol of, **11** 257;
as soul-symbol, **9ii** 187;
southern, **9ii** 173*n*, 174;
starfish, **9ii** 197–9, 239*n*;
star of the sea/*stella marina*/*stella
maris*, **9ii** 210;
symbols, **8** 816, 827; **9i** 247*n*;
9ii (*p*ix), 127;
and synchronicity, *see above*
April;
Tobit and, **9ii** 174;
and transformation, **9i** 248;
two, **9ii** 172, 173, 177, 225,
228–9; **11** 257, (*p*357); as
mother and son, **9ii** 177;
as unborn child, **5** 290;
as unconscious content(s), **5**
290*n*; **8** 827; **9i** 245, 248; **13**
241;
Vishnu as, **5** 449, pl. XLVII; **9ii**
176; **12** 533, *fig.* 255;
voracious, **5** 369; **9ii** 174, 187;
see also catfish; crayfish; dolphin; herring; jellyfish
fowl, **11** 361
fox, as Mercurius, **13** 241*n*
frog(s), **7** 8/417
gazelle, horn of, **12** 534
gibbon, **12** 164, 175, 181;
goat, **9i** 597, 603; **12** 105; **16** 340;
black, blood of, **14** 77–8;
as evil, image of, **6** 389;
in fairytale, **9i** 413;
-fish, **5** 290;
one-footed, **14** 735;
as sexual symbol, **14** 735*n*;
golden plover, **5** 439–40
goose, **12** 561;
of Hermes/*anser Hermetis* (*avis
Hermetis*), **9i** 686; **12** 457*n*, *fig.*
198; **14** 727*n*;

Mercurius as, **14** 637;
tree-, **15** 25
grasshopper, **13** *fig.* 25
griffin, **9i** 407*n*; **12** *fig.* 246; **13**
(*p*63*n*); **14** 407*n*
hamsa, see swan *s.v.*
hare: as Mercurius, **13** 241*n*;
as mother archetype, **9i** 156;
motif, in mandala, **9i** 694, *fig.*
39;
as redeemer-figure, **8** 229; **10**
679; **16** 254;
as self, symbol of, **10** 779
hawk, **13** 360;
and trickster-figure, **9i** 473;
sea-, **9ii** 292*n*, 296
hen/chicken/chick, **10** 636; **12** 83,
512; **14** 147;
chick as bird of Hermes, *see*
bird *s.v.* of Hermes;
chicken, as alchemical symbol,
13 188; **14** 41;
and cock, **12** *fig.* 167; **13** 278;
herring, **5** 367*n*
hoopoe, **11** 362
horse(s), **12** 494, 526*n*, 535, 548, *fig.*
206; **14** 407*n*; **16** 353;
as animal instinct in man, **5**
421; **16** 347;
as archetype, **16** 347–8;
belly of, in alchemy, **14** 360;
black: Apaosha, **5** 395; of
death, **16** 347; in dreams, *see
below s.v.;*
changing into, **5** 421*n*;
as death/herald of death, **5**
427–8; **16** 347;
and devil, **5** 421;
in dreams, **3** 123–9; **4** 218–21,
300, 356, 361; **7** 8, 10/419; **16**
343–7; black, **9i** 71–2, 74, 398;
17 208;
as fire and light symbol, **5** 423;
in Freud's case, **17** 47;
goddess of, **5** 577;
head of, **5** 421*n*;
hero and, **5** 421, 616, 679;
hoof(s) of, *see below* sexual;

human-footed, **5** 421;
as libido-symbol, **5** 421, 658;
as lower part of body, **16** 347;
man-eating, **5** 427*n*;
as mother-symbol, **5** 302, 373,
421, 658; **16** 347–8;
as movement/energy, symbol
of, **5** 302, 658; **16** 347;
in mythology, **5** 421–8; **16** 347;
and nightmares, **5** 370, 421;
Odin's, **13** 461*n*;
one-horned, **12** 518;
and rider, **5** 370, 421, 678;
and *rta,* **6** 349*n*, 353;
-sacrifice, **5** 424, 657–9, 675;
as self, symbol of, **9ii** 356;
as sexual symbol/horse's hoofs
as, **3** 289; **5** 370, 421–2, 638; **16**
340;
snake and, **5** (*p*459);
symbolism, **5** 421–8;
three-legged, **5** 427–8; in
fairytales, **9i** 423–5;
thunder-, **5** 421, 423;
white, **5** 421, 439*n*; **11** 725;
black and, *see* Plato, parables;
witches and, **5** 421*n*;
of Wotan, **10** 373;
see also mare
hyenas, **10** 126
ibex, **12** 183
ibis: and *avis Hermetis,* **14** 250;
and Mercurius, **12** 530; **13** 359
insects, **8** 673, 674, 955;
symbiotic functions of, **18** 540;
and Ufos, **10** 667;
see also bees; beetle; butterfly;
cockchafer; cockroach; grasshopper; rose-chafer; spider;
wasp
invertebrates, **8** 322
jackal, **13** 360
jellyfish/scyphomedusa, **5** 500, 501;
9ii 196, 208, 213, 239*n*;
see also fish(es): "round" *s.v.*
kartazonon, *see* unicorn *s.v.*
kingfisher, **13** *fig.* 32
lamb/Lamb, **6** 312; **8** 229; **9i** 424;

lamb (*cont.*):
  9ii 162; 12 *fig.* 62; 13 *fig.* 22; 15 175; 16 254;
    in Apocalypse/Revelation, 9i 14; 9ii 147*n*, 167; 11 708, 712–13, 715–16; 12 139; marriage of, 5 316–17, 330; 9ii 22, 68, 425; 11 726, 743–4, 748; 13 225, 227; 14 200, 412, 524–5, 528, 664;
    Christ as, 5 659, 667, 668*n*;
    Christian sacrifice of, 5 294; 12 417*n*;
    Church as bride of, 9ii 319;
    of God, 5 41*n*; 10 679; 12 417;
    sacred in early Church, 18 222;
    sacrifice, in fairy tale, 9i 433*n*;
    as symbol of spirit, 11 276
leopard, 9i 352; 13 365;
  -woman, 10 129, 133
Leviathan, 6 444; 9i 553*n*, 673; 9ii 188, 228*n*, 285; 11 599, 681; 12 547, *fig.* 28; 13 334, 450; 14 255, 277, 338, 574, 637; 16 560;
    as animal force, 5 87–9, 173–4, 383–6;
    and Behemoth, *see* Behemoth *s.v.*;
    as devil, 9i 559*n*; 11 250;
    fish and, 9ii 185;
    Jewish, as eucharistic food in Paradise, 9ii 174, 185; 14 338;
    male and female, 9ii 181
lion(s), 9i 267, 588*n*; 13 182&*n*, 228, *figs.* 22, 25; 14 405, 512–13, 573*n*; 16 533; 18 1827;
    "antiquus," 14 405;
    arcane substance as, 13 97*n*; 14 147, 404&*n*;
    as Archangel Michael, 9ii 128;
    in astrology, 5 600*n*; 14 493*n* (*see also* zodiac, twelve signs of: Leo);
    blood of, *see* blood *s.v.*
    as Christ, symbol of, 12 547; 13 275&*n*; 14 147, 429, 454;
    as Christ and devil/Satan, 9ii

127; 10 846 (*see also below* devil);
corruption of, 14 21;
in Daniel's vision, 13 365;
deus leontocephalus (Aion), 5 163*n*, 425, pl. XLIV;
devil as, 5 525; 12 84, 173, 277; 13 246; 14 408, 467 (*see also above* as Christ and devil);
and dog, 14 407;
and dragon, 14 404, 493;
in dreams, 7 45;
dung of, 14 403*n*;
erotic aspect of, 14 408, 416, 426;
in II Esdras, 9ii 185;
and evangelists, four, 8 559*n*;
as evil passions/violence, 14 140, 188, 404;
in Ezekiel's vision, 13 361;
in fairytales, 9i 405, 423, 424;
fighting, 14 405, 415, 506*n*;
in Gnosticism, 13 275;
golden, 12 *fig.* 142a;
green, in alchemy, 9i 246*n*; 12 491&*n*, 498, 519, *figs.* 142E, 169; 13 275; 14 404–5, 415*n*, 416, 419, 453; 16 453, 454*n*;
blood of, *see* blood *s.v.*; and red, 13 267, 275; 14 405&*n*, 473;
as heat of midsummer, 5 600*n*, 671*n*;
and heroes, 5 600*n*;
-hunt, of Marchos, 14 386, 409, 412*n*;
of Judah, tribe of/Messiah as, 5 524; 9ii 167; 13 275, 390*n*;
King and/Rex and Leo, 14 405, 416, 467;
as latent affects, 12 277;
as libido symbol, 18 1078;
and lioness, winged and wingless, 14 3, 404, 408;
and Luna, 14 24;
in mandalas, 9i 660;
man-faced, 9i 660;
Mercurius as, *see* Mercurius *s.v.*;

and hero, **5** 540, 594, 596, 598, 615–16, 662*n*, 671, 677, (*p* 459); **8** 555; **14** 481; **17** 298, 321; eyes of, *see above* eyes;

Hopi Indians and, **13** 270;

horned, **9i** 623; **18** 525, 533 (*see also above* four-horned);

of Ignatius Loyola, *see* Ignatius Loyola;

in initiation ceremonies, **5** 530; **12** 184;

as instinct, **5** 615; **9ii** 370, 385;

as instrument of regeneration, **5** 677;

as instrument of sacrifice, **5** 676;

Isis and, **5** 351, 374, 451–3, pl. LIII;

ithyphallic, **9i** 556, 561;

kiss of, **5** 581*n*, 584;

as Kore, **9i** 311;

Kundalini, **5** 676; **12** 184, 246; **16** 380, 562;

as libido symbol, **5** 146, 149; **18** 1078;

Lilith as, **13** 460;

lion and, *see* lion *s.v.*;

as Logos, **9ii** 293, 367;

as magnetic agent, **9ii** 293;

mamba, **10** 126;

Melusina as, **13** 218, 288, 416;

Mercurius and, *see* Mercurius *s.v.* snake;

Midgard, **5** 681*n*;

and moon, **14** 216, 437; as orbit of moon, **5** 163*n*, *fig.* 10;

of Moses, **9i** 533&*n*; **11** 349; **12** *figs.* 217, 238; **13** 137; **14** 251;

as mother, attribute/numen of, **5** 452, 541;

mystery, **5** 584, pl. LXI*a*;

in mythology, **5** 681*n*;

Naassene/Naas, **9i** 560; **9ii** 311, 365, 367; **12** 527; **13** 420&*n*, 427, 448; **14** 41*n*;

naked, **13** 400;

Negroes and, *see below* primitives;

in Nietzsche, *Zarathustra:* in shepherd vision, **5** 585–6; **12** 184, 201; **14** 483*n*; Zarathustra bitten by, **14** 483*n*;

Nous as, **9i** 554; **9ii** 291, 293, 366, 367; **11** 276, 380, 619; **13** 448; **14** 266;

as numina/souls/spirits of dead, **5** 578; **13** 416–17; **14** 75&*n*, 78, 85*n*, 481;

Ophitic, **5** 584, 593; **9i** 74; **9ii** 294; **12** 184;

and opposites: pair of, **9ii** 181*n*; **13** 462; tension between, **9ii** 390&*n*;

in paradise/paradisal, **5** 8, 155, *fig.* 8; **9i** 74, 554, 560; **9ii** 371; **10** 288; **11** 291, 438, 458*n*, 619; **13** 110, 180, 288, 399, 400; **14** 104, 141, 437; **18** 1555, 1593, 1610, 1631;

-path, **16** 381;

in Peratic doctrine, **9ii** 290–1;

phallic significance of, *see below* sexual;

in pictures and mandalas, **9i** 545, 560–1, 576, 604, 611, 613, 646, 648, 660, 667–8, 671, 685, 705; **11** 136; **12** 217; **13** 331; **16** 380, 533, *fig.* 10; **18** 412;

-pit, as "poor-box," **5** 577;

poisonous, **5** 351, 374, 459&*n*, 540, 596; **13** 170; **14** 58, 607;

"Power," **16** 561;

with Priapus, *see above* -bite *s.v.* phallus;

as *prima materia*, **14** 261;

primitives/Negroes and "my snake," **7** 323, 374; **9ii** 293; **17** 300; **18** 275;

puff-adder, **10** 126;

python at Delphi/in Greek myth, **5** 316*n*, 396, 577; **9ii** 163; **13** 263; **17** 321; **18** 258;

in quaternios: Anthropos, **9ii** 369; Paradise, **9ii** 386; Shadow, **9ii** 369–71, 385;

quicksilver as, **13** 105*n*;

serpent (*cont.*):
    and Ra's night sea journey, **5**
    362; **14** 482*n*;
    rattlesnake, **5** 677; **7** 150; **8**
    609;
    redemptive/as Redeemer, **9i**
    74, 374; **9ii** 291; **16** 254;
    "rejoicing in itself," **14** 718;
    as renewal, symbol of, **5** 410,
    592; **11** 348; **12** 184;
    ritual, **16** 533*n*;
    sacred, **5** 577&*n*
    sacrifice, **5** pl. LVII*b*; **13** 449;
    as Saviour, **9i** 74; **13** 137;
    sea-, **8** 335;
    as self, symbol of, **9i** 315; **9ii**
    356;
    as sexual/phallic symbol, **3**
    284–5; **5** 8, 584, 585, pls. LXI*b*,
    LXIV; **8** 332;
    as shadow, personification of,
    9i 567; **9ii** 390*n*;
    shakti-as, **18** 263;
    and shepherd, *see above*
    Nietzsche;
    sign:Ω, **13** 263;
    Son as, **9ii** 293;
    as spinal cord, *see above* cere-
    brospinal system;
    as spiral rotation, **13** 349*n*;
    as spirit symbol, **11** 276; **13** 219
    (*see also above* numina);
    spirituality of, **9ii** 369; **13** 448;
    stag swallowing, **8** 559*n*; **14**
    188*n*;
    and stone/lapis, **9ii** 386–7; **13**
    182*n*; in head of snake, **13**
    381*n*;
    as *summa summarum*, **14** 473;
    as sun/sun-disc, **5** 146, 149;
    swallowing, **5** 549*n*;
    symbolism, **12** 184;
    tail of: Melusina with, **13** 218;
    virgin with, **14** 23&*n*;
    three in chalice, as Trinity, **16**
    533, *fig.* 10;
    three-headed, **16** 533;

    train's movement and, **18** 169,
    181;
    trampler of, **16** 517;
    as transformative substance/
    symbol of transformation; **5**
    676; **12** 173, 184, *fig.* 70;
    and treasure/as guardian of
    hoard, **5** 541, 577, 578; **8** 555;
    9ii 370; **13** 314;
    and tree, **13** 416, 461, *fig.* 12;
    14 483*n*; chthonic numen of,
    13 416, 417; **14** 85*n*; in
    paradise, **13** 247, 288, 460 (*see
    also above* paradise); in philo-
    sophical tree, **13** 288; union of,
    13 316, 317, *fig.* 12;
    two fighting, **9ii** 181; **14** 408;
    as the unconscious, **5** 458, 580,
    586–7, 679; **9i** 282, 651; **9ii**
    370, 390; **12** 203; **13** 448; col-
    lective, **9ii** 370;
    as unconsciousness, **13** 118,
    449;
    of underworld, **5** 577;
    Uraeus (Egyptian), **5** 146, 149;
    viper, **9ii** 127; **11** 361;
    in visions/visual impressions, **7**
    6/415; **9i** 330–1 (*see also above*
    Nietzsche);
    in the wilderness, **13** 137;
    winged, **14** 352; **16** 380; and
    wingless, in alchemy, **9ii** 181;
    as winter, symbol of, **18** 266;
    wisdom of, **7** 395; **9ii** 369, 370,
    385; **13** 448; **14** 347;
    and witches, **14** 77&*n*, 78;
    world-, **9i** 559*n*;
    worship, **16** 533*n*;
    and zodiac, **5** 163*n*; **8** 394;
    see also basilisk
shark, **10** 712
sheep, **12** 535, *fig.* 17;
    Christian symbol of, **12** 72*n*,
    417*n*;
    land of, **9ii** 32; **12** 71–3;
    in mandala, **9i** 660;
    sacrifice of, **9i** 329; **10** 375;

symbol of good, **6** 389;
see also lamb; ram
snail: shell of, as proof of God's
existence, **18** 1360;
as symbol of self, **9ii** 356
spider(s), **12** 325, *fig.* 108;
black, in dream, **13** 449;
flying, Ufo as, **10** 666–8, 679;
as symbol of self, **9i** 315; **9ii**
356
squirrel, **13** 461*n*
stag, *see* deer
starfish, *see* fish(es) *s.v.*
steeds, in mythology, **5** 421
stork(s), **4** 481, 501, 506–7;
Adebar (Teutonic), bringer of
souls, **13** 417;
as Anthropos, **13** 417;
as *avis Hermetis*, **12** 457*n*;
as bringers of children, **4** 479,
498; **17** 6, 11, 18, 22, 26, 61;
as Christ symbol, **13** 417;
as "circle of moon," **14** 157,
167, 498*n*;
and tree, **13** 343*n*, 415–17, 459
sucking-fish, *see* fish *s.v. echeneis*
sun-beetle, *see* beetle *s.v.*
swallow, **5** 367*n*;
swan, **9i** 560, 580*n*; **9ii** 134; **12** *figs.*
142T, 200; **13** *fig.* 32; **16** 515;
anser/cygnus Hermetis, **12** *fig.*
198;
hamsa, **12** 446*n*;
maiden myth, **5** 332*n*, 392*n*,
494*n*;
Mercurius as, **14** 637;
singing, **5** 235*n*, 538;
as sun, **5** 235*n*
tapeworm, as image of Joyce's style,
15 166, 169, 194
tiger(s), **14** 216, 403*n*;
as anima, **9i** 358;
in dreams, **7** 45;
winged, **13** 460
toad(s), **7** 37, 437; **12** 518*n*; **14** 30,
172;
and eagle, alchemical, as oppo-

sites, **14** 2, 172;
Nietzsche and, *see* Nietzsche *s.v.*
tortoise, **9i** 604*n*; **12** 203, 548, *figs.*
75–6; **13** 132, *fig.* 25; **14** 573;
as avatar of Vishnu, **9ii** 272;
as symbol of self, **9ii** 356
unicorn(s), **12** 491*n*, 498*n*, 518–54,
figs. 239, 243, 248, 249, 250, 252;
in alchemical writing, **12** 518–
19;
in China (*ch'i-lin*), **12** 548–9,
figs. 259, 260; **14** 573; androgyny of, **12** 548;
Christ as, **12** 519–21, 523–4,
547;
as *complexio oppositorum*, **12** 526;
as creation of Eve, **12** *fig.* 248;
and cross, **12** 521, 523*n*, 549;
and cup, **12** 526*n*, 550–3;
as demon, **12** 525, *fig.* 249;
as ecclesiastical symbol, **12**
250–6;
in Gnosticism, **12** 527–9, 554;
God of Old Testament as, **11**
259, 408; **12** 522;
as Holy Ghost, **5** 492; **12** 519,
fig. 261;
horn of, **12** 518, 520–1&*nn*,
526*n*, 532–3; as alexipharmic,
12 522*n*, 526*n*, 529, 549; **14**
608*n*; as symbol of cross, **12**
521, 523*n*, 549; as uniting
symbol, **12** 553;
"kartazonon," **12** 526*n*;
lion and, *see* lion *s.v.*;
lunar, **12** *fig.* 262;
and Mary, *see* Mary *s.v.*;
Mercurius as, *see* Mercurius *s.v.*;
monoceros/monodon/sea-uni-
corn, **11** 259; **12** 524, *fig.* 254;
as *monstrum*, **12** 526, 547;
in Persia, **12** 535–9;
as power of evil, **12** 520, 525–6;
re'em, in Jewish tradition, **12**
540, 545–6;
and his reflection, **12** *fig.* 265;
sea-, *see above* monoceros;

unicorn (*cont.*):
    and stag, as symbol of soul and
    spirit, **9ii** 234; **12** 518, *fig.* 240;
    14 3;
    and tree of life, **12** 518, *fig.*
    264;
    in Vedas, **12** 532–4;
    and virgin, **12** 498*n*, 519,
    522&*n*, 524, 534, *figs.* 241–2,
    245, 247; **14** 375;
    white, **12** 518;
    wild, **12** *fig.* 249
uroboros/tail-eater, **8** 394, 416; **9i**
    537; **9ii** 297, 389, 391, 407, 410,
    418; **11** 109*n*, 161*n*, 351*n*, 353,
    359, 420; **12** 165, 404, 460, 496,
    figs. 7, 46–7, 108, 147, 253; **13**
    105, 111, 137, 168*n*, 272, *fig.* 17;
    14 41, 86, 123*n*, 139*n*, 140, 296,
    402, 404, 423–4, 429, 483*n*; **16**
    454, 527; **18** 1235;
    Agathodaimon as, **14** 6*n*;
    alchemical, and egg, **13** 109*n*;
    as *prima materia*, **12** *fig.* 13;
    and Christ, analogy, **14** 423;
    and Leviathan, **14** 637;
    in mandala symbolism, **9i** 646,
    690;
    Mercurius as, *see* Mercurius
    s.v.;
    -motif, in *Faust,* **13** 120;
    Nous as, **12** 447;
    as opus, symbol of, **12** 404;
    salt as, **14** 338;
    as spirit, **12** 447
vampire, **7** 370
vertebrates: aquatic, **8** 323;
    higher, **8** 605; as symbols of af-
    fects, **9i** 282*n*;
    lower, as symbols of collective
    psychic substratum, **9i** 282;
    sympathetic system in, **8** 957
viper, *see* serpent *s.v.*
vulture(s), **5** 358; **12** 220&*n*, 305,
    536; **16** 494*n*;
    Egyptian legend of, **5** 150*n*, 335;
    and Leonardo da Vinci, **9i** 95,
    100;

Mercurius as, **14** 637;
    mother as, **5** 354; **9i** 95
wasp(s), **10** 636; **18** 1228
weaver-bird, **8** 435; **18** 1260, 1271
whale/whale-dragon, **5** 369; **9ii**
    181; **13** 180, 398; **18** 80;
    hero and, **5** 374, 538; **6** 444–5;
    12 440; **14** 277; **16** 455;
    Jonah and, **12** figs. 170, 172,
    174, 176, 177;
    myths of, **5** 374*n*; **14** 482*n*;
    night sea journey in, **5** 310–11,
    526*n*; **9ii** 173; **12** *figs.* 170, 172;
    14 262;
    sperm, **13** 193*n*;
    as symbol: of unconscious, **6**
    458; **12** *fig.* 222; **14** 277; of
    womb, **16** 560
wolf/wolves, **13** 176&*n*; **14** 3, 506*n*;
    16 353*n*;
    in child's dream, **4** 475, 478,
    480–2;
    as Mercurius, **9ii** 234; **13** 359;
    as *prima materia*, **12** 440*n*, *fig.*
    175;
    in fairytales, **4** 476; **9i** 421, 423,
    426;
    Fenris-, **5** 681*n*, *fig.* 33;
    in legend/myth, **5** 681*n*, pl. II;
    signifying devil, and Saint
    Paul, **14** 147;
    as symbol of unconsciousness,
    14 172, 277, 511;
    were-, **7** 150; **9i** 405; **14** 336*n*
woodpecker, **5** 547
worm(s), **12** 215, 365; **13** 182&*n*; **14**
    482, 483*n*, 484, 493&*n*;
    in child's dream, **5** 365;
    palolo-, (wawo) time-orienta-
    tion of, **8** 842&*n*;
    phoenix and, **9i** 685; **14** 472,
    474, 476, 483;
    poisonous, in Egyptian mythol-
    ogy, **5** 451, 567; **18** 230;
    as theriomorphic symbol of
    self, **9i** 315
yucca moth, **8** 268, 277; **10** 547; **18**
    1260

74

* *

animality, primordial, **12** 29, 242
animate stone, *see* stone, alchemical *s.v.*
animation: of body, **13** 316;
of environment, **12** 57;
of psychic atmosphere, **12** 57,
59, 61, 118;
suffix of, **11** 389;
of unconscious, **12** 201
animism, **11** 140*n*; **18** 1368;
primitive, **7** 108; **10** 431; **13**
247; **15** 16
animosity, **9i** 175; **9ii** 32, 424; **10**
78; **13** 59;
manifestation of animus/an-
ima, **11** 48
animus (J.'s term), **6** 803*n*, 808–11
(def.); **7** 328, 341, 384, 507; **8**
845; **9i** 53*n*, 63, 296, 309, 444,
525, 545, 559, 561, 585, 592, 706;
10 81–6, 246–7; **12** 9*n*, *fig.* 132;
13 342, 346; **14** 159; **16** 432–3,
441; **17** 338; **18** 150*n*, 187, 1158,
1262;
TITLES: "Anima and Animus,"
7 296–340; "Animus and
Anima," **13** 57–63; "The
Syzygy: Anima and Animus,"
9ii 20–42;
activity of, **7** 341, 370;
and anima, relationship, *see*
anima *s.v.*;
a priori assumptions of, **10** 90;
as archetype, **5** 83*n*, 611; **7** 185;
9i 634; **9ii** 13, 19, 27, 40; **10**
71; of Terrible Mother, **5** 543;
and argument, **9ii** 29; **10** 80;
11 48;
autonomous, **7** 370; **9ii** 40, 53,
422;
as Chinese *hun* soul, **13** 57, 59;
compensating, **7** 328;
danger from, **9i** 606*n*;
definition, **7** 141*n*; **9i** 512; **9ii**
29;
derivation, **9i** 387;
in dreams, **9ii** 39; **11** 48;

and ego, **9ii** 34;
and evil, **9ii** 423;
expressed by dogma, **16** 442;
extraversion of, **7** 328, 336;
-fantasy, **9i** 518*n*;
fear of, **9ii** 62;
feeling quality, **9ii** 53;
-figure, **5** 462, 675; **9i** 326;
mythological, **5** 566*n*;
first formulation, **7** (*p*296*n*);
as function, **7** 336; **9ii** 40; as-
sociative, **7** 336; discriminative,
16 505, 519, 522; mediating
between conscious and unconscious, **9i** 350; **9ii** 40; of relationship to the unconscious, **7**
387;
-hero, **5** 465, 615;
historical element, **10** 89, 91;
-hound, **7** 336;
illusions, **16** 504*n*;
-image, father as first carrier
of, **14** 232;
incubators, **18** 339;
and integration, **9ii** 40;
intellectual, **9ii** 58;
as jealous lover, **7** 334;
localization of, **9i** 518;
as Logos, **9ii** 29, 33, 41; **13** 60;
as mediator, **9ii** 33;
as neologist, **7** 333;
as numen/numinous, **9ii** 425;
old man as, **9i** 417;
opinions, **5** 458; **7** 331, 334; **11**
48; **13** 60; **16** 504, 521;
personification of, **7** 332; of
masculine component of
woman, **5** 267; **11** 48; **13** 339;
14 616; of the unconscious, **8**
945*n*; **9ii** 40; **11** 48;
in place of self, *see* self *s.v.*;
plays up anima, **7** 334;
plurality, **7** 332, 338; **10** 81,
698; **16** 538*n*;
polymorphism, **10** 81;
positive, **9i** 396; and negative,
9ii 33, 425; **11** 48*n*;

75

animus (*cont.*):
    possession, **5** 272; **7** 337; **9i**
    223, 417; **13** 339; **14** 225; **16**
    504;
    prima materia as, **16** 519;
    projection, **7** 333; **9ii** 35, 39,
    57, 381; **16** 442, 521; **17** 338–
    40;
    psychology of, **7** 328;
    as psychopomp, **9ii** 33;
    quicksilver as, **9i** 555;
    recognition of, **9ii** 42, 424;
    -ridden, **9ii** 29;
    and shadow, differentiated, **9ii**
    19;
    "son"-hero, **5** 466;
    and soul-image, **6** 803*n*, 808;
    and spirit, **9i** 439; **9ii** 33;
    -thinking, **10** 80 (*see also above*
    opinions);
    see also anima; hero(es); lover
animus (spirit), **8** 664; **14** 670
ankh/ankhi, **5** 410; **14** 352
Anna, imaginary twin sister, **17** 225,
    227
Anna, J.'s case, *see* Jung: CASES, **17**
    case (1)
Anna O., *see* Breuer *s.v.* case of
    Anna O.
Anne, St., **9i** 93–5
L'Année psychologique, **18** 961*n*
Annunciation: of Christ-figure, **9ii**
    295;
    of the Virgin, **4** 148; **11** 744*n*;
    16 380
Anquetil du Perron, A. H., **6** 193;
    10 175, 176; **14** 735; **15** 87;
    his tr. of Upanishads, *see* Up-
    anishads *s.v.*
Anselm, St., Archbishop of Canter-
    bury, **6** 59–60, 62–3;
    and ontological argument, **6**
    59, 62;
    Proslogion, **6** 59*n*, 62*n*
anser Hermetis, *see* ANIMALS *s.v.* swan
Anshen, Ruth Nanda, **8** 232*n*
answer(s): irrelevant, **1** 164; **3** 179;
    senseless, **1** 236*f*, 278*f*, 320&*n*,

324, 346, 369–84
ant(s), *see* ANIMALS *s.v.*
Antaeus, **5** 259
Antarctic, **10** 603
anteaters, *see* ANIMALS *s.v.*
antelope, *see* ANIMALS *s.v.*
Anthera, *see* Paracelsus *s.v.* ARCANA
Anthonius de Abbatia; *Epistolae*
    duae, **14** 31*n*
Anthony (of Egypt), St., **6** 82&*n*; **11**
    32*n*, 953; **12** 59; **16** 384; *see also*
    Athanasius, St.
Anthony (of Padua), St.;
    "Sermo in Assumptione
    Sanctae Mariae Virginis," **14**
    201*n*;
    Sermones dominicales et in solem-
    nitatibus, **11** 743*n*
Anthos, *see* Paracelsus *s.v.* ARCANA
anthracites, in Böhme's symbolism,
    9i 537;
    and anthrax, **9i** 537*n*, 580*n*
anthrax, *see* anthracites
Anthroparion/ἀνθρωπάριον,
    metal-man, **8** 945*n*; **9i** 268; **13**
    (*pp*60, 62), 121; **14** 304;
    leaden, **9i** 408; **13** (*p*60*n*);
    see also homunculus *s.v.*
anthropoid(s): African, **11** 460;
    pre-Adamic, **11** 576, 618*n*;
    psyche, **5** 506
anthropology, **9i** 318
anthropomorphic: ideas, **11** 223,
    276;
    images of God, **11** 556;
    projections, **11** 375;
    vision, **5** 158*n*
anthropomorphism, **13** 356;
    in antiquity, **5** 24;
    and God-image, **5** 97, 98;
    love as extreme example of, **5**
    97;
    in symbolism of the Mass, **11**
    307;
    tree-, **5** 545
anthropophagy, **6** 43;
    ritual, **11** 339
Anthropophyteia, **10** 177; **16** 66

Anthropos/First/Original/Primordial
Man, **5** 313, 668*n*; **9i** 146, 660,
690; **9ii** 304, 389; **10** 733; **11** 400,
401, 437; **12** 139, 410, 411, 533,
figs. 82, 196; **13** 116*n*, 165–8, 173,
209, 210, 215, 220, 450, 452,
458&*n*; **14** 5, 50, 209, 323, 443,
487, 567, 573; **18** 269;
  Adam as, *see* Adam *s.v.*;
  alchemical, **12** 426, 456–61,
  476; **13** 252; **14** 354, 487,
  490–3, 590, 748;
  androgynous / feminine / hermaphrodite, **9i** 138*n*; **11** 711;
  12 209; **13** 173; **14** 8, 276, 526,
  610; **16** 416, 471, 481;
  as *anima mundi*, **9ii** 308; **11** 711;
  12 *fig*. 117; **13** 173; **14** 323; redemption of, **12** 306; **14** 238;
  as archetype, **9ii** 318; **10** 767;
  11 419; **13** 210; **14** 488, 600,
  748;
  in Cabala, **14** 18;
  Chinese doctrine of, *see chên-
  yên s.v.*;
  Christ and, **9ii** (*p*ix), 69, 304,
  318, 320; **10** 751; **11** 276, 414,
  425; **12** 412, 457, 476, *fig*. 64;
  13 210, 456; **14** 12, 33, 285,
  397, 520, 607; **16** 418; **18** 1687;
  descent into Physis, **5** 113; **9ii**
  308, 390, 391, 410; **12** 306; **14**
  600; **16** 416, 481;
  as *filius: macrocosmi*, **14** 238;
  philosophorum, **14** 304, 487; **16**
  473; *regius*, **14** 443:
  four and, **12** 210; **13** 173, 215;
  elements and, *see* elements,
  four, in alchemy, *s.v.* Adam
  Gnostic, **9ii** 296, 308; **11** 97; **12**
  138, 209; **13** 168, 252, 268,
  459; **14** 12 1*n*, 304, 354, 490; **16**
  417;
  and God-image, **18** 1511;
  homo altus, **9i** 555;
  homo maximus, **9i** 555; **9ii** 310;
  10 733; **11** 419; **13** 372; **14** 573,
  590;

homo   philosophicus/Philosophic
Man, **12** 209, 476;
as homunculus, **9i** 529;
king as, **9ii** 310; **14** 450, 484–
97;
and lapis, **9i** 555; **12** 335; **13**
133; **14** 397, 412; **16** 527;
Manichaean, *see* Manichaean
s.v.;
as Mercurius, *see* Mercurius
s.v.;
and Monad, *see* Monad *s.v.*
Gnostic;
and Nous, **12** 410;
and Oceanus, **16** 525*n*;
Original Man, **5** 478*n*; **9ii** 313,
331, 335, 338, 375, 388; **11**
356, 380, 420, 895&*n*; **12** 109*n*,
173, 209, 283, 335; **13** 203; **14**
5, 8, 12, 18, 21*n*, 44, 592; **18**
638;
Primordial Man, **10** 622, 767;
11 711; **13** 168&*n*, 173, *fig*. B4;
14 159*n* (*see also* Paracelsus:
ARCANA *s.v.* Original/etc.); as
world soul, **13** 450;
quadripartite, **12** 173;
quaternio, *see* quaternity/etc.
s.v.;
and rotundum, *see* rotundum
s.v.;
as self/wholeness in men, **9i**
529, 550; **9ii** 296; **11** 444; **12**
210; **13** 173, 220, 268, 372,
458; **14** 152–3, 209, 498;
and serpent, *see* ANIMALS: serpent *s.v.*;
and sonship, third/threefold,
of God (Basilides), **9ii** 118; **14**
397;
tetramorph as, *see* tetramorph
s.v. Anthropos;
trichotomy of, **9ii** 118;
as vessel, **9ii** 380;
Yima, **9ii** 389*n*; **14** 640*n*;
in *Zohar,* as Metatron, **13** 168;
see also Archanthropos; Protanthropos; Purusha

Apollo (*cont.*):
　Delos, birth place of, **5** 577; **14** 261;
　and Diana, **16** 410;
　and Leto, **5** 316*n*, 577; **11** 711, 713;
　and Linus, **5** 316*n*;
　Nietzsche on, **6** 225–6, 228, 231, 876 (*see also* Apollinian);
　and python, **5** 316*n*, 396, 577; **17** 321; **18** 258;
　and raven, **9i** 428*n*;
　see also Helios
Apollonius, **13** 103
Apollonius of Tyana, *see* ALCHEMICAL WRITERS *s.v.*
apologetics, Christian, **9i** 267
Apophis-serpent, Egyptian, **5** 425; **9ii** 366
apostasies, **7** 115
apostle(s), **13** 148*n*;
　at Pentecost, **8** 596;
　zodiacal symbols of, *see* zodiac: twelve signs of *s.v.*
Apostles' Creed, *see* Creeds
apothecary (-ies), **13** 252;
　"messes," **4** 588
apotheosis, **11** 154, 161*n*, 448; **14** 498;
　of Virgin Mother, **14** 664*n*;
　see also Mary *s.v.* Assumption of
apotropaic/apotropaism, **5** 576; **13** 36;
　　charms, **13** 66;
　　euphemism, **7** 400; **13** 435;
　　significance of quaternity, **13** 363
apparatus, distilling, **13** 117, 417; see also *vas*/vessel *s.v.* Hermetic, "philosophical Pelican"
apparition(s), **7** 295; **9i** 395*n*; *see also* ghost(s); hallucinations; vision(s)
Appenzell, **10** 930;
apperception(s), **2** 385; **6** 683 (Def.); **8** 288, 937; **9i** 135; **9ii** 259; **12** 372; **18** 22, 419, 873;
　　in alchemist's work, **16** 486, 488;

anticipatory, **5** 11*n*;
　degeneration of, **1** 395; **3** 29, 30, 103; and dementia praecox, **3** 19, 24;
　directed and undirected, **8** 294;
　disturbance of, **3** 56, 59;
　fantastic, **18** 877;
　schizophrenic, **3** 569;
　state of, **18** 874;
　in unconscious, **8** 362; **10** 9; **11** 776, 781;
　see also Wundt, W. *s.v.*
appetite(s): feature of impulses and automatisms, **5** 185;
　lack of, **1** 330;
　loss of, **4** 569; **17** 216;
　and passions, **14** 171;
　as psychic energy, **5** 195
appetition, **8** 937
apple(s), **8** 457–60, 476, 751; **9i** 56, 407, 416; **13** 398, 403–4;
　forbidden, **13** 288;
　of Hesperides, *see* Hesperides *s.v.*;
　of the Holy Spirit, **13** 407*n*;
apprehension, **7** 184; **16** 373*n*;
　archetypes of, **8** 270, 278–80;
　conscious and unconscious, **8** 277;
　and impulse to act, **8** 282;
　total, **8** 356;
approfondissement, **6** 467, 471
apraxia, **18** 908
April fish, *see* ANIMALS *s.v.* fish
a priori: assumptions, *see* assumptions *s.v.*;
　categories, **7** 300;
　existence: of archetypes, *see* archetypes *s.v. a priori*; of ideas, see ideas *s.v. a priori*
Apsu, **5** 375;
aptitudes/potentialities: mental/psychic, **7** 300; **17** 257;
　unconscious, **7** 300; **17** 185
Aptowitzer, V.: "Arabisch-Jüdische Schöpfungstheorien," **9i** 580*n*; **14** 587*n*, 590*n*

Aquinas (cont.):
  (Quaestiones) de veritate, in:
  Sancti Thomas Aquinas quaes-
  tiones disputate, 11 289n;
  Scriptum supra libros Senten-
  tiarum Magistri Petri Lom-
  bardi, 6 62n;
  Summa contra Gentiles, tr. by
  the English Domican Fa-
  thers, 9ii 91n;
  Summa theologica, tr. by the
  Fathers of the English Dominican Province, 9ii 91n,
  92, 276n; 11 276n, 289n; 14
  570n, 760n; 16 559; 18
  1551n
Aquinas, Thomas, pseudo: Aurora
  consurgens, see ALCHEMICAL
  WRITERS: Aurora consurgens;
  "De alchimia," see ALCHEMICAL
  WRITERS; Thomas Aquinas
Arab(s), 13 254; 14 154, 170, 326;
  and alchemy, 12 375, 403,
  462n, 473, 536–7; 13 187n,
  278; 14 158; 16 455n (see also
  ALCHEMICAL WRITERS: Abu'l
  Qāsim; El-Ḥabib; Geber;
  Kalid; Magus; Nadim; Rhazes;
  Senior);
  fish-tradition, 9ii 189
  see also Sabaean(s)
Arabia: Abraham legend in, 5 515;
  Felix, 14 280, 281;
  Mary cult in, 11 194;
  phoenix of, 14 281&n
Aranyaka, Taittiriya, 6 331n
Aratus: citations of Hippolytus, 8
  394;
  on fish-symbol, 9ii 147n;
  Phaenomena, 9ii 147n
arbiter mundi, 12 8, 18
arbor: aurea, 13 409n, fig. 4;
  immortalis, 12 451;
  inversa, see tree, inverted;
  philosophica, see below;
  sapientiae, 12 298
arbor philosophica, 9i 452n, 582; 13

119, 288; 14 157, 158, 181n; 16
  519, 533;
  as alchemical symbol, 12 499,
  figs. 122, 131, 221, 231;
  and Cross, 18 1360;
  see also tree, philosophical
"Arca arcani," see ALCHEMICAL COL-
  LECTIONS: Theatr. chem. s.v. Grasseus
Arcadia, 13 278; see also Monakris
arcane substance/arcanum(-a), 5
  276; 9ii 376, 377; 10 728; 13 109,
  136, 231, 234n, 289, 367, 424; 14
  58–9, 674, 713, 772; 15 26, 37; 16
  413, 529;
  as Adam, 13 110n; 14 544–58,
  570;
  aqua permanens as, 9ii 234;
  as archetype, 12 472;
  artifex as, 9ii 239; 13 408;
  artis, 16 410;
  ascent and descent of, 13 137n;
  bloody sweat of, 13 381, 390;
  brain/corpus rotundum as, 14
  626;
  Cheiri as, 13 171n;
  and Christ, 14 145; Passion of,
  18 1360;
  corrupt (through original sin),
  14 375;
  "dead," 14 401&n;
  devaluation of, 12 503;
  divine nature of, 13 97;
  dogmatic mystery, 14 120;
  as earth, 14 244, 632;
  as earthy water/watery earth, 8
  388;
  as egg, 13 109;
  extraction of, from ray, 9ii
  292n;
  filius produced from, 5 276; 13
  177;
  filius regius as, 13 181–4;
  as fish, 9ii 224, 234, 245; 13
  101;
  as flesh, 14 181n;
  four-square, 8 932;

as God/*res simplex,* **13** 264;
golden, **14** 626;
as head, **13** 95, 107;
healing power of, **9ii** 281;
heart (*cor*) as, **14** 493*n*;
hermaphroditic, **14** 195, 472;
as idea, **9ii** 247;
initiate as, **13** 95;
as inner/Primordial Man, **14** 548;
Isis as, **14** 14;
as King/Rex, **14** 181*n*, 354*n*, 466, 472, 720;
as *laudanum,* **13** 193*n*;
lapis as, see *lapis philosophorum s.v.*;
as lead, **9ii** 215; **13** 97, 251, 445; **14** 329, 493*n*, 726;
as lion, **14** 147, 404;
as magnesia, **9ii** 241, 245; **12** 165*n*; **13** 273*n*, 278; **14** 321&*n*;
as magnet, **9ii** 244, 245;
in man and outside man, **9ii** 249;
Mercurius as, *see* Mercurius *s.v.*;
as Monad, **14** 38;
as moon, **14** 154;
in *nigredo,* **9i** 452; **14** 43, 739;
Nostoch as, **12** 244; **13** 190*n*;
nostra, **13** 262;
One and All, **14** 36;
one and only, **10** 633;
opposites united in, **14** 36, 291;
as *para-da,* **9ii** 237;
paradox of, **14** 36, 57–9;
physical nature of, **14** 773;
pneuma as, **11** 359;
prima materia as, **14** 36, 62;
production of, **9ii** 250;
and projection of unconscious, **9ii** 242;
psychic nature of, **9ii** 247; **12** 376; **13** 107, 260, 266;
as remedies, **13** 158;
as *res,* **13** 440;
rotating, **12** 472;

as *rotundum*/round element, **11** 152; **13** 95;
as salt, **9i** 575; **14** 234–44, 318, 322, 329; double nature of, **14** 337;
as saltpetre, **9i** 535*n*;
scintillae/sparks in, **8** 388;
as scorpion, **14** 58;
as self, **9ii** 224;
separatio, solutio and *digestio* of, **18** 1360;
as serpent-chariot, **14** 270;
as soul, **14** 321; spiritual martyrdom of, **13** 442;
splitting, significance of, **14** 195;
sponsus and sponsa in, **14** 57;
as stone, **9ii** 244 (see also *lapis philosophorum s.v.*);
as sulphur, **13** 97, 177; **14** 144, 145, 151;
symbolic character of, **14** 147, 680;
symbols of, **14** 147;
tartarus as, **9i** 535*n*;
thousand names of, **10** 633;
tincture as, **14** 57;
tormenting of, **13** 440;
transformations of, **9ii** 194; **13** 424; **14** 290–3, 321, 492; **16** 398;
as tree, *see* tree(s) *s.v.*;
unity of, **14** 181*n*, 772;
Venus in, **14** 415;
as *veritas,* **9ii** 264; **12** 377;
vessel/*vas* as, **9ii** 377; **13** 113;
Virgin as, **12** 483;
water as, **9ii** 245; **13** 97;
whore as, **14** 415;
see also Paracelsus *s.v.* ARCANA
"Arcanum hermeticae philosophiae," *see* ALCHEMICAL COLLECTIONS: *Bibl. chem. s.v.* Espagnet
Archa, see Paracelsus *s.v.* ARCANA
archaeologist, J.'s case, **3** 341–53
archaeology, **16** 96, 111

Arch(a)eus, *see* Paracelsus *s.v.* AR-
CANA
archai, Gnostic, **13** 31
archaic/archaism(s), **3** 563, 565–8; **6**
684 (Def.);
    TITLE: "Archaic Man," **10**
    104–47;
    collective contents, **7** 150;
    colour hearing, **6** 684;
    features of schizophrenia, *see*
    schizophrenia *s.v.* mythologi-
    cal/archaic images;
    functions, **7** 520;
    god-image, **7** 217; **13** 475;
    idea of God, **7** 219;
    man, in ourselves, **6** 129;
    mentality, **7** 217;
    modes of functioning, **7** 159;
    psyche, **5** 258;
    psychology, **7** 471;
    residues in dreams, **13** 478;
    smile, **7** 437;
    substitute, in loss of reality, **5**
    201;
    unconscious fantasies, **7** 263;
    vestiges, Freud on, *see* Freud
    s.v. archaic;
    see also archetypes
archangels, *see* angel(s)
Archanthropos: Adam as, **9ii** 307;
    Christ as, **9ii** 326;
    God as, **9ii** 318;
    see also Anthropos; Protan-
    thropos
Archasius, *see* Paracelsus *s.v.* ARCANA
Archegonos, **9ii** 313*n*
Archelaos (alchemist), *see* ALCHEMI-
CAL WRITERS *s.v.*
Archelaos, Roman governor of
Palestine, **18** 241, 242, 243, 244
Archelaus of Miletus, pupil of
Anaxagoras, **12** 410*n*
archer: death as, **5** pl. XLV; Mer-
curius as, *see* Mercurius *s.v.*
Cupid
archetic appetite (Paracelsus), **9ii**
205, 208; *see also* Paracelsus: AR-
CANA *s.v.* Archeus

archetype(s)/archetypal, **3** 413*n*,
549–50, 565, 575, 582–3; **4** 729,
741, 743–4; **5** 62*n*, 89*n*, 154,
224–5, 349, 351, 462, 466, 607; **6**
624–5, 629, 684&*n*, 747 (Def.); **7**
(*p*v), 118–19, 129, 151&*n*, 155,
179, 184, 196, 219–20; **8** 229,
254, 276–7, 334, 342, 353, 390,
435, 840–1; **9i** 4, 88–90, 118, 260,
297, 634, 711, 714; **9ii** 13; **10**
593, 622, 635, 656, 694, 780; **11**
146, 165, 195, 454, 533–4, 555,
557, 648, 845; **13** 111, 174*n*, 210,
336, 357, 367–8, 382, 397, 448;
14 123*n*, 125, 356, 474*n*, 501,
517, 647–8, 744–5; **15** 12, 127–9;
16 15, 25, 61, 184, 254, 533–4; **17**
97, 338, 341; **18** 80, 543, 1208,
1244, 1323;
    TITLES: *The Archetypes and the
    Collective Unconscious,* **9i**; "The
    Archetypes of the Collective
    Unconscious," **7** 141–91; "Ar-
    chetypes of the Collective Un-
    conscious," **9i** 1–86; "The Ar-
    chetype in Dream Symbolism,"
    18 521–59; "Christ as Ar-
    chetype," **11** 226–33; "Con-
    cerning the Archetypes, with
    Special Reference to the Anima
    Concept," **9i** 111–47; "The
    Hypothesis of the Archetype,"
    11 222–5; "Patterns of Behav-
    iour and Archetypes," **8** 397–
    420; "Psychological Aspects of
    the Mother Archetype," **9i**
    148–98; "The Psychology of
    the Child Archetype," **9i** 259–
    305; "The Tree as an Arche-
    typal Image." **13** 350–3;
    absorptive power of, **16** 501;
    and acausal orderedness, **8**
    964–5;
    activation of, **9i** 98–9; **9ii** 257;
    10 850; **11** 223&*n*; **12** 38, 42;
    14 488, 505; **15** 130;
    as active personalities, **5** 388; **9i**
    80;

and affect, **8** 841;
amorality of, **10** 845;
amplification of, **8** 403, 404;
analogy with river-bed, **10** 395;
15 127;
as Antichrist, **11** 178;
and apprehension, **8** 270, 277,
279–80;
a priori existence of, **5** 505*n*; **6**
659; **8** 270&*n*, 871, 965; **9i**
309*n*; **9ii** 34; **11** 222*n*, 280; **18**
1183, 1488;
arcane substance as, **12** 472;
and archetypal idea(s), *see*
idea(s) *s.v.*;
in art history, **9ii** 123;
assimilation of, **9ii** 347;
Augustine's concept, **8** 275; **9i**
5; **11** 845;
autonomy of, **5** 259–60, 467; **7**
104, 184; **9i** 85, 406; **9ii** 40; **10**
847; **11** 557, 758; **13** 298; **14**
668, 746; **18** 560, 1686;
an auxiliary idea, **11** 460;
bipolarity of, **12** 553;
can rearise spontaneously, **9i**
153;
cannot be fully explained, **9i**
271;
child, **7** 185; **9i** 260, 268–76,
309; and animals, **9i** 270, 273*n*;
divine child as, **9i** 268; **12** 215;
16 533 (see also *filius; infans*);
choice of, **18** 1529–30;
claims of, **8** 725–6;
compensatory and curative
meaning, **5** 655;
as completeness, **9ii** 123;
concept of perfect being, **13**
39;
concretization of, **9i** 406;
configurations of the unconscious, **13** 304;
and the conscious mind, **5** 101,
344, 450, 467, 617; **10** 53; **11**
758;
of consciousness, **14** 504;
constellation of, **8** 847; **10** 589;

11 223; **16** 367; **18** 1492, 1529;
in neuroses, **9i** 98;
contents; not determined, **9i**
155; spontaneity of, **12** 19;
of demiurge, **11** 470;
deviation from, **8** 724;
discovered and invented, **8**
871;
of divine son, **14** 744;
as dominants, **5** 611; **7** 102,
151; **8** 423; **11** 845;
and dualism, **11** 557;
as dynamism, **8** 414; **9i** 187; **10**
846;
emotional value of, **18** 596;
enrichment through introversion, **5** 450;
equivalents of dogmas, **12** 20;
establishing existence of, **18**
1518–31;
as eternal presence/timeless-
ness of, **12** 329; **18** 1572;
etymology of, **18** 523*n*;
existence of, denied, **18** 595,
596;
and Ezekiel's visions, **11** 665;
family, **8** 336;
and fantasies, *see* fantasies *s.v.*
mythological/primordial images;
fascination of, **11** 223; **18** 547;
a *fascinosum*, **13** 207;
feeling-value of, **8** 411;
first use of term by J., **8** 270&*n*;
15 126*n*;
as foundation of consciousness,
10 656;
Freud and, **10** 830–1; **16** 381*n*
(*see also* Freud *s.v.* archaic vestiges);
function of, **9i** 276–7;
and function, transcendent, **7**
184;
futurity of, **9i** 278;
and Germany, **18** 1329;
gods as, **9i** 50;
of healing serpent, **12** 184;
hierarchy of, **8** 931;

archetype (*cont.*):
  Hiranyagharba as, **12** 20;
  and historical factor, **7** 303;
  and history, **18** 371, 372;
  identification with, **7** 389; **8** 254; **9i** 189, 621; **11** 472; **12** 41, 43; **18** 354, 1333;
  as image and emotion, **18** 589, 1589;
  Imago Dei, *see* God-image *s.v.*;
  indefiniteness of, **8** 964; **12** 20; **16** 497;
  and individuation process, **8** 554; **11** 281; **18** 1162;
  inexhaustibility of, **14** 777;
  as inherited tendency to form mythological motifs, **18** 523;
  not inherited ideas, **18** 524, 1127, 1228;
  initiative of, **18** 546;
  and instinct, **3** 550; **4** 729; **5** 225; **8** 270–1, 277, 281, 282*n*, 339, 404, 406, 415–16, 425*n*, 856; **9i** 91, **9ii** 13, 278; **10** 547; **16** 185; **18** 1263, 1271;
  integration of, **14** 746;
  interpretation of, **14** 745;
  intervention of, **18** 368;
  and intuition, **8** 270; **12** 175;
  invasion by, **16** 188;
  irrepresentable, **11** 222–3;
  of jesters, **11** 470;
  and Joyce, **15** 185;
  Kant's conception (*Urbild*), **6** 519, 733; **8** 276 (*see also* primordial image(s));
  Karma and, **7** 118*n*;
  of king's renewal/sacrifice, **14** 507, 525;
  of life, anima as, *see* anima *s.v.* archetype;
  light, **9i** 5, 149;
  as link with the past, **9i** 271–5;
  as living matter, **18** 589;
  loss of, **9i** 141;
  of lover in a remote land, **18** 366;

luminosity of, **8** 388, 392; **11** 707*n*;
magic demon, **7** 153;
mana-personality as, **7** 377, 380, 388–9, 393, 395;
manifestation in child, **10** 58–61;
many or few, **8** 274; **11** 440;
of meaning, **9i** 66, 79, 682; **14** 313;
as mediator, **9i** 293;
metaphysical significance, **11** 295; **18** 1229;
as models, **8** 275;
and motifs, **7** 129; **9i** 89, 260; **16** 15, 254;
as myths/mythological, *see* myth(s) *s.v.*;
nature of, **8** 417; **10** 53–4, 447, 847; **11** 88;
in neurosis, **9i** 98;
noumenon of the image, **6** 659;
numinosity of, **5** 225, 450, 467; **7** 109; **8** 388, 392, 405, 411, 590*n*, 841; **9i** 82; **9ii** 287*n*, 305; **10** 530, 646, 652, 713, 854; **11** 102, 222, 472, 556; **12** 41; **14** 312, 411*n*, 558, 787; **18** 547, 595, 596, 1160, 1229, 1273, 1492;
of opposites, their union, **16** 354;
opposites united in, **5** 576; **9i** 293;
of order, **10** 624;
and organic illness, **18** 231, 299, 300;
as organizers, **8** 440;
origin, **7** 109; **9i** 187; **11** 222*n*;
parallels of *pramantha*, **5** 208;
as patterns of behaviour, pre-existent/innate, **3** 565; **5** 337, 467, 474; **8** 352, 398, 404, 528*n*, 841, 931*n*; **9i** 6*n*, 91; **10** 831, 846–7; **11** 222*n*; **16** 254*n*; **18** 1158, 1228, 1273, 1389, 1488, 1492–3, 1830;

philosophy and, **8** 342;

Plato and, **8** 275; **9i** 5;

play of, **14** 401;

positive and negative sides, **9i** 413; **9ii** 423; **10** 461, 474;

possession by, **7** 390; **11** 223, 648; **12** 41, 558; **14** 746, 787;

in practical experience, **18** 589;

preconscious, **8** 412;

production of, **12** 19;

and projection, **18** 324, 353, 360, 361;

projection of, **5** 83n, 576; **7** 152; **12** 12, 40, 43, 557; **13** 395; **16** 407, 501;

proofs of, **9i** 100–3;

psychic and non-psychic, **8** 419–20, 439–40, 964;

psychic life of, is timeless, **11** 149;

psychic premises, **13** 378;

psychoid, **8** 419–20, 964; **10** 849, 851–2, 854;

quasi-personal, **5** 388;

no "rational" substitute for, **9i** 272;

reality of, **7** 158;

recognition of, **10** 56–7;

as scintillae, **8** 388; **14** 700;

of situations, **7** 185; **9i** 80;

soul and, **9i** 74;

specific energy of, **18** 546, 547;

spontaneous activity of, **18** 1161;

stability of, **14** 660;

in Tanguy picture, **10** 755;

term used by other authors, **8** 275n; **9i** 5&n; **11** 89n; **14** 761;

in *Corpus Hermeticum*, **8** 275n; **9i** 5, 149; **11** 89n;

"that which is believed," **11** 178;

totality of, **9ii** 305;

and transference, *see* transference *s.v.*;

of transformation, **9i** 80, 258; **11** 758;

transgressiveness of, **10** 660;

trans-subjective union of, **16** 469;

treasure-house of, **14** 744;

unconscious organizers of our ideas, **9ii** 278;

unity of, **14** 661;

of unity, **14** 772;

and violet (colour), **8** 414, 416–17, 420;

of witch, **5** 611; **10** 60;

Wotan, **10** 391, 394;

wrathful form, **11** 178;

see also under anima; animal(s); animus; Anthropus; brothers; hostile; Christ; coniunctio; dreams; ego; energy; engram; fairytales; father; God; God-image; God-man; hero; hierosgamos; Holy Ghost; horse; image(s); incest; maiden; mandala; mother; mother-son marriage; Mother, Earth-; number(s); parent; persona; primitive(s); psyche; quaternity; rebirth; Redeemer; religion; *Sapientia Dei*; schizophrenia; self; shadow; Son of Man; spirit; spirit of gravity; sun; symbol/symbolism; synchronicity; tree; triad; Trinity; types; unconscious; unconscious, collective; wholeness; wise old man; *and see also* primordial image(s)

Archeus, *see* Paracelsus *s.v.* ARCANA

Archidoxis magicae, see Paracelsus: WORKS *s.v.*

archigallos, **5** 662

Archimedean point, **13** 144; **16** 254; **17** 163, 164

architecture, **15** 174;

Indian, **10** 983, 989; **11** 908

archon(s)/Archons, **11** 429, 446; **12** 456(7)n, 468; **13** 129n; **14** 34, 308, 309;

Gnostic/in Gnosticism, **7** 104;

mutilated, **5** 356*n*;
outstretched on cross, **5** 402;
wing-shaped, **5** 403
Armenian(s), **11** 312;
"bitch," *see* ANIMALS *s.v.* dog;
cave worship by, **5** 528
Armilus/Armillus, **9ii** 168&*n*; **14** 640*n*
army: commander, ego as, **8** 692–3;
general's dream, **17** 187;
J.'s experience as medical officer in, **17** 177–8;
and psyche, compared, **8** 690
army with banners (*acies castrorum*), **13** 389
Arnaldus of Villanova, *see* ALCHEMICAL WRITERS *s.v.*
Arndt, E.: "Über die Geschichte der Katatonie," **3** 1*n*
Arnobius, **5** 530;
Adversus gentes, **5** 530*n*; **12** 184*n*; tr. A. H. Bryce and H. Campbell, **5** 530*n*
Arnold, Sir Edwin: *The Light of Asia*, **5** 362, 490; see also under *Bhagavad Gita*
Arnold of Villanova, *see* ALCHEMICAL WRITERS *s.v.* Arnaldus de Villanova
"Arnolde the great Clerke," *see* ALCHEMICAL WRITERS *s.v.* Arnaldus de Villanova
Aros, **12** 209, 422*n*
Arran, green stone of, **13** 129
arrangement(s), **8** 527;
Adler's term, *see* Adler, A. *s.v.*;
in J.'s case, **7** 75;
meaningful, and synchronicity, **8** 967;
of psychic process, **8** 860;
unconscious, **8** 832; **10** 680
Arrhetophoria festival, **5** 530
arrogance, **7** 224–5, 283
arrow(s), **10** 638; **13** 278; **14** 23, 144*n*; **16** 519;
Cupid's, **8** 627; **16** 500; see also below *s.v. telum passionis;*
death by, **5** 434, pl. XLV;

and moon, **14** 20;
-shot, **5** 400, 420, 462, 547&*n*, 585*n*;
-smith, **5** 515;
of the sun, **5** 439;
symbolism, **5** 438&*n*; of direction, **9i** 667, 705; libido, **5** 447;
masculine, **5** 439; phallic, **13** 343, *fig.* 30; in stigmata, **5** 435–8;
and *telum passionis*/passion, dart of: Cupid's as, **13** 110, 278; **14** 23, 426; of Mercurius, **11** 420; **12** *figs.* 80, 131; **14** 144*n*, 550; **16** 500*n*, 519*n*;
see also Adam *s.v.*; Mercurius *s.v.* as Cupid/archer
ars aurifera, **13** 158, 414
Ars chemica, *see* ALCHEMICAL COLLECTIONS
arsenic, in alchemy, **12** *fig.* 142T; **14** 31*n*, 195;
"theft" of, **14** 186–7, 193–6
Ars Geomantica/Art of Punctuation, **8** 866
art(s), **7** 298; **11** 906; **17** 157, 206, 210, 266;
TITLE: *The Spirit in Man, Art, and Literature*, **15**;
as alchemical term, *see* alchemy *s.v.*;
analysis as, **7** 502;
Apollinian/Dionysian, **6** 225;
contemporary, **6** 645; **8** 176; **10** 290, 430, 584, 724; **11** 722; **15** 178; and neurosis, **18** 1724;
psychology of, **10** 307; and unconscious, **10** 754;
ecclesiastical, **5** 163, 332*n*;
as end in itself, **8** 731;
expressionism in, **10** 167;
galleries, **18** 626;
of healing, *see* healing *s.v.*;
history of, archetype in, **9ii** 123;
Indian, **11** 933;
introverted and extraverted, **15** 111, 117;

art (*cont.*):
  magic, **13** 156;
  mediating role of, **6** 230;
  medieval, **5** 368;
  non-objective, **15** 206;
  Oriental, **6** 493–4;
  of primitives, **6** 493;
  psychoanalysis and, **7** 224; **8** 702;
  and psychology, **15** 97–103, 111–18, 133–5;
  sexuality and sensuality as basis of, **5** 332*n*;
  social significance of, **15** 130;
  and subjective factor, **6** 647;
  sublimation and, **7** 71;
  "symbol" of, **10** 24;
  Western, **6** 487;
  works of, meaning, **3** 398; **15** 121, 161;
  see also artist(s); artistic; arts and sciences; painting
art (of alchemy), *see* alchemy/alchemist(s)
Artefius, *see* ALCHEMICAL COLLECTIONS: *Bibl. chem. cur. s.v.* and *Theatr. chem. s.v.*
Artemidorus of Daldis, **14** 474; **17** 262; **18** 544, 546;
  dream-book of, **5** 4;
  Onirocriticon, **14** 474*n*
Artemis, **14** 144*n*, 607;
  bear and, **5** 89*n*, 496*n*;
  Chitone, **14** 75*n*;
  on coin from Perga, **5** 298;
  Cybele-, **9i** 339;
  Orthia, as *Lygodesma*, **5** 364;
  temple in Ephesus, **10** 725*n*; **11** 734*n*;
  veiled, **14** 75*n*;
  see also Diana
arthropods, **9i** 114
artifex, **12** 43, 306, 358&*n*, 388, 558, *figs.* 17, 136, 140, 141, 216; **13** 88*n*, 117, 173, 177, 414, 429, 435, 439; **16** 414;
  and arcanum, *see* arcane substance;
  and lapis, **18** 1631&*n*;

Mercurius as, **13** 284; **14** 401*n*;
  qualities of, **12** 382–9, 394; **13** 212;
  servant of the work, **16** 471;
  and *soror mystica*, **12** *figs* 132, 140, 215, 237, 269 (*see also* ALCHEMICAL WRITERS: Flamel *s.v.* Peronelle; Pordage *s.v.* Jane Leade
  transformation of, **13** 277;
  see also adept
Artio, **5** 496*n*; **9i** 341;
  with bear, **5** pl. I*b*
artisan, as hero's father, **5** 515
Artis auriferae, see ALCHEMICAL COLLECTIONS: *Art. aurif.*
artist(s), **1** 34, 186, 219; **3** 171, 355, 385, 520; **7** 510; **17** 312;
  TITLE: "The Artist," **15** 155–62;
  and abstract sensation, **6** 794;
  and creative urge, **15** 115, 135, 143, 155;
  detachment of, **15** 188*n*;
  difficulty of thinking, **18** 392;
  duality of, **15** 157;
  and experience of unconscious, **7** 342;
  and introverted intuitive type, **6** 661;
  Miller and, **5** (*p*449);
  pathological fantasy of, **5** 277;
  psychology of, **15** 147;
  and repression, **15** 156;
  role of, **5** 500*n*;
  vision of, **7** 289;
  would-be, **17** 206;
  see also art(s); Leonardo; Picasso
artistic: capacity, unconscious, **7** 136, 137&*n*, 140; on pathology of, **15** 122, 144; and the unconscious, **15** 141–3, 159, 162;
  creation, and schizophrenia, **15** 208&*n*, 209;
  experience of the unconscious, **7** 342;
  inspiration and invasion, **18** 71, 72;
  instinct, in animals, **4** 279;
  temperament, **7** 375;

Ashburnham Codex (*cont.*):
AND MSS *s.v.* Florence
"Ash Metsareph," *see* ALCHEMICAL WRITERS *s.v.*
ash-tree, see TREES *s.v.*
Ashvaghosha: *Buddha-Carita*, **13** 458*n*
ashvattha (Ficus religiosa), see TREES *s.v.*
Asia/Asiatic, **7** 326;
    central, **10** 927;
    cults, **9i** 25;
    Europe as peninsula of, **18** 139
"as-if," **9i** 265; **9ii** 315
Ask, **13** 458*n*
askesis, **11** 776; *see also* ascetics/asceticism
Asklepios, *see* Aesculapius
Asmodeus, **4** 743, 744*n*
Asophol (gold), **14** 624&*n*
asparagus plant, **13** 413
aspects, astrological, **8** 867, 869*n*;
    and marriage, **8** 868, 878–901;
    and mortality rate, **8** 987;
    and radio weather, **8** 875
aspersion, **9ii** 293
ass(es), see ANIMALS *s.v.*; Apuleius *s.v. Golden Ass*
Assagioli, R., **18** (*p*398*n*)
assault motif, **5** 8
assertions, delusional, *see* delusional *s.v.*
Ass Festival (*Zarathustra*), *see* Nietzsche *s.v.*
assimilation, **1** 357; **3** 31; **5** 11; **6** 685–6 (Def.); **11** 2, 400, 439; **13** 12, 55; **18** 1515–17, 1529;
    TITLE: "Phenomena Resulting from the Assimilation of the Unconscious," **7** 221–42/451–63;
    in alchemy, **14** 455–7;
    of anima/animus, **7** 384; **13** 223*n*;
    of archetypes, **9ii** 347;
    and associations, **1** 317; **8** 195–8;

of Christ through symbols, *see* Christ *s.v.*;
Christian doctrine and, **14** 455*n*;
by church, **14** 455*n*;
of collective psyche, **7** 237/458, 480;
of complexes, *see* complex(es) *s.v.*
of doctor by patient, **16** 164;
of ego/self, **9ii** 9, 43, 45, 47;
and Gnosticism, **18** 1516–17; 1827–8, 1830;
of irrational ideas, **18** 837;
of lost contents, **18** 595;
of man to country, **10** 968, 971;
of mana-personality, **7** 398;
of object, empathy and, **6** 486, 489 (*see also* extraverted type *s.v.* object);
of opposites, **14** 513;
phenomena of, **18** 1515, 1517, 1529, 1827, 1830–1;
by projection-making factor, **9ii** 44;
of *représentations collectives*, **11** 453;
symbols and phenomena of, **9ii** 295;
of the unconscious, **7** 221, 365;
of unconscious contents by conscious, **5** 631, 683; **7** 205/446, 218/450, 253, 361, 365, 384, 505; **8** 430; **16** 26–7, 326–9;
of vision/God-experience, **11** 478, 480;
work of, **18** 595
association(s), **1** 75–6, 139, 147*n*, 340; **3** 215; **5** 16*n*, 25, 91, 280–1, 468; **6** 463–5, 467, 469, 481, 966; **17** 207, 270;
    TITLES: "An Analysis of the Associations of an Epileptic," **2** 499–559; "Association, Dream, and Hysterical Symptoms," **2** 793–862; "The Association

92

Method," **2** 939–98; "The Associations of Normal Subjects," **2** 3–495; "Studies in Word Association," **2** 1–1014;
assimilation and, **1** 317; **8** 195–8;
"astrological," **7** 250;
and attention, **1** 73, 314–17; **3** 24, 108, 300, 544 (see also *abaissement du niveau mental*);
blocking of, **16** 320;
categories/classification of, **18** 155;
chains of, **3** 56–8; **4** 43; **5** 65–6, 79, 128, 166 (see also sep. entry below);
clang, **3** 11&*n*, 23–4, 41*n*, 157, 265, 267, 291, 294, 544 (see also clang);
classification of, see sep. entry below;
compulsive, **3** 218;
concord/parallelism of, **1** 148; **10** 608;
concordant, in families, **4** 309; **8** 228, 503;
and consciousness, **1** 87, 166–9, 279, 290; **2** 608, (*p*253); **17** 207;
co-ordination in, **2** 939–98;
definition, **2** 20, 730&*n*;
in dementia praecox/schizophrenia, **3** 8–11, 22–4, 41, 505, 544, 563, 565, 568–9;
dream-, **3** 126, 129–30, 137*n*, 505, 544, 563, 568; **4** 46, 324, 326, 542–6; **7** 21/434, 45, 129, 139, 170–1, 210; **8** 148–50; **12** 48, 403; **16** 95–6, 319–20; **17** 114; numbers in, **4** 131–2;
duration of, **2** 568–76;
experiments, see below;
and extremes of feeling, **1** 142, 184;
father in, see father *s.v.*;
and feeling-toned complex, **1** 478–84; **3** 82, 107–42, 175,

218; **4** 41, 43, 211; **7** 20/432;
free, **2** 640, 662, 704; **4** 40, 42, 157; **6** 702; **8** 167, 179, 453; **9i** 101; **16** 100, 319–20; **17** 114; **18** 171, 172, 175, 422, 424–5, 430, 432–4;
of ideas, **5** 639; **18** 833;
inhibited by embarrassment, **1** 311–17;
laws of, **2** 868–9, 883; **3** 37, 41;
mediate, **3** 37, 44–5, 47, 134–5&*n*, 218;
memory and, **9i** 504; **11** 776;
method, **17** 128, 175; **18** 4;
negative/contrasting, **3** 27–30, 138;
primitive/archaic, **3** 563, 565; **7** 101;
and repression, **1** 73; **4** 211; **8** 372;
sound (sound reactions), **2** 76–80, 385, 388–9, 391, 394, 403–5, 407, 446–51, 731, 874, 881–2;
symbolical, **7** 341;
see also Aschaffenburg; thinking *s.v.* non-directed/associative
association-chains; INSTANCES:
"affirm," **3** 236–9;
"Alexander, Empress," **3** 290–1;
"amphi," **3** 282–4;
"bazaar," **3** 293–4;
bone/bed, **2** 605;
"Bunau-Varilla cigar," **2** 451; **3** 110;
in case of B. St, **3** 203–7;
"crown," **3** 228–9;
"discord," **3** 262–3;
"establish," **3** 236–7;
"finality," **3** 243–4;
"Gessler," **3** 272–3;
"hero," **3** 241–2;
"hieroglyphical," **3** 260–1;
"Hufeland," **3** 270–1, 377;
in hysteria, **2** 816;
"interest-draughts," **3** 234–5;
"Lorelei," **3** 225–7, 373;

nosis of;
in dementia praecox/schizo-
phrenia, **2** 1157–78; **3** 215–95,
506, 554; **18** 107, 832; and dis-
tracted attention, **3** 37–47, 52;
educated men, **2** 165–266, 441,
477–8; subjects, **2** 13–14, 20,
398–411, 577–82; women, **2**
115–66, 439–41, 462–3;
in epilepsy, **2** 499–559;
failure in, *see* failure;
and familes, **2** 135, 144, 151–2,
158; **4** 309, 695, 780; **8** 228,
503; **18** 1137;
and family constellation, **2**
999–1014;
and feeling-toned complexes, **3**
92–6, 106, 107–10, 175, 203–8,
210–11, 554; **5** 219; **8** 253, 365,
592–3; **11** 21, 37; **17** 128, 199a
(*see also* feeling-tone);
and Freudian unconscious, **18**
121;
and galvanometer, *see* galvanometer *s.v.*;
historical development of, **2**
730;
in hysteria, **2** 793–822, 943,
946–54; **18** 973;
men and women compared, **2**
399–400, 434–44, 456–68,
577–8, 904–6;
and neurosis, **2** 1351; **3** 506; **4**
408;
participation in, **18** 159;
potentialities of, **18** 1137;
and practice, effects of, **1** 316;
procedure, **2** 7–19, 761;
and psychoanalysis, **4** 18–19;
reaction time in, *see* reaction
time;
respiration in, **18** 129–34;
simple, **3** 203–14;
sound, *see* association(s) *s.v.*;
stimulus words in, **1** 483; **2**
730; attitudes towards, **2** 384,
408–19; choice of, and com-
plex, **3** 93–5; **8** 592–3; **11** 21,

37; defining of, **2** 408n, 513,
984–5; emotionally charged, **2**
157; experimental procedure,
2 8–9, 12; explanation of, **2**
525–9, 539, 947–8, 984; forgetting, **2** 639; grammatical
form, influence of, **2** 475–87,
585–92; language problems, **2**
10–11; not understanding, **2**
286–90; and reaction, as association, **2** 20; reaction-time
and, **2** 584–93, 622–32; repetition of, **2** 95, 454–5, 539,
541–3, 545–6, 555&n, 954–5;
and subjective factor, **10**
753–4;
and unconscious, **4** 335–9; **10**
50; **14** 181, 272;
uneducated men, **2** 358–81,
397, 439; subjects, **2** 10–11, 20,
270, 392–3, 397, 400–11, 523,
577–82, 589–600, 633–4,
884–5, 1080; women, **2** 267–
357, 393–7, 438, 462, 475–80;
vowel sequences in, **18** 944
assonance(s), **3** 22n, 41, 578; **6** 463
Assumption of Mary/*Assumptio Mar-*
iae, see Mary/Mother of God *s.v.*
assumptions: *a priori*, **9ii** 29;
basic, **4** 784;
false, **8** 761; **16** 237;
historical, **7** 310;
prior, **16** 543;
unconscious, **4** 776; **7** 331
Assurbanipal, *see* Assyria *s.v.*
Assyria: Assurbanipal/Asurbanipal,
King of, **5** 280, 375, 659n; **14**
384;
God of, **5** 403;
and sun-god, **5** 600n
Ast the Shepherd, **18** 797
Astanus, *see* ALCHEMICAL WRITERS:
Ostanes
Astarte, **5** 321n, 353n;
Canaanite, **18** 1529;
doves of, **8** 336; **14** 80n;
love-goddess, **9ii** 174; **13** 226,
278;

Astarte (*cont.*):
  Semitic, **13** 407*n*;
  in Spitteler, **6** 456*n*
Asterius, Bishop of Amasea, **5** 528;
  9i 297*n*; **18** 264&*n*;
  Homilia X in sanctos martyres, **5**
  528*n*
asthma, nervous, **4** 365; **7** 44, 69
Astrampsychos, **9i** 238*n*; **13** 359–61
astrolabe, **14** 270
astrologer(s), **6** 933; **10** 172, 682,
  687; **11** 970
astrology/astrological, **5** 421*n*; **6**
  917, 934; **8** 405*n*, 829, 867–9,
  916, 944, 987–94; **9i** 605, 607*n*;
  10 169, 176, 590, 687, 914; **11**
  390, 654, 714; **12** 314; **13** 49,
  151; **14** 180*n*, 493*n*; **15** 19–20,
  29–30; **16** 410;
  TITLE: "An Astrological Experiment," **8** 872–915; **18** 1174–
  92;
  and alchemy, **9ii** 415; **12** 40,
  346, 524; **13** 154, 285; **14** 222,
  476*n*;
  birth data and, **15** 82;
  and characterology, *see* char-
  acter/etc. *s.v.*;
  and collective unconscious, **8**
  325, 392;
  colours and, **14** 390;
  current, **7** 494; **10** 700;
  earthly, **13** 355;
  fishes in, **9ii** 128, 173 (*see also*
  zodiac: twelve signs of *s.v.*
  Pisces);
  J.'s experiment, **8** 872–915; **18**
  1174–92;
  and mandala, **12** 314;
  mantic character of, **8** 994;
  morphomata and, **9ii** 136;
  Oriental, **9ii** 148; **10** 188;
  Paracelsus and, **12** 210; **13**
  355*n*; **15** 22;
  Platonic months in, **9i** 551;
  possible causal laws in, **8** 876,
  987;
  Saturn in, **9ii** 128–30;

  science, in antiquity, **10** 121; **11**
  257*n*; **15** 81;
  and statistics, **18** 1175;
  temperaments, **13** 355;
  unconscious, **18** 412;
  see also aspects, astrological; associations, "astrological;" horo-
  scope(s); planets; zodiac;
  see also under Antichrist; as-
  cendent and descendent; character; Christianity; Mercury,
  planet; synchronicity
astro-mythology, *see* mythology *s.v.*
Astronomia (Paracelsus, arcana), **8**
  390
astronomy(-er), **1** 144; **13** 148*n*,
  154, 285; **14** 571; **15** 38;
  laws of, **11** 140;
  as source of names in S. W.'s
  metric system, **1** 144
astrophysics, **8** 987
astrum, eternal, **12** 214; *see also*
  Paracelsus *s.v.* ARCANA; star *s.v.*
  man
Asurabama (Miller fantasies), **5**
  280–81, (*p*460)
Asuras, **12** 533
Asurbanipal, *see* Assyria
Aswan, **9i** 239
aswatha, *see* TREES *s.v.*
asylum, **1** 477;
  fear of, **1** 356;
  modern, **3** 472
asymmetry, of fourth dimension,
  10 742
Atarah, **14** 652
Atargatis, **9ii** 127, 163, 173, 174;
  fish cult of, **9ii** 186;
  see also Derceto
atavism, **3** 529
ataxia, **3** 33, 35;
  intrapsychic, **3** 37
ataxia-abasia, **18** 876
Athanasian creed, *see* creed(s)
Athanasius, St., Bishop of Alexandria, **6** 82; **16** 384;
  "Life of St. Anthony," in *The
  Book of Paradise or Garden of the*

Holy Fathers, tr. E. A. Wallis Budge, **6** 82*n*; **11** 32*n*
athanor (melting pot/furnace), **5** 245; **13** *fig.* B4; **16** 538*n*
Atharva Veda, see Vedas *s.v.*
atheism, **9i** 125; **9ii** 170; **10** 510; **11** 34, 140, 285; **18** 1658, 1660;
   and theism, as opposites, **8** 712
Athenaeus, A., **5** 321; **14** 96;
   Deipnosophists, tr. C. B. Gulick, **14** 90*n*, 96*n*
Athenagoras, **14** 14;
   Legatio pro Christianis, **14** 14*n*
Athene/Pallas/Minerva, **4** 511, 760; **5** 321, 372; **9i** 95, 368; **10** 731; **12** *fig.* 187; **18** 250;
   in Goethe, **6** 289, 291, 295, 302;
   Phidias' statue of, **6** 44
Athens, **6** 42, 43, 44; **13** 92; **14** 154; **18** 195, 260, 264;
   chasm on the Areopagus, **5** 572;
   classical, **5** 36;
   Little Metropolis, **5** 460*n*; **9ii** 147;
   sacred precinct, **5** 570;
   sacred tree, **5** 392*n*;
   St. Paul and, **9ii** 274, 299
Athi plains, **9i** 177
athista/adhista, **8** 329, 411
athla/ἄθλα, *see* Heracles *s.v.* labours of
Athos, Mount, **14** 328; **18** 1536
Atlantic Ocean, **7** 326
L'Atlantide, see Benoît *s.v.*
Atlantis, **6** 594; **9i** 471; **11** 190
Atlases, **12** *fig.* 142BB
Atman/*atman*, **5** 227, 550; **6** 188, 415; **7** 303; **9i** 248, 289(b), 408, 572; **9ii** 60, 124, 223, 257, 303, 348; **10** 65, 779, 873, 875; **11** 231, 433, 955–6, 959; **12** 16, 20, 209; **13** 210, 268; **14** 132, 133, 145, 273, 711; **16** 474; **18** 638, 1567;
   Brahman and, **6** 189, 190;
   Elijah as, **18** 1526;

hermaphroditic nature, **5** 227*n*;
personal and supra-/trans-personal, **5** 296*n*, 596*n*, 612*n*; **12** 137; **13** 287; **14** 133; of tree, *see* Mercurius (1) *s.v.* tree; *purusha-, see* Purusha *s.v.*;
   self as, **6** 189, 330–2, 361; **7** 303; **9ii** 223, 348; **11** 231; **12** 9, 137; **16** 474;
   see also *anātman*
Atninga ceremony, *see* Australian aborigines *s.v.* Aruntas
atom(s)/atomic, **7** 405; **8** 278&*n*, 417; **9i** 117; **9ii** 376, 380, 391, 411; **13** 143, 248;
   bomb, **8** 424, 426, 428; **11** 733, 747, 751, 768; **18** 1407, 1505;
   chain reactions, **10** 611;
   of Democritus, **10** 766;
   energy, **10** 485, 611;
   fission, **8** 422, 967; **9i** 454(b);
   theory, **9i** 117;
   world/age, **9i** 408; **18** 1666;
   see also microphysics; physics, atomic *and* nuclear
Aton, **14** 356*n*
atonement, **11** 661;
   Day of, **18** 1551
at-one-ment, **11** 799, 817–18
Atreus, **6** 43*n*
Atrides/House of Atreus, curse of, **6** 223; **17** 88, 154; **18** 1374
atrophy, instinctual, **13** 13
attachments, infantile, **14** 750
attainable, restriction to the, **8** 768, 770–1
attention, **1** 119&*nn*; **2** 3–5, 382–3, 882, 1080–1; **8** 690; **9ii** 46; **11** 897; **14** 180;
   and affectivity, **3** 83&*n*;
   and apperception, **3** 19;
   and association(s), *see* association(s) *s.v.*;
   blunting of, **2** 133, 138, 151, 165, 169–78;
   concentration of, **17** 343; and automatic actions, **1** 119; and

attention (*cont.*):
  new ideas, **1** 147*n*;
  directed, and thought, **5** 11–14; **8** 294;
  distraction of, and association, *see* distraction *s.v.*;
  disturbances of, **1** 43, 73, 277, 338–40; **2** 120, 132–4, 136, 168–9, 378–9, 731, 1322; **3** 1–3, 12, 14–15, 17, 24, 26, 30, 52–3, 162, 300, 434, 544; in dementia praecox, **2** 1067;
  and fatiguability, **1** 254 (*see also* Aschaffenburg);
  in galvanometer and pneumograph experiments, **2** 1048, 1187;
  inhibition of, **3** 135;
  oscillating, **18** 445;
  phenomenon, **2** 419;
  subliminal, **1** 119*n*;
  -tone, **3** 83–4, 86–7;
  withdrawal of, **3** 137; **17** 199;
  see also distractibility
attentive reaction, **2** 119
attic, in dream, **10** 671
Attic: bas-relief, **5** 298, pl. XXI*a*; fertility and rebirth ceremonies, **13** 92
Attis/Atys, **5** 183, 321, 330*n*, 392; **9ii** 334, 339*n*; **11** 10, 348, 612, 718*n*, 828*n*; **12** 26, 416, 529; **14** 27*n*, 64*n*, 510*n*, 627*n*, 653*n*;
  Adonis, **5** 165&*n*;
  archigallos, **5** 662;
  and Christ, affinities, **13** 92&*n*;
  cult/legend, **5** 659–62; **18** 1287;
  -Cybele cult, *see* Rhea/Cybele *s.v.*;
  "holy shepherd," **9ii** 145*n*;
  as Ichthys, **9ii** 237*n*;
  and Men, **5** 299;
  and Mithras, **5** 165*n*;
  mystery of, **5** 535;
  polymorphous, **9ii** 310;
  and sacred pine-tree, **5** 321,

349, 659, 661–2, *fig.* 42; **13** 401*n*;
  self-castration of, **5** 356*n*, 392, 585;
  and shepherd, **9ii** 162;
  see also Adonis
attitude(s), **6** 687–91 (Def.); **8** 49; **11** 245; **16** 79, 81, 236, 419;
  abstracting, *see* abstracting *s.v.*;
  and adaptation, **8** 60;
  aesthetic, **6** 173, 194, 232, 485;
  and affect, **8** 630–1;
  apotropaic, **16** 365;
  authoritarian, **17** 211;
  bad effects of, **8** 630;
  basis of, **8** 631;
  breakdown of, in individual, **8** 594;
  change of, **7** 252; **8** 845; **13** 473; **18** 1391–5, 1402; and conflict, **4** 606; social or national, **8** 594;
  collective, **6** 12, 311–12; **7** 240, 459; **8** 142; introverted, **11** 800; national, **10** 972; as religion, **6** 313; undifferentiated, **6** 311;
  conscious, **6** 571–2; **7** 63, 78, 88, 159, 338, 344, 347, 359, 371, 391; **8** 497; **9i** 431; **11** 56, 517, 783; **12** 48, 95, 247; **15** 152; **16** 26, 366, 381; **17** 194, 281, 282; aberrations of, **13** 229; and archetypal images, **5** 264; badly adapted, **8** 494; collapse of, **7** 254; and dreams, **8** 546; **17** 187; failure of, **8** 65; and godlikeness, **6** 150; Goethe's, **15** 153; and neurosis, **16** 12, 26; one-sidedness of, **10** 20; **13** 223; and works of art, **15** 160;
  of consciousness, **6** 563–7; abstracting. *see* abstracting, attitude; and dying. **8** 809;
  contemplative, **11** 797;
  contents of, **8** 692–3;

gelium/Tractates on the Gospel According to Saint John, tr. J. Innes, **5** 162*n*; **9ii** 71*n*; **11** 313*n*; **12** 112*n*; **14** 256*n*; **18** 16*n*, 688*n*

Augustine, pseudo-: *Liber de spiritu et anima,* **11** 221&*n*; **13** 301*nn*

Augustus, **9ii** 223; **18** 241;
   era of, **10** 293, 488

aurea apprehensio (golden understanding), **12** 381

Aurea catena Homeri, **12** 148*n*

"Aurea hora," *see* ALCHEMICAL COLLECTIONS: *Art. aurif. s.v.* "Aurora consurgens"

"Aurelia occulta," *see* ALCHEMICAL COLLECTIONS: *Theatr. chem. s.v.* Beatus

aureole of sun, **13** 107

"Aureum saeculum redivivum," *see* ALCHEMICAL COLLECTIONS: *Mus. herm. s.v.* Madathanus

aureum vellus, see golden fleece

Aureum vellus (text), *see* ALCHEMICAL COLLECTIONS; *see also Theatr. chem.:* Mennens, "De aureo vellere libri tres"

Aurobindo, Shri, **10** 875

Aurora, **13** 215

aurora borealis, **10** 389

Aurora consurgens, see ALCHEMICAL WRITERS *s.v.*

aurum, see gold

Aurum hermeticum, see ALCHEMICAL WRITERS *s.v.* Balduinus

Auschwitz, **10** 404; *see also* concentration camps

auster (south wind), **12** 480&*n*; *see also* wind

austerity, optimum of, **18** 1348

Australasian Medical Congress (1911), **2** 1349*n*

Australian aborigines/primitives, **6** 431, 496; **8** 119, 570; **10** 103; **14** 162*n*; **18** 84, 649;
   alchera(bugari)/alcheringa, alcheringamijini (identification with ancestral souls), **9i** 84, 224,

226*n*, 260; **12** 171; **13** 130*n*;
   arunquiltha (mana), **8** 120; **13** 128;
   Aruntas, *atninga* ceremony of, **8** 86;
   and children's souls, **13** 128;
   churingas (ancestral stones), **6** 325, 496; **8** 92, 119&*n*; **13** 128–9, 132;
   hierosgamos amongst, **5** 215, 220, 226;
   renewal rites among, **5** 671;
   and soul-atoms/sparks, **8** 278*n*; **9i** 116;
   totem-ancestor, **13** 128;
   Wachandi tribe, rites of, **5** 213, 220, 226; **8** 83–5, 88;
   world of ancestors and dreams, **13** 130*n*;
   zogo concept, **8** 120;
   see also Spencer and Gillen

Austria/Austrian, **10** 908, 975, 1055, 1060; **18** 1311;
   legendary sign of rain in, **5** 421

Authades, demon, **9ii** 307*n*

author, and public, **7** 406

"Authoris ignoti opusculum," *see* ALCHEMICAL COLLECTIONS: *Art. aurif. s.v.* "Opusculum authoris ignoti"

authoritarian principle, **10** 326

authority (-ies), **7** 389; **13** 25, 148, 150;
   alchemical, slaying of, **13** 427;
   and children, **17** 211;
   of the Church, **10** 326;
   dialects and, **16** 2;
   faith in, **4** 653, 655;
   inner, **9ii** 48, 49;
   of *lumen naturae,* **13** 151;
   magic of female, **9i** 158;
   parental, **7** 97; lack of, **17** 107a; unwillingness to abandon, **17** 107a;
   political/religious, **16** 227;
   reaction to, **1** 193;
   search for, **16** 227;
   submission to, **4** 658;

authority (*cont.*):
    and therapist, **16** 2, 23;
    of tradition, **13** 149
autism/autistic: and autoeroticism, **3**
    429*n*, 430;
    in schizophrenia, **5** 37;
    withdrawal, in negativism, **3**
    428, 429
autochthonous image, **13** 352
autoerotic/autoerotism/autoeroticism,
    4 246; **6** 403, 621; **8** 432; **11** 770;
    12 5; **15** 158;
    and autism, **3** 429*n*, 430;
    infantile, **5** 37; **6** 898;
    insulation, **18** 343;
    isolation, **13** 307;
    projections and, **9ii** 17;
    type, **17** 136
autofécondation intérieure, **7** 233*n*
Autogenes, **9ii** 307*n*; **11** 60; **13** 419;
    see also under Barbelo; Monogenes
autogenic training, **11** 874; **16** 1,
    230
auto-hypnosis, **1** 354, 422;
    drowsiness as, **2** 134
automata, reflex, **8** 955
automatic phenomena, **3** 56;
    memory of, **1** 58;
    misreading as, **1** 155
automatic writing, *see* psychography
automatism(s)/automatization, **2**
    847–9, 857; **3** 32, 71, 182, 196; **4**
    615; **8** 22, 383, 384; **14** 225; **18**
    560;
    and auto-suggestion, **1** 100; **2**
    847;
    catatonic, **3** 7, 187–93;
    command, **3** 17, 27, 30;
    creative force of, **1** 184–5;
    and distractibility, **1** 339;
    dream role, **1** 119, 304;
    and feeling of strangeness, **1**
    87, 93, 99;
    linguistic, **2** 136;
    melodic, **3** 117;
    motor/automatic movement(s),
    1 85–6, 129; **2** 136; **3** 196; **18**

729, 730, 733; and partial hyp-
    nosis, **1** 82;
    psychic, sexual theory of, **5**
    185;
    and semi-somnambulism, **1** 29,
    41–2, 77–9; table-turning in, **1**
    49, 80–95, 126;
    unconscious/unconscious con-
    trol, **1** 82; **4** 28; **17** 296;
    verbal, **1** 98;
    visual, **1** 98;
    see also feeling-tone(d) *s.v.*
    ideas; Janet
automatisme ambulatoire, **1** 1, 18; **8**
    383;
    and vagrancy, **1** 19
automatisme téléologique, *see* Flournoy
    s.v. WORKS
automatons, children treated as, **17**
    16
automobiles, dream-motif, **8** 535
autonomism, God as, *see* God *s.v.*
autonomous/autonomy, **7** 85, 302;
    13 12, 437;
    activity, of the unconscious, *see*
    unconscious *s.v.* autonomous;
    conscious, **18** 154;
    in divine process, **11** 290;
    individual, **4** 655, 657;
    of matter, **13** 286;
    moral, **4** 667;
    of naive intellect, **5** 95;
    psychic contents, **13** 48, 54;
    God/God-image as, **7** 402; **18**
    1507;
    primitives and, *see* primitive(s)
    s.v.
    see also under affect(s); anima;
    animus; archetype(s); com-
    plex(es); image(s); psyche;
    shadow; symbol; unconscious;
    unconscious contents, collec-
    tive
Autopator, **9ii** 298&*n*; **18** 1481
autos-da-fé, **11** 291
auto-suggestion/ -suggestibility, **1**
    25–9, 82; **4** 17–20, 206; **5** 55; **7**

267, 344; **9i** 130n; **11** 888, 907; **18** 725;
    and dreams, **1** 117; **12** 327;
    hypnosis through, **1** 96;
    "Instantaneous," *see* Miller, Miss F., "Phenomena of Transitory Suggestion. . . ";
    and malingerers, **1** 305;
    and motor area, **1** 85, 86;
    and self-deception, **1** 438
autumn, **5** 408, 665n
Autun, **9ii** 145n
auxiliary function, *see* function(s) *s.v.*
Avalokiteshvara, **12** 125
Avalon, A. (pseud. of Sir J. Woodroffe):
    The Serpent Power, **9i** 81n, 142n, 312n, 467n; **12** 123n, 184n, 246n, 397n, *fig.* 39; **13** 35n, 334n; **14** 580n; **16** 380n, 558; **18** 1331n;
    (ed.) *Shri-Chakra-Sambhara Tantra*, **9i** 142n; **11** 113n, 791n; *see also* Woodroffe
Avantius, Josephus, **12** 356n
avarice, **13** 355
avatar(s), *see* Hindu/Hinduism *s.v.*
Avenarius, Richard, **6** 767;
    Der menschliche Weltbegriff, **6** 767n
"Ave Praeclara," *see* ALCHEMICAL COLLECTIONS: *Theatr. chem. s.v.* Melchior Cibinensis

average, statistical, **10** 744
Avesta, **5** 243
Avicenna, *see* ALCHEMICAL WRITERS *s.v.*
avidyā, **11** 775; **12** 123
avis Hermetis, *see* ANIMALS *s.v.* bird, of Hermes
awareness, **11** 774;
    mind and, **11** 804;
    unreflecting, **11** 272;
    see also consciousness
Axiom of Maria, *see* ALCHEMICAL WRITERS *s.v.* Maria Prophetissa
ayami, *see* shaman(ism) *s.v.*
Ayesha, *see* Haggard, H. Rider
ayik, *see* Elgonyi
Azael, *see* Azaziel
Azam, C.M.E.E.: case of Felida, **1** 110, 136;
    on periodic amnesia, **1** 17;
    on spontaneous somnambulism, **1** 110, 136, 280;
    Hypnotisme, double conscience, et altérations de la personnalité, **1** 17n, 110n, 280n; **6** 797n
Azaziel/Azazel/Azael (angel), **11** 669, 670, 680; **12** 543;
    in Byron's poem, *see* Byron *s.v.*
Azi-Dahaka, **14** 640n
Azoch/Azot/Azoth, **8** 388n; **12** 207n, *fig.* 142O, 537n; *see also* Mercurius
Aztec(s), *see* American Indians: NORTH *s.v.*

B

ba (soul) (Egyptian), **7** 295; **8** 845;
10 84
Baader, F. von, **4** 748;
Sämmtliche Werke, **14** 581*n*
Baal, **9ii** 182; **11** 350; **18** 1529;
of Edessa, **5** 294;
and Shemesh, **5** 460*n*
Baba Bathra (Talmud), **9ii** 181*n*
Baba Kamma (Talmud), **9ii** 106*n*
Baba Yaga, **9i** 435
Babbitt, F. C., *see under* Plutarch
Babbitt (Sinclair Lewis), **10** 927
babe, *see* infancy; infant
Babel, *see* Babylon *s.v.*
Babinski, J., **16** 1; **18** 943
baboon, *see* ANIMALS *s.v.*
baby, *see* infancy; infant
Babylon(-ia), **11** 612
and Babel: dragon of, in alchemy, **14** 140, 408, 420; tower
of, as symbol, **5** 171;
civilization of, **16** 223;
Creation Epic, **5** 375–9; **18**
234; battle of gods in, **5**
375–8 (*see also* Marduk; Tiamat);
cup of, in alchemy, **14** 387,
414, 426;
gods of, **9ii** 186, 189 (*see also*
Adad; Marduk; Oannes;
triad(s) *s.v.* Trinity);
rite of temple prostitution in,
18 365, 366;
symbolism of, **5** 303, 304, 313;
underworld, **5** 315*n*;
"whore of," **5** 313, *fig.* 22; **11**
721, 723–4; in alchemy, **14**
420; patient's nickname, **18**
335;
see also Gilgamesh Epic
Bacchus, *see* Dionysus
Baccius, Andreas, **12** 518*n*
Bach, J. S., **10** 158; **12** 176; **14** 754
Bachofen, J. J., **15** (*p*84);
Versuch über die Gräbersymbolik,
5 *fig.* 43

backward children, *see* child(ren)
s.v.
Bacon, Francis, **8** 275
Bacon, Josephine D.: "Woman of
the Bees" in *In the Border Country,*
9i 312*n*
Bacon, Roger, **9ii** 143, 154, 404; **16**
221; **18** 1530
Bactria, **9ii** 128
Badenweiler, **13** 169
badi (Malayan), **8** 120
Bad Nauheim: Congresses of
General Medical Society for
Psychotherapy:
4th Congress (1929), 16 (*p*36*n*);
7th Congress (1934), **8** (*p*92*n*);
10 1016*n*, 1035*n*, 1039&*n*;
8th Congress (1935), **10** 1035*n*,
(*p*554)
Badrutt, H., **10** 909
Baechtold-Stäubli, H., and E. Hoff-
mann-Krayer; *Handwörterbuch des
deutschen Aberglaubens,* **9i** 605*n*; **14**
214*n*, 698*n*, 701*n*
baetylus, **14** 770
Baetz, E. von: on "emotional
paralysis," **1** 123*n*, 307; **3** 147;
"Über Emotionslähmung, " **1**
123*n*, 307*n*; **3** 147*n*
Bahaism, **11** 861
Bahamas, **10** 603
"Bahir, Book," *see* Scholem
Bahman Yast, **9ii** 169
Bahr, H., **3** 105
bailiffs, four, **12** 214
Bain, A.: "The Senses and the Intel-
lect," **1** 86*n*
Baïs, **14** 317
Baït, **14** 352
Bakairi Indians, *see* American In-
dians: SOUTH *s.v.*
Bakcheus, **14** 510*n*
Balaam, **5** 421; **9ii** 106, 179
Balak, **9ii** 106
balance: centre of, **7** 311;
loss of, **7** 252–3;

baptism (*cont.*):
336; **14** 75*n*; **17** 270;
as initiation, **18** 256, 361;
initiation rites and, **4** 330; **7**
384, 393;
mass-, **10** 516;
meaning of ceremony, analogy
with psychoanalysis, **4** 330–1;
as mysteria, **18** 255;
pre-Christian, **13** 89*n*;
as rebirth, **5** 494;
Red Sea, as water of, **14** 256–7;
salt/*sal sapientiae* in, **12** 360*n*; **14**
318;
and sprinkling, **4** 330;
symbolism, **18** 364;
transformation through, **10**
136; **11** 335;
water in, **4** 330; **5** 320, pl.
XXVII; **9ii** 281; **11** 161; **12**
455; **13** 89, 104, 111; **14** 319;
and *aqua permanens,* **18** 1360
Barabbas, **9ii** 147; **11** 406
barbarians/barbarism, **4** 550; **6** 118,
150, 172, 173, 178, 346, 357, 453;
11 463; **13** 7, 14;
and Germanic mentality, **10**
19;
untamed energy as, **6** 160
Barbarus Hermolaus, *see* ALCHEMI-
CAL WRITERS: Hermolaus
barbel, *see* ANIMALS *s.v.* fish
Barbelo, **9ii** 307*n*; **14** 34*n*;
Barbeliots, **13** 419, 459; **14**
589*n*;
-gnosis, **9i** 564; **11** 60, 400; Autogenes in, **9ii** 307*n*; **13** 419 (*see
also* Monogenes);
"God is four" in, **9ii** 304; **10**
751; **11** 152*n*, 281, 332, 672; **13**
168*n*;
Metra (uterus) in, **9i** 564
barber: in ancient Egypt, **11**
348&*n*;
in vision of Zosimos, **11** 347,
348; **13** 86&*n*
Barchusen, J. K., *see* ALCHEMICAL
WRITERS *s.v.*

Barcius/Barchius, *see* ALCHEMICAL
COLLECTIONS: *Mus. herm.* and
Theatr. chem. s.v. "Gloria mundi"
Bardesanes (Gnostic), **9ii** 99; **12**
436*n*; **13** 458; **14** 32*n*, 80*n*, 526*n*;
"The Hymn to the Soul," **9i** 38
Bardo Thödol/Book of the Dead (Tibe-
tan), ed. W. Y. Evans-Wentz, **9i**
630&*n*; **11** 905; **13** 37&*n*, 47, 50,
334*n*; **18** 204*n*
"Psychological Commentary of
The Tibetan Book of the Dead," **11**
831–58;
Bardo body, **11** 848;
Bardo existence, **18** 204;
Bardo state, **11** 620, 629, 831,
837–56; **13** 334;
see also Chikhai Bardo; Chön-
yid Bardo; Sidpa Bardo
bariaua (Melanesia), **8** 123*n*
Baring-Gould, S.: *Curious Myths of
the Middle Ages,* **13** 218*n*
Barker, M., **18** (*pp*3–4)
Bar-kuni, *see* Theodore Bar-kuni
Barlach, Ernst: *Der tote Tag/The
Dead Day,* **4** 780; **5** 566*n*, 569*n*; **6**
426*n*; **9i** 396; **15** 142; Old Kule
in, **6** 436, 445&*n*
Barmen, Pomerania, **18** 702
barn, in dream of J.'s patient, **4**
96–9
Barnabas, Epistle of, **13** 116
Barnabus, **11** 656
Barnaud, N., *see* ALCHEMICAL
WRITERS *s.v.*
Baroldus, Wilhelmus, **14** 67*n*
Baroncini, L., **2** (*p*586*nn*)
Baroque, **14** 199;
art, **15** 176
Barth, K., **18** 1674&*n*; *Bibelstunden
über Luk,* **11** 177*n*; *Credo,* tr. J. S.
McNab, **11** 177&*n*
Bartholomaeus Anglicus, *see* Glan-
ville, Bartholomew de
Bartholomew, Book of, *see* BIBLE:
Apocrypha etc. *s.v.*
Bartsch, Karl, see *Meisterlieder der
Kolmarer Handschrift*

bathing (*cont.*):
-place, in dream of J.'s patient, **4** 96–9;
surprise in, **14** 144&*n*, 188
bath kol, **9ii** 167
Batiffol, P.: "Le Livre de la Prière d'Asenath," **12** 456*n*
"battle of the faculties," **7** 302
battle of the gods, **5** 375–7
Baubo, **9i** 167, 312, 313;
chthonic, **9ii** 24
Baucis, *see* Goethe: *Faust:* Characters *s.v.* Philemon
Baudouin, C., **10** 1052; **18** (*pp*673*n*, 765*n*)
Bauer, W.: *Griechisch-Deutsches Wörterbuch zu den Schriften des neuen Testaments,* **9ii** 333*n*
"Baumann, August," in hysterical patient's fantasy, **1** 435–8, 444, 466, 474
Baumann, J., **1** 220&*n*; "Über Willens- und Charakterbildung auf physiologisch-psychologischer Grundlage," **1** 220*n*
Baumgartner, M.: *Die Philosophie des Alanus de Insulis,* **9i** 572*n*; **11** 229*n*
Bavarian Board of Physicians, **18** 740
"bay," *see* etymologies *s.v.*
Bayle, A., and Esquirol, **3** 322&*n*
Baynes, Cary F., **1** 168*n*; **7** (*pp*v, 6*n*, 124*n*); **13** (*pl*); **15** 77*n*; tr. into English of *I Ching,* see under *I Ching*
Baynes, Charlotte A.: *A Coptic Gnostic Treatise,* **11** 62*n*, 97*n*; **12** 138*n*, 139*nn*, 140*n*, 458*n*; **13** 212*n*; **16** 378*n*
Baynes, H. G., **1** 168*n*; **6** (*p*v); **7** (*pp*v, 6*n*, 124*n*); **10** 1052, 1069; **13** 460*n*; **18** 384, (*p*623*n*);
Analytical Psychology and the English Mind, J.'s foreword, **18** 1421–7;
Germany Possessed, **18** 1422, 1424;
Mythology of the Soul, **9i** 319*n*;

18 1134, 1402*n*, 1422, 1423;
"On the Psychological Origins of Divine Kingship," **14** 351*n*
"bazaar," *see* association-chain(s) *s.v.*
bear/bearskin etc., *see* ANIMALS: bear
Bear, constellations of, **5** 155; **9i** 342; **9ii** 190;
Great Bear/Ursa Major/Big Dipper/Charles' Wain, **5** 156*n*; **9ii** 188; **13** 176*n*; **14** 265*n*; Little Bear, **14** 176&*n*
beard, man with: in dream, *see* "Pointed Beard;"
in hallucination of boy who stabbed his sister, **17** 137; **18** 810–14
bearings, taking one's, **12** 132; *see also* centre *s.v.* finding of
beast(s), *see* ANIMALS *s.v.*; *see also* blond beast; Nietzsche *s.v.* blond beast
Beatrice (Dante), **13** 215
Beatus, Giorgius, *see* ALCHEMICAL COLLECTIONS: *Theatr. chem. s.v.*
Beauchamp, C. L., **10** 257
"beautiful and good," **9i** 60
beauty, **10** 135, 139; **11** 954;
in Mass ritual, **11** 379
Schiller on, **6** 126–8; aesthetic mood, and concept of, **6** 206–9; play instinct and, **6** 171–3; as religious ideal, **6** 195;
in Western art, **6** 488; **10** 724
Beauvais, **9i** 461
beaver, *see* ANIMALS *s.v.*
Bechterew, W. von: *Psyche und Leben,* J.'s review, **18** 915;
"Über die Geschwindigkeitsveränderungen der psychischen Prozesse zu verschiedenen Tageszeiten," **2** (*p*270);
"Über zeitliche Verhältnisse der psychischen Prozesse bei in Hypnose befindlichen Personen," **2** (*p*270)
Becker, Ferdinand: *Die Darstellung Jesu Christi unter dem Bilde des Fisches,* **14** 238*n*

Becker, Th.: *Einführung in die Psychiatrie,* J.'s review, **18** 919
bed(s): bridal, *see* bridal bed;
   in dreams, **9i** 584; **16** 310;
   as symbol of alchemical vessel, **14** 438–40
Bede, **12** 522*n*
Bedford College, London, **8** 660
bed-wetting, *see* enuresis
Beelzebub, **7** 111; **10** 536; **13** 180; *see also* Saturn *s.v.*
Beer, P.: *Geschichte, Lehre und Meinungen aller bestandenen und noch bestehenden religiösen Sekten der Juden und der Geheimlehre oder Cabbalah,* **14** 572*n*
bees, *see* ANIMALS *s.v.*
Beeson, C. H., **13** 419*n*
Beethoven, Ludwig van, **17** 206
beetle, *see* ANIMALS *s.v.*
Beghards and Béguin(e)s, **9ii** 139, 235; **16** 517*n*;
   and Schwestrones, **9ii** 139*n*
beginning, **13** 34;
   of work, Mercurius as, **13** 283
behaviour:
   TITLE: "Psychological Factors Determining Human Behaviour," **8** 232–62;
   American, *see* America(n) *s.v.* way of life;
   causality and, **8** 41;
   and instincts, **8** 272;
   outward, and mental activity, **1** 339*n*;
   pattern of, and archetypes, **3** 565; **5** 337, 467, 474; **8** 352, 398, 404, 528*n*, 841, 931*n*; **9i** 6*n*, 91; **10** 831, 846–7; **11** 222*n*; **16** 254*n*;
   psychic, sudden alterations in, **1** 357;
   and real man, **10** 967;
   rules for, **5** 673;
   typology of, **10** 890
behaviourism(-ists), **10** 141, 928–9
beheading/decapitation, **13** 95; **14** 730;

see also cutting off
Behemoth, *see* ANIMALS *s.v.*
"behind," as region of unconscious, **12** 55
Behr, A.: "Erinnerungsfälschungen und pathologische Traumzustände," **1** 117*n*
Being/being: Eleatic principle of, **6** 52;
   God as, **9ii** 301; **13** 256*n*;
   and not-being, **12** 557;
   unitary idea of, **8** 960; **13** 43;
   Universal, **11** 952; **13** 59
Beit, H. von (H. von Roques), **18** 1134;
   Gegensatz und Erneuerung im Märchen, **18** 1134*n*;
   Symbolik des Märchens, **18** 1134*n*
Bel, **11** 173–6
Belenius, *see* ALCHEMICAL WRITERS: Apollonius of Tyana
belief, **8** 804;
   Christian, **17** 292; in Jesus Christ, **13** 207;
   collective, **11** 463;
   content of, and psychology, **11** 376;
   difficulty of, **8** 790;
   and doubt, **11** 294; **14** 651;
   and illusion, **18** 566
   "invention" of, **11** 339;
   and reality, **10** 1005;
   uncompellable, **11** 516;
   unreflecting, **10** 521
Belilios, A. D., **18** 681
Belinus, *see* ALCHEMICAL WRITERS: Apollonius of Tyana
bell(s): in Mithraic ritual, **11** 342; **18** 616;
   -ringing, **3** 81–2
Bellator ignis, **13** 184*n*
"belle indifférence," *see* hysterical subjects/hysterics
Belletête,—.: tr., *Contes turcs,* **13** 278*n*
Bellus, *see* ALCHEMICAL WRITERS: Apollonius of Tyana
belly, **7** 110, 111;

BIBLE

Textual citations are drawn from the following versions: AV: Authorized ("King James") Version, cited unless otherwise indicated; DV: Douay-Reims Version; RSV: Revised Standard Version (1952); RV: Revised Version (**5** 231, 439); Septuagint: Karl von Weizsäcker version (1875) referred to in **11** 298n; ZB: Zürcher Bible (first tr. 16th cent.); Luther's version is referred to in **14** 624n. Books are arranged below according to the order in AV.

Psalms (*cont.*):
18:10), **12** 397*n*;
(18:6–7) (DV and Vulgate, = AV 19:4–6), **12** 469*n*;
13 384*n*; (18:9) (AV), *see* (17:10) (DV); (18:10) (AV) *see* (17:11) (Vulgate);
(19:4–6) (AV), *see* (18:6–7) (DV);
(21:7) (DV), *see* (22:6) (AV);
(21:22) (DV), *see* (22:21) (AV);
(22:6) (AV), **14** 146&*n*; (= DV 21:7), **14** 484*n*; (22:21) (AV and Vulgate, = DV 21:22), **12** 520&*n*, 545*n*; (DV), **13** 182*n*;
(23:7ff.) (DV), *see* (24:7ff.) (AV);
(24:7) (AV), **14** 146&*n*;
(24:7ff.) (AV), **14** 484; (= DV 23:7ff.), **13** 182;
(27:8), **11** 326;
(28:3) (DV), *see* (29:3) (AV);
(29:3) (AV), **14** 627*n*; (= DV 28:3), **13** 182*n*; (29:6) (AV and Vulgate, = DV 28:6), **12** 520&*n*; (29:7) (RV), **5** 231; (29:10), **13** 182*n*; **14** 627*n*;
(33:6) (DV and Vulgate, = AV 34:5), **12** 465*n*;
(34:17) (DV, = AV 35:17), **13** 182*n*;
(37:4) (DV, = AV 38:3), **16** 420*n*;
(44) (DV, = AV 45), **12** 474*n*;
(44:3) (DV), **12** 474;
(45:5) (DV, = AV 46:4), **12** 475*n*;
(51:7), **14** 644;
(54:7) (Vulgate, = AV 55:6), **12** 518*n*;
(61:3), **6** 390;
(68:3) (DV), *see* (69:2) (AV);
(69:2) (AV), **14** 465*n*, 469; (= DV 68: 3), **12** 434*n*; **13** 183; (= Vulgate 68:3), **14** 469;
(69:14f.), **14** 465*n*;
(71:6) (DV and Vulgate, = AV 72:6), **14** 288*n*; (71:7) (?, DV

and Vulgate, = AV 72:7), **14** 20&*n*, 28*n*;
(74:13ff.) (RSV), **5** 384;
(78:69) (AV, = DV 77:69), **12** 522*n*;
(82 (Vulgate 81) :6), **5** 132; **9ii** 327*n*; (RSV), **11** 692;
(89), **11** 575, 578&*n*, 661, 685; (89:10) (RSV), **5** 381; (89:28, 34, 35) (RSV), **11** 569&*n*; (89:33ff.) (RSV), **9ii** 169&*n*; (89:46, 47, 49) (AV and RSV), **11** 571&*n*;
(92:10) (AV and Vulgate, = DV 91:11), **12** 520&*n*;
(102:6), **14** 728*n*;
(104:4), **10** 728;
(105:38) (= AV 106:38), **12** 434*n*;
(113:14), **8** 967*n*;
(118:22), **14** 640*n*;
(127:4) (RV), **5** 439;
(129:1) (DV), *see* (130:1) (AV);
(130:1) (AV), **14** 469; (= DV 129:1), **12** 434*n*; **13** 181*n*;
(139:5), **14** 588;
(139:7–9), **15** 196*n*;
(147:3), **16** 249*n*; (147:9), **9i** 428*n*
Proverbs: dating of, **11** 609;
(1:20–1) (DV and Vulgate), **12** 465;
(6:12), **9i** 576*n*;
(8:22–35), **11** 126*n*, 609&*n*, 634&*n*; (8:29–30) (RSV), **11** 634&*n*;
(10:25), **14** 636*n*
Ecclesiastes: (9:16), **11** 615*n*
Song of Songs/of Solomon/*Cantica Canticorum*, **3** 279; **6** 392; **14** 44, 154&*n*, 185, 592, 625*n*; **16** 361, 438, 460;
(1:1) (DV), **6** 394; **9ii** 320; **14** 565*n*; (AV and RSV), **14** 565*n*; (1:4), **14** 24; (1:4–5), **14** 30; (1:5), **9ii** 329; **12** 434*n*; **14** 24, 172*n*; (1:6), **14** 172*n*;
(2:1), **6** 392; **14** 73*n*; (2:2), **14**

(26), **13** 267; **14** 485; (26:26ff.),
13 384*n*; (26:39), **11** 659&*n*;
(27), **14** 485; (27:15ff.), **9ii** 147;
(27:46), **11** 204; **14** 484*n*;
(28), **14** 485; (28:2), **14** 186*n*,
475
Mark, **11** 299; **18** 568;
(1:6), **18** 1521; (1:23), **18** 1473;
(3:21), **11** 647*n*; **14** 782&*n*;
(5:2), **18** 1473;
(9:49), **14** 319&*n*; (9:50), **14**
324–5, 327;
(10:7), **14** 583; (10:18), **9ii**
105*n*;
(16), **14** 485; (16:9ff.) (given as
11:19 in error), **18** 1560&*n*
Luke, **11** 299; **14** pl. II;
(1:37), **4** 148; (1:78f.), **11** 177;
(2:35), **5** 435*n*; (2:49), **11** 197;
(4), **13** *fig.* B6; (4:1f.), **14** 494*n*;
(4:34), **18** 1473;
(5:10), **9ii** 145;
(6:4) (Apocryphal insertion of
Codex Bezae), **10** 676; **11** 416,
696*n*, 745*n*; **13** 292; (6:35), **9ii**
144, 327*n*;
(7:12–14), **4** 150;
(10:18), **9i** 534*n*; **11** 650*n*; **13**
171*n*; **18** 1617; (10:42) (DV),
12 488*n*;
(11), **13** 141; (11:29f.), **9ii**
173*n*; (11:31), **12** 466*n*; **14** 535;
(11:33ff.), **9i** 593;
(12:24), **9i** 428*n*; (12:49), **8**
391*n*; **10** 733*n*; (12:58f.), **11**
133;
(13:3), **14** 268; (13:7), **4** 149;
(15:22f.), **10** 480*n*;
(16), **11** 416; (16:8), **9ii** 225*n*;
11 620*n*; (16:17), **9ii** 340*n*;
(17), **13** 141; (17:20f.), **9ii** 69*n*;
(17:21f.) (various trs.), **14** 9&*n*;
(17:24), **9i** 533*n*; (17:33), **14**
671*n*;
(18:19), **18** 298*n*;
(19), **14** 158*n*; (19:12), **14** 258;
(19:12ff.), **9ii** 255; (19:27), **9ii**
167*n*;

(21:26), **14** 472*n*;
(22), **14** 485; (22:44), **13** 390*n*;
(23:42), **14** 41*n*; (23:43), **14**
475; (23:44), **12** 434*n*;
(24:42), **9ii** 186*n*; **18** 1561;
(24:43), **9ii** 174
John, Gospel of, **8** 395; **11** 179,
210*n*, 228, 418, 445; **13** 366; **16**
458; **18** 1549;
(1), **9ii** 340*n*; **11** 657; (1:1–3), **5**
496; **14** 397; (1:1), **9ii** 330; **11**
212; **12** 497*n*; (1:2), **9ii** 230;
(1:3), **11** 173, 628&*n*; **12**
550&*n*; **13** 116*n*; **14** 653*n*; (1:4,
5), **8** 389*n*; **9i** 536; **9ii** 330; **14**
48*n*; (1:5), **14** 476; (1:9), **14**
124*n*, 337*n*; (1:9–11), **12** 356*n*;
(1:14), **12** 497*n*, *fig.* 158; (1:18),
11 174*n*; (1:30), **5** 496; (1:46), **6**
438&*n*; **14** 344*n*;
(2:4), **11** 197;
(3), **13** 136–7&*n*; **14** 178*n*;
(3:4), **4** 782; (3:4ff.) (AV and
Greek), **5** 332–4; (3:8), **18**
1532*n*; (3:12) (RSV), **9ii** 314,
316; (3:13) (DV), **14** 291*n*,
294*n*; (3:14), **5** 163*n*, 575; **9ii**
291&*n*; **11** 349; **12** 517; **13** 137,
449; **14** 251, 483, 607*n*; (3:30),
5 288*n*;
(4:10), **9ii** 288*n*, 289, 312*n*;
(4:13–14), **16** 485*n*; (4:14), **11**
313; **13** 137; (4:24) (RSV), **5**
99&*n*; **13** 137; **14** 9; (Greek),
14 9*n*;
(5:2), **9ii** 200*n*; (5:2ff.), **14**
187*n*; (5:37), **14** 627;
(6:35), **13** 403; **14** 181*n*; (6:44),
11 379*n*; (6:53, given as 6:54 in
error) (RSV), **9ii** 314;
(7:37–9), **11** 313; (7:38), **9ii**
336; **11** 935; **12** 155; **14** 372*n*;
(8:58) (DV), **12** 431;
(9:1), **9ii** 299*n*;
(10:9), **9ii** 290*n*; (10:30) (AV),
11 380; (RSV), **5** 134*n*; (10:34),
5 132; **9ii** 144, 327*n*; **11** 235,
416, 438*n*, 655&*n*; (10:35), **11**

John (*cont.*):
692&*n*;
(12:25), **14** 671*n*; (12:31), **8**
426; **11** 250; **14** 27*n*; (12:32),
12 492*n*;
(14), **14** 530; (14:6) (RSV), **11**
647&*n*; (14:9) (AV), **11** 380;
(RSV), **5** 134*n*; (14:11) (RSV), **5**
134*n*; (14:12), **11** 204; **14** 529;
(RSV), **11** 655&*n*, 692&*n*;
(14:16f.), **11** 655*n*, 691*n*;
(14:26), **11** 655&*n*; (14:30), **11**
250;
(15:1), **13** 458*n*; **14** 181*n*; (15:1,
4, 5), **11** 299; (15:5), **11** 418; **14**
181*n*;
(16:11), **8** 426; (16:13), **11**
655&*n*; (16:15), **11** 173*n*;
(16:28) (RSV), **5** 134*n*;
(18:36), **9ii** 69*n*;
(19:34), **11** 315;
(20:17) (RSV), **5** 134*n*;
(20:24ff.), **18** 1561;
(21:21ff.), **5** 287
Acts of the Apostles: (1), **14** 485;
(1:7), **4** 148; (1:9), **14** 288*n*;
(2:3–4), **5** 232; **9ii** 210*n*; (2:13),
8 596;
(3:21), **6** 444; **14** 474; **18** 527;
(5:29), **10** 840;
(7:43), **9ii** 128*n*;
(8:9–24), **10** 75&*n*; (8:30), **10**
544;
(9:3ff.), **6** 712*n*;
(10:10ff.), **6** 717*n*; (10:19) (DV,
Latin and Greek), **11** 421;
(10:28), **6** 719;
(11:4ff.), **6** 717*n*;
(14:11), **11** 656&*n*;
(17), **14** 485; (17:29) (AV and
Greek), **9ii** 299&*n*; (17:30), **9i**
470; (Vulgate), **9ii** 299&*n*
Romans: (3:19), **5** 89;
(6:6), **14** 596;
(7:19), **10** 834; (7:21), **9ii**
123&*n*; (7:24), **14** 774&*n*;
(8:17) (RSV), **11** 655&*n*;

(8:19ff.), **14** 474*n*; (8:22), **10**
679;
(12:2) (RSV), **9ii** 73;
(13:1), **10** 521;
(14), **14** 485;
(15:7) (RSV), **5** 100&*n*;
Corinthians, St. Paul's First Epistle
to, **7** 243*n*;
(1:23), **18** 1515;
(2), **13** 141; (2:10), **14** 9*n*;
(RSV), **11** 659*n*; (2:11), **14** 9*n*;
(5:2) (AV and Latin), **9ii** 44*n*;
(10:4), **9ii** 143; (10:16) (DV),
9ii 178*n*;
(11:3) (DV), **14** 626*n*; (11:7), **14**
626*n*; (11:23ff.) (Karl von
Weizsäcker version, Greek and
Vulgate), **11** 298&*n*;
(12:4–6), **11** 207;
(13), **18** 1710; (13:4ff.), **13**
391*n*; (13:12), **14** 745*n*;
(15:5ff.), **18** 1561; (15:8), **14**
68*n*; (15:14ff.), **18** 1561,
1563*n*; (15:22), **18** 527, 529;
(15:37–55), **18** 1710; (15:45),
14 592; (15:47), **9ii** 71*n*; (DV),
14 554&*n*, 592; (15:53f.) (DV),
12 475*n*
Corinthians, St. Paul's Second Epistle to: (3:5) (Greek, Latin, DV),
11 421;
(3:6), **14** 10*n*; (3:17) (DV), **11**
212;
(4:16), **14** 28*n*;
(6:15), **9i** 576*n*;
(10:7) (AV, DV, RSV), **11** 421;
(11:2), **14** 568;
(12:7), **10** 843; **14** 206*n*;
(13:14), **11** 207&*n*
Galatians, **5** 318
(2:20), **11** 890*n*, 949; **14** 520;
(3:27) (RSV), **5** 594*n*;
(4:4) (DV), **12** 474&*n*; (4:9), **12**
456(7)*n*; (4:26–5:1), **5** 312;
(5:13), **5** 95*n*;
(6:2) (RSV), **5** 95*n*
Ephesians: (1), **14** 485; (1:7), **5** 95*n*;

*   *

bin, **9ii** 185
Binah, **9i** 576*n*, 588*n*; **12** 313; **13**
411; **14** 643*n*
binarius, **11** 122; **12** *fig.* 185; **14** 659;
as Eve, **11** 104&*n*, 262;
evil/devilish, **8** 962; **11** 104&*n*,
120*n*, 180, 256; **14** 238, 554; **16**
403, 525*n*;
see also NUMBERS *s.v.* TWO
Bi-neb-did, **5** 358
Binet, Alfred, **1** 24*n*, 339; **3** 55; **4**
155&*n*; **6** 863; **7** 408; **10** 2; **18**
798;
on attention, **3** 12*n*, 19;
on automatism, **1** 119, 339;
and Féré, **1** 28, 96*n*;
and hysterical patients, **1** 75,
97, 117*n*; **3** 35*n*; experiments
with, **1** 98, 138, 160;
and Janet's experiment, **1** 93;
on somnambulism, semi-, **1** 5,
78;
WORKS:
*Alterations of Personality (Les
Altérations de la personnalité),* **1**
5*n*, 21*n*, 75*n*, 78*n*, 93*n*, 97*n*,
117*n*, 119*n*, 138*n*, 280*n*,
339*n*; **3** 35*n*;
"Attention et Adaptation," **3**
12*n*;
ed., *L'Année psychologique,* **18**
961*n*
Bin Gorion, Josef: *Der Born Judas,* **9i**
253*n*;
Die Sagen der Juden, **11** 368&*n*;
12 542*n*
Binswanger, L., **2** 1035, 1044,
1094&*n*, 1136, 1182&*n*; **18**
1027&*n*;
Die Hysterie, **4** 159;
"Freud'sche Mechanismen in
der Symptomatologie von
Psychosen," **4** 28*n*;
"On the Psychogalvanic Phenomenon in Association Exper-
iments," **2** 1035*n*, 1044*n*, 1326*n*;
6 681*n*; **8** 23*n*; **18** 978

biochemical processes, psyche and,
8 660
biography, **4** 745;
TITLE: "The Type Problem in
Biography," **6** 542–55;
psychological, **18** 1130
biological: phenomena, changes in,
5 194;
process, individuation as, **11**
460;
and sexual processes, **17** 79
and spiritual view-points, **17**
160, 161; as opposites, **17** 160;
biology, **4** 777; **11** 488, 491;
causality in, **8** 822;
energic standpoint and, **8** 30;
human—, aim of, **13** 291;
inadequate basis for therapy,
11 450;
knowledge and, **10** 548, 636;
and the psyche, **8** 232; **10** 6, 23;
and psychology, **8** 232; **17** 157;
and purpose, **9i** 465;
and the "unique," **8** 821
Bion, W. R., **18** 55, 135, 137
Bircher, **4** 604
bird, soul-, *see* soul *s.v.*
birds, *see* ANIMALS *s.v.*
Birkhäuser, P., **10** 736, pl. III
Birs river, **13** 129
birth, **7** 300; **8** 662; **13** 69; **17** 10;
alchemical, **16** 509; and germi-
nation of stone, **13** 392; new,
16 516, 525–37 (*see also* rebirth);
anal, **5** 279;
of Buddha, *see* Buddha *s.v.*
conception and birth;
-chamber, baptismal font as, **18**
364; Egyptian, **18** 361;
of child, **17** 134, 224, 226; archetype, **9i** 290; in case of
Anna, **17** 6–10; conflict in, **17**
11–60;
child's ideas of, *see* child *s.v.*
birth, theories of;
of Christ, *see* Christ *s.v.*;

control, *see* contraception;
in cowshed, **5** 291*n*;
data, *see* astrology;
and death, *see* death *s.v.*;
divine, **6** 319;
of divine child, **16** 482&*n*;
dual/second, **5** 494; **9i** 94, 140;
of Leonardo da Vinci, **9i** 93–5,
140*n*;
-giving: in Egyptian mythol-
ogy, **5** 359,*fig.* 24; orifice (Mexican), **5** *fig.* 12;
of God, in Eckhart, **6** 427–8;
of god(s), **6** 448 (*see also* lotus
s.v. birthplace);
goddess of, *see* Hecate;
of hero, *see* hero *s.v.*;
of lapis, *see* lapis *s.v.*;
miraculous, **9i** 282, 285;
of Mithras, *see* Mithras *s.v.*;
pangs of, **5** 438*n*;
place of, **5** 291*n*, 579*n*; **10** 969;
stone as, **13** 128 (*see also* lotus);
psychic, **8** 756;
of Redeemer, **13** 393;
rites at, **11** 287; **16** 214;
of saviour, *see* saviour *s.v.*;
in stable, **5** 579*n*;
stone-, **13** 128, 132;
of symbol, **6** 445;
theories of, *see* child *s.v.* birth,
theories of;
through water and spirit, **5**
333–5;
through wind, **5** 334, 335;
trauma of, **11** 842;
tree-, *see* tree;
twice-born, *see* twice-born;
virgin, *see* Christ *s.v.* birth;
water and, *see* water *s.v.*;
see also rebirth
birth control, *see* contraception
Bischoff, E.: *Elemente der Kabbalah,*
12 313*n*; **14** 158*n*
bisexuality, **5** 324;
in libido myth, **5** 441;
of tree, **5** 324;

see also androgyne; hermaphrodite
bishop, children's/*episcopus puerorum,* **9i** 458, 460
Bismarck, Prince Otto E. L. von, **7**
279, 306; **10** 425
bitch, *see* ANIMALS: dog(s)/bitch
Bithus of Dyrrhachium, **12** 456*n*
Bithynia: Attis/Cybele cult, **5** 662*n*
biting by animals, *see* animal(s) *s.v.*
Bitos (in Zosimos), **12** 456
bitterness/*amaritudo,* **14** 245–55,
330, 333–4;
and wisdom, as opposites, **14**
330;
see also under colour(s); *lapis
philosophorum;* salt
Bitys, prophet at court of King
Ammon, **12** 456*n*
Bjerre, P. C.: **10** 1049, 1055, 1068;
"Zur Radikalbehandlung der
chronischen Paranoia," **6** 467*n*
black, *see* COLOURS *s.v.*
"black, going," *see* Negro(es) *s.v.*
European assimilation
Black Elk (Sioux holy man), vision
of, **14** 266*n*
Blackfoot, *see* Melampus
blackmail, between children, **4** 462,
472, 474
Blackman, A. M., *see under* Erman
blackness, *see* COLOURS: black/etc.
blacksmith, in Rig-Veda, **5** 556
bladder: disturbances of, **18** 884;
hyperaesthesia of (in J.'s patient), **16** 554;
irritation of, and dreams, **4** 83,
736
Blake, W., **6** 422*n*; **11** 905*n*; **12** *figs.*
14, 19; **15** 142, 151;
"devouring" and "prolific"
types in, **6** 460, 559;
"The Marriage of Heaven and
Hell," **6** 460*n*
Bland, C.C.S., and H. von E. Scott,
see under Caesarius of Heisterbach
Blanke, F., **9i** 16;

light of, **13** 141;

living, **8** 604, 605; **13** 76;

marks inflicted on, **8** 725 (*see also* circumcision; scars);

of Mary, **13** 174, 175 (*see also below* transfiguration);

microcosmic, **13** 171;

and mind, **12** 377, 396, 450; **18** 69, 135; cofunctioning/inter-action, **8** 33; duality, **8** 606; pair of opposites, **8** 619; separation of, **14** 671; two aspects of single fact, **8** 619, 621; **18** 70;

mortal, **13** 170;

mortified, **13** 137;

mystical, **11** 229, 337; **12** 478; **13** 142*n*;

-openings, **4** 291; **5** 206;

as personification of shadow of ego, **18** 40;

pneumatic, **5** 513; **13** 77;

proportions, **7** 250;

protruding parts and concavities, **5** 208*n*;

and psyche, **7** 194; **8** 618; **10** 780; **12** 562; **13** 11, 475–6; **16** 1, 386; causal relation, **14** 767; coalescence, **12** 327; cofunctioning, **8** 502, 605, 657;

and psychic representatives of organs, **12** 440;

purified, **13** 190, 201*n*; **16** 495;

reconstituted, **5** 356;

rediscovery of, **10** 195;

relics, **13** 128;

resurrection of, **9i** 202, 637; **11** 855; **12** 475, 511; **13** 127, 205; **14** 763;

rights of, **7** 504;

round, **13** 173;

in sacramental meal, **11** 304;

secretions, **5** 458 (*see also* spittle);

self rooted in, **13** 242;

sensations, **13** 43; and affects, **3** 86, 87; in "godlikeness," **7** 467;

peculiar, **7** 75;

separation of consciousness

from, **8** 954–5;

shining, **13** 188; 194;

soul and, **12** 327, 396, 397–9, 460, 492, 512–13; **13** 126, 157, 316; **14** 670, 674, 685, 742; as animation/life of, **8** 662; **14** 670, 673, 742; of Antimimos, **12** 456; coniunctio/union of, **12** 417, 462, 500, *fig.* 159; **13** *fig.* B5; **14** 475, 476, 681*n*, 685, 693, 742; **16** 503; as opposites, **14** 31; problem, **8** 948; separation/freeing from, **12** 165; **13** 287; **14** 673, 691, 696, 699, 710, 722, 739, 742, 773, 774; **16** 190; unity of, **14** 664, 670, 673, 696;

soul/body/spirit, **12** 165*n*, 327, 474, *figs.* 142K, 196; **13** 176*n*, 381; *anima* as *ligamentum corporis et spiritus*, **9i** 555; *lapis* as, see *lapis philosophorum s.v.* body/etc.; Mercurius as, *see* Mercurius *s.v.*; spirit as *ligamentum animae et corporis*, **9i** 386; trichotomy of, in three sonships, **9ii** 118; union of, **14** 663–4, 774; —, in stone, **13** 283*n*; unity of, **14** 66;

spirit and, **9i** 572; **9ii** 118; **10** 195; **13** 103, 126, 137*n*, 263; **14** 41&*n*, 175, 328, 722; are one in God, **9i** 572; as opposites, **14** 1, 3, 655, 658; separation of, **12** 165, 366*n*, 377, 511*n*; **14** 293, 664, 722; as triads, **9ii** 100; union of, **13** 261; **14** 635, 677, 679, 681*n*, 736, 742; **16** 499;

spirit-, **13** 69, 266 (*p*32);

spiritualization of, *see* spiritualization *s.v.* alchemical;

-stimulus, and dreams, **7** 21;

stone-, motif of, **13** 132;

or substance, **13** 168*n*;

subtle, **5** 513; **9i** 202, 392; **11** 160, 848; **12** 394, 417; **13** 137*n*, 262; **16** 486 (see also *corpus subtile*);

boredom (*cont.*):
and telepathic experiments, 8 838
Borges, J. L.: "Pascal's Sphere," 6 791*n*
Borgias, 10 809
Borgnet, A. and E.: eds, *Beati Alberti Magni Opera omnia*, 13 173*n*
boring: finger gesture, 5 204;
and fire-making, 5 208, 210, 217, 227;
masturbatory, 5 227;
see also etymologies *s.v.* "to bore/born"
Börner, C. G.: *Auctions-Katalog 184*, 12 *fig.* 244
Borobudur, India, 11 908; 18 409
Bororos (of central Brazil), 13 253
Boschius, *see* ALCHEMICAL WRITERS *s.v.*
Boss, Medard, 18 (*p*347), 822, 824, 825
Bostonians, 6 527&*n*
Bostra, Titus of, 13 450
Botho, C.: *Sachsisch Chronicon*, 5 *fig.* 4
bottle, spirit in, *see* Grimm brothers *s.v.* fairytale
Bouché-Leclercq, A., 9ii 129;
L'Astrologie grècque, 9i 604*n*, 605*n*; 9ii 129*n*, 136*n*, 163*n*, 174*n*; 11 356*n*; 14 140*n*, 493*nn*
Bouelles, Charles de, *see* Bovillus
boulders, in paintings of J.'s patient, 9i 526, 529, 531
boundary(-ies), 7 124, 132, 159, 225;
cross as, 11 429, 434, 445
Bourdon, B., 2 24, 105–6;
"Recherches sur la succession des phénomènes psychologiques," 2 105
Bourget, P., 17 233;
L'Étape, 18 185
Bourne, Rev. A., 1 20
Bourru, H., and F. Burot: *Variations de la personnalité*, 1 110&*n*
Bousset, W., 9ii 171;

The Antichrist Legend, 5 576*n*;
9ii 168*n*; 14 14*n*;
Hauptprobleme der Gnosis, 9i 242*n*; 9ii 128*n*, 307*n*, 308*n*, 325*n*, 344*nn*; 11 350*n*; 12 456*nn*, 458*n*; 13 168*n*, 275*n*, 278*n*, 450*n*; 14 32*n*, 42*n*, 80*n*, 160*n*, 498*n*, 566*n*, 576*n*, 585*n*, 587*n*, 595*n*; 16 355*n*, 378*n*;
"Die Himmelsreise der Seele," 14 299*n*, 300*n*; 18 1528
Bovillus, K. (Charles de Bouelles):
Ein gesichte Bruder Clausen ynn Schweytz und seine deutunge, 9i 14&*n*; 11 478&*n*
bow and arrow symbolism, 5 439&*n*; *see also* arrow
bowl(s)/goblet(s): four, containing coloured water, in dream, 11 128; 12 286–7;
golden, in dream, 8 555; 18 251–2, 260, 261, 265, 375;
in mandalas, 11 136;
in schizophrenic patient's picture, 18 407;
silver, with nuts, in dream, 11 90, 109; 12 299
boy/Boy, 9i 279; 13 228, 314;
charioteer/Charioteer, *see* Goethe: *Faust:* Characters *s.v.*;
crowned, 13 *fig.* 32;
in dream, 12 196–7;
in golden clothes, 10 730;
naked, 9i 268, 396*n*;
radiant, 9i 268;
sacrificed, 11 370;
spirit as, 9i 396;
see also *puer*
Bozzano, E.: *Popoli primitivi e manifestazioni supernormali*, 9i 532*n*
Braceschus, Johannes, *see* ALCHEMICAL COLLECTIONS: *Bibl. chem. s.v.*
Bradford, R., 11 266*n*
Brahe, Tycho, 9ii 136*n*
Brahma, 5 177, 449, 545, 620, pl. XLVI*a*; 11 890*n*; 12 533, *fig.* 75;
and lotus, 5 449, pl. XLVI*a*;
and sun, 6 331–2;

bread (*cont.*):
 of life, **13** 403;
 in the Mass, **11** 310, 381–4;
 consecration formula, **11** 322;
 and wine, **11** 337; **12** 417–18,
 475 (*see also* Eucharist);
 in Mithraic ritual, **11** 342; **18**
 616;
 superessential, **10** 651;
 "through God," **9ii** 139
breakdown, nervous, *see* nervous
 disorders/etc.
breaking lines, **18** 407
breakthrough: beyond intellect, **11**
 892;
 in Goethe and Nietzsche, **10**
 657; **11** 905;
 Greeks and, **11** 905*n*;
 in satori, **11** 887
break-up, radioactive, *see* radioactive decay
breast(s), **9i** 605;
 -beating, **5** 390;
 Christ's, **9ii** 320;
 drink of immortality from, **5**
 581*n*;
 exposed to arrow shot, **5** 429;
 as "mama," **5** 26*n*, 373;
 multiple, **9i** 312
Breasted, J. H.: *Development of Religion and Thought in Ancient Egypt,*
14 356*n*
breath, **7** 151, 217; **8** 601, 662;
 -body(ies), **8** 390, 664; **13** 69,
 286; **14** 748; **16** 486; as carrier
 of life, **13** 76*n*; incorruptible,
 13 76; (*see also* Chinese alchemy
 s.v. diamond body);
 and consciousness, **11** 373;
 control of, **11** 867; **13** 41, 76*n*;
 of God, **13** 174;
 Holy Ghost as, **11** 235, 237, 276;
 as psyche, **11** 771;
 soul, **13** 262; higher, **13** 57;
 as spirit, **5** 334; **10** 146;
 of spirit, **12** *figs.* 115, 142 I;
 subtle, **13** 104
breathing, *see* respiration

Bremen, **18** 486
Brendan, St., **12** 417*n*
Brenner, A., **5** 45*n*
Brentano, Bettina, **1** 123
Bresler, J.: "Kulturhistorischer
 Beitrag zur Hysterie," **1** 143*n*; **3**
 321*n*
Brethren of the Free Spirit, **9ii**
 139&*n*, 235; **14** 646; **18** 1530;
 and Eckhart, **9ii** 302
Breuer, Joseph, **2** 640; **4** 30; **16**
 143; **18** 421, 922, 1223;
 and hysteria, **18** 1147; case of
 Anna O., **4** 30, 205; **7** 4–
 7/413–15, 199; conversion, **1**
 298; and Freud, theory, **3** 55; **4**
 28, 29, 34–5, 207–9, 577; **15**
 62; **16** 33, 231, 256; trauma
 theory, **7** 10/417; **15** 62;
 and S. Freud, *Studies on Hysteria, see* Freud: WORKS *s.v.*
Breukink, H., **2** 501; **3** 10;
 "Über eknoische Zustände," **3**
 10*n*;
 "Über Ermüdungskurven bei
 Gesunden und bei einigen
 Neurosen und Psychosen," **2**
 501*n*
"Brevis manuductio," *see* ALCHEMI-
 CAL COLLECTIONS: *Mus. herm. s.v.*
 Philalethes
brh, **9ii** 181, 182
bridal bed: cross as, **13** 457;
 in the field, **5** 214*n*; **8** 85
bride/bride and bridegroom, **9i**
 453; **13** 124, 268, 273*n*, 384*n*,
 457; **16** 410, 508;
 atomization of, **16** 398;
 of Christ, *see* Christ *s.v.*;
 heavenly bride, tree and, **13**
 460;
 heavenly bridegroom, Christ
 as, *see* Christ *s.v.* bridegroom;
 Mercurius as, **13** 268;
 sun as bridegroom, **14** 30,
 568&*n*
"Bride of Corinth," **5** 577
bridge, **4** 321; **7** 8/417, 123;

Christ's life as, **11** 272;
intellectual function as, **7** 206;
man as, *see* man *s.v.*;
see also rainbow
"bright," *see* etymology(-ies) *s.v.*
bright and dark, as opposites, **14** 1
brightness, hypnagogic, **1** 43
Brihadāranyaka Upanishad, *see* Upanishads *s.v.*
Brill, A. A., **2** (*pp*vi, 439*n*, 466*n*, 492*n*), 1000*n*; **18** 1027&*n*;
"Psychological Factors in Dementia Praecox," **4** 744*n*
Brimo/Brimos, **5** 577; **9ii** 339
Brinktrine, J.: *Die Heilige Messe in ihrem Werden und Wesen,* **11** 309*n*, 324*n*
British and American Society for Psychical Research, **18** 758
British Anthropological Society, **15** 80; **18** 141
British Broadcasting Corporation, **18** 1689
British Empire, *see* India
British Medical Journal, **18** 135, 1502
British Museum, **7** 394*n*; **18** 139, 266
British Psychological Society, **8** 660
British Union of Fascists ("Blackshirts"), **18** 1327*n*
broadsheets, illustrating Ufos, *see* Ufo(s) *s.v.*
Broca's convolution, **1** 186
Brocken, spectre of, **10** 727
Brody, D., **15** (*pp*132-3)
Broglie, L. de, **9i** 490*n*; **18** 69&*n*
bronchi, **13** 379
Brons (Grail legend), **6** 401*n*
Bronze Age, **11** 484; **18** 81
bronze, leprous (alchemical), **12** 207
brooch, lost and found, **1** 146
brooding, **1** 320*n*; **4** 417; **18** 1810, 1811;
heat of, **12** 441;
of Holy Spirit, **13** 104
brook, **9i** 336;
symbol in Zen Buddhism, **11** 878, 891
brother(s), **1** 7; **7** 279-83; **17** 12,
28-9, 213-14;
big, fantasy of, **17** 29, 54;
in dreams, **2** 840-4;
fellow men as, **5** 104&*n*;
hostile, **8** 712; **9ii** 133&*n*, 134, 142, 401; **11** 254*n*, 629; **13** 29*n*; **18** 523 (*see also* Abel; Cain; fratricide);
monsters as, **9ii** 184;
mortal and immortal, **5** 596*n*;
neurotic attachment to, **2** 1008;
sinister, *see* Medardus;
and sister, *see below*;
unequal, motif of, **5** 356
brother-sister pair, **12** 336, 404, *fig.* 118; **16** 410, 419;
hierosgamos of, **18** 1692;
incestuous, *see* incest *s.v.* brother/sister;
marriages, **5** 350, 458;
as opposites, **12** 436, 438;
royal, **5** 676; **9i** 442, 445, 449&*n*; **9ii** 59, 329; **16** 401;
see also *coniunctio;* incest
Brother Klaus/Nicholas of Flüe/Niklaus von der Flüe, **3** 562; **9i** 12-19, 131, 133; **9ii** 47; **13** 477; **14** 220; **18** 221;
TITLES: "Brother Klaus," **11** 474-87; "The Miraculous Fast of Brother Klaus," **18** 1497-8;
fast of, **18** 1497-8;
God in, **9i** 16, 131; **11** 486;
(Trinity) vision of, **3** 562; **7** 119; **8** 413; **9i** 12-18, 131; **10** 643; **11** 476-9, 483-6, 947; **18** 1538; Gnostic parallel to, **11** 486; painting of, in Sachseln parish church, **3** 562; **9i** 12, 16; **11** 478, 479, 947; —, mandala form of, **9i** 12, 16; of threefold fountain of God, **16** 378*n*, 403*n*;
see also Blanke; Bovillus; Dürrer; Gundolfingen; Lavaud; "Pilgrim's Tract;" Stoeckli; wheel(s); Wölflin
Brown, G. Spencer, *see* Spencer Brown

Brown, W. Norman: "The Sources and Nature of Pūrusa in the Pūrusasukta" (includes tr. of Rig-Veda), **5** 648*n*, 656*n*

Brown, William, **16** 255; "The Revival of Emotional Memories and its Therapeutic Value," **16** 255

Browne, L. F., **18** 206, 208

brownies, **9i** 408

Bruce MS., *see* CODICES AND MSS.: Oxford *s.v.*

Bruchmann, C.F.H.: *Epitheta deorum quae apud poetas Graecos leguntur*, **12** 172*n*; **14** 420*n*

Brüel, O., **10** 1048, 1055, 1068

Brugsch, H.: *Adonisklage und Linosliede*, **5** 316*n*;
Dictionnaire hiéroglyphique, **5** 235*n*;
Religion und Mythologie der alten Aegypter, **5** 235*n*, 357*nn*, 358*nn*, 359*n*, 367*n*, 389*n*, 408*n*, 410*n*; **9ii** 322*n*; **14** 14*n*, 25*n*, 483*n*

Brünhilde, *see* Wagner: *Der Ring;* Wotan

Brunner, C.: *Die Anima als Schicksalsproblem des Mannes*, J.'s foreword, **18** 1276–83

Bruno, Bishop of Würzburg, **12** 524;
Expositio Psalmorum, **11** 161*n*; **12** 524*n*

Bruno, Père, J.'s letter to, **18** 1518–31;
ed., *Élie le prophète*, **18** (*p*673*n*)

Bruno, Giordano, **5** 24; **8** 696

Bruns, Gerda, *see* Wolters

Bruns, L.: *Die Hysterie im Kindesalter*, J.'s review, **18** 884–7

Brunton, C., **18** 202

brutality, *see* Christian/Christianity *s.v.* early

Brutus, and Cassius, **5** 429–31, (*p*461)

Bry, J.-T. de, **12** *fig.* 8

Bubastis, *see* Isis *s.v.* festival of

Buber, Martin, **18** 1536;

Ekstatische Konfessionen, **5** 139*n*, 140*n*, 141*n*; **6** 47*n*;
Die Erzählungen der Chassidim, **18** 1526;
"Religion und modernes Denken," J.'s "Reply," **18** 1499–1513;
Tales of the Hasidim, **18** 1526*n*

Buber, Salomon: ed., *Midrash Tehillim*, **12** 545*n*

Buch der Alaune und Salze/Liber de aluminibus et salibus, ed. J. Ruska, **14** 320*n*, 472*n*

"Buch der heiligen Dreifaltigkeit," *see* CODICES AND MSS: Munich

Buchenwald, **10** 404; *see also* concentration camps

Bücher, K.: *Arbeit und Rhythmus*, **5** 218*n*;
Die Aufstände der unfreien Arbeiter, **5** 104*n*

Buchman, Frank, **11** 275*n*; **18** 1676; *see also* Oxford Group(s)

Büchner, L.: *Kraft und Stoff/Force and Matter*, **11** 508&*n*; **18** 1383&*n*

bud/budding: imagery of, *see* Hölderlin;
tree, symbol, **5** 368*n*

Buddha, **5** 437, 470; **6** 453; **8** 705; **9i** 248, 517, 587, 638; **10** 192, 779, 986, 992, 1002–6; **11** 10, 516, 518, 666, 879, 896, 919–26, 952; **12** 20, 22, 169; **14** 520; **15** 191; **17** 311; **18** 409, 745;
TITLE: "On the Discourses of the Buddha," **18** 1575–80;
Adi-, **11** 912;
Amitābha, **11** 839, 852, 912–16, 920; **12** 125; **14** 14*n*; land, **9ii** 236*n*; **11** 913, 919, 931–2, 942; sun and, **11** 915; water and, **11** 915–19; —, in yoga exercise, **11** 929;
Amitāyus, **11** 912, 921, 926; **14** 14*n*;
Bodhisattva, **5** 492; **6** 298; **12** 169;
-child, **12** 313;

C

cab, **4** 218–19
Cabala/Kabbala, **9i** 576&n, 579&n,
588; **9ii** 111, 191, 340n; **11** 595n,
727; **12** 313, 427n; **13** 152, 167–8,
173n, 401, 411, 420, 460; **14** 2n,
6n, 14n, 18–19, 25n, 266, 548,
572n, 591, 592&n; **18** 1480,
1516–17, 1666, 1830–1;
  and alchemy, **14** 18–19&n,
652;
  Anthropos/etc. in, **14** 18;
  "Gabal" (Paracelsus), **13** 167;
15 40
  hierosgamos in, **14** 18–19, 568;
  lapis/stone in, **14** 45n, 568,
640–3;
  see also Knorr von Rosenroth:
Kabbala Denudata
cabalism, **9ii** 105, 267; **10** 779; **14**
551, 558, 566, 569, 634&n;
  cabalistic arts, **13** 148n
  number in, **12** 313;
  tree in, see *sefiroth* s.v.; Yesod
s.v.
cabalists, **8** 735; **9ii** 425; **14** 592n;
  Satan as, **13** 148n
Cabasilas/Kabasilas, N., **11** 324; **12**
417, 421;
  "De divino altaris sacrificio," **11**
324n
cabinets, natural history, **8** 821
Cabir/Cabiros/Cabiri, **5** 183&n, 184,
299, *figs.* 13, 14; **12** 273, 302,
308; **14** 589;
  Gnostic, **9ii** 313, 332;
  phallic aspect of, **5** 180;
  Telesphoros (Aesculapius), **12**
fig. 77; **14** 304n; **17** 300;
  see also Goethe: *Faust* s.v.
Characters
Cabrol, F., and H. Leclercq: *Diction-
naire d'archéologie chrétienne et de
liturgie*, **9ii** 145n
Cacodaimon, **5** 593
Cadmia, **14** 87n
Cadmus, **5** 306; **14** 85–7&n, 483n

caduceus, **9i** 533n; **11** 160n; **12** 6,
fig. 23; *see also* Mercurius *s.v.*
caelum/coelum, **13** 171n; **14** 46, 691,
698, 703–5, 757, 763, 770, 774;
  Mercurius as, **13** 268;
Caesar, as god, **5** 133n; **18** 373,
1342, 1568–9; *see also* Julius
Caesar
Caesarian section, **17** 23
Caesarism, **7** 395; **17** 311;
  and Jesus, **17** 309
Caesarius (Monk) of Heisterbach,
9i 532; **13** 114, 245; **14** 167;
  *Dialogus miraculorum/The Dia-
logue on Miracles*, tr. H. von
E. Scott, and C. C. S. Bland, **9i**
532n; **9ii** 377n; **13** 114n, 245n;
14 167n, 404n
Caetani-Lovatelli, E.: *Antichi monumenti illustrati*, **5** 530n
Cagastrum/cagastric, *see* Paracelsus:
ARCANA *s.v.*
Cagliostro, Alessandro di, **5** 282n
Cahen (Cahen-Salabelle), R., ed.
and tr. of J.'s essays, in *L'Homme à
la découverte de son âme*, **18** (*p*3),
1357&n
Cain, **11** 576, 619, 629, 654, 669; **14**
555; as copy of Satan, **11** 254n,
618, 619, 628;
  see also Abel; Byron
Cairo, **12** 155;
  tombs of Khalifs, **18** 753
calcinatio, *see* opus, alchemical,
stages in *s.v.*
Calcutta: Indian Science Congress
in, **10** 993;
  University, **10** 1006
calendar: Aztec, **12** *fig.* 41;
  ecclesiastical, **11** 118; **12** 314,
317–18;
  Mexican, **12** *fig.* 44;
  revolutionary, **9ii** 156
Calid, *see* ALCHEMICAL WRITERS:
Kalid
"Calidis liber secretorum," *see* AL-

CHEMICAL COLLECTIONS: *Art. aurif. s.v.* Kalid
California, **10** 704
Caligula, **9ii** 223
Calixtus I, **6** 19
Callistus, catacomb of, **5** 163*n*
Callot, J., **9i** 464
calves, two-headed, **10** 608
calx, **13** 173*n*;
    viva, **12** 446*n*
Calypso, **7** 338
cambar, **12** 336
Cambodia: goddess in the lingam, **5** pl. XXIX;
    lingam with yoni, **5** pl. XXV
camel, *see* ANIMALS *s.v.*
Camerarius, Georgius, **14** 421*n*
Campbell, C.: *The Miraculous Birth of King Amon-Hotep III*, **9ii** 309&*n*; **11** 348*nn*; **14** 46*n*, 64*n*, 356*nn*
Campion Pendant, **12** *fig.* 263
Camps, P.W.L., **18** 285
Camuset, L., **1** 110
Cana, miracle of, **9ii** 331; **11** 197, 384; **12** 550; **14** 454
Canaanite(s), **5** 280; **14** 350*n*; deities, **18** 1529
Canada, Nootka Indians, *see* American Indians: NORTH
"Canadians who know not . . . ," **7** 318
Cancer (zodiacal sign), *see* zodiac, twelve signs *s.v.*
cancer/carcinoma, **3** 319; **7** 126, 129, 133, 159; **18** 766;
    imaginary, **9i** 190; **11** 12–13, 22, 26, 35; **17** 313;
    neurotic's fear of, **17** 315;
    phobia, **18** 467, 556;
    of stomach, **17** 178
candelabrum, **13** 308
candelulae, **14** 139&*n*
candle(s): and baptism, **14** 316; **18** 364;
    in dream, **11** 58, 60, 90;
    four, **11** 60*n*;
    as phallic symbol, **8** 336

candlesticks, seven, Son of Man between, **5** pl. V*b*
canicula, *see* ANIMALS: dog(s)/bitch *s.v.*
Cannegieter, Hendrik, **5** 370;
    Epistola de ara ad Noviomagum reperta, **5** 370*n*
cannons, **10** 761
Canon of the Mass, **11** 321–30
Canopic: Gate, **14** 287;
    jars, four, **9ii** 187; **13** 360
Canticles, *see* BIBLE: Song of Songs
Cantilena Riplaei, see ALCHEMICAL WRITERS: Ripley *s.v.*
Cantril, H.: *The Invasion from Mars*, **9i** 227*n*
cap, magic, **5** 569; *see also* pileus
Capelle, P.: *De luna stellis lacteo orbe animarum sedibus*, **14** 155*n*
capital, living on one's, **10** 910*n*
capitalists, **10** 610
capitelum, **14** 81*n*; *see also vas*/vessel
Capitol, **14** 70*n*
Capricorn, *see* zodiac, twelve signs *s.v.*
Capron, E. W.: *Modern Spiritualism, its Facts and Fanaticisms*, **18** 698*n*
capsule of heart/*capsula cordis*, **13** 201, 202
captivation ("*Bannung*"), **3** 177&*n*
Capuchins, **6** 316*n*
caput corporum, **12** 491
caput corvi (raven/crow's head), *see* ANIMALS: raven *s.v.*
caput draconis, see ANIMALS: dragon *s.v.* head
caput mortuum, **10** 363; **14** 729; **16** 512;
    in alchemy, as head of black Osiris, **12** 484*n*; **14** 727–30;
    see also head
carbon(s), **9i** 537; **12** 327;
    -nitrogen cycle, **9ii** 411
carboniferous era, **13** 336
carbuncle, **8** 384*n*; **13** 183; **14** 608;
    lapis as, **9i** 580*n*; **12** 552&*n*; **14** 608;
    Mercurius as, **13** 282;

carbuncle (*cont.*):
of sun, **13** 267
Carcassonne, **9ii** 225
carcinoma, *see* cancer
Cardan, Jerome (Hieronymus Cardanus), **9i** 436; **9ii** 130*nn*, 136; **14** 474; **15** 36; **16** 410*n*, 486;
Commentaria in Ptolomaeum de astrorum iudiciis, **8** 869*n*; **9ii** 151*n*;
De subtilitate rerum, **1** 100*n*; **14** 474*n*;
Somniorum synesiorum, **16** 486*n*
cardiac disorder, **18** 839; *see also* heart
cardinal points, four, **7** 367; **12** 282, 299, 457; *see also* quarters
cards for ESP experiments, **8** 833–4, 836, 975
career, transition to, **8** 761
caritas, **5** 129*n*
Carlyle, T.: "Heroes and Hero-worship," **5** 140*n*
Carmel, **13** 411; Elijah and, **18** 1521, 1523, 1526, 1529, 1530;
pagan sanctuary on, **18** 1521
"Carmen," *see* ALCHEMICAL COLLECTIONS: *Theatr. chem. s.v.* Arnaldus de Villa Nova
Carmen Archelai, see Heliodorus *s.v.*
Carmina Heliodori, see Heliodorus *s.v.*
Carnal Pleasure, statue of, **7** 437
Carnitolus, Josephus, **13** 411
carnival(s), **5** 214*n*; **9i** 456;
customs, **9i** 469;
mediaeval, **12** 182;
in Rome, **5** 156*n*
Carnot's law, **8** 48
Carpenter, W. B.: *Principles of Mental Physiology,* **8** 371*n*
carpenter, as hero's father, **5** 515
Carpocrates/Carpocratians, **10** 271: **11** 133; **14** 284
carriage, golden, **9i** 325
carrus navalis, **5** 214*n*
carrying: burden, **5** 460&*n*;
the cross, **5** 460&*n*, 526&*n*;

transitus, **5** 526
Cartari, V., **12** 172;
Le Imagini de i dei/Les Images des dieux, **12** 172*n*, *fig.* 165
Carter, J. B.: *Epitheta Deorum,* **13** 234*n*
Carter, R. K.: *Pastor Blumhardt,* **3** 321*n*
Cartesian philosophy, **8** 845;
and perception, **8** 937;
see also Descartes
Carthage, **9ii** 186
Carus, K. G./C. G., **4** 748; **5** 258; **8** 212, 355, 358, 359, 361; **9i** 1, 259, 492; **9ii** 11; **11** 141, 375; **14** 791; **15** (*p*84) 157; **16** 204, 294; **18** 1070, 1223, 1295, 1732, 1739;
Psyche, **9i** 259; **15** 157*n*
Casaralta, **14** 72
case-histories, **9i** 319; **10** 1042
CASES IN SUMMARY, *listed alphabetically by reporting physician:*
Azam: boy 12½, illustrating periodic amnesia, **1** 17, 280*n*;
Felida, somnambulistic girl whose second state became dominant, **1** 110, 136;
Bleuler: male, middle aged, suddenly attempting suicide without prodromal symptoms, **1** 32;
Boeteau: widow 22, with somnambulism and amnesia, **1** 19;
Bourru and Burot: Louis V., male hysteric with amnesic alternating character, **1** 110;
Fürstner: Sabina S., case of simulation, **1** 352;
Guinon and Woltke: hysterical female, illustrating associations with colour, **1** 22;
James: male, 30, of "ambulatory sort," a psychopath with amnesia, **1** 20;
Krafft-Ebing: servant-girl aged 24 with hallucinations, **18** 712;
Landgraf: male, habitual thief

who simulated imbecility, **1** 344;

Leppmann: mentally defective murderer who simulated imbecility, **1** 343;

MacNish: young female showing sleep disorder followed by amnesia, **1** 24, 280;

Maeder: apprentice locksmith with megalomania, **7** 228–9/ 447–8;

Marandon de Montyel:psychopathic woman who drowned her child and shammed amnesia,**1** 345;

Mesnet: soldier, 27, with somnambulistic attacks with restriction of consciousness, **1** 21;

Mitchell: Mary Reynolds, young woman with character change after deep sleep of 20 hours, **1** 107–8, 136, 280n;

Naef: male, 32, illustrating retrograde amnesia, **1** 17;

Pick: young girl whose daydream passed into twilight state, **1** 117, 304;

Proust: male, 30, with *automatisme ambulatoire*, **1** 18;

Renaudin: character change in young man with periodic anaesthesia of entire body surface, **1** 112;

Richer: woman, 30, a hysteric with hallucinations of children being devoured, **1** 13; hysterical girl, 17, with hallucinations of dead mother, **1** 14;

Rüdin: male, convicted of theft and offences against decency and declared irresponsible because of epileptic stupor, **1** 342;

Schroeder van der Kolk: girl, 15, exhibiting change of character in periods separated by amnesia, **1** 109, 280;

Siefert: male, 36, illustrating

chronic manic state, **1** 187;

Siemens: young male, daylabourer, falsely accused of murder, **1** 348;

Spielrein: schizophrenic woman, *see* Spielrein

Van Deventer: male with hereditary taint, illustrating sanguine inferiority, **1** 187;

see also under Breuer; Flournoy; Freud; Janet; Jung; Riklin

Caspari, C. P.: *Alte und neue Quellen zur Geschichte des Taufsymbols*, **11** 213n

Cassandra, **10** 713

Cassell, P. S.: *Aus Literatur und Symbolik*, **14** 13n

Cassian, J., **9i** 295; **11** 32n

Cassini, Jacques Dominique, comte de Thury ("Professor Thury"): *Les Tables parlantes au point de vue de la physique générale*, **18** 704

Cassino, Monte, **9ii** 139

Cassiodorus, Marcus Aurelius, **13** 401;
   Expositio in Cantica Canticorum, **14** 394n

Cassius, and Brutus, **5** 430–1, (*p*461)

Castalia, fountain of, **18** 258, 259

Castel, W., **18** 708

castes, four, **11** 246

castigation, self-, **5** 589–90

castle, **9i** 646; **12** 166n, 438;
   dragon, **13** 33;
   dream of, **7** 189, 281;
   impregnable, **12** *fig.* 50;
   as symbol, **9ii** 352;
   yellow, **13** 33

Castor, **9ii** 134

castration, **11** 718n;
   TITLE: "A Case of Transvestism Treated by Castration," **18** 822–5;
   complex, *see* complex *s.v.*;
   of mother, **9i** 139;
   motif of, **5** 392; **18** 1057–8,

castration (*cont.*):
1062–3; by snake, **5** 681; **18** 1062;
myth, **17** 200;
as numinous mutilation, **18** 823;
ritual, and incest problem, **5** 299;
as sacrifice of instinctuality, **5** 299;
self-, **5** 530*n*; **9i** 82, 162, 297*n*; of Attis, **5** 392, 585, 659; as ideal sacrifice, **5** 671; of Origen, *see* Origen *s.v.*;
substitution for, in Attis/Cybele cult, **5** 662;
tree-felling as, **5** 659, 662
casuistry, **13** 229
cat(s), see ANIMALS *s.v.*
catacombs, **5** 536, 577;
sun symbolism of pictures in, **5** 163*n*
catalepsy, **1** 39, 40, 50, 262; **3** 3, 12, 13, 161, 182, 193; **18** 780, 820;
psychology of, **18** 1013–20
catamnesis, **1** 338;
in doubtful cases of simulation, **1** 306
cataract, of Nile, **13** 360*n*
catastrophe(s):
TITLE: "After the Catastrophe," **10** 400–43;
cosmic, **3** 523, 559; **10** 694, 696; **18** 754;
personal, **10** 696;
psychic, **10** 673
catatonia/catatonic, **1** 279, 367; **2** 116, 450*n*, 659; **3** 1–15, 57, 173, 315, 346, 471, 473–5, 503, 571, 577; **18** 908;
associations in, **3** 9–11, 22;
automatisms in, **3** 193;
consciousness, **3** 12; **18** 874;
depression, **5** 204;
galvanometer and pneumograph experiments in, **2** 1062–5 *fig.* 9, 1076, 1248–56;
hallucinations, **3** 150;

in hysteria, **2** 1067; **18** 893;
imitation of, **1** 309;
as motility psychosis, akinetic, **18** 895, 908;
negativism, **1** 279; **3** 179;
pathological ideas of, **3** 7;
perseveration in, **3** 12, 22;
and psychological influence of milieu, **3** 472;
stupor, **2** 1072;
suggestibility, **3** 160;
categorical imperative (Kant), **15** 31
category(-ies): *a priori,* **7** 300; **9i** 136*n*;
of the imagination, **9i** 153;
inherited, **7** 220; (*see also* archetype(s));
Kantian, *see* Kant *s.v.*;
mental, **11** 845
Catelanus, L.: *Ein schöner newer historischer Discurs,* **12** 518*n*
caterpillar, *see* ANIMALS *s.v.*
catfish, *see* ANIMALS *s.v.*
Cathari/Cathars/Catharists, **9ii** 105, 139, 226, 229; **11** 470; **13** 277&*n*;
and alchemy, **9ii** 234, 235;
Summa Fratris Reineri, **9ii** 226*n*
catharsis, **7** 437; **16** 137, 230;
cathartic method, **4** 39, 208, 577–8, 622; **16** 33, 134, 138, 154, 274; **18** 893, 935, 947;
psychocatharsis, **4** 577
cathedra, **12** 349&*n*
cathedral, **7** 167–71; **17** 266–9
Gothic, **3** 396; **7** 175; **8** 973; **17** 275; **18** 253; collapsed, **12** 180; tower, **17** 7;
see also Basel; Chartres; Cologne; Lourdes; Notre Dame (Paris); Pesaro; Toledo
Catherine of Alexandria, St., **14** 227; **18** 1751
Catherine of Siena, St., **3** 279; **4** 72
cathexis(-es): ego-, **5** 190;
libidinal, **5** 185*n*, 190
Catholic/Catholicism, **3** 462; **7** 118, 156; **9i** 21; **12** 24, 93, 420; **16** 392; **18** 565;

TITLE: "Why I am Not a Catholic," **18** 1466–72;
and collective unconscious, **8** 338;
and complexes, *see* complex(es) *s.v.*;
J. and, **18** 1466–72;
Monad, **13** 187*n*;
mysticism, **9i** 292;
as patients, **18** 370;
and psychology/psychological analysis, **11** 76, 509, 511, 548–9;
and truth, **18** 1470;
see also Church (Catholic)
Cattell, J. McK.: "Psychometrische Untersuchungen," **2** (*p*270)
cattle, *see* ANIMALS *s.v.*
Caucasus, **7** 224, 243*n*
cauda pavonis, see ANIMALS: peacock
caul, **5** 291*n*
cauldron, **11** 976, 986–92, 1015;
magic, **6** 401*n*;
see also *ting*
causa efficiens/causa finalis, **8** 530
causa instrumentalis, **11** 7*n*
causal: philosophy, **7** 72;
point of view, **7** 88; **8** 471;
-reductive interpretations, **7** 128; Freud and, *see* Freud *s.v.*
causalism, **3** 420, 480; **4** 658; **17** 200;
reductive, in Freud, *see* Freud *s.v.*
causality, **3** 392; **8** 819, 855, 917, 939, 958, 995; **10** 113; **11** 967, 1017; **15** 81, 135; **17** 163; **18** 1187–8;
and behaviour, **8** 41;
and dreams, **4** 67;
and finality, **8** 4–5, 41, 456;
Freud and, *see* Freud *s.v.* reductive causalism;
importance of, **17** 85;
law of, **14** 662; **18** 1471;
life process and, **10** 636;
limits of, **7** 344;
magical, **8** 915, 939;

need for, and fantasy formation, **4** 389;
objective, **7** 210; **8** 5;
opposed viewpoint, **11** 972–4;
and physics, **7** 72*n*;
primitives and, *see* primitives *s.v.*;
psychiatry and, **8** 51;
psychic, **10** 841; **16** 295; and heredity, **17** 85; law of, **5** 69;
psychology and, **4** 679, 687; **7** 501*n*;
relativeness of, **8** 424, 814; **18** 141, 142;
of schizophrenia, **3** 498;
and symbol formation, **5** 332;
and synchronicity, compared, *see* synchronicity *s.v.*;
Western concept of, **18** 1485
causa ministerialis, **11** 7*n*
causation: material, **8** 649, 657; **11** 490;
physical, **3** 467;
psychological, **9ii** 114
cause(s), **9ii** 253;
and aims, **4** 674;
divine belief in, **11** 7;
and effect, **8** 58;
external, **17** 259;
final, **8** 931; and mechanical, **8** 4*n*;
first, **4** 687; **8** 677, 828; **13** 278*n*;
material, **3** 466, **8** 653;
mechanistic and energic views and, **8** 3;
natural, primitives and, **8** 941;
of neurosis, **11** 517; **17** 99;
transcendental, **8** 856
Caussin, N., **9i** 573, 604*n*; **14** 326;
Polyhistor symbolicus, **9ii** 197&*n*, 299*n*; **11** 408&*n*; **14** 326*n*, 344*n*, 728*n*;
De symbolica Aegyptiorum sapientia, **12** 498*n*, 522; **14** 474*n*, 476*n*
Cautopates, **5** 299;
and Cautes, see Mithras *s.v.*

cautopates (*cont.*):
  bull-sacrifice
Caux, *see* Moral Re-Armament
cave/cavern, **5** 579&*n*; **8** 558, 945;
  9i 156; **12** 196–7, 258;
    Cos, in temple at, **5** 577;
    of death and rebirth, **5** 577;
    descent into, **18** 80, 252, 264;
    dream of, **4** 185;
    and grave, **5** 526;
    and hero, **8** 555;
    -man, **12** 117;
    as maternal womb, **5** 659;
    meaning of, **5** 450*n*; **9i** 241,
    247; **12** 438;
    Plato's, **8** 416*n*;
    serpent/dragon in, *see* ANIMALS
    s.v. dragon; serpent;
    seven sleepers in, **5** 282;
    spelaeum, **5** 165*n*, 528, 536;
    worship in cult, **5** 528, 536,
    577
caviar, suggestibility *re*, **5** (*p*447)
Cecrops, myth of, **5** 594; **18** 195,
  260, 262
cedar-tree, *see* TREES *s.v.*
Cedrenus, G.: *Historiarum compendium,* **14** 31*n*
Cedurini (Paracelsus), **13** 210
Celandine, *see* Paracelsus: ARCANA
  s.v. Chelidonia
celestial: Aquaster, *see* Paracelsus:
  s.v. Aquaster;
    family reunion, **13** 290;
    harmony, **5** 235;
    man, **13** 168;
    spirit, **13** 384
Celestius, **6** 34
celibacy, of priesthood, **11** 197; **14**
  106
cell/cellular: degeneration, **13** 48;
    destruction, **3** 471, 493;
    see also brain
Cellini, Benvenuto, **7** 100; **9i** 94,
  311*n*;
    father's vision, **12** 404*n*;
    sun vision of, **1** 101;
    "The Life of Cellini," tr. J. A.

Symonds, **1** 101*n*; **12** 404*n*
Celsus, diagram of the Ophites,
  9ii 128; **14** 574–8, 592*n*;
    "accursed God" in, **14** 575;
    see also Origen
Celts, **13** 154;
    mythology of, **5** 371; **6** 401*n*
cemetery: Miss E's behaviour in,
  1 7;
    walk in, **1** 26
cenobite, **17** 298
censing, **11** 307, 318–19
censor (Freud's concept), *see* Freud
  s.v.
censorship, in modern Switzerland,
  10 427
censure, angry reaction to, **1** 203,
  204
centaurs, **5** 422&*n*;
    origin, **5** 460*n*
centre(s), **7** 398; **11** 435; **12** 310; **13**
  173&*n*, 201, 334, 348*n*; **14** 10,
  555;
    in alchemy, **9ii** 261, 263, 264;
    13 186&*n*, 187;
    in body, **13** 337;
    of/with circle, **9ii** 352; **13** 280;
    allegory of God, **12** 137; **13**
    457*n* (*see also* circle *s.v.* God);
    circular movement and, **13**
    31–45;
    command of, **13** 38;
    concentration on, **12** 186–7,
    200, 211, 273;
    of consciousness, *see* ego *s.v.*
    centre;
    dark, **12** 258–9, 263;
    deity in, *see* deity(-ies) *s.v.*;
    development of psychic, **12** 34,
    35;
    dissolution of, **12** 243;
    of earth, *see* earth *s.v.*;
    ego as, *see* ego *s.v.*;
    of emptiness, **13** 56;
    finding the, **12** 132–3, 148,
    213, 217, 237, 244, 269;
    flowerlike, in patient's picture,
    13 345–6, *fig.* 31;

gibbon and, in dream, **12** 164, 175;
giving life to, **12** 244;
healing significance of, **12** 35, 125;
heart as, *see* heart *s.v.*;
lapis as, see *lapis philosophorum s.v.;*
in man and God-image, **9ii** 265;
of mandala, *see* mandala *s.v.*;
as mediator, **12** 167n;
midpoint of, **13** 187–8; fire in, **13** 186, 188, 257;
of natural wisdom, **13** 187;
non-ego, **18** 379, 401, 408;
objective, **12** 133;
of personality, *see* personality *s.v.*;
place of creative change, **12** 186;
point of reflection, **12** 223–4;
quaternity of, *see* quaternity *s.v.*;
self as, **7** 399; **9i** 248, 634; **12** 44, 137, 310, 327; **13** 67, 189;
of collective unconscious, **12** 265;
soul and (Plotinus), **9ii** 342–3;
spiral movement round, **12** 34, 325–6;
subordinate, **3** 4;
symbols of, **12** 35, 44–5, 325–7;
timelessness of, **12** 135;
of tree, **13** 243;
in unconscious, **7** 509; **9i** 492;
and unconscious contents, **11** 774;
of universal system, **13** 40;
unknown, **12** 327;
as *vitrum*, **12** 224
centrencephalic system, **3** 582n
centrifugal/centripetal sound-shift, **2** 85–9
centring process, **8** 401; **16** 111, 219
"century of the child," **17** 284
Cerberus, **5** 265, 577
cerebellum, **9i** 282;

"son" and, **9ii** 291
cerebrospinal system, **8** 955, 957; **9i** 41; **10** 671;
serpent as, **18** 194
cerebrum, **3** 196; **8** 955; **9i** 42;
and consciousness, **8** 955;
"Father" and, **9ii** 291;
origin of, **18** 14;
removal of, **3** 193
ceremonies: for canalizing libido, **8** 86–7;
cleansing, **7** 286;
puberty and initiation, **8** 725;
religious, and sand-paintings, **13** 31
Ceres, *see* Demeter
certainties, **8** 751
Cervula/Cervulus, **9i** 459n
cervus fugitivus, *see* ANIMALS: deer/ stag *s.v.*
cesspits of medieval magic, **13** 295
Cetonia aurata, *see* ANIMALS *s.v.* beetle/scarab
Ceylon, **10** 877, 1002
Chaeronea, **8** 394
chain, Homeric, **12** 148&n
chain of ideas, and feeling-value, **1** 221; *see also* association-chains
chain-reactions, atomic, *see* atom *s.v.*
chairs, four, in dreams, **9i** 581, 582; **11** 90; **12** 260
chakra(s), *see* Tantra/etc. *s.v.*
Chalcedon, Council of, *see* Church, Councils of
Chaldea/Chaldeans, **5** 303; **9ii** 172; **12** 375n, 456(5); **14** 570n;
dream-interpreters of, **5** 4
Chalewsky, F.: "Heilung eines hysterischen Bellens durch Psychoanalyse," **18** 941
chalice, **5** 626; **9i** 270; **12** 550–1, *fig.* 158; **16** 533;
consecration formula, in Mass, **11** 322;
Damascus, **12** 177;
elevation of, **11** 317;
as mother-symbol, **5** 450n;
preparation of, **11** 311–16

chalybs (steel), **9ii** 204; *see also* steel
Cham (blackness), **14** 43&*n*
chamaeleon, see ANIMALS *s.v.*
Chamberlain, Houston Stewart, **10** 389;
    Foundations of the Nineteenth Century, **5** 119*n*;
    Goethe, **8** 70*n*
Chamberlain, Neville, **10** 420, 421
Champollion, J. F.: *Panthéon égyptien,* **12** *fig.* 66
Champs Élysées, **10** 627
chance, **7** 8, 417, 11/420, 72, 501; **8** 856, 964, 967; **10** 114, 135;
    Chinese mind and, **11** 968–9;
    and explanation, **8** 821;
    groupings, **8** 846&*n*; of occurrences, **10** 124;
    laws of, **8** 819*n*;
    and natural law, **11** 968;
    primitives and, **10** 836;
    and psychoanalysis, **4** 625, 634, 643, 653;
    and synchronicity, **11** 972;
    and telepathic dreams, **8** 504;
    world of, **8** 823
chancefulness, **8** 826
change: of attitude, **13** 473;
    cycle of, **13** 14
    from father to son, **11** 242;
    law of, **14** 503;
    love of, **8** 240;
    psychic, in middle life, **8** 773, 778–83
"Ch'ang Sheng Shu: The Art of Prolonging Life," *see* Wilhelm, R. *s.v.*
Chantepie de la Saussaye, P. D.: *Lehrbuch der Religionsgeschichte,* **5** 395*n*; **9i** 119*n*
chaos, **8** 388; **9ii** 132, 230, 240, 304, 371, 375; **10** 725; **11** 160*n*, 531; **12** 96, 185&*n*, 306, 334, 410*n*, 433, 446, *figs.* 4, 125, 142I, 164, 199; **13** 104, 111, 176*n*; **14** 87, 264, 365*n*, 477, 494, 511*n*, 573, 656; **16** 402, 404;
    and cosmos, **5** 74 (*p*453); **9i**

66; **9ii** 60, 187; as opposites, **9ii** 187;
feeling of, **7** 254;
inner, **14** 388;
magnesia as, **9ii** 241;
maternal aspect of, **14** 415, 505–6;
Mercurius as, **13** 275, 282;
as *nigredo, see* COLOURS *s.v. nigredo;*
original, **11** 92, 160, 357; **14** 373; **16** 363, 375, 462;
polytheistic, **7** 17, 427;
as *prima materia,* **11** 160&*n*; **12** 306, 334, 356, 366*n*, 425, 426*n*, 433*n*, 442, *fig.* 162; **13** 157, 171*n*, 433; **14** 6, 183, 246, 552, 570*n*;
return to, **14** 252–3, 381;
and schizophrenia, **16** 363;
spirit of, **14** 253;
"strange son of," **12** 119; **13** 171*n*;
of Tiamat, **13** 286;
unconsciousness as, **14** 342, 696;
see also *massa confusa/informis;* Tiamat
Chapman, P. F., and Nierenstein, M.: "Enquiry into the Authorship of the *Ordinall of Alchimy,*" **12** 404*n*
Chapouthier, F.: *Les Dioscures,* **5** *fig.* 31
character/characterology, **13** 58;
    TITLE: "The Type Problem in the Discernment of Human Character," **6** 243–74;
    affective, of man, **13** 58;
    without amnesic split, **1** 111;
    astrological, **8** 868, 934; constituents of, **13** 286;
    change in, **1** 77, 107–20; **8** 773; **10** 286; from uprush of collective forces, **11** 25;
    displacement and, **3** 105;
    disturbances of, **3** 153;
    hysteria and, **3** 152;

of God, **18** 636;
hallucinations of, **1** 7, 13, 26;
and hatred of next baby, **17** 7, 213;
hermaphroditism of, **9i** 292–7;
-hero, *see* hero *s.v.*;
illegitimate/adopted, **1** 227; **15** 158; **17** 136;
introversion of, **6** 897;
invincibility of, **9i** 289–91;
Lamia and, **5** 369, 396, pl. XXXVIII*a*;
libido of, *see* libido *s.v.*;
"of light," **7** 395; **13** 299;
and man, as opposites, **11** 742;
in mandala(s), *see* mandalas *s.v.*;
of Mars and Venus, **16** 508–10;
Mercurius as, *see* Mercurius *s.v.*;
-mother relationship, *see* mother *s.v.*
motif, **9i** 268, 270, 273&*n*, 276, 280; **9ii** 304; in mythology, **9i** 259; as quaternity, **9i** 270, 278; unity and plurality of, **9i** 279–80;
myths, **9i** 289;
neuroses, *see* neurosis(-es) *s.v.* of childhood;
numinosity of, **9i** 285;
and parent(s), *see* parents;
and parental imagos, **5** 263–4, 431, 456–7, 505; **7** 88, 99, 294, 296; **16** 212–13 (*see also* imago *s.v.* parental);
personality of, *see* personality *s.v.*;
"polymorphous perverse," *see* Freud *s.v.*;
psyche of, *see* psyche *s.v.*;
psychology, **8** 98; **17** 80, 100–1, 108, 142–3, 284, 286; and individual potential, **17** 106;
psychopathic, **17** 135–6;
quickening of, in womb, **10** 765–6, pl. 8;
-sacrifice, **9i** 324;
sexual precocity in, **4** 216, 228;

17 (*p*5), 136, 145, 222; **18** 1794 (*see also* Freud *s.v.* infantile sexuality);
spoilt, **4** 312; **17** 226, 256, 286;
-stone, **13** 128;
substitution, **18** 1492;
sun-moon-, **11** 717;
Sunday's, **13** 250;
as symbol, **9** 286–7;
as symbol for God, **9ii** 304;
torn out of mother's womb, **5** 316*n*;
unborn, fish symbol of, **5** 290;
unconscious in, **18** 288;
and use of first or third person, **8** 755;
witch thief of, **5** pl. XLVIII;
wonder-, *see* Spitteler *s.v.*;
see also infant(s)
childhood, **1** 210; **7** 202/443;
complex, **6** 201;
customs of, **6** 313;
early, unconscious, **18** 9, 15;
failure to develop from state of, **7** 401; **12** 74, 227, 233, 273;
fantasies, **6** 436;
libido in, *see* libido *s.v.*;
longing to return to, **5** 448, 501, 618–20, 624*n*, 643; **17** 95 (*see also* womb fantasies);
memories, *see* memories *s.v.*;
and neurosis, *see* neurosis *s.v.*;
overemphasized, **10** 932; **17** 284;
patient's psychological state of, **7** 27; **16** 101, 106;
personality disorder and, **7** 270; **16** 44;
psychosis in, **17** 139;
regression/return to, **12** 72–81, 152, 156; **17** 330;
religion and, **11** 762–3; **16** 216;
separation from, and parents, **5** 351; **7** 314, 393; **8** 725; **16** 212;
thinking in, *see* thinking *s.v.*;
see also infancy
childishness, *see* infantilism
childlikeness, **6** 422, 442;

248&*n*, 401*n*;
and Western, **13** 432–4; **14** 249*n*;
see also ALCHEMICAL WRITERS: Wei Po-yang: *chên-yên*; *ch'i*
ching (unchangeable power), **9i** 640
ching (the well), hexagram from *I Ching*, **11** 1011
chirographum (handwriting), **9ii** 366&*n*
chirology, **18** 1818
Chiron, **14** 144*n*; **15** 159
Chiun (Saturn), **9ii** 128&*n*
Chiwantopel, *see* Miller, Miss F. *s.v.*
Chladni, E.F.F., **18** 740&*n*
chlamys, **13** (*p* 192)
Chnuphis serpent, *see* ANIMALS: serpent/snake *s.v.*
Chochma(h)/Hokhmah, **9i** 588*n*; **11** 610; **12** 313; **14** 619*n*, 643*n*
choice: four elements and, **9ii** 100; free, **9ii** 9
choking, **10** 3;
-fits, **7** 45, 47, 52
cholera, **7** 385
choleric temperament, **6** 547, 883, 933, 960
Chönyid Bardo (second part of *Bardo Thödol*), **11** 831, 842–5, 846–52, 854;
chönyid state, torture of, **11** 847–8
chorea: hysterical, *see* hysteria *s.v.*; St. Vitus's dance, **13** 156*n*
chörtens, **9i** 564
Chou, Duke of, **8** 865; **15** 83
Chrétien de Troyes: *Contes del Graal*, **13** 272*n*
Christ/Jesus Christ, **3** 482; **4** 738*n*; **5** 21, 392; **7** 66, 365, 397; **9i** 195, 560, 582; **9ii** 66, 127; **10** 151, 434, 536, 622, 634, 676, 733; **11** 10, 137, 226, 554, 647, 706, 713, 762; **12** 12, 20, 26, 176, 253, 475, 550, *figs.* 18, 101, 197; **13** 77, 111*n*, 137*n*, 141, 148*n*, 168*n*, 174, 201*n*, 207, 277, 372, 393, 450; **14** 14*n*, 158*n*, 206, 520, 555*n*, 607,

726, 782; **15** 105, 159, 191; **16** 400, 485;
TITLES: "Christ as Archetype," **11** 226–33; "Christ, a Symbol of the Self," **9ii** 68–126; "If Christ Walked the Earth Today," **18** 1461; "The Lapis-Christ Parallel," **12** 447–515;
and Adam, Adam Kadmon, *see* Adam *s.v.*;
alchemists and/in alchemy, **9i** 555*n*; **12** 451–2; **14** 12 (*see also below* lapis; *opus;* and passim);
allegoriae/allegories of, **10** 808; **11** 60; **12** 20, 21; **13** 139*n*, 158, 417, 448, *fig.* B4; **14** 6*n*, 121, 146, 147, 148, 188*n*, 205, 429, 454, 465, 474, 484, 627*n*, 728; **16** 525*n*; and devil's, **9ii** 127 (*see also sep. entry below* Christ, animal allegories of)
as alpha and omega, and uroboros, **14** 423;
androgyny of, **9i** 292; **9ii** 319, 320; **10** 772; **11** 337; **12** 22, 25, 547; **14** 235, 524, 527–8, 536, 565; **16** 525; and Christianity, **14** 527; "virgin, in mind," **14** 580;
animal(s) as, *see sep. entry below*;
as Anthropos, *see* Anthropos *s.v.*;
Antichrist, *see* Antichrist *s.v.*;
Apocalyptic, **9i** 106; **14** 524, 633 (*see also* ANIMALS: lamb *s.v.*);
and archetype, **5** 576, 641; **9ii** 70, 123; **11** 146, 226–33, 648; **12** 20, 22; **14** 146; **18** 1648–50, 1669; of consciousness, **13** 299; God-man, **9ii** 283–4; as half-, **9ii** 79; life of, as, **11** 146, 233; of Redeemer, **18** 1676; of wholeness, **9ii** (*p*x), 73 (*see also below* hero);
ascension of, **5** 289; **9i** 204; **9ii** 118; and descent of, **13** 137&*n*; **14** 124;

Christ (*cont.*):

assimilation of, through symbolism, **9ii** 147, 172, 283, 346; **11** 418;

astrological assimilation of, **18** 1520;

and Attis, affinities, **13** 92&*n*;

baptism of, **5** 292, 349; **12** 522*n*; **16** 473; mythological parallels, **5** 288; "twice-born," through, **9i** 93;

Barabbas and, **9ii** 147; **11** 406;

beyond good and evil, **18** 1629–30;

birth of/Nativity, **5** 492; **6** 395&*n*, 436; **8** 388; **9i** 248; **11** 629, 637, 644, 657, 690, 712, 713, 727, 738; **14** 498*n*; as hero, *see below* hero *s.v.*; and medieval festivities, **9i** 458–64; Virgin-, **9i** 11, 22; **11** 81, 553; **18** 1619–20;

birthplace, in cave/stable, **5** 165*n*, 528, 579*n*;

blood of, *see* blood *s.v.*;

body of, **12** 417; **13** 127; in alchemy, **13** 116, 175; **14** 632; Paracelsan, **13** 174; pierced, **14** 23, 25, 144, 372, 631;

as "branch" or "rod," **5** 368*n*;

as bread, **9i** 248; **11** 229;

bride of, **11** 743, 753; human soul as, **9ii** 72 (*see also below* Church);

as bridegroom, **6** 392; **8** 336; **12** 474; "heavenly," **11** 752; *sponsus*, **9i** 450; **12** 478; **14** 106; **16** 355, 438;

as brother, **18** 638;

-child, **9i** 108, 229, 268, 287; **12** *fig.* 42; **13** 132; **18** 1537;

Christification, **7** 43; **11** 758; **14** 530;

and Church, **11** 146, 727; **12** 477; **14** 25; **16** 438; as bride of/*sponsa*, **5** 318*n*, 411&*n*; **8** 336; **9i** 450, 677; **9ii** 41&*n*, 319; **14** 106, 582, 592; **16** 355,

438, 496*n*, 525; as calendar, **12** 314; *corpus mysticum* of, **5** 672; **8** 927; **9ii** 60; **11** 122, 323; **16** 392 (*see also* Church *s.v.*); head of, **10** 751; hierosgamos of, **9ii** 72; marriage of, **6** 392; **9ii** 72&*n*; —, alchemical, as Sol and Luna, **16** 355;

circle as symbol of, **11** 229;

coming of, **8** 388; **14** 277, 282, 285; second, **5** 287; **9ii** (φix), 403; **11** 713, 725; **14** 777; **16** 481;

-complex, **8** 582, 584; **10** 963; as *complexio oppositorum*, **18** 1632, 1650, 1668;

conception of, by wind, **9i** 108–9;

coniunctio/intercourse of, on mountain, **9ii** 314; **12** 209;

and consciousness, *see* consciousness *s.v.*;

as cornerstone/*lapis angularis*/rock, **8** 314; **9ii** 143, 326; **12** 41, 451, 485, 509, 521, *fig.* 172; **13** 134; **14** 10, 11, 643, 685;

and cross, *see* cross *s.v.*;

and crown/diadem, **14** 6*n*;

crucifixion/death of, **5** 368, 398, 445, pl. IX*b*; **11** 378, 406–7, 431, 516, 650, 693; **12** 177; **13** 331, 363; **14** 555*n*; **16** 470; **18** 1661; on Adam's grave, **5** pl. XXXVII; between two thieves, **5** 294; **9ii** 79, 123, 402; **11** 342, 407, 739; **18** 210, 1539; as conflict of divine opposites, **18** 1551; and man's redemption, **18** 1079; mock, *see* ANIMALS *s.v.* ass; parallel in human suffering, **12** 24; perfect man and, **9ii** 124; **16** 470; Peter and, **5** 289; **11** 437; as punishment for slaves, **9ii** 130*n*; symbolism of, **9ii** 125; **12** *figs.* 28, 53; **13** 450 (*see also* ANIMALS: serpent/snake *s.v.*);

demythologization of, **11** 647;
and denarius, as Son of God,
16 525&*n*;
descent into hell/*descensus ad in-
feros*, **5** 512; **9ii** 72; **12** 61*n*, 440,
451; **14** 207, 475; **16** 455 (see
also *descensus ad inferos*);
and devil/Satan, *see* devil *s.v.*;
and Dionysus, *see* Dionysus
s.v.;
disciples of, and dance, **11** 415,
418;
divine/divinity of, **5** 132, 536;
9i 22; **13** 127, 154, 165; **17** 311;
and human, **5** 42*n*; **11** 647,
690; as mystical food, **5** 526;
personal, **5** 259; **17** 311;
dogmatic, **11** 228; **12** 20, 253;
double of, see below *ka*;
dual form/nature of, **6** 31–4;
11 380; **14** 33, 124, 146 (*see also
above s.v.* androgyny of);
as dying and self-transforming
god, **11** 146;
and Elijah, **18** 1521, 1529;
and Evangelists, **5** pl. LX;
evil and, **18** 1633–4;
and family, separation from, **5**
470, 644;
fast of, as *nigredo*, **14** 729;
and fig-tree, **18** 1468;
-figure, **9i** 14; **9ii** 122, 283,
293, 295, 318; **11** 232, 283,
715; **13** 127, 295; **16** 525; dual
aspects of, **9ii** 172; as self, **9i**
661; **13** 296 (*see also below* self;
and *see also* Gnosticism *s.v.*
Christ-figure);
as filius, *see* filius *s.v.*;
as fire, **5** 245; **12** 157, 297&*n*,
451,*fig.* 58; -ball, **10** 766; "life"
as, **11** 60; and nature of, **9i**
288*n*; Son of God in, **5** 244–5;
as fish, *see* Ichthys;
as fisher, **9ii** 174;
future, **13** 390;
genealogy of, **13** 404; **14** 351*n*
(*see also* Adam *s.v.* Christ);

in Gnosticism, *see* Gnosticism
s.v.;
and God, **11** 229, 663; as deliv-
erer from sin, **5** 95; -image, *see*
God-image *s.v.*; as right hand
of, **11** 470, (*p*358); **18** 1526;
Son of, *see separate entry below;*
and healing the sick, **18** 1578;
as hero, **11** 229, 644, 648, 690;
13 79; archetype of, **5** 576*n*,
641; **11** 146, 229, 648; birth/
childhood of, **9ii** 163; **11** 644,
690;
historical/historicity of, and
personal, **5** 259; **9i** 216; **9ii**
123, 277; **10** 551, 751; **11** 648;
12 41, 253; **13** 80; **14** 146, 206,
488, 507; **16** 473; **17** 309; archetype of God-man, **9ii** 283;
and dogmatic, **11** 228; **14** 507,
509; and "inner" Christ, **11**
446; **13** 81;
as Holy Spirit, **18** 1549, 1551,
1553;
as *homo philosophicus*, **12** 476;
as *homo purissimus*, **13** 390;
and horoscope, **9ii** 130*n*;
Host, *corpus Christi*, **14** 639;
humanity of, **9ii** 71; **13** 137*n*,
165; as suffering servant, **14**
145, 494;
as Ichthys, *see* Ichthys;
-image, **5** 536; **13** 127, 295; in
alchemy, **9ii** 122; anthropomorphic, **9ii** 122; as archetype of self, **9ii** 123; of God,
14 586; perfection of, **9ii** 123,
124; in religious art, **14** 526&*n*;
vision of, in Apocalypse, **9i** 14;
imitatio Christi/imitation of, **6**
531; **11** 413, 446, 717, 762,
773; **12** 25, 37, 41, 417; **14** 27,
283, 492; **18** 271, 1553; and alchemist, **12** 452; **13** 433; demands of, in daily life, **11** 522,
524; **12** 7–8; **13** 80–1;
incarnation of, **11** 233, 655,
744; **12** 253, 464; **13** 384*n*; **14**

Christ (*cont.*):
   288, 491, 570, 574;
   inner, **5** 612; **9i** 229, 237; **9ii** 318; **11** 231, 446; **13** 41, 127; **14** 488, 586, 700;
   innocent victim, **18** 1620, 1680;
   and Jewish law, **5** 287, 396;
   as Jewish prophet, **11** 647, 688;
   as *Judex mundi*, **11** 229;
   and *ka*, **5** 318*n*; **11** 177;
   as king and priest, **9ii** 72, 228&*n*;
   as Kyrios, **9ii** 283; **11** 432;
   as *lapis angularis, see above* cornerstone;
   and *lapis philosophorum/*
   philosophers' stone, **9ii** 122, 143, 216, 284, 326, 375; **10** 806; **11** 93, 150, 160*n*, 738; **12** 40, 173, 451, 453, 461, 463, 474, 476, 480, 504, 508, 509–10, 515, 517, 556, 557,*fig.* 99; **13** 127, 134, 158, 162, 289, 384&*n*, 386, 387, 390, 392–5, 437; **14** 45, 144, 146, 150, 186*n*, 235, 295, 355, 397, 419, 485, 508, 567, 643&*n*, 677, 747, 770; **16** 533; and earthly stone, **13** 384*n*; as transforming substance, **12** 517;
   and Last Supper, *see* Last Supper;
   as light-bringer, **18** 1515, 1827;
   as Logos/Nous, **11** 212, 229, 254, 400, 422, 628; **12** 412; **13** 110, 271, 294, 366, 447, 448; **14** 170, 397, 476, 507;
   as man, **11** 645, 647; "encompassed by woman," **9i** 677; **14** 147, 235, 534; inner man as, **14** 700; prototype and goal of, **10** 751;
   in mandala(s), *see* mandalas *s.v.*;
   man's identification with, **11** 105&*n*;
   and Mary, **11** 627, 628; relationship with, **11** 197; in Virgin's womb, **5** pl. III; **12** 139*n* (*see also* Mary/etc. *s.v.* Mother of Christ);
   in Mass: death of, as sacrifice, **12** 415, 417, 419, 451; **14** 423, 474, 631 (*see also below* sacrifice); life represented in, **11** 146, 336, 378, 406; mystical unity of, **11** 337; as offerer and offering, **11** 337; presence of, **11** 307, 323; as priest sacrificer, **11** 307, 388; transformation in, **9i** 209;
   as mediator/redeemer/Saviour, **5** 41&*n*, 246; **11** 202, 229, 420, 658, 659, 661, 684, 690, 693, 695, 739, 754; **12** 252, 415, 417, 452, 453,*fig.* 182; **13** 127, 390, 393; **14** 27, 146, 237, 285, 298; **18** 530, 1687; crucified between two thieves, **18** 210; and death of, **9ii** 66, 402; of man, **11** 643, 688; of Microcosm, **14** 676;
   Mercurius and, *see* Mercurius *s.v.*;
   as Microcosm, **12** 476;
   miracles of, **11** 229;
   as/on mountain, *see* mountain *s.v.*;
   mystic union/*unio mystica*, and stigmata, **5** 438;
   and myth, **10** 551; **11** 648; **18** 568;
   myth-motifs and, **11** 146;
   name of, not to be mentioned, **18** 255;
   and Nicodémus dialogue, **5** 644; **14** 178*n*; and alchemy, **13** 136–7; rebirth symbolism in, **5** 332–7, 510;
   numinosity of, **11** 663;
   opposites contained/united in, **11** 690; **18** 1650;
   and *opus*, alchemical, **13** 393 (*see also below s.v.* Passion);
   "outward uncomeliness" of, **9ii** 216;

Christ (*cont.*):
as Son of Man, *see* Son of Man;
and Sophia, *see* Sophia *s.v.*
sources for, **18** 1656;
as *sponsus, see above* bridegroom;
stigmata/stigmatization, **5** 438; **6** 531; **10** 806; **11** 276; **12** 7, 452,*fig.* 58; **14** 530;
as sulphur, **14** 145, 147, 153;
as sun/*Sol novus*/rising sun, **5** 158, 159, 638; **6** 395; **10** 808; **11** 935; **12** 112, 314, 497; **13** 290; **14** 25, 121; **16** 355; "introitus solis," **5** 496; sungod parallel, **9i** 106;
as sword, **5** 557, pl. V*b*; **11** 357;
on tree, **13** 448;
symbol(s)/symbolism, **8** 559; **9i** 218; **10** 846; **11** 229, 232, 648, 713; **13** 79, 81, 289; **14** 121, 465; alchemical, **14** 507, 642, 704; animal, *see separate entry below;*
in the temple, **5** 531;
temptation(s) of, **5** 523*n*; **10** 733; **13** *fig.* B6; **17** 309, 319; alchemical parallel, **16** 512;
totality/wholeness of, **9ii** 70–1, 74; **11** 229, 414, 446, 667, 690; **14** 652; **18** 271;
Transfiguration of, **5** 244, 286; **9ii** 187*n*; and ascension, **9i** 204; and Peter, **5** 289;
as tree, **13** 401, 458; **18** 550; of life, **13** 243*n*; of Paradise, **13** 243, 419, 453*n*; **14** 75*n*; philosophical, **13** 407&*n*; vine, **11** 229, 299, 384, 418; **12** 478; **13** 458; **14** 181*n* (*see also* cross);
and triad, *see* triad *s.v.*;
trichotomy of, **9ii** 118;
"twice-born," **9i** 93;
Ufo pilot and, **10** 797;
as union of opposites, **11** 690;
and unjust steward, **18** 1642;
virginity of, **14** 527*n*;
as Vishnu, avatar of, **9ii** 272;

visions of: Brother Klaus, **9i** 15; St. Paul, **8** 582;
within, **18** 638;
as Wotan, **10** 373;
yoke of, **12** 24*n*, 25;
as Zeus/Helios, **5** 163*n*;
see also God-man; Son of Man
Christ, animal allegories/symbols of: ass, **9i** 463;
birds, **9ii** 127;
bull, **12** 520–1;
dragon, **5** 576; **13** 416; **14** 141;
eagle, **9ii** 127;
fish, *see* ANIMALS: fish *s.v.*;
lamb, *see* ANIMALS: lamb *s.v.*;
lion, *see* ANIMALS: lion *s.v.*;
peacock, **12** 498;
pelican, *see* ANIMALS: pelican *s.v.*;
phoenix, **12** 498; **14** 285, 474–5;
ram, **9ii** 147&*n*, 148;
raven/crow, **9ii** 127; **10** 846; **14** 728;
serpent/snake, *see* ANIMALS: serpent *s.v.*;
stag, **8** 559&*n*;
stork, **13** 417;
unicorn, **12** 519–23, 547;
uroboros, **14** 423
Christ, Son of God, **9i** 74; **11** 229, 628, 645, 651, 654, 658, 663, 689, 693, 694; **12** 18, 41, 412, 457;
and God as father, **11** 407, 651–2, 659, 689, 691, 694; as love, **4** 738*n*;
as second/younger son, **9ii** 103, 105, 118, 229; **11** 249, 470, 684;
third sonship of, **9ii** 118; *filius regius* and, **14** 124*n*;
see also Basilides; devil *s.v.* God; Ebionites
Christendom, ills of, **13** 147
christening, *see* baptism
Christensen, A. E.: *Les Types du premier homme et du premier roi dans l'histoire légendaire des Iraniens,* **9ii**

130n, 389n; **13** 268n, 458n; **14** 34n; **16** 458n

Christian/Christianity, **3** 279; **4** 640, 662, 668, 750; **5** 119, 615, 683; **6** 964; **7** (p5), 41, 97, 118, 159; **9i** 229, 455; **9ii** 267, 272; **10** 185, 189, 193, 238, 542, 623, 1006; **11** 35, 413, 754; **12** 7, 9, 18–19, 24, 40, 182; **14** 124, 251, 286, 520, 744, 777; **15** 87, 154, 159, 176; **16** 387; **17** 292; **18** 279, 1584;

TITLE: "Background to the Psychology of Christian Alchemical Symbolism," **9ii** 267–86;

in Africa, **9i** 25; **10** 185;

and alchemy, *see* alchemy *s.v.*;

androgyny, *see* Christ *s.v.*;

anima Christiana, **9ii** 68;

ascetic tendency in, **5** 339, 392n; **6** 346; **7** 35; **11** 43; **13** 69;

astrology and, **9ii** 130; **10** 589; **11** 725n;

and Buddhism, **8** 804;

Caesar and, **17** 309;

charity/love, **13** 71, 230, 234, 391;

civilization, *see* civilization *s.v.*;

and collective culture, **6** 107–10;

compensatory relation with, **6** 229;

and consciousness, **8** 751; **13** 164; development of, **18** 1516–17; Goethe's, **13** 295;

conversion, **6** 27;

cross, *see* cross *s.v.*;

devil, as Mercurius, **13** 300;

devitalization of, **18** 1665–6;

dogma, *see* dogma *s.v.*;

dominants, *see* dominants *s.v.*;

dualism of, **18** 1553;

early, **5** 102, 104, 105; **6** 31; **11** 206, 223; **13** 76n; **14** 325; and contemporary brutality, **5** 341, 667; **6** 114; doctrine, rationalizing of, **11** 444; and Jewish law, **5** 396; motif, **13** *fig.* B1; and

slavery, **10** 250; spirit of, transformation through, **5** 667; **8** 644;

education, *see* education *s.v.*;

and end of the world, **18** 564;

esoteric meaning of, **18** (p267), 638;

ethics of, **11** 659; **12** 13;

European developments: French Revolution, **10** 22; German(ic), **9i** 25; **10** 17, 391, 397&n; Western, **11** 772, 779;

evangelical, **11** 736;

and evil, *see* evil *s.v.*;

expansion of, **18** 1389;

extraverted, **6** 191;

and fantasy, **6** 86;

Father, Son in, **9i** 20;

and functions, conflict of, **6** 114–15, 167, 314–16;

and God, relationship with, **5** 130; **10** 507;

and *Gottesminne,* **8** 36; **10** 199;

hermeneutics, **14** 474&n;

hierosgamos in, **5** 411;

Hitler and, **18** 1329;

and *homoousia,* see *homoousia;*

idea(s)/ideal/ideology, **7** 373; **13** 31, 212, 366;

imagery/images in, **11** 81; **13** 228;

and immortality, **16** 223;

impotence of, **18** 1364&n;

Indian influences on, **11** 713;

and individuality, violation of, **6** 110;

and individuation, *see* individuation *s.v.*;

initiation rites, survival of, **7** 384, 393;

Jewish monotheism in, **9i** 189;

"joyful," **16** 400;

and knowledge, **6** 14; **13** 148n;

love, *see* love *s.v.*;

and mandalas, *see* mandalas *s.v.* Christ etc.;

medieval, **6** 231; **11** 463; **13** 25, 399; **15** 154;

Christopher of Paris, *see* ALCHEMICAL
COLLECTIONS: *Theatr. chem. s.v.*
Chronicles of Lanercost, **5** 212
chronograph, Jaquet, **2** 1018, 1181
Chronos, *see* Kronos/etc.
chronoscope, **2** 593
χρνσάνθεμον, **12** 99*n*
Chryse, **5** 450
chrysopoea, see gold *s.v.* -making
Chrysostom, John, *see* John
Chrysostom
Chthonia, temple of, **5** 572
chthonic: bear, *see* ANIMALS *s.v.*;
= dark, **12** 240;
femininity of unconscious, **12**
26;
gods, **12** 204, 435*n*;
Mercurius, *see* Mercurius *s.v.*;
numen of tree as snake, dragon, *see* ANIMALS *s.v.*;
portion of psyche, **10** 53;
prison, **12** 277;
quality, in man, **10** 18–19;
serpent, *see* ANIMALS *s.v.*;
triad, *see* triad *s.v.* lower/
chthonic;
trinity, **12** 539;
underworld, **12** 29;
world, shadow and, **9ii** 64
Chuang-tzu, **5** 663; **6** 95; **8** 917*n*,
923
Chu-hi school of philosophy, **6** 370
Chu-niao, see Chinese alchemy *s.v.*
scarlet bird
Ch'un-ts'iu, see Confusius/Confu-
cianism *s.v.*
Church/Ecclesia, **7** 111, 172, 176; **9i**
156; **11** 778, 903; **12** 3, 32, 36, 37,
93, 176–9, 315, 417; **13** 120, 151,
155, 195, 198, 427; **14** 9, 347,
455*n*, 524; **16** 397, 502, 525; **17**
271;
alchemists/alchemy and, *see*
alchemy *s.v.*;
androgyny of, **14** 527, 528;
assimilation by, **14** 455*n*;
authority of, **10** 654; **11** 273;
loss of, in modern world, **9i** 23;

mass exodus from, **11** 507;
Protestantism and, **11** 862,
864; and State, **10** 516; **16** 221,
222; —, and politics, **10** 520;
—, totalitarianism and, **10**
1019; **11** 83–4;
and Christ/bride of Christ, *see*
Christ *s.v.*;
Christian, **10** 155, 326, 404,
905; **15** 154;
as communion of saints, **5** 335;
corpus mysticum/mystical body,
and, **5** 672; **9i** 279, 661; **11**
337; **14** 528, 535, 631; **16** 525,
526 (*see also* Christ *s.v.* Church);
doctrines of, **11** 685; of Holy
Ghost, **11** 289, 695;
Ecclesia spiritualis, **9i** 164; **14**
9, 12, 22, 27;
and eternal images, **9i** 11;
and evil, **11** 248;
experience of God and, **11** 481;
extra ecclesiam, **18** 632; *nulla
salus*, **7** 325; **12** 96; **18** 663, 669;
fanatical sects in, **18** 355;
Fathers, *see sep. entry below*;
and fear of God, **18** 1539;
Hermas' vision of, *see* Hermas
s.v.;
as hero's grave, **5** 536;
as instrument of redemption,
11 770;
Luna/moon and, **14** 19–20,
218, 436, 524;
mass-action by, **10** 536–7;
and mass education, **18** 1383;
as mother/Mater Ecclesia, **5**
313, 318*n*, 351, 411*n*, *fig.*
XXX*a*; **7** 171, 369; **8** 336, 426;
9i 61; **10** 64; **13** 147, 153; **16**
215, 218; **17** 270; substitution
of, for family/parents, **7** 172;
17 158;
as mother-archetype, **5** 351;
as mother-wife, **5** 318*n*;
Paracelsus and, *see* Paracelsus
s.v. Christianity/Church;
and philosophy, **14** 325, 326;

Church (*cont.*):
  priest, role of, *see* priest/-hood
  s.v.;
  protective function of, **7** 394*n*;
  11 32; **14** 100;
  and psyche, **10** 529; **11** 778;
  dogmas and, **16** 391;
  return to, **12** 40; **16** 218;
  riding animal of, **13** 366;
  schism in, **12** 503; and intercession between God and man, **11**
  82;
  seven, **12** 468;
  soul as, **9ii** 321
  symbol(s)/-ism, **9ii** 352*n*; **14**
  100;
  theocracy and, **16** 222;
  as widow, **14** 17;
  as womb, **5** 536; baptismal font
  as, **5** pl. XXVII; **7** 171; **8** 336;
  17 270;
  see also Christian/Christianity;
  Church (Catholic); Prot-
  estant(-ism)
church(-es), buildings: crooked, in
  fairytale, **9i** 405;
  robbed of magical images, **18**
  626;
  -spire, dream of, **4** 488;
  -warden, **8** 775
Church (Catholic), **4** 658; **5** 101,
  259, 332*n*; **11** 457, 537, 547; **18**
  565, 603;
  absolutism of, **11** 34;
  and analysis, **18** 618;
  and *benedictio fontis*, *see* baptism
  s.v. font;
  and complexes, **16** 218;
  confession(-al), **4** 433; **10** 1045;
  11 86, 285, 542, 547, 549; **16**
  21, 215;
  and cure, **18** 622;
  and departed souls, **11** 855;
  dogma in, **7** 118, 156; **11** 10,
  285; of infallibility, **18** 660 (*see
  also* Mary *s.v.* Assumption);
  in dreams, **11** 32, 40, 43–4;
  and Fascism, **10** 396;

and fire, in Easter rite, **5** 248;
and Holy Spirit, **18** 1534;
marriage rite in, **18** 362;
Mass, *see* Mass;
and meaningful life, **18** 631;
and neurosis, **18** (*p*267), 609,
  615;
and Nicene creed, **11** 215;
and Paracelsus, *see* Paracelsus *s.v.*;
Pax Romana/Imperium
  Romanum in, **11** 82;
and priest/-hood, *see* priest/-
  hood;
quaternity in, **18** 1602,
  1606–7;
rite/ritual of, **7** 118; **9i** 48, 230;
  9ii 403; **11** 285, 778; **16** 215;
  Rituale Romanum, **6** 379*n*; **11**
  242*n*;
and sacrament(s), **11** 7, 862;
  13 232;
and sexuality, **10** 654; **18** 1684;
and sin, **10** 654;
and spiritualism, **18** 700;
and symbols, **7** 118; **8** 110;
  11 75, 547
Church, Councils of, **11** 227;
  Chalcedon, **6** 31
Church, Eastern Orthodox, **10** 372;
  Greek *see* Greece/Greek *s.v.*; Russian, **18** 644–8
Church of England, **18** 640, 641,
  643
Church Fathers, **5** 76, 669&*n*; **6**
  395; **12** 20, 473, *fig.* 197; **13**
  384*n*; **14** 457; **18** 1639–40;
  Desert, **5** 119*n*;
  Gnostic influence on, **6** 398;
  Greek, **18** 527;
  on knowledge and ignorance,
  11 271&*n*;
  patristic allegories, **9ii** 336*n*; **11**
  229; **12** 453;
  and Trinity, **11** 222, 250
Church(-es), Free, **18** 656
churinga(s), *see* Australian aborigines *s.v.*

Chinese, *see* China *s.v.*;
Christian, **11** 292; **12** 12; **16** 225;
collapse of, **10** 295;
conflict with instincts, **7** 17;
consciousness, **13** 229;
and culture, **6** 110&*n*, 477&*n*;
16 227*n*;
errors of our, **6** 665;
history of symbols in, **4** 680;
man, *see* man *s.v.*;
modern, and symbols, **5** 683;
and morality, **7** 30;
and neurosis, **7** 16;
peoples, **13** 83;
and permanence, **10** 923;
regeneration of, **10** 299;
Western, **11** 778; **13** 5; and
war, **7** 74
Civitas Dei, and State, **18** 1324
clairvoyance, **8** 440, 974, 983; **14**
662; **18** 701, 705, 706, 732, 735,
736;
spatial, **8** 862*n*
Clairvoyante of Prevorst (Frau
Hauffe), *see under* Kerner
clan, **7** 238; **8** 725
clang, **2** 76*n*;
displacements, **3** 218;
reactions, **1** 312, tables I–III; **2**
76; **3** 37, 108–9;
see also association(s) *s.v.*
"Clangor buccinae," *see* ALCHEMICAL
COLLECTIONS: *Art. aurif. s.v.*
Claparède, E., **2** 23, 451, 560, 564,
1354; **3** 418, **4** 125, 137*n*, 273,
569;
WORKS:
L'Association des idées, **2** 23*n*,
451*n*, 560*n*, 564*n*, 868*n*,
(*p*270);
"Association médiate dans
l'évocation volontaire," **2**
451*n*;
"Classification et plan des
méthodes psychologiques,"
18 (*p*421);
"Esquisse d'une théorie
biologique du sommeil," **3**

137*nn*;
"Quelques mots sur la défini-
tion de l'hystérie," **5** 26*n*; **18**
(*p*420); J.'s abstract, **18** 943;
with D. Israïlovitch: "Influence du tabac sur l'association des idées," **2** (*p*270)
clarity, lack of, **3** 434
Clark University, Worcester, Mass.,
2 939&*n*, 1356; **4** 154; **17** (*p*1)
classes, marriage, *see* marriage *s.v.*
classical:
TITLE: "The Problem of Types
in the History of Classical and
Medieval Thought," **6** 8–100;
culture, **7** 17/427;
mind, and mythology, **5** 23; **6**
314;
and romantic, as opposites, **7**
80;
spirit, understanding of, **5** 1;
type, *see* Ostwald *s.v.*
*Classicorum auctorum e Vaticanis
codicibus editorum*, **9i** 553*n*
classification(s): of contents of consciousness, **8** 287;
"natural," **8** 226
Claus, — (Sachsenberg): "Ein Fall
von simulierter Geistesstörung,"
1 351*n*
Claus, A.: *Catatonie et stupeur*, **3**
175*n*
Clausura, **18** 619
"Clavis maioris sapientiae," *see* AL-
CHEMICAL COLLECTIONS: *Bibl.
chem. cur. s.v.* Artefius; *Theatr.
chem. s.v.* Artefius
clay: in alchemy, **13** 358, 375&*n*;
in rituals, **11** 370, 371
cleanliness compulsion, **2** 793, 839
Cleanthes, **4** 693
cleft, mother-symbol, **5** 577
Clemen, P.: *Die romanische Monumen-
talmalerei*, **12** *fig.* 101;
Die romanischen Wandmalereien,
5 pl. XIV*a*
Clement of Alexandria, **9i** 295,
573; **9ii** 42, 186; **11** 170*n*;

Clement of Alexandria (*cont.*):
on Eleusinian mysteries, **5** 529, 530;
WORKS
Paedagogus, **9ii** 347;
Protrepticus, **5** 530*n*;
Stromata, **9i** 295*n*; **9ii** 370*nn*; **11** 271*n*; **12** 139*n*; **14** 174*n*, 528&*n* ["Clement of Rome" in error], 630*n*;
The Writings of Clement of Alexandria, tr. W. Wilson, **5** 530*n*; **9i** 573*n*; **9ii** 175*n*, 370*n*; **11** 271*n*; **14** 174*n*
Clement of Rome/pseudo-Clement/ Pope Clement I, **9i** 295; **9ii** 191; **14** 528, 583;
identity, **9ii** 99*n*, 103*n*; **11** 207*n*;
on right and left hands of God, **9ii** 99; **11** 470, (*p*358); **18** 1537;
WORKS:
The Apostolic Constitutions, **14** 474&*n*;
Clementine *Homilies,* **5** 163*n*; **9i** 572; **9ii** 99–103, 158*n*, 299*n*, 400; **12** 469; **14** 573&*n*; Ethiopic *Clementines,* **14** 556;
Epistles/Letters to the Corinthians, in *The Apostolic Fathers,* ed. and tr. K. Lake: First, **11** 207&*n*; Second, **9i** 295; **9ii** 41*n*; **11** 212; **14** 200*n*;
Recognitiones, **14** 160*n*
Cleomenes, **11** 373
Cleopatra, **5** 8; and Comarius, *see* ALCHEMICAL WRITERS: Comarius/ Komarios *s.v.*;
and Ostanes, *see* ALCHEMICAL WRITERS: Ostanes *s.v.*
clergyman/minister/parson, **11** 499– 507, 511–12;
TITLE: "Psychotherapists or the Clergy," **11** 488–538;
and ethical and religious questions, **11** 515, 546, 547;

Protestant, limitations as mediator, **11** 76, 543, 547, 549, 550, 551; and spiritual suffering, **11** 505–10;
and psychotherapy/doctor, **10** 1070; **11** 499, 502, 504–6, 511, 518, 537, 538, 548, 550;
see also cure of souls; director of conscience; priest
climacteric, **4** 703–6; **7** 184; *see also* life, stages of; menopause
climax of life, **9i** 548, 549
climbing as dream-motif, **8** 535; **16** 303–4, 323
clock, **9i** 315; **11** 90, 112, 114;
cosmic, **12** 135;
pendulum, **12** 134–5, 146, 157, 246;
as *perpetuum mobile,* **11** 109, 125; **12** 246;
synchronized (metaphor), **8** 937;
world clock, in patient's vision, **11** 111, 128, 138, 158, 164; **12** 307–14;
in Zurich, **12** 137
clothing, insufficient, as dream-motif, **8** 535;
cloud(s), **9ii** 240; **12** *fig.* 142O:
black, **10** 811–12; **14** 727*n*;
-demon, **13** 57;
images in, **12** 349, 351;
as *prima materia,* **12** 425
clover, in dream, **12** 212, 220
clown, **9i** 474
clubs, battle with, **5** 390
Clytemnestra, **4** 347
Cnidaria, **9ii** 196
coagulatio/coagulation (alchemical), *see* opus, alchemical, stages in *s.v.*
coagulation (Masselon's term), **3** 74, 75
coal, **12** 327
cobalt, **14** 87*n*
Coblenz bas-relief, **5** 662
Coccius, S., **10** 758
cock, *see* ANIMALS *s.v.*
cockatoo, *see* ANIMALS *s.v.*

cockchafer, *see* ANIMALS *s.v.*
Cockin, F. A., **18** 1689*n*
cockroach, *see* ANIMALS *s.v.*

code: moral, **7** 30; **13** 229;
   penal, **13** 229
Code Napoléon, **18** 622, 623

CODICES AND MANUSCRIPTS

Akhmim: Elijah, Apocalypse of, **13** 93;
   Peter, Gospel of, **12** 61*n*;
Appenzell, MS. (18th cent.), in coll. Dr. C. Rusch, **12** *fig.* 230;
Aschaffenburg: Evangeliary, **12** *fig.* 109;
Basel: "Alchymistisches MS.," **13** 180*n*;
   "De arbore contemplationis," AX. 128b: **13** 414&*n*;
Berlin: Cod. Berol. Lat. 532: **13** 188*n*; **14** 41*n*, 113*n*;
   Cod. Berol. Lat. Q. 584, "Visio Arislei," **12** 449&*n*; **13** 88*n*, 403&*n*;
Bezae, **11** 416, 696, 745*n*; **13** 292; **18** 1415, 1628*n*, 1642;
Bingen: *Scivias* (Hildegard), **12** *fig.* 126 [*same MS. as Wiesbaden Codex*];
Chantilly: *Les Très Riches Heures,* **12** *fig.* 156;
Dresden, **12** *fig.* 190;
Florence: Ashburnham 1166, *Miscellanea d'alchimia,* **9ii** 367; **12** *figs.* 131, 135; **14** 23; **16** 519&*n*;
   Biblioteca Medicea-Laurenziana, Cod. Laur. 71, 33: **11** 47*n*;
Heidelberg: "Scivias" (Hildegard), **11** 62*n* [*same MS. as Wiesbaden Codex*];
Jung (Coptic Gnostic Papyrus), **18** (*p*671&*n*), 1826–34;
Küsnacht: *see below,* manuscripts in author's possession
Leiden: Cod. Vossianus Chem. 520 (29); *De Alchimia,* **5** pl. XVIII; **12** *figs.* 9, 17, 20, 38, 90, 99, 129, 140, 152, 201, 241; **13** 110*n*, 278*n*;
Liverpool Public Museum: Fejérváry MS., **5** 400;

London: BM MS. Add. 1316, "Emblemetical Figures," **12** *fig.* 15;
   BM MS. Add. 10302/Sloane 5025, "Ripley Scrowle," **12** 433*n figs.* 30, 92, 196, 228, 251, 257; **13** 261*n*, 374*n*, *fig.* B5;
   BM MS. Add. 5245, "Cabala mineralis," **12** *fig.* 121;
   BM MS. Add. 15268, "Livre des ansienes histoires," **13** *fig.* B1;
   BM MS. Add. 19352, "Theodore Psalter," **12** *fig.* 206;
   BM MS. Harley 3469, "Splendor solis," **12** *figs.* 32, 95, 134, 166, 219; **13** 95;
   BM MS. Harley 4751, "Historia animalium," **12** *fig.* 242;
Lucca: Biblioteca governativa, Codex 1942, Hildegarde of Bingen, "Liber divinorum operum," **9i** 703*n*, *fig.* 48; **11** 62*n*; **12** *fig.* 195; **18** 1225;
Manuscripts in author's possession: "Figurarum Aegyptiorum," **12** 336*n*, 391*n*, *figs.* 23, 148, 157, 164; **14** 4*n*, 44*n*, 134*n*, 395*n*, 549*n*, 720*n*, pls. 4–7;
   "La Sagesse des anciens," **12** *fig.* 149;
Milan: Bibl. Ambrosiana, Codex I: **12** *fig.* 27;
Modena: Est. Lat. 209, "De sphaera," **12** *fig.* 56;
Munich: SB. Cod. Germ. 598, "Book of the Holy Trinity"/ "Buch der hlg. Dreifaltigkeit"/ Drifaltigkeitsbuch, **11** 47*n*, 62*n*; **12** 500*n*, 505*n*, *fig.* 224; **13** 180*n*, *fig.* B3; **14** 23*n*;
   SB Cod. Lat. 15713, Lectionary (*Perikopenbuch*), **12** *fig.* 191;

165

Munich (*cont.*):

Cod. Lat. 4453: **14** 526n;

New Haven: German alch. MS. (Mellon Coll.), **13** *frontisp.*;

Oxford: BL: MSS Ashmole 1394, 1445, 1479: **14** 370n;

BL Cod. Brucianus (Bruce MS. 96), Coptic Gnostic treatise, **11** 60, 62n, 97; **12** 138; **14** 41n; **18** 269&n;

BL MS. 270b, "Bible moralisée," **12** *fig.* 213;

BL MS. Digby 65 (by Godfrey, Prior of St. Swithin's, Winchester), **6** 74n;

BL MS. Digby 83: **14** 626n;

Paris: Arsenal MS 973: **12** 391n;

Arsenal MS. 974: **12** *fig.* 178;

Arsenal MS. 975: **12** *figs.* 193, 226;

Arsenal MS. 3022: **14** 80n;

Arsenal MS. 5061: **12** *figs.* 6, 74;

Arsenal MS. 5076: **12** *fig.* 248;

Arsenal MS. 6577: **12** *fig.* 116;

BN Cod. Lat. 511: **12** *fig.* 67;

BN Cod. Lat. 512: **12** *fig.* 172;

BN Cod. Lat. 7171: "Turba philosophorum," **12** *fig.* 208;

BN MS. Lat. 919, "Grandes heures du duc de Berry," **12** *fig.* 159; **16** 454;

BN Cod. Lat. 11534, Bible of Manerius, **5** pl. LVI;

BN MS. Lat. 14006: **11** 93n; **12** 465;

BN Cod. Par. 6319, "Liber Hermetis Trismegisti," **9i** 572n; **11** 229n;

BN Par. Gr. 1220: **11** 47n;

BN MS. Fr. 116: **12** *fig.* 88;

BN MS. Fr. 594: **12** *fig.* 252;

BN MS. Fr. 2327: **14** 58n, 353n;

BN MS. Fr. 14765: Abraham le Juif, "Livre des figures hiéroglifiques," **12** *fig.* 217; **14** 18n, 634&n, 720, pl. 3; "Pratique"

or "Alchimie de Flamel," **12** 391n;

BN MS. Fr. 14770: **12** *fig.* 85;

BN MS. Gr. 2250: **13** 191n;

BN MS. Gr. 2252: **13** 87n; **14** 36n;

BN MS. Gr. 2419: **13** 276n;

Library of the Palais Bourbon, Cod. Borbonicus, **5** *fig.* 30;

Ste. Gen. MS 2263-4 "Lapidis philosophorum nomina," **13** 203n;

Preobrazhensk, Russia: Khludov Psalter, **12** *figs.* 176, 247;

Reims: Bibl., **12** *fig.* 211;

Rome: Bibl. Angelica, Cod. 1474: **12** *fig.* 57;

Rupertsberg: "Scivias" (Hildegard), **10** 765, pl. VIII [*same MS. as Wiesbaden Codex*];

Sachse Codex, **12** 332n;

St. Gall: Cod. Germ. Alch. Vad. (16th cent.), **13** 180n; **14** 23n;

Cod. N. Vad. 390 (15th cent.), **13** 101n;

Bibliothek: Alch. MS. (17th cent.), **5** pl. XXXIIb;

Tübingen UB MS. (*c.* 1400): **12** *fig.* 24;

UB MS. Theol. Lat. fol. 561 "Beatus Commentary" (mid 12th cent.), **5** pl. Vb;

Vatican: BV Cod. Graec. 190: **5** 163n; BV Cod. Graec. 237: **11** 47n;

BV Cod. Graec. 951: **11** 47n;

BV Cod. Lat. 3060, "Liber Hermetis Trismegisti," **9i** 572n; **11** 229n;

BV Pal. Lat. 412: **12** *figs.* 73, 98, 266;

BV Pal. Lat. 413: **12** *figs.* 105, 107;

BV Pal. Lat. 565: **12** *fig.* 197;

BV Pal. Lat. 1993, Opicinus de Canistris, **11** 62n;

BV Reg. Lat. 1458: **12** *fig.* 106;

BV Urb. Lat. 365: **12** *figs.* 69, 83;

BV Urb. Lat. 899: **12** *figs.* 35, 220;

BV Vat. Lat. 681: **12** *fig.* 104;

BV Vat. Lat. 7286: **12** *figs.* 80, 150; **13** 110*n*;

Venice: Cod. Marcianus, **11** 344, 348*n*; **12** 404, *fig.* 147;

Vienna: NB Cod. Med. Gr. I: **12** *fig.* 186;

NB "Moysis Prophetae . . . secretum Chimicum," **9i** 579*n*;

Wiesbaden, Nassauische Landesbibliothek: "Scivias," Hildegarde of

*

"Codicillus," *see* ALCHEMICAL COLLECTIONS: *Bibl. chem. cur. s.v.* Lully

Codrington, R. H.: *The Melanesians,* **8** 123&*n*

coeducation, **10** 994; *see also* education

coelum, see caelum

coenaesthetic perception, extinction of, **8** 955

coercion, **4** 658

coetaneum, see ANIMALS: dog/bitch *s.v.*

coffer, **13** 319, 320, *figs.* 14, 15

coffin/bier: Osiris in, **5** *fig.* 23;

symbol in Nietzsche, **10** 377;

as tree of death, **5** 349; **13** 401;

wooden horse as, **5** 427

cogitatio, **11** 421; **12** 375&*n*, 390, 405*n*

cognitio: matutina, **13** 299–301;

sui ipsius, **13** 301; **18** 1655 (*see also* self-knowledge);

vespertina, **13** 299–301, 303

cognition, **7** 158; **9i** 150, 289; **9ii** 112, 124; **11** 459; **12** 462*n*; **18** 51, 419;

essential to consciousness, **11** 238;

a mental faculty, **11** 765;

mind the condition of, **11** 768;

mystic powers of, **18** 736;

mythological stage of, **18** 1061;

philosophical, **15** 39;

Bingen (destroyed in World War II), **5** pl. XXX*a*; **11** 62*n* [*Bingen, Heidelberg and Rupertsberg refer to same MS.*];

Zürich: ZB Rhenoviensis/Rhenovacensis 172, "Aurora consurgens," **9i** 686, 707, *figs.* 32, 54; **11** 93*n*; **12** 464; **13** 180*n*, 269*n*, 278*n*; **16** 401;

see also above Jung (Coptic Gnostic Papyrus)

Zwiefalten Abbey: Breviary No. 128: **12** *fig.* 62

*

process of, **13** 378;

theory of, **4** 371, 688; **18** 120;

transcendental subject of, **9i** 289

cohabitation, **10** 751;

continuous, **5** 306, 317*n*;

with god, **5** 438;

of Sol and Luna, **13** 157

Cohen, H., **6** 735;

Logik der reinen Erkenntnis, **6** 735*n*

Cohn, Paul V., *see* Nietzsche *s.v. Human, All-too-Human*

Cohn, William: *Buddha in der Kunst des Ostens,* **5** pl. LV

coincidence, **8** 823, 843, 971;

meaningful, **8** 827, 840, 845–6, 866, 941, 946, 965, 969, 995; **10** 593, 682, 789; **11** 968–72; **14** 662 (*see also* synchronicity)

coincidentia oppositorum, **10** 674; **11** 881; **14** 176, 258, 540; **16** 502;

Cusanus on, **14** 200;

danger of, **8** 679;

God as, **13** 256; in Nicholas Cusanus, *see* Cusanus *s.v.*;

self as, *see* self *s.v.*;

as symbol of wholeness, **16** 537;

see also *complexio oppositorum; coniunctio oppositorum;* opposites *s.v.* coincidence of

coins, **8** 865–6, 986; **11** 970, 974;

falling from sky, **10** 730;

golden, **12** 103–4, 127, 348&*n*;

coins (*cont.*):
symbols on, **10** 99; sexual, **5** 298
coitus, **12** 334, 436, 484*n*; **17** 79;
child's ignorance of, **17** 48;
ritual, **5** 215;
"upward displacement" of (Freud), **5** 204*n*
Colchis, **14** 85*n*
colcothar, **14** 729; see also *caput mortuum*
cold/warm, **13** 359
Coleridge, S. T., **5** 169; **10** 334; **13** 190*n*; **16** 70;
"Kubla Khan," in *Poems*, **5** 169*n*
collaboration of conscious and unconscious, *see* unconscious and conscious, relationship *s.v.*
collecting, mania for, **1** 21; **3** 105
collective, **6** 692 (Def.);
belief, **11** 463;
and collectivistic, **7** 462*n*;
compensation, **7** 283, 285;
compromise, **7** 237;
culture, and Christianity, **6** 107–10;
dangers, **10** 608;
delusions, **13** 52;
element, **7** 223; in individual, **7** 484;
factors, **7** 227, 240, 241/462, 311;
feeling, Epimetheus and, **6** 293;
figure(s), **7** 378;
identity, **7** 480–502;
melting of individual in, **7** 240;
mentality, **7** 237/458; primitive, **6** 123 (see also *participation mystique*);
nature of self, **13** 287; **16** 474;
obligations, **7** 267;
opinions, **7** 334;
psychic phenomena, **13** 51;
psychology, *see* psychology *s.v.*;
religious phenomena/worship, **6** 204, 399, 400;
representations, *see* Lévy–Bruhl

s.v. représentations collectives;
and self-alienation, **7** 267;
sensuous feeling as, **6** 146;
state, and identification with differentiated function, **6** 161;
symbols, **13** 395;
see also under attitude; conscience; consciousness; dream(s); ego; feeling; function; idea(s); image(s); individual; instinct; man; psyche; soul; thinking; truth; unconscious
collectiveness, American, **10** 967–9
collectivism, **12** 557, 559; **16** 227
collectivity, **6** 12, 123; **7** 268, 374, 504, 506; **17** 297, 303;
TITLE: "Adaptation, Individuation, Collectivity," **18** 1084–1106;
Christian, **18** 1539;
individuation and, **18** 1099–1106
collectivization, **7** 236
Collesson, Johannes, *see* ALCHEMICAL COLLECTIONS: *Theatr. chem. s.v.*
collision: of conscious and unconscious, **9ii** 304;
of opposites, *see* opposites *s.v.*;
with the shadow, **7** 42;
with the unconscious, **7** 41
colloquy (internal), **9i** 236&*n*, 237
Collyridians, and Mary worship, **11** 194
collyrium, **9ii** 195; **13** 101
Cologne cathedral, **7** 171, 173;
as mother substitute, **17** 269–72
Colonna, Francesco, *see* ALCHEMICAL WRITERS *s.v.*
Colossians, Epistle to, *see* BIBLE: N.T. *s.v.*
colour(s) (*topics*): **8** 680; **11** 118; **13** 33, 86, 141, 190&*n*, 267, 380; **14** 306, 392, 394, 577, 591*n*, 723–4;
and Adam, in creation of, *see* Adam *s.v.* (*see also below* red *s.v.* earth);

COLOUR(S)

71; plant, **12** 198; tree, **12** 232;
in fairytale, **9i** 406;
and Holy Ghost, **11** 118; **12**
319; **14** 395;
as life and hope, **5** 615; **9i** 566;
9ii 57; **14** 395, 624;
as perfection, **14** 624;
as sensation function, **9i** 582,
588*n*;
sulphur, **14** 136, 140*n*;
and Venus, **14** 140*n*, 393;
womb, **12** 199;
and yellow, as opposites, **14** 31;
see also below *viriditas;*
grey, **12** 353;
iosis, **12** 333; *see also* red; *rubefactio;*
iridescent, **12** 353;
kermes, see above *chermes;*
leukosis, **12** 333; see also *dealbatio;*
white;
melanosis, **12** 333; **13** 444; *see also*
black; *nigredo;*
nigredo, **5** 83*n*; **9ii** 329; **10** 814; **12**
333, 404, 433, 484*n*, 496,*figs.* 34,
115, 137, 142RR, 219, 223; **13**
105*n*, 279, 337*n*; **14** 24, 44*n*,
144*n*, 607, 729, 733, pl. 10; **16**
398, 468&*n*, 484;
and arcane substance, **9i** 452;
"black blacker than black," **14**
741;
as chaos/*massa confusa,* **9ii** 230,
304; **13** 433; **14** 253–4, 708; **16**
381, 383;
dog as, **14** 27*n*;
dragon as, **14** 493&*n*, 733;
interment as, **14** 65;
as melancholia, **10** 811; **12** 41,
383; **13** 445; **14** 390*n*, 446, 493,
496*n*, 607, 708, 727, 733, 741;
16 479;
as projection, **13** 444;
as putrefaction, **14** 714, 721;
16 376*n*;
raven/raven's head as, **14** 727,
729, 741;
salt as, **14** 244;
as sin, **11** 423;

sol niger/black sun, *see* sun *s.v.*
black;
as stage of alchemical work, **9i**
246&*n*; **9ii** 231; **11** 98; **12** 333,
353, 389; **13** 201*n*; **14** 183, 346,
464, 592, 708, 722;
as symbol of psychic suffering,
14 493, 494;
and *tenebrositas,* **14** 708; **16** 398,
468;
transformation into *albedo,* **13**
89; **14** 82, 253, 264;
as the unconscious, **14** 646;
as unconsciousness, **14** 696;
see also above black/etc.;
melanosis; salt;
purple, **11** 118; **13** 184, 411*n*; **14**
393, 394; **16** 497*n*;
chermes/kermes, **13** 184&*n*;
king, **12** 454,*fig.* 142a;
phoenix, **14** 281*n*;
robe, **11** 406;
spirits, **12** 317;
red/reddening/redness, **12** 220; **13**
459; **14** 420;
and affectivity, **9i** 565;
in alchemical process, **12** 165*n*,
353, 365; **14** 415; **16** 512;
cockatoo, **13** 253;
daughter, **12** 454;
in dreams/visions: ball, **12** 107,
108, 112, 127; Earth Mother,
9i 312, 331; fruits of tree of
life, **13** 459; **14** 73*n*; -haired
man, **12** 200, 211;
earth, **12** 456; **13** 418; **14** 552,
639;
flowers, **13** *fig.* 5;
garment, **12** 454&*n*;
God the Son as, **12** 319;
gum, **12** 209, 484*n*;
-haired: man, **12** 200, 211, 365;
woman, as professorial anima,
9i 62;
instinct and, **8** 384, 414;
lily, **12** *fig.* 142a; **14** 683, 702;
lion, *see* ANIMALS: lion;
man, **13** 123&*n*;

171

red (*cont.*):
    masculine colour, **10** 790;
    in pictures, **13** *figs.* 5, 6;
    sepulchre, **16** 495;
    sin as, **14** 420;
    stone, **13** 392;
    sulphur, **14** 16*n*, 21*n*, 110, 118,
    134, 135, 140*n*, 404, 405*n*, 720,
    734; as masculine, **14** 135, 720;
    symbolism of, **9i** 68o*n*;
    tincture, see below *tinctura s.v.*;
red-green blindness, **1** 395, 415;
red and white, **10** 790; **14** 139,
757*n*;
    double eagle, **12** *fig.* 20;
    flowers: lilies, **12** *fig.* 142a; **14**
    73&*n*, 689; roses, **12** *figs.* 13,
    20, 193; **14** 419&*n*;
    King and Queen, **12** 334;
    of Mercurius, **14** 12, 757;
    as opposites, **14** 655;
    red man/slave *and* white wo-
    man, *vir rubeus/servus* and *mu-
    lier candida*, **10** 790; **12** 193*n*;
    13 124; **14** 2&*n*, 16*n*, 73, 154*n*,
    174, 307, 655*n*, 702
    sea, **12** *fig.* 142K;
    of sun and moon, **13** 459; **14**
    134;
rose-coloured blood:
    ch'i (Chinese) as, **13** 433;
    of *filius macrocosmi*/Christ, **14**
    419;
    of lion, **13** 383, 390&*n*; **14** 419;
rubedo, alchemical term, stage in
    transformation, **9i** 537, 58o*n*; **12**
    269, 271, 334; **14** 7, 118, 307,
    419, 434, 441;
rubefactio in alchemical work, **11** 98;
rubeus, see red and white *s.v.* red
    man/slave;
saffron, **13** 366; **14** 725; see also *cit-
    rinitas; xanthosis;* yellow;
sapphire/sapphirine: circle, **12** 316;
    flower, **13** 234*n*, 346; **14** 641;
    stone, **13** 234*n*, 321, 322, *figs.*
    16, 17; **14** 640, 642;
scarlet, **14** 420;

bird, *see* Chinese alchemy *s.v.*;
silver: bowl, in dream, **12** 299;
    eagle, *see* ANIMALS *s.v.*;
    and gold, *see above* gold(en);
    man, **13** 87;
    rain, **12** *fig.* 142O;
    water, **13** 371;
    white elixir of, *see below* white;
tinctura/-e, in alchemy, **11** 160; **13**
    282;
    alba, **12** 334;
    black, **14** 259; **16** 510;
    blue/*caelum*, **14** 703;
    golden, **12** 462, 505; **13** 255;
    red, **8** 384*n*; **12** 335, 454; **13**
    196, 384, 390; **14** 690;
    roseate, **14** 485&*n*;
    rubea, **12** 165; **14** 110;
    white, **12** 335; **16** 495, 514,
    515;
violet: as archetype, **8** 414, 416–17,
    420;
    darkness, **12** 379;
viriditas/greenness, **12** 333;
    benedicta/blessed, **9i** 566; **9ii**
    386&*n*; **11** 151, 16o*n*; **13** 102,
    299, 374*n*; **14** 391, 623;
    gloriosa, **13** 415;
    and Holy Ghost, **11** 118*n*;
    and verdigris, **12** 207; **14** 623;
    see also above green;
white/whiteness/whitening, **9ii** 230;
    12 165*n*, 220, 333, 334, 349*n*,
    379, 383; **13** 459; **16** 512, 514–
    15;
    animals, *see* ANIMALS: dove;
    eagle; unicorn;
    and black, *see* black *s.v.*;
    blossoms, in patient's picture,
    13 *fig.* 1;
    dove, **13** 123*n*;
    earth, see *terra alba;*
    elixir/fermentation, **12** *fig.*
    142T; **13** 171*n*;
    as feminine colour, **10** 790; **14**
    154*n*;
    ghost, of anima, **13** 57;
    gum, **12** 484*n*;

head (Cabalistic), **12** 313;
lily, **12** *fig.* 142a;
magician, in dream, *see* magician *s.v.* black and white;
man, **13** 124; Pueblo view of, **10** 184, 431;
moon, full, **14** 21;
in ritual transformation process, **11** 371;
sulphur, **14** 134, 404, 405*n*; as lapis, **12** 475*n*;
symbolism of, **9i** 680*n*;
tincture, see above *tinctura s.v.*;
tree, **13** 401*n*;
water/stream, **12** *fig.* 142L; as

*

coloured races, **10** 568, 571;
and Americans, **10** 963–7;
reactions to, **10** 962–7;
see also Negro
colour hearing/*audition colorée* (synesthesia), **2** 139; **5** 237; **6** 180, 684
Colson, T. H., *see* Philo
Colucci, Cesare, **2** 501;
"L'Allenamento ergografico nei normali e negli epilettici," **2** 501*n*
Columbus, Christopher, **4** 230; **6** 936
columns, in dream, **8** 945
coma, **8** 950–5;
consciousness during, **8** 957
Comarius/Komarios, *see* ALCHEMICAL WRITERS *s.v.*
combination(s): chemical, *see* chemical *s.v.*;
conscious/unconscious, **7** 197
combustible liquid, **13** 424
comet(s), **5** 481; **10** 608;
Ishkoodah, **5** 478
comic-strips, **9i** 465*n*
"Comma Johanneum," and Trinity, **11** 207*n*
"Commentarius," *see* ALCHEMICAL COLLECTIONS: *De alchemia s.v.* Hortulanus
commissure, **9ii** 149, 230

Mercurial fluid, **12** *fig.* 142G;
see also above *albedo; dealbatio; leukosis;* red and white;
xanthos/xanthosis, **5** 423; **9ii** 195; **12** 333; **14** 281*n; see also below* yellow;
yellow/yellowing, **12** 270;
in alchemy, **12** 165*n;* castle, **13** 33; man, **13** 123; wallflower (*cheyri*), **13** 171*n;*
in dream(s)/vision(s): balls, **12** 266; light, **12** 270;
emperor, **12** 548;
and fire/light, **5** 423;
and green, as opposites, **14** 31

*

Commixtio, in the Mass, **11** 334–5; **16** 454
common sense, **7** 207, 209, 214, 290, 332; **8** 742
communication(s): automatic, **1** 39, 45–62, 73;
impression of, **5** (*p*458);
irruption of collective contents in, **8** 599;
mediumistic/spiritualistic, **8** 599; origin of, **1** 55;
role of speech in, **5** 14;
in twilight state, of information, **8** 956
communio, among Aztecs, **11** 341
Communion/Holy Communion/ Lord's Supper, **5** 526; **11** 76, 418, 543; **13** 194;
blasphemy on, **5** 581;
in Church of England, **18** 640;
contróversy on, **6** 36, 40; Luther/Zwingli, **6** 96–100; and cure, **18** 622;
pagan ritual and, **7** 159; survival of, in Christian, **7** 384;
in Protestant Church, **18** 625;
substances, **13** 193; **14** 631; in Greek Uniate rite, **11** 311*n;*
symbol, of family and Church, **16** 215;
see also consubstantiation;

Communion (*cont.*):
Mass; transubstantiation; volipresence
"communion of saints," Church as, **5** 335
Communism, **9i** 228; **10** 559, 1019; **11** 222–4, 688; **18** 1320, 1324, 1335–6, 1661;
archaic social order, **10** 541, 818; **18** 1272;
Bolshevism and, **10** 932;
idea of community, **10** 516;
ideology of, **10** 523, 568; **11** 778;
primitive, **10** 504;
revolution, **10** 559;
as State prison, **10** 653;
as substitute for God, **18** 1568–9
community, **7** 113, 240, 247, 278;
archetypal, **5** 101;
differentiated personalities and, **17** 248;
and divine experience, **18** 1637;
idea of, **10** 516;
individual and, **18** 1351–5, 1676;
political, **17** 231;
primitive, **7** 173;
structure of, **17** 248
companion, theme of, **12** 154–5; *see also* friend(s)
comparative: anatomy, **13** 353*n*;
method, *see* method *s.v.*;
procedure: as used by J., **5** (*pp*xxvi, xxviii), 3, 575;
research into symbols/symbolism, **13** 353, 463
comparison(s): by analogy, **5** 146–7;
causative, **5** 146;
choice of, **5** 57*n*;
functional, **5** 147;
in libido-symbolizing, **5** 147
compass: eight points of, **9i** 607&*n*;
turning to the north, **9ii** 206
compassion: of Buddha, **10** 200; **11** 921, 932;

of Paracelsus, **13** 146
"Compendium artis alchemiae," *see* ALCHEMICAL COLLECTIONS: *Bibl. chem. cur. s.v.* Lully
Compendium theologicae veritatis (attrib. Hugh of Strasbourg), **9ii** 133*n*
compensation(s), **4** 349; **6** 693–5 (Def.); **7** 265, 495; **9i** 277; **12** 26, 32, 48, 51, 61, 63, 106, 155, 230; **16** 12, 81, 252, 336; **17** 18, 25, 153;
Adler and, **7** 170&*n*;
animus as, **7** 328;
archetypal, **18** 1232;
of basic type, **7** 63;
biological, by dreams, **13** 90;
childish, **17** 24;
collective, **7** 283, 285;
between conscious and unconscious, *see* unconscious, the *s.v.* compensatory relation;
and creation of wholeness, **5** 614;
downward, **12** 230;
and dreams, *see* dream(s) *s.v.*;
Elijah as, **18** 1529;
through fantasy, **5** 33;
feminine, **18** 1233;
goal of, **18** 1138;
humility and pride, **7** 225;
instincts, **5** 625;
for latent psychosis, **7** 192;
law of, **13** 295; **16** 330;
in man and woman, **9ii** 27;
between man's animal and evolutionary instincts, **5** 653;
mythological, **7** 284;
and neurosis, *see* neurosis *s.v.*;
office as, **7** 230;
and one-sided attitude, **6** 28, 30;
by opposites, **7** 78, 80;
optimism as unsuccessful, **7** 222, 452;
persona and anima, **7** 304; and feminine weakness, **7** 309;
personal, **7** 275, 288;

principle of, **6** 294;
psychic, **8** 489, 545; and psychological, **10** 292, 448, 650; in history, **10** 250, 295;
of relationships, **7** 278;
of religious problem, **7** 287;
schizophrenic, **3** 567;
self as, **7** 404;
of self-confidence, by inferiority, **7** 457;
transference as, **16** 282;
unconscious, *see* unconscious, the *s.v.*;
wrought by fate, **17** 90
complementarity, **8** 439*n*, 440, 545*n*; **18** 1133;
human-divine, **11** 233
complementation, **8** 545
completeness, **7** 186; **11** 246;
as feminine, **11** 620, 627;
and perfection, **9ii** 123, 171; **12** 208;
voluntary, **9ii** 125;
see also totality; wholeness
complex(es), **1** 93, 132*n*; **2** 357, 378–9, 664, 733–6, 740, 742–7, 1082–7; **3** 181, 218, 263, 429, 434, 521; **5** 122, 202, 259, 505; **6** 175, 384; **7** 137, 432*n*; **8** 255, 856; **10** 456, 1034*n*; **11** 143; **12** 439; **17** 170, 200, 204, 211; **18** 424, 548, 908, 922, 1223;
TITLES: "The Complex of Being Wronged," **3** 258–70; "On the Doctrine of Complexes," **2** 1349–56; "A Review of the Complex Theory," **8** 194–219;
in animals, **10** 842;
assimilation of, **8** 197, 204–9; **16** 273;
and association experiments, **3** 506; **4** 408; **7** 20/432; **8** 18, 196, 199, 253, 365, 821; **11** 21; **17** 175; **18** 147, 832;
attention-toned, **3** 87;
autonomous/autonomy of, **1** 93; **2** 1352–4; **3** 74, 183; **5** 95; **6**

419–21, 923; **7** 27/438, 295; **8** 203–6, 255, 582, 584, 587, 593, 710–11; **11** 21, 26, 223; **12** 410; **13** 47, 75; **16** 266–8, 271, 438; **18** 151, 546, 1256–7; anima/-us as, **7** 295, 339, 374, 387; and art, **15** 115, 122–4, 174; identification with, **7** 329; **8** 204; overcoming of, **14** 308; painfulness of, **8** 205, 207; personification of, **7** 312–3, 339; **18** 150; in schizophrenia, **3** 498, 506, 521; **15** 174;
blocking of, **3** 146;
castration-, **4** 342; **9i** 138; **13** 401*n*; **18** 111, 113, 122;
Catholics and, **16** 218; **18** 612, 615;
-characteristics, **2** 621, 640, 649, 659, 675, 817, 819, 919–21, 1324&*n*, 1363–5, 1369–70; in children (childhood), **3** 90; **6** 201;
Christ-, **8** 582, 584;
of collective/personal unconscious, **8** 590; **9i** 88;
collision of, **6** 468;
compensatory function of, **8** 488;
concealed, **2** 419–20, 983;
"conflict," **6** 467*n*;
in conscious and unconscious, **8** 383–4;
consciousness of, **18** 153, 154;
constellating power of, **2** 182, 198, 664; **3** 92; **4** 43–4, 335; **8** 19–21;
-constellation(s), **2** 236, 239, 265, 271–2, 289, 337, 339, 348, 372, 378, 607, 734, 742, 919; **4** 44; **8** 198–200; **9ii** 54; in hysteria, **2** 818–19; reaction-time and, **2** 290–4, 339, 548*n*, 552, 606–7, 621, 645, 650, 743–51; type, **2** 210, 414&*n*, 429–31, 520, 984, 990; **18** 963;
constellations and, **2** 182–4, 198, 664, 733–6; **4** 44;

complex (*cont.*):
    definition of, **2** 733, 1350–1;
    -delirium, **3** 163&*n*, 164&*n*;
    in demonism, **18** 1473;
    as demons, **7** 293–5; **8** 204, 712;
    and dream-formations, **3** 133, 298; **8** 210; **11** 37; **17** 38;
    and dreams, **3** 122, 181; **18** 150, 171, 172, 432, 433;
    effects of, **3** 88–106; **8** 209; exteriorized, **8** 600;
    ego-, **2** 610, (*pp* 250, 251), 664, 1352; **3** 102; **8** 208, 582, 611, 613–14, 758; **14** 47; **18** 18, 19, 149; associations and, **3** 82, 86&*n*, 135, 218; conscious, **18** 90, 153; and cryptomnesic idea, **1** 138–9; dreams and, **14** 502; energy of, **18** 91; in hysterical splits of consciousness, **1** 130, 133, 157–63; in schizophrenia, **3** 180, 521–2; sleep and, **3** 137 (*see also* ego);
    Electra-, *see* Oedipus complex *s.v.*;
    emotionally charged, **2** 167&*n*, 178, 198, 237–8, 270, 319, 329–30, 337, 529, 602, 664, 718, 733*n*, 892, 1363; in hysteria, **2** 798; slips of tongue and, **2** 547; in value judgements, **2** 146, 156;
    endogamy, **3** 564;
    erotic, *see below* sexual;
    and extraversion/introversion, **5** 259;
    family-/love-, **2** 270–1, 616, 618;
    and fantasy, **16** 125;
    father-, **2** 692; **4** 738; **7** 294; **9i** 162*n*; **11** 24; **18** 635; and Freudian school, **4** 781; of J., **10** 1026; of man, **3** 401; **9i** 396; of woman/girl, **7** 206; **9i** 168*n*, 396, 525; **17** 216;
    fear of, **8** 207–15;
    feeling-toned,   *see*   feeling-

tone(d) complex;
    fixation of, **3** 75–6;
    free association and, **16** 320;
    functional-, crime and, **1** 479–80;
    fusion of, **3** 133–4&*n*;
    house-, *see above* family-;
    in hysteria/hysterogenic, *see* hysteria *s.v.*;
    of ideas, **1** 139; **3** 56, 59, 71; **4** 43; **5** 95; **7** 21/434; **13** 437;
    identification with, *see above* autonomous;
    -image, **2** 891;
    and imago, differentiated, **5** 62*n*;
    incest, **3** 564; **4** 470, 477; **10** 659; **18** 113, 175, 276;
    incompatibility of, **3** 427;
    -indicator(s), **2** 1082; **3** 109; **4** 335; **8** 62; **10** 753*n*; **18** 1155;
    infantile, **8** 712;
    inferiority, **10** 655; **11** 791; **16** 216, (*p*165); **18** 332, 509;
    intelligence-, **2** 985–6;
    and Jewish problems, **10** 963, 1024;
    in Jews/Protestants/Catholics, **16** 218; **18** 612;
    and "life-wound," *see* Bleuler;
    loss and revival of, **8** 590&*n*;
    love-, *see above* family-;
    love as obsessional c., **3** 102, 104;
    luminosity of, **14** 47, 270, 502;
    masked reactions, **2** 290;
    masturbation-, **2** 698;
    memory-, **2** 612; **6** 201; **7** 130;
    modern art and, **10** 755;
    money-, **2** 611; **18** 99;
    mother-, **4** 150*n*; **5** 392*n*, 569*n*, 585; **7** 173, 294; **8** 711, 721; **9i** 96, 138–9, 141; TITLES: "The Mother-Complex," **9i** 161–71; "Positive Aspects of the Mother-Complex," **9i** 172–86; in America, **5** 272; of daughter/feminine, **9i** 163,

167–71, 175; Goethe's, **8** 707; in man, **9i** 162–6, 175; **13** 131; negative, **9i** 170, 184–6, 311*n*; positive, **9i** 172–82; of son, **9i** 162–6; types of, **9i** (*p*87*n*); and neuroses, *see* neurosis *s.v.* nuclear, **4** 354, 562–3; **8** 18, 19; numinosity of, **13** 437; of observer/analyst, **8** 213; **16** 8; obsessional, **3** 104; Oedipus-, *see* Oedipus complex; origin of, **6** 924–6; **8** 594; "over-valued," **6** 467&*n*; in paranoia, **3** 73; parents' own, **4** 729*n*; **10** 62; **17** 107, 219, 330; patient's parental, **4** 303–6, 409; **6** 201, 927–9; **7** 293–4; **16** 357; of personal grandeur, **3** 211, 214; personality-, **3** 17, 83; as a personality(-ies), **18** 149, 153; personification of, **18** 150 (*see also above* autonomous); possession and, **8** 204; **9i** 220; **16** 196; power, **6** 344, 625, 782; **16** 542; **17** 215; **18** 275, 276, 279 (*see also* Adler, A. *s.v.*); pregnancy-, **2** 605, 610; prison-, **1** 218; projection of, **5** 644; -proneness, **10** 62; psychology, **9i** 84; **10** 887; **13** 435; **14** 686; **16** 115; **18** 1298 (*see also* analytical psychology); racial and national, **5** 45; repressed, **3** 70, 76, 93, 141; **8** 590; **11** 22; resistance to, **4** 43, 80, 349; **resolution/transformation/dis-solution/reintegration of, 4** 41; **5** 48; **7** 341; **14** 308; **16** 268, 273; Saviour, **18** 352, 354, 358, 359, 369;

schizophrenia and, *see* schizophrenia *s.v.*; school-, **2** 816, 847; sejunction of, **6** 467; -sensitiveness, **3** 87, 104, 106, 141, 433; sexual/erotic, **2** 198, 245–8, 381, 610, 612–14, 619, 676, 679, 680, 682, 685–6, 695–702, 851, 891, 906; **3** 92, 102, 104–5, 140, 213, 277–96, 436; **6** 344–5, 471; **8** 209; in dreams, **2** 716, 823–44; in hysteria, **2** 816, 845–62; reaction-time in, **2** 295, 610–12, 614; and sleep disturbances, **3** 137, 181; social, **18** 547; soul-, *see* soul *s.v.*; spirit-, **8** 587; as splinter psyche, **8** 203–4; split-off, **3** 59; **5** 39; **6** 923; **11** 22; **13** 48; **16** 134; **18** 383; stability of, **5** 117*n*; subjective, **7** 141; suppression of, **2** 417–19; tendency to self-normalization, **3** 581; theory, **7** 432; **8** 582; **17** 128*n*; **18** 1155; thought-, **3** 256, 435; tormenting, **18** 1080; traumatic, **16** 262, 266; unconscious(ness) and, **1** 172; **2** 208–14; **6** 175; **8** 19*n*; **11** 22; "wave-like" character of, **8** 201; working through, **17** 38, 49
complexio oppositorum, **9i** 257, 555; **9ii** 112*n*, 237, 245; **11** (*p*358); androgyne as, **14** 528; Christ as, **18** 1632, 1650, 1668; God as, **18** 1640, 1668; in Nicholas Cusanus, *see* Cusanus *s.v.*; Holy Ghost as, **11** 277–9; **18** 1553; Mercurius as, **10** 727; self as, *see* self *s.v.*;

complexio oppositorum (cont.):
son of heavenly nuptials as, **11** 712;
Star of David as, **18** 1617;
in a third, **8** 401;
unicorn as, **12** 526;
see also *coincidentia oppositorum; coniunctio* s.v. *oppositorum*
components of sexuality, **4** 248, 253
composition: of liquids, **13** (*p*62);
literary, of manic patient, **1** 214, 216;
patient's autobiographical, **1** 399;
process of, **9i** 582;
of the waters, **13** 86, 88, 121, 135, 139, 143
compound words as reactions, **2** 73
"comprehend," *see* etymology *s.v.*
comprehension, **3** 31, 393; **8** 454;
and association, **1** 317;
and distractibility, **1** 240;
etymology, *see* etymology *s.v.*;
faulty, **1** 338;
reduced, **1** 333;
retention of, despite loss of knowledge, **1** 285;
and senseless answers, **1** 371
compromise: collective, **7** 237;
formation(s), **3** 141; **7** 246
compulsion(s), **3** 539; **6** 146, 615, 684; **7** 373; **9ii** 216; **14** 151, 225;
automatic, **3** 539; **5** 185; **6** 472, 609, 654, 663;
cleanliness, **2** 793, 839;
conscience and, **10** 843;
in love, **17** 327;
negative, **1** 279;
neurosis, **6** 472, 609, 654, 663; **7** 285–6; **8** 297, 702; **9ii** 17; **16** 3, 372; **17** 182; **18** 282, 284 (*see also* obsessional neurosis);
pathological, **1** 460;
of stars (Heimarmene), **5** 102&*n*, 644; **6** 355;
in types: extraverted intuitive, **6** 615; sensation, **6** 609
compulsive/-ness, **6** 670; **8** 293;

associations, *see* association(s) *s.v.*;
feelings, **6** 306;
one-sidedness of, **6** 347;
thinking, *see* thinking *s.v.*
Conan Doyle, Sir Arthur, **15** 137
conation, **4** 282; **18** 51, 1601
concentration, **9i** 710; **11** 63, 942; **13** 38;
among primitives, **10** 111;
Eastern, **11** 827;
failure of, **11** 784;
see also attention
concentration camps, **9ii** 96; **10** 404, 479, 1019; **13** 466; **18** 1374&*n*, 1379; *see also* Maidenek
concept(s), **5** 201;
abstract, **2** 47–8;
building, **17** (*pp*4–5);
common intermediate, **2** 83–4;
concrete, **2** 47–8;
and experience, **9ii** 60, 63, 65;
and feelings, **1** 148;
generic, **6** 44–5, 48–50, 55;
meaning of term, **10** 1012; **11** 981&*n*, 991, 1013
conceptio, **16** 467
conception (biological), **17** 40;
by breath/wind, **5** 488; **8** 662; **9i** 107;
of Christ, by wind, **9i** 108–9;
failure of, **9i** 170;
Immaculate, *see* Mary/Mother of God *s.v.*;
miraculous, **9i** 282;
virgin, **5** 497
conceptions, general, spiritual, *see* life *s.v.* spiritual
conceptualism, **16** 498; *see also* Abelard *s.v.*
concert, unpleasant episode at, **1** 267, 297
concordance(s), psychic, **8** 228, 229
Concorricci, **9ii** 139, 226*n*
concretism(-ization), **6** 29, 36, 52, 57, 516, 696–9 (Def.); **7** 389; **13** 140, 220; **18** 1564;
Bolshevistic, **18** 1569;

in Communion, **6** 96;
of God, **7** 395, 403;
of intellect, **7** 361;
of memory, **6** 201;
as primitive superstition, **7** 352
concubine, **11** 986
concupiscentia/concupiscence, **9i** 630;
9ii 174, 199; **10** 340–2, 555; **16** 361;
effrenata, **5** 425;
and natural instincts, **5** 223
concussion, **17** 199a
condemnation, **11** 519
condensation(s), **3** 109, 218; **4** 91, 165;
in dream, **3** 50&*n*;
of ideas, **3** 44, 267, 300;
verbal, **3** 157
condensing apparatus, **13** 117; see also *vas*/vessel
Condillac, E. B. de, **8** 197; **10** 370
conditionalism, **3** 480, 533
conduct, principles of, **13** 433
confession (psychological), **7** 278;
16 24, 135, 153, 503; **17** 154;
in analysis, parallel to religious c., **3** 152; **4** 431–5; **7** 218; **11** 873; **16** 123;
analytical psychology and, **18** 1811;
patient's, **1** 53; **4** 462–3; **11** 519; **12** 3; **16** 138, 150; of simulation, **1** 329, 391;
psychology as subjective-, **4** 774;
public, **17** 154
confession (religious), **4** 434; **11** 448; **12** 24; **18** 513, 613, 618;
in Catholic Church, *see* Church, Catholic *s.v.*;
formulae of, **4** 106;
in Mass, **11** 390; decline of, **11** 862;
negative, in Egypt, **6** 962; **10** 158;
and Protestants, **11** 33, 78, 86, 544;
public, **17** 154; **18** 558;

see also confession (psychological) *s.v.* in analysis
confessional, *see* Church, Catholic *s.v.*
confessionalism, **18** 1466, 1468
confidence: need of mutual, in analysis, **17** 181;
in self, *see* self (1) *s.v.*
configurations, archetypal, of the unconscious, **13** 304
confirmamentum (Paracelsan neologism), **13** 173
confirmation, **7** 384; **16** 215;
lessons, **9i** 30
Confiteor, **10** 674
conflagration, hysteric's vision of, **1** 130
conflict, **4** 295, 353–4; **5** 175; **7** 16–19/432–4, 27/438, 49, 95, 116, 218/450, 253, 257, 359, 382; **9i** 522–3; **11** 443, 522, 532, 779–80; **12** 32, 37, 193, 195, 231, 233, 251, 259; **13** 15, 17–18, 149, 155, 163, 238, 293; **16** 392, 398–9, 470; **17** (*p*5), 11, 16, 204, 249;
actual, **4** 407;
body/spirit, **14** 672;
child/adult, **4** 354;
with collectivity, **7** 504;
of conscience, **12** 489;
conscious realization of, **14** 514;
conscious transference of, **5** 95;
of conscious and unconscious mind, **3** 529; **7** 18, 27; **10** 558; **11** 392; **12** 59, 186, 188, 193; **14** 705; (*see also below* unconscious);
in dreams, **7** 21–2, 277; **8** 491; **11** 37;
of duty, **13** 229–30;
East/West, **11** 770;
ego/instinct, **7** 43;
ego/unconscious, **8** 706;
erotic, *see* erotic/eroticism *s.v.*;
father/mother world, **12** 27;
Faustian, **7** 43;
fundamental human, **5** 1;

in Gnosticism, **9i** 295, 297;
heaven/earth, **12** *fig.* 74;
as *hierosgamos*, **8** 900; **16** 401, 458, 500;
in horoscopes, **8** 879–83, 989;
image (alchemical) of, **16** 355;
king/daughter, **12** 454;
king/queen, **9i** 612; **12** *fig.* 116; **16** 410, 414, 415;
king/son, **12** 210*n*;
lapis/son, **12** 140&*n*, *fig.* 13;
maxima, see sep. entry below;
Mercurius and, *see* Mercurius *s.v.*;
mother/son, *see* mother and son *s.v.* incest;
on mountain, **12** 209;
mysterium of, **9ii** 117; **14** 200, 662, 664;
Nous/Physis, **12** 410, 436, 438, 440; **14** 548;
oppositorum/of opposites, **8** 900; **9ii** 58, 72, 124, 130, 256, 304, 425; **10** 767, 801; **11** 716, 738; **12** 436, *figs.* 167, 226; **18** 1627; on animal level, **14** 338*n*;
as psychic synthesis, **14** 657;
of red man and white woman, **14** 174, 307;
in the retort, **14** 657;
of royal pair, **9i** 612;
Sol/Luna, sun/moon, marriage/union, **8** 869, 880, 899, 988; **12** 475*n*, 484*n*, 558, *figs.* 13, 23, 27, 32, 113, 141, 223; **13** 105*n*, 157; **14** 2*n*, 21, 25, 27, 44, 87, 106, 134, 161, 163, 171, 174, 177, 180*n*, 188, 195, 276, 307, 436, 517, 532, 625&*n*, 630&*n*, 631; **16** 401, 410, 421*n*, 451, 454, 457–68, 538*n*; ascendent/descendent in, **8** 869&*n*; at new moon, **14** 293;
soul/body, *see* body *s.v.* soul and;
spirituum, **12** *fig.* 268;
stages of, **14** 669–80;
and suffering, **13** 450;

supracelestial, **13** 190;
symbolism of, **14** 523*n*, 669, 670;
tetraptiva/fourfold/noblest, **13** 357&*n*;
and transference neurosis, **16** 533;
tree as medium of, **13** 457;
triptativa/threefold, of Trinity, **13** 357&*n*;
two Mercurii, **12** 484*n*;
of two and three, **9i** 679;
upper/lower, **12** *fig.* 78;
of woman with dragon, **14** 15, 30, 168, 293, 657*n*, 669;
see also *hierosgamos;* incest; marriage; opposites, union of; syzygy
coniunctio(nes)/maxima(-ae), **9ii** 130*n*, 136, 137*n*, 153, 154, 156, 172; **11** 92
Connelly, Marc: *The Green Pastures*, **11** 266*n*
connoisseurs, **11** 970
Connolly, R. Hugh (ed.): *The So-called Egyptian Church Order and Derived Documents,* **11** 313*n*;
Church Order of Hippolytus in, **11** 313
Conrad of Würzburg, **9i** 653
conscience, **7** 311, 401; **10** 563, 807; **12** 8, 24*n*; **16** 390;
TITLE: "A Psychological View of Conscience," **10** 825–57;
collective, **6** 306, 318; **7** 333;
conflict of, **12** 489;
"Court of", **7** 332;
effect on psychic life, **1** 320*n*;
of Epimetheus, **6** 284–5, 299&*n*, 311, 318, 450;
exploration of, **18** 561;
intellectual, **7** 159;
moral and ethical, **10** 856–7;
morality of, **10** 855;
nature of, **10** 825–7;
and neurosis, **18** 1408;
paradox of, **10** 835;
Protestant, **11** 86;

conscience (*cont.*):
    relation to moral precepts, **10** 836;
    "right" and "false," **10** 840;
    scientific, **7** 365;
    and synchronicity, **10** 850;
    want of, and neurosis, **8** 685;
    see also voice/vox s.v. *Dei*
conscientia peccati, **10** 827
conscientiousness, **9ii** 46
conscious:
    TITLE: "Conscious, Unconscious and Individuation," **9i** 489–524;
    attitude, *see* attitude *s.v.*;
    contents, **7** 511–19; in dreams, **5** 261; and sacrifice of primal beings, **5** 650;
    differentiation, **6** 179; **13** 395;
    discrimination, **13** 287;
    expectations, **13** 19;
    fear of becoming, **8** 244;
    judgement, **13** 23;
    morality, **13** 434;
    motives, Freud and, **17** 17n;
    processes, adaptation and, **5** 258;
    psyche, **7** 27, 234, 274, 438; **13** 478; —, conscious activity, **5** 10; —, conscious image, **13** 75;
    as psychic modality, **8** 249;
    psychic processes, causally explicable, **15** 135;
    realization, **13** 293;
    self becoming, **12** 105n;
    and unconscious, *see* unconscious and conscious;
    way, **13** 28;
    will, **13** 13, 44;
    willing, **13** 18
conscious mind, **7** 27, 110, 344; **13** 20–1, 229, 307; **16** 51, 62, 84, 88, 111, 201, 406; **17** 189, 199*a*, 200, 281, 313;
    Adlerian psychology and, **11** 539;
    of alchemist, **16** 440;
    animus and, **5** 615;

archetype and, *see* archetype(s) *s.v.*;
and articulation of unconscious contents, **16** 26;
assimilation of contents from unconscious, **5** 631;
and associations, **1** 172;
attitude of, *see* attitude *s.v.* conscious;
characteristics of, **16** 317;
and collective unconscious, **5** 683;
and compensation, **5** 9; by unconscious, **12** 26;
complexes and, **11** 22;
cramp in, **13** 23;
directedness of, **8** 132, 135;
and dreams, **16** 334;
and ego, *see* ego *s.v.*;
energy attracted by unconscious from, **5** 671;
and fantasy-products, **5** 39, 468, 683;
gets stuck, **5** 617;
hybris of, **16** 216;
impatience of, **13** 21;
individual differences in content, **5** 258;
inhibitive action of, **16** 125;
removed in mania, **18** 830;
and instinct, conflict, **5** 615;
instinctive roots of, **16** 251;
integrative powers of, **16** 270;
intervention of, **12** 111, 438;
language of, **13** 44;
lopsidedness of, **18** 429;
and loss of energy, **16** 372;
and mana-personality, **5** 612;
narrowness of, **18** 13, 755;
and objective psyche, **12** 48;
one-sidedness of, *see* one-sidedness;
overvaluation of, **16** 51, 108;
in primitives, *see* primitive(s) *s.v.* consciousness;
and primordial image, **5** 260, 681;
and projected content, **12** 436;

psyche not identical with, **16**
201, 204; **17** 302;
rejection of unconscious, **5** 450,
462;
secrets and, **16** 125;
not totality of man, **11** 390;
and transformation, **5** 351; **14**
503;
tyrannized by memories, **1** 176;
and unconscious, *see* unconscious and conscious mind;
whims of, **7** 243*n*;
widening of, **9i** 316
consciousness, **6** 700 (Def.); **7** 41,
235/456, 236, 243/464, 244, 270,
366, 389, 500, 507; **9i** 634; **11**
658, 839, 897–900; **13** 11–17, 20,
28, 53, 55, 62, 119, 126, 187*n*,
244, 324, 396; **14** 117&n, 125,
141, 261, 330; **17** 169; **18** 542;
TITLES: "The Detachment of
Consciousness from the Object," **13** 64–71; "The Disintegration of Consciousness," **13**
46–56; "The Effects of the Unconscious upon Conscious-
ness," **7** 202–65; "The Relation
of the King-Symbol to Consciousness," **14** 498–513;
absolute, **7** 292;
abstracting attitude of, *see*
abstracting *s.v.*;
and adaptation, **4** 553; to present, **8** 324;
adaptive function of, **10** 14;
alteration(s) of, **17** 137; **18** 725;
caused by *numinosum*, **11** 6;
alternating states of, **1** 25, 279,
280;
always ego-consciousness, **17**
326;
amnesic split, **1** 130;
anomalies of, in dementia
praecox, **3** 160;
approximative, **8** 387;
archetype as foundation of, **10**
656;
archetype of, **14** 504;

articulated, **8** 687;
and artistic creation, **15** 139;
and assimilation of unconscious
material, **6** 184*n*;
association and, *see* association
s.v.;
assumed unity of, **8** 200;
attitude of, *see* attitude *s.v.*;
autarky of, **12** 174;
in Autopator, **9ii** 298;
beginnings of, **17** 83; **18** 297;
beyond, **7** 302;
and the "Beyond," **18** 752;
not biochemically explicable,
10 655;
birth of, **5** 500;
broadening of, **13** 291 (*see also
below* extension; widening); and
opus, **9ii** 230;
as Buddha, **11** 839;
cannot comprehend whole, **9ii**
171;
catatonic, **3** 12; **18** 844;
categories of, seven, **8** 293–4;
and causes and ends, **9ii** 253;
and cerebrum, **9i** 42;
and change, **17** 260;
in child, *see* child *s.v.*;
childish, **12** 74–5, 79;
Chinese, **13** 57;
Christ, as archetype of, **13** 299;
Christian, *see* Christian/Chris-
tianity *s.v.*;
circumferential, **13** 40;
civilized, **13** 229;
clarification of, **13** 291;
clarity of, **13** 43, 59;
clouding of, **18** 732;
collective, **7** 229; **8** 405, 423–4;
9i 2*n*; **12** 92; **13** 463; of our
time, **18** 5;
coming of, **14** 129*n*;
coming to, **14** 6, 152, 180&n,
309, 318, 486;
and compensation of instinctive certainty, **5** 673;
and complexes, **7** 295;
conflict within, **9i** 483;

consciousness (*cont.*):
of consciousness, **11** 890;
consolidation of, **5** 553; **9i** 47;
contemporary hypertrophy of, **11** 442;
contents of, **3** 56, 443; **17** 185;
continuity of, **11** 53;
cosmic, **10** 281;
cramp of, **12** 201; **13** 20;
created by psyche, **17** 165;
creative, **13** 59;
cult of, **13** 51;
and cure of neurosis, **16** 53;
dark background of, **11** 776;
dawn of, **8** 751; **10** 288; **12** 556; **13** 118; **18** 204;
dawning and extinction, **5** 425;
daylight of, **13** 290;
daytime, **7** 273;
and death, **8** 801;
deep and restricted (Gross), **3** 419;
defective, **7** 253;
defensive, **3** 530;
definition of, **6** 700; **14** 522*n*; **18** 18;
deflection of, **16** 395;
depotentiated, **16** 399;
descendant of unconscious, **8** 676;
detached/detachment of, **11** 816; **13** 43, 65–6, 68–9, 78; **15** 186–8, 191–3; in yoga, **11** 871;
development of, **5** 674; **11** 442; **13** 90; **14** 338*n*, 773; **17** 130, 144, 211; **18** 439, 1493; in Buddhism, **18** 1578; in child, **17** 103; and separation from mother, **5** 351;
differentiation of, **7** 329; **8** 344, 345; **9i** 565; **9ii** 298; **10** 280, 281, 284; **11** 245, 268, 758; **12** 60, 77, 84; **13** 247, 291, 453; **14** 603, 672; **16** 387; **18** 361; Trinity and, **11** 268;
dimming of, **18** 787;
as discrimination, **6** 179; **9ii** 410; **10** 657; **12** 30, 563;

disintegration of, **3** 55, 59, 76; **10** 286; **13** 46; **17** 260;
disorientation of, **16** 476;
dissociability of, **1** 423; **8** 202; **9i** 190; **18** 447;
dissociated, and memory, **1** 110;
dissociation of, *see* dissociation *s.v.*;
dissolution of, **9i** 254; **11** 829; **12** 116;
disturbances of, **1** 305, 425; **8** 639;
diurnal, **14** 128;
division of/divided, **1** 119; **7** 305; **13** 324;
dominants of, *see* dominants *s.v.*;
double, **1** 1, 25; **3** 105; **8** 351–2, 365, 396; and amnesia, **1** 130; and new character formation, **1** 136; and submersion in role, **1** 304;
in dreams, **8** 580; **17** 113–14;
dreams as compensators of, **7** 489; **12** 26;
Eastern view of, **11** 774;
eclipse of, **18** 65, 447;
ectopsychic contents of, **18** 77;
ego, *see* ego-consciousness; as centre of, *see* ego *s.v.* centre;
egocentric nature of, **14** 660;
as effect of anima, **13** 62;
emancipation of, **11** 245, 442; **18** 1658;
emptying/empty state of, **6** 187, 199, 201; **7** 357; **11** 890, 898; **18** 874;
an end result, **17** 102;
energy of, **9i** 248;
enhancement of, **11** 245;
enlargement/extension of/widened, **7** 243*n*, 275, 292;
enlargers of, **9i** 288;
entry of cryptomnesic image, **1** 139–48, 166;
essential to man, **8** 412;
evolution of, **18** 1235;

consciousness (*cont.*):
lapses of, **16** 126;
levels of, **11** 891; new level of, **11** 779;
Leviathan and development of, **9ii** 185;
libido tendencies and, **5** 659;
and life, **13** 28–30, 33; separation of, **13** 30; union of, **13** 29–30, 33–7;
and light, *see* light *s.v.*;
limits of, **12** 247;
localization of, **13** 334; **18** 17, 1331; in cerebrum, **18** 14;
longing for nature, **5** 299; **8** 750;
loss of, **8** 949;
its loss: of numinous symbols, **18** 583; of previous impressions, **1** 183;
lowered threshold of, **18** 829;
lucidity of, **3** 161;
maladaptation of, **9i** 61;
man more than, **11** 140;
masculine/male, **7** 330; **9i** 296; **11** 711; **12** 26, 192; **13** 453; **14** 221–2, 224, 619; compensated by anima, **7** 328; union with feminine unconscious, **5** 672; **14** 181;
and material objects, **8** 745;
modern, **13** 437; low level of, **11** 442;
monotheism of, **13** 51;
moon as, in woman, **14** 159, 227;
moral, **7** 218; **11** 390; **13** 244; **14** 607;
as moral criterion, **11** 696;
most individual part of man, **16** 254;
motor automatism, **1** 146;
and moulding of human nature, **5** 674;
myths and coming of, **9ii** 230;
narrowing of, **3** 160;
narrowness/narrow: intensive (Gross), *see* introverted type

s.v.; limits of, **8** 812; **13** 53;
natural, **13** 299;
nature of, **8** 610; **11** 897;
new and universal, **15** 201;
normal, **17** 102;
one-sidedness of, *see* one-sidedness *s.v.*;
ordering principles of, **13** 433;
origin of, **8** 754;
overvaluation of, **17** 343;
and Pandora's jewel, **6** 300;
is partisan, **13** 44;
passion for, **11** 542;
penumbra of, **7** 330;
perception of life-process, **8** 277;
personal and supra-personal, **16** 99;
phenomena of, **8** 10;
and physical world, **18** 12;
possession by, **13** 51;
precariousness of, **11** 29;
precondition: of being, **10** 528; of ego, **8** 611;
present-day, **10** 150; **12** 74; **13** 45;
present level of, **13** 248;
primitive, **4** 738; **11** 29, 339; **13** 341; **14** 657; **18** 15, 754; lacks coherence, **9i** 213; and myths, **9i** 264;
primordial night of, **10** 282;
problematical state of, **6** 886–7;
processes of, and instinct, **8** 264;
and projection, **11** 140; **14** 129, 520, 696–7, 742;
Protestant cult of, **13** 71;
psyche and, **3** 6; **4** 175, 317, 782; **8** 362, 380, 385, 397; **9i** 490; **11** 21, 68–9, 141, 389, 441–2, 906; **12** 562; **14** 274, 501; **16** 201; **17** 112; **18** 439, 601, 798, 1230;
as psychic existence, **11** 21;
and psychic otherness, **9i** 289;
psychological determinants of, **4** 525;

consciousness (*cont.*):
    twilight state of, **13** 122;
    two attitudes of (Promethean and Epimethean) **6** 310;
    tyrannized by the unconscious, **1** 184;
    and unconscious, *see* unconscious and consciousness;
    unconscious elements and, **3** 439, 440;
    undifferentiated, **6** 199;
    union: with collective/unconscious psyche, **12** 68, 115; with Orthos, **18** 755;
    unity of, **8** 365; **13** 47; **18** 151, 443; only a desideratum, **9i** 190;
    universal, **9i** 520;
    uprooted, **13** 13, 30, 72;
    urge of, **9i** 563;
    value of, **18** 754;
    weakening of, **3** 1, 2, 56;
    and *Weltanschauung*, **8** 695–6;
    Western, **7** 317; **13** 84; **18** 562;
    whence it comes, **11** 533;
    why it exists, **8** 695;
    widening of/wider, **8** 615, 637, 638, 639, 641, 642, 645, 695, 751, 767; **13** 7, 84, 391; **14** 205, 209, 297, 306, 342, 426–8, 779;
    woman's different from man's, **7** 330; **14** 222–4;
    world's, splitting of, **11** 443;
    Yahweh's, **11** 638
consecration, in the Mass, **11** 307, 322–5, 334; **12** 417, 486–9; **13** 110;
    inner meaning, **11** 307;
    as miracle, **11** 379;
    and shaving the head, **11** 348;
    words of, **11** 378
consensus gentium, **7** 110; **18** 632;
    and death, **8** 804;
    and religion, **8** 807
consensus omnium/generalis, **8** 821; **9ii** 54, 57, 84, 276; **10** 563; **11** 294; **18** 567
conservatism, psychic, **13** 12

conservatives, **7** 198
consideratio, **13** 201*n*
consideration, lack of, **3** 158
Consignatio, **11** 333, 336
"Consilium coniugii," *see* ALCHEMICAL COLLECTIONS: *Ars. chem. s.v.*; *Bibl chem. cur. s.v.*; *Theatr. chem. s.v.*
constancy: principle of, **8** 34;
    virtue of sapphire, **13** 321
Constantine, Arch of, in dream, **5** 9
Constantine, Emperor, **13** 157
constellation(s), **2** 186&*n*, 191–3, 226, 243–4, 258, 312, 340, 363, 607; **8** 198; **9ii** 54;
    TITLE: "The Family Constellation," **2** 999–1014;
    of archetype, *see* archetype *s.v.*;
    in association experiments, **4** 47;
    celestial, *see sep. entry below;*
    of childhood sexuality, **4** 224;
    definitions of, **2** 733;
    in epilepsy, **2** 539, 555;
    family, **2** 999–1014;
    in feeble-minded, **2** 193, 509;
    in hysteria, **2** 192, 210;
    increase of, **2** 337;
    reaction time and, *see* complex *s.v.* constellation;
    theriomorphic, **4** 335; **5** 145;
    type: complex, *see* complex *s.v.* constellation, type; simple, **2** 414, 427–8;
    unconscious, **4** 335; **5** 92, 681; **11** 780;
    see also complex
constellation(s), heavenly/celestial, **8** 325;
    Bear, *see* Bear;
    Dragon, **8** 394; **14** 176;
    Engonasi (The Kneeler), **14** 493*n*;
    Orion, *see* Orion
constipation, **17** 141
constitution:
    TITLE: "The Significance of Constitution and Heredity in

Psychology," **8** 220–31;
inherited, **17** 228;
and psyche, **8** 220–1;
psychopathic, **17** 245
constructive method/standpoint, *see*
method(s) *s.v.* constructive
consubstantiation, doctrine of, **6** 96
consultation, reactions after, **3** 494
consummation of universe, **9ii** 400
contagion: by example, **17** 253;
mental, **18** 46, 156, 318; attitude and, **8** 630;
psychic, **4** 701;
unconscious, **17** 255
"contained" and "container," **10**
253, 255; **17** 331c–4
containment, motif of, **5** 351
contamination(s), **3** 39, 42–4, 49; **7**
144, 373; **16** 501, 503;
"all-", **11** 817;
and images, **11** 783;
of opposites, *see* opposites *s.v.*;
through mutual unconsciousness, **18** 323, 345;
by unconscious, **12** 31, 145,
192, 204, 242*n*, 295;
of unconscious, **14** 401
contemplatio, **13** 201*n*
contemplation, **9i** 562, 633; **13** 46*n*,
64, *fig.* A5; **14** 709; **16** 134; **17**
207;
Christian and yogic, **11** 937;
of life of Jesus, **13** 201*n*;
sage in, **13** 46;
tree of, **13** 414;
see also *meditatio;* meditation
contemporary events:
TITLES: Preface and Epilogue
to *Essays on Contemporary Events,*
10 (*pp*177–8), 458–87; "Marginalia on Contemporary
Events," **18** 1360–83;
content(s):
TITLE: "The Content of the
Psychoses," **3** 320–87;
autonomous, **7** 400, 402, 403;
psychic, **3** 56;
repressed, **13** 51;

unconscious, *see* unconscious
contents
see also under conscious; consciousness; unconscious
context: in dream(s), **12** 38, 49,
403; **18** 248, 485, 1380; interpretation of, **12** 48–50; **16** 319,
321–2; **17** 114; **18** 1391;
importance in psychology, **4**
14;
taking up, **8** 542
contiguity, **3** 22*n*, 41
continents, four, **14** 283
contingent, the, **8** 964, 968
continuum, **8** 812; *see also* spacetime
contraception/birth-control, **10** 210,
253;
labour camps and, **10** 615
contract/covenant, between Yahweh
and man, **11** 569–73, 577, 599,
620, 637
"contraction," **8** 856
contradictio in adiecto, **18** 1606
contradictions, **3** 263;
logical and moral, **13** 294–5;
in psychology, **16** 1
contraries, *see* opposites
contrasexual (-ity), *see* sexual *s.v.*
contrasts: of associations, **3** 138;
verbal, **3** 29
contritio, **12** 36&*n*
control, mediumistic, **1** 54–62
controversies, spiritual, **7** 80
Conventi, Italian murderer, somnambulistic personality, **1** 60
convention(s)/conventionality, **10**
962; **17** 296–9, 305;
a collective necessity, **17** 297;
mechanism of, **17** 305
conversation, trance, **1** 40–1, 50, 51;
impression of wilful deception,
1 71;
by means of intended tremors,
1 94;
memory of, **1** 48;
with somnambulistic personality, **1** 55–8

conversing with oneself, art of, **7** 323
conversion(s): of excitation, **4** 31, 208;
    and hysterical symptom, **18** 1047;
    into opposite, **7** 115–16;
    principle of, **3** 76;
    religious, **3** 483, 489, 491, 493; **7** 110, 270; **9ii** 73; **10** 566; **11** 110, 274; **12** 3; **14** 514; **18** 594;
    of St. Paul, *see* Paul, St.;
    sudden, **7** 233; **8** 582
converts, **3** 462
conviction(s): hardening of, **8** 773;
    inward, **13** 81
convulsion(s): hysterical attacks of, **1** 197;
    religious, **7** 115;
    symptom of childhood neurosis, **17** 141;
    therapy, **14** 680;
    see also epilepsy
Conybeare, F.C.C.: "Die jungfräuliche Kirche und die jungfräuliche Mutter," **5** 318n
Cook, Florence, medium, **1** 63
cooking, **13** 101;
    in alchemy, **13** 89;
    symbolism of, **5** 200;
    vessel, and mother archetype, **9i** 156
Coolidge, C., **11** 518
Coomaraswamy, A.: "The Inverted Tree," **13** 408n, 412n, 458n;
    Journal of the American Oriental Society, **8** 395n
co-operation: of individual and collective, **7** 486;
    in individuation, **7** 268
co-ordinates/co-ordination: in association, *see* association(s) *s.v.*;
    conceptual, **8** 855;
    of psychic and physical processes, **8** 948
Copenhagen, **10** 1048, 1055, 1064
Copernicus, **10** 527
copper, **13** 118, 228, 267, 357;

leprosy of (Paracelsus), **15** 25–7;
sign for, in alchemy, **9i** 537, 575;
and sun, **14** 110
Coptic: myth of the Father-Creator, **5** 479;
    Gnostic papyrus (Jung Codex), **18** (*p*671&*n*);
    Gnostic treatise, *see* CODICES AND MSS: Oxford *s.v.* Brucianus
copulation, **9ii** 322;
    self-, **9ii** 322
cor, **14** 493n, 568;
    altum, **13** 301n;
    see also heart
coral, **9ii** 192n;
    tree of, *see* tree(s) *s.v.*
corascenum, see ANIMALS: dog/bitch *s.v.* Corascene
Corbin, H.: *Creative Imagination in the Sufism of Ibn 'Arabi,* **18** 1279n
Cordes, G., **2** 14&n, 20, 86, 730;
    "Experimentelle Untersuchungen über Assoziationen," **2** 14n, 451n, 730n
Cordovero, M.: *Pardes Rimmonim,* **14** 18n
Co-Redemptrix, dogma of, **18** 1607, 1652
Corinthians: Clement's Epistles to, *see* Clement of Rome/etc. *s.v.*;
    St Paul's Epistles to, *see* BIBLE: N.T. *s.v.*
corn, **9i** 288;
    cobs, **13** 331, *fig.* 25;
    ear of, **5** 530, pl. IV*b*;
    mortar, **5** 298n;
    seed of, **13** 322
Cornarius, **9ii** 298
Cornell, J. H.: *Iconography of the Nativity of Christ,* **12** *fig.* 42
corners, four, of heavens, **13** 359
cornerstone, *see* Christ *s.v.; lapis angularis;* stone *s.v.*
Cornford, F. M., *see* Plato: *Timaeus*
corn-god/spirit, **11** 385;
    Adonis as, **5** 530n;

creation, **9i** 631, 632; **10** 623; **11** 565, 619, 630, 631; **12** 30, *fig.* 126; **13** 168;
  TITLE: "The Hymn of Creation," **5** 56–114;
  acts of, **8** 965, 967;
  alchemical, **9i** 550; **12** 347, 429, 433; opus as, *see* opus *s.v.* creation;
  continuous/*creatio continua,* **8** 967&*n*; **18** 1630;
  cruel aspect of, **18** 1654;
  days of, **13** 301, 334; second, **11** 180, 256, 262;
  of a god, **11** 143;
  ideal, and real, **5** 77;
  imperfection of, **11** 201;
  of man, **11** 574, 631; **13** 113;
  in Miller fantasies, **5** 67–8;
  myth, **6** 366–7; **13** 132;
  original, **1** 66, 139;
  regression and, **4** 406;
  and repression, **5** 95;
  and sacrifice, **5** 646–7;
  self-copulation (Egyptian) and, **9ii** 322&*n*;
  of souls, **13** 113;
  through thought, **5** 72–4;
  and Trinity, **11** 290;
  of world, *see* world
Creation Epic, Babylonian, *see* Babylon *s.v.*
creative: achievements, **8** 702;
  complex, *see* complex, autonomous;
  fantasy, *see* fantasy *s.v.*;
  force, **5** 198; symbols of, **5** 180;
  imagination, subsconscious (Miller fantasies), **5** (*pp*446–62);
  impulses, **3** 531;
  instinct, *see* instinct(s);
  possibilities, **16** 82;
  powers, and unconscious, **5** 523;
  processes, of artist, **15** 109–12, 130, 135, 155; and collective unconscious, **15** 153, 159–61,

174; feminine quality of, **15** 159; Freud on, **15** 155–6; of Picasso, **15** 204–14; psychological and visionary, **15** 139&*n*, 140–4;
  secret, **11** 906;
  spiritual activity, **5** 588;
  thought, **5** 449; **7** 292;
  word, **5** 65;
  work, **16** 373; and disease, **17** 206
creativeness, **11** 497, 782; and primordial experience, **15** 151
creativity: and ecstasy, **1** 184, 185;
  of hallucinations, **1** 25; impulses of, **3** 531;
  and memory-complex, **1** 177–8;
  and morbidity, **17** 206;
  Promethean, **6** 291–2, 294
  and sexuality, **8** 245, 709;
  and unconscious, *see* unconscious *s.v.*;
  and wish-fulfilment, **1** 172;
  see also originality
creator, **12** *figs.* 1, 195; **13** 248;
  and creation/creature, **5** 95, 588; **13** 299&*n*;
  and father-imago, **5** 63;
  Gnostic symbolism for, **9ii** 306–8;
  -God, in Hindu literature, **9ii** 300;
  "of the nations," **5** 478
Creator Spiritus, **5** 678
creatum/increatum, lapis/Mercurius as, **16** 527
creatures, four, *see* Ezekiel *s.v.* vision
"Crede mihi, seu Ordinale," *see* ALCHEMICAL COLLECTIONS: *Mus. herm. s.v.* Norton
credulity, **10** 554
creed(s), **9ii** 277; **10** 509; **12** 3, 17, 19;
  ambivalence of, **10** 520;
  Apostles', **11** 211–14;
  Athanasian/Symbolum Quicunque, **11** 171, 218&*n*, 226;

crowd (*cont.*):
 dream-motif, **8** 535;
 emotion in, **18** 318;
 individual in, **9i** 225;
 psychology of, *see* psychology
  svv. collective; mob/mass/herd
crowfoot, *see* flame/*flammula s.v.*
crown/*corona*/diadem/*diadema*, -*cordis tui*, **8** 229; **9i** 573; **11** 230; **12**
  53, 138, 157*n*, 467, 499; **13** 346,
  416,*fig.* 31; **14** 6; **16** 495, 497*n*;
  in alchemy, **5** 268*n*; **14** 319*n*;
  hermaphrodite with, **5** pl.
  XVIII; king's, **13** 107*n*, 183; **14**
  499;
  in association-chain, **3** 228,
  229;
  of eternal life, **5** 397;
  and foul deposit, **16** 496;
  gold, and silver, see COLOURS
  s.v.;
  "of the heart," **13** 346; **16** 496,
  497&*n* (*see also* ash(es));
  in Mithraic mysteries, **5** 288;
  mural, **5** 303, pl. XXIVb; **13**
  399*n*;
  Solomon's, **16** 496*n*;
  symbolism of, **5** 671*n*;
  of victory, **14** 12, 319&*n*; **16**
  496;
  see also Atarah; Kether
crowned: boy, **13** *fig.* 32;
  dragon, **13** *fig.* 14;
  Maid, **12** 491, 499;
  serpent, **13** *fig.* 32
Crucifix, *see* cross
crucifixion, **7** 224; **9i** 240, 311, 705;
  9ii 124, 125; **11** 406, 430; **12** 24,
  177,*figs.* 28, 53; **14** 555*n*; **16** 470;
  Aztec, **5** 445;
  of Christ, *see* Christ *s.v.*;
  of evil spirit, **9i** 434, 446–8;
  mock, **5** 421, 622, pl. XLIII; **12**
  539;
  of Peter, **11** 436–7;
  as punishment for slaves, **9ii**
  130&*n*;
  quaternity, **11** 430, 677;

of raven, **9i** 427–8, 434;
  and serpent, *see* ANIMALS *s.v.*
  serpent/snake;
  of soul, **7** 36;
  symbol, **5** 575;
  on wheel, **18** 81
cruelty: as dream symbol, **10** 447,
  449;
  and sadism, **17** 145;
  of transformative process, **11**
  410
Crusaders, **5** 276; **10** 597
crux ansata (Egyptian), **5** 401*n*, 408,
  fig. 27;
  meaning of forms of, **5** 411
crying, fits of, **3** 468
crypt, **18** 254, 255, 256
cryptomnesia, **1** 138–48; **4** 152; **5**
  474, 682*n*; **6** 839; **7** 219; **8** 311,
  319, 503, 599, 845; **9i** 92, 549*n*;
  13 352*n*; **17** 200; **18** 26, 454, 457;
  TITLE: "Cryptomnesia," **1** 166–
  86; **6** 839*n*;
  definition of, **1** 180;
  enrichment of conscious memory, **1** 146;
  verbal correspondences, in
  works of Nietzsche and Kerner,
  1 140–2, 180–3;
  see also Flournoy
crystal(s), **7** 398; **8** 221, 589*n*, 945;
  9i 155; **9ii** 352; **11** 122, 968; **12**
  221–4, 327, *fig.* 142K; **14** 329,
  642;
  brown, see COLOURS *s.v.*;
  lapis as, **12** 221–2;
  terrible, **13** 362;
  throne, **12** 315, 322; and minis-
  tering spirits, **13** 132
Ctesias, **12** 536;
  Ἰνδικά/*Ancient India*, tr. J. W.
  McCrindle, **12** 526*n*
cube, **11** 247*n*; **13** 348*n*
cubism, **15** 174
Cubricus, **14** 31&*n*; *see also* Kybric
Cucorogna, **9i** 464
cucullatus, **9i** 298
cucumber, association to, **4** 337

cucurbita, see *vas*/vessel *s.v.* Hermetic
Cuesta, bishop of Leon, **11** 324
cul de Paris, **18** 1315
Cullerre, A.: "Un cas de somnam-
bulisme hystérique," **1** 14*n*
culmination, of dream, **8** 563
cult(s), **13** 55;
> ancient, sexual content of, **5**
> 339;
> basis in relationship of son to
> mother, **5** 330*n;*
> of consciousness, **13** 51;
> of the dead, **13** 360;
> mystery, **16** 124; confession in,
> **16** 133;
> personality, **17** 311;
> stone-, **13** 132
cultural: activities, and sexual libido, **5** 219;
> aim, **7** 114;
> development, and psychic en-
> ergy, **5** 17;
> phase, **7** 114
culture, **4** 444, 664; **5** 506;
> adult as upholder of, **17** 109;
> aetiological c.-myth, **17** 200;
> beginnings of, **8** 726;
> bread and wine as expression
> of, **11** 382–3;
> Chinese, **13** 6;
> Christian, **13** 7;
> and civilization, *see* civilization
> *s.v.;*
> classical, **7** 17/427;
> collective, and Christianity, **6**
> 107–10;
> as continuity, **17** 250;
> creation of, **10** 272; **17** 200,
> 206 (*see also* spirit *s.v.* living);
> essence of, **18** 1344;
> externalization of, **11** 962;
> Freudian view, **16** 232; **18**
> 1150;
> growth/development of, **7** 17/
> 427; **10** 16;
> hero(es), **5** 42, 259; **13** 132;
> chauffeur as, **10** 195; child as,
> **9i** 288; Christ as, **9ii** 69; of

Natchez Indians, **13** 132;
> individual, **8** 113; and collec-
> tive, **6** 107–11;
> introverted side of spiritual, **7**
> 303;
> irrational devastation of, **7**
> 111&*n;*
> meaning of, **17** 159;
> megalithic, **13** 132;
> modern/present day/contem-
> porary, **6** 106–12, 172; **7** 26/
> 437; **17** 11*n*, 200; and extra-
> verted attitude, **6** 619; patho-
> logical, **18** 1494;
> natural, **8** 81;
> and nature, **4** 486; **6** 133–5; **7**
> 16, 41; **8** 787; **9i** 680; **17** 159,
> 335;
> negroid, **7** 156;
> psychological, **12** 12;
> reflection and, **8** 243;
> self-, **7** 327;
> teacher and, **17** 110;
> and war, **7** 72
Cumaean Sybil, **5** 119
Cumont, F., **5** 109, 288, 294–5,
666–7; **6** 395; **8** 394; **9ii** 186;
> *The Mysteries of Mithra,* tr. T.
> McCormack, **5** 102*n*, 104*n*,
> 109*n*, 149*n*, 289*n*, 423*n;*
> *Les Religions orientales dans le
> paganisme romain,* **9ii** 178*n*,
> 186*n;*
> *Textes et monuments figurés relatifs
> aux mystères de Mithra,* **5** 150*n*,
> 158*nn*, 160*n*, 161*n*, 163*n*, 165*n*,
> 288*n*, 294*nn*, 319*n*, 425*nn*,
> 439*n*, 460*n*, 528*n*, 572*n*, 574*n*,
> 577*n*, 666*n*, 671*n*, *fig.* 9, pls
> XXXIII, XL, LXIII*b;* **8** 394*n;*
> **9i** 240*n*, 553*n;* **9ii** 147*n;* **11**
> 342*n;* **12** 469*nn;* **13** 404*n;* **14**
> 300*n;* **18** 1528
cup: golden, **14** 414, 426;
> of Joseph and Anacreon, **12**
> 550;
> poison-proof, **12** 550;
> unicorn, **12** 550–3

D

Dacqué, E., **8** 652&*n*
dactyl(s)/Dactyl(s), **9i** 408; **9ii** 332; **12** 223;
  birth of, **5** 279;
  Idaean (fingers, thumbs), **5** 183&*n*;
  phallic aspect, **5** 180; **9i** 298
Dadaism, **10** 44
dadophors, *see* Mithras/Mithraic *s.v.* bull-sacrifice
Daemogorgon, **13** 176*n*
daemon/daimon(-ion), **4** 727, 743; **5** 553; **7** 33, 108, 111*n*, 403; **9i** 454; **9ii** 51, 311, 356; **10** 843; **11** 8, 20, 141; **13** 51, 251, 278, 343, 372*n*; **14** 6*n*, 251; **17** 244, 298;
  archetype "daemonic," **11** 223;
  autonomous dynamism of, **10** 843; **13** 51;
  conquered, **13** 437;
  Eros as, *see* Eros/Cupid *s.v.*;
  as a familiar, **13** 437;
  and hero, **5** 548; **14** 6*n*; **17** 298;
  is an illusion, **13** 55;
  intellect as, **12** 88;
  masculine, **13** 339;
  Mercurius as: serpent-daemon, **13** 288; storm-, **13** 250;
  nature-, **7** 217;
  nous as, **12** 410;
  possession by, **8** 627;
  private, **17** 300;
  psychic activity, **11** 242;
  of revelation, **13** 218;
  of scientific spirit, **13** 163;
  self as, **11** 154;
  serpent-, female, **13** 288;
  of Socrates, **3** 308; **10** 843, 853; **17** 300;
  transformation of, **5** 548;
  tree, **13** 247–8;
  triunus, ass as, **12** 539;
  voice of, **17** 302;
  see also demon
daemonic: agencies, **13** 430;
  forces of life, **13** 55

daemonization of man, **13** 365
Dagda (Irish god), **6** 401*n*
dagger, **8** 151;
  in dream of Toledo cathedral, **18** 251–2, 260–1, 265–6, 375;
  -symbol, **5** 577;
  see also sword
Dagon, **9ii** 178*n*, 186
Dahns, F.: "Das Schwärmen des Palolo," **8** 842*n*
daimon(ion), see daemon/etc.
Daimorgon, **13** 176*n*
Dakota Indians, *see* American Indians: NORTH *s.v.*
Dalai Lama, **11** 149
Dalcq, A. M., **8** 959;
  "La Morphogénèse dans le cadre de la biologie générale," **8** 959*n*
Dale, A. van: *Dissertationes de origine ac progressu idololatriae et superstitionum,* **14** 589*n*
Daltonism, **1** 415
Damascene earth, **13** 418
Damascius, Diadochus: *De principiis,* **14** 576&*n*
Damascus: chalice, **11** 384;
  Paul's journey to, *see* Paul *s.v.*
Damdad-Nashk, **9ii** 389*n*
Dame à la Licorne, **12** *fig.* 258
damnation, everlasting/eternal, **8** 736; **9ii** 112*n*; **11** 28, 291; **18** 1553, 1564, 1641
Dana, M., **18** (*p* 692*n*)
Danae, **9i** 560
dance(s)/dancing/dancer(s), **8** 400; **9i** 311, 312*n*, 458;
  African, **10** 964;
  American Indian: Navaho, *yaibichy,* **18** 1225; New Mexico, **5** pl. XXI*b*; Pueblo, **5** 480; **8** 86;
  American (jazz), **10** 964;
  of Australian Wachandi, **8** 83–5;
  of bees, **8** 956;
  couples, Kekulé's, **16** 353;

"De alchimia" (Thomas Aquinas, pseud.), *see* ALCHEMICAL WRITERS: Thomas Aquinas

dea mater, **12** 431

Dea Natura, **13** 130; *see also* nature *s.v.* deity

"De arbore contemplationis," *see* CODICES AND MSS: Basel *s.v.*

"De arte chymica," *see* ALCHEMICAL COLLECTIONS: *Art. aurif. s.v.*

death, **7** 293, 300, 302; **8** 796–7; **9i** 256; **12** 165, 334, 436–7, 475*n*; **13** 57, 69, 139, 201&*n*, 203, 267, 276, 429, 434; **17** 5, 6, 8, 17, 119;
TITLE: "The Soul and Death," **8** 796–815;
acceptance of, **8** 790;
actual, **14** 675;
in African Negro myth, **5** 538;
as archer, **5** pl. XLV;
as archetype, **16** 469;
-bed and cryptomnesic reproduction, **1** 143, 183;
birds as omens of, **8** 844–5, 850&*n*, 851, 857;
birth and, **18** 564; (*see also below* rebirth);
child's conception of, **17** 10–11;
consensus gentium and, **8** 804;
-dealing poison, **13** 429*n*;
departure of spirit at, **8** 662;
and dragon, **5** 394; **13** 416;
dreams: anticipating, **16** 323; of death, **8** 852; **17** 223; of own death, **16** 349;
and dying, **8** 809;
early, **9i** 162;
emblem of, **5** 324*n*;
-expectation, **3** 271, 276;
-fantasies, and renunciation of desire, **5** 165–6;
fear of, **5** 681; **8** 778, 792, 797, 800; **10** 696; **18** 239; ransom from, **5** 671;
figurative, **13** (*p*63*n*);
followed by new life, **16** 467, 511;

fruitfulness from, **5** 526;
gesture of self-exposure to, **5** 429, 462, 465;
as goal, **8** 792, 797, 807; **13** 68; **18** 1706;
-heads, **7** 6, 415;
horse, as herald of, **16** 347;
instinct, *see* Freud *s.v.* death;
irrationalism and, **10** 375*n*;
life and, *see* life *s.v.*;
longing for, **5** 432, 434, 553, 596;
meaning of, **16** 468;
moon and, **14** 20;
and mother: as re-entry into, **5** 354, 682*n*; as source of, **5** 504, 571; as womb of, **5** 319;
of mother, **17** 10–11, 223;
obsession with, **2** 666, 692, 713–15, 722;
as omen, **5** 552;
origin of, **5** 415, 538;
as perfection, **10** 695;
philosophy and, **18** 753;
precognitions of, **8** 844, 974;
preparation for, **8** 804, 808; **18** 538, 753;
presentiments of, **5** 432;
primitives and, **10** 106;
punishment for incest, **16** 468;
-ray, red, **13** 401;
and rebirth, **5** 355, 363, 364, 592, 638, 644*n*; **16** 471; in alchemy, **13** 96, 135, 139; cycle of birth and death, **13** 105, 135; of philosophical tree, **13** 376 (*see also* rebirth); symbols of, **5** 644*n*; **8** 809;
reiterated, **16** 478;
ritual/sacrificial, **12** 171, 415, 417; **16** 214, 223;
as sequela of insanity, **3** 322;
ship of, **10** 702; and tree of, **5** 368;
shrinking from, **16** 75;
spectre of, **18** 565;
spiritual, **12** 105–6;
state of, **16** 493;

survival after, **13** 76*n*;
as symbol/symbolic, **9i** 158,
231; **18** 1661;
symbols of, *see above* and rebirth;
synchronistic phenomena and,
10 849;
as telepathic dreams, **8** 504;
thoughts of, **1** 40;
tree of, *see* tree *s.v.*;
and Ufos, **10** 699;
unknown approach of, **18** 537;
victory over, **12** 416–17, 436,
440, 454, 475;
voluntary, **5** 601; **9i** 66;
water(s) of, **5** 293, 319, 541,
542, 548;
zenith of the sun, **5** 354;
see also dead; dying
debility: mental, **3** 21;
physical, **8** 598;
"debraining," **3** 196
decad/δεκάς, Pythagorean view of,
16 525*n*
decapitation, *see* beheading
decay, radioactive, **8** 959, 966
deceit, **7** 497
"decent," **4** 579
deception: of analyst, **4** 636, 650;
in hallucinatory phenomena, **1**
134;
see also malingering; self-
deception
De chemia, see ALCHEMICAL
WRITERS: Senior *s.v.*
decisions: and feeling-values, **1** 221;
making of, and conscious
mind, **5** 462;
voluntary, and feeling tone, **1**
220
Decius, **6** 23; **9i** 242*n*
"Declaratio et Explicatio Adolphi,"
see ALCHEMICAL COLLECTIONS:
Theatr. chem. s.v. Beatus: "Aurelia
occulta"
decoctio, **12** 353
decomposition, **13** 170*n*
"decoy mechanisms," **5** 219

Dedalus, Stephen, *see* Joyce, James:
Ulysses
Dedu, god of, **5** 148*n*
Dee, John, *see* ALCHEMICAL WRITERS
s.v.
deep heart, *see* heart *s.v.*
deer, *see* ANIMALS *s.v.*
Déesse Raison, see Reason, Goddess of
defecation: act of, **5** 275; **13** 269*n*;
see also anal; excrement
defence: aggressive, German, **10**
482;
dogma as, **11** 81;
homosexuality as, **7** 134;
mechanism(s), **7** 148; **8** 488; instinctive, **11** 533;
resentment as, **10** 915;
scientific theory as, **11** 81;
and truth, **11** 79
defensiveness, in neurosis, **6** 469
definition(s): tendency to give, **3**
208;
type, *see* type(s) *s.v.*
"De flavo et rubeo viro," *see* AL-
CHEMICAL COLLECTIONS: *Aureum
vellus,* Melchior *s.v.* "Von dem
gelben und rotten Mann"
deformity motif in Cabiric cult, **5**
184; *see also* dwarfs
degeneracy: congenital, **1** 425; **4**
296;
effect of detention on, **1** 317;
hereditary, **1** 113; **4** 209, 296;
and hypalgesia, **1** 338;
hysteria as mark of, **1** 175;
and malingering, **1** 302;
mental states in, **1** 357;
psychic, symptoms of, **1** 218;
signs/symptoms of, **1** 191, 417;
and simulation, **1** 356
degenerate(s), **11** 516;
case of simulation, **1** 345–7;
energy and self-control of, **1**
303;
"syndromes épisodiques des
dégénérés," **1** 218
degeneration, **3** 141, 142, 471; **8** 69,
687; **15** 123;

degeneration (*cont.*):
    in cancer cells, **3** 319;
    in epilepsy, **3** 326;
    mass-, **16** 502;
    pathological, **17** 257;
    secondary symptoms of, **3** 318, 503
Degenhardus, **9ii** 215; **12** 443*n*
de Goeje, M. J., *see under* Dozy
degradation, in dream, **8** 567
De Gubernatis, A., **9i** 605;
    Zoological Mythology, **5** 276*n*, 450*n*; **9i** 605*n*; **9ii** 176*n*; **14** 398&*n*
Deianeira/Deianira, **5** 34;
    robe of, **9i** 221, 571
deification: of the believer, **5** 132;
    of doctor, **7** 110, 214;
    of hero figures, **17** 311;
    of man, **7** 400;
    of master, by disciple, **7** 263;
    rites, **9i** 249;
    self, **7** 110
"De igne et sale," *see* ALCHEMICAL COLLECTIONS: *Theatr. chem. s.v.* Vigenerus
dei infernales, **14** 216
De incertitudine et vanitate scientiarum, *see* Agrippa von Nettesheim
deipnon, **11** 302–4, 307, 346
deisidaimonia (δεισιδαιμονία), **11** 23
Deity: bisexual nature of the, **11** 47;
    circle as symbol of, **11** 92;
    life process within, **11** 206;
    see also God
deity(-ies): in centre, **12** 125, 139*n*, *figs.* 42, 62, 109;
    feminine element in, **12** 192;
    as hermaphrodite, **11** 47*n*; **12** 410*n*, 436*n*, *fig.* 183;
    in lotus, **12** 139&*n*, 246*n*;
    male-female pairs, **9i** 120;
    and mandala, **11** 139;
    nature, **13** 247, 299; Dea Natura, **13** 130 (*see also* god(s) *s.v.* nature);
    peaceful and wrathful, **11** 833;

symbols for, **9i** 572;
    see also god(s)
déja-vu, see foreknowledge
dejection, **1** 320*n*
De Jong, K.H.E.: *Das antike Mysterienwesen,* **5** 528*n*, 530*n*
Delabarre, E. B., **2** 1058, 1187&*n*;
    Über Bewegungsempfindungen, **2** 1058*n*, (*p*580)
Delacotte, J., *see under* Guillaume de Digulleville
Delacroix, E., **12** *fig.* 36
"De lapide philosophico figurae et emblemata," *see* ALCHEMICAL COLLECTIONS: *Mus. herm. s.v.* Lambspringk
Delatte, L., *see under* Cyranides
Delbrück, A., **1** 117, 304; *Die pathologische Lüge und die psychisch abnormen Schwindler,* **1** 117*n*, 118*n*, 304*n*
Delhi, **10** 983
deliberation, **8** 241; **9ii** 33;
    unconscious, **11** 63
delight-maker, **9i** 469
Delilah, **5** 458
delinquency, juvenile, **10** 897; *see also* criminal(s) *s.v.* children
delirium, **1** 285; **3** 346; **9i** 263;
    delusions of grandeur in, **1** 213;
    hallucinatory, **3** 61, 164;
    hysterical, **1** 7, 11, 117; **3** 164–5;
    induced by intoxicants, **16** 501*n*;
    with motor excitement, **1** 283;
    syndromes of degeneracy, **1** 218
delirium tremens, **1** 199, 203
deliverance: archetype of, **10** 624;
    and Greek mysteries, **6** 229;
    Schopenhauer's doctrine of, **6** 223
Delos, birthplace of Apollo, **5** 577; **14** 261
Delphi/Delphic, **18** 258;
    crevice and Castalian spring, **5** 577;

gorge, **5** 369*n*, 371n;
oracle, **5** 450*n*; **18** 548
Delphinas, *see* ALCHEMICAL COLLEC-
TIONS: *Theatr. chem. s.v.*
Deluge/Flood, the, **5** 167; **9ii** 330;
11 577, 653, 669; **14** 571;
Deucalion and, **5** 279, 570;
in Jewish tradition, **12** 540–2;
Noah and, *see* Noah *s.v.*;
Ogygian, **5** 306;
symbolism of, **5** 570–1
delusion(s), **1** 11, 283; **3** 72, 166–9,
175, 200–7, 498, 565; **4** 256; **7**
110, 381; **9i** 309; **10** 714; **11** 557;
13 47, 55, 139*n*, 298, 454; **15** 152;
17 250–1;
aims of, **3** 410–12;
collective, **13** 52;
comparative study of, **3** 414;
as expressions of complex, **3**
204;
of grandeur, *see* grandeur;
Mercurius a god of, **13** 299;
and mythological motifs, **18**
833;
paranoid, **3** 147; **5** 185*n*; **7** 470;
9i 103;
of reference, **3** 169;
schizophrenic, **11** 454; **15** 65;
of self as Messiah/pope, **1** 213,
214;
social and political, **13** 5;
and unconscious processes, **3**
452–3;
wish-fulfilling, **1** 283–4;
see also hallucination(s)
delusional: assertions, **3** 168;
ideas, **1** 466; **3** 190, 200–7; **8**
581, 584, 747; **11** 222, 899; **18**
1478; and archetypal motifs,
18 1480
demand(s): contrasexual, **7** 297;
infantile sexual, **7** 256;
outer and inner, **7** 311
Demant, V. A., **18** 1586; *The Religious Prospect*, **18** 1586*n*
dementia, **2** 1302, 1307, 1354;
acute juvenile, **3** 9*n*;

epileptic, **3** 471;
and outer associations, **1** 317;
paralytica, **1** 283;
paranoides, *see* paranoia;
praecox, *see* schizophrenia;
sejunctiva, see Gross, O.;
senile, **1** 154; **2** 1295; **3** 471–2
(*see also* deterioration *s.v.*
senile)
Demeter/Ceres, **5** 354*n*, 355, 421*n*,
528&*n*, 530*n*; **9i** 167, 310, 317,
339; **16** 518; **18** 264&*n*;
Homeric hymn to, **5** 533; **9i**
205*n*;
and Kore, see Kore *s.v.*;
and Persephone, **5** 526; **9i** 169;
9ii 23; **12** 26;
of Pharos, **5** 321;
serpent of, in Eleusinian mysteries, **5** 530, 584;
and tree, **5** 526*n*
demigod, **7** 206, 380; *see also*
superman
demiurge, **5** 163*n*, 665*n*; **6** 141; **9ii**
296, 299, 306, 308, 366; **11** 133;
12 126, 410, 413; **13** 96, 116, 276,
278; **15** 11, 192, 199;
as *anima mundi*, **11** 160;
devil as, **9ii** 233, 367; **11** 255,
470;
Gnostic, **7** 212; **9ii** 75*n*, 233&*n*,
306, 308; **11** 160, 408, 470; **14**
522*n*; **18** 1419; and highest
God, **9ii** 296, 366; Ialdabaoth,
9ii 128, 325; **11** 350; —, and
Jehovah, **12** 539; **13** 270*n*; imprisoned in matter, **10** 633; **11**
92, 94; Naassene/Esaldaios, **9ii**
128, 307, 325; and Ogdoad, **9ii**
297;
Platonic, **11** 186
democracy, **10** 326, 456; **18** 1317–
20, 1324, 1337, 1569;
social, **10** 155
Democritus of Abdera (philosopher), **9i** 573; **14** 41;
atomic theory of, **8** 278*n*; **9i**
116–17; **10** 766

detachment, **13** 60;
  Christian ideal of, **11** 539;
  of consciousness, *see* conscious-
    ness *s.v.*;
  from father, **11** 271;
  inner, **13** 55;
  in yoga, **11** 826, 890
details, importance of, **8** 863, 924
detective story(-ies), **10** 195; **15** 137
detention: characteristic states of
  prisoners in, **1** 277–81;
    fear of, **1** 356;
    and hysterical psychoses, **1** 302;
    hysterical stupor in, **1** 226–300;
    influence of, **1** 283;
    and patient's affect, **1** 245, 317
deterioration: apperceptive, **3** 19,
  20, 30–2, 74, 76;
    emotional, **3** 33, 144;
    senile, **3** 327, 497 (*see also* de-
      mentia *s.v.* senile)
determinant(s): of function, **8** 377;
    producing human culture, **4**
    665
determination: causal and final, **4**
  688;
    over-, **3** 133; **4** 44;
    principle of, **18** 1041;
    unconscious, **4** 355–64
determinism, **3** 90; **11** 391;
    and James's typology, **6** 531–5;
    Schopenhauer and, **8** 828;
    and synchronicity, **8** 944
De triplici habitaculo (anon.), **8** 967*n*
Deubner, L.: *Attische Feste,* **5** pl.
  LXIII*a*
Deucalion, **5** 570;
    and Pyrrha, **5** 279; **13** 132
Deursen, A. van: *Der Heilbringer,* **13**
  132*n*
deus absconditus, **6** 150, 427; **9ii** 209;
  11 259, 289, 358; **13** 138–9; **18**
  1531, 1535, 1537;
    as *lapis*/philosophers' stone, **13**
    127;
    Mercurius as, *see* Mercurius
deus terrenus/terrestris, **12** 335, 445;
  14 676, 779; **13** 203;

as *lapis*/philosophers' stone, **9i**
  289; **11** 150; **12** 471;
  Mercurius as, *see* Mercurius *s.v.*
deus ultionum, **18** 1539
Deussen, Paul, **5** 589, 658; **6** 336,
  337*n*; **10** 189;
    *Allgemeine Geschichte der Philos-
    ophie,* **5** 556*n*, 588*n*, 589*nn*,
    590*n*, 646*n*; **6** 328*n*, 329*n*,
    336*n*, 349*n*; **9ii** 237*n*; **12** 137*n*;
    13 254*n*; **14** 131*n*, 595*n*; tr. of
    Rig Veda in, **9i** 671*n*;
    Die Geheimlehre des Veda, **14**
    131*n*;
    Sechzig Upanishads des Veda, **5**
    658*n*
Deuteronomy, see BIBLE: O.T. *s.v.*
deuteros theos, **11** 594
Deutsche Märchen seit Grimm, ed. P.
  Zaunert, **9i** 404*n*, 405*n*, 412*n*,
  421*n*, 427*n*
devaluation, **12** 11*n*;
    of religious function, **7** 150;
    of sexuality, **9ii** 357;
    see also "nothing but"
Devas, angel/devil, **18** 1077
Dev Azur, **5** 664
development(s): abnormal, **7** 270;
    arrested, **3** 529;
    Christian, **13** 71;
    collective, **17** 297;
    conscious, **7** 290; **16** 387;
    of dream, **8** 562;
    embryonic, **17** 105;
    final, **8** 40, 42;
    human, **7** 482; **10** 678;
    man's, **10** 678;
    of meaning, **13** 350;
    of neurosis, **17** 177;
    ontogenetic, **7** 235/456, 457;
    pace of, **7** 159;
    personal/of personality, **7** 237/
    458–9, 239, 241*n*, 247, 267,
    364, 461–2*n*, 504; **13** 24, 31; **17**
    331c;
    precocious, of Christ, **11** 229;
    of progression, **8** 70;
    progressive, **7** 373;

diabolus, sulphur as, **13** 276; *see also* devil

diadem/*diadema cordis tue, see* crown

diagnosis(-es)/diagnostic:
TITLES: "On the Psychological Diagnosis of Facts," **1** 478–84; "The Psychological Diagnosis of Evidence," **2** 728–92; "A Third and Final Opinion on Two Contradictory Psychiatric Diagnoses," **1** 430–77; "On Pictures in Psychiatric Diagnosis," **18** 1792;
an art, **17** 198;
contradictory psychiatric, two, **1** 430–62; final opinion on, **1** 463–77;
difficulty of differentiation, in certain states, **1** 29–31;
of facts: experimental, **4** 19; psychological, **1** 478–84;
modern requirements for, **1** 302;
optimistic, danger of, **1** 351;
and paintings of patients, **18** 414;
Paracelsan concepts of, **15** 29, 32;
of problem child, **17** 228;
in psychotherapy, **16** 540; and clinical, contrasted, **16** 195–8; knowledge of symbols in, **16** 343;
of rare states of consciousness, **1** 1–4

dialectic/dialectical: conscious/unconscious, **12** 3–4, 36;
meaning, **16** 1;
philosophical, **13** 286;
procedure/process, **7** 339; **16** 9, 11, 21, 23, 25, 239, 240, 535; analytical treatment as **10** 888; psychotherapy as, **16** 1–12, 239, 544; **18** 1504, 1509;
and suggestion methods, **16** 10;
see also unconscious *s.v.*

dialect word, **1** 73(2); *see also* word substitution

dialogue, **8** 199;
inner, **8** 186;
of observer and observed, **8** 214

"Dialogus inter naturam et filii," *see* ALCHEMICAL COLLECTIONS: *Theatr. chem. s.v.* Aegidius de Vadis

"Dialogus Mercurii," *see* ALCHEMICAL COLLECTIONS: *Theatr. chem. s.v.* Sendivogius

diamond, **11** 276; **12** 221, 327, 511;
in dream, **12** 258, 273–5

diamond body, *see* Chinese alchemy *s.v.*

Diana, **9i** 341; **14** 187, 188, 203, 360;
and Actaeon, **14** 188&*n*;
as anima, **14** 193;
Apollo and, **16** 410;
at Aricia, **5** 250;
bathing in river, **14** 144&*n*, 157*n*;
of Caria, **5** 321;
dog of, **14** 188;
doves of, **14** 182, 185&*n*, 187, 408&*n*, 410;
of Ephesus, **5** pl. XXIV*b*; **11** 194;
grove of, **14** 182;
moon goddess, **13** 398; **14** 188; **16** 410;
with mural crown, **5** 303, pl. XXIV*b*;
see also Artemis

diaphragm: seat of fourth *chakra,* **16** 560;
seat of psychic activity, **18** 16

diaschisis, **3** 497

diastole, **6** 4–6;
and systole, **6** 4, 356, 428; **7** 514(5); **8** 70&*n*; as opposites, **7** 87;
see also Goethe *s.v.* systole

dice, game of, **13** 340–1; and ESP, **8** 837, 977

dichotomy: of God, **11** 380;
of universe, **11** 435

Dicks, H. V., **18** 47, 386, 387
"Dicta Alani," *see* ALCHEMICAL COL-
LECTIONS: *Theatr. chem. s.v.*
"Dicta Belini," *see* ALCHEMICAL COL-
LECTIONS: *Art. aurif. s.v.* "Rosarium philosophorum"; *Bibl. chem.
cur. s.v.* "Allegoriae sapientum";
Theatr. chem. s.v. "Allegoriae
sapientum"
dictators/dictatorship, **9ii** 96; **17**
284&n; **18** 759, 1336–7, 1341–2;
deification of, **10** 514;
and external solemnities, **10**
512
Dictionary of Goldmaking, **13** 97
didactic poetry, **15** 140
Didymus of Alexandria, **12** 522*n*;
De trinitate, **9ii** 373*n*
Diehl, A.: "Neurasthenische Kri-
sen," **1** 31&n
Diels, H.: *Fragmente der Vorsokratiker,*
9i 573*n*; **12** 435*n*; **14** 75*n*
Diem, O.: "Die einfach demente
Form der Dementia praecox," **3**
10&n
Dieterich, A., **5** 138*n*, 144*n*, 149*n*,
153*n*, 155*n*, 530&*nn*, 536*n*, 581*n*,
596*n*; **8** 318; **18** 85–6;
on Apollo and Python, **5** 316*n*;
on cista, **5** 530;
magic papyrus, **5** 130, 135; **8**
228;
on primitive forces and religion, **5** 411*n*;
on solar phallus, **5** 223;
WORKS:
*Abraxas: Studien zur Reli-
gionsgeschichte des späteren Al-
tertums,* **5** 65*n*, 316*n*;
Die Grabschrift des Aberkios, **9ii**
145*n*;
Eine Mithrasliturgie, **5** 102*n*,
130*n*, 274*n*, 297*n*, 391*n*,
411*n*, 526*n*, 664*n*; **8** 318*n*,
929*n*; **9i** 105&*n*; **9ii** 190*n*; **11**
353*n*; **13** 91*n*; **18** 85*n*, 86;
Mutter Erde, **5** 214*n*, *fig.* 15;
Nekyia: Beiträge zur Erklärung

*der neuentdeckten Petrusapoka-
lypse,* **12** 61*n*;
"Papyrus magica Musei
Lugdunensis Batavi," **12**
456*n*
Dietrich of Berne, **5** 283*n*, 585*n*
Diez, F. C.: *Wörterbuch der romanischen Sprachen,* **5** 416*n*
difference(s): individual, **7** 240,
329;
numerical, **14** 594*n*;
racial, **7** 240; **13** 11
"Different, the," in *Timaeus,* **11** 186,
188
differentiated: function, *see* func-
tion(s) *s.v.*;
type, *see* type(s) *s.v.*
differentiation, **6** 415, 705 (Def.); **7**
80, 236, 241*n*, 372–3; **13** 456; **16**
124, 503; **18** 1418;
from collective psyche, **7** 240,
515, 519;
conscious, **6** 179; **13** 395;
of consciousness, *see* consciousness *s.v.*;
and deliverance, **6** 176;
of ego, *see* ego *s.v.*;
of feelings, **14** 334;
of functions, *see* function(s) *s.v.*;
higher, **7** 198;
of human brain, **7** 235/456;
individual, **6** 88, 105, 399; **8**
523; **16** 124;
of instinct, **6** 405;
of intellect, **12** 112;
non-, *see* non-differentiation;
one-sided, **6** 130, 346;
of opposites, **13** 291;
of persona from anima, **7** 317,
504;
personal, **7** 237/459, 242/463,
456;
of personality, *see* personality
s.v.;
psychological, of man, **6** 12,
107;
racial, **7** 240*n*;
of self, **6** 183;

of typical attitudes, **6** 101;
in unconscious, **11** 440;
of unconscious from conscious products, **6** 268; **11** 64;
of Western intellect, **13** 8;
of whole man, **10** 1010

difficulties: psychic, **8** 762;
underestimation of, **8** 761

digestive disorders, **4** 569; **17** 141

Digulleville, *see* Guillaume de Digulleville

Dike, **11** 606

dilemma, of one and three, see NUMBERS *s.v.* one

dimension, fourth, *see* NUMBERS *s.v.* four

diminutives, **9i** 408

din, **9ii** 105

Ding an sich, self as, **12** 247

dinner party, **4** 86

dinner table, dream of, **2** 838–43, 856

Dio Chrysostom: on mystic quadriga, **5** 423;
Opera, **5** 423*n*

Diocletian, **18** 257

Diodoros (Megarian philosopher), **9ii** 129*n*

Diodorus Siculus, **9ii** 129; **14** 63*n*;
Bibliotheca historica, ed. and tr. C. H. Oldfather and R. M. Geer, **5** 354*n*; **12** 457*n*; **14** 14*nn*, 46*n*, 383*n*

Diogenes, **6** 43, 55

Diogenes, Fossor, **5** 163*n*

Diogenes Laertius: "Lives of Eminent Philosophers," tr. R. D. Hicks, **11** 350*n*; **12** 370*n*

Diomedes, **12** 457*n*

Dionysia, **5** 156*n*

Dionysius (pseudo-), the Areopagite, **6** 62; **7** 104; **8** 275*n*; **9i** 5, 603*n*; **9ii** 80, 87, 91; **11** 170*n*; **14** 564&*n*, 644;
WORKS:
De coelesti hierarchia/The Celestial Hierarchies, **9i** 5; **14** 644*n*;
Pachymeres' paraphrase of,

14 564*n*;
De divinis nominibus, **9i** 5; **9ii** 87–8; **14** 568;
On the Divine Names and the Mystical Theology, tr. C. E. Rolt, **14** 568*n*;
Works of Dionysius the Areopagite, tr. J. Parker, **9ii** 88*n*

Dionysius I (Jacobite patriarch), **11** 365

Dionysius the Elder (of Syracuse), **11** 184

Dionysius Thrax, **9i** 573*n*

Dionysius the Younger (of Syracuse), **11** 184

Dionysus, Dionysian/Bacchus, **5** 36, 184, 264, 274*n*, 299*n*, 330*n*; **6** 225, 228, 231&*n*, 232, 877; **9i** 128, 195; **9ii** 134, 243*n*; **11** 44*n*, 204*n*, 612, 639*n*; **12** 416; **14** 5*n*, 379, 589; **16** 388; **18** 258, 264*n*;
TITLE: "The Apollinian and the Dionysian," **6** 223–40;
and Agni, **5** 246*n*;
-bull, Argive, **5** 184;
Christ/Christian parallels, **5** 622; **6** 314*n*, 316; **11** 206, 384;
consecrations to, **5** 536;
cult, *see below* mysteries;
dismembered, **5** 354*n*; **11** 353, 400; **14** 350*n*, 365;
as dissolution, **12** 118;
double figure of, **5** 184;
enkolpios, **10** 638*n*;
fig-tree, phallic symbol, **5** 324*n*;
fluid of, **12** 210*n*;
-impulse, **5** 623, 624; **6** 225–7, 230–2, 238, 877, 908; **10** 375*n*, 657; as expansion, **6** 234–5; as intoxication, **6** 226, 230, 876; **12** 182 (*see also* Apollinian impulse);
and Korybas, **9ii** 332; **14** 589;
Lysius, **5** 198;
Messiah and, **12** 416*n*;
mysteries/cult of, **5** 184, 662*n*; **6** 231; **12** 118–19, 169, 177–82, 191; **13** 91:

Dionysus (*cont.*):
Nietzsche and, **5** 623; **7** 40; **8** 162; **9i** 210; **11** 44, 142; **12** 118; **15** 142;
orgies, **6** 227; **7** 17/427; **11** 353; **12** 171; **13** 91; prayer during, **5** 421;
penis/Phales/*phallos* of, **4** 106; **5** 184;
as pneuma, **11** 387;
satyr play, **12** 105, 118, 170;
Semele and, **9i** 195;
as spirit, divided and undivided, **13** 91;
train of, **4** 106;
and tree (Dendrites), **5** 526*n*, 662;
Wotan and, **10** 373, 375, 386, 394; **11** 44;
-Zagreus, **5** 659, 665; **7** 113; **10** 434, 436; **11** 142, 353, 387; **12** 118; sacrifice and rebirth, **5** 526&*n*, 527; **9i** 210
Diorphos, **9ii** 186
Dioscorides, **5** 208*n*; **9ii** 241*n*;
"De materia medica," **12** *fig.* 186; **13** 193*nn*; **14** 157*nn*, 683*nn*
Dioscorus/Dioskoros, priest of Serapis, **9ii** 244*n*; **13** 173*n*
Dioscuri, **5** 183; **9i** 253, 256*n*;
dual motif of, **5** 294, 296, 596*n*; **6** 339*n*; **9i** 218, 235, 256*n*; **9ii** 134; **15** 159*n*
Dioskoros, *see* Dioscorus
Diotima, **5** 242; **6** 56; **7** 33; **9ii** 51
diphtheria, in case history, **1** 193, 195
Dirac, P.A.M., **8** 962*n*
directedness: and unconscious, **8** 158;
value of, **8** 136
directeur de conscience, *see* director of conscience
direction(s): four, **9i** 701; **14** 1, 248, 276, 555, 607&*n*;
sense of, in primitives, **10** 110
directional idea, *see* idea(s) *s.v.*

director of conscience/*directeur de conscience*, **10** 533, 555; **11** 76, 273*n*, 285; **18** 613, 614, 671
Dirr, A.: *Kaukasishe Märchen*, **14** 273*n*, 279*n*
disappointment(s), **14** 332, 334;
professional, **17** 109
disc(s): blue, dream of, **12** 307, 318; starry, **10** 740*n*
disciple(s), **7** 263, 265;
and dance-round with Christ, **11** 415, 418–19;
see also Emmaus
discontent, **8** 169; **9i** 144;
cultural, **17** 200;
sources of, in modern life, **7** 428, 429
discontinuity(-ies): of physics, **8** 965, 966, 967; **9i** 490*n*; principle of, **18** 1198
"discord," *see* association-chain(s) *s.v.*
discovery, age of, **10** 172
discretion, years of, **8** 776
discrimination, **9ii** 185, 409–10; **12** 30, 367, 563; **13** 247, 291, 456;
in alchemy, **11** 411;
conscious, **13** 287;
consciousness as, *see* consciousness *s.v.*;
deficient, **3** 136, 217–18;
Logos as, **13** 60;
of the natures, **9ii** 133
discussion, effect of complexes on, **8** 199
disease(s): and creative activity, **17** 206;
as disturbed normal processes, **18** 5;
"ens spirituale" of, **13** 148*n*;
as *entia*, **17** 203;
gods as, **13** 54;
mental, *see* mental illness;
multiplicity of causes, **3** 480;
names of, **15** 34;
as obscurity/darkness, **13** 444;
Paracelsus' attitude to, **15** 13;
and patient's psychology, **11** 15;

psychic realities and, **8** 686
disembowelling, **13** 441
disequilibrium, psychic, **7** 252, 262
disgust, **4** 51, 56–61
disharmony with oneself, **7** 373
disintegration, **11** 930; **16** 219; **17** 334;
  chemical, **4** 293;
  in painting, **10** 724;
  pathological, **7** 229;
  of persona, *see* persona *s.v.*;
  of personality, *see* personality *s.v.*;
  psychic, **8** 202; **12** 79;
  in schizophrenic complex, **3** 546–8, 569;
  see also under consciousness
disiunctio, **16** 397, 398
disks, *see* disc(s)
dislike, **16** (*p* 165*n*)
dismemberment, **11** 346&*n*, 410; **12** 118, 416*n*, 469, 530; **13** (*p* 60), 89, 91&*n*, 93, 111, 116*n*, 121, 401*n*; **14** 179, 216*n*, 238, 350*n*, 361, 493, 494, 607; **16** 398; motif of, **5** 354, 556; **14** 64;
  see also cutting; mutilation; torture
disobedience, shadow and, **11** 292
disorder, infernal, **13** 156
disorientation, **7** 250/467, 254; **8** 815; **12** 74; **13** 15;
  of consciousness, **16** 476;
  of patients, **1** 230, 237–9, 266;
  philosophical, **13** 5;
  in place, **1** 385–7, 401;
  worldwide, **18** 581;
  see also orientation
disparagement, euphemistic, **10** 365
dispersions, **8** 846*n*
displacement, **3** 109, 141, 166, 168; **7** 162; **17** 282;
  downwards, **13** 334, 337–8;
  nursing as, **3** 105;
  replacing character, **3** 106;
  upwards, **13** 334
disposition(s), **11** 491;

hysterical, **1** 423, 451;
individual, **13** 464;
inherited, **7** 359; or acquired pathological, **7** 269; and universal psychic, **7** 234;
instinctive, **13** 355;
mental, **1** 317; and simulation, **1** 320;
pleasure-seeking, **1** 220, 438;
psychic, **7** 9;
unconscious, **7** 137;
see also attitude(s)
disproportion, **7** 504
"Dispute between Mary and the Cross," **14** 26
Disraeli, B., **10** 292
dissenters, fate of, **11** 23
dissimilation, **6** 531, 688 (Def.)
dissociation/dissociability, **4** 678; **6** 344, 631; **10** 476; **11** 272, 698; **13** 473–4; **18** 741;
  and affects, **1** 318, 339, 423; **10** 286;
  from anima, **13** 454;
  and autonomous fragmentary systems, **13** 51, 55;
  of basic functions, **6** 113;
  between conscious and unconscious, **4** 761; **6** 204; **8** 724; **10** 608, 1008; **11** 280, 688; **16** 26, 394, 476; **18** 1389;
  of consciousness, **3** 55–6, 304; **8** 378; **9i** 83, 244; **14** 772; **18** 440, 1418;
  in dementia praecox/schizophrenia, **3** 55, 76, 428, 507–8, 544; **5** 58, 193; **8** 254, 383–4&*n*; **9i** 279; **11** 848; **18** 223–4;
  of differentiated and undifferentiated functions, **6** 314;
  and fourth "inferior" function, **11** 292;
  in hysteria, **1** 318, 423; **3** 304, 509; **4** 28; **10** 417, 424; **18** 223–4;
  of individual ego and collective psyche, **7** 156;

dissociation (*cont.*):

inner, **6** 92;

and "loss of soul," **10** 287; **11** 688;

multiple, **8** 253, 255;

neurotic/and neurosis, **3** 506, 544; **4** 761; **5** 683; **8** 61; **9i** 244, **9ii** 280; **10** 546; **11** 274, 285; **14** 494; **16** 26, 271, 452, 490; **18** 382, 474, 1390, 1554;

of personality, *see* personality *s.v.*;

and primitive man, **10** 130, 287;

of psyche, **8** 365–6; **10** 540–1; **14** 494; **16** 266; **18** 442, 1504;

and repression, **13** 108, 332; **16** 452;

and symbols, **11** 285;

treatment of, **5** 683; **11** 285; **13** 464; **16** 271–3;

in Western/modern society, **10** 290–1, 552, 1008; **11** 443; **18** 559;

worldwide, **18** 581;

see also split *s.v.* of psyche

dissolution, **16** 454;

alchemical, **12** *fig.* 142L;

of centre, **12** 243;

of compromise, **7** 504;

of consciousness, *see* consciousness *s.v.*;

Dionysus as, **12** 118;

of ego, *see* ego *s.v.*;

of infantile ties, **7** 91;

of mana-personality, **7** 398;

of persona, **7** 251/468, 260/476;

of personality, **7** 466; in collective psyche, **7** 238; into paired opposites, **7** 237/458;

of prestige, **7** 239;

regressive, **7** 239

distaff, in Estonian fairytale, **9i** 410;

distance, and ESP experiments, **8** 834–5;

distillation, **13** 185, 222; **16** 503, 515;

apparatus of, **13** 417;

circular, **9ii** 420; **12** 165, 167*n*; **13** 185; **14** 303;

thousandfold, **13** 185; **16** 400;

vessel of, **13** 117, 214, *fig.* B7

distinction(s), vanish in the unconscious, **11** 817

distortion: and the creative process, **15** 175;

dream mechanism of, *see* dream(s) *s.v.*

distractibility, **1** 73, 190, 204; **2** 132; **6** 464, 481;

and catalepsy, **3** 13;

effect on comprehension, **1** 240;

and faulty memory, **1** 246;

and interest, **1** 139;

and lethargy, **1** 125;

low-grade states of, **1** 76;

self-, **3** 16;

see also automatization; misreading

distractio, **14** 671, 674*n*

distraction(s): of attention, and association experiments, **2** 286–9; **3** 108, 134, 135; averages, **2** 436–51; effects of, **2** 382; and perseveration, **3** 37;

in hysteria, **2** 797, 803;

inner, **3** 108;

and mediate associations, **3** 135;

motor excitation and, **2** 132;

outer, experiments with, **1** 315; **2** 267–9;

of uneducated subjects, **2** 269

distress, situation of, **10** 615

disturbance(s): of attention, **1** 73;

digestive, **4** 569; **17** 141;

of emotions, **1** 11;

in erotic sphere, **7** 13/422;

of memory, **1** 9;

mental/psychic, **13** 47, 431, 464;

psychogenic, **1** 349;

psychotic, **7** 252;

reaction, **8** 821;

of sensibility, **1** 281;
symptoms of, **9ii** 54;
of thinking, **1** 189;
of writing, **1** 237;
see also aberration; disease
disunion/disunity: inner, **7** 16, 27/
438, 206;
   with self, **3** 427
Dittus sisters, *see under* Blumhardt
divans, **10** 990
divided, *see* division
Divina Commedia, see Dante
divination, **10** 121; **12** 550;
   experiments in, **18** 702
divine: archetype as, **11** 223;
   attributes of stone, **13** 437;
   child, *see below;*
   concept of the, **5** 471*n*;
   dynamism of self, **13** 372&*n*;
   experience of the, **9i** 18; **17**
330;
   and father-imago, **4** 728;
   fire, in alchemy, **13** 256, 257,
404;
   harlot, *see* harlot;
   light, *see* light *s.v.*;
   love, *see* love *s.v.*;
   magic, **13** 174;
   mother, *see* mother(s) *s.v.*;
   mysteries, **13** 236;
   myth, **13** 331–2;
   nature, *see* nature (2) *s.v.*;
   numen, *see* numen *s.v.*;
   office of physician, **13** 151;
   pair, **9i** 121;
   revelation, **13** 151, 283;
   secrets, Mercurius as revealer
of, **13** 278;
   spark, **13** 197;
   spirit, **13** 40;
   water, *see* water *s.v.*;
   will, **11** 519; **13** 236;
   youth, **11** 715
divine child/children, **9i** 273*n*, 289;
11 714; **12** *fig.* 87; **16** 378, 379,
482, 533;
   as archetype, **12** 215; **16** 533;
   as future saviour, **11** 741;

golden, **12** 215; **16** 379;
mythologem of, **9i** 692;
as symbol of: self, **11** 713, 755;
16 378; unity, **9ii** 59;
   see also *puer aeternus;* Spitteler
Divine Comedy, see Dante
divining rod, **8** 966; **18** 702, 704,
727
divinity, **13** 186*n*;
   of Christ, **13** 127, 154, 165;
   eating of, **5** 526;
   idea of, **7** 403;
   itself, Mercurius as, **13** 282;
   "ocean" of, **7** 476;
   splitting of, **9i** 189;
   symbols of, **10** 644;
   theriomorphic element in, **5**
89;
   triune, Mercurius as, **13** 271
divinus ternarius, Mercurius as, **13**
278
divisio, see opus, alchemical, stages in
s.v.
division/divided, **13** 125;
   consciousness, *see* consciousness
s.v.;
   into four, **13** 89*n*, 109*n*, 207;
   by sex, **13** 173
divorce, **7** 115, 320; **9i** 61, 714; **10**
248, 958; **17** 216, 343; **18** 1343
dizziness, **1** 266–8; *see also* fainting-
fits; giddiness
Djabir, *see* ALCHEMICAL WRITERS:
Geber
dmigs-pa, **12** 123
Docetism/ists, **6** 15, 31, 32; **9i** 533*n*;
   in Apocryphal *Acts of John,* **11**
428–31
doctor(s), **7** 369, 499; **9i** 398; **13** 14;
   advice and reproof by, **17** 178;
   aim of, **16** 81;
   analysis of/as analysand, **4** 627;
10 339; **16** 237, 287; **16** 239
(see also analysis *s.v.* training;
analyst *s.v.* analysis of);
   animals as, *see* animal(s) *s.v.*;
   and clergyman, *see* clergyman
s.v. psychotherapy/doctor;

doctor (*cont.*):
a complete human being, **16** 158;
and correct interpretations, **7** 189;
as demon, **7** 99, 145;
desirable for analysis, **17** 261;
in dreams, **12** 136–7, 147–8;
empirical and phenomenological outlook, **17** 160;
ethical attitude of, **16** 173;
ethics and, **11** 547;
and faith, **18** 1511;
as father-lover, **7** 98, 206, 211–13;
and Freud's theory, **7** 411;
function in analysis, **17** 261;
as God/deification of, **7** 110, 207, 214, 217;
as image, **7** 145, 157;
and incurable disease, **18** 1575;
and the individual, **10** 532, 881–2; **14** 125;
involvement of, **10** 337;
jargon of, **13** 155;
lack of understanding/insight in, **16** 312, 365;
as lover, **7** 98, 206;
as magician, **7** 99, 143;
as mana-personality, **7** 38–9;
maternal significance of, **7** 98;
and meaning of life, **11** 515;
as mediator, **16** 374;
and misunderstanding, **17** 181;
necessity of intervention, **16** 270;
neurotic's attitude to, **11** 12;
Paracelsus and, **13** 154;
and patient, relationship, **5** 62, 683; **7** 58 61, 93–4, 110, 143, 206, 255; **8** 421; **10** 352, 532; **11** 904; **16** 1, 163, 239, 270–1, 273, 276, 364–5; assimilation of, **16** 164; mutual transformation, **16** 164, 166–7, 170, 399; mutual imprisonment, **16** 365; patient's behaviour to, **7** 221/451;

as patient, **4** 627;
patient in love with, **2** 833, 835–43;
and patient's shadow, **12** 36;
persona of, **16** 365;
personality of, **7** 110; **10** 338, 340; **16** 10, 23, 170, 172, 198; **17** 240; patient's evaluation, **5** 62;
personification of goodness, **7** 99;
and psychiatry, **8** 526;
psychological training of, **7** 1/409, 65;
and reductive theories, **7** 259;
and religion, **11** 452, 548, 738;
as research workers, **5** 685;
as saviour, **7** 99; **18** 1330;
self criticism by, **16** 236;
somatic, **11** 466;
as sorcerer, **18** 1330;
subjective possibilities of, **16** 400;
takes over patient's conflicts/suffering, **5** 95; **16** 364;
transference to, **2** 816*n*; **7** 94, 97, 163, 214; **16** 275, 357, 363; of father-imago, **7** 206; **16** 139; **17** 158;
and treatment of dissociation, **5** 683;
and treatment of unconscious, **7** 342;
words of, **11** 494;
see also analyst; physician; psychotherapist; therapist
doctrinairism, **9i** 173; **9ii** 141;
Freudian, **13** 465
doctrine:
TITLE: "An Exposition of the Secret Doctrine," **13** 169–93;
Buddhist yoga, **13** 51;
Christian: early, rationalizing of, **11** 444; and nature, **9ii** 267; and psyche, **9ii** 270
Gnostic, of Anthropos, **13** 210;
of redemption, in alchemy, **13** 252;

secret/arcane, **13** 73, 165, 236, 290

Doelger, F. J., **9ii** 127, 145, 175*n*, 176*n*, 177, 186;
 Antike und Christentum, **14** 256*n*;
 Das Fischsymbol in frühchristlicher Zeit, **9ii** 127*n*, 145*n*;
 Die Sonne der Gerechtigkeit und der Schwarze, **14** 726*n*

doer and deed, **12** 36

dog(s), *see* ANIMALS *s.v.*

Doggeli, **10** 701

dogma, **4** 751; **9i** 19; **9ii** 259, 271; **11** 75, 172; **12** 11, 14, 17, 40, 93; **13** 290, 384*n*; **14** 488; **16** 198; **18** 1511;
 TITLE: "A Psychological Approach to the Dogma of the Trinity." **11** 169–295;
 alchemy and, **12** 41, 403, 453; **14** 425;
 and archetypes, **11** 148, 459;
 of Assumption, *see* Mary/ Mother of God *s.v.* Assumption;
 barbarian peoples and, **9ii** 272;
 becomes soulless, **14** 488;
 "belief" in, **9ii** 276&*n*;
 believers and, **9ii** 276&*n*;
 Christian, **5** 339; **9i** 17; **13** 120, 270; truth of, **18** 688; and unconscious (Walpurgisnacht), **13** 120;
 and collective unconscious, **9i** 21, 47; **9ii** 271;
 as defence, **11** 81;
 development of, **11** 88, 469; **14** 744–5, 777;
 drift from/loss of, **4** 434; **9ii** 271, 276, 278; materialistic criticism of, **5** 674;
 history of, **11** 222, 469;
 Holy Ghost and, **11** 222;
 as mental hygiene, **11** 76;
 and paradox, **12** 19;
 and practice, in religion, **12** 25;
 Protestantism and, *see* Protestantism *s.v.*;

as expression of psyche, **11** 81, 778; **14** 489, 650; **16** 391;
 psychology and, **11** 294;
 and punishment, **9i** 56;
 religious/philosophical, value of, **4** 555, 746; **9ii** 276*n*; **11** 81, 294;
 Roman Catholic, *see* Church, Catholic *s.v.*;
 science and, **4** 746;
 symbolism/as symbol, **5** 113; **9i** 18–19; **9ii** 271, 278; **11** 171, 293; **12** 253; **14** 667;
 and truth, **10** 335; **18** 617

dogmatism, **4** 746; **7** 467; **8** 214, 216;
 and scepticism, **6** 537

dog's mercury, *see* mercury (plant)

dog-star, **5** 354; **14** 176

doll(s), **13** 326, *fig.* 20; **17** 40;
 children as, **17** 222;
 four, **16** 427, 428, 430;
 as "grandmothers," **17** 54

"doll woman," **12** 136–7

dolphin, *see* ANIMALS *s.v.*

Domaldi, Swedish king, **5** 306

domestication, and incest-taboo, **5** 415

Domina, **14** 18

dominants, **8** 403, 423, 718;
 Christian, **12** 41; **14** 466;
 collective, **12** 41;
 conscious/of consciousness, **12** 41; **14** 455, 498, 504–6, 516–17, 519–21, 536; binding force of, **14** 517; decay of, **14** 510; historical, **14** 521; mythical, **14** 520; negative aspect of, **14** 539; relativization of, **14** 455; renewal of, **14** 498, 504, 525;
 of mana-personality, **7** 391;
 organising, among archetypes, **5** 611;
 psychic, **11** 849;
 unconscious, **11** 850; **12** 346, 391;
 see also archetypes

domination, infantile desire for, **7** 471

Dominic, St., **5** 530*n*
Dominican order, **9ii** 138
Domitian, **9ii** 171
domus: ignis, **13** 257*n*;
    sapientiae, **13** 212;
    thesaurorum or *gazophylacium*
    (treasure house), **13** 112
Donath, J.: "Über Suggestibilität," **1**
    109*n*
Don Juan, **10** 248;
    Don Juanism, **9i** 162, 165
donkey, *see* ANIMALS: ass
donum amoris, **5** 101
donum gratiae, **5** 101
donum Spiritus sancti, in alchemy, **16**
    389, 411, 413, 486
doodles, **3** 109
door, **11** 427
Dora, case of, *see* Freud: CASES
dorje, **11** 113;
    in mandala symbolism, **9i** 636;
    12 125, 139*n*;
    twelve, **12** 139*n*
Dorn, G., *see* ALCHEMICAL WRITERS
    s.v.
Dornach, **10** 176
Dost, M.: *Kurzer Abriss der Psychologie, Psychiatrie und gerichtlichen
Psychiatrie,* J.'s review, **18** 913
double: consciousness, *see* con-
    sciousness *s.v.*;
    contrary nature of Mercurius,
    see Mercurius *s.v.* dual/double
    nature of;
    dyads, unification of, **13** 358;
    life, of S. W., **1** 44;
    psychic, **17** 227 (*see also* person-
    ality)
doubt, **8** 750–1; **14** 238, 314, 362;
    and belief, **11** 294; **14** 651; as
    opposites, **11** 791;
    precious gift, **12** 8
dove, *see* ANIMALS *s.v.*
Dowding, Lord: *God's Magic, Lych-
gate, Many Mansions,* **11** 855*n*
downwards, *see* displacement *s.v.*
Dozy, R., and M. J. de Goeje:
    "Nouveaux documents pour

l'étude de la religion des Harra-
niens," **9ii** 128*n*; **11** 350*n*, 365*n*;
13 273&*n*
drachates/draconites/dracontias, **9ii**
    214–16
draco viridis, see ANIMALS: dragon
Dragomanov, M.: "Zabelezhki
    vrkhy slavyanskite religioznoe-
    ticheski Legendi," **9ii** 227*n*
dragon, *see* ANIMALS *s.v.*
Dragon constellation, *see* constella-
    tion(s) *s.v.*
drama(s), **15** 140;
    archetypal, **5** 466;
    mystery-, **9i** 208, 209;
    and rebirth, **18** 1245
drawing(s), **8** 168, 180, 400;
    by children and artists, phallic
    symbolism in, **5** 183;
    by patients, **14** 333, 757; **16** 401
drawing water as individual experi-
    ence and archetype, **5** 349
dread, holy, **11** 222, 375
dreams(s) *(topics)*: **1** 116–17; **3** 174
    565; **5** 20; **6** 47, 79, 694, 701, 715;
    7 98, 119, 134, 187, 209–10,
    289–90, 501, 520; **8** 270, 296,
    573–4, 580, 671–2, 674, 702–3; **9i**
    44, 211, 299, 309, 318, 506–7,
    509; **9ii** 47, 57, 66, 351; **10** 15,
    301, 304–6, 351; **11** 87, 90, 128,
    738, 746, 781; **12** 48; **13** 121, 127,
    148*n*, 216, 219, 240–1, 298, 368,
    385, 395–6, 463; **14** 180, 306,
    335, 454, 502, 505, 598, 668, 736,
    749; **15** 57, 64, 154; **16** 12, 85–95,
    125, 252, 254, 501; **17** 112–16,
    162, 167, 184–98; **18** 141;
    TITLES: "The Analysis of
    Dreams," **4** 64–94; "The Ar-
    chetype in Dream Symbolism,"
    18 521; "Association, Dream,
    and Hysterical Symptom, **2**
    793–862; "The Dream," **4**
    323–5; "General Aspects of
    Dream Psychology," **8** 443–
    529; "Individual Dream Sym-
    bolism in Relation to Al-

chemy," **12** 44–331; "The Language of Dreams," **18** 461–94; "The Mechanism and Interpretation of Dreams: A Critical Review," *see* Prince, Morton; "The Method of Dream-Interpretation," **4** 326–34; "On the Nature of Dreams," **8** 530–69; "The Practical Use of Dream Analysis," **16** 294–352; "The Problem of Types in Dream Interpretation," **18** 495–559; "The Prospective Function of Dreams," **4** 452–4; "Self-representation of the Spirit in Dreams," **9i** 396–9; "The Significance of Dreams," **18** 416–43; "On the Significance of Number Dreams," **4** 129–53; "Symbolism and the Interpretation of Dreams," **18** 416–607; "Ufos in Dreams," **10** 626–723;

active imagination and, **8** 400; **9i** 101; **14** 706, 708;

actor in, **12** 254;

aetiological significance, **16** 295–6, 304–6;

affects in, **18** 855, 858;

of Africans, stopped by white man's arrival, **18** 1291, 1438;

aircraft/airplane in, **8** 535; **11** 90; **12** 147, 153; **18** 471, 477; rocket-propelled, **13** 466, 472; during alchemical opus, **13** 88&*n*;

alchemical parallels, **11** 105; **12** 39, 448; **13** 396;

alleged absence of, **4** 536, 628; **7** 273;

of American Negroes, **8** 228;

of Americans, Indian/Negro symbols, **10** 99;

and analogies, **17** 44;

analogy with psychotic thinking, **3** 297–8;

analysis of, *see sep. entry below;*

analysts and own, **8** 141;

analyst's, of patient, **18** 333, 337;

and anima, *see* anima *s.v.*;

animals in, *see* animal(s) *s.v.*;

and animus, *see* animus *s.v.*;

anticipatory, **18** 26, 545;

in antiquity, **17** 262; **18** 240, 250;

anxiety, *see* anxiety *s.v.*;

and Apollinian impulse, **6** 226, 236, 876;

apparent disguise in, **13** 479;

apparently accidental, **8** 443;

arcanum revealed in, **11** 152;

archaic thinking in, **4** 553;

archetypes and/archetypal, **7** 109; **8** 554, 559, 847; **9i** 100, 110, 319, 546; **11** 146, 222, 450, 757; **13** 90*n*; **15** 160; **17** 106, 209; **18** 233, 521, 595, 1469; of children, *see* child(ren) *s.v.* dream(s); in middle life, **8** 556;

ascent/descent in, **12** 201–2; **13** 399; **14** 296;

associations, *see* associations *s.v.*;

automobiles in, **8** 535;

autonomy of, **8** 580;

and autosuggestion, **12** 327;

balloons in, **18** 471, 477;

banal, **7** 288;

at beginning of analysis, **5** 62; **16** 87, 296, 306, 307, 313;

and belief in spirits, **8** 574, 579;

"big," **3** 525, 528, 549; **7** 276–7; **8** 554–5, 558; **9i** 70*n*, 546, 549; **10** 324; **17** 106, 208–9; **18** 176, 250, 436, 1159, 1291;

black man in, **2** 832–5, 856; **4** 733, 737;

blood in, **2** 823, 833, 850–1;

-book, **8** 537, 543; Arabic, **18** 1290; of Artemidorus, **5** 4; **18** 545; of Jagaddeva, **5** 542;

breakdown of ideas in, **3** 557;

as category of conscious contents, **8** 294;

Catholic Church in, *see* Church,

dream(s) (*cont.*):
Catholic *s.v.*;
and causality, **4** 67;
censorship in, *see* Freud *s.v.*;
chairs, four in, **9i** 581, 582; **11** 90; **12** 260;
child as symbol in, **8** 451; **9i** 323–4; **16** 92–3, 377–9;
children's, *see* child(ren) *s.v.*;
Church's views on, **11** 32&*n*;
circle in, **11** 90, 109;
-city, vision of, **5** (*pp* 458, 461);
classification, **8** 474;
climbing in, **8** 535; **16** 303–4, 323;
clothing, insufficient in, **8** 535;
collective, **7** 250*n*, 277; **10** 323; **18** 249; myth as, **5** 28–9 (*see also below* dream symbols *s.v.* collective);
colours in, **14** 140*n*, 333;
compensatory function, **3** 450; **4** 490; **5** 9, 469, 611; **7** 170, 182, 190, 489, 501*n*; **8** 469, 483–92, 495, 549–50; **10** 29, 732; **11** 731, 780; **12** 26, 63, 230; **14** 124, 425; **15** 152; **16** 330–4; **17** 185–6, 269, 281–2; **18** 247, 471, 507, 521, 535, 1391, 1487, 1489;
and complex(es), *see* complex(es) *s.v.*;
composition of, **18** 861;
condensations in, **3** 50&*n*; **18** 852–3, 856, 870;
conflict in, *see* conflict *s.v.*;
conscious(ness) and unconscious in, **8** 299–300, 580; **14** 501; in hysteria, **1** 15;
and conscious mind, **16** 334;
contamination in, **11** 783; **14** 601, 660;
context, *see* context *s.v.*;
continuity in, **8** 444;
contradiction in, **5** (*p*451);
of convenience, **18** 848–9;
cosmic element in, **7** 250/467;
and creative process, **18** 1766;

cross in, **9i** 354–5; **18** 589;
crowds in, **8** 535;
death in, *see* death *s.v.*;
and dementia praecox, **2** 839; **3** 22, 181, 523, 525, 544–5, 557;
destruction and restoration in, **18** 529;
destructive, **3** 561–2;
devil in, *see* devil *s.v.*;
and diagnosis of physical disorder, **5** 681; **16** 343–6; **18** 135&*n*, 136, 138, 299–302;
difficulty in remembering, **8** 445;
displacement in, **3** 111; **17** 282; **18** 857, 870;
and distortion, **10** 320; **14** 454; **17** 282; **18** 175, 178;
dogma compared to, **11** 81;
dramatic structure of, **8** 565;
dreamer as several figures/whole dream, **5** 288*n*; **7** 129; **10** 321; **17** 39;
of J. W. Dunne, **11** 815;
-ego, **8** 580;
-elements, **18** 854, 856, 861;
among Elgonyi, **10** 128;
endogenous and exogenous, **3** 163*n*;
erotic/sexual, **2** 716; **3** 140; **4** 548–51; **5** 7–8; **17** 189; **18** 572;
-experiences, **13** 88*n*, 106;
exposition of, **8** 561;
façade, **7** 21/434, 162; **16** 54–5, 319; **18** 861;
fantasies in, **8** 449;
fantastic, **8** 445;
fear in, **18** 867, 869;
feeling-values of, **17** 198;
fire in, *see* fire *s.v.*;
fish in, **5** 290;
flowers in, *see* flowers *s.v.*;
flying in, *see* flying *s.v.*;
foot in, *see* foot/feet *s.v.*;
foreknowledge in, **8** 974;
form of, **8** 561;
Freud and, **3** (*p*3–4), 50, 92,

-series/sequences, **7** 386; **8** 550–2; **11** 53; **12** 48–50; **16** 13–16, 322, 556; **18** 83, 162, 403–6, 525; and catastrophe, **18** 543; and death, **8** 809; and enantiodromia, **12** 111; and individuation, **8** 550–3; **9i** 235; and symbols, **9i** 110; unconscious in relation to, **11** 39; sexuality in, *see* sexuality *s.v.*; shadow in, **7** 103; **9ii** 185; "shocking" surprises in, **9ii** 315&*n*; shows inner truth, **16** 304; similes in, **8** 474; snakes in, *see* ANIMALS: serpent/ snake *s.v.*; solution of problems in, **7** 166; **8** 299, 564; somatic stimuli in, **8** 502; **17** 189; somnambulistic, **1** 58, 76, 117; as source of natural symbols, **18** 497; specialism of, **10** 678; spirality of motifs, **12** 34, 242, 245–6, 325; -state, **3** 525; **5** (*pp* 455, 457); **14** 457; pathological, **1** 74; somnambulistic, **1** 26; statement, manifest, **18** 430; as statements about the unconscious, **18** 748; a subliminal process, **18** 511; subliminal understanding of, **18** 476; suggested, **4** 636–7; -symbols/symbolism in, *see sep. entry below;* technique of elucidation, **4** 325; teleological significance, **4** 452, 454, 490; **7** 501*n*; **18** 869, 870; telepathic, **8** 503–4; **18** 1487; theories of, **18** 841; theriomorphic representations in, **5** 261, 505; -thinking/thoughts, **5** 25, 28; **7**

162, 210; **8** 474; **18** 854, 865; analogical, **7** 219; origin of, **18** 1487; vagueness of, **3** 133; trains in, **8** 535; **17** 51; and transcendent function, **8** 152–3; transcerebral nature of, **8** 957; and transference, **16** 376; **18** 342; Trinity and, **11** 269, 281; at turning-points in life, **3** 525; **17** 210; two aspects of, **18** 595; typical, **8** 535; **9i** 309; Ufos in, **10** 626–723, 770; unconscious in, **1** 172; **3** 518; **4** 158, 324; **5** 38; **7** 20–5/432–7; **8** 152–3, 301–2, 477; **10** 320, 446; **14** 401*n*; **15** 105; **17** 112–13, 262 (*see also above* -series *s.v.*); undisguised, **4** 649; -vision, **13** 106 visual, and light sensations of retina, **1** 101; voice in, *see* voice *s.v.*; waking, *see sep. entry below;* water in, *see* water *s.v.*; as wish-fulfilment, *see* wish-fulfilment *s.v.*; women's, **5** 8; **13** 479; -work, **18** 844, 859, 862; world of, **13** 130*n*; -world, reality of, **1** 43; of Zosimos, *see* ALCHEMICAL WRITERS: Zosimos *s.v.* visions; *see also* day dream(s); visions dream(s), analysis/interpretation of, **4** 81, 85, 125; **5** 4; **7** 20–1/432–4, 25–6, 192, 199, 213–14, 218; **8** 450, 498, 529, 533–43; **9i** 101; **9ii** 316; **10** 319–20; **13** 88; **14** 410, 705, 752, 755, 772; **16** 55, 95, 144, 277, 294*ff*, 321–3, 334–5; **17** 115, 162, 199–200, 262–3, 282; **18** 4, 83, 160*ff*, 1809–10; TITLES: "The Analysis of Dreams," **4** 64–94; "The

dream(s), analysis (*cont.*):
Mechanism and Interpretation of Dreams: A Critical Review," *see* Prince, Morton; "The Method of Dream-Interpretation," **4** 326–34; "The Practical Use of Dream Analysis," **16** 294–352; "The Problem of Types in Dream Interpretation," **18** 495–559; "Symbolism and the Interpretation of Dreams," **18** 416–607;
and amplification, **12** 403; **13** 467; **14** 189;
analyst and, **8** 498;
in analytical psychology, **12** 403;
in antiquity, **18** 240;
and archetypal image, **18** 229;
an art, **17** 198;
before Freud, **18** 431;
in children, **17** 179, 211;
complexes in, **18** 154;
and confrontation of two minds, **18** 497, 498;
and context, *see* context *s.v.*;
criteria for correctness of, **7** 189;
educational, **17** 125, 192;
and feelings, **18** 856;
incompetent application of, **18** 476;
and individuality of dreamer, **18** 573;
interpretation of one's own, **18** 244;
intricacies of, **18** 7;
and intuitive attitude, **18** 1283;
method of, **4** 326–34, 533–4; **17** 263;
and mutual dream of interpreter and dreamer, **18** 577;
oneiromancy, **4** 533; **11** 105;
and "personalistic" approach, **9i** 311*n*;
psychoanalysis and, **4** 157–8;
qualifications for, **8** 543; **17** 198;

reductive *vs.* constructive, **17** 194–5; **18** 1147;
rules of, **5** 611; **7** 434*n*;
as self-awareness of interpreter, **18** 573;
on subjective level, **8** 509&*n*; **13** 88

dream symbols/symbolism, **1** 97, 176; **3** 26, 51, 291, 298, 400–1; **4** 158, 457, 539, 549–51, 761, (*p* 252); **5** 4, 7; **6** 671; **7** 176, 434*n*, 435; **8** 92, 388, 470; **9ii** 219, 383; **11** 390; **13** 90, 478; **14** 128, 558; **17** 115, 196–7; **18** 83, 418, 431–2, 512, 568, 591;
TITLE: "The Archetype in Dream Symbolism," **18** 521–59;
analysis of, **5** 9–11;
animals in, **10** 679;
and archetypal motifs, **18** 1480;
child as, *see* dream(s) *s.v.* child;
collective, **7** 122; **10** 323;
fire as, *see* fire *s.v.*;
of image of self, **9ii** 120; **11** 808; **14** 146, 283*n*;
of individuation, **12** 44;
modern, **10** 635;
of mother-image, **5** 569;
quaternary/quaternity, *see* quaternity *s.v.* dream symbols;
sexual, **1** 172; **4** 541, 551, 649, (*p*252); **5** 7, 8;
of subjective contents, **7** 130;
theriomorphic, **9ii** 291;
of unity, **14** 294

DREAMS; INSTANCES OF (in order of occurrence in volumes);
of black and white figures, **1** 43;
of kittens and cats, **1** 253;
of blood, **2** 823, 833;
of fire, **2** 823, 833, 834;
of cats, **2** 825–7, 829;
of mice, **2** 828–9;
of dogs, **2** 829–33;
of black man, **2** 831–2, 835, 856;

Völker und des Christentums, **9ii** 146*n*

Drexel, F.: "Das Kastell Stockstadt," **5** pl. XLIX*a*

Drexelius, Hieremias: *Opera,* **14** 67*n*

Dreyfus,—, M. O., **18** 916

Dreyfuss, J.: *Adam und Eva nach der Auffassung des Midrasch,* **12** 185*n*

Driesch, H.: *The Science and Philosophy of the Organism,* **8** 368*n*;
Die "Seele" als elementarer Naturfaktor, **8** 380*n*, 843*n*, 931*n*

drink: of immortality, *see* immortality *s.v.*;
symbolism of, **5** 246–7, 315;
see also soma

"Drivaltigkeitsbuch," *see* CODICES AND MSS: Munich *s.v.* Cod. Germ. 598

drive(s), **8** 51, 653–4; **11** 492; **14** 602;
energy as a, **8** 52;
Freud's use of term, **8** 54;
power, **13** 323;
psychology of, **11** 452;
sexual, plurality of, **4** 244

droits de l'homme, **16** 502

Dromard, G.: "De la dissociation de la mimique chez les aliénés," **18** (*p*421)

dromenon, **9i** 230

drop, Ufo as, *see* Ufo(s) *s.v.*

dropsy, **14** 358, 360; **15** 41; **16** 472

Drosselbart, **5** 421

drowning: in dream/fantasy, **4** 508; **17** 49–52, 221;
motif, **14** 360;
see also association-chains: INSTANCES: water

drowsiness, **2** 165, 259;
and darkness, **1** 97;
see also auto-hypnosis

drugs, **3** 569; **13** 252; **18** 1373;
medicinal, **13** 190&*n*;
see also mescalin

Druids, **13** 154;
and cross, **5** 402;
sacred oak and mistletoe, **5** 392

Drummond, H., **7** 306; **11** 130;
The Greatest Thing in the World, and other addresses, **11** 130*n*;
Natural Law in the Spiritual World, **11** 130*n*

drunkenness, *see* alcohol; alcoholic/ alcoholism

Druses, **18** 1521, 1530

Drusiana, **11** 419*n*

dry/damp, as opposites, **12** 192, 436; **13** 359; **18** 1078

dryads, **14** 69–71

Dryden, H. L., **10** 606

Dryden, J., **7** 494

dual: mother, *see* mother *s.v.*;
motif, **16** 16

dualism, **5** 446;
in archetypal self, **9ii** 76;
in Christ-figure, **9ii** 172; **14** 33;
in Christianity, **11** (*p*358); **18** 1593, 1650;
cosmic, **11** 798;
derivation of ideas of, **1** 148;
God's humanity and, **9ii** 171;
Manichaean, **9i** 189; **9ii** 89, 99, 103*n*, 104, 112*n*, 427; **14** 32, 86; **18** 1639;
Persian, **11** 254, 279; **13** 291 (*see also* Cathars);
psychological, **10** 573, 576;
and *vox Dei* conception, **10** 844;
see also duality

dualistic phase, **8** 765

duality, **8** 401; **11** 557; **12** 310–11, 413, 436*n*; **13** 226, 263, 315, 456;
in alchemy, **12** 26; **16** 398;
Christian, **12** 25;
man's, **9ii** 402;
of Mercurius, *see* Mercurius *s.v.*;
of psychic life, **14** 117;
of self, **13** 297;
of soul, **13** 263;
symbol for God, **9ii** 304;
tension of, **11** 236;
in world and soul, **13** 150;
see also dualism; God; opposites

Dublin, in *Ulysses,* **15** 164, 197

E

E., Miss, *see* Jung: CASES, vol. 1 case
(1); vol. 2 case (1a) (*different
patient*)
E. S., monogrammist, **12** *fig.* 250
Ea, **5** 375; **9ii** 186; **11** 173
eagle, *see* ANIMALS *s.v.*
ear(s), **5** 311n;
  picking, **5** 549n;
  piercing of, **5** 545
earth, **7** 366; **9i** 156; **9ii** 420; **12** 84,
  112, 148, 165n, 310, 366, 433,
  475, *figs.* 81, 142A; **13** 57, 73, 81
  122, 267, 268, 280, 283n, 301,
  358, *fig.* 8; **14** 2, 354, 552;
    TITLE: "Mind and Earth," **10**
    49–103;
    acceleration of, **8** 842;
    Adam as, *see* Adam *s.v.* earthly;
    adamah, **14** 585, 624&n, 632;
    as arcane substance, **14** 404,
    632 (*see also below* watery);
    black, **8** 396; **12** 426, 433; **13**
    334, 337; **14** 183, 264, 537n,
    552, 691n, 724, 725n, 729;
    burial in, **5** 676; and rebirth
    from, **5** 638;
    centre of, **13** 186, 257; **14** 248,
    293, 321;
    as centre of universe, **14** 576;
    and correspondences, **8** 933;
    as cube (Platonic), **11** 247n;
    Damascene, **13** 418;
    descent into, and womb sym-
    bolism, **5** 528; |
    feminine, **12** 26, 192&n, 447;
    fertilization/fertility of, **12** 105,
    fig. 74;
    and fire, in alchemy, *see* fire *s.v.*
    in alchemy;
    glorified, **13** 410;
    gods, **12** 240n;
    goddesses, **13** *fig.* 8;
    and heaven, *see* heaven *s.v.*;
    libido, transference to, **8** 86;
    man bound to, **10** 913; **12** 148;

Mercurius as, *see* Mercurius
s.v.;
metallic, **13** 409;
and moon, *see* moon *s.v.*;
-Mother, *see* Mother *s.v.*;
mother, symbolized by, *see*
mother, symbols of;
of paradise/paradisal (alchemical), **11** 92; **12** 433, 529; **13**
410; **14** 632;
philosophic, **13** 380; **14** 2;
as *prima materia*, **12** 425, 444,
fig. 163;
red, *see* COLOURS;
snake as symbol of, **5** 155;
-soul, **8** 935;
-spirit, *see* spirit(s) (2) *s.v.*;
spiritualizing of, **14** 207;
splitting of, **5** 439&n, 480, 638;
as square, **10** 767; **11** 136;
-square, Chinese, **12** 169, 192;
theriomorphic symbols of, **14**
427;
toad as, **14** 2;
two (alchemical), **13** 358n;
Ufos' low opinion of, **10** 796–7;
virginal, **14** 23;
Virgin Mary as, *see* Mary;
and water, *see* water *s.v.* air/
earth/fire;
watery, as arcane substance, **8**
388; **14** 726;
white, see *terra alba;*
woman as, **16** 361;
-world, **13** *fig.* A4;
see also sal/salt; stone,
alchemical/philosophical; *terra*
earthly, *see* Adam; paradise
earthquake(s), **1** 319; **5** 613, (*p* 460);
8 331;
animal warnings of, **10** 636;
child's fear of, **17** 19, 29, 35–6;
at Christ's death and resurrection, **14** 207, 209, 475;
emotional paralysis during, **1**

307; **3** 147;
East/Eastern/Oriental, **5** 309; **13** 15,
31, 63;
 TITLE: "The Psychology of Eastern Meditation," **11** 908–49;
 aim of detachment, **18** 377;
 enlightenment, **13** 81;
 European fear of, **18** 1253;
 European invasion of, **13** 84;
 and Golden Age, **18** 563;
 ideas, **13** 3, 9;
 intellect, **13** 8, 84;
 mandalas in, **13** (*p*56); **18** 271,
 409;
 mind of, **7** 304; **11** 759, 768,
 773; **13** 10, 83, (*p* 56); **18** 143,
 534;
 occultism, **13** 3;
 philosophical, **9ii** 204;
 philosophy/philosophers of, *see*
 philosophy *s.v.*;
 polytheism, **13** 50;
 practices of, **13** 36;
 and psyche/spirit, **8** 682, 748;
 psychology of, **11** 759, **13** 5, 9;
 quietism, **10** 190;
 realism, **13** 2;
 religions, *see* religion(s) *s.v.*;
 sages, **13** 55;
 significance of, **10** 237;
 spirit of, **13** 72;
 symbolism of, **9i** 11; **18** 139; of
 greeting, **18** 35;
 therapy, **18** 231;
 thinking, **18** 142;
 view of the world, **7** 304; **8** 743;
 and West/Western, *see sep. entry
 below;*
 white man in, **18** 334;
 will to power of, **18** 561;
 wisdom, **13** 2, 10
East and West/Eastern and Western:
 TITLE: *Psychology and Religion:
 West and East,* **11**
 difference between, **10** 237; **12**
 8; **13** 80; **18** 142–3;
 hero in, **12** 469;
 images, **9i** 24–5;

in labours of Hercules, **12**
416*n*, 457*n*;
 as opposites, **14** 1;
 psychology of, **18** 1483–5;
 religious experiences of, **13** 79;
 in ten numbers, **12** 313;
 thought, **9ii** 273; **11** 770,
 772–3, 778, 785, 907; **12** 8; **13**
 55, 83–4
Easter, **12** 454; **14** 729;
 candle, **9i** 312*n*;
 consecration of fire, **12** 451; **14**
 45*n*;
 consecration of font, *see* baptism *s.v. benedictio fontis;*
 Day, **14** 476;
 eggs, **9i** 22; **10** 145; **18** 540;
 Eve, **13** 104; **14** 45*n*;
 see also Holy Saturday
Eastern, *see* East/Eastern
eating, **11** 420;
 symbolism of, **2** 838–9
Ebbinghaus, H.: *Grundzüge der
 Psychologie,* **6** 687&*n*;
 Kultur der Gegenwart, **5** 11*n*
Ebers, G., **15** 41;
 *Papyros Ebers, Das hermetische
 Buch über die Arzneimittel der
 alten Aegypter,* **15** 41*n*
Eberschweiler, A., **5** 16*n*;
 "Untersuchungen über die
 sprachliche Komponente der
 Assoziation," **5** 219*n*; **6** 463&*n*;
 J.'s abstract, **18** 944–5
Ebionites (Gnostic sect), **6** 31–2;
 Adam as Christ in, **9ii** 307;
 Christ and Satan as two sons of
 God in, **9ii** 78, 103, 134, 229;
 13 271*n*; **14** 123*n*, 124*n*, 728
 (*see also* devil *s.v.* God)
Ecbatana, **14** 577
"Ecce Homo," *see* Nietzsche *s.v.*
eccentricity/eccentric(s), **3** 154; **7**
 254; **11** 516
Ecclesia, *see* Church; *see also* woman
 s.v. old
Ecclesiastes, *see* BIBLE: O.T.
ecclesiastical: allegory, **13** 321;

237

ecclesiastical (*cont.*):
 art, *see* art(s);
 sacrament, **13** 231–36;
 symbols, **10** 700; **16** 471 (*see also*
  religious symbols);
 terminology, **13** 194;
 tradition, **13** 393, 427
Ecclesiasticus/Wisdom of Jesus, Son
 of Sirach, *see* BIBLE: Apocrypha/
 etc. *s.v.*
echeneis/echinus, see ANIMALS: fish
 s.v.
Echidna, **5** 315;
 and Mercurius, **13** 180*n*;
 mother of Sphinx, **5** 265
echinus, see ANIMALS: fish *s.v. echeneis*
Echion, adder, **5** 662*n*
echolalia, **3** 160; **18** 893
echopraxia, **3** 27, 160
Eckermann, J. P.: *Conversations with*
 Goethe, **1** 143*n*, 183&*n*; **7** 306; **8**
 860&*n*; **15** 159*n*
Eckert, E. E.: *Die Mysterien der*
 Heidenkirche, erhalten und fortgebil-
 det im Bunde der alten und der neuen
 Kinder der Wittwe, **14** 14*n*
Eckhart, Meister, **6** 193, 410–11,
 415–18, 421, 423–33, 457; **7** 397;
 9ii 143, 209, 295, 301–3, 321; **10**
 397&*n*, 440, 1026; **11** 733, 887,
 893; **12** 10; **13** 20, 75, 148*n*, 372;
 14 102–3, 258, 444&*n*, 447, 472*n*,
 782; **15** 10; **17** 320; **18** 638, 1375;
 "little sparks of soul," **9ii** 344;
 14 42;
 visions of, **9i** 268, 396*n*; **11** 741,
 882; **14** 103, 379;
 WORKS, tr. C. de B. Evans, **6**
  411*n*, 415*n*, 416*n*, 417*n*, 418*n*,
  423*n*, 425*n*, 426*n*, 427*n*, 428*nn*,
  429*n*, 457*n*; **9i** 396*n*; **9ii** 295*n*,
  301*n*; **10** 440*n*; **11** 773*n*, 882*n*,
  887*n*; **12** 126*n*, 152*n*; **14** 102*n*,
  258*n*, 261*n*, 444*n*, 447*n*, 472*n*;
  18 1375*n*;
  Meister Eckhart: A Modern
  Translation, R. B. Blakney, **11**
  887*n*; *see also* Meerpohl;

H. Büttner, ed.: *Meister Eck-*
 hart's Schriften und Predigten,
 11 773*n*
eclecticism, **18** 1512
eclipse: alchemists' representation,
 14 23;
 at Crucifixion, **14** 26;
 mental, *see* Janet;
 of sun, moon, **12** *fig.* 142V,YY;
 13 105*n*; **14** 21
ecliptic, **9ii** 149, 190
ecphoration, **7** 219; **16** 251
"Ecrasez l'infâme," **6** 314, 320
ecstasy/ecstatic, **7** 41, 108; **9i** 520;
 10 375*n*, 434; **11** 387; **18** 731;
 and creativity, **1** 184;
 cult of, **10** 375*n*;
 drunken, **10** 434; **12** 177*n*,
  182;
 experience, **13** 58;
 fantasy activity in, **1** 58;
 and glossolalia, **1** 143–4;
 and intellectual exaltation, **1**
  148;
 journey, **13** 462;
 in manic mood disorder, **1** 214;
 Nietzsche on, **1** 142&*n*;
 poetic, **1** 142;
 religious, **16** 501;
 in somnambulistic states, **1** 40;
 and table turning experiments,
  1 44
The Ecstatic Virgins of the Tyrol/Die
 Tyroler ekstatischen Jungfrauen
 (anon.), **18** 700&*n*
ectoderm and brain, **17** (*p*5)
ectoplasm, **18** 1498
ectopsyche, **18** 20, 89
Edda, **4** 494; **5** 170*n*; **10** 397–9; **13**
 458*n*; **14** 482;
 Hovamol, **5** 399
Eddington, Sir Arthur, **8** 441
Eddy, Mary Baker, *see* Christian
 Science
Edem, **9i** 571, 579*n*; **12** 529; **14**
 144;
 and androgynous Mercurius,
  9i 560; **13** 427;

with four rivers of Paradise, *see* Paradise *s.v.*;
and Leda, **9i** 560;
snake-maiden/Mercurius, **9i** 552; **12** 413&*n*;
see also Elohim

Eden, Garden of, **5** 668*n*; **8** 458, 476; **9i** 56, 73; **9ii** 353, 371; **10** 677; **11** 291, 438, 579, 619; **14** 276;
see also Paradise

Eden, river of, **13** 420*n*

Eder, M. D., **1** 1*n*; **2** (*p*vi); **7** 20*n*/432*n*; **18** 97*n*

Edfu, **13** 97; **14** 359

Edmond, Laura, daughter of judge, **1** 143

Edochinum, *see* Paracelsus *s.v.* ARCANA

Edom, **14** 396*n*

Edomites, **10** 398

education/pedagogics, **6** 125, 131, 665; **7** 173, 332, 426; **8** 720; **10** 1045; **17** 282, 284;
  TITLES: "Analytical Psychology and Education," **17** 127–229; "Child Development and Education," **17** 98–126; "The Significance of the Unconscious in Individual Education," **17** Adler's method as, *see* Adler, A. *s.v.* (*see also below* analytical psychology);
  of adults/for life, **7** 114; **8** 113; **10** 1045; **12** 14; **17** 109–10, 191, 284, 286–9;
  aim/task of, **3** 90; **6** 760; **7** 203/444; **12** 14; among primitives, **7** 314–16; **8** 766;
  American, **10** 523, 928–9;
  analytical psychology/psychoanalysis and, **4** 41, 200, 422; **7** 26/437; **10** 1070; **16** 122, 150–3, 158, 169–70; **17** 98, 130, 211 (*see also* Adler, A. *s.v.* educational method);
  253–83;
  of anima, **7** 323;

of children, **17** 107a, 284–8, 292; exceptional/difficult/gifted, **17** 228, 233–47, 257; necessity for balance in, **17** 250–2;
Christianity/religion and, **5** 107; **6** 888; **8** 766; **10** 326, 1045; **11** 513–14; **12** 7, 12–14; **18** 1380&*n*;
coeducation, **10** 994;
collective, **17** 254–6;
of common man, **6** 198;
Dubois' method as, **4** 41&*n*;
and educator, **9i** 293; **10** 896; **16** 169–70, 172, 174; **17** 108–10, 155, 229, 240–1, 284 (*see also below* self; transformation);
enthusiasm for, **17** 287;
by example, **17** 107a, 229, 253;
experimental, **7** 408;
for fuller consciousness, **18** 1387;
German, **10** 453;
historical/humanistic, **10** 523;
individual, **17** 257–9;
and leadership, **18** 1383;
Marxist, **10** 549;
modern/scientific, **9ii** 282; **10** 498, 523; **16** 5; **17** 191, 250, 288; one-sidedness of, **10** 326; **17** 284;
moral, **4** 485–6;
patient's, and prognosis, **3** 575;
of personality/and personality development, **10** 897; **17** 284, 286, 288–9;
and psychology, **11** 508;
religious, **8** 766;
self-, **16** 172, 174; **17** 110–11, 240; of educator, *see above;* possibilities of continued, **17** 111;
and somnambulistic states, **1** 38, 40, 149;
see also school; teacher/teaching

Edwards, H. M., **18** 677, 679

effect: cause and, **8** 2, 57, 840;
and energy, **8** 840;
numinous, **7** 109; of archetypal

effect (*cont.*):
    symbols, **13** 396;
    therapeutic, of detachment, **13** 66
effeminacy, **7** 337; **10** 79, 220;
    in Wagner, **15** 134;
"efficacity of things," **13** 190, 194, 214
efflorescence, of metallic salts, **13** 183*n*;
Egeria, **5** 457*n*
egg(s), **9i** 526, 543, 564*n*; **10** 145; **12** 512; **13** *fig.* 32;
    arcane substance as, **14** 180*n*;
    basilisk's (Nietzsche), **5** 592;
    Easter, *see* Easter *s.v.*;
    and gods, self-creation of, **5** 389, 547*n* (*see also* Khnum);
    golden, and child motif, **9i** 270, 290 (see also *hiranyagarbha*);
    in mandala(s), **9i** 646, 677, *fig.* 5; **12** 303–5;
    Mercurius as, **13** 267;
    as mother, **5** 550;
    of nature, **13** 267;
    nomenclature, and writers, **13** 109*n*;
    Orphic, **5** pl. XII; **9i** 529, 646;
    peacock's, *see* ANIMALS *s.v.*;
    philosophical, **9i** 529; **11** 357; **12** *figs.* 22, 98; **14** 734; division of, **13** 109;
    and point/*punctum solis*/yolk, **9ii** 345&*n*; **11** 92, 109; **12** 325; **13** 188&*n*; **14** 41&*n*;
    silver, **14** 734;
    symbol(ism), **9i** 529; alchemical, **9ii** 377*n*; **11** 361; **12** 306, 441*n*; **13** 109*n*, 115, 381;
    vas/vessel as, see *vas*/vessel *s.v.*;
    and water, **13** 109&*n*;
    world- (cosmic), **5** 550, 589, 592, 659, *fig.* 36, pl. XLI*b*; **8** 932; **9i** 290, 554; **13** 109; **14** 472
Eggeling, J., *see* Brahmanas *s.v.* Shatapatha
L'Eglise gnostique de la France, **7** 385; **10** 169

ego, **3** 82–3, 86*n*; **5** 660; **6** 706 (Def.); **7** 51, 111, 115, 235/457, 236, 275, 312, 323, 365, 374, 388, 466; **8** 352, 755; **9i** 279; **12** 8, 36*n*, 104, 411, 562; **13** 48, 75–6, 120, 221, 287, 298, 307, 372*n*; **14** 129–33, 192, 265, 492*n*, 538–40, 778; **16** 111, 231, 361, 399, 454*n*, 469, 500; **17** 166–7, 189, 248;
    TITLES: "The Ego," **9ii** 1–12; "The Relations between the Ego and the Unconscious," **7** 202–406;
    abstraction and conservation of, **6** 141;
    acquired during lifetime, **9ii** 6;
    affect-, *see* affect *s.v.*;
    and affectivity, *see* affectivity *s.v.*;
    and anima/animus, *see* anima; animus *s.v.*;
    archetypes and, **5** 101; **9ii** 13; **11** 534;
    as army commander, **8** 692–3;
    awareness of body, **11** 774;
    centre of consciousness, **9i** 506; **9ii** 1, 2, 3; **12** 44; **13** 67; **14** 133, 501; **18** 19 (*see also below* and consciousness);
    not centre of personality, **12** 126, 129, 135; **16** 219;
    -centredness, **8** 432;
    child's struggle for, **8** 771;
    Christ's correspondence to, **9ii** 171;
    and collective, **6** 138; **8** 590;
    -complex, *see* complex *s.v.*;
    and complex, **11** 21; **18** 18, 19 (*see also* complex *s.v.* ego); as shadow-government of, **16** 196;
    conscious, **16** 108–9; produced in analysis, **11** 904; and psychic contents, **8** 383; and unconscious, **7** 512, 517; **9i** 503; **11** 774;
    and conscious mind, **9i** 315; **16** 108;

primitive, **10** 285
egoistic instincts, **4** 654
ego-personality, **9ii** 43, 185; **10** 491;
11 140; **12** 242*n*, 563; **13** 307; **14**
4, 501, 778; **16** 472, 474; **18** 459;
and anima/animus, **9ii** 34;
depotentiation of, **3** 579–80;
and shadow, **9ii** 14; **12** 242*n*;
transformation of, **8** 430
egotism, **1** 451; **7** 267;
in children, **17** 136;
direct and indirect, **18** 1398;
of introvert, **6** 646
Egypt/Egyptians, **5** 316*n*; **6** 396–7;
8 411; **9i** 605*n*; **9ii** 328&*n*; **12**
175; **14** 6*n*, 22, 25*n*, 34*n*, 46&*n*,
287; **15** 41; **16** 223; **18** 245;
and alchemy, **12** 173;
angelology of, **13** 107;
ankh/ankhi, **5** 410; **14** 352;
barbers in, **11** 348&*n*;
Book of the Dead, see sep. entry
below;
burial ladder in, **12** 66;
cat sculpture, **18** 325;
and Christian ideas, **11** 178; **18**
1569*n*;
concept of soul(s) in, **7** 295; **8**
845; **10** 84;
Coptic ideas of fertility, **5** 479;
crux ansata, see *crux ansata;*
decline of civilization, **14** 743;
dream-interpreters of, **5** 4;
Essene sect in, *see* Essene sect;
fantasy of rejuvenated mother,
5 496;
fish-cult in, **9ii** 186–7;
and Gnostic hymn, **9i** 37;
gods of, **11** 600, 624, 631;
god's incarnation in Pharaoh,
11 624–5, 631, 748;
Hellenism, **13** 360;
and Horus, *see* Horus;
hymn(s), **5** 351, 408, 451–2;
incest in, **16** 418, 438;
infant in tomb, and sun-barge,
9i 239;
initiation in, **9i** 25;

and Israel, common symbols,
9ii 189;
Jews in, **9ii** 130;
kingship in, **11** 197; **14** 350–2;
Mary's/Christ's flight into, **9i**
461; **9ii** 163;
medical lore of, **11** 287; **18** 230;
Mithraism and, **10** 189;
mummies, **13** 170;
mysteries, **11** 841; Iamblichus
on, **9i** 573; **12** 456(5)*n* (*see also*
Isis *s.v.*);
myth of Apis bull, **5** 579*n*;
mythology, **10** 645; **13** 178;
negative confession in, **6** 962;
10 158;
"Osirification" in, **11** 448;
polytheism in, **5** 147–9;
Ptah shaping world-egg, **5** pl.
XLI*b*;
pyramid(s) in, **9i** 526, 543; **10**
158;
Pyramid inscriptions, **12** 84;
texts, **5** 391, 526*n*; **9ii** 187; **13**
360&*n*;
quaternity, **13** 360;
rebirth ritual, **9i** 93;
representation of God, **9i** 573;
royal ancestors in, **11** 209*n*;
and sea, **14** 246, 257;
significance of water in, **13** 97;
slaying of first-born in, **9ii**
106*n*;
and snake-bite, treatment for,
8 307, 313; **18** 230–1;
statue, Miller's fantasy of, **5** 52,
261,(*p*448);
symbolism, **18** 401;
symbol of sun-disc, **5** 146,
159*n*, pl. VII;
tale of Bata, **13** 401, 458*n*;
temples, **18** 361;
text on becoming a god, **5** 133;
theology, **11** 222, 748;
triads of gods in, **11** 177–8;
vessel with tree of life, **5** pl.
XXXI;
young man born in, **13** 424–5

Egypt (*cont.*):
(*see also* Budge; Erman);
Egyptian *Book of the Dead,* **5** 367, 389, 425; **8** 845; **11** 833; **12** 173, 314*n, fig.* 102; **13** 360; **14** 482*n*;
Papyrus of Hunefer, **12** 314*n*;
see also Budge
Egyptians, Gospel of the, *see* BIBLE: Apocrypha/etc. *s.v.*
Ehrenfels, C. von: *Grundbegriffe der Ethik,* J.'s review, **18** 911;
Sexualethik, J.'s review, **18** 912
Ehrenstein, T.: "Das Alte Testament im Bilde," **5** *fig.* 21; **12** *figs.* 184, 207, 213
Eid, Albert, Estate, **18** (*p*826*n*)
eida/eidola/eidos, ειδος, *see* Plato s.v. *eidos/*etc.
Eidgenössische Technische Hochschule, *see* Zurich, Federal Polytechnic Institute
eidolon of Satan, Cain as, **11** 628
Eidolos (in papyrus text), **14** 727
eight, *see* NUMBERS *s.v.*
Eileithyia, **5** 355, 577;
darts of, **5** 438*n*
Einfall, **1** 168; **17** 167&*n*; **18** 26, 398
Einherier, **10** 393
Einsiedeln, **15** 2, 4
Einstein, A., **10** 182, 1020; **16** 146; **18** 140, 1187*n*
Eirenaeus Orandus, *see* ALCHEMICAL WRITERS: Flamel
Eisenstein, J. D.: *Ozar Midrashim,* **12** 546*n*
Eisleben, **10** 382
Eisler, R., **8** 394&*n*;
"Der Fisch als Sexualsymbol," **9ii** 147*n*;
Orpheus–The Fisher, **9ii** 147*n*, 162n, 178*n*, 186*n*; **11** 384*n*; **12** 177*n, figs.* 174, 202;
The Royal Art of Astrology, **9ii** 147*n*, 163*n*;
Weltenmantel und Himmelszelt, **9i** 553*n*; **11** 123*n*; **13** 404*n*; **14** 14*nn*, 154*nn*, 185*n*

"Zur Terminologie und Geschichte der jüdischen Alchemie," **14** 610*n*;
Ekasringa, **12** 534
Ekoi, **8** 125
élan vital, **6** 871; **8** 678; *see also* Bergson *s.v.*
elasticity, of unconscious time, **16** 468*n*
elation, **1** 204, 212;
of body and spirit, **11** 866;
in chronic mania, **1** 189;
continuous state of, **1** 213
Elbo Interfector, **14** 316; **16** 484*n*
El-chai, **14** 634*n*
elders, surrounding Christ, **11** 229
Eleatic principle of "being," *see* Being/being
Eleazar, *see* ALCHEMICAL WRITERS *s.v.*
Electra-complex, *see* Oedipus complex *s.v.*
electrical resistance, **2** 1015, 1180–5
electricity, **4** 612; **7** 1/409; **8** 90; **10** 7
electrocardiogram experiments, **18** 57*n*
electromagnetism, **4** 282
electron(s), **8** 650; **9ii** 292*n*; **11** 279; **18** 69*n*
electron-microscope, **8** 357
El'Elyon, **11** 328; **18** 1529
element(s), **13** 186, 193; **14** 353;
ascent of, **13** 187;
chemical, **13** 195; as roots of self, **13** 242;
as circles, **14** 450;
"cosmic," **7** 250;
decomposition of, and ego-consciousness, **16** 476;
five, **14** 450;
four, **6** 960; **11** 246; in alchemy, *see sep. entry below;*
hate and love of, **9ii** 35;
head-, **13** 381*n*;
masculine, **13** 97; and feminine, **16** 411;
ogdoad of, **13** 359;
omega, *see* omega *s.v.*;

psychic, **7** 258/473;
quaternity of, *see* quaternity *s.v.*
alchemical;
round, *see* round *s.v.*;
of stone, **13** 414*n*;
"supermonic," (Paracelsan), **13** 222;
transmutation of, **8** 90, 962;
transubstantiation of, Eucharistic, **13** 196;
unity of, **16** 403; and *ordo compositionis*, **14** 655*n*; partial, **16** 451;
see also air; earth; fire; water
elements, four, in alchemy, **9i** 578, 588; **9ii** 393, 395, 420, pl. I; **11** 62*n*; **12** 109, 165, 167*n*, 214, 333, 366–72, 491, *figs.* 46, 47, 64, 66, 82, 93, 114, 117, 178; **13** 87, 122, 148, 168, 171&*n*, 176, 204, 268, 274; **14** 1, 7, 43, 68, 143, 261, 290, 294, 341, 354, 450, 553, 655; **16** 402, 404, 529;
as Achurayim, **9i** 579;
and Adam/Anthropos/first man, **11** 94; **12** 456, 457, *figs.* 82, 117; **14** 552, 570;
as components of opus, **9i** 564; **13** 402;
creation of, **11** 97;
as cross/intercrossing, **14** 607, 719*n*; **16** 523;
dissolution and synthesis of, **14** 657;
dissolution/division into, **13** 89&*n*, 109;
as functions of consciousness, **14** 265, 276;
hostility between, **14** 104, 552;
at initiations, **9ii** 400;
in lapis/stone, **9ii** 256, 375, 376&*n*; **12** 220, 449, 457; **13** 125, 207*n*, 336, 385; **14** 719; **16** 529;
mystery of, **14** 41;
One divides into, **12** 529;
in *prima materia*, **12** 433*n*; **14** 552;

as quaternary system, **13** 207;
as *radices*/"roots," **13** 89, 242;
separation of, **12** 334, 367, 530; **14** 365*n*;
separation of spirit from, **13** 165;
synthesis of, **14** 5, 389*n*;
in totality, **12** 173;
transformation/transmutation of, **8** 90, 962; **10** 629;
two active and two passive, **16** 410;
two higher and two lower, **14** 7*n*;
union of, **13** 357*n*, 446;
unity of, **12** 31;
in World-Egg, **13** 109, 188;
see also water *s.v.* air/earth/fire
elementum primordiale, see *prima materia*
elephant, *see* ANIMALS *s.v.*
Elephantine, inhabitants of, **9ii** 186
Eleusinian mysteries, **5** 526, pl. IV*b*; **7** 384; **9ii** 339; **11** 828*n*, 841; **12** 105; **18** 548, 615;
god-eating in, **5** 526; **8** 333;
immortality through, **9i** 205, 208, 241;
invocation for rain, **14** 727*n*;
priests of, **9ii** 339*n*;
psychic effects of, **14** 312;
serpent of Demeter in, **5** 530, 584;
symbolism in, **5** 526–33
Eleusis, **18** 264
elevation, in Mass, **11** 325, 326
eleven, *see* NUMBERS *s.v.*
elf/elves, **8** 202; **9i** 268
Elgon, Mount, **7** 293*n*; **8** 411; **9i** 288; **10** 118, 126; **11** 30; **18** 551
Elgonyi tribe, **7** 276; **8** 129*n*; **10** 128, 143, 144; **18** 1288;
adhista/athista (God, sun), **8** 329, 411; and *mungu*, **8** 411;
Ayik/nocturnal god/"maker of fear," **8** 129*n*; **9i** 35, 288; **11** 200;
dreams among, **18** 436, 674;

Elgonyi (*cont.*):
  and "ghost-trap"/-house, **8** 575*n*; **9i** 481; **10** 128; **11** 30; and religion, **9i** 288; **10** 144–6; *selelteni* (ghost), **11** 30; **18** 759; and sun worship, **18** 551
El-Ḥabib, Book of, *see* ALCHEMICAL WRITERS *s.v.*
Eliade, M., **18** 578, 1250;
  Shamanism: Archaic Techniques of Ecstasy (Le Chamanisme), **9i** 115*n*; **11** 346*n*, 410*n*, 447*n*; **13** 91*n*, 132*n*, 402*n*, 404*n*, 407*n*, 460*n*, 462&*n*; **14** 2*n*, 34*n*; **18** 578*n*
Elias, *see* Elijah
Eliezer ben Hyrcanus, pseud., *Pirkê de Rabbi Eliezer*, **5** 509; **12** 541; **13** 420, 458*n*; **14** 552, 555*n*, 556, 571; **18** 1522;
  tr. and ed. G. Friedlander, **5** 509*n*; **12** 541*n*; **13** 420*n*, 458*n*; **14** 552*n*, 571*n*
Elihu the Buzite, **11** 566
Elijah/Elias, **5** 285–7; **9i** 247, 253; **9ii** 167, 187*n*; **10** 622&*n*, 733; **11** 251*n*; **12** 469, *fig.* 207; **13** 171*n*, 206;
  in alchemy, **18** 1528&*n*;
  as angel, **18** 1522–3, 1526;
  Apocalypse of, **13** 93, 133;
  ascension of, **5** 158*n*, 285; **6** 395; **10** 622; **11** 686; **12** 469, *fig.* 207; **13** 206; **18** 1528;
  and Elisha, **18** 1521, 1523;
  fed by ravens, **9i** 428*n*;
  as "hairy" man, **18** 1521;
  as mythical/archetypal figure, **18** 1518–31;
  two souls of, **18** 1521;
  in *Ulysses*, **15** 190;
  walking on the water, **18** 1521;
  see also Khidr *s.v.*
Elimelekh of Lizhensk: "Elijah," **18** 1526*n*
elixir: alchemists and, **12** 224, 531, 537, 538; **13** 203, 212; **14** 50; **16** 408;

as arcane substance, **8** 388;
as *homo philosophicus*, the "One," **12** 476;
human, **13** 125;
as *lapis philosophorum*, **9ii** 194; **12** 245*n*; **13** 203;
of life/-*vitae*, **9ii** 281; **10** 727, 741; **11** 161; **12** 125, 245*n*, 335, 476, 498; **13** 76*n*, 103&*n*, 191; **14** 14, 15, 443; **16** 516, 531;
natural, **13** 170;
as panacea, **10** 727; **12** 335;
synonyms for, **16** 408;
white, **12** *fig.* 142T
Elizabeth, St., **14** 421
elk, *see* ANIMALS *s.v.*
Elkesaites, **14** 653*n*
El-Khidr, *see* Khidr
Ellenberger, H. F.: *The Discovery of the Unconscious*, **18** (*pp*374*n*, 427*n*)
ellipsis, **3** 50*n*
Ellis, H. Havelock, **2** 1349*n*; **10** 177; **16** 66; **18** 904
Ellmann, R., **15** 196*n*, (*p*133)
Elogabal, **9ii** 145*n*
Elohim, **12** 512;
  and Edem, in Justin's gnosis, **9i** 552, 560, 571;
  Ruach-, **11** 611, 619; **14** 355, 391; **18** 1361, 1549;
  Yahweh and, **11** 576
"Elucidarius artis transmutatoriae," *see* ALCHEMICAL COLLECTIONS: *Theatr. chem. s.v.* Christopher
elucidation, **16** 122, 136, 139–41; effects of, **16** 148, 153
elves, *see* elf/elves
Elysian Fields, **9ii** 56
embalming, **13** (*pp*61, 64)
embarrassment: and attention, **1** 314;
  and inhibited association, **1** 312
Embla, **13** 458*n*
emblems, national aircraft, **10** 790
embracing, **5** 682
embryo, **13** 76
Ememqut, **9i** 415
Emerson, R. W., **10** 928;

The Conduct of Life, **5** 102*n*;
Essays, **11** 92&*n*; **12** 445*n*
Emmaus: disciples at, **9ii** 174;
Jesus as magical travelling
companion, **12** 155
Emmel, Samuel, **14** 3*n*
Emmerich, Anna Catherina/Kath-
arina, **1** 352; **5** 435–8; **18** 700;
stigmatization, **5** 438;
T.a.V. Wegener, *Leben der
Dienerin Gottes Anna Catherina
Emmerich,* **5** 435*n*, 438*n*
Emmerich, Count of Poitiers, **13**
217
Emminghaus, H.: *Allgemeine Psychopathologie,* **1** 109*n*
emotion(s)/emotional, **8** 667, 846;
9i 179, 387, 497; **13** 17; **14** 405;
15 128; **17** 221; **18** 42, 44–6;
affects and, *see* affects *s.v.*;
in association, **2** (*p*210);
and attitudes, **8** 634; classified,
2 984; infantile, and neurosis, **4**
312;
changes in, in feebleminded-
ness, **1** 357;
collective, **8** 555;
contagious, **18** 318, 322 (*see also*
contagion, mental);
in dementia praecox, **2** 1066,
1071;
disturbances of, in dementia
praecox, **3** 145, 330, 510; and
hysterical delirium, **1** 11;
domination over intellect, **1**
219;
and feeling, differentiated, **18**
46–51, 57, 502;
fluctuations of, **6** 329;
in galvanometer experiments,
2 1049, 1054;
impoverishment, **3** 74, 76, 103;
inadequate, in neurosis, **3** 547;
influence on actions, **1** 220;
insight and, **4** 312;
intensity of, **13** 341;
mass, **9i** 97;
needs, evasion of, **11** 72;

not an activity, **9ii** 15;
Ossianic, **18** 700;
overwhelming, **18** 316;
and paralysis, **1** 307;
and psychogenic disturbances,
1 349;
rapport, lack of, **4** 272;
repressed, **1** 97; **16** 130–1;
and shadow, **9ii** 15–16;
signs of, infective, **10** 965;
stupidity, **2** 207, 455, 504,
13 13*n*;
suppressed, **17** 177;
and symbols, **18** 570;
unusual, **10** 598;
value of, **13** 341;
violent, **9i** 214; after-effect of, **1**
354;
see also affect(s); feeling(s)
emotionality, **13** 7, 316; **14** 404–5;
female, **9ii** 100
emotionally charged complex, *see*
complex(es) *s.v.*
empathetic type, *see* type(s) *s.v.*
empathy, **4** 640, 661; **6** 485–95, 707
(Def.), 871–3; **8** 5, 61; **12** 23; **13**
199;
abstraction, and, **6** 493, 496;
as extraversion, **6** 486, 493;
into individual object, **6** 70,
485–6, 489–92, 497, 500–1,
511–15, 531–2; **17** 242;
introvert's lack of, **6** 551–2;
and transference, **4** 427, 601*n*,
663
Empedocles, **6** 960; **8** 55; **9ii** 35; **11**
62*n*, 93, 104*n*, 246*n*; **12** 109*n*,
433, 436*n*; **13** 242; **15** 11
Emperor/Empress, **14** 2; **16** 520;
clothes of, fable, **17** 286;
Roman, **14** 349
empiricism/empirical, **3** 420, 423; **6**
516, 518–22; **8** 750; **9i** 149; **18**
1116;
J.'s, **18** 1507, 1510;
man, **14** 601, 647, 765;
nominalist, **13** 378;
and philosophy, **18** 1730–3;

discharge of, **6** 463;
disposable, **6** 183; **7** 74–7, 93–6;
emotional, of numinous phenomena, **18** 583;
and ESP, **8** 840;
and force, differentiated, **8** 26–7, 52;
and God, **5** 129; **8** 678;
gradient, **6** 130; **7** 76–8, 93–6; **8** 3, 80;
libido as psychic, *see* libido *s.v.* energic theory;
life as, **8** 80, 798;
life-, **8** 31–2; **13** 37;
and opposites: tension of/polarity, **4** 779; **6** 337; **7** 34, 78, 115, 121; **11** 291; **13** 147, 154; **14** 603, 707; **18** 1640; union of, **5** 671;
paralysis of, **5** 459;
primitive concept of, and mana, **8** 124–30, 278*n*; **10** 139;
primordial, **6** 571; **8** 278; **11** 279;
and psyche, relation, **18** 915;
psychic, **4** 275, 278; **5** 17, 296, 683; **8** 56; **11** 460; **16** 438; **18** 1110; and complexes, **3** 103, 137–8; **8** 19;
"reality" of, **6** 45, 51;
release of, **6** 351, 371–2, 391, 435;
Schiller on, **6** 165;
sexual components and/sexual, **4** 246, 250; **7** 71;
specific, of functions, **18** 27;
and substance, **8** 41, 51–2;
symbol as transformer of, **8** 92; **11** 810; **16** 460;
symbols of, **5** 180, 388, 658;
tension, **6** 351; **7** 382; **8** 152–3; **11** 479; **17** 199, 200, 207; **18** 511;
transformation of, **5** 669; **8** 79–80;
unconscious, **7** 159–60, 195,

258/473, 349; **12** 118; contents and, **6** 180; **9i** 248; **11** 793; and neurosis, **7** 192, 206, 291, 345;
untamed, **6** 159–60;
value(s): of conscious contents, **6** 180; depotentiation of, **6** 199; of relations to object, **6** 191;
water and, **16** 15
enfant terrible, **17** 63
Engels, F., **11** 222
engineers, and philosophy, **18** 1406
England, Canon H., **18** 640, 654
England/English, **18** 23, 24, 84, 100, 287, 369, 416;
archbishops, **11** 749;
as "beast-man," **10** 908;
Church of, *see* Church of England;
gentleman, **10** 974, 976;
German attitude to, **10** 478;
national character of, **10** 921;
national idea, **10** 974;
"rescue circles," **13** 76*n*;
theosophy in, **18** 1287; *see also* United Kingdom
English language, "boy's-love" plant, **5** 212
Engonasi, **14** 493*n*
engourdissement, hysterical, **6** 199
engrams, **7** 159;
or imprints, **6** 281, 405; as God-image, **6** 412;
see also Semon
"Enigma of Bologna," *see* Aelia Laelia Crispis Inscription
Enkekalymmenos (veiled man) fallacy, **6** 48; **9ii** 37
Enkidu, *see* Gilgamesh Epic
enlightenment/Enlightenment, **6** 313; **8** 598; **9i** 267; **12** 409,*fig.* 136; **13** 112, 231, 248, 361*n*;
Age of, **6** 117, 314, 516, 966; **7** 150; **8** 516, 805; **9ii** 78, 235; **10** 22, 471; **11** 48*n*, 471; **12** 19, 562; **14** 147, 509; **17** 302; **18** 1368;
of civilization, **8** 572;

enlightenment (*cont.*):
Eastern, **11** 880–1; **13** 81 (*see also* koan; satori; Zen Buddhism);
effect of, on children, **17** 75–7;
intellectual, **12** 68;
sexual, **4** 22, 503, 517, 518, 519;
tree as symbol of, **5** pl. LV; **13** 413
enlistment, study of, **2** 1312–15
enmity, male/female, **14** 104
Ennemoser, J., **4** 748; **18** 797&*n*
Ennoia (ἔννοια), **9ii** 298, 307*n*; **14** 160–1;
in Barbelo-Gnosis, **11** 152*n*; **14** 589*n*;
see also consciousness
ennui, **8** 693
Enoch (patriarch), **10** 733; **11** 251*n*; **12** 457, 458, 543; **13** 257*n*, 366; **14** 6*n*, 571*n*;
and Elijah, **18** 1526;
and Ilyās, **18** 1527;
vision of, **9i** 715; **11** 671–81, 698; **12** 72*n*, 74*n*, 298; **13** 168, 215*n*
Enoch, Book of, see BIBLE: Apocrypha/etc. *s.v.*
Enochdianus, *see* Paracelsus *s.v.* ARCANA
Enōš, **12** 458; **13** 173*n*
ens/entia, **15** 13;
absolutum, **11** 454;
astrorum, **15** 13;
ideale, **15** 13;
naturale, **15** 13;
primum, **12** 436*n*;
realissimum, **11** 558;
spirituale, **15** 13; of diseases, **13** 148*n*;
veneni, **15** 13
En Soph, **14** 592&*n*, 594, 600
entanglement(s): in the ego, **13** 397;
emotional and intellectual, **13** 43
entelechy(-ies), **9i** 278, 282;
of Aristotle, **13** 41;

Faust's, *see* Goethe: *Faust s.v.* Characters/themes;
in Leibniz, **8** 937;
of self, **11** 960; **12** 248
enthusiasm: dangers of, **8** 595; **11** 960;
in ESP experiments, **8** 838;
and psychotherapist, **3** 539; **4** 634;
sources of, **8** 668; **9i** 393
entia, see *ens*
enticement(s), divine, **8** 930
Entkrist, *see* Antichrist
ἐντὸπᾶν, **11** 440; **12** 404, 427
entoptic phenomena, **1** 99–100
entropy, **8** 3, 48, 375;
psychological, **8** 50
entwining: and devouring, **5** 365, 425;
etymology of, **5** 366;
motif of, **5** 362, 367, 542;
and motif of clashing rocks, **5** 367&*n*
Enuma Elish, **9ii** 189;
enuresis/bedwetting, **4** 580, 592, 731, 737*n*
environment, **16** 194; **17** 312;
adaptation to, **17** 203, 294;
children and, **17** 81;
and creation of God-image, **5** 128;
culture and, **4** 665;
and extraversion, **10** 658;
falsified perception of, **1** 419;
family, **17** 260;
hostility to, **3** 428;
importance of rapport with, **5** 300;
influence of, **7** 202/443; **9ii** 40;
misapprehension of, **3** 428;
and neurosis, **5** 199;
organism and, **8** 323;
and origin of psychic contents, **11** 223;
patient's influence on, **7** 240/460;
projections and, **9ii** 17;
psyche and, **8** 324;

and psychology, **4** 209;
suggestive power of, **5** 223;
see also child(ren) *s.v.*
envy/envious, **11** 980;
in alchemy/*invidi*, **11** 980*n*;
among Megarians, *see* Megara;
patient's, of analyst, **4** 138;
in Tibetan "World Wheel," **9i**
644
Ephedra vulgaris, **5** 636*n*
Ephesians, St. Paul's Epistle to, *see*
BIBLE: N.T. *s.v.*
Ephesus/Ephesian(s), **9i** 242*n*;
Council of, **11** 194; **14** 744*n*;
Diana, goddess of, **5** pl.
XXIV *b*; **11** 194, 469;
letter to church of, in *Revelation,* **11** 700;
letter to, by Ignatius, *see* Ignatius of Antioch
Ephraem Syrus, St./Ephrem the Sy-
rian, St., **9ii** 216; **14** 29, 123*n*,
377;
"De poenitentia," **14** 567*n*;
Hymni et sermones, **9ii** 216*n*; **14**
7*n*, 29*n*, 377&*n*;
Opera omnia, **14** 567*n*
epiclesis, **11** 321; **12** 450
Epictetus: *Enchiridion,* **9ii** 333*n*
Epicurus/Epicureanism, **6** 18; **11**
43; **14** 47
Epidaurus, **9ii** 294; **18** 257;
serpent of, **17** 300
epidemic(s), psychic, **5** 221; **9i** 227,
267, 496; **10** 471, 490, 519, 721;
13 54; **18** 93, 696, 1161, 1358,
1385, 1389, 1495;
demonism as, **18** 1474
Epigoni (alchemical authors of 17th
century), **12** 502–15
"Epigramma Mercurio philosophico dicatum," *see* ALCHEMICAL
COLLECTIONS: *Mus herm. s.v.*
Maier
epilepsy(-tic/-toid), **7** 389*n*;
TITLE: "An Analysis of the Associations of an Epileptic," **2**
499–559;

attacks, and neuropathy, **1** 29;
brain function and, **3** 326, 497;
children, **17** 137–8; psychotherapy and, **17** 138;
constellations in, **2** 539, 555;
depression, **1** 311*n*;
ego-synthesis disturbed in, **3**
151;
flight of ideas in, **2** 116;
galvanometer experiments in,
2 1232–46;
hereditary, **9i** 151;
and hysteria, **1** 2, 4–5, 29–30
(*see also* hystero-epilepsy);
indirect associations, **2** 450;
petit mal, **17** 137;
prodromal symptoms of, **18**
203;
and psychopathic inferiority, **1**
1–2, 5, 29;
reaction-time in, **2** 541, 550–5;
as repression of criminal instinct, **18** 815;
St. Paul and, **8** 582;
and somnambulism, **1** 30;
stupor, **1** 342;
traits of character, **2** 499–500;
twilight states, *see* twilight
states;
visions, antecedent to attack, **3**
582; **17** 137
"Epilogus et recapitulatio in novum
lumen Sendivogii," *see* ALCHEMI-
CAL COLLECTIONS: *Bibl. chem. s.v.*
Orthelius
Epimeleia (Care), **6** 304, 308
Epimethean: function, **6** 592;
mentality, **6** 318–20;
principle, **6** 315;
thinking, **6** 586;
see also attitude, extraverted
Epimetheus, **6** 456, 563; **12** 456(7),
459; **13** 126;
Adam and, **12** 456(10);
"Afterthinker," **5** 209;
conscience of, *see* conscience
s.v.;
Goethe on, **6** 293, 302–8, 310–

Epimetheus (*cont.*):
11, 314–15; as introvert in, **6** 306;
and jewel symbol, **6** 437;
see also extraverted type, *s.v.*;
Spitteler: *Prometheus and Epimetheus*

Epimetheus, Franciscus, pseud. of Reusner, *see* ALCHEMICAL WRITERS: Reusner

Epinoia, **14** 160, 161, 166, 170

epiousios, **11** 779&*n*

Epiphanius, St., **9ii** 103, 119, 164, 165, 176, 229, 298, 307, 314, 326; **11** 194, 207, 208; **12** 209; **13** 183, 231; **14** 14, 31, 285*n*, 469, 476&*n*, 484, 718*n*; **18** 1607;
on cult of Virgin Mary, **11** 194;
WORKS:
Ancoratus, **9ii** 127*n*, 143, 326*n*; **13** 275*n*, 407*n*; **14** 14*n*, 469*n*, 472, 484*n*, 727*n*;
Panarium: Adversus octoginta haereses, in Migne, **5** 487*n*; —, ed. F. Oehler, **9ii** 78*n*, 103*n*, 119*n*, 129*n*, 134*n*, 164*n*, 243*n*, 298*n*, 307*n*, 314*n*; **11** 194*n*, 207*n*, 249*n*, 360*n*; **12** 209*n*, 469*n*; **13** 116*n*, 183*n*, 271*n*; **14** 6*n*, 31*nn*, 32*n*, 68*n*, 124*n*, 469*n*, 653*n*; **18** 1481*n*

Epiphany, **9ii** 164; **10** 770–1

epiphenomenalism, **8** 10

epiphenomenon, psyche as, **9ii** 268

Epirus, love-song of, **5** 81*n*

episcopus puerorum, *see* bishop, children's

epistemology/epistemological:
criticism, **8** 358, 359, 625, 828, 915;
India and, **11** 956

Epistle of Barnabas, **13** 116

epistles to Seven Churches (Apocalypse), **11** 700–6

"Epistola ad Hermannum," *see* ALCHEMICAL COLLECTIONS: *Theatr. chem. s.v.*

Epistolae Apostolorum, **11** 329

Epona, **9i** 450

equality, **10** 326;
psychic, **10** 283

equation(s), **10** 777;
quaternio as, **9ii** 408–11

equilibrium, **8** 657;
of ego/non-ego, **16** 395;
left/right, **13** 343;
psychic, **7** 111, 170, 218/450, 252, 365; **13** 68; **16** 330; disturbed, **8** 762

equinoctial point, **9ii** 130&*n*

equinox(es), precession of, **8** 987

equivalence, **8** 962, 996;
in Freud, **8** 35; and psychic substitutes, **8** 39; psychic and psychophysical, **8** 964–5;
principle of, **8** 34, 73

Eranos Conferences/lectures/Tagung (Ascona), **8** (*p*520*n*), 986*n*; **9i** (*p*387*n*); **18** 139*n*, 1250

Eranos-Jahrbuch: 1933–5: **7** (*p*7*n*);
1935: **12** (*p*x); **14** (*p*xiii*n*); **18** 673*n*;
1936: **12** (*p*x); **13** (*pp*4*n*, 57); **14** (*p*xiii*n*);
1937: **13** (*pp*4*n*, 57);
1939: **9i** (*p*111*n*);
1940–1: **11** 169*n*, (*p*201);
1942: **13** (*p*191);
1945: **13** (*p*409*n*);
1946: **8** (*p*159*n*);
1951: **8** (*p*520*n*)

Eranos Yearbooks, Papers from:
1. *Spirit and Nature*, **8** (*p*159*n*);
2. *The Mysteries*, **11** (*p*201), 415*n*;
4. *Spiritual Disciplines*, **7** (*p*7*n*)

Erasmus, **3** (*p*4)

Erataoth, **14** 575

Erdmann, B., **5** 15

Erechtheus, **5** 594; **14** 481*n*; **18** 260

erection: in children, **4** 228;
see also tower, as symbol of

ergograph, **2** 1018, 1181

Ergreifer/Ergriffener/Ergriffenheit, **10** 386, 388, 394, 397

escapism, **12** 5
eschatological state, **9ii** 260
eschatology, **11** 645, 856;
    and Antichrist, **9ii** 68, 170; **11**
    743;
    in New Testament, **9ii** 68
Eschenmayer, K. A., **18** 797&*n*
Eschimayer, **4** 748
Eschle, F.C.R.: *Grundzüge der Psy-*
chiatrie, J.'s review, **18** 900–2
Escobar, **12** 24*n*
II Esdras/IV Ezra, visions in, **9ii**
    178*n*, 185&*n*; **12** 57*n*, 551; **13**
    168, 183*n*, 268; **14** 39*n*; *see also*
    BIBLE: Apocrypha/etc. *s.v.*
Esenephys, **14** 317
Eskimo(s): myth, **5** 526*n*;
    Polar, **18** 674;
    primitive languages of, **6** 878;
    sungod, **5** pl. I*b*
Esne, **5** 358
esoteric/esotericism, **10** 886;
    teaching, **9i** 10; archetypes in,
    9i 6
ESP, *see* extra-sensory perception
Espagnet, Jean d', *see* ALCHEMICAL
    WRITERS *s.v.*
esprit and spirit, **10** 935
Esquirol, J.E.D., *see* Bayle
essence/Essence: ethereal, **13** 433;
    fifth, **13** 166;
    God's, *see* God *s.v.*;
    mercurial, **13** 244;
    salamandrine, **13** 173, 177;
    triune, **13** 384&*n*
Essene sect (Therapeutai), **5** 594; **17**
    262; **18** 242
"establish," *see* association-chain(s)
    s.v.
Estsánatlehi, **13** 130
état prélogique (Lévy-Bruhl), **14**
    336*n*
eternal: blessedness, **13** 227;
    ideas, **13** 378;
    man, **13** 403*n*; **16** 502;
    principle(s), **13** 208;
    water, **13** 274
Eternal Feminine, *see* Goethe: *Faust:*

Characters/themes *s.v.*
eternity, **8** 739, 815; **9i** 258; **12** 135,
    315–18; **13** 176*n*;
    circle as symbol of, **14** 41;
    divine attribute, **11** 454, 785;
    feeling of, **13** 223;
    of hell, **9ii** 171;
    hieroglyph of, uroboros as, **13**
    322;
    longing for, **5** 635;
    the Mass and, **11** 307;
    signified by four, **11** 332;
    and stars, **9i** 343
E.T.H., *see* Zurich, Federal Poly-
    technic Institute
ether, **8** 53, 278; **12** 371, 410*n*
ethics/ethical: of action and convic-
    tion, **10** 871;
    and archetypes, **8** 342;
    Christian, **12** 13;
    differentiation of, **18** 1417;
    feelings, effect of lack of, **1** 220;
    and individual, **10** 912;
    Judaeo-Christian, **10** 517;
    "new," **18** 1416, 1420;
    "old," **18** 1413–17;
    primitive and civilized, **10** 108;
    problems, **7** 289; **18** 1412; doc-
    tor and, **11** 547;
    and psychology, **18** 1408–9;
    sense, **16** 315;
    and sex, conflict, **8** 107;
    standards of, **16** 489;
    of Victorian age, **15** 48;
    and *Weltanschauung*, **8** 736,
    740;
    see also morality
Ethiopian(s), **9ii** 329; **12** 484–6, *fig.*
    219; **13** (*p*60*n*), 416; **14** 32&*n*,
    731;
    man and woman, **12** *fig.* 142
    RR;
    treatise, *see* Jurain;
    woman, **9ii** 329, 361, 396, 397;
    see also Aithiops
Ethiopic Book of Enoch, *see* BIBLE:
    Apocrypha/etc. *s.v.* Enoch
ethnology/ethnologist(s), **7** (*p*123),

Europe (*cont.*):
    influence of the East on, **15** 78, 88–90;
    invasion of the East, **13** 84; **15** 90;
    man, mental state of, **11** 514;
    mandalas, **13** (*p*2), 31&*n*, 34, (*p*56);
    mother of dragons, **11** 82;
    neo-paganism in, **16** 397;
    non-European view of, **10** 431;
    occultism in, **15** 86;
    and patriarchal order, **16** 222;
    a peninsula of Asia, **18** 139;
    philosophy, **15** 85;
    plight of, **16** 212;
    and primitive conditions, **8** 573;
    relation of East and West, **10** 237;
    relation of Switzerland to, **10** 920

Eurydice, **10** 434

Eurystheus, **5** 450*n*; **12** 416*n*

Eusebius of Alexandria, **5** 161; **12** 112*n*;
    "Constantini oratio ad sanctorum coelum," **12** 112*n*; **14** 277;
    Oratio VI, **5** 161*n*

Eusebius (Bishop of Caesarea), **14** 353*n*;
    The Ecclesiastical History and the Martyrs of Palestine, tr. H. J. Lawlor and J.E.L. Oulton, **6** 21*n*;
    Evangelica praeparatio, **11** 328*n*; **12** 456(5)*n*

Eustachius, Brother, **9i** 268

Eustathius Macrembolites: *Aenigmata*, **14** 91*n*

Euthicia, **16** 505*n*

Euthymios Zigabenos: *Panoplia dogmatica*, **9ii** 229; **13** 271*n*; **14** 589*n*

Eutychius, Patriarch of Alexandria: *Annales*, **13** (*p*60*n*)

Euxine (ευξεινος), **8** 206

evaluation: process of, **8** 291;
    in reaction, **2** 539;

    see also value judgments

evangelical principle, **6** 96, 97, 98

evangelist(s): four, **5** pl. LX; **9i** 603*n*, 611*n*; **9ii** 304; **11** 97, 113&*n*, 123, 727; **12** 139, *figs.* 158, 197; **13** 31; symbols of, **8** 559; **9i** 425*n*; **9ii** 69, 188; **10** 738; **11** 176, 229, 281, 946; **12** 314, *figs.* 99, 109, 232; **14** 188*n*, 267, 454, pls. 1, 2; —, in mandala(s), **9i** 660; **12** 169, 500, *figs.* 62, 101;
    Matthew, St., **6** 80;
    three, **13** 228*n*

Evangelium aeternum, *see* gospel *s.v.* e·ernal/everlasting

Evans, C. de B., *see under* Eckhart, Meister

Evans, E.: *The Problem of the Nervous Child*, J.'s foreword, **18** 1793–4

Evans-Wentz, W. Y.: ed., *The Tibetan Book of the Great Liberation*, **11** (*p*475*n*);
    see also *Bardo Thödol*/*Book of the Dead*

evaporation, **14** 263, 318

evasion, **7** 259

Eve, **8** 307; **9i** 56, 554; **11** 619; **12** 192*n*; **13** *fig.* B4; **14** 34, 104, 348*n*, 589; **16** 361;
    Adam and, *see* Adam and Eve;
    in alchemy, **11** 47&*n*; **13** 110*n*; **14** 587; and Adamic Mercurius, **13** 282*n*; as binarius, **11** 104&*n*, 262; as earth, **14** 545; as feminine element, **14** 235*n*, 321*n*, 652; *mortificatio* of, **12** *fig.* 135; as Shulamite, **14** 592;
    sin of, **14** 592, 607, 609;
    as anima, **16** 519;
    burial place of, **14** 556;
    children of, **14** 555; Shem, **14** 556;
    creation of, **9ii** 321; **11** 618; **12** *fig.* 248; **13** 327; **14** 581;
    Gnostic, **6** 317; **9i** 560; **9ii** 319; **15** 211;
    "hidden in the body," **18** 429;
    and Lilith, **11** 624;

as Pandora, **12** 456(7); **13** 126;
as people of Israel, **11** 619;
Second, **9ii** 321; **11** 625;
as Sophia, **11** 624;
tempting of, **5** *fig.* 8; **9ii** 372; **13** 400; **14** 554
evening: knowledge, **13** 301*n*;
of life, *see* life, stages of
Evensen, H.: "Die psychologische Grundlage der katatonischen Krankheitszeichen," **3** 13&*n*
events: acausal, *see* synchronicity *s.v.*;
affective, and complexes, **3** 140;
immediacy of, **8** 856;
and mental activities, **8** 962*n*;
psychic, **11** 5; and physical, relation, **11** 972–3;
unique/rare, **8** 821
everlasting gospel, *see* gospel *s.v.* eternal/everlasting
everlasting hills, **13** 403
evidence, psychological diagnosis of, **2** 664, 956, 1023, 1317–47;
TITLES: "The Psychological Diagnosis of Evidence," **2** 728–92; "On the Psychological Diagnosis of Evidence: the Evidence-Experiment in the Näf trial," **2** 1357–88;
nurse suspected of theft, **2** 957–81, 1332–45;
young man suspected of theft, **2** 769–92, 907;
see also facts, psychological diagnosis
evil, **5** 351; **7** (*p*4), 395, 400; **10** 409; **11** 618, 631, 651, 690, 693, 696, 747; **12** 26, 29, 36, 37, 126, 192; **13** 70, 201*n*, 228*n*, 234, 245, 248, 271; **14** 33, 86, 203; **17** 319;
absolute, **9ii** 19;
anima/animus and, **9ii** 423; **12** 192, 273;
in Christ, **18** 1633–4;
Christianity and, **6** 314; **9ii** 170; **11** 247–8; **17** 292;

and chthonic triad, **9i** 425;
contagion of, **10** 410;
devil and, *see* devil *s.v.*;
eye, *see* eye *s.v.*;
Gnostic(s) and, *see* Gnostic *s.v.*;
goat as image of, **6** 389;
good and, *see* good and evil;
individuation as source of, **13** 244;
integration of, in alchemy, **14** 644;
man and, **11** 291, 739; **17** 292;
matter and, **9i** 197, 603*n*; **12** 413;
moral values and, **11** 696, 742;
in nature, question of, **11** 942;
"non-existing," **6** 52; **18** 1593, 1639;
and north, **9ii** 191;
origin of, **9ii** 114; **11** 201, 249;
overcoming of, **10** 883;
pact with, **6** 311, 318; **7** 286;
as positive factor, **18** 1592;
principle of, **5** 662; **7** 240; **9i** 567; **11** 107, 470; **12** 460, 469; **16** 388, 533; as world creator, **9ii** 403;
reality of, **9i** 567; **9ii** 113; **10** 879; **11** 247, 248; **12** 19, 24;
"imagination for," **10** 559, 572;
and rebirth, **5** 351;
relativity of, **9ii** 85; **11** 291, 516;
shadow as, **9i** 567; **9ii** 423; **11** 528;
spirit(s), *see* spirit(s) *s.v.*;
symbolism of, **9i** 157, 425;
and totality, **11** 232;
and unconscious, **5** 569; **10** 165; **11** 291;
unicorn as power of, **12** 520, 525–6
"Evil One," **11** (*p*357)
Evola, J.: *La Tradizione ermetica*, **12** 332*n*, 342*n*
evolution, **4** 279; **9ii** 279;
and instinct, **5** 653;
and progression, **8** 70;

of supernatural events, **10** 623; unconscious, **5** 273

expediency, **4** 599, 602, 607, 613

experience(s), **7** 199, 341, 364; **8** 604, 623; **11** 501;
 and abreaction, **16** 270;
 communal, **10** 516;
 critical, **8** 855;
 destructive, **7** 254;
 of fantasy, **7** 342, 350, 359;
 of God, validity of, **8** 625;
 immediate, **11** 148; defence against, **11** 81, 85; dreams and, **11** 88; replacement by symbols, **11** 75; risks of, **11** 76, 77; individual and collective truths, **11** 463;
 inner, **3** 176; **4** 738*n*; **12** 14, 17, 41, 219; **13** 18;
 intersexual, **9ii** 41*n*;
 of life, **12** 59, 81, 564–5;
 psychic, **7** 354; **8** 680, 682; **13** 42*n*, 77;
 and reflection, **11** 2;
 rehearsal of, **16** 269;
 religious, *see* religious experience;
 sensory and immediate, **9ii** 2–3;
 and thought, **11** 469;
 of unconscious, **7** 292;
 and understanding, **12** 564;
 see also abreaction *s.v.*

experimental psychology, *see* psychology *s.v.*

expiation, **10** 410; **18** 1094–5, 1103

explanation(s), **16** 158, 240; **17** 70;
 fantastic, children's preference for, **17** 76;
 limits of, **16** 153;
 reductive, **16** 146, 150;
 "right," **17** 78;
 of stimulus word, *see* association experiments/tests *s.v.* stimulus

explosion(s), atomic, **10** 611; *see also* atom(s) *s.v.* bomb

exposition of dream, **8** 561

exposure of child, **9i** 285

expression: and reflection, **8** 242; true, **4** 771

expressionism in art, **10** 167; *see also* art(s)

extension of personality, *see* personality *s.v.* enlargement

extensity, **13** 37;
 factor of, **5** 226*n*; **8** 37

exteriorizations, **8** 600

external: and internal, **16** 497*n*;
 object, *see* object *s.v.*;
 world, *see* world *s.v.*

externalization (Jodl), **6** 485&*n*

extractio, **14** 700;
 animae, **16** 486

extra ecclesiam, *see* Church/Ecclesia

extra-human, **7** 159

extra-sensory perception/ESP, **8** 913, 954, 955, 966; **16** 254; **18** 1198;
 and archetypes, **18** 1190;
 and psychic factors, **8** 838, 848, 907, 994; **9ii** 287*n*, 743;
 psychokinetic experiments, with dice, **8** 837, 977;
 and synchronicity, **8** 840, 855, 863, 947;
 transmission in, **8** 840;
 see also Rhine

extraversion/extravert, **3** 418, 420; **5** 259; **6** 459, 478–9, 710 (Def.), 943–4, 975; **7** 356, 373, 462*n*; **9i** 431; **10** 296, 658, 890; **11** 777, 797, 803; **16** 59, 242; **18** 1157, 1259;
 and aesthetic standpoint, **6** 239;
 affectivity of, *see* affectivity *s.v.*;
 of animus, **7** 328, 336;
 in children, **6** 896–7;
 empathy as, *see* empathy *s.v.*;
 and feeling, **6** 235, 595–6;
 and Freudian theory, **6** 91;
 hysterical, **6** 861–2;
 inferior, **6** 163; **7** 84;
 introjection as, **6** 768;
 and introversion, **4** 763; **6** 4, 7, 78, 872, 944, 981; **8** 77, 250; as opposites, **7** 80–2; **11** 803;

extraversion (*cont.*):
   and intuition, **6** 610–12;
   and Luther, **6** 99;
   among mystics, **6** 47;
   and object, **6** 4, 145, 238, 972;
   7 62;
   and pluralism, **6** 536;
   regressive, **6** 860; **8** 77;
   thinking and, *see* thinking
   unconscious in, *see* unconscious
   s.v.;
   unconscious contents and, **7**
   373;
   vac and, **6** 343;
   Western, **11** 770, 785;
   see also affectivity; attitude *s.v.*
   extraverted
extraverted feeling type, *see* type(s)
   s.v. feeling
extraverted thinking type, *see*
   type(s) *s.v.* thinking
extraverted type, **3** 418–21; **4** 763;
   6 38, 39, 55, 249, 520, 913, 972; **7**
   80–4, 462n, 482; **16** 241–2; **18**
   496;
      TITLE: "The Extraverted
      Type," **6** 562–619;
      adjustment of, **6** 564–5;
      empathy with, *see* empathy *s.v.*;
      Epimetheus as, in Spitteler, **6**
      276, 283–6, 592; **7** 82;
      and feeling, **7** 482;
      Goethe as, **6** 103, 142, 148&n,
      288, 309;
      and Gross's typology, **6** 466,
      471, 473, 476, 483, 879;
      hysteria and, **6** 306, 566, 600;
      and introvert, **6** 163–4, 264,
      270–1; **7** 81–4, 86;
      irrational, **6** 616–19;
      and Jordan's typology, **6** 244–
      50, 252, 255, 265–8, 285, 466,
      471n;
      neurosis of, *see* neurosis *s.v.*;
      and object, **6** 4–5, 77, 145, 155,
      164, 213, 250, 266, 557, 563,
      897, 937–8, 982; **7** 62, 81–4; as-
      similation to, **6** 4, 531, 535,

569–71, 596, 599; danger of
surrender to, **6** 4, 284, 565; in
feeling function, **6** 595; identification with, **6** 500–1, 535;
projection of contents/idea
into, **6** 498, 521, 548; **7** 373; in
thinking function, **6** 580–1,
630;
   Origen as, **6** 24;
   Prometheus as, in Goethe, **6**
   306;
   psychoanalysis and, **6** 92;
   rational, **6** 601–3;
   and romantic type, **6** 548, 555;
   "tough-minded," James's term,
   see James;
   of woman, **6** 260–4; social usefulness of, **6** 261–2, 266
eye(s), **5** 574&n; **10** 670, 807; **13** 37,
   57, 377, 471; **14** 24, 45, pls. 8, 9;
   17 55;
   in alchemy, **14** 46, 117n,
   389&n;
   of animals, *see* ANIMALS: fish;
   peacock; serpent/snake;
   in dreams: "eagle," **13** 472;
   blue and white, and Ufo, **10**
   627, 640;
   evil, **9i** 350, 699; **10** 431;
   fiery (Böhme's), as soul, **9i**
   592–3, 704;
   of fish, *see* ANIMALS: fish *s.v.*;
   of God, **5** *fig.* 2; **9i** 594; **10** 639,
   645, 729, 766, 807; **14** 45, 46;
   seven, **8** 394; **9ii** 167n; **10** 766;
   14 45, 627n;
   hero's, and snake's eyes, **5** 575,
   593; **17** 298; **18** 195;
   Hildegarde of Bingen, vision of,
   see Hildegarde *s.v.*;
   Holy Ghost as, **14** 46;
   of Horus, *see* Horus *s.v.*;
   mandala as, **9i** 593, 646, 690,
   698; Böhme's, **13** 31;
   as mind/spirit/understanding,
   12 350, 352, 357, 381, 431; **13**
   377;
   multiple/polyophthalmia

motif, **8** 394–5; **9i** 532, 614, 690, *picture* 17; **13** 114, 267*n*; **14** 270, 627*n* (*see also* Ignatius Loyola);
of Osiris, *see* Osiris *s.v.*;
-personality, **8** 638, 641;
philosophic, **13** 31;
of Rudra, **5** 176;
-salve, **14** 683*n*;
spiritual, **13** 377;
symbolism, **5** 408; **8** 396; **14** 46;
of consciousness, see consciousness *s.v.* eye;
-wash, of the philosophers, see *collyrium;*
of Wotan, **9i** 413

Ezekiel/Ezechiel: the prophet, **11** 665, 667, 681, 686, 690;

vision of, **5** pl. LVI; **9i** 425*n*, 715; **9ii** 188; **11** 100, 431*n*, 600, 665, 698, 727; **13** 361&*n*, 362–3; **14** 269; four cherubim/seraphim in, **9i** 564, 588*n*, 660; **9ii** 188; **11** 176, 667, 675, 727; **13** 361–3, *fig.* 32; **14** 634; **16** 378*n*; four creatures in, **9i** 425*n*, 611*n*; **11** 727; **14** 266–7, 285; as mandala, **9ii** 379; **11** 100; wheel(s) in, **8** 394; **9i** 578*n*; **10** 764; **12** 214, 471&*n*, *fig.* 109; —, four, **11** 727; **12** 471*n*; **13** 362; **14** 266;
see also BIBLE: O.T.

Ezra, *see* BIBLE: Apocrypha/etc. *s.v.* Esdras/Ezra;
visions of, *see* Esdras

F

fables: Aesop's, *see* Aesop's fables;
  didactic, **13** 88
façade of dream, *see* dream *s.v.*
face(s), **13** 37;
  distorted, **8** 590;
  in dreams/visions: of Brother
  Klaus, **11** 477–8; burned, **10**
  627, 642, 643, 664;
  four: of cherubim, **13** 361 (*see
  also* Ezekiel *s.v.* vision); of god
  (Egyptian), **13** 360; of God (in
  Enoch), **11** 673–4; **13** 215*n*
facial expression: of patients, **1** 50,
  311, 326, 337, 368;
  of sacrificer and sacrificed, **5**
  665, 666
facility, verbal, **17** 238
factor(s): aetiological, **7** 270; **11**
  490;
  anima as, **9i** 57;
  causal and final, of psychic experience, **9ii** 253;
  collective, *see* collective *s.v.*;
  constituting unconscious, **11**
  66;
  erotic, **17** 194;
  of extensity, **5** 226*n*; **8** 37;
  gods as, **9i** 49, 50;
  historical, in Buddhism, **7** 303;
  individual, **7** 240;
  karmic, **7** 118*n*;
  ordering / transcending consciousness, **11** 447;
  pathogenic, **11** 491;
  psychic, **11** 67, 491; and freedom, **11** 143; inherited, **11**
  845;
  social, **7** 227;
  subjective, *see* subjective *s.v.*;
  universal, **7** 267
facts:
  TITLE: "On the Psychological
  Diagnosis of Facts," **1** 478–84;
  irrational, **8** 625;
  physiological, **8** 780;

psychic, validity of, **8** 625; **11**
  454, 553;
  psychological diagnosis of, **1**
  478–84 (*see also* evidence);
  rational, **11** 228;
  Western belief in, **11** 767,
  800–1
faculties: battle of, **7** 302;
  differentiation of, **8** 256;
  human, mysterious evolution
  of, **17** 100;
  psychic, **4** 253, 258
faeces, **12** 365; *see also* defecation;
  dung; excrement
faiblesse de la volonté, **3** 505
failure in association experiment, **2**
  94, 419, 453, 455, 473(3), 946,
  951;
  in hysteria, **2** 803, 807, 812–13,
  946
fainting-fits, **1** 6, 37, 328, 337, 419;
  see also giddiness
Fairclough, H. Rushton, *see under*
  Horace
fairy(-ies): child's fantasy of, **5** 277;
  in dreams, **10** 619; **12** 61;
  motif, **16** 17
fairytales/folktales, **3** 565; **4** 493–7;
  6 512; **8** 325, 476, 555; **9i** 51, 263,
  310; **9ii** 232, 259; **10** 58–9, 629;
  11 738; **16** 254, 538; **17** 44; **18** 80,
  249, 526, 1475;
  TITLE: "The Phenomenology of
  the Spirit in Fairytales," **9i**
  384–455;
  alchemical, **14** 420*n*;
  animals in, *see* animal(s) *s.v.*;
  archetypes in, **9i** 6–7, 400, 406,
  409, 433–4, 451; **10** 60, 847;
  and dreams, **5** 29; **18** 1488;
  evil mother in, **5** 369;
  foster-parents in, **5** 34;
  Hanswurst in, **9i** 456;
  hero's father in, as woodcutter,
  5 515;

fairytales (*cont.*):
  Oriental: of Crusaders and Pope's excrement, **5** 276;
  Russian: The girl with no hands, **9i** 404*n*;
    King of the Forest, **9i** 406;
    Maria Morevna, **9i** 435&*n*;
    Prince Danila Govorila, **16** 427–30;
  Siberian: Ememqut and the Creator, **9i** 415;
    The girl and the skull, **16** 519*n*;
    The man turned to stone, **9i** 408*n*;
    The one-sided old man, **9i** 413;
  Spanish and Portuguese: Queen Rose, or Little Tom, **9i** 404*n*, 405*n*;
    The white parrot, **9i** 404*n*, 405*n*;
  Swiss, of peasant boy and little iron man, **9i** 407;
  Unknown origin: diagrams on wall, **9i** 233
faith/*fides*, **9i** 384, 619; **11** 765; **12** 35, 415, 417; **13** 2, 47, 69, 82, 289; **18** 1538–9;
  absolute, **9ii** 269;
  alchemical confession of, **13** 166;
  basis in experience and tradition, **5** 345;
  blind, danger of, **5** 339; **10** 521; a charisma, **5** 342; **11** 285, 864; **13** 73; **18** 1470;
  confession of, **11** 539;
  and consolation, **18** 1576;
  and criticism, **11** 227;
  crumbling away of content, **9ii** 277;
  demythologization of, **10** 551;
  doctor and, **11** 499, 502;
  and dogma, **9ii** 276;
  in God, **13** 146;
  grace of, **13** 197;
  healing/cures, **15** 20; **16** 3, 73;

justification by, **12** 37;
and knowledge, **9ii** 268, 269; **10** 171, 551, 853; **11** 864; **12** 41; **13** 149, 238; **14** 150; **18** 1511;
organ of, **11** 762;
patient's **4** 577, 591;
and projection, **18** 1635, 1648;
religious/Christian, **4** 780; **10** 521, 563; **11** 285; **13** 234, 236;
return to, **14** 751;
Scaiolae as *fides*, **13** 215;
and symbolical truth, **5** 336, 346;
and thought, **18** 582;
and tradition, **5** 345;
and work, **12** 37
faithfulness in marriage, **10** 270
fake, spiritual, Yoga in West as, **11** 802
falcon, *see* ANIMALS *s.v.*
Falke, Jakob von: *Geschichte des deutschen Kunstgewerbes*, **12** *fig.* 158
Falke, K., **4** 199
fall/Fall: of the angels, *see* angel(s) *s.v.*;
  of man, **8** 460, 751; **9i** 420, 576*n*; **9ii** 70, 71; **11** 579, 618, 619, 624; **12** 347, 430; **13** 381, 390, 400; **14** 206, 585;
  of Satan, *see* devil/Satan *s.v.*
Fallopius, Gabriel, **9ii** 243
familiar(-is)/paredros(-oi)πάρεδρος, **12** 88, *fig.* 77; **13** 437; **14** 177, 727;
  in alchemy, **11** 344, 347, 363; **12** 351; **13** 162&*n*, 219, 250, 273, 319, *fig.* B5; **14** 391*n*, 707;
  daemon as, **13** 437; Holy Ghost as, **12** 187, 420&*n*; Mercurius as, **12** 84;
  Mephistopheles as, **12** 88; **13** 120, 295; **14** 177;
  and Semitic gods, **5** 294;
  in shamanism, *ayami*/guardian spirit, **13** 460, 462
family, **7** 278, 320, 338;
  TITLE: "The Family Constella-

tion," **2** 999–1014;
analyst assimilated to, **4** 436;
archetype of, **8** 336;
and association reactions, *see* association experiments *s.v.*;
and collective psyche, **7** 235/456;
complex, *see* complex(es) *s.v.*;
constellation, **2** 999–1014;
father's significance in, **4** 695;
Indian, **10** 997, 999;
milieu, and neurosis, **2** 1009; **4** 307–8, 311–12, 700–1; **17** 107;
Mother Church substituted for, **17** 158;
murder, **18** 918;
and need for independence, **5** 461, 470, 644; **17** 107a, 158–9, 271;
and psychological kinship, **17** 107*n*;
research into, **18** 155;
reunion, celestial, **13** 290;
romance, **4** 780, (*p*301); **7** 508; **10** 352; **18** 1151;
taboo, **7** 508
fanaticism, **3** 456, 462, 513; **4** 613; **8** 582, 773; **10** 511; **17** 156; **18** 1375
Fanianus, Joannes Chrysippus, *see* ALCHEMICAL WRITERS *s.v.*
fantasy (-ies), **1** 304; **5** 465; **6** 711–22 (Def.); **7** 75, 142, 206, 228, 270, 278, 307, 323, 355, 362, 369; **8** 294, 573, 667, 719; **9i** 135, 309; **10** 593; **11** 533–4; **12** 34, 305; **13** 20, 31, 36, 459, 464–5, 470; **14** 275, 306, 335, 424; **15** 105; **17** (*p*3), 76, 102, 281;
TITLE: "Active Participation in the Fantasy," **4** 415–18;
"The Fantasies of the Unconscious," **4** 314–39;
and active imagination/conscious participation, **4** 415–18; **7** 342, 350–1, 357–9; **9i** 101, 319; **14** 706, 736, 749, 752–3; **16** 97–9, 106; **18** 396, 397;

activity, **5** 465*n*; **17** 13&*n*, 77;
aetiological significance of, **4** 353, 411, 422, 561, 570; **9i** 290;
of alchemy, **13** 253, 356, 373, 385; **14** 686–7, 693–4; and *opus*, **12** 394;
in analytical situation, **4** 316, 393–5, 413, 415–18; **7** 192 (*see also below* infantile sexual; transference);
and anticipations, **8** 808;
archaic, **7** 256, 263;
archetypal images in, *see below* mythological;
artificial aids to production of, **8** 155, 166–7; **14** 706;
of ascetics, **10** 649;
autoerotic, **16** 476;
bases/source of, **5** 34–5, 38; **8** 71;
bondage to, **4** 410;
childhood, **7** 88, 99;
childish, **7** 171;
child's, **17** 28–9;
collective/of collective unconscious, **7** 247, 250–1/468, 387;
as compensation, **5** 33, 469;
conscious, **4** 315, 341; **5** 44–5;
creative, **3** 385; **5** (*p*xxix); **6** 84–6, 174, 185, 187; **8** 709; **9i** 153; **10** 13, 355; **13** 63, 305; **16** 62, 98, 277, 353; **18** 481; Miss Miller's term, **5** 616 (*p*448); as unifying/mediating function, **6** 78, 89, 171; **7** 490–1;
defecation, **4** 55–60;
in dementia praecox/schizophrenia, **4** 272; **5** 200 (*see also below* insanity);
disciple-, **7** 265;
dramatic, **14** 753;
erotic, *see below* sexual;
of father: on commode, **5** 276;
in obscene attitude, **4** 389;
hermeneutic treatment of, **7** 497;
in hypnotism, **7** 20/432;
in hysterics, **4** 51, 60–1, 217,

265

fantasy (*cont.*):
221, 298–300, 303, 387; **5** 654; **6** 306; **7** 5/414, 11/420; **15** 103; **17** 128;
ideas born of, **13** 357;
-image, **7** 344–5, 349; **9i** 135; **13** 221; **14** 736;
incest, *see* incest *s.v.*
of Indian mother-figure, **9i** 311*n*;
infantile, **3** 407, 463; **6** 93; **10** 545–7; sexual, **7** 446; **16** 277; **11** 842; —, and neurosis, **4** 313–14, 409–10, 559–62, 569–70, 573–5; **5** 654; **9i** 159; **10** 345, 355, 545–6; **17** 13*n*; —, and transference, **4** 657, 662; **7** 94–8; **16** 140, 153, 276–7, 360 (*see also below* neurosis; transference);
in insanity, **8** 719; **15** 144 (*see also above* dementia praecox);
intensification of, **9i** 303;
involuntary product, **5** 432*n*;
karmic illusion as, **11** 846;
lack of, **14** 190;
-life, **7** 161;
light-motif in, **8** 396;
localized "down below," **18** 16;
Miller's, **5** (*pp*xxviii–xxix), 46, 67, 461–2, 468–9, 474–5, 684–5; **9i** 319;
modern, **14** 736; of tree, **13** 462;
and mythological/primordial images/archetypes, **5** (*pp*xxix), 38, 75, 474–5; **7** 99–102, 109–10; **8** 71, 334; **9i** 102, 262–3, 319; **10** 11–12; **11** 781; **12** 38; **13** 319, 368; **14** 736; **16** 254, 501;
neurosis and/neurotic, **4** 353, 416; **7** 115, 386; **10** 546–7; **17** 13*n* (*see also above under* infantile);
night-world of, **7** 325;
-occurrences, **7** 121;

pathological, **1** 117; **15** 144;
patients' translation of, **5** 19*n*;
perverse, **10** 160;
phobia of, **7** 353;
positive aspect of, **18** 1249;
powers of, **7** 161;
as prima materia, **14** 752;
products, **13** 31, 240, 253, 304;
of "rays of God," *see* Schreber;
"reality" of, **4** 412;
schizoid, **3** 560;
secondary, **13** 323;
-sequences, **7** 134, 386; **9i** 101; **14** 706;
sexual/erotic/of sexuality, **3** 105; **7** 42, 128, 144; **8** 332, 709; **9i** 54; **10** 217; **11** 843; **17** 158; in children, **4** 232 (*see also above under* infantile);
and sexual function, **4** 234;
of snake, *see* ANIMALS: serpent/ snake *s.v.*;
in somnambulistic states, **1** 58, 62–4, 118;
spontaneous, **8** 155; **14** 693; **16** 13, 125;
of stone, *see* stone *s.v.*;
subjective, **11** 939;
symbolical, **5** 83; **7** 122, 241/ 462;
and symptom-formation, **7** 47;
systems, unconscious, **4** 256;
-thinking, **5** 19*n*, 20*n*, 36–7, 39; **6** 830;
transference, **4** 645–6, 662; **7** 213–14 (*see also above under* infantile);
unawareness of, **11** 805;
unconscious, **4** 314–17, 323, 340–2; **6** 171, 183, 355; **7** 344, 445; and decisions, **5** 462; origin of, **4** 342;
and the unconscious, **6** 79–80;
"nothing but fantasy," **17** 302;
uncontrollable, **7** 192;
useless, **7** 439;
visions and, **17** 193;

visual, **8** 388; **16** 13;
waking, **14** 668; and dreams, **8** 449;
wish-, *see* wish *s.v.*
Faraday, M., **6** 547, 548
Faria, —, **10** 366
Farnese: Atlas (Naples), **9ii** 147; stucco-relief, **5** 536
fasces, **9i** 98; *see also* Fascism
fascination, **7** 136, 142; **9i** 690, 693; **12** 326;
    by archetypal contents, **3** 575; **9i** 141;
    and captivation/interdiction, **3** 177–8;
    of mescalin, **3** 569;
    by nixie, **9i** 54;
    of psychic truth, **13** 210;
    of unconscious, **7** 344; **12** 436, 439, 448
fascinosum, **10** 864, 874
Fascism, **10** 396; **11** 224; **18** 372, 373, 1324, 1335–6; *see also* fasces; Hitler; Mussolini
fasting: of Brother Klaus, **18** 1497–8;
    Hiawatha's, **5** 517
fatalism, Islamic, **16** 186
fate, **7** 61, 72–5, 208, 221/451, 236, 254, 258, 438; **8** 828–9; **12** 23, 36*n*; **13** 18, 60, 210, 332; **17** 294;
    aesthetic flirtations with, **13** 25;
    of child, restricted to parents, **4** 343;
    dreams and, **7** 21/433; **18** 1490;
    eternal images as, **7** 183;
    fear of, **5** 165;
    goddess(es) of, **12** *figs.* 6, 205; Ananke, **5** 426*n*; Graeae, **9i** 157; Moira, **5** 371; **9i** 157; Norns, **5** 371; **9i** 157; Heimarmene, **12** 456*n*;
    human, **16** 365;
    personifications of, **5** 371;
    power of, **5** 102*n*; **7** 108;
    propitiation of, **11** 29;

of psyche, **13** 482;
religious attitude to, **7** 164;
Stoic conception of, **5** 102*n*, 423; **7** 108;
symbol of, **5** 426;
web of, **5** 102*n*; **13** 228*n*;
see also destiny
Fatehpur-Sikri, **10** 983
father, **5** 76; **7** 88–90, 389; **8** 720, 774; **9i** 315; **11** 270; **13** 147, 203; **17** 330;
    TITLE: "The Significance of the Father in the Destiny of the Individual," **4** 693–744;
    animal, **4** 737;
    -animus, **9ii** 329; **14** 232;
    archetypal role of, **5** 396; **9i** 187, 273*n*; **12** 159;
    archetype of, **4** 739, 743–4; **10** 65–6, 396;
    in associations, **2** 671, 679–81, 692, 698, 699;
    as body, **12** 436;
    in Breuer's case (Anna), **7** 6/415;
    and child's birth theories, **17** 45–8;
    -complex, *see* complex *s.v.*;
    as consciousness, **11** 270;
    and daughter: incestuous relationship, **9i** 168&*n*; influence on, **5** 272; **9ii** 28–9, 32; **14** 232; **17** 218–19; her love for, **7** 22;
    demiurge as, **9ii** 297;
    differentiation from, **11** 271;
    divinities, **6** 201;
    doctor/analyst as, **4** 657–8; **7** 97–8, 206, 213–14, 248, 255; **16** 139; **17** 158; **18** 1330;
    in dreams, **2** 836–7, 1011–12; **12** 58, 78, 82, 91, 151, 158, 162;
    embodies tradition/collective consciousness, **12** 59, 83, 92, 159;
    in family constellation, **2** 1006, 1008–9, 1011–12;

father (*cont.*):
    and father-in-law, **5** 515;
    fear of, **4** 482–5, 487, 489, 738;
    5 396; **17** 52;
    -figure: in dreams, **9i** 396; ma-
    gician as, **5** 543, 548;
    -fixation, **7** 247; **17** 220; **18**
    633;
    four, **13** 186;
    in Freudian theory, **7** 58;
    and hero, **5** 515–16; **11** 229;
    hysterical symptoms related to,
    2 911–12;
    idea of, **9ii** 37;
    identification with, **11** 271;
    -image: projection of, **18** 365,
    366, 634, 1330; —, onto hus-
    band, **18** 365; and teachers, **17**
    107a;
    -imago, *see* imago *s.v.*;
    "informing spirit," **12** 159;
    in J.'s case-histories, **7** 45–53,
    206; **12** 58–9, 151–2, 162–3; **17**
    29–32, 216–17a;
    liberation from, **7** 393;
    of lies, Lucifer as, **13** 303;
    -lover, **7** 206, 212–13, 216, 248,
    255;
    -mask, **7** 390;
    of all metals, **13** 282;
    as model persona, **7** 315;
    in Moses quaternio, **9ii** 328–9,
    360;
    -mother, symbol for God, **9ii**
    304;
    as obstacle to regression, **5** 511;
    and personification of destiny,
    4 728;
    pneuma as, **9i** 571;
    primitive side of, **5** 267;
    primordial, **5** 216; **7** 217; **17**
    97;
    relation to, and neurosis, **4**
    693–5;
    return to, **12** 79;
    self as the, **11** 400;
    "signs of," **9ii** 297;
    and son, **5** 184, 497; **11** 197–8;

12 26; **13** 77; **16** 336–7; as begetter of excellent sons, **5** 515;
cult of, **5** 184; fight/conquest, **5**
375, 511–12; **11** 271; identical,
5 497, 516; neurotic fear of, **5**
396; as subjective psychic factor in son, **5** 396; **12** 84; symbolism, **5** 356, 439;
symbol(s) of, **5** 396, 504; bull
as, **5** 396; wolf as, **4** 478, 480–2,
484–5;
-transference, **18** 366, 634;
tribal, **9i** 126; **11** 328;
unknown/unknowable, **9ii** 298;
16 378*n*;
wicked, **8** 99; **12** 152;
-world, **11** 200; **12** 26–7, 30, 93
Father: of All, **18** 584; Gnostic,
    see Gnostic(-ism) *s.v.*;
    -Creator, in Coptic myth, **5**
    479;
    "devoid of consciousness" (in
    Gnosticism), **18** 1481;
    God as, *see* God *s.v.*;
    in Heaven, *see* God *s.v.* Father;
    -Mother, Gnostic, *see* Gnostic
    (-ism) *s.v.* Father;
    paradoxical nature of, **18** 1552,
    1556;
    Sun, *see* sun *s.v.*
Fathers of the Church, *see* Church
    Fathers
fatigue, **1** 248; **2** 388, 491, 731; **3**
    16, 184, 569; **9i** 214, 245;
    in hysteria, **2** 813–14, 816;
    and thinking, **5** 11, 32;
    see also Aschaffenburg *s.v.*
Fatima, **10** 597
Faust (Rembrandt etching), **12** *fig.*
    55
Faust, see Goethe: *Faust*
fear/fright, **3** 86–7; **4** 736; **5** 167; **7**
    258/473, 285, 369; **8** 750; **12** 240;
    15 161;
    abstracting type and, **6** 490,
    497;
    "animal," **5** 530;
    of asylum, **1** 309, 348;

collective, **10** 731;
of collective unconscious, **7** 157;
of complexes, **8** 207–15;
of concretization, **7** 352;
in contemporary world, **10** 724–5; **11** 84–5;
of death, *see* death *s.v.*;
of decision, **12** 285;
of detention/jailer, **1** 229, 345;
dream as fulfilment of, **4** 160, 167 (*see also* anxiety *s.v.* dreams);
"examination," **1** 307;
expression in art, **10** 724–5;
of father, *see* father *s.v.*;
"first brought gods into world," **6** 488&*n*;
of ghosts, *see* ghosts *s.v.*;
of God, *see* God *s.v.*;
of going mad, **12** 38, 60; **16** 374;
and hypnosis, **4** 591;
of incest, *see* incest *s.v.*;
instinct-inhibiting, **5** 216, 221;
of life, *see* life *s.v.*;
"maker of," **9i** 35, 288;
of new relationship, **7** 179, 181;
night-, **10** 60; **15** 148;
of people, **6** 468;
in primitives, *see* primitives *s.v.*;
projection and, **10** 572, 616; **11** 85;
of psychology, **12** 19;
of reality, **7** 510;
snake as symbol of, **5** 395, 671, 681;
of snakes, **8** 266;
spirit of evil, **5** 551;
sudden, **4** 218, 355; **7** 8/417 (*see also* trauma);
of unconscious/inner side, **7** 316, 323–4; **9ii** 62; **10** 530; **11** 23, 28; **12** 60, 325, 439; **16** 374;
of women, **6** 637
feast, ritual, **8** 738; see also *festum*
feather(s), **14** 637;

-dress, **5** 315*n*, 369*n*; **8** 845;
symbol of power, **5** 133*n*
features: feminine, in men, **8** 780;
hardening of, **8** 780
Fechner, G. T., **8** 354&*n*, 364*n*, 426; **9i** 111; **12** 372*n*; **17** 162; **18** 1144;
Elemente der Psychophysik, **7** 407; **8** 352&*n*; **9i** 111*n*; **12** 372*n*
"fedeli d'amore," **13** 389; **18** 1279
Federal Polytechnic, *see* Zurich
feebleminded/feeblemindedness, *see* mental defectives
feeling(s), **5** 431; **6** 723–30 (Def.); **7** 201, 206, 216, 289, 307, 323, 482–3, 501, 507; **8** 291, 683, 705; **9ii** 58, 275; **13** 7; **16** 59; **17** 240, 280;
and affects, **18** 47, 502;
atrophy of, in pictures of schizophrenics, **15** 208; in work of Joyce, **15** 173, 183;
collective, **7** 239, 241/462, 459, 514;
and concepts, **1** 148;
consolidation of, **13** 222;
differentiation of, **14** 334;
directed, **8** 50;
emotion and, *see* emotion(s) *s.v.*;
and extraverted attitude, **6** 595–6;
faith and, **11** 763;
function, *see* function(s) *s.v.*;
and immortality, **16** 531;
and intellect, *see* intellect *s.v.*;
and introverted attitude, **6** 638–9;
J.'s use of term, **1** 168*n*;
lesion of, **18** 839;
man's, **17** 222;
meaning of, in psychology, **8** 223;
of moral resentment, **7** 218/450;
mythological, **7** 468;
need of, in dream analysis, **17** 198;
negative, **7** 344;

feeling (*cont.*):
    neurotic, **17** 172;
    personal, **6** 54–5;
    projection of, **7** 513;
    realization through, **16** 491;
    release of, in early Christianity, **5** 667;
    in Schiller, **6** 117–18, 153–4;
    -sensation, **6** 154–63, 171, 235, 726 (*see also* affectivity);
    site of, **8** 669;
    subliminal, **7** 520; **8** 362; **17** 199;
    suppression of, **2** 417;
    and thought, as opposites, **6** 85;
    -thoughts, **7** 473;
    type, *see* type(s) *s.v.*;
    -values, **18** 23, 29;
    in woman, **7** 296; **10** 79
feeling-tone(d), **1** 168&*n*, 220; **2** 413, 1322; **3** 103, 170; **5** 128; **8** 291; **9ii** 53, 61; **13** 341; **18** 23;
    ambivalence in, **3** 425;
    complex, *see sep. entry below;*
    galvanometer recording of, **2** 1015–20, 1025, 1027, 1043;
    ideas, **1** 119, 298, 304; **6** 239; **7** 20; **18** 1389; complex of, **4** 67;
    inadequate, in dementia praecox, **3** 70–1;
    memories, **1** 176, 264, 298;
    motivations, **1** 305;
    perseveration of, **2** 620–1, 638, 645;
    resistance and, **3** 428;
    stimulus words and, **2** 396;
    subjective and objective, **9ii** 54–5;
    thought-processes, **1** 423;
    train of thought, **1** 168–9
feeling-toned complex, **1** 168*n*, 170, 478–80; **2** 315–29, 352, 396–7, 456, 473(3), 509, 539, 675; **4** 67; **5** 203; **8** 18, 592; **9i** 4; **17** 128, 199a; **18** 959, 1130;
    TITLES: "The Feeling-toned Complex and its General Effect on the Psyche," **3** 77–106; "The Influence of the Feeling-toned Complex on the Valency of Associations," **3** 107–42;
    crime and, **1** 478–80;
    in criminal investigation, **2** 1322–4;
    definition of, **1** 168*n*; **2** 167*n*, 733;
    discovery of, **8** 196;
    and ego-centred attitude, **2** 417;
    in hysteria, **2** 908–15, 917;
    nature of, **8** 201;
    persistence of, **3** 90;
    reaction-time in, **2** 548*n*, 602–3, 606–8, (*p*253), 616, 645, 1084–5;
    repeated words and, **2** 541*n*;
    repressed, **18** 922, 1155;
    in reproduction, **2** 991;
    stimulus-words in, **2** 396, 413–14, 430, 455;
    in unconscious, **8** 383;
    see also under association(s); association experiments; complex *s.v.* emotionally charged
feeling-values, **1** 221; **9i** 189; **9ii** 53, 58;
    of archetypes, **8** 411;
    as function, *see* function(s) *s.v.* feeling;
    and intellect, **17** 183
feet, *see* foot/feet
Feindel, E., *see under* Meige
Fejérváry Manuscript, *see* CODICES AND MSS; *s.v.* Liverpool
Felida, *see* CASES IN SUMMARY: Azam *s.v.*
felix culpa, **10** 677, 868; **12** 36; **18** 1594
felling of tree, *see* tree(s) *s.v.*
female, *see* feminine
femina candida/alba, see woman *s.v.* white
feminine/female: anima, *see* anima *s.v.*;
    archetype of, **5** 514;

non-Christian, **12** 20;
sacred, **12** 9, 12, 14, 20–2;
Fihrist, see ALCHEMICAL WRITERS:
Nadim *s.v.*
Fiji, kingship in, **14** 350*n*
filia mystica, **9i** 372; **14** 161
filiatio, **11** 272, 289
filiation, third, *see* Basilides *s.v.*
filioque clause, *see* homoousia *s.v.*
filius, **13** 177, 186*n*, 207*n*, *fig.* B2;
Mercurius as, *see* Mercurius *s.v.*
filius canis coelici coloris, see ANI-
MALS: dog/bitch
filius Dei, see Son of God
filius hermaphroditus: as arcane substance, **10** 629;
Hermes Psychopompos as, **12**
fig. 23
filius hominis, **10** 733
filius ignis, **13** 163*n*
*filius macrocosmi/mundi maioris/*Son of
the Macrocosm, **12** 162, 335; **13**
162, 384*n*; **14** 15, 124, 141, 150,
163, 238, 355, 373, 419, 460, 700,
704; **18** 1631, 1684;
as Anthropos, **14** 238;
as arcane substance, **10** 629;
as Christ, **9ii** 239; **12** 506;
as *lapis philosophorum,* **9ii** 194,
375; **12** 335; **13** 127, 384, 386;
Mercurius as, *see* Mercurius
s.v.;
as *salvator,* **12** 26;
as self, **16** 220;
symbolism of, **9ii** 120; **12** 26,
420; **13** 203, 287
filius microcosmi: Christ as, **11** 357;
13 384, 386;
"Son of Man" as, **13** 127; **14**
150
filius noster rex genitus, **13** 184
filius philosophorum, **9i** 246; **11** 470;
12 215, 537*n*, 558, *figs.* 30, 153,
155; **13** 162, 165, 187, 371; **14** 62,
124*n*, 177, 290; **16** 474; **18** 1631;
as Anthropos, *see* Anthropos
s.v.;
as bird of Hermes, **14** 6;

Christ as, **12** 474, *fig.* 234; **13**
158, 162, 163, 166; **16** 525;
God as, **13** 162;
hermaphrodite, **12** 29, *fig.* 23;
16 398;
as lapis, **14** 14; **16** 458;
light as, **13** 161–3; **14** 34;
Mercurius as, **13** 157;
as self, **9ii** 194;
symbolism of, **9ii** 120, 334; **11**
400; **13** 161–2, 168; **16** 404
filius regis, **13** *fig.* B6
filius regius, **12** 436, 440; **13** 181,
183, 184; **14** 185, 443, 460, 475,
488, 507, 524; **16** 404, 407, 496;
Anthropos/Primordial Man as,
14 443; **16** 481;
as son of whore, **14** 420;
as symbol of self, **9i** 396; **14**
548;
"third sonship," **14** 124, 397;
16 481 (*see also* Basilides *s.v.*
third sonship);
see also king *s.v.* son
filius sapientiae, **9i** 193; **11** 714*n*, 738,
739; **13** 157, 406;
Christ as, **11** 748;
lapis as, **9i** 289
filius solis et lunae, **11** 748, 756
filius unicus, as goal of *opus,* **13** 212
filius unigenitus, **13** 212*n*
*filius unius diei/*son of one day:
arcane substance as, **14** 472;
lapis as, **13** 301*n*; **14** 171*n*, 718;
Logos/light/Christ as, **14** 476;
Mercurius as, **14** 718
film producers, in dream, **10** 704
fils à papa, **16** 196
filth, **13** 290;
as alchemical substance, **12**
365, 421; **13** 182*n*, 209;
see also dunghill
fimarium, **14** 261*n*
finality, **4** 687; **7** 501*n*; **8** 4–5, 43–5;
association-chain, *see* associa-
tion chain(s) *s.v.*;
and dreams, **8** 456;
importance of, **8** 472;

music, *see* Wagner;
of nature, **9i** 536; **9ii** 397*n*;
New, **12** 451&*n*;
Nodfyr/Niedfyr, **5** 212&*n*;
in the north, **9ii** 158, 190,
203*n*;
"of the Philosophers," **10**
726–7; **16** 507;
"our," **13** 184;
pillar of, **13** (*p*62);
pneuma, **12** 370, 451;
as *prima materia*, **12** 336, 425;
Prometheus and, *see* Prometheus *s.v.* theft of fire;
and quaternity, **9ii** 203&*n* (*see
also above* four kinds of);
and sacrifice, **5** 210, 240, 663;
11 302;
salamander as, **13** 177;
and salt, see *sal*/salt;
-Sermon, *see* Buddha *s.v.*;
and soul, **8** 665; **12** 370*n*;
"south wind," **12** 473&*n*;
and speech, **5** 230–3; **6** 338&*n*;
spirit as, in alchemy, **12** 449; **13**
103*n*;
spirit-, **13** 46, 54;
-spirits, **5** 663; Salamandrini as,
13 177;
spiritual, **13** 187*n*;
sprite, **9i** 705;
-stick/*pramantha*, **5** 208–12,
215, 404, pl. XIII*b*;
in sun, **13** 187&*n*;
supracelestial, **13** 408;
symbol(s)(-ism), **10** 726, 734;
11 276; **13** 185; of emotion, **10**
643, 745; and light, **5** 163, 423;
-temple, **12** 17;
tongues of, **13** 46 (*see also* Holy
Ghost *s.v.* fire);
torment of, **13** 89, 94, 183;
-totem, **5** 208*n*;
-tree, *see* tree(s) *s.v.*;
unnatural, **13** 444;
unquenchable, **11** 60, 74;
vessel, *vas* as, **12** 338&*nn*;
warrior, **12** 454; **13** 184;

and water, **9ii** 353; **12** 313,
377, 436, 469, 551, *fig.* 1; **13**
98, 103*n*, 266; in alchemy, **9ii**
393; **11** 355; **12** 336, 338&*n*,
551*n*; **13** 187&*n*, 408*n*; **16** 509;
as opposites, **10** 771; **12** 336,
436; **13** 98, 266; **14** 1, 4, 10*n*;
union of, **12** *figs.* 72, 160; **13**
310; —, in star of David, **10**
771; **18** 1617 (see also *aqua permanens*);
"water that is fire," **10** 727, 746;
-wood, **4** 165;
"wrath-," *see* Böhme;
see also Easter; *ignis;* incendiarism; mountain, in alchemy
s.v. burning
fireballs, **10** 766–9;
green, **10** 602*n*, 792
Fire Sower, **10** 725–34, 770–1, pl. II
firestone, **8** 314; **12** 451
firewood, as dream symbol, **4** 165
firmament, **9i** 315; **13** 173, 301,
362, *fig.* A6; **15** 29;
interior, **8** 392;
in man, **13** 188;
Paracelsus on, **8** 390; **9ii** 251;
13 355*n*; **14** 171*n*
firmamental body, **15** 29
firmamentum, **13** 268
Firmicus Maternus, J., **9ii** 143; **12**
66; **14** 14, 45, 726;
on Attis mystery, **5** 535;
on bridegroom, **5** 274*n*;
on tree and effigy, **5** 662;
WORKS:
    *De errore profanarum reli-
    gionum,* **5** 274*n*, 535*n*, 596*n*,
    662*n*; **9ii** 143*n*; **11** 400*n*; **12**
    66*n*; **13** 91*n*; **14** 14*n*, 45*n*,
    58*n*, 65*n*, 350*n*, 726*n*;
    Matheseos libri octo, **5** 487*n*; **14**
    154*n*, 630*n*, **16** 454*n*
firm-rootedness, **13** 350
first-born, slaying of the, **9ii** 106*n*;
see also Innocents, massacre of
First Cause, *see* cause *s.v.*
first fruits, **11** 387

first half of life, *see* life, stages of
First Man, *see* Anthropos
first parents, *see* parent(s) *s.v.*
First Thomas, **13** 168*n*
fir-tree, *see* TREES *s.v.*
fish, *see* ANIMALS *s.v.*
fisherman, **9ii** 174
fishing: rod, God's, **13** 456;
    for sea-monster, motif of, **5**
    387;
fission, nuclear, **10** 575, 600, 813,
    879
fists, beating to death by, among
    Mamba clan, **5** 594
Fitch, C., **5** (*p*456*n*);
    The Moth and the Flame, **5**
    (*p*456&*n*)
fitness, in biology, **13** 464
fits, St. Paul and, **8** 582; *see also*
    epilepsy
five, *see* NUMBERS *s.v.*
fixation, **3** 196; **7** 501*n*; **8** 724; **9ii**
    259; **13** 38, 222; **16** 148;
    of affects, **3** 73–4, 76, 211;
    father-, *see* father *s.v.*;
    infantile, *see* infantile *s.v.*;
    and transference, **16** 139;
    visual, **3** 3, 16, 177
Flaccianus, **9ii** 127*n*
flagstaff, missionary's, **10** 119
Flambart, P.: *Preuves et bases de l'astrologie scientifique*, **8** 868*n*
flame/*flammula*, **13** 193, 194;
    blue, in patient's vision, **7** 366,
    368;
    crowfoot, name for, **13** 193&*n*;
    imagery of, **5** 140*n*, 149;
    sacrificial, god as, **5** 246;
    soul as, **8** 665
Flamel, Nicholas, *see* ALCHEMICAL
    WRITERS *s.v.*
Flammarion, C., **8** 830, 974; **18**
    750;
    The Unknown, **8** 830*n*
flash, *see* lightning *s.v.*
flattery, **13** 441
flatus vocis, **6** 65; **13** 378;
    universals/*universalia* as, **6** 40,

58, 73; **9i** 149; **9ii** 60
Flaubert, Gustave: *Salammbô*, **1**
    123*n*;
    La Tentation de Saint Antoine, **12** 59
flaying, **11** 348; **13** 93, 116*n*;
    motif, **5** 595*n*;
    see also god(s) *s.v.*
Fledermäuse (Meyrink), **7** 153
fleece, *see* golden fleece
Fleischer, H. L.: *see* ALCHEMICAL
    WRITERS: Hermes Trismegistus
    s.v. WORKS
flesh, **9ii** 369; **13** (*pp*60, 63), 111,
    122, 127, 133, 137*nn*, 148*n*, 149,
    276, 408;
    as arcane substance, **14** 181*n*;
    Christ's, **13** 137*n*; **14** 11;
    as *prima materia*, **14** 11&*n*;
    in sacramental meal, **11** 304;
    and spirit, balance, **4** 783;
    as "world," **14** 354
fleshly: eyes, **13** 377;
    man, **13** 126
Fletcher, A., **8** 122
flexibilitas cerea, **1** 40
flight: of ideas, *see* idea(s) *s.v.*;
    of Ufos, *see* Ufos *s.v.*
Flinker, M., **18** (*p*789*n*)
Flinker Almanac, **18** (*p*789*n*)
flint, **13** 141, 148*n*;
    body, **13** 132;
    man, **13** 132
flirting, **10** 227–8
Flood/flood, *see* Deluge
flos/flores, alchemical, **11** 161*n*; **12**
    99*n*; **13** 160;
    cheiri, **13** 171*n*;
    sapientum, **12** *fig.* 13;
    see also flower
Flournoy, T., **1** 126*n*, 143, 180; **3**
    10, 58*n*, 164*n*, 298, 304, 308; **4**
    152, 155&*n*; **6** 509, 967; **8** 488,
    503; **9i** 113, 263*n*; **16** 294; **17**
    129; **18** 1130, 1223;
    case of Hélène Smith, **1** 98,
    101, 105, 106&*n*, 119, 136&*n*,
    145; **3** 157&*n*, 298; **10** 257; automatic speech, **1** 126*n*; —,

Psychology, J.'s foreword, **18** 1 168–73

Fordham University, **4** (*pp*83, 87);

foreigners, **10** 162

foreknowledge/precognition, **8** 930–1, 972–3; **10** 636, 849; **14** 662;

  and *déjà-vu*, **8** 974; **11** 640

Forel, A. H., **3** 137*n*, 157*n*, 275, 279, 496; **4** (*p*252); **10** 366; **16** 66, 231; **17** 129; **18** 798&*n*;

  ant experiments, **3** 193;

  on dissociation, **1** 339;

  on ellipses, **3** 50*n*;

  on pathological cheating and daydreaming, **1** 117;

  Ethische und rechtliche Konflikte im Sexualleben in- und ausserhalb der Ehe, J.'s review, **18** 921;

  Hypnotism, **1** 1 17*n*; **4** 637;

  "Selbstbiographie eines Falles von Mania acuta," **3** 150*n*;

  The Sexual Question, **7** 425; **10** 213

forest/Forest, **12** 438;

  demon of, Wotan as, **13** 246;

  King/king of: as tree numen, **9i** 406; oak tree as, **13** 241, 247;

  of mares'-tails, **13** *fig.* 27;

  maternal significance of, **5** 420;

  primeval, as dream motif, **12** 117, 245;

  as synonym for the unconscious, **13** 241;

  see also tree(s)

forethought (προνοίᾳ), **13** 270*n*

forgetfulness, **8** 610;

  hysterical, **1** 119&*n*;

  and inhibition, **4** 89;

  see also amnesia

forgetting, **4** 15, 210; **17** 102;

  definition of, **18** 450;

  Freud's concept, **2** 639, 657; **3** 92;

  idea of, **1** 298;

  normal, **17** 199a, 200;

  and suppression, **17** 199a;

  of unpleasant experiences, **2** 900

forgiveness:

  Christian virtue of, **11** 523;

  in Protestantism, **11** 547;

  of sin, **5** 95; **11** 537;

  trance pantomime of, **1** 53

form(s), **8** 959; **12** 366;

  actual and ideal, **11** 968;

  disintegration of, **10** 724;

  an image and a mode of manifestation, **5** 128;

  and matter, union, **14** 654&*n*;

  Platonic, *see* Plato *s.v. eidos*/etc.;

  psychoid, **13** 350;

  "severe," **12** 203;

  sexual significance of, **10** 637;

  unity of, **12** 427;

  Universal Mind source of all, **11** 782;

  see also image

formae essentiales, **8** 388

formal instinct (Schiller), **6** 157&*n*

formlessness, **9ii** 119

formulation of unconscious material, **8** 176;

  aesthetic, **8** 175, 177;

  creative, **8** 172, 173

fornication, **11** 721

Förster, F. W., **7** 411

Förster, M.: "Adams Erschaffung und Namengebung," **12** 328*n*

Förster-Nietzsche, E., **1** 141, 182; **10** 382; **18** 456;

  ed., *Der werdende Nietzsche,* **10** 382*n*; **11** 44*n*

Fortgibu, M. de, and plum-pudding, **8** 830&*n*

fortress, **13** 389

fortune teller(s), **7** 489; **8** 479, 481

forty, *see* NUMBERS *s.v.*

forward striving: and libido, **5** 617, 680;

  taken over by unconscious, **5** 617

Fossor Diogenes, **5** 163*n*

foster: children, **4** 377;

  mother, animal as, *see* animal(s) *s.v.* mother;

  parents, *see* parent(s) *s.v.*

FREUD, SIGMUND

on abreaction, **2** 725;

and A. Adler, conflicting/contrasted theories, **3** 411, 419; **6** 88, 90, 91; **7** 44, 57–60, 92, 466; **8** 44; **10** 342–3, 352–3, 556; **16** 24, 67–9, 151–2, 234, 243–4; **17** 156; **18** 275–6, 278;

on ambivalence in language, **18** 1077;

and analysis of therapist, **10** 339; **16** 8, 165, 237;

on archaic vestiges, **8** 373; **9i** 2; **10** 530, 831; **13** 478; **16** 205, 246, 38*n*; **18** 468, 521, 1261;

on artist and work of art, **15** 155–6;

on autoeroticism, **3** 429*n*;

"biological" orientation of his school, **5** 507; **18** 1074;

on castration complex, **18** 122;

causalism of, *see below s.v.* reductive;

and causes of psychosis, **18** 905;

on censor/censorship, **2** 611; **3** 137, 434; **4** 73, 80, 112; **7** 21; **8** 62, 132, 461, 486; **13** 467; **15** 64, 106; **16** 54–5, 231, 245; **18** 510, 864–5, 1149, 1150, 1152;

on choice of neurosis, **6** 929–30;

on compulsive thinking, **3** 435;

concretism of his theory, **12** 171;

on condensation, **2** 323; **3** 50&*n*;

and counter-transference, **16** 358*n*; **18** 322;

on death instinct, **5** 504*n*; **7** 33&*n*, 79; **18** 1150;

on determination, **18** 1041;

development of his views, **4** 48;

on displacement from below upwards, **2** 839, 851; **3** 285;

dogmatism of, **17** 128, 180, 203;

on dreams, **5** 25; **6** 701; **7** 3/411; analysis of, **1** 97, 133, 172; **3** 112, 122; **4** 64–73, 552; **5** 18*n*, 28; **7** 21/432, 25–6/437; **8** 447–50, 461–2, 473, 485–7, 497, 539, 541; **10** 319, 351; **11** 41; **13** 396; **15** 64–5; **16** 35, 144; **17** 129–30, 262; **18** 175, 176, 421, 893 (*see also* dreams); *s.v.*
  analysis of one's own, **4** (*p*252);
  façade unlike dream thought, **4** 66, 171, 452; **7** 21, 162; **9ii** 316*n*, **11** 41; **16** 54; **17** 162;
  importance of, **3** 450; **4** 334;
  of "Irma's injection," **10** 351;
  as *via regia* to the unconscious, **7** 437;
  as wish fulfilment, **17** 185, 282;

on ego as seat of anxiety, **10** 360; **11** 849;

on ego-ideal, **18** 1152;

on ego-instincts, **7** 43, 58; **10** 556; **18** 1150;

and equivalence, *see* equivalence *s.v.*

and evil nature of psyche, **10** 173, 177; **17** 292;

and extraversion, **3** 419; **6** 91;

and fantasy, **7** 490–1;

and forgetting, **2** 639–40, 657;

on free association, **2** 451, 640, 662, 704; **8** 167, 179; **9i** 101; **16** 100; **18** 1147;

Freudian error, **3** 109;

German criticism of, **4** 156;

on hypermnesia, **2** 712;

and hypnosis, **17** 99, 128, 176;

hysteria, theory of, **1** 318; **2** 660–1, 1067, 1354; **3** 55; **4** 1, 6–7, 27–30, 61–2, 207–9; **7** 8/417, 10/419; **15** 63; **17** 176; **18** 871, 880, 887, 906, 922 (*see also* Breuer);

on hysterical identification, **1** 117;

on Id, **9i** 2*n*; **18** 121, 123, 281, 289, 1152;

on incest: barrier, **4** 351–2; **5** 332, 652, 654; **6** 201; **10** 61; **16** 415; problem, **5** 253; **10** 659; **13** 396;
wish, **6** 572; **7** 22–3, 261/477; **16** 140, 368; **18** 192, 201;

on infantile fixation, **7** 202/443, 261/477; **16** 139 (*see also* infantile *s.v.*);

on infantile sexuality, **4** 37, 50–1, (*p*76), 224, 226, 258, 268–9, 368, 370–2; **7** 256; **8** 97, 497; **15** 50–1, 63, 104 (*see also below* sexuality);

on instinct theories, **5** 199; **18** 1494;

on introversion, **11** 770; **18** 498;

and J., personal relationship: analysis of J.'s dream, **18** 483–91; collaboration, **4** (*pp*v–vi); **10** 1034*n*; **17** 128; **18** 274, 832, (*p*374*n*);
parting of ways, **4** (*pp*v–vi); **5** (*p*xxvi); **6** (*p*499*n*); **17** 180; **18** 274, 487, 1156;

J.'s answers to questions on, **18** 1065–76;

on latency period, **4** 370–2;

and lay therapy, **10** 1062;

on Leonardo, see WORKS: "Leonardo da Vinci";

libido theory of, *see* libido *s.v.*;

and materialism, **7** 33; **8** 705; **10** 352; **11** 541; **15** 46, 70; **16** 41, 50; **18** 1074, 1150;

and memories, **18** 593;

misunderstandings of, **4** 375;

and morality, **7** 28–30; **15** 48;

on Moses, **15** 67;

on myth(s), **5** 28, 396;

on narcissism, **6** 810;

neurosis theory, **4** 216, 558–61, 583; **5** 190*n*, 655; **7** 33, 256; **9i** 113, 159; **11** 492; **16** 66, 256; **18** 1030, 1042, 1480;

and "nothing-but" explanation, *see* "nothing-but" *s.v.*;

and number symbolism, **4** 129;

and objective side, **18** 367;

on obsessional neurosis, **2** 726; **18** 922;

and occultism, **10** 530;

on Oedipus complex, **3** 564; **4** 351–2; **9i** 259*n*; **10** 658–9; **14** 107; **17** 97; **18** 1261, 1492;

onesidedness of, **15** 56–7; **17** 180; **18** 1067, 1069;

on overdetermination, **3** 133; **4** 44;

on paranoia, **3** 61 (*see also below* CASES: paranoid woman; Schreber);

and parental complex, **4** 307;

personalism of, **5** (*p*xxiv); **11** 452; **16** 381*n*;

on personal nature of psyche, **9i** 91, 540;

and pleasure principle, **7** 58; **8** 95; **10** 340, 658; **15** 57; **16** 24, 76, 151, 234; **17** (*p*3), 203; **18** 1150;

"polymorphous-perverse" concept of childhood, **4** 228; **17** (*p*5);

on preconscious, **18** 111;

on primal horde, **5** 396;

on primitive mind, **18** 1298;

psychoanalytic method, **2** 660–2, 761, 765–6; **3** 298; **7** 2/410, 293; **8** 93; **9ii** 316*n*; **10** 169, 173, 350, 658, 842; **11** 531, 540; **15** 44, 52, 56; **16** 115; **17** 99, 180; **18** 1146;

psychology, **6** 601; **10** 186; **15** 44–7, 144, 179; **17** (*p*3), 156; **18** 276;

on psychology of the individual, **3** 406;

psychology of instinct, **6** 88; **8** 104;

reductive causalism/causality of, **5** (*p*xxiii); **6** 88, 716, 788, 880; **7** 44, 58, 88, 113; **8** 40; **10** 19; **11** 875; **15** 46, 103–4; **16** 146; **17** 195; **18** 1153 (*see also* reduction);

and reductive function of unconscious, **8** 497;

and regression, **4** 367, 376–7;

on relationship to father, **4** 693–4, 728;

on religion, **9i** 140*n*; **10** 1042; **15** 47, 67; **16** 249; **18** 1455;

on repression, *see* repression *s.v.*;

on resistance, **2** 859;

on screen memories, **2** 658;

sectarianism of, **18** 1239;

on separation of pairs of opposites, **3** 427*n*;

and sexuality, his concept of, **3** (*p*4); **4** 49&*n*, 50–1, 215; **5** 190*n*, 193–4; **6** 91; **7** 3/411, 31, 39, 199, 466; **8** 35, 40, 54, 105–7; **9i** 61; **9ii** 357; **10** 5–6, 257, 340, 362, 659; **11** 507, 517, 541; **14** 98; **15** 45–6; **16** 1, 39, 115, 241, 340; **17** 156–8, 180, 282; **18** 493, 1150;

sexual trauma theory of, **3** 140; **4** 36–7, 205–9, 213–16, 224, 559; **7** 8/417, 10/419, 13/422, 293; **8** 46; **10** 362; **15** 63; **16** 33–4; **18** 1042; criticism of, **4** 299–302;

and shadow-side, **10** 353; **11** 531, 941; **14** 342; **16** 145, 173; **18** 1830;

static view of, **18** 126;

on sublimation, **3** 105*n*; **10** 365; **11** 541; **15** 53; **16** 328;

on super-ego, **4** 760, 781; **9i** 2*n*; **10** 659, 828, 830–1; **11** 390, 393, 396; **14** 673; **16** 245; **18** 1152;

on symbols, **5** 332; **6** 93*n*, 201; **8** 366; **13** 396;

on symptomatic action, **1** 170; **2** 733*n*; **3** 92, 449; **6** 821; **10** 50;

therapy of, **3** (*p*4);

three-dimensional, **18** 115;

totem and taboo theory of, **18** 1074;

and transference, **4** 427, 657; **6** 486, 860; **7** 58, 94*n*, 206, 256; **14** 751; **16** 10, 41, 139, 276, (*p*164), 358&*n*, 359*n*, 381*n*; **17** 260; **18** 310, 324, 351, 1151, 1162, 1278; technique of handling, **16** 358&*n*;

and transference-neurosis, **16** 357&*nn*;

and unconscious, **4** 318–19, 760; **7** 202/443, 205, 212, 247; **8** 141, 210, 372–3, 383, 397*n*, 398, 676; **9i** 2&*n*, 492–3, 513; **10** 3, 50, 352; **11** 531, 540–1, 875; **16** 51, 61, 65, 328; **17** 128–9; **18** 121, 123–

5, 273, 280, 281, 607, 893, 1223–4;

  derivation from conscious, **18** 14;

on unconscious contents, **18** 1150;

on unconscious motives, **5** 37;

on wish-fulfilment, **7** 21; **15** 64;

on youth trauma, **2** 717;

see also psychoanalysis;

CASES:

  Dora, **4** 25*n*;

  Little Hans, **5** 277; **17** 2, 7, 9, 38, 47, 52 (*see also below* WORKS: "Analysis of a Phobia in a Five-Year-Old Boy");

  Lucy R., **4** 213;

  paranoid woman, **3** 61–72;

  rat-man, **18** 1056;

  Schreber, **3** 389, 408, 411; **4** 271; **5** 185*n*, 192*n*, 458*n*;

WORKS:

  "Analysis of a Phobia in a Five-Year-Old Boy," **2** 1013*n*, 1014*n*; **4** 730*n*; **5** 26*n*, 76*n*, 277*n*, 370*n*; **17** 1*n* (*see also above* CASES: Little Hans);

  "The Antithetical Meaning of Primal Words," **3** 427;

  "Beyond the Pleasure Principle," **7** 33*n*;

  "Character and Anal Erotism," **4** (*p*76);

  Civilization and its Discontents, **17** 200*n*;

  "Creative Writers and Day-Dreaming," **5** 28*n*;

  "The Defence Neuropsychoses," **4** 32, 36;

  "Delusions and Dreams in Jensen's *Gradiva,*" **15** 155*n*;

  "The Dynamics of the Transference," **5** 652*n*;

  Early Psycho-Analytic Publications, **7** 411*n*;

  The Ego and the Id, **4** 782;

  "Five Lectures on Psycho-Analysis," **2** (*p*439*n*); **4** 154*n*, 205*n*;

WORKS (*cont.*):
Die Suggestion und ihre Heilwirkung, **17** 128*n*;

*   *

Freudlicher,—, **18** 57
Freusberg,—, **3** 1–3;
"Über motorische Symptome bei einfachen Psychosen," **3** 1*n*
Frey/Freya/Freia, **5** 421; **18** 1077;
god of fertility, **5** pl. XI*b*;
sword of, **8** 966*n*
Frey-Rohn, L., **8** 896, 936*n*, 989; **18** 1177
Fribourg, Bishop of, **18** 616
Frictes, *see* Socrates, pseudo-
Friday: day of Redeemer's, and Adam's, death, **14** 555;
day of Venus, **13** 301
Friedenskaiser, **10** 452
Friedländer, G., *see under* Eliezer ben Hyrcanus
Friedländer, S.: *Jugend,* **5** 140*n*;
friend(s), **9i** 238;
dreamer's, **12** 162, 252;
Khidr as, **9i** 251–2;
lapis as, **12** 155;
of man, **5** 522&*n*; Hiawatha as, **5** 476;
mother as, *see* mother *s.v.*;
two/pair of, **9i** 218, 253–4, 256, 258
friendship, **9i** 164;
homosexual, **10** 220;
of Mithras and sun-god, **9i** 235;
patient's, for analyst, **4** 663;
platonic, **7** 180; **10** 225, 227;
of two birds, **9i** 218
Friends of God, **11** 474, 484
Frigg, **5** 422
fright, *see* fear/fright
frigidity, sexual, **10** 217; animus and, **10** 246
Frisch, K. von, **8** 956–7;
The Dancing Bees, **8** 956*n*
Fritsch,—, investigation of malingerers, **1** 303

preface to W. Stekel, *Nervöse Angstzustände und ihre Behandlung,* **18** (*p*390*n*)

frivolity, and evil, **9ii** 114
Frobenius, L., **5** 387; **8** 474; **17** 219*n*; **18** 1140;
on clashing (and magic) rocks, **5** 367*n*;
on missing limbs, **5** 356*n*;
on mythological journeys, diagram of, **5** 309–10;
on night sea journey, **5** 308–11; **7** 160; **12** 440; imprisonment during, **5** 308, 374; loss of hair in, **11** 348; **12** 440; slipping out (of fish), **5** 309, 310, 311; **6** 444; and sun-gods, **5** 307–8;
on transitus, **13** 133;
on whale-dragon, **5** 369, 374&*n*, 526*n*, 538*n*; **8** 68; **9ii** 173;
WORKS:
Schicksalskunde, **9i** 552*n*;
Das Zeitalter des Sonnengottes, **4** 478; **5** 248*n*, 289*n*, 291*n*, 298*n*, 321*n*, 352*n*, 362*n*, 369*n*, 392*n*, 396*n*, 487*n*, 526*n*, 528*n*, 538*n*, 574*n*, 579*n*, 662*n*, 681*n*; **6** 444*n*; **7** 160*n*; **8** 68*n*; **9ii** 173*n*; **12** 416*n*, 440*n*; **13** 133*n*; **14** 277*n*; **16** 455*n*; **17** 219*n*
Froboese-Thiele, F.: *Träume—eine Quelle religiöser Erfahrung?,* J.'s foreword, **18** 1581–3
frog, *see* ANIMALS *s.v.*
Fromer, J., and M. Schnitzer: *Legenden aus dem Talmud,* **11** 406*n*
Fromm, E., **18** (*p*634*n*), 1584;
Psychoanalysis and Religion, **18** 1584*n*
frontier, dreams of, **16** 307–10, 546–8; **18** 346–7
fructificatio, **9ii** 139
fructification of Virgin Mary, *see* Mary *s.v.*

fruit(s), **13** 76, 350;
-bearing tree, *see* tree(s) *s.v.*;
first, **11** 387;
forbidden, **13** 400;
and herbs of paradise, **13** 403*n*;
holy, **13** 68;
pregnancy by swallowing, **17** 43-5;
sun-and-moon, *see* tree(s) *s.v.*;
see also pomegranate
fruitfulness: concept of, in Mithraic sacrifice, **5** 354, pl. XXXIII; **8** 333;
spiritual, **5** 78
frumentum nostrum, lapis as, **13** 408
frustrations, **17** 224
fugitive slave, *see servus fugitivus*
fugues, **3** 105
Fuhrmann, E.: *Reich der Inka,* **5** pl. LII
Fuhrmann, M., **2** 501-6, 539;
Analyse des Vorstellungsmaterials bei epileptischen Schwachsinn, **2** 501*n*;
"Über acute juvenile Verblödung," **3** 9*n*
fulfilment/Fulfilment, **13** 65, 72-82;
great, **10** 423
fulmination, metallic, **13** 190*n*
fulness of life, **12** 18, 296-7;
in dream, **12** 293
function(s)/functional, **5** 261; **6** 731 (Def.); **7** 237, 305, 505; **10** 657; **16** 59;
TITLE: "The Function of Religious Symbols," **18** 560-77;
adaptation, **7** 81, 507(2);
biological, **8** 368; by differentiated function, *see* adaptation *s.v.*;
of anima/animus, *see* anima, animus *s.v.*;
archaic, **6** 149, 503; **7** 520; **8** 65;
and archetypes, *see* archetype(s) *s.v.*;
and attitudes, *see* attitude(s) *s.v.*;

auxiliary/secondary, **6** 666-9; **12** 137, 192, 197, 295;
Christianity and, *see* Christianity *s.v.*;
collective, **6** 111, 113, 306; **7** 235/455, 456*n*; **18** 1101;
sensation/thinking as, **6** 176;
compensatory, **10** 25-7, 446; **15** 152-3;
conscious, **7** 63; and adaptation to reality, **7** 462*n*; **8** 64-5, 67;
subjective components of, **18** 40;
in consciousness, **18** 20, 75;
counter-, **7** 85;
creative, **17** 206;
cross of, **18** 29;
devaluation of, **3** 324;
differentiated, **6** 84, 171, 446, 666, 898, 905, 953; **7** 267, 360; **9i** 431; **10** 657, 677-8, 751; **12** 137, 148, 192, 197; **16** 393, 490; **18** 830; adaptation by, *see* adaptation *s.v.*; autonomy of, **10** 657; of extravert, **6** 575; identification with, **6** 109, 161-2, 344-5, 739; and inferior/undifferentiated, **8** 64; **9ii** 305; **11** 184, 244-5;—, harmony/unity with, **6** 105, 130-1, 301, 314, 471-2; **7** 360; **9i** 541;—, suppression of, **6** 93, 105, 109, 112, 167; onesidedness of, **7** 504, 505;
differentiation of, and culture, **6** 105-9, 113, 123;
directed ("valuable"), **6** 502-4;
disturbance(s) of, **4** 278; **5** 194;
psychological, and degeneration, **3** 318;
dominating, **8** 588; **10** 657;
domination and repression of, **7** 505;
ectopsychic, **18** 21;
endopsychic, **18** 37, 39, 40, 77;
Epimethean, **6** 592;
evolution of, from reproductive instinct, **4** 279; **5** 194;

function (*cont.*):

feeling, **6** 7, 899–900, 953, 983; **7** 64*n*, 347, 462*n*, 505; **9i** 541*n*; **10** 626, 657, 774; **11** 184, 245–6; **12** 150, 204; **13** 207; **14** 330, 332–4; **16** 77*n*, 486; **18** 23, 24, 28, 89; and adaptation, **8** 64; of evaluation/value, **8** 17, 256, 441; **9ii** 61; **18** 45, 58, 502; inferior, **18** 185;—, of extraverted intuitive type, **6** 613;—, of extraverted thinking type, **6** 588–9;—, in Germans, **18** 96; and intellect, **8** 600; rational, **18** 57, 502; specific content of, **6** 730; and thinking, **18** 29;

four basic/orienting psychological, of consciousness, **4** 763; **6** 7, 14, 28, 900–1, 953, 958, 983–4; **7** 63, 64*n*, 235; **8** 256–7; **9i** 430, 565, 582; **9ii** 409, 410; **10** 626, 738, 774; **11** 184, 245, 246, 281; **12** 137, 192, 195, 287, *fig.* 49; **13** 111, 207; **14** 261, 265, 272, 276, 557; **16** 77*n*, 236, 405, 486; **18** 53, 89, 110, 269, 1157, 1601; antitheses and, **8** 259; and colours, *see* colour(s) *s.v.* psychological significance of; equally differentiated, **18** 211, 212; of extravert, **6** 567, 577; fourth, *see below* inferior; gods as, *see* god(s) *s.v.*; and introvert, **6** 913; as quaternity, **9ii** 305, 398; **14** 261; Scaiolae as, **13** 215; and types, **7** 64*n*; **8** 258; **13** 111; **16** 236;

God as, *see* God *s.v.*; guiding, and energy, **7** 216; Holy Ghost as, *see* Holy Ghost *s.v.*;

hypertrophy of, **6** 105;

immature and developed, **4** 261;

indirect failure of, **3** 497;

inferior/feminine/fourth/re-

pressed/undifferentiated, **6** 149–50, 175, 763–4 (Def.), 905–8, 953, 955–6; **7** 85–6, 359, 360; **9i** 222, 430–1, 434, 582; **11** 130&*n*, 184, 245; **12** 31, 137, 145, 150, 192–3, 201, 220, 295; **14** 282, 288; **18** 35, 36, 1653; autonomy of, **7** 85; **11** 292; **14** 272; as dark side of personality/ shadow, **9i** 222, 439; **12** 240; **14** 257, 276; of extravert, **6** 164, 575–6; of extraverted thinking type, **6** 587–8; need to accept/ develop, **6** 113–15, 130, 444, 504; soul and, **6** 306; and symbol, **6** 453; and the unconscious, **6** 171; **18** 212;

intellectual, **7** 110, 206; **12** 88, 166;

intuition, **6** 7, 610–11, 899–900, 953, 983; **7** 64*n*, 505; **8** 257, 292; **10** 626, 657, 774; **11** 245–6; **13** 207; **16** 77*n*, 492; as inferior function, **9i** 541;

of the irrational, **7** 150;

Janet on, *see* Janet *s.v. fonction du réel*;

libido and, **4** 280; **8** 91;

loss of, hysterical, **9i** 213;

and meaning, **4** 688;

mediating, **6** 171;

mental, **7** 110, 456; higher, **13** 174*n*; personal, **7** 455;

moral, **7** 498, 501*n*;

nation as (Keyserling), **10** 922;

neurosis and, **5** 26*n*;

nutritive: importance of, **4** 237–42; libido and, **4** 290; and pleasure, **4** 239; in presexual stage, **4** 262, 263; and sexual, **4** 238, 291; **10** 5;

opposition between, **6** 171–4, 325;

pairs of, **9i** 541*n*;

perceptive, **7** 507(2);

polarity of, **12** 300;

primary and secondary (Gross on), **6** 463–7, 468, 471–83, 879;

psychic, **7** 219, 237; **8** 63, 375–9, 702; **9i** 150, 260, 430–1, 565; **11** 759; **12** 88; **13** 8, 208, 215; **16** 77, 486; automatization of, **1** 158; in unicellular organisms, **8** 233;

psychological, **4** 682; **6** 7; **7** 505; **18** 27; God as, **7** 110;

quaternity of, *see above* four;

rational, **9ii** 52; **18** 23;

reality, **6** 171; **7** 469; disturbance of, **5** 200; and sexuality, **4** 278;

reflex, **9ii** 369;

of relationships, *see* relationship *s.v.*;

religious, **4** 781; **6** 231*n*, 411, 529; **7** 150; **16** 99; **18** 560–77; of soul, **12** 14;

of religious symbols, **18** 560–77;

self-regulating, **6** 370;

sensation, **6** 7, 899–900, 953, 983; **7** 64*n*; **8** 256, 863; **9i** 541&*n*, 582&*n*, 588&*n*; **10** 626, 657, 774; **11** 245–6; **13** 207; **16** 77*n*, 486; **18** 21, 24, 28, 53, 89, 502; and frigidity, **10** 217; and intuition, **10** 918; **18** 30;

sense-: and consciousness, **8** 367;—paralysis of, **1** 21;

sensory, *see* Paradise, four rivers of;

sexual, **7** 471; **17** (*p*5) (*see also above* nutritive;

social, **7** 235/455;

spiritual, and infantile sexuality, **17** (*p*5);

subjective components of, **18** 90;

superior, **9i** 431; and inferior, **9i** 541;

symbol-creating, **6** 171; **10** 25, 27, 34;

of symbols, **4** 680; **5** 343*n*; **8** 92; **9i** 103;

as "teleological" concept, **4** 688;

thinking, **6** 7, 158–9, 162, 830,

899–900, 981, 983–4; **7** 63, 64*n*, 505; **8** 256; **9i** 541*n*; **10** 774; **11** 184, 244–6; **13** 207; **16** 77*n*; **17** (*p*5), 79; **18** 22, 24, 28–9, 89, 502; as inferior, repressed function, **6** 598, 600, 613; and adaptation, **8** 64, 67; differentiated, **6** 953; and feeling, **18** 29; in Goethe, **11** 244; **12** 204; medical man and, **8** 526;

transcendent(-al), *see* transcendent function;

triads of, **9i** 579*n*; **9ii** 100*n*;

-types, **6** 103, 248, 556, 835, 902, 985; **8** 258; **18** 503, 1130, 1259; (*see also* type(s) *s.vv.* feeling; intuitive; sensation; thinking);

unifying, of creative fantasy, **7** 490;

universal, **7** 267

functioning: collective, **7** 239, 462*n*, 514, 519;

individual, **7** 239, 459;

mental, **7** 235/455

funeral: monuments, **11** 855;

rites, **16** 215

Funk, P.: *Ignatius von Loyola*, **8** 395*n*

"funny," child's use of term, **17** 23–4

Fürer,—, **2** 116*n*

"Furies," *see* Erinyes

furnace, **12** 338*n*, 404, *figs.* 2, 113, 119; **13** *fig.* B4; **16** 538*n*;

fiery, **5** 243–5; **9ii** 188*n*; **11** 122*n*; **12** 449, *fig.* 184;

great book of, **12** 456;

sacred, **16** 507;

three youths in, **12** *fig.* 184

furor teutonicus, **10** 388; **17** 284

furrow, **5** 291*n*, 306, 528; **12** 63;

cohabitation in, **16** 340;

symbol of woman, **5** 527

Fürst, E., **2** 886*n*, 999&*n*, 1001; **4** 309, 695–9; **8** 228;

"Statistical Investigations on Word Associations and on Fa-

G

Gabal, *see* Cabala *s.v.*
Gabbatha (Golgotha), **14** 556
Gabir, *see* ALCHEMICAL WRITERS: Geber
Gabricus/Gabritius/Thabritius, and Beya, **11** 164; **13** 124, 125; **14** 2, 16*n*, 18*n*, 23, 31, 57, 64, 140, 181, 316*n*, 365*n*, 409, 547; **16** 455, 457;
    death of, **12** 436, 437, 449;
    gestation in brain, **12** 435, 496;
    hierosgamos of, **5** 676;
    incest, **5** 676; **12** 193*n*, 355, 436, 439&*n*, 450, 496, *fig.* 225; **14** 14, 381; **16** 453, 467;
    rebirth, **12** 436, 449, 498;
    in triple glass house, **12** 437, 449; **16** 455;
    variant spellings of, **12** 435*n*; **14** 31
Gabriel, **11** 681; **14** 570, 575, 584
Gachnang, von, family crest, **12** *fig.* 243
Gaedechens, R.: *Der marmorne Himmelsglobus,* **9ii** 147*n*
Gaia, **5** 265, 577; **14** 734
gaiety, aggressive, **3** 105
Gaillac, **10** 668
gain, lust for, **8** 236
gait of Americans, **10** 956
galactophagy, **11** 314
Galatea (Goethe's *Faust*), **9i** 680; **12** 243; **13** 220
Galatians, Epistle to, *see* BIBLE: N.T.
galaxy(-ies), **10** 635, 636
Galen, Claudius, **14** 156; **16** 22;
    on four temperaments, **6** 883–4, 960;
    Paracelsus on, **13** 150; **15** 19, 24;
    pseudo-, on *arbor philosophica,* **13** 374*n*; **14** 157&*n*
    De simplicium medicamentorum facultatibus, **13** 171*n*; **14** 87*n*, 157*n*

Galilee, marriage in (Pordage), **16** 508
Galileo, **4** 230; **5** 195; **8** 861; **9ii** 63; **10** 1020
Gall, F. J., **3** 323; **6** 917
Galla Placidia, **12** *fig.* 18
Galli, **11** 718*n*
Gallican liturgy, **11** 321
Galton, F., **1** 479; **2** 569, 730, 868, 1079;
    "Psychometric Experiments," **2** 569*n*, 730*n*, 868*n*, (*p*270)
galvanic:
    TITLE: "Further Investigations on the Galvanic Phenomenon and Respiration in Normal and Insane Individuals," **2** 1180–1311;
    reflex, *see* psychophysical *s.v.*
galvanometer:
    TITLE: "Psychophysical Investigations with the Galvanometer and Pneumograph in Normal and Insane Individuals," **2** 1036–1179;
    Deprez-d'Arsonval, **2** 1015, 1043, 1045, 1181;
    Meissner and Meyerstein, **2** 1038;
    technique of use, **2** 1018–24, 1038–45, 1181
galvanometer experiments: in alcoholism, **2** 1033, 1271–81;
    association with, **2** 1079–1179;
    coughing in, **2** 1047;
    emotion in, **2** 1049–50, 1054–5;
    in epilepsy, **2** 1232–46;
    expectation in, **2** 1048;
    latent time, **2** 1056, 1074–7;
    in mental disorders, **2** 1045, *fig.* 8, 1066–78, 1157–79, 1230–1311;
    reaction-time in, **2** 1020, 1092–1117, 1125–79;

galvanometer (*cont.*):
    repetition in, **2** 1054–5;
    respiration in, **2** 1047, 1059–
    64, 1197–1217;
    of Tarchanoff, **2** 1035, 1038–
    43, 1048, 1056, 1179, 1181;
    of Veraguth, **2** 1015–17, 1043,
    1181, 1182*n*
galvano-psychophysical reflex, *see*
    psychophysical galvanic reflex
Gamaliel the Elder, **9ii** 175*n*
Game, Margaret, **18** (*pp*3,4)
Gamelion, wedding month, **5** 363
game of dice, *see* dice
gametes, reduction in number, **4**
    279
gamonymus (Paracelsus), **13** 171,
    198; **14** 663, 689; see also *hieros-
    gamos*
Gamow, G.: *Atomic Energy*, **9ii** 411*n*
gana (loss), in South America, **9i**
    213*n*; **17** 204*n*;
    -world, **10** 937
Ganesha, **10** 989
ganglia: basal, **3** 582*n*;
    ganglion cells, **8** 607;
    in insects, **8** 955–6
Ganser, S., **1** 226, 296;
    on hysterical ailments, **1** 349;
    and "senseless answers," **1** 278,
    279, 320;
    syndrome, **1** 349, 354; **2**
    (*p*252); **3** 164*n*, 179, 271; **18**
    999, 1000;
    twilight states of prisoners, **1**
    278–9, 302, 320, 337; **2** 657;
    "Über einen eigenartigen hys-
    terischen Dämmerzustand," **1**
    278*n*, 349*n*
Ganz, H.: *Das Unbewusste bei Leibniz
    in Beziehung zu modernen Theorien*,
    7 159*n*
Gaokerena, *see* TREES *s.v.*
Garbe, R.: *Die Samkhya Philosophie*,
    9i 158*n*
garbha griha, **9ii** 339*n*
garden, **9i** 156; **12** 154;
    ascetic, **13** 407*n*;

of the gods, **5** 364;
of Hesperides, **12** 457*n*;
Mary as, *see* Mary *s.v.*;
of philosophers, **13** 407;
philosophical, **12** 155, 235,
    338*n*;
of spices, **13** 389;
symmetrical, **11** 90;
walled/enclosed, **8** 558; **12** 257,
    figs. 84, 245;
see also *hortus*
Garden of Eden, **11** 291, 438, 579,
    619; **13** 400, 420;
    see also Paradise
Garden of Gethsemane, *see* Geth-
    semane
Gargantua, **5** 311*n*
Gargaros, **9ii** 322*n*
Garlandia, Joannes de, **16** 498*n*
Garlandus, **14** 320*n*
garment, purple, **13** (*p* 62)
Garnerius of St. Victor, **9ii** 192*n*; **11**
    161*n*;
    *Sancti Victoris Parisiensis Gre-
    gorianum*, **9ii** 158&*n*; **14** 46*n*
garnet, **9i** 537
Garotman, anus of, **13** 269
Garrett, E. J., **8** 838
Garuda Purana, *see* Puranas *s.v.*
gas(es), **13** 262, 434;
    poison, **13** 358*n*; **18** 1306
Gast, Peter, *see* Nietzsche: *Thus
    Spake Zarathustra*
gastro-enteritis, **3** 180*n*
gate(s)/Gate: attribute of Virgin
    Mary, **5** 577*n*; **12** *fig.* 26;
    of city, four, **12** 139&*n*; **13**
    212&*n*; twelve, **12** 138;
    of Hades, **5** 577;
    strait, **9ii** 312&*n*;
    of Victory (India), **10** 983
Gateway of India, **10** 983
"Gathering, House of the," **12** 293,
    295, *fig.* 93
Gatschet, A. S.: "The Klamath In-
    dians of South-Western Oregon,"
    8 92*n*
Gatti, A.: *South of the Sahara*, **5** 452*n*

genius (*cont.*):
 unconscious dynamism of, **1**
 184; **3** 135*n*; **15** 157; **17** 248
Gensha (Buddhist), **11** 878
Gentiles, **7** 264; **11** 576;
 gods of, **13** 176*n*;
 numen of, **11** 576
gentleman, English, **10** 974, 976
Genza (holy book of the Mandaeans), **14** 566*n*
Geoffrey of Monmouth: *Histories of
 the Kings of Britain,* **14** 357*n*
geomancy, **13** 154;
 Rubeus in, **14** 704*n*
geomantic experiments, **8** 986
geometria, **8** 933
geometry/geometrical, **8** 935;
 pattern, of mandala symbol, **13**
 33;
 progression, **11** 181–2;
 symbols of self, **9i** 315; **9ii** 358;
 11 276
George, St., **18** 1527
George, Stefan, **10** 375&*n*
Georgian fairytale, *see* fairytales; IN-
 STANCES *s.v.* Caucasian/Georgian
Gerard of Borgo San Donnino, **9ii**
 137
Gerbenstein, U. von (somnambulistic personality), **1** 51, 57, 62, 63,
 71, 132, 134
Gerbert of Rheims, *see* Sylvester II
Gerhardt, O., **9ii** 130;
 Der Stern des Messias, **9ii** 128*nn,*
 130*n*
Gering, H., **5** 170*n*
germ, golden, **9i** 664, 674
German Congress for Experimental
 Psychology (Würzburg, 1906), **2**
 1015, 1043*n*
Germanic: Christ as, **10** 389;
 hanging rites, **5** 349, 399;
 man, Faustian split in, **13** 70;
 peoples, **9ii** 272;
 sacred trees, **5** 368*n*;
 soul, **9i** 254;
 tribes, and Christianity, **9i** 25;
 11 82;

unconscious, tensions in, **10**
 354, 447–8;
 women, Tacitus on, **7** 296&*n*
Germany/German(s), **4** 354, 373,
 687; **7** 440; **8** 359; **9i** 227; **10**
 389–94, 452–60; **18** 96, 369, 372,
 1311, 1322–3, 1368, 1371, 1375;
 alchemists, **18** 17;
 army, **4** 730*n*;
 Christians, **16** 20;
 and classical culture, **6** 110;
 and collective guilt, **18** 1609;
 collective hysteria, **10** 419,
 424–8;
 collective unconscious, **10** 448;
 and coloured man, **10** 963;
 critics, **4** 184;
 and dream symbols of violence,
 10 447–9;
 Faith movement, **10** 397&*n*; **16**
 20;
 folklore, devil in, **5** 421;
 France and, **18** 92–3;
 Freudian theory and, **4** 156,
 215;
 Gleichschaltung, **10** 1018–20,
 1060;
 Gnosticism in, **10** 169;
 inferiority feelings in, **10** 417;
 18 1385, 1389;
 Keyserling and, **10** 908;
 language, **2** 10–11; **18** 24, 26,
 59, 184, 311, 407; colloquial, **5**
 212;
 legends, of hero and snake, **5**
 593; of saviour's birth, **5** 368*n*;
 and mass psychology, *see* psychology *s.v.* mob/mass;
 national character of, **18** 1382;
 national keynote, **10** 973;
 Nazism in, *see* National
 Socialism;
 paganism in, **11** 44;
 philosophy, **8** 359, 360; **18** 124;
 political tensions in, **15** (*p*132);
 primitivity of, **18** 581;
 psyche, *see* psyche *s.v.*;
 psychiatry, **3** 322;

psychic phenomena in, **8** 430;
psychological problem of, **10** 458–85;
psychology, *see* psychology *s.v.*;
psychopathology in, **10** 2;
Reich, *see* Reich;
sentimentality of, **18** 95, 351;
southern, **18** 264;
S. S. in, **18** 1336, 1378;
and triadic mandalas, **10** 775; **18** 1609;
and victims, **10** 398;
Wotan and, **10** 389

germinal vesicle, **13** 33, 34, *figs.* A8, A9

germination, and birth of stone, **13** 392

Gerry, P., **18** (*p*692*n*)

Gerster, G., **10** 591*n*; **18** (*p*626*n*)

Geryon, **5** 265, 288; **9ii** 330; **14** 652;
oxen of, **5** 250, 288; **12** 457*n*;
of threefold body, **12** 550, 551; **14** 652

Gesangbuch der evangelisch-reformierten Kirchen . . . , **6** 437*n*
see also *Lyra Germanica*

"Gessler," association-chain, *see* association-chain(s) *s.v.*

Gessmann, G. W.: *Die Geheimsymbole der Alchymie, Arzneikunde, und Astrologie des Mittelalters,* **9i** 537*n*

Gessner, C., **12** 462*n*; **13** 154, 165; **15** 21–3;
Epistolarum medicinalium Conradi Gessneri, **13** 154*n*, 165*n*; **15** 21*n*

Gestalt psychology, **16** 245

Gestapo, **10** 464

gesture, use of, **2** 526, 536, 541

Gethsemane: Christ's prayer in, **11** 395, 659;
garden of, **13** 390

"getting stuck," **3** 416, 567; **4** 303, 405, 408, 424, 449, 536; **8** 847; **9i** 82, 525, 561; **11** 276, 292, 843, 900; **16** 85, 218, 319, 342, 488, 490, 545, 549; **17** 226, 296;
of soul, **12** 11;

universalism and, **12** 36

Geulincx, A., **8** 860, 948; **10** 593;
Metaphysica vera, **8** 860*n*, 937*n*

Gevartius, J. C., **14** 67, 96;
Electorum Libri III, **14** 96*n*

Ghana (Gold Coast), **8** 118

Ghāya al-hakīm, **11** 364–5

Ghazali, Al-: *Die kostbare Perle im Wissen des Jenseits,* **14** 587*n*

ghost(s), **8** 625; **9i** 396; **11** 20, 845; **18** 762, 784;
anima and, **13** 57–8;
explanation of, **18** 781;
fear of, **8** 681; **12** 437&*n*; **15** 149; **18** 759, 760;
haunted house, **18** 764–81;
haunting, **8** 598; **18** 784;
land of, **16** 455;
mother as (in dream), **7** 280;
primitive belief in, **6** 46; **8** 573, 598; **10** 140; **11** 245, 777, 800; **13** 66; **17** 312;
seleteni, see Elgonyi;
-stories, **9i** 268; **18** 758, 761, 781, 783–4;
as symbol, **18** 786;
-trap, *see* Elgonyi *s.v.*;
unconscious imago as, **8** 522

giant(s), **9i** 273*n*; **10** 603; **11** 669–70; **12** 469&*n*, 484, 543*n*, *fig.* 142BB; **13** 384*n*;
father as, in dream, **7** 211;
of twofold substance, **13** 267, 384*n*

gibberish, **1** 144*n*; **17** 224

gibbon, *see* ANIMALS *s.v.*

Gibil, *see* Girru

giddiness, **1** 6; *see also* fainting-fits

Gideon, *see* dew of Gideon

Giedion-Welcker, C.: *Neue Schweizer Rundschau,* **15** 165*n*

Gierlich, N.: "Über periodische Paranoia und die Entstehung der paranoischen Wahnideen," **3** 169*n*, 169*n*

gift(s): compensated by inferiority, **17** 245;
dangers of, **17** 244;

gift (*cont.*):
    diagnosis of, **17** 237;
    of head and heart, **17** 242;
    musical and mathematical, **17** 239;
    and pathological variant, **17** 245;
    relation to ego, **11** 390
"Gift of Love" (Miller), **5** 74, (*p*454);
    creation through, **5** 74
gifted child, *see* child(ren) *s.v.*
Gihon, **9ii** 311, 353, 372
Gikatila, J., **14** 158*n*;
    Shaare ora, **14** 19*n*
Gilbert, J. A., **18** (*p*767*n*);
    "The Curse of Intellect" (unpublished), J.'s preface, **18** 1725–6
Gilbert, S., **15** (*p*132);
    James Joyce's "Ulysses": A Study, **15** 166*n*, 170*n*, 186*n*, 191
Gilbert Islands, **13** 458*n*
Gilgamesh Epic, **5** 315*n*, 396, 506, 512*n*, 513, 552; **6** 346; **8** 209; **13** 425, 428; **18** 235–9;
    bull in, **18** 237, 238;
    Eabani/Enkidu in, **5** 288, 293, 506, 552, 659, 678; **9i** 253; **13** 425, 428; **18** 235–9, 1721;
    Gilgamesh, **5** 251*n*, 288, 293, 299*n*, 396, 450, 457, 459, 513, 642, 659, 678, pl. XIX; **18** 235–9;
    gods in, **5** 457; **11** 27, 28, 173, 176;
    heroic journey in, **5** 293;
    Humbaba, giant, in, **5** 396, 504; **18** 236, 246;
    Ishtar, **5** 396, 450, 577*n*; **13** 425; **18** 237–8;
    magic herb in, **5** 293, 513, 642, pl. XIX;
    regression in, **5** 506;
    sun-hero in, **5** 251*n*;
    Utnapishtim in, **5** 293, 513;
    Heidel, A.: *The Gilgamesh Epic and Old Testament Parallels*, **5** 293*n*;

Jensen, P.: *Gilgamesh-Epos*, **5** 251*n*, 293&*n*, 396*n*, 577*n*;
Schott, A.: *Das Gilgamesh-Epos*, **5** 293*n*;
Speiser, E. A., in Pritchard, ed., *Ancient Near Eastern Texts*, **5** 293*n*;
Thompson, R. C.: *The Epic of Gilgamish*, **5** 293*n*; **18** 235*n*
Gillen, F. J., *see under* Spencer, W. B.
Gillen, Otto: *Ikonographische Studien*, **12** *fig*. 65
Gilles de la Tourette, G., **1** 148*n*
Gilli, G.: *Der dunkle Bruder*, J.'s foreword, **18** 1742–7;
    "C. G. Jung in seiner Handschrift," **18** (*p*776*n*)
girl(s): death-wish, **5** 432;
    defence of innocence, **5** 69&*n*;
    and father-imago, **5** 62;
    hysteria in, **4** 384;
    Oedipus complex in, **4** 345;
    sacrificed to dragon, **5** 574;
    unconscious fantasies of 15-year-old, **5** 75 (*see also* Jung, CASES, vol. **1** case (2));
    unknown young, **9i** 311;
    virginity test, **5** 572;
    wanton, **12** 439*n*
Girru/Gibil, god of fire, **11** 176
Givry, G. de: *Le Musée des Sorciers*, **5** *fig*. 29
glacier, in dream, **12** 245
glands, **8** 652, 657, 658; **11** 493;
    genital, **4** 687;
    hormone-producing, **8** 233;
    instincts and, **8** 374;
    thyroid, **8** 794;
    see also endocrine, disorders
Glanville, Bartholomew de/Bartholomaeus Anglicus: *Le Propriétaire des choses*, **12** *fig*. 64
Glaphyra, **18** 243
glass, **14** 319, 404*n*;
    broken, **10** 123;
    filled with gelatinous mass, **12** 241–4;
    gold, *see* gold *s.v. aurum vitreum*;

-house, **16** 453, 455;
transparent, **13** 245; **14** 319;
tumbler, as "psychograph," **1**
45, 49;
see also *vitrum*
glasses (spectacles), **17** 225
Glauber, Johann, *see* ALCHEMICAL
WRITERS *s.v.*
Gleichschaltung, see Germany *s.v.*
Gley, M.E.E., **1** 82
globe(s), **9i** 682; **11** 90, 93, 109,
123; **12** 112, 116, 127, *figs.* 64,
165, 199;
black, **10** 758, 760;
luminous, **8** 396
globulus, **10** 811
globus hystericus, **8** 303
gloire, la, **10** 972
"Gloria mundi," *see* ALCHEMICAL
COLLECTIONS: *Mus. herm. s.v.;*
Theatr. chem. s.v.
glorified: body, *see* body *s.v.* glorifi-
cation of;
earth, **13** 410
Glory, king of, **13** 182
glory of the Lord, **11** 212
"Glory to God: A Dream Poem," *see*
Miller, Miss F. *s.v.*
glossolalia, **1** 144; **11** 433*n*; *see also*
Flournoy
Glover, A.S.B., **6** 379*n*, 392*n*, 393*n*;
9i 462*n*; **13** (*p*vi), 86*n*, 384*n*,
390*n*; **18** (*pp*589*n*, 673*n*, 679*n*)
Glover, E.: *Freud or Jung,* **18** (*p*706)
glue, **12** 244;
"of the world" (*glutinum mundi*),
12 209
gnomes, **4** 185; **13** *fig.* B5;
create Gulliver situation, **4** 185,
190
gnosis/Gnosis, **6** 14–16, 18, 25–6; **11**
202, 271*n*, 439, 861, **13** (*p*4); **18**
1647;
Barbelo, *see* Barbelo *s.v.*;
Cabalistic, **12** 414*n*;
Coptic, **11** 60;
of empirical method, **18** 1511;
of Justin, **9i** 552, 579*n*; **9ii**

366*n*; **12** 413; **13** 420; Baruch,
9i 560, 571; **13** 459;
Naassene, **9i** 665;
of Ophites, **11** 359;
as psychological/revealed
knowledge, **9ii** 350; **11** 81&*n*,
127, 272; **12** 28; **14** 257; loss of,
11 285;
and tree, **13** 419, 459
Gnosius, Dominicus, *see* ALCHEMI-
CAL WRITERS *s.v.*
Gnostic(s)-ism, **1** 149; **5** 487, 622; **6**
25–6, 347, 398, 409; **8** 102,
388*n*; **9i** 20, 37, 142, 324; **9ii** 80,
105, 148, 281, 302, 310; **11** 153,
160, 399, 438–9, 460, 841; **12** 40,
138, 209, 408, 410, 422*n*, 517; **13**
85, 273; **14** 41*n*, 42*n*, 46, 576*n*,
626*n*; **15** 10, 16; **16** 378*n*, 458; **18**
638, 1419, 1478–82, 1499;
TITLE: "Gnostic Symbols of the
Self," **9ii** 287–346;
and Adam, **9i** 560; **14** 570*n*,
589; as "cornerstone"/"rock"
(Naassene), **9ii** 143, 326; **14**
627 (*see also* Adamas);
and alchemy, *see* alchemy *s.v.*;
amulet, **12** *fig.* 204;
angels in, *see* angel(s) *s.v.*
"fatherly," "motherly";
Anthropos in, *see* Anthropos/
etc. *s.v.*;
archai, **13** 31;
archons, *see* archon(s) *s.v.*;
and assimilation, **18** 1516–17,
1827–8, 1830;
Christ-figure in, **9ii** 75*n*; **11**
228, 245*n*, 255, 263, 422,
445–6; **12** 314, 457; **13** 456; **14**
526; **16** 473; as Man and Son of
Man, **9i** 318; and Mary, *see*
Mary *s.v.* Gnostic; and Physis,
14 124; his shadow/*umbra*, **9ii**
75&*n*, 167, 171; **11** 245*n*, 263;
18 1617, 1633;
Christianity and, **6** 14–16, 30,
81; **11** 160, 431, 444; **12** 41,
453; **13** 236; **14** 455*n*, 643; **15** 16;

Gnostic (*cont.*):

"circular" thinking in, **11** 159*n*, 229*n*; **13** 110–11; **14** 123&*n*;

and collective unconscious, **18** 1480, 1501;

coniunctio in, **9i** 295, 297;

cross, **11** 433, 435;

demiurge, *see* demiurge *s.v.*;

and devil, **11** 255, 263;

dragon in, **14** 627;

l'Eglise gnostique de la France, **7** 385; **10** 169;

Elohim and Edem, *see* Elohim *s.v.*;

Eve in, *see* Eve;

and evil, **9ii** 75, 83, 171, 366; **10** 677; **18** 1642; dualism and, **11** 249;

Father in, "devoid of consciousness," **18** 1481;

"Father of All," as Bythos (abyss), **14** 8;

"Father-Mother," **13** 269*n*; **14** 220, 476*n* (*see also below* masculine-feminine);

four in, *see* Barbelo *s.v.* "God is four";

gem(s), **5** *fig.* 34; **9i** 573*n*; **12** *figs.* 52, 203, 253;

and gnosis, **11** 81*n*, 127;

God-image in, **8** 102; **9ii** 105, 299;

Holy Ghost in, **9ii** 141; **11** 236, 240; **14** 432, 701; as feminine, **18** 221;

hymn to the soul, **9i** 37–8;

in John's Gospel, **18** 1480, 1549, 1642;

Jung and, **11** 460; **18** 1499–1502, 1507, (*p*727), 1642–3, 1647;

Logos/*canis* parallel, **14** 174*n*;

and magnet, **9ii** 239, 288, 291–3, 295, 296;

Mary in, *see* Mary *s.v.*;

masculine-feminine / hermaphrodite in, **9i** 292; **10** 772; **14** 8, 327, 526 (*see also above* "Father-Mother");

modern, **7** 118; **10** 21, 169; **15** 91, 195;

morality, **18** 1629;

mysteries, **10** 21;

Naas, *see* Naas;

Nous in, **11** 276, 380;

ogdoad, *see* ogdoad *s.v.*;

Original/Primordial man, *see* Anthropos;

paradox in, **11** 417;

and peacock, **9i** 685;

and philosophical tree, **13** 242*n*, 422; "great," of Simon Magus, **13** 408;

"philosophoumena" of, **18** 1511;

philosophy of, **7** 104; **12** 41, 410 (*see also* Irenaeus);

pneumatikos and *sarkikos* in, **11** 153;

psychology/integration in, **9ii** 269, 347, 350; **11** 399, 444, 460; **12** 41; **13** (*pp*3–4), 408; **18** 1514, 1827–34;

quaternio, *see* quaternio/quaternity *s.v.*;

Reedemer/redemption, **9ii** 133, 287; **11** 133, 202; **12** 461; **13** 280; **14** 308; Naassene, **14** 146;

Saturn (Kronos) in, **11** 400; as Esaldaios, **9ii** 307, 325; as Ialdabaoth/supreme archon, **9ii** 128, 325; **11** 255, 350, 403, 607*n*; **13** 270*n*, 274–5, 276; **14** 476; in Peratic sect, **14** 257; "power of the colour of water" (Hippolytus), **9ii** 215; **13** 101&*n*, 274; as Primas, **11** 350; as "primus Anthropus," **9ii** 307; as Yahweh, **9ii** 128, 307; **11** 607*n*;

sects/schools/systems, **7** 104; **9ii** 267; **10** 21; **13** (*p*3); **14** 47; Antitactae and Encratites, **6** 25, 426 (*see also* Bardesanes; Basilides/Basilidians; Ebionites; Euchites; Mandaeans; Marcus; Naas/Naassenes; Ophites; Peratics; Sethians; Valentinians; Valentinus); and seeds of light, 8 388*n*; and serpent, *see* ANIMALS *s.v.*; and sin, 11 133; Sophia in, 6 398; 11 240; 14 498, 648*n*, 699; -Achamoth, 9ii 307*n*; 13 451–4; 14 576; and Christ, 12 487; as divine harlot, 6 317; Sapientia, 9i 93; 14 576; *spinther,* see *spinther;* symbol(ism), 9ii 306–8, 428; 12 518, 527; 16 458; and alchemical symbols, 12 40; of Paradise, *see* Paradise *s.v.*; of self, 9ii 358, 428; and syzygies, 9i 120, 142; "Trinity" in, 11 486; and unconscious, 9ii 298–9; 10 676; 11 440–1; 14 660; collective, 18 1480, 1501; symbolism and, 9ii 350; and unicorn, 12 527–9, 554; vessel/Grail in, 6 396–8, 401, 409; *see also* Bousset; King, C. W.; Matter; Schultz, W.

goal(s), 13 22, 27, 334, 354; 16 407; of alchemist, *see* alchemy *s.v.*: of analysis, *see* analysis *s.v.* aims; antithetical nature of, 16 533; conquest of anima as, 7 374; conscious, 7 346; death as, *see* death *s.v.*; of developmental process, 7 185; of dreams, 7 501*n*; of Eastern and Western religion, 11 958; of fantasies, 7 384; hermaphrodite as synonym for, 16 533; higher consciousness as, 7 87; highest, 13 34; as an idea, 16 400; images of, 12 328; 16 535;

of individual's development, 7 241/462; of individuation, *see* individuation *s.v.*; instinctive, 17 331; of life, 8 797, 803–4; first half of, 13 69; second half, 8 789; of man, wholeness as, 12 6, 36, 210, 328; Mercurius is, of his own transformation, 13 282; midpoint of personality as, 7 364; of opus, *see* opus *s.v.*; lapis as, see *lapis philosophorum s.v.* opus; psychic/of psyche, 7 346; 11 958; 12 3–4, 328; 13 36; of psychoanalysis, 4 640; 18 930; of psychotherapy, *see* psychotherapy *s.v.*; self as, 7 404; 11 960; sexual, 17 (*p*4); social, 8 772; spiritual, 5 674; 13 69; 16 486; necessity of, 17 159; symbols of, 12 35, 335; 16 398; of unconscious, 7 216

goat/goat-fish, *see* ANIMALS *s.v.*

Goblet d'Almellas, E., Count: *Migration of Symbols,* 8 228

goblets, *see* bowl(s)

goblins, 13 124; goddess of, 5 pl. XVI

Goclenius, Rodolphus: *Uranoscopiae, chiroscopiae, metoposcopiae,* 18 1818&*n*

God, 4 751, 783, 741*n*; 5 95, 283; 7 243*n*, 377, 394*n*, 395, 397, 427; 8 805; 9i 390; 9ii 300; 10 1020; 11 95, 142, 555, 561; 12 11, 15, 139, 214, 356, 456; 13 28, 50, 53, 75, 103, 113, 117*n*, 141, 146, 151, 164, 168, 201*n*, 244, 342, 395, 416, 433; 14 143, 781, 784; 17 298; TITLE: "Answer to Job," 11 560–758;

God (*cont.*):

766; liberation from, **12** 420, 451–2; projection into, **12** 432; male and female in, **13** 40; **14** 630*n*;

metaphysical, **18** 1511;

Mother of, *see* Mary;

as mother, *see* mother *s.v.*;

name of, four letter, **16** 497*n*, 533*n* (*see also* tetragrammaton): nationalist, **10** 397;

Nietzsche on, **11** 142, 145; **13** 163;

and "nothing-but" psychology, **11** 242*n*;

as Nothingness, **11** 893;

of Old and New Testament, **9ii** 299; **11** 358; **12** 522; **14** 375, 507, 781; **18** 1533–4, 1645; alchemical idea of, **11** 350; of New Testament, **9i** 18; paternalism in, **5** 89;

omnipotence of, **14** 785;

One, **13** 117*n*;

One and Many, **5** 423;

as one-horned/unicorn, **12** 521, 522; **13** 134;

ontological proof of (Anselm), **6** 59;

"outside" man, **12** 10, 12;

paradox/ambivalence of, **8** 103; **11** 738; **18** 1537–9, 1545, 1551, 1556, 1593, 1680–1;

pneuma and soma, **9ii** 400; **18** 1553;

as point, **14** 41;

polarity of, **12** 547;

positive and negative concept of, **11** 738&*n*;

presence of, **14** 374, 392;

as *prima materia*, **12** 431; **16** 533*n*;

as primal cause, **18** 1471;

primitive concept of, **7** 108;

as primordial experience, **5** 260; **11** 480;

as principle of existence, **11** 763;

projection and, **7** 333;

Prometheus and, **6** 296, 301;

psyche and, **11** 142; in collective unconscious, **17** 207; fear of, and, **17** 302;

psychic: in fact, **11** 751; factor, **11** 137; quantity, **11** 463;

as psychological function, *see* function(s);

quaternary vision of, **9ii** 397*n*; **11** 101 (*see also* NUMBERS: four);

as quaternity, *see* quaternity *s.v.*;

as reality, *see* reality *s.v.*;

-redeemer, **6** 297;

relationship/"relativity" of, **6** 411–15, 431–2; **7** 394*n*; **11** 279, 454;

renewal of, **6** 325–6;

as *res/res simplex*, **12** 372, 431; **13** 117*n*, 264;

right and left hands of, **9ii** 99, 107; **11** 470, (p358); **18** 1537;

Schiller's view of, **6** 141;

and self, **7** 399, 400; **10** 644; **14** 129*n*, 273, 558, 711; **18** 1419; -atman, **11** 956–7; -offering, in Mass, **11** 378;

self-transforming, **11** 146;

shadow of, **9ii** 183;

sons of, **13** 107; **14** 355, 704; **18** 1553; devil as, *see* devil *s.v.* God; Mercurius as second, **13** 271; **14** 22; quaternity of, **13** 366 (*see also* Son, The);

sonship of: double/two, *see* Ebionites; man's inclusion in, **11** 235; threefold, *see* Basilides; and Sophia/wisdom, *see* Sophia *s.v.*;

and soul, **6** 423–4, 428–9; **8** 677; **11** 124; **12** 11, 19, 215; as impulse of the soul, **13** 82; as master of souls, **13** 244; true, **13** 174; as vice-regent of, **12** 396;

speaks through dreams and visions, **18** 601, 603;

as sphere, **14** 41;

as Spirit/spirit of, **5** 583; **7** 217; **8** 102, 359, 653; **9i** 385, 394; **11** 152; **12** 313, 512; **13** 137, 171n; **14** 10; **18** 359;

and state, **10** 510;

as *summum bonum, see* Summum Bonum *s.v.*;

as sun, **5** 128, 135, 138, 163, 176, 178; **12** 445, *fig.* 181; **14** 130, 568n; in Augustine, *see* Augustine *s.v.* God; primitive view of, **8** 329, 411;

sun as eye of, **8** 394;

symbol(s)/symbolism, **6** 310; **9ii** 304; **13** 363; of symbols, **18** 657;

terrenus/terrestris, see *deus;*

is terrible, **18** 690;

as *tetraktys,* **11** 95;

as totality, **10** 622; **11** 740n;

transcendent, **14** 785;

transformation of, in Mass, **11** 338;

triadic conceptions of, **11** 222; Trinity, **11** 103, 289; threefold nature of, **12** 98;

as ultimate principle, **10** 864;

and the unconscious, **11** 757; unconsciousness of, **11** 560, 575, 597, 600, 638, 659;

unio mentalis in, see *unio mentalis;*

union with, **5** 102n, 339, 672; **13** 301n; **16** 381;

unity of, **12** 31; **13** 150; **14** 41; as value, **6** 417, 421;

vision of, **7** 217; **13** 477;

voice of, *see* voice/*vox s.v.* Dei; wager with, **7** 311;

will of/act of, **9ii** 48–51; **11** 524–5, 539; **12** 36n; **16** 393, 517; **18** 1627, 1637, 1667; and fate, **12** 36n;

"within," **6** 370; **11** 101, 105; word of, **13** 110, 116n, 148, 242n;

world as visible, **8** 927;

world-system and, **8** 677;

wrath of/wrathful, **7** 430; **12** 215; **13** 110; **16** 511, 513;

see also Godhead; God-image; Godless; God-man; God-substitute; Son, The; Yahweh/Jehovah

god(s)/divinity, **4** 350; **5** 133, 388, 438, 574; **6** 324, 435; **7** 105, 111, 150, 151, 164, 326, 389, 466; **9i** 356; **9ii** 321; **10** 394, 566; **11** 8; **12** 40&n, 246, 346; **13** 57, 66, 91, 130, 340n, 341; **14** 787;

absolute, **11** 771;

"accursed," *see* Celsus;

acknowledgement of, **13** 55–6;

of air, **9i** 702;

"all things full of," **8** 930;

ancient, degradation of, **9i** 26; **12** 84; **13** 49, 54; as unconscious powers, **9ii** 41;

androgyny of, **5** 662, *fig.* 19;

animal/theriomorphic attributes/representation, **5** 36, 144; **9ii** 55; **14** 601; ithyphallic, **9ii** 331; snake-, **14** 266;

archaic, **11** 571;

as archetypes, **9i** 50;

in Babylonian epics, *see* Babylon;

Buddha(-ism), and, **10** 1003; **13** 47; Tibetan, **11** 380, 791;

Celtic, **6** 401n;

child-, **9i** 259, 281; **18** 1552; as archetype, **9i** 268;

chthonic, **5** 183, 594; Mercurius as, *see* Mercurius *s.v.*; pair of, **12** 435n; seven (in *Faust*), **12** 204–5;

circle of, *see* circle *s.v.*;

company of, see below *paut neteru;*

and consciousness, **11** 231;

corn-, *see* corn *s.v.*;

of destruction and salvation, **14** 257, 274;

dismembered (Osiris), **13** 97;

doctor as, **7** 206, 214, 217;

god(s) (*cont.*):

dreams as messengers of, **7** 21/433;

dying, **9ii** 321; **11** 612, 641, 718; **18** 550; Christ as, **11** 146, 650; mother of, **11** 646; and rebirth/renewal, **5** 165, 175, 494, 526, 534–5; **6** 435; **18** 1566;

earth, **12** 240*n*;

eating of, **5** 522, 526&*n* (*see also* American Indians: NORTH: Aztec(s) *s.v. teoqualo*); as food, **8** 333;

and father-imago, **5** 63&*n*;

fire-, **9i** 106;

fish-, *see* ANIMALS: fish *s.v.*;

flaying of, **5** 594, 595; **13** 92;

four: faces, **13** 360; functions as, **7** 366–7; in vision, **7** 366; of Gentiles, **13** 176*n*;

and goddesses: bisexuality of, **5** 358; as libido-symbols, **5** 321–4; as opposites, **14** 655;

Greek, *see* Greece/Greek *s.v.*;

-hero, symbolized by spring zodion, **5** 596;

hidden, see *deus absconditus*;

hierosgamos of, see *hierosgamos s.v.*;

-images, archaic, **7** 217, 219, 248; **12** 12; Ufos as, **10** 622 (*see also* God-image);

as immortal part of man, **5** 296;

Indian, *see* India *s.v.*;

kinship with, **7** 398;

lapis as, **14** 607;

as libido-analogues, **8** 92;

of light, *see* light *s.v.*;

"metamorphosis of," **10** 1020;

names of, *see* name(s) *s.v.* god(s);

of nature, **13** 186*n*; pagan, **5** 113, 600*n*; Sol and Luna as, **13** 186 (*see also* deity *s.v.* nature);

and opposites, **7** 111, 113;

paut neteru (Egyptian), **12** 84;

of planets, *see* planets;

as psychic: factors, **9i** 49; **13** 54; forces, personified, **10** 387, 431;

and psychological change, agents of, **11** 20;

psychopompic, **18** 267;

quaternio of, **9ii** 397;

relativity of, **11** 140&*n*;

of revelation, **13** 219;

ritual communion with, **7** 159;

sacrifice and, **5** 650, 656; **11** 339; **13** 107*n*; **18** 1083; by hanging, **5** 349, 594;

seven, *see* planet(s); star(s);

solar/sun, *see* sun *s.v.*;

son-, **5** 392;

of spring, **18** 1083;

stone as birthplace of, **13** 128;

symbol(s)/-ism, **8** 92; of self, **9i** 315;

transformation: Greek, **8** 655; self-, **5** 389; through man, **5** 524, 612;

turned into philosophical ideas, **18** 756;

as the unconscious, **5** 457; **10** 681;

unconscious contents and, **11** 242;

unconscious need for, **18** 634;

world of, **13** 193;

yoga and, **13** 56;

see also Mithras; triad(s) *s.v.* Trinity

"God(god)-Almightiness," **10** 437; **12** 563; **18** 1643; *see also* inflation

Goddard, Air Marshall Sir Victor, **8** 983

goddess(es), **5** *fig.* 3; **9i** 579*n*; **6** 383, 398; **9ii** 24;

as anima, **9i** 61; matriarchal, **13** 131;

animal attributes of, **5** 421*n* (*see also* Hecate);

black, **14** 607;

earth (Mexican), **13** *fig.* 8;

of fate, *see* fate *s.v.*;

immortality by suckling, **5** 581*n*;
as libido-symbols, **5** 324;
of love, *see* love *s.v.*;
moon-, *see* moon *s.v.*;
mother-, *see* mother *s.v.*;
as mother-symbol, **9i** 156;
numen of, **16** 438;
phallic symbolism of, **5** 324, pl. XXIX;
of Reason, *see* Reason, Goddess of;
sun-, *see* sun *s.v.*;
as symbols of self, **9i** 315;
"thought-forms" (Tibetan), as, **11** 850;
turquoise (Navaho), **13** 130
Godefridus, *see* Godfrey, Abbot of Admont
godfather, *see* godparents
Godfernaux, A.: *Le Sentiment et la pensée et leurs principaux aspects physiologiques,* **3** 78*n*, 166*n*
Godfrey, Abbot of Admont, and allegories of Mary, **13** 389; **14** 731*n*;
    Homiliae Dominicales: Homilia III, **13** 389*n*; **14** 731*n*; *Homilia IV,* **14** 73*n*; *Homilia LXIII,* **13** 389*n*
Godfrey, Prior of St. Swithin's, epitaph on Abelard, **6** 74*n*
Godhead, **9ii** 305;
    essence of, in Brother Klaus's vision, **11** 476;
    and mystical unity of Mass, **11** 378;
    priest in, **18** 627;
    as soul, **11** 840;
    and transcendent spirit, **9i** 390;
    unconscious, in Eckhart's theology, **9ii** 301
God-image/*imago Dei*, **5** 97; **6** 319, 412; **8** 528; **9ii** 70&*n*; **11** 192, 558, 656, 660, 740; **13** 416; **14** 140, 269–70, 427, 569, 681, 704, 718, 736, 748, 770; **18** 1589;
amoral, **18** 1688;

anthropomorphic, **9ii** 99, 122; **10** 847;
archaic, **18** 359;
archetype/archetypal ideas, **5** 89, 129, 497; **8** 390; **9i** 5; **11** 102, 238; **12** 11&*n*, 14; **14** 48*n*; **18** 1495, 1508–9, 1688; incarnation of, **5** 497;
as autonomous psychic content, **18** 1507;
in Cain and Abel, **11** 628;
as "centre of all things," **9ii** 343;
in Christ, and man, **9ii** 70–2; Christian doctrine as expression of, **9ii** 270;
complexes transferred to, **5** 95;
creation of, **5** 95;
destruction of, and effects on man, **9ii** 170;
eagle as, **13** 475;
evolution of, **18** 1681;
father as, **10** 66;
human element in, **9ii** 185;
incomplete, **9ii** 185;
in man, **9i** 626; **9ii** 265; **13** 160; **18** 1556; and in Christ, *see above;* reformation, renewal of, **9ii** 73; spontaneous experience, **9ii** 303;
mandala as, **9i** 572, 626;
numinosity of, **11** 454, 558;
prayer and, **5** 257, 260;
self as, **5** 612; **9ii** 42, 73, 116, 170, 320; **10** 806; **11** 231, 233, 238, 281, 289; **13** 289, 301*n*; **18** 1495;
stone as, **13** 128;
as a symbol, **6** 201–2;
transformation of, **5** 396*n*; and changes in consciousness, **9ii** 303;
two sides of, **18** 1537;
unconscious and, **5** 98; **10** 746; **18** 1511;
and world-soul, **11** 187;
Wotan as, **9i** 442;
Yahwistic, *see* Yahweh;

462, 475, 557; **13** 80, 143, 234;
of the Church, **10** 651;
divine, **7** 108; **9i** 205, 208–9,
237, 239; **9ii** 198; **11** 7, 28;
external origin of, **11** 771;
gift of, **9i** 205; **11** 501;
gratia adiuvans and *sanctificans,*
11 7*n*;
"of Heaven," **5** 149*n*;
in magic rites, **9i** 232;
man's dependence on, **11** 770;
and the Mass, **11** 307*n*, 403;
means of, **11** 542;
restoration through, **9ii** 72;
state of, **9ii** 65;
water of, **13** 110
"Gracious One" *(vena),* **6** 331–2
gradient: energy, *see* energy *s.v.*;
of libido, *see* libido *s.v.*
Graeae, **9i** 157; *see also* Gorgon
Graeter, C.: "Ein Fall von epilep-
tischer Amnesie durch Hyper-
mnesie beseitigt," **1** 130*n*
Graf, M.: *Richard Wagner im Fliegen-
den Holländer,* **5** 299*n*
Graham, B., **18** 1461*n*
Grail, **6** 407; **9i** 40, 51; **12** *fig.* 88; **18**
1684, 1783;
as feminine religious symbol,
18 1530;
as Hermetic vessel, **6** 371*n*; **12**
245*n*, 246*n*;
king, **5** 450*n*; **14** 375;
legend of, **6** 401&*n*; **14** 188*n*,
357*n*, 369;
messenger of, anima-figure, **7**
374; **10** 713; **16** 504;
and opposites, **6** 371–3;
Saint-Graal, **8** 559*n*;
and spear, **18** 261, 263;
-stone, **12** 246*n*, 263;
of Wolfram von Eschenbach,
see Wolfram von Eschenbach;
see also Gnostic(-ism) *s.v.* vessel
grain: field of, **9i** 333;
of mustard seed, **13** 321;
regenerative power of, **5** 676;
sowing of, **13** 97*n*;

of wheat/*granum frumenti,* **12**
103, 357, 433, 490; **13** 403
grana (grape-pips), **14** 683
grande hystérie, **1** 13, 18
"Grandes heures du duc de Berry,"
12 *fig.* 159; **16** 454
grandeur, delusions/ideas of, **1** 213,
214, 215, 283; **3** 211, 291, 309,
343–6
grandfather(s), **4** 744*n*; **9i** 398;
J.'s, in S. W.'s séances, **1** 45, 97
S. W.'s, as spiritualistic control,
1 39, 46, 55, 126, 127–9, 132
grandmother/"granny," **9i** 156,
188, 189; **11** 997; **17** 216–17, 219;
and death, **17** 5–6;
devil's, **9i** 189;
game of, **17** 54;
as "mouth," **17** 219
Granet, M., **8** 924;
La Pensée chinoise, **8** 924*n*
grape(s), **9ii** 312; **11** 612; **13** 359*n*,
403, 419;
harvest, **11** 720;
-pips *(grana),* **14** 683;
see also TREES: vine
graphite, **12** 327
graphology, **6** 917; **8** 867; **18** 159
"graphomaniacs," *see* Lombroso *s.v.*
grass, **9i** 250
Grasseus, Johannes, *see* ALCHEMICAL
COLLECTIONS: *Bibl. chem. cur. s.v.;
Theatr. chem. s.v.*
grasshopper, *see* ANIMALS *s.v.*
Gratarolus, Gulielmus, *see* ALCHEM-
ICAL WRITERS *s.v.*
Gratianus, **13** 445
grave(s), **9i** 157; **13** 128;
stench of/*odor sepulchrorum,* **14**
658*n*, 701
Graves, R., **13** (*p*63*n*)
gravitation, **10** 611, 624, 667; *see
also* Ufo(s) *s.v.* weightlessness
gravity, spirit of, **10** 939; **11** 245; **12**
79
Gray, L. H., and J. MacCulloch:
The Mythology of All Races, **5** *figs.*
28, 33

Gray, Ronald D.: *Goethe the Alchemist,* **13** 90*n*
Great Bear, *see* Bear, constellations of
Great Magic Papyrus of Paris, *see* ALCHEMICAL WRITERS: Magic Papyri
Great Mother, *see* Mother *s.v.*
greatness, national, **10** 976
Great War, *see* War *s.v.* World War I
Grebelskaja, S., **3** 390;
  "Psychologische Analyse eines Paranoiden," **3** 390*n*
Greece/Greek(s)/Hellenistic, **10** 908;
  alchemy, *see* alchemy *s.v.*;
  character, dichotomy of, **6** 964;
  Nietzsche on, **6** 223, 228–30;
  child-motif in, **9i** 259;
  consciousness, **11** 373;
  and dreams, **3** 525;
  essence and spirit of, **18** 548;
  executions in, **5** 415*n*;
  folksongs, **5** 81*n*, 170*n*;
  gods, **9i** 26; **11** 607; **18** 568;
  triads of, **11** 179–93 (*see also sep. entry below* Greek mythology);
  Greco-Roman: religions, and Christianity, **10** 1006; world, **8** 649, 683; **15** 150;
  heroes of, **17** 298;
  homosexuality in, **7** 173; **17** 272;
  influence, **11** 609, 905;
  intellect, **8** 743;
  language, **1** 144, 183; **18** 172;
  and literature, **11** 860;
  Magic Papyri, *see* ALCHEMICAL WRITERS *s.v.*;
  medicine in, **14** 367; **18** 231;
  and moderns, contrasted, **6** 107;
  mysteries, *see* mystery(-ies) *s.v.*;
  mythology, *see sep. entry below;*
  oracle head in, **11** 373;
  Orthodox Church, **11** 283*n*, 324; **14** 631;
  philosophy, *see* philosophy *s.v.*;
  Satan, **13** 377;

and the soul, **8** 663–4;
sun-wheel in, **5** 460*n*;
syncretism, *see* syncretism *s.v.* Hellenistic;
temperament, and Germanic, **10** 394;
tragedy, **6** 231
greed, **8** 236; egotism and, **18** 1398–9; of a nation, **18** 1401
Greek mythology/myths, **5** 24; **13** 178; **14** 735; **18** 82, 260, 1132;
  matriarchal-patriarchal elements in, **11** 711;
  see also individual names of deities and mythological beings; and see Greece *s.v.* gods
green, *see* COLOURS *s.v.*
Gregory the Great, St. (Pope Gregory IX), **9ii** 158; **11** 152; **14** 17, 255, 579, 582, 642;
  Dialogorum libri IV, **11** 32*n*;
  Epistolae, **16** 468*n*;
  Expositiones in librum I Regum, **9ii** 320*n*, 321*n*; **11** 152*n*; **14** 235*n*, 534*n*, 643*n*;
  Homiliae in Evangelia, **14** 255*n*;
  Homiliae in Ezechielem, **14** 17*n*, 642*n*;
  Moralia in Job, **9ii** 158*n*; **13** 407*n*; **14** 174*n*, 579*n*, 642*n*;
  In septem psalmos penitentiales expositio, **13** 275*n*; **14** 582*n*;
  Super Cantica Canticorum, **13** 458*n*; **14** 181*n*; **16** 496*n*
Gregory XII, Pope, **12** 362*n*
Gregory XIV, Pope, **12** 478; **13** 281
Gregory, Dr., **4** (*p*87)
Gregory of Nyssa, St.: *De vita S. Gregorii Thaumaturgi,* **11** 213*n*
Gregory Thaumaturgus, St., **11** 213–14
gremlins, **9i** 408
Grenfell, B. P., *see* Christ/Jesus *s.v.* sayings of/etc.
Gressmann, H.: *Altorientalische Texte,* **5** 375*n*, 659*n*;
  Die orientalischen Religionen, **5** *fig.* 42

Gretchen, *see* Goethe's *Faust:* CHARACTERS *s.v.*

Greverus, Jodocus, *see* ALCHEMICAL WRITERS *s.v.*

grex segregatus, **10** 384

greybeard, **13** 276

Griesinger, W., **7** 106

griffin, *see* ANIMALS *s.v.*

Griffith, F. L.: *A Collection of Hieroglyphs,* **11** 190n

Griffith, R.H.T., *see* Vedas *s.v.* Hymns

Grill, J.: *Hundert Lieder des Atharva-Veda,* **14** 735n

Grimm, J.: *Teutonic Mythology,* **5** 212n, 362n, 367n, 368nn, 370n, 395n, 566nn, 581n, 585n, 593n; **8** 966n; **13** 218n; **14** 482n, 552n; on eating lentils, **5** 276n; and "Stempe," **5** 370n

Grimm brothers (Jacob, Wilhelm), **5** 34; **9i** 412n; **14** 574n; fairytale of spirit in bottle, **9i** 456; **13** 239–46, 247, 250–1, 287–8, 321; **14** 75, 416n; *Fairy Tales,* tr. M. Hunt; revised J. Stern, **9i** 407n; **13** 239n; **18** 230

Groddeck, G., **18** 1152

Gross, —, on perseveration, **2** 100n

Gross, Alfred, **2** 791, 907; "Die Associationsmethode in Strafprozess," **2** 664n, (p491); "Kriminalpsychologische Tatbestandsforschung," **2** 918n, 1317n; "Zur psychologischen Tatbestandsdiagnostik als kriminalistisches Hilfsmittel," **2** 640n, 765n, (p491)

Gross, Hans: *Criminal Psychology,* **1** 303n; "Zur Frage des Wahrnehmungsproblems," **2** 758n; "Zur psychologischen Tatbestandsdiagnostik," **2** 640n, 664n, 758n, (p491)

Gross, Otto, **2** 662; **3** 70, 76, 299; **4** 695n; **6** 693n; on *dementia sejunctiva,* **3** 55–60; and two psychological types, **6** 462–3, 465–7, 470–80, 879 (*see also* extraverted type; introverted type) on functions, *see* function(s) *s.v.* primary and secondary; and "sejunctive" personality, **6** 467, 472;

WORKS: "Beitrag zur Pathologie des Negativismus," **3** 55n; "Über Bewusstseinzerfall," **3** 55n; *Über psychopathische Minderwertigkeit,* **6** 462n, 467nn, 480n; *Die zerebrale Sekundärfunktion,* **3** 419n; **6** 462, 471n, 473nn, 475n, 480n, 879n; "Zur Differentialdiagnostik negativistischer Phänomene," **3** 55n, 57n; "Zur Nomenklatur 'Dementia sejunctiva'," **3** 55nn

Grot, N. von, **8** 8, 10, 11, 12n, 26; "Die Begriffe der Seele und der psychischen Energie in der Psychologie," **8** 8n, 26n

ground, **11** 949; **12** 8; divine, **11** 486; Gnostic symbols for, **9ii** 306; of lapis lazuli, **11** 917, 929, 937; universal, **9ii** 304, 313

group: analysis, **14** 125n; -consciousness, **10** 280; effects on members, **10** 891–2; factors influencing, **10** 891; formations, **18** 1313–14; identification with, **9i** 225–8; **17** 303; Imperator, **13** 60; inferiority to individuals, **10** 722; psychology, **10** 889; and psychotherapeutic method, **18** 1392–3;

H

Habakkuk/Habacuc, *see* BIBLE: O.T. *s.v.*

"Ḥabib, Book of al-," *see* ALCHEMI-CAL WRITERS:El-Ḥabib

habit(s), **11** 270–1;
    bad, in children, see child(ren) *s.v.*;
    and neuroses, **16** 152

Hades, **9i** 246*n*, 311; **11** 671; **12** 61*n*, 182, 406, 409*n*, 426, 438–9, 457*n*, *fig.* 21; **13** 103&*n*, 191, 380*n*; **14** 80*n*, 316; **15** 210, 214; **16** 418, 455, 468; **18** 243;
    Babylonian, **8** 845;
    descent to, **12** 438;
    entrances to, **5** 572;
    journey to, *see* journey *s.v.*;
    as quaternity, **11** 672;
    see also hell; nekyia; night sea journey; underworld

Hadfield, J. A., **18** (*p*1), 44, 74, 390

haemoptysis, simulation of, **1** 305

Haeussermann, F.: *Wortempfang und Symbol in der alttestamentlichen Prophetie*, **11** 32*n*

Hagar, **11** 713

Hagen, **5** 611

Hagen, F. W.: "Zur Theorie der Hallucination," **1** 97*n*, 100*nn*, 101*nn*, 124*n*

Haggadah, **14** 590*n*

Haggadic tradition, **13** 417; **14** 585

Haggard, H. Rider, **5** 678; **9i** 60*n*, 145; **10** 85, 87; **15** 137, 143;
    "She," and anima-figure, **7** 298–9; **9i** 60, 64, 145, 356, 516, 518*n*; **9ii** 424*n*; **10** 75; **17** 339*n*, 341; **18** 1279–81; *coniunctio* of, **16** 421*n*; mana-personality of, **7** 375; soul, immortality of, **7** 303;
    WORKS:
        Ayesha: The Return of She, **9i** 145, 356; **10** 88; **15** 142; **16** 421*n*;
        She, **7** 298*n*, 303; **9i** 145, 356; **9ii** 424*n*; **10** 88, **13** 131*n*; **15** 142; **16** 421*n*; **17** 339*n*; **18** 457, 1280, 1281;
        Wisdom's Daughter, **9i** 145; **10** 75

Hagia Sophia, **11** 40; **12** 181;
    in dream, **12** 176

Hahn, C. H., **9ii** 139;
    Geschichte der Ketzer im Mittelalter, **9ii** 139*nn*, 225*n*, 226*n*

Hahn, E.: *Demeter und Baubo*, **5** 214*n*

Hahn, R., **1** 151–65;
    review of J.'s "Zur Psychologie und Pathologie sogenannter occulter Phänomene," **1** 151&*n*

Haida Indians, Northwest America, **5** *fig.* 32

hair, **13** 122, 360, 375*n*, 381, 411, 462;
    at birth, **17** 56;
    curly, **14** 98, 625&*n*;
    -dresser, analyst as, **13** 479;
    and heat, **5** 366;
    of hero, loss of, **5** 366; **11** 348; **12** 440; **14** 277; **16** 455;
    red, *see* COLOURS: red *s.v.*;
    woman's, **13** 107

Hajós, L., *see under* Ranschburg

half-life, **8** 959

Hali, *see* Haly

Halirrhothios, **5** 372, 392*n*

Hall, G. Stanley, **8** 552; **18** 399;
    autobiography, **15** 52

Hall, M. P.: *Codex Rosae Crucis*, **12** 332*n*

Haller, M.: *Das Hohe Lied*, **14** 24*n*

hallucination(s), **1** 11, 34; **3** 72, 166, 180–1; **6** 47; **7** 312; **8** 584; **9i** 395*n*; **10** 597*n*, 609, 714; **11** 474; **12** 57, 59, 353; **13** 47, 374; **16** 501; **18** 711, 922, 1113–14;
    TITLE: "On Hallucination," **18** 1113–14;

auditory/of voices/verbal, *see* voice/vox *s.v.* hallucinatory;
body-, **7** 469;
complexes and, **8** 593;
creative, **1** 25;
in dementia praecox, *see* schizophrenia *s.v.*;
in *grande hystérie*, **1** 13;
hypnagogic, **1** 28, 43, 100–1; **18** 778;
incipient, **3** 457;
induced, **1** 21–2;
intuitive, **1** 106;
and neologisms, **3** 157;
olfactory, **18** 767, 780;
among primitives, **6** 46, 254;
in prodromal stage, **1** 281;
psychogenic, **1** 29;
of saints, **1** 117;
of all the senses/sense organs, **1** 11, 43;
of skeletons, **1** 7, 26;
Socrates and, **6** 240;
and somnambulism, **1** 97–8; **3** 161;
systematic nature of, **1** 43;
teleological, **1** 136; **3** 304;
and unconscious, **3** 452–3;
verbal, *see* voice/vox *s.v.* hallucinatory;
waking, **1** 37;
INSTANCES: of dead people and skeletons, **1** 7–8; of female genitals, **3** 63–4; of snake, **7** 6/415; of levitation, **8** 949; of solar phallus, *see* solar phallus; of theft of money, **1** 252; *see also* visions
Halm, K. F., **13** 91*n*;
ed., *Rhetores Latini minores*, **12** 457*n*
halo/nimbus, **7** 108;
at finger-ends, **5** 271;
meaning of, **5** 133*n*;
snake wearing, **13** *fig.* 12;
as symbol, **5** 163
Haloa festival, **18** 264*n*;
regenerative symbol of, **5** pl.

LXIII*a*
Hal Saflieni, **9i** 312
Haly/Hali, King of Arabia, **9ii** 377*n*; **13** 162, 271*n*, 429; **14** 174
hamadryad, **14** 69, 85*n*
Hamann, J. G., **5** 12*n*;
Schriften, **5** 12*n*, 14*n*
Hambruch, P.: *Südseemärchen*, **12** 416*n*
Hamburger, J.: *Encyclopädie des Judentums*, **14** 158*n*
Hamelin, Pied Piper of, **18** 1364
Hamlet, **12** 108
hammer, Thor's, **8** 966*n*
hammering, in dream, **4** 170, 172–3, 190
Hammer-Purgstall, J.:
Mémoire sur deux coffrets gnostiques du moyen âge, **12** 184*n*, *fig.* 70; **16** 533*n*;
Mysterium Baphometis, **16** 533*n*
Hammurabi, **11** 173, 174
hamsa, see ANIMALS: swan
han, **8** 125
Hanan ben Tahlifa, Rabbi, **9ii** 133*n*
hand(s), **4** 291; **13** 22;
anaesthetic, **1** 98, 138, 160;
as auxiliary organ, in rhythmic activity, **5** 206;
baby's gesture with, involving mouth, **5** 228;
and character, **18** 1819;
and feet, cutting off of, **13** 441;
phallic meaning of, **5** 271;
right and left, *see* right and left;
of sun, **5** *fig.* 7;
symbolism of, **5** 271;
thrust into fire, **1** 305*n*;
and unconscious, **8** 171, 180
Handel, G. F., **3** 114
Händler, O.: *Die Predigt*, **12** 6*n*
handwriting, *see* writing
hanging, **5** pl. XXVIII;
on tree, **5** 398–9, 594, 659; as sacrifice, **5** 349
"hanging on" to analysis, **12** 5, 33
"Hans, Clever" (talking dog), **8** 364*n*; **18** 893&*n*

head (*cont.*):
    377; **11** 366; **12** 109*n*; **13** 95; **14**
    626, 732; as alchemical vessel,
    11 366; **12** 116; **13** 113, 117; **14**
    731, 732;
    as seat of consciousness, **8** 669;
    13 107;
    skinning of, as spiritual trans-
    formation, **11** 348; **13** 93, 95;
    of snake, **13** 381*n*;
    symbolism, **13** 117;
    as teraphim, **11** 368;
    three in one, **12** 313;
    and tree, **13** *figs.* 28–9;
    white, of Ancient of Days, **12**
    313;
    see also beheading; skull
headache(s), **7** 206;
    in patients, **1** 6, 8, 29, 33, 49,
    51, 246, 258; **4** 461
healing:
    TITLE: "Healing the Split," **18**
    578–607;
    art of, **13** 146, 152;
    initiation as, **11** 410;
    mental, *see* mental *s.v.*;
    money-offering for, **5** 571;
    need of, **4** 754;
    psychic systems of, **13** 478;
    a religious problem, **11** 523;
    snake of Moses, **13** 137;
    symptomatology and, **8** 312;
    water, **12** 475*n*
health, **7** 108
Heard, G.: *Is Another World Watch-
    ing? The Riddle of the Flying Sauc-
    ers,* **10** 667*n*
hearing: extinction of, **8** 955;
    hysterical loss of, **7** 4/413;
    spiritual/bodily, **12** 456
heart, **9i** 42, 535; **10** 843; **12** 445&*n*,
    462&*n*, *fig.* 149; **13** 91, 97, 174,
    188, 197, 201, (*p*192), 300, 322,
    339, 388; **14** 41;
    bodily, fleshly, **13** 57;
    body and, **13** 202; **16** 495;
    capsule of/*capsula cordis,* **13**
    201–2;

centre/midpoint of, **13** 174; **14**
    41;
    as centre, **13** 349;
    as consciousness, **12** 462*n*;
    cutting off of, **5** 310;
    cutting out, and eating, **13** 93;
    of the dead, **13** 348*n*;
    deep, **13** 301*n*;
    diadem of the, **13** 183, 346; **16**
    495–7;
    eating of, **5** 569;
    fire of, **13** 201; **14** 41;
    of heaven, **13** 64;
    heavenly, **13** 33, 57;
    high, **13** 301*n*;
    and memory, **18** 744;
    of Mercurius, at North Pole, **13**
    256&*n*;
    of the microcosm, **13** 268;
    pierced by arrows, **5** 435;
    region, **13** 202;
    -shaped, **13** 349*n*; blossoms, **13**
    322;
    of statue, **14** 560, 568;
    thinking in, **18** 15–16;
    troubles, **3** 87;
    see also *cor*
heartache, **8** 303
hearth spirit (*ch'i*), **5** 663
heat/heating, **13** 29;
    alchemical, **7** 368;
    creative, **5** 589–90*n*;
    emitted by Ufos, **10** 641;
    four degrees of, **14** 5;
    hair and, **5** 366;
    magical, **10** 643;
    original, **7** 108;
    sensations, **2** 793, 850–6;
    of underworld, **12** 437, 440,
    449
Heath, Sir Thomas, **11** 182;
    A History of Greek Mathematics,
    11 182*n*
heathen, **13** 25
heathenism, **12** 12;
    see also paganism
heaven/Heaven, **9i** 50, 56, 156; **9ii**
    240; **12** 347–8; **14** 292, 554, 573,

St. Basil on, **9ii** 199;
serpent and, **14** 482;
see also Hades; underworld
hellebore, lapis as, **18** 1631
Hellenistic, *see* Greece/Greek(s)
Hellpach, W., **2** 662&*n*;
*Grundlinien einer Psychologie der
Hysterie,* J.'s review, **18** 871–83
Hellwig, C. von, *see* ALCHEMICAL
WRITERS *s.v.*
Helm, G. F., **7** 107;
*Die Energetik nach ihrer geschicht-
lichen Entwicklung,* **7** 107*n*
Helmholtz, H. von, **6** 544, 551
Héloise, *see* Abelard
Helsdingen, R. J. van: *Beelden uit
het onbewuste,* J.'s foreword, **18**
1252–5
Helvetius, *see* ALCHEMICAL COLLEC-
TIONS: *Mus. herm. s.v.*
hematite, **9i** 575
hemispheres, **9ii** 206
hemlock, **9i** 297*n*; **9ii** 339*n*
hemorrhage, **9i** 170
hen, *see* ANIMALS *s.v.*
Hendy, B. D., **18** 68
heng (all-pervading power), **9i** 640,
fig. 2
Hennecke, E., ed. *Neutestamentliche
Apokryphen,* **9ii** 104*n*; **11** 429*n*
Henning, W.: "Ein Manichäisches
Henochbuch," **12** 458*n*
henosis, **13** 357; *see also* unification
Henry II of France, **9ii** 151
Henry III of France, **14** 19*n*
Henry, Victor: *Antinomies linguis-
tiques,* **3** 303*n*
Hephaistos/Hephaestus/Vulcan, **5**
364*n*, 515; **6** 295, 302, 304; **9i**
682; **9ii** 393, 396; **12** 215, 484*n*;
15 39*n*; **18** 1697
heptad, **9ii** 307*n*; *see also* NUMBERS:
seven
Hera/Juno, **5** 264, 321, 460*n*; **9i** 93,
604; **9ii** 322*n*; **12** 436*n*; **13** 91; **14**
2, 70, 154*n*; **17** 321;
of Argos, **5** 363;
Babylonian, **9ii** 178;

Heracles and, **5** 540; **14** 384,
652;
Iamia as, **5** 450*n*;
Ludovici (Schiller), **6** 200, 202;
peacock, attribute of, **14** 398;
Samian, **5** 363;
vengeful, **5** 459
Heracles/Hercules/Herakles, **5** 183,
299*n*, 396, 449*n*, 581*n*, 600*n*; **6**
437; **7** 224; **9i** 93, 221, 283, 604;
9ii 134; **12** 416&*n*, 513, *figs.* 171,
215; **13** 131; **14** 166, 384, 652; **17**
321; **18** 250;
and Cerberus, **5** 572;
cross of, **5** 460*n*;
cycle, **9i** 433*n*;
labours, twelve of, **5** *fig.* 17; **12**
119, 457, 469; *athla,* **9i** 289,
433&*n*;
legend of, **5** 450*n*;
and Mithras, **5** 288;
Morbicida, as antimony, **9i**
537*n*;
and Nemean lion, **5** 450*n*;
Omphale and, **5** 451*n*, 458*n*; **9i**
571; **12** 416*n*; **13** 131;
pillars of, **5** 460*n*;
"Prophet," **9i** 571;
and the sun, **5** 288, 600*n*;
taskmaster of, *see* Eurystheus;
two mothers of, **5** 450*n*
Heraclitus/Heraclitean, **3** 424; **6**
87*n*; **8** 99, 278, 916; **9i** 32; **9ii**
394*n*; **10** 695; **11** 60, 151; **12** 157,
182, 333, 435*n*; **14** 192*n*, 251,
503; **15** 85;
on enantiodromia, **6** 150,
708&*n*; **7** 111; **10** 164, 630; **18**
(*p*711);
on ever-living fire, **7** 108; **9i** 68;
12 297; **13** 408;
on soul, **9i** 55; **9ii** 344; **14** 42;
16 455
Heraclius, Emperor, **12** 404*n*, 449*n*;
13 414*n*; **16** 529
Herakleon, **13** 116&*n*
Herakles, *see* Heracles
herb(s): of immortality, *see* immor-

herb (*cont.*):
  tality *s.v.*;
    magic, *see* magic *s.v.*
Herbart, J. F., **2** 128; **6** 180, 518; **8**
  350; **10** 370;
    Psychologie als Wissenschaft, **6**
    518*n*
Herbert of Cherbury, Lord, **8** 275;
  De veritate, tr. M. H. Carré, **8**
  275*n*
Hercules, *see* Heracles
herd, **7** 30, 37–8, 430; **17** 298;
  instinct, **10** 448; **16** 41, 222;
  psychology, *see* psychology *s.v.*
  mob/mass;
  "soul," in individual, **7** 462*n*;
  see also mass(es)/mob
hereafter, the, **10** 1005
heredity/hereditary, **8** 248, 657; **10**
  646, 961; **12** 148; **14** 308; **16** 194;
  17 85, 89, 312, 331c;
  TITLE: "The Significance of
  Constitution and Heredity in
  Psychology," **8** 220–31;
  of behaviour patterns, **8** 673; **9i**
  151–2; **11** 88;
  and degeneracy, **1** 113, 416–
  17;
  in fraud case, **1** 451;
  and hysterical stupor, **1** 227;
  and introversion, **10** 658;
  manic mood disorder and, **1**
  193, 197, 206, 212, 218;
  psychic, **11** 491, 845;
  and psychopathic inferiority, **1**
  6;
  and simulated insanity, **1** 322,
  361
heresiologists, **11** 360; **13** (*p*3), 184,
  231
heresy(-ies), **6** 31–2, 81, 400–1, 409,
  426; **9ii** 233; **10** 529; **11** 485; **12**
  144, 431*n*; **13** 277; **16** 418; **18**
  1512;
  alchemy and, *see* alchemy *s.v.*;
  s.v.;
  in Christianity, **11** 279, 470;
  unconscious, **11** 483;

  see also Cathars: Harran School;
  Manichaeans; Scythians
heretics: religious geniuses as, **18**
  1539;
  saints as, **11** 481
Hermann, —.: "Gefühlsbetonte
  Komplexe im Seelenleben des
  Kindes, im Alltagsleben und im
  Wahnsinn," **18** 949
hermaphrodite / hermaphroditism /
  hermaphroditic, **9i** 140*n*, 682; **9ii**
  245, 330, 371, 390; **10** 772; **12**
  101, 311, 335, 426, 447, 470, 517,
  550, *figs.* 54, 123, 125, 199; **13**
  157, 203, *figs.* B1–4; **14** 22, 57,
  89, 162*n*, 168, 180*n*, 225, 389,
  391, 416, 523, 607, 654, 770; **16**
  468, 494, 533;
  Adam as, *see* Adam *s.v.* androgyny;
  alchemical symbols as, **16** 398;
  alchemists and, **9i** 326, 682;
  anima as, *see* anima *s.v.*;
  Anthropos as, *see* Anthropos
  s.v. androgynous;
  aspect of arcane substance, **14**
  195, 472;
  and Atman, **5** 227*n*;
  child/infant, **9i** 292–7; **14**
  27&*n*, 182;
  creator as, **11** 47;
  crucified, **12** 436*n*;
  deity as, *see* deity(-ies) *s.v.*;
  double eagles as, **12** *fig.* 20;
  and elevated places, **9ii** 322;
  epigram of the, **14** 89;
  filius as, **10** 629; **12** 29, *fig.* 23;
  and Gnosticism, *see* Gnostic(s)
  s.v. masculine-feminine;
  homunculus, *see* homunculus
  s.v.;
  lapis as, *see* lapis *s.v.*;
  Mercurius as, *see* Mercurius
  s.v.;
  monster, **13** 173, 268;
  of nature, **14** 472, 476;
  Nous as, **12** 436*n*, 447;
  Original/primordial man as, **9ii**

319; **16** 416;
Platonic, **9i** 326;
prima materia as, **12** 427*n*, 517;
of primordial divine being, **11** 748;
rebis as, **12** 305, *fig.* 199;
statue of, **14** 80*n*, 526*n*;
stone as, **9ii** 387; philosopher's, **11** 93, 152; **12** 335;
symbol for God, **9ii** 304;
synonym for goal of opus, **16** 533;
and tree-symbol, **5** 325&*n*;
two-headed, **14** 11;
type, **9i** 140*n*;
of the unconscious, **14** 220;
unicorn as, **12** 526;
union, **13** 171; of opposites, **16** 454;
uroboros as, **12** 496;
Venus as, **13** 234*n*;
of Yahweh/Sophia, **11** 727;
see also androgyne; bisexuality
Hermaphroditisches Sonn- und Monds-kind, see ALCHEMICAL WRITERS *s.v.*
hermaphroditosis, **10** 994
Hermaphroditus, **9ii** 194; **11** 359*n*; **16** 468, 525, 527, 529
Hermas, *The Shepherd,* **6** 381&*n*-2, 385-7; **9i** 79*n*; **9ii** 162; **14** 301-2, 305; **15** 142, 148, 153; **18** 255;
and Muratori Canon, **6** 381;
vision of Church/Ecclesia, **6** 388-91, 402; **9ii** 144*n*, 352*n*; **14** 11, 303, 770; as old woman, **6** 388-91, 402;
vision of monster and maiden, **14** 301
hermeneut(ic(s)), **6** 22; **7** 491;
Christian, **14** 474&*n*;
method, **7** 131*n*, 493, 497, 501;
see also Mercurius
Hermes, *see* Mercurius (in alchemy); Mercury (god)
"Hermes Bird," *see* ALCHEMICAL COLLECTIONS: *Theatr. chem. brit.*
Hermes Trismegistus, *see* ALCHEMICAL WRITERS *s.v.*

Hermetic philosophy, **9i** 120*n*; **9ii** 266; **11** 47, 261; **12** 222, 403, 503; **13** 281, 353, 378; **18** 532, 1517, 1554, 1700, 1831;
and Christianity, **12** 478;
coniunctio in, **9i** 295;
four elements in, **11** 62*n*;
fourteen principal virtues in, **12** 382;
and Paracelsus, **13** 158;
quaternity, *see* quaternity *s.v.*;
Timaeus and, **11** 92;
and totality/wholeness, **10** 621, 633; **11** 738, 755; **13** 378;
tree symbolism in, **12** 34;
see also *Corpus Hermeticum*; *krater*; *vas Hermetis* (Hermetic vessel)
Hermetica, see Corpus Hermeticum
hermit(s), **10** 648; **11** 475, 786
Hermogenes, **14** 32*n*
Hermolaus Barbarus, *see* ALCHEMICAL WRITERS *s.v.*
hero/-es, **5** 259, 390, 421, 433, 460, 615; **7** 248, 261/477, 283, 306, 310, 377, 389; **9i** 350, 356, 418, 515; **13** 133, 152, 164, 228*n*, 241, 276, 278, 384, 401, 425, 457, *fig.* 15; **17** 207, 298, 311;
TITLE: "The Origin of the Hero," **5** 251-99;
and animal(s), magic, **5** 503 (*see also* ANIMALS: birds *s.v.* helpful; bull; dragon; horse; serpent);
animus-figure and, **5** 462, 465; **7** 341;
archetype/motif, **5** 516; **10** 90, 100-1; **12** 15; **18** 80, 191, 196, 530; wise old man, **9i** 401;
in association-chain, *see* association-chain(s) *s.v.*;
battles of, **5** 523; **17** 303; with dragon; Gilgamesh Epic);
s.v. hero; with magician, **5** 544;
with monster, **5** 538; **7** 160, 261/477; for rebirth, **5** 511;
birth of, **5** 487, 493; **6** 806; **9i** 248; **11** 293; **14** 630*n*; **17** 318,

hesed, **9ii** 105
Hesiod, **12** 456; **5** 198, 577;
  Theogony, **5** 198*n*; **12** 456*n*;
  see also Homeric Hymns
Hesperides: apples of, **5** 250; **13**
  404; **14** 85*n*;
  dragon of, **5** 577;
  garden of, **12** 457*n*;
  see also tree(s) *s.v.*
Hesperus, evening star, **16** 451*n*
Hesychius, **12** 456(5)*n*;
  gloss of, **5** 208
hetaira, transformation into, **18**
  1525, 1529
heterosuggestion, **9i** 130*n*
Heterwick, Alexander, **8** 117;
  "Some Animistic Beliefs among
  the Yaos of Central Africa," **8**
  117*n*
heuristic: principle, **7** 139;
  value, **7** 216
hexad, **9i** 679; **9ii** 361; **10** 771; **16**
  451
hexagram(s), see *I Ching*
Heyer, G. R., **10** 1060; **18** 1227,
  1737;
  The Organism of the Mind, **18**
  278*n*;
  Der Organismus der Seele, **18**
  1776: J.'s review, **18** 1774;
  Praktische Seelenheilkunde, J.'s
  review, **18** 1775–9
Heyer, Lucy, **18** 1778
Hiawatha (Longfellow's hero):
  antecendents and family of, **5**
  482–8;
  battles: with father, **5** 504, 511;
  with magician, **5** 544 (*see also*
  below corn-god, Mondamin);
  birth and childhood of, **5**
  487–9, 498–502;
  and corn-god, Mondamin, vi-
  sion of, **5** 520–1; **9i** 248&*n*; **10**
  779; battle with, **5** 522–3;
  deeds of, **5** 502–4, 537, 540;
  and father-in-law, **5** 515–16;
  grandmother of, **5** 487;
  historical, **5** 474*n*;

loss of friends, **5** 552;
  and Minnehaha, **5** 513–14,
  517–18;
  mother of, **5** 487;
  retreat into forest, **5** 517–20;
  wampum belt, "treasure hard
  to attain," **5** 482, 547;
  writing, invention of, **5** 549–50
Hiawatha, Song of (Longfellow's
  poem), **5** 474–554, 614 (*p*461); **7**
  160;
  mythological motifs, **5** 475–8;
  origin of, **5** 474*n*
Hibil Ziwa, **11** 173
Hibis, hymn of, **5** 357
Hicks, R. D., *see under* Diogenes
  Laertius
Hiddekel, **9ii** 353, 372
Hierapolis, temple, **5** 577; **14** 701*n*
Hiereus, *see* priest *s.v.* Zosimos
hierogamy, *see hierosgamos*
hieroglyph, **9i** 538;
  of eternity, uroborus as, **13** 322
"hieroglyphical," *see* association-
  chain(s) *s.v.*
hierosgamos (sacred marriage)/hi-
  erogamy, **5** 364&*n*, 531; **9i** 197,
  295, 297; **9ii** 22, 145*n*; **10** 751; **11**
  711, 748; **12** 435*n*; **14** 19, 207,
  356, 551, 664; **16** 355, 458, 534;
  18 264&*n*;
  aboriginals and, *see* Australian
  aborigines *s.v.*;
  alchemical, **12** 43; **14** 412; **16**
  538;
  archetypal, **14** 664; incestuous,
  14 178 (*see also* Gabricus/
  Thabritius);
  Assumption as, *see* Mary *s.v.*;
  in Cabala, **14** 18–19, 568;
  of Christ and Church, **9ii** 72;
  in Christianity, **5** 411;
  coniunctio as, see *coniunctio*
  s.v.;
  in earth, **14** 154;
  of gods/divine pair, **14** 689; eye
  and, **14** 25*n*; incest in, **14** 107,
  412;

offerings tossed into, **5** 570;
sacramental mating with spear,
5 214
holidays, **8** 685
holiness, **11** 225;
see also holy *s.v.* man
Holl, K., **13** 183*n*
Holland, *see* Netherlands
Hollandus, Joannes Isaacus, *see* AL-
CHEMICAL WRITERS *s.v.*
Holmberg, U., **13** 354;
Der Baum des Lebens, **13** 354*n*,
381*n*
Holmyard, E. J., *see under* ALCHEMI-
CAL WRITERS: Abu'l Qāsim
Holobolus, **14** 91*n*
Holstein-Augustenburg, Duke of, **6**
101
Holtzmann, A.: *Indische Sagen*, **12**
534*n*
holy: dread, **13** 210;
Indian, **11** 950–63;
man, **11** 786;
sacraments, **13** 194;
scripture, **13** 374*n*;
trees of India, **13** 461
Holy City, The (cantata), **15** 196*n*
Holy Ghost/Spirit, **5** 232; **8** 391; **9ii**
210, 249; **10** 766; **11** 126, 160*n*,
204, 276, 690–2, 743, 746; **12** 26,
347, 470, 505, *figs.* 180, 191; **13**
104&*n*, 194, 263, 288, 407*n*, 451;
14 22, 487, 516*n*, 530, 667; **16**
462, 498; **18** 1532–57;
TITLE: "The Holy Ghost," **11**
234–42;
age of, *see* Joachim of Flora;
and alchemy, **10** 768; **12** 187;
13 263; **14** 444; **16** 413, 416,
455; as *paredros*, **12** 420; religion of, **14** 286*n*, 531, 646;
Spiritus Sanctus, **14** 235*n*;
sweet smell of, **14** 432, 701;
water of, **11** 151; **13** 103;
as *anima mundi*, **8** 393;
archetypal basis of, **11** 197; **14**
579;
as breath, **11** 235, 237, 276;

as Christ's father, **18** 1619;
Church and, **11** 289, 695;
as *complexio oppositorum*, **11**
277–9; **18** 1553;
concept of, **11** 237, 239, 241,
267; disappearance of, **11** 242;
as life, **11** 197;
descent of, **9ii** 144; **10** 767; **11**
161, 289;
dogma, **11** 222;
dove as symbol of, *see* ANIMALS:
dove *s.v.*;
and dream-interpretation, **11**
32*n*;
enthusiasm of, **10** 733;
as eye, **14** 46;
feminine, *see* Sapientia; Sophia
as fire, **5** 149*n*; **9ii** 200; **10** 733;
12 446, 473, *fig.* 191; **16** 484;
-flash (Böhme), **9i** 535; tongues
of, **7** 108; **9ii** 210*n*; **10** 728; **11**
232, 276; **14** 251;
as function, **11** 236;
gifts of, **11** 289; **13** 136, 142; **14**
253, 443; grace of, **13** 197;
in Gnosticism, *see* Gnosticism
s.v.;
and God, continuing incarnation of, **11** 655–8, 693, 741,
746, 749, 758;
green/*viriditas* of, **11** 118&*n*; **12**
319;
as hypothesis, **11** 222;
identification with, **18** 1662;
invocation of, **18** 1536;
as *ka*, **11** 177;
light of, **13** 149;
maternal significance of, **5** 198;
11 126, 236, 240; in *Acts of
Thomas*, **5** 558, 561; **11** 175*n*,
236*n*;
as mediator, **12** 192;
Mercurius and, *see* Mercurius
s.v.;
-movement, *see* Joachim of
Flora;
nature of, Origen on , **11** 214,
276;

Holy Ghost (*cont.*):
and opposites, union of, **18** 1553, 1556;
Paraclete, **13** 277; **14** 73*n*; alchemy and, **14** 22, 27; as Comforter, **11** 260; in individuals, **11** 696; as legacy of the Son, **11** 205, 235, 267, 655–7, 691–2; sending of, **9i** 247; **11** 741; **14** 444; as spirit: of procreation, **11** 197, 692; —, of truth, **11** 655, 692, 696; —, and wisdom, **11** 612;
personal quality absent, **11** 276; procession of, **11** 197, 218, 289; "vera persona"/real person, **11** 197;
as progenitor of Son, **11** 205, 420;
as psychic experience, **18** 1555; and redemption, **11** 205;
as revolutionary, **18** 1541; saints as symbols of its working, **11** 276;
as Sapientia, *see* Sapientia *s.v.*;
sevenfold, **14** 579;
sin against, **16** 392; as Sophia, *see* Sophia *s.v.*;
spiration of, **11** 197, 204; **14** 701; active and passive, **11** 235*n*; **14** 286*n*;
spontaneous revelation of, **11** 260;
sweet odor, **14** 432, 658, 701; symbols of, *see* ANIMALS: dove; unicorn; *and see above* breath; eye; fire; *see below* water; wind; as third person with Father and Son, **11** 232, 235; **14** 286*n*; as transcendental fact, **18** 1536; two aspects of, **18** 1545;
as Ufo, **10** 618*n*; as water, **11** 151, 161*n*; as wind, **8** 319; **9i** 108; **11** 197; **14** 531; south-, **12** 473;
as winged old man, **12** 446; wisdom of, **12** 466;
as world-soul, **5** 198

Holy Ghost Movement (age of the Holy Ghost), *see* Joachim of Flora
Holy Roman Empire, **18** 1329
Holy Saturday, **8** 314, 336; **9i** 93; *see also* Easter
Holy Sepulchre, worship of, **5** 536
Holy Spirit, *see* Holy Ghost
Holy Trinity, *see* Trinity
Home, —, spiritualistic medium, **18** 715, 719, 720, 721
home: atmosphere, teacher and, **17** 259;
-sickness, **17** 13
homelessness, **10** 999
Homer, **6** 963*n*; **8** 318, 845*n*; **14** 119*n*; **16** 560; Schiller on, **6** 213, 875;
Iliad, **5** 363, 571*n*; **9ii** 322*n*, 340*n*; **14** 18*n*, 38*n*, 174*n*;
Odyssey, **5** 634*n*; **6** 60; **8** 845*n*; **9i** 538; **9ii** 326*n*, 327, 338*n*; **12** 61*n*, 456*n*, **14** 77*n*; **18** 80;
see also Odysseus
Homeric: age, **18** 16;
chain, **12** 148;
imagery, **15** 186;
μωλυ, **13** 409*n*
Homeric Hymns, **5** 567*n*;
to Demeter, **5** 533; **9i** 205*n*;
tr. H. G. Evelyn-White, *Hesiod, the Homeric Hymns and Homerica*, **9i** 205*n*
homilectics, **12** 6*n*
homo Adamicus, **11** 47
homo albus, **11** 371*n*
homo altus, **11** 738; **13** 203;
Anthropos as, **9i** 555;
Mercurius as, *see* Mercurius *s.v.* high man;
stone/no stone, **11** 707;
see also man *s.v.* high
homo coelestis, of St. Paul, **9ii** 71
Homoforus, **12** 469*n*
homo interior: Christ as, **18** 1570;
Mercurius as, **9i** 550*n*
homoiousia, **11** 226;
and *homoousia*, see *homoousia s.v.*

homo maior, **13** 185;
    Adech as, **13** 226;
    as individuation, **13** 220
homo maximus, **10** 175, 727; **12** 173;
    13 381*n*; **14** 593, 605; **15** 12;
    Adech as, **13** 168&*n*, 203;
    as Anthropos, *see* Anthropos
    s.v.;
    Heaven as, **15** 31;
    inner, **13** 203;
    invisibilis, **13** 208;
    and planet Mercury, **9i** 557;
    quaternity of, **13** 206–9;
    Son of Man as, **11** 419;
    spiritual forces from, **13** 220;
    union with, **13** 205
homoousia, **5** 612; **9i** 11; **11** 209, 219,
    287, 289, 628; **14** 377, 423;
    archetype of, **11** 222;
    and *homoiousia* formula, **6**
    31–2; **11** 194, 215–16, 628;
    filioque clause, **11** 217*n*, 218,
    289; **18** 1549, 1550
homo philosophicus: and Anthropos,
    see Anthropos *s.v.*;
    Christ as, **12** 476;
    as Mercurius, **12** *fig.* 214; **13**
    268;
    as Second Adam, **9i** 238*n*; **11**
    94
homo purissimus, Christ the, **13** 390
homo putissimus, as arcane substance,
    13 390
homo quadratus, **9i** 549; **9ii** 418
homo religiosus, **11** 11
homo sapiens, **10** 822; **18** 494;
    individuals representative of,
    10 888;
    place in biology, **10** 548
homosexuality/homosexual, **4** 247,
    254; **6** 809; **7** 127–9; **9i** 356; **16**
    357*n*, 419*n*;
    of adolescence, **7** 173–81; **17**
    221–2, 266, 268, 272–3, 277–
    80;
    and anima, **9i** 146;
    children and, **4** 243;
    as component of normal sexu-

ality, **4** 246–9;
    as defence, **7** 134;
    female, **10** 203, 221–2, 246;
    in Greece, *see* Greece *s.v.*;
    and heterosexual, as opposites,
    7 179;
    and law in Germany, **18** 907;
    and mother, **9i** 162, 164; **9ii**
    22; **17** 328;
    among students, **10** 203, 208,
    217, 220
homo totus, **12** 6; **13** 372;
    lapis/stone as, **13** 390; **14** 86
homunculus, **9i** 270, 279, 408, 541,
    (*p*315), 686, 692, 707; **9ii** 387; **11**
    345, 420, 738; **12** 302, *figs.* 22,
    121, 153; **13** (*p*60*n*), 111, 118,
    120, 134, 158, 175, 195, 220; **14**
    364, 412, 433, 445, 490; **16** 402;
    Anthroparion as, **14** 412 (*see
    also below* leaden/metal man);
    Anthropos as, **9i** 529;
    in *Faust, see* Goethe: *Faust s.v.*
    Characters;
    hermaphroditic, **14** 700; **16**
    398;
    lapis as, **14** 552, 770;
    leaden/metal man, **11** 350; **12**
    210; **13** 93, 246 (*see also above*
    Anthroparion);
    pissing manikin, **12** *fig.* 121;
    as product of unconscious, **11**
    411;
    soul as, **16** 481
Honegger, J., **5** 200; **18** 1033&*n*
honesty, **7** 323
honey, **11** 334; **14** 683&*n*, 687, 698,
    704;
    -cakes, to pacify Cerberus, **5**
    577;
    -dew, **13** 190*n*
Honorius of Autun, **11** 358; **12** 523;
    14 24, 25, 256, 268, 408, 536;
    WORKS:
      Elucidarium, **14** 420;
      Expositio in Cantica canticorum,
      9i 403*n*; **14** 25*n*, 268*n*;
      Liber duodecim quaestionum, **14**

Honorius of Autun (*cont.*):
732*n*;
Sacramentarium, **14** 732*n*;
Sermo in Dominica in Palmis,
14 408*n*;
Sermo in Epiphania Domini, **14**
188*n*;
Speculum de mysteriis, **8** ̄559*n*;
9ii 158*n*; **12** 523&*n*; **13** 116*n*;
14 10*n*, 121*n*, 256*n*, 396,
482*n*, 483*n*, 535&*n*
hooded man, **9i** 408
hoof and hoofmarks, **5** 421, 638
hook: fish-, **9ii** 174&*n*;
for hanging, **5** pl. XXVIII;
three-pronged, **13** 447, 450 (*see
also* trident)
hoopoe, *see* ANIMALS *s.v.*
hope, **4** 663; **11** 499
Hopfer, H., **10** 696
Hopi Indians, *see* American Indians: NORTH *s.v.*
Hopkins, W., **18** 691, 693, 695
Horace, **4** 744*n*; **5** 626; **9i** 464*n*;
Odes, **5** 480*n*;
Satires, Epistles and Ars Poetica,
tr. H. Rushton Fairclough, **4**
(*p*302), 743*n*; **11** 96*n*, 742*n*; **13**
229*n*; **14** 62*n*, 280*n*; **15** 198*n*
Horapollo, **8** 394; **9i** 95, 100; **14**
712*n*;
Hieroglyphica, tr. G. Boas, **8**
392*n*; **9i** 95, 553*n*; **12** 530, *fig.*
7; **13** 322&*n*; **14** 174*n*, 474&*n*
horde, primal, **5** 396; **9i** 126
Horfoltus, **12** 449*n*; **13** 88*n*
horizon, quartering of, **12** 137
horizontal/vertical, **12** 287–91, 320;
circle/disc, **12** 307, 316, 320–1
Hormanuthi, **13** 99
hormé, **3** 418*n*
hormones, **8** 374, 376, 653; **14** 680
horn(s): animal with, in dream, **9i**
623;
fish with, **5** 290*n*;
of moon, **12** 529, 550–3; **13**
193*n*;
of narwhal, *see* ANIMALS *s.v.*;

in pictures, **9i** 689;
of plenty, **12** *fig.* 165;
two-horned, **5** 283*n*, 290*n*, pl.
XX*a*;
of unicorn, *see* ANIMALS *s.v.*
Horneffer, E.: *Nietzsche's Lehre von
der ewigen Wiederkunft,* **9i** 210*n*; **14**
483*n*
Horos, *see* ALCHEMICAL WRITERS:
Maria Prophetissa *s.v.* Aros
horos doctrine of Valentinians, **9ii**
118*n*
horoscope(s), **7** 494; **8** 868, 869*n*; **9i**
7, 606; **10** 173; **11** 114, 115; **13**
154; **14** 298, 308; **15** 22;
of Christ, **9ii** 130*n*;
conjunction in, **8** 878–83, 989;
as mandala, **12** 314, *fig.* 100;
marriage, *see* marriage *s.v.*;
and medicine, **15** 36;
as wheel of birth, **9ii** 212, 352;
zodiac in, **9ii** 230; **15** 82;
see also astrology
horoscopum, **13** 167*n*
Horpi-chrud, **5** 357
horror novi, **17** 146
horse, *see* ANIMALS *s.v.*
Horst, G. C., **18** 797&*n*
Horstmann, C.: *Sammlung alt-
englischer Legenden,* **13** 400*n*
Horton, —, **18** 1534, 1545–6
Hortulanus, *see* ALCHEMICAL WRIT-
ERS *s.v.*
hortus: aromatum, **13** 389;
conclusus, **11** 126; **12** 257; **13**
389;
see also garden
Hortus deliciarum, see Herrad of
Landsberg
Horus, **11** 600, 641, 711; **18** 416;
and Artus, **14** 357*n*; **16** 472*n*;
-/Arueris, **5** 349;
-child, **9i** 195, 576, 652*n*, 661;
14 379;
of the East, **5** 147;
of Edfu, **5** 147;
eyes of, **5** *fig.* 11; **10** 645; **11**
177; **14** 64*n*; Osiris in, **14** 46;

four sons of (Amset, Hapi, Qebhsennuf, Tuamutef), **6** 905; **9i** 425*n*, 564, 611*n*, 660, 715; **9ii** 187, 188, 189, 203, 378, 383; **10** 738; **11** 113, 176, 600; **12** 314, *fig.* 102; **13** 31, 360, 363; **18** 1617, 1656;
names and functions of, **9ii** 188; **13** 360;
-/Harus, **14** 587;
and Isis, **5** 396, 471&*n*; **9i** 195; **9ii** 163; **14** 14; **18** 548;
and Osiris, **5** 356–7, 566; **12** *fig.* 102, 314; **14** 14*n*, 46&*n*; **18** 548;
quaternio of, *see* quaternity *s.v.* marriage;
and Set, **5** 374; **11** 641; **13** 362;
"son of Hathor," **14** 350*n*, 352;
-sun, **5** 131*n*, 356; **13** 361*n*;
as sun-hero, **5** 374 (*see also* Heru-ur)
Hosea, **18** 1541, 1629, 1637;
Book of, *see* BIBLE: O.T. *s.v.*;
marriage of, **11** 32, 394
Hosius, Bishop of Cordoba, **11** 216
hospital(s): in Dorn's treatise, **9i** 335;
in dream, **8** 478–9;
mental, change in, **3** 539
Host (Eucharistic), **8** 333; **13** 403; **14** 639;
and Mithras cult, **18** 616
hostility, **12** 29
hot/cold, as opposites, **7** 78, 115; **12** 192, 436; **14** 1, 7, 330, 607; **18** 1625
hotel, in dream(s), **4** 537, 538; **8** 535; **12** 200
Hottentots, **18** 363;
idea of sun, **5** 487
house(s), **8** 571;
astrological, **8** 866, 869*n*, 987; **12** 314, 348;
-complex, *see* complex *s.v.* family;
"of the Creative," **13** 57;
of fire, **13** 186;

with historic layers, dream/analogy of, **10** 54; **18** 484–91;
planetary, descent of soul through, **14** 299, 309;
symbolism of, **9ii** 352–3; alchemical, **14** 2&*n*, 180&*n*, 181&*n*
"House of the Gathering" (dream), **11** 58–63, 140;
and anima, **11** 128;
four/quaternity in, **11** 58, 60–3, 90, 136; **12** 293–4, *fig.* 93;
ritual in, **11** 63
Hovamol (Edda), **9i** 442*n*
Howe, E. G., **18** 50, 52, 115, 116, 117, 119, 126
Howitt, A. W., **16** 433;
The Native Tribes of South-East Australia, **16** 433*n*
Hoyle, F., **10** 810–20;
The Black Cloud, **10** 810;
Frontiers of Astronomy, **10** 810;
The Nature of the Universe, **10** 810
Hrungnir, **5** 585*n*
h.sien-yên ("immortals"), **14** 574
hsing (human nature), **13** 28*n*, 37, 46, 59–60;
-*ming* (human nature and life), **13** 34
Huang Shan-ku, *see* Kozankoku
Hubert, H., and Mauss, M., **8** 254; **9i** 89, 153; **11** 89; **16** 15;
Mélanges d'histoire des religions, **7** 220*n*; **8** 52*n*; **9i** 136*n*; **11** 89*n*; **18** 81&*n*
Hubur, **5** 375
Huch, R., **5** 140*n*
Hudibras, **8** 63*n*
Hufeland, C. W., **3** 271*n*; *see also* association-chain(s) *s.v.*
Hugh of St. Victor, **5** 97; **14** 550;
De laude caritatis, **5** 97*n*; **14** 550*n*
Hugh of Strasbourg: attrib., *Compendium theologicae veritatis,* **9ii** 133*n*, 159*n*
hui (consciousness), **13** 28*n*, 37
Huichol Indians, **8** 121

and evil inclinations, **1** 467, 474;

extraverted type and, *see* extraversion;

failure in, *see* failure *s.v.*;

in family constellation, **2** 1008;

and feeling-tone, **1** 170; complex, **2** 908, 915, 917;

forgetting in, **2** 207, 639–40, 657–8;

Freud on, *see* Freud *s.v.*;

"grande hystérie," **1** 13, 18;

indirect associations in, **2** 450*n*;

as latent psychosis, **3** 539, 558;

among mediums, **18** 725;

a "metaphysical problem," **18** 1119;

and moral defect, **1** 457–75;

paralysis in, **2** 911, 913;

pathological ideas in, **3** 7, 10;

periodic changes in personality in, **1** 110, 112;

psychogenesis of/as psychogenetic illness, **3** 75, 505–6; **4** 5, 28, 207, 231; **7** 1/409, 4–5/ 413–14; **13** 48; **18** 885, 922;

psychology of, **18** 871;

reaction-time in, **2** 799–807, 813, 944;

reinforced object-libido in, **2** 950–3;

repression in, **2** 639–40, 657, 661–2, 800; **4** 51, 60;

riddle of, **18** 871;

root phenomenon of, **18** 879;

screen memories in, **2** 658;

and sexuality, **4** 5–8, 36–8, 51, 215; **15** 63;

and simulation, **1** 304–5, 338, 353;

sociological and historical aspects, **18** 882;

stereotypies in, **3** 183;

symptoms of, **1** 417; **7** 4/413; **8** 702; **15** 62; **16** 231; psychic, **18** 884–5; as symbolism, **4** 159; and unconscious psychic activity, **8** 297;

theory(-ies), **18** 872–3;

trauma theory of, **4** 206–9; **5** 654; **7** 8/417; **17** 176; **18** 1148;

traumatic, **3** 162; **4** 10–11;

treatment for, **18** 886;

Ufos and, **10** 631;

wrongly diagnosed as sarcoma of spine, **3** 468–9; **18** 114;

in young girls, **4** 384, 386

hysterical:

TITLES: "Association, Dream and Hysterical Symptoms," **2** 793–862; "A Case of Hysterical Stupor in a Prisoner in Detention," **1** 226–300; "On Hysterical Misreading," **1** 151–65;

amnesia, *see* amnesia *s.v.*;

anaesthesia, **1** 73; **18** 421;

anxiety states, **7** 69; **15** 64;

behaviour, and infantile disposition, **5** 430–1;

blindness, *see* blindness *s.v.*;

conversion, **1** 298;

deafness, **7** 4/413;

delirium, *see* delirium *s.v.*;

distractibility, **1** 73;

disturbance of sensation, **18** 876;

dream-state, **5** 204;

engourdissement, **6** 199;

fantasies, *see* fantasy(-ies) *s.v.* in hysterics;

fever, case of, **11** 15;

hyperaesthesias, **18** 876;

intellect, **18** 877;

misreading, *see* misreading *s.v.*;

pain-apraxia, **18** 876;

pains, **16** 185; **18** 50;

paralysis, **18** 876, 884;

reaction-type, **2** 943–4;

self-deceivers, **13** 142;

symptoms, **2** 793, 794, 816, 833, 845–62; psychogenesis of, **18** 922, 1147;

twilight states, *see* twilight states

hysterical subjects/hysterics, **1** 97, 114, 138, 280, 340; **3** 141;

analysis of, **18** 1045–50;

hysterical subjects (*cont.*):
    belle indifference of, **3** 35, 145–6;
    fantasies of, *see* fantasy(-ies)
    s.v.;
    and forgetfulness, **1** 119&*n*;
    hypnosis of, **3** 137, 163, 181;
    influence of affects on, **1** 318–
    19, 475;
    irrelevant answers of, **1** 164;
    lying/deception in, **1** 302, 420,
    441; **18** 447 (see also *pseudologia*
    phantastica);
    and secrets, **16** 131;
    spontaneous phenomena in, **18**
    728;
    substitution of physical for psy-
    chic pain, **5** 436;
    vision of conflagration, **1** 130
hystero-epilepsy, **1** 12, 130; *see also*
    epilepsy *s.v.* hysteria
hysterogenic: complexes, **2** 798;
    mechanism, **5** 26*n*
hystero-hypnosis, **1** 128; **3** 160&*n*

idea (*cont.*):

512, 520–1, 533, 536, 733, 751;
archetypal, **9i** 6*n*, 45, 117; **11**
222; **13** 476; **14** 673–4;
and archetypes, distinction, **8**
417; **9i** 6*n*; **15** 126&*n*;
ascent to (Augustine), **5** 104*n*;
association of, *see* association;
"big," **7** 289;
chain of, **1** 221 (*see also* association-chains);
and changelessness, **6** 153;
collective, **6** 164, 373; **7** 122,
520; **11** 222; **16** 248; God as, **6**
176;
and complexes, *see* complex(es)
s.v.;
condensation of, **3** 44, 267,
300;
confusion of, **3** 135, 346;
delusional, *see* delusion(s); delusional;
depersonalized, **6** 54;
depressive, **7** 344;
directional, **2** 383–4;
dissociated/repressive, **3** 56, 70,
76;
elementary, **8** 353; **9i** 153;
as entity, **18** 742;
and fantasy, **13** 356–7;
feeling-toned, **1** 119, 298, 304;
6 239; **7** 20 (*see also* feeling-
toned complex);
flight of, **1** 189, 190, 194, 199,
208–9, 213, 216, 219; **2** 28,
116, 132, 388, 450*n*; **3** 21–2,
37; **6** 481; **18** 829;
formation of, **5** 474;
German, **10** 973;
as golden vessels, **18** 745;
as higher reality, **6** 59;
hypostatizing of, **6** 62;
inborn, **8** 352–3, 435, 589; **11**
461;
inherited, **3** 565; **5** 154; **7** 101,
219; **8** 229, 718; **9i** 136; **10** 14,
831; **11** 165; **16** 61, 206, 254*n*;
introvert's relation to, **6** 103,

629, 633–4;
intuitive, **7** 107, 151; **12** 305;
13 7, 59;
lucky, **10** 305;
morbid, **7** 254; **11** 22;
mythical/mythological, **5** 629; **7**
109; **8** 589; **18** 742;
neurotic, **5** 655;
new, **10** 463; **11** 23; combinations of, **1** 172–5; developed in
somnambulism, **1** 147*n*; fear
of, **10** 916; **17** 146; spread of, **8**
594, 597; spirits as, **8** 596;
numinous, **13** 393, 396;
obsessive, *see* obsessions *s.v.*;
over-valued, **6** 467&*n*;
pathological, **3** 7, 9–10, 218,
361–2;
as phenomenon, **18** 742;
Platonic, *see* Plato;
predominant, **1** 82*n*, 101, 117;
pressure of, **3** 428, 434–5;
primordial, **7** 217–18/448–9;
16 206; adaptation of, **10**
548–9 (*see also* archetypes;
primordial image(s));
ruling, **5** 11, 18; **8** 633–4;
sovereignty of, **5** 113;
spontaneously creative, **5** 74,
(*p*453);
subjective, **4** 768–70;
symbolic, **5** 683; **18** 570;
symptom-producing, **15** 62;
and thing, united, **6** 72–3, 77;
unconscious, **18** 728;
unconscious activities of, and
idealism, **6** 525, 533;
unity of, **6** 158;
universal, **18** 742, 744, 745;
world of, **10** 38; **13** 168*n*
ideal(s), **7** 65, 150, 254, 462*n*, 482;
11 8;
Christian/Christ as, **7** 373; **12**
7–9;
collective, **7** 240, 519; **9ii** 54; **15**
128;
cultural, **6** 110;
delusive, **7** 93;

342

343

identity (*cont.*):
    original, **7** 329; **13** 122; **17** 331;
    of priest and Christ, **11** 413;
    of psyche and matter, **12** 376,
    378, 410;
    psychic, **18** 440&*n*, 465;
    psychology of, **17** 93;
    secret, **12** 451;
    of stone and man, **13** 394;
    unconscious, **7** 172; **10** 69; **11**
    375*n*, 389, 817; **13** 66, 122,
    125; **14** 336; **16** 504; **17** 83,
    271, 330; of child with parents,
    16 142; **17** 83–4, 107, 253 (*see
    also* Lévy-Bruhl *s.v. participation
    mystique*);
    of uroboros and egg, **13** 109*n*
ideologism, **6** 518, 522, 523
ideology(-ies), **11** 778;
    Christian, **13** 366
Ides/Ideus (Paracelsus), **9ii** 334; **13**
    168, 193
idiosyncrasy(-ies), **7** 267; **9ii** 259,
    312
ἰδιῶται, **17** 298
idiots, **2** 408*n*, 506, 509, 523; **17**
    292; *see also* imbecility; mental
    deficiency
idleness, La Rochefoucauld on, **5**
    253; **9i** 56
idols: reason for, **18** 413;
    repression of, **7** 115
Idris, **18** 1527–8
Ignatius (of Antioch), **8** 388;
    Epistle to the Ephesians, tr. K.
    Lake, **8** 388&*n*
Ignatius Loyola, St., **10** 522; **13**
    293; **14** 283;
    and spiritual exercises/*exercitia
    spiritualia,* **9i** 232, 237;
    terms used by, **13** 201*n*;
    vision of polyophthalmia in
    snake/*serpens oculatus,* **5** 177*n*; **7**
    119; **8** 395; **11** 957; **13** 114,
    267*n*; **18** 1538;
    vision of round golden object, **8**
    395*n*;
    WORKS:

Exercitia spiritualia, **9i** 236;
    9ii 252&*n*; **11** 150*n*, 391,
    778, 793, 854, 864, 873, 893,
    937–40, 958; **12** 166, 390*n*;
    14 708; **18** 1536, 1548,
    1590&*n*;
    The Spiritual Exercises, tr. J.
    Rickaby, **13** 201*n*, 293*n*; **14**
    255&*n*, 283*n*;
    see also Funk; Gonzales
ignis: Bellator, **13** 184*n*;
    coelestis, **13** 103*n*;
    elementaris, **13** 256;
    fatuus, **13** 303;
    gehennalis/fire of Gehenna, **9ii**
    201; **12** 433, 440, 451, 470; **14**
    113, 631 (*see also* hell *s.v.* fire);
    mercurialis, **13** 256 (*see also* Mer-
    curius *s.v.* fire);
    noster, **12** 336&*n*;
    see also fire
ignition, **13** 173*n*
ignorance, **9ii** 299; **11** 271;
    in Yoga (avidyā), **11** 775; **12**
    123
Ikhnaton, **15** 175
Ila, **5** 211&*n*
Iliad, see Homer *s.v.*
Iliaster, iliastic, *see* Paracelsus *s.v.*
    ARCANA
illatio, **11** 321
ills, *see* illness *s.v.*
illness, **9i** 214;
    association and, **2** 881–2;
    as defence, **10** 881;
    "ills" and, **11** 248;
    mental, *see* mental illness/
    disease;
    physical, schizophrenia and, **3**
    180&*n*, 360;
    primitives and, *see* primitive(s)
    s.v.;
    psychic, attachment to dead
    and, **8** 598;
    soul-complexes and, *see* soul-
    complex;
    treatment of, **8** 684
illuminatio/illumination(s), **9i** 82; **12**

11, 68, 83, 120, 188, 356, 451, 456; **13** 107, 112, 119, 148, 219, 417; **17** 318–19;
  of consciousness, *see* consciousness *s.v.*;
  of initiate, **5** 553*n*; **12** 83;
  as spiritual transformation, **11** 274;
    three stages of, **14** 718;
    two sources of, **13** 263;
  see also light; revelation
illusion(s), **7** 26, 90, 189, 325, 373, 400, 437; **8** 682, 802; **9i** 353; **9ii** 20, 32; **10** 608, 672; **11** 494; **12** 57, 353–5; **13** 24, 47, 56, 391; **15** 69, 71; **16** 111, 149; **17** 228;
  of anchorites, **10** 651;
  of conscious mind, **5** 95&*n*;
  daemon is, **13** 55;
  descent into, after death, **11** 856;
  and ego, **17** 167;
  enjoyment of, **5** 432;
  hypochondriacal, **7** 75;
  infantile, **7** 88, 91;
  karmic, *see* karmic illusions;
  Mercurius as god of, **13** 299;
  of participation in story or play, **5** (*p*448);
  of personal God, **13** 50;
  and poetic creation, **15** 113, 118;
  projected, **11** 140;
  in puberty, **10** 217;
  reality as, **10** 986;
  and religious experience, **11** 167;
  transcendental, **13** 47;
  of youth, **7** 90, 113;
  see also *maya*
Iloch, *see* Paracelsus: ARCANA *s.v.*
image(s)/imagery, **1** 28; **7** 151, 231–2, 236, 289, 323, 386, 405, 507; **8** 510, 931; **9i** 21–2, 152; **11** 893, 896–7; **12** 15; **13** 77, 88; **14** 603, 753–4; **16** 246, 465–6;
  TITLES: "The Image of Wholeness," **13** 369–73; "The Tree

as an Archetypal Image," **13** 350–3;
  in active fantasy, **8** 170, 399–403;
  of alchemy, **16** (*p*165), 471;
  anima-, *see* anima *s.v.*;
  animus, *see* animus *s.v.*;
  anthropomorphic, **5** 145;
  archetypal, **7** 151; **8** 279, 417; **9i** 22, 82; **11** 845; **12** 32, 38; **13** 350; **14** 401; **15** 11; **17** 337;
  part animal, part human, **5** 264;
  "austere," **10** 730 (*see also below* "severe");
  autochthonous, **13** 352;
  autonomous, **8** 521; **13** 299;
  Christ-, *see* Christ *s.v.*;
  in Christianity, *see* Christian *s.v.*;
  collective/of collective unconscious, **5** 655; **7** 184, 219, 233, 250, 283–4, 287, 301; **13** 353;
  complex-, **2** 891;
  contamination of, **11** 783; **14** 454;
  creation of new, **5** 553–4;
  cryptomnesic, **1** 138–9, 145–6;
  definition, **6** 743–54;
  displacement of, **14** 401–2;
  divine/heavenly, **7** 150, 217; **12** 12; **13** 215;
  doctor as, **7** 145, 157;
  dream-, *see* dream(s) *s.v.*;
  eschatological, **13** 294;
  eternal, **7** 183, 232; **9i** 11; **13** 457; **14** 510; **17** 338;
  fantasy-, *see* fantasy *s.v.*;
  of the goal, **12** 328; **16** 535;
  God-, *see* God-image;
  helpful, **11** 533;
  of Hera, **5** 363;
  hypnagogic, **1** 101;
  ideal, **7** 244, 388;
  ideas as, **9i** 68;
  inborn, **7** 300; **8** 398; **17** 338;
  infantile, **7** 217;
  inner, **12** 17, 123, 219;

image (*cont.*):
    magical, of childhood, **5** 631;
    memory-, *see* memory-image
    metaphysical, **11** 469;
    mythological/myth-creating, **6** 280–1; **7** 118; **9i** 8; **10** 646; **11** 781;
    neurotic, **3** 560;
    parental, **18** 361, 362, 366;
    plastic, **2** 471&*n*, 473;
    Plato on, **6** 512;
    among primitives, **8** 278;
    primordial, *see* primordial image;
    projected, **7** 294;
    psyche and, **8** 607–11, 615–18; **13** 75;
    psychic, **4** 764; **6** 46; **8** 680–1, 745–7; **9i** 135; **11** 16, 777; **16** 201;
    in psychoses, **5** 474;
    regulating, **13** 396;
    religious, **13** 77;
    sacred, **11** 82, 893; **12** 19;
    of sacrificial death and resurrection, **5** 638;
    sequence/trains of, **5** 18; **16** 13;
    "severe," **12** 203, 205, 211, 308;
    soul-, *see* soul-image;
    spirits as, **8** 628;
    in stone, **12** 406;
    symbolical, **8** 388; **9i** 82;
    totality, *see* totality *s.v.*;
    unconscious, **5** 258; **12** 14;
    universal, **7** 372;
    visual, **2** 127–8, 130, 143, 204, 206, 246; objectified as hallucination, **1** 98;
    vividness of, **2** 462, 471–3, 485*n*;
    of women, **12** 293, 295; **17** 338–40;
    see also anima
imagination/*imaginatio*, **7** 274; **12** 219, 350; **13** 176, 193, 195, 201–4, 207, 220, 393; **17** 225;
    TITLES: "Meditation and Imagination," **12** 390–6; "Some

Instances of Subconscious Creative Imagination" (Miss Miller), **5** (*pp*447–62);
    active, *see* active imagination;
    fantasy *s.v.* active imagination;
    and alchemy, **11** 793; analytical psychology/analysis and, **11** 793; **14** 333, 705; and dream-series, **18** 403, 406;
    a priori categories of, **18** 81;
    categories of, **8** 254; **11** 845; **16** 15;
    creative, **16** 98;
    and hypnagogic images, **1** 100;
    imaginatio sensus, **13** 201*n*;
    inherited possibilities of, **7** 101;
    masculine, **14** 619;
    moral, **16** 150;
    and neurosis, **11** 12, 17; **16** 32; **17** 313;
    pathological effects of, **18** 903;
    principle of, **6** 93;
    a psychic process, **11** 889;
    in unconscious, **8** 362;
    and visions, **1** 106;
    see also Paracelsus *s.v. imaginatio*
imagines, **8** 628
Imago (periodical), ed. O. Rank and H. Sachs, **18** 1031*n*
imago, **5** 62*n*; **6** 812 (Def.); **7** 223, 296–7;
    of daughter, **9ii** 24;
    dream-, **8** 524;
    father-, **4** 728, 740–2; **7** 88, 113, 380; **10** 66; **14** 232; and God-image/religion, **5** 63, 89, 93–4, 134; reactivation of, **5** 62, 134; and transference, **7** 206; **9i** 122; **16** 218;
    mother-, **5** 406, 468, 555; **7** 88, 113; **9ii** 26; anima as, *see* anima *s.v.* mother; dragon as negative, **5** 395; hero and, **5** 558, 606; libido's regression to, **5** 329–30, 450*n*, 508; religion and, **5** 89, 94, 134; son and, **9ii** 20, 24, 26; **13** 147; symbols of, **5** 261, 265, 318, 320, 395, 457,

impossibility of task/situation, **8** 847–8

impostors, intentional fraud of, **1** 474

impotence, **4** 150–1; **7** 308; **9i** 162; sense of, **7** 222, 452

impoverishment, emotional, **3** 74, 76, 103

impression(s), **4** 399, 401–2; **8** 264; conditioned by predisposition, **4** 400;
early, **4** 310;
effects of, **3** 90;
first, **11** 776, 821;
forgotten, reappearance of, in cryptomnesia, **1** 183;
pleasing, transmission of, **5** (*p*447);
re-animation of, **5** (*p*461);
subjective, of the malingerer, **1** 301;
subliminal, **8** 588;
suspect reality of, **4** 403

imprint, *see* engram; *typos*

improbable, occurrence of the, **10** 744

improvement, patient's, **14** 614, 615

impulse(s), **9ii** 51; **17** 102;
and attitude, **8** 692;
exaggerated, **8** 264;
instinctive, *see* instinctual *s.v.*
natural, **8** 423;
repressed, **16** 115;
unexpected, **1** 25–6;
vital, **13** 64

impure metals, **13** 381*n*

inattentiveness, **17** 237

incantation, for producing *numinosum*, **11** 7

Incarnation/incarnation/*incarnatio*, **1** 64; **9ii** 277; **11** 626, 628, 631, 655, 678; **12** 11*n*, 26; **17** 96; **18** 1511, 1664;
cause of, **11** 642;
of Christ, *see* Christ *s.v.*;
continuing, *see* Holy Ghost *s.v.* God;
and creed, **12** 253;

devil/Satan and, **11** 248, 650;
earlier, revealed in meditation, **7** 303; **13** 46*n*;
further, **18** 1660–1;
of God, *see* God *s.v.*;
hierosgamos, as first step towards, **11** 748, 755; in Egyptian theology, **11** 624;
incompleteness of, **18** 1645, 1660; and individuation, **18** 1624;
and Mass, commemoration of, **11** 338, 378;
among primitives, *see* primitive(s) *s.v.* children;
of Yahweh, *see* Yahweh *s.v.*

Incas, *see* American Indians: SOUTH *s.v.*

incendiarism, **5** 271*n*;
psychology of, **5** 249

incense, representing prayer, **11** 319&*n*; *see also* censing

incest, **3** 421; **4** 350–3, 512; **5** 507; **7** 22; **9i** 449, 516; **9ii** 322, 329, 361, 363; **11** 528, 576; **13** 360; **14** 107, 506, 523*n*, 664; **16** 55–6, 64, 75, 140, 362, 368, 410, 415, 419, 452, 471; **17** 220;
in alchemy, **14** 106, 610, 664;
in ancient Egypt, **16** 419, 438;
and anima/animus, **16** 521;
archetype of, **5** 299*n*; **10** 659; **13** 396; **14** 107, 178; **16** 368, 533;
barrier/prohibition, **4** 352, 565; **5** 652; and canalization of libido, **5** 332; and creation of self-consciousness, **5** 415; by danger of regression, **5** 335; Freud on, *see* Freud *s.v.*; as impulse to domestication, **5** 415; motif of father and, **5** 396; origin of, **5** 332; *re* son and mother, **5** 388 (*see also below* taboo);
brother/sister, **5** 555; **9ii** 329; **12** 140*n*, 193*n*, 436, 439&*n*, 496, *figs.* 118, 225; **14** 188, 669,

735; **16** 426;
and civilization, **8** 44;
complex, *see* complex(es) *s.v.*;
death as punishment for, **16** 468;
definition of, **5** 351*n*, 415;
dream of, **14** 178;
in fairytales, **16** 430–1;
fantasies of, **4** 470, 540, 550; **5** 67*n*, 655; **9i** 122, 130, 135; **14** 410; **17** 220;
fear of, **7** 173; and devouring mother, **5** 654; and horror of, **16** 55, 415;
Freud on, *see* Freud *s.v.*;
of the gods, **5** 390&*n*;
Greek myths and, **16** 146;
among Hottentots, **18** 363;
as individuation, **16** 419;
and inertia, **5** 253;
as instinct, **16** 368, 438;
king/daughter, **12** 454;
magical, **5** 394;
matriarchal, in Oedipus legend, **5** 264;
misleading use of term, **17** 144;
mother/son, *see* mother and son *s.v.*;
motif, **13** 278, 360, 396;
in mythology, **5** 253; **9i** 140*n*, 449*n*; **16** 146;
and natural love of father, **5** 76;
and Oedipus complex, **4** 343, 562, 565;
primal, **13** 396;
and primitives, **4** 349, 352, 470, 565;
problem: Freud on, *see* Freud *s.v.* incest; and reactivation of mother-imago, **5** 313;
procreation through, **16** 473;
prohibition, *see above* barrier;
regression to, **12** 171; **14** 86;
and religious instinct, **10** 659;
repression and, **6** 201;
and ritual castration, **5** 299;
"royal," **14** 104, 410;

royal or divine prerogative, **16** 419, 473;
sacred, **9i** 417;
sin of, **5** 555;
symbolical, **5** 299, 313, 565; conquest of, **5** 530; of union with one's own being, **16** 419;
-taboo, **4** 565; **5** 450, 487; **7** 239; **16** 369, 438, 443; effect of, **5** 216; and infantile regression, **5** 351; *vs.* libido, **5** 313; in marriage class system, **5** 415*n*; in Wachandi rite, **5** 226 (*see also above* barrier);
tendency, **10** 61; as desire of the mother or the anima, **5** 450; libido freed from, through symbolical truths, **5** 357;
theory, **9i** 140*n*;
unconscious, **17** 218;
variants of, **14** 402;
-wish, *see* Freud *s.v.* incest
incestuous: desire, basis of, **5** 332;
energy, desexualization of, **5** 226;
fixation, **15** 49;
hierosgamos, **16** 438;
instinct, **16** 368, 438
incineratio, **13** 163*n*; **16** 398, 467
inclinations, evil, *see* hysteria *s.v.* evil
incongruity, of idea and affect, *see* affect *s.v.*
inconscient supérieur, **5** 78
incorporation motif, **12** 440*n*; *see also* devouring; swallowing
incorporeal, *see* corporeal
incorruptibility, **13** 170–1*n*, 177;
of Mercurius, **13** 264, 295
incorruptible substance, **12** 43, 558
Increatum/Uncreated, **11** 60; **13** 283; **14** 32, 143; **16** 402*n*, 454; *see also* Paracelsus: ARCANA *s.v.*
incubation: in alchemy, **14** 262&*n*;
dreams, in temples of Aesculapius, **8** 549;
period, **17** 200;
self-, **5** 589–90; **14** 262;

incubation (*cont.*):
    sleep of, **12** 171;
    in temple of Oropos, **5** 571;
    warmth of, **12** 441
incubus, **5** 577; **7** 370
indecision, neurotic, **17** 150
indefiniteness, **11** 785, 792
independence: adult, **5** 461;
    battle for, **5** 470;
    and development of consciousness, **5** 351;
    of mind, importance of, **17** 173;
    social, women and, **10** 242–3;
    of unconscious, **7** (*p*123)
indeterminacy / indeterminism, **8** 376*n*, 828; **10** 188
Index, the, **11** 172
India/Indian, **8** 672; **9i** 11, 193, 398&*n*; **10** 962; **11** 610, 666, 860–1, 908–11, 933, 961; **12** 9, 192, 209; **13** 168, 218, 362*n*; **14** 131; **15** 91, 151; **18** 91, 141;
    TITLES: "The Dreamlike World of India," **10** 981–1001; "The Holy Men of India," **11** 950–63; "What India Can Teach Us," **10** 1002–13;
    and alchemy, **10** 631; **13** 278;
    American, *see* American Indians;
    art, **11** 933;
    astrology, **7** 494;
    and birth control, **10** 615;
    Bombay Parsis, **5** 354;
    British Empire and, **10** 984;
    castes in, **18** 361;
    child motif in, **9i** 259;
    and Christian culture, **10** 404;
    civilization and primitivity in, **10** 1011;
    development of symbol in, **9ii** 271–2;
    Eckhart and, **9ii** 302;
    fish symbol in, **9ii** 176;
    god(s), **13** 458; Adityas, solar gods, **13** 339; lotus and, **13** 345; Parjanya, rain-, **13** 341&*n*;

Varuna, sky-, **13** 341*n*;
    influence on Christianity, **11** 713;
    insights in, **9ii** 350;
    Jains, **5** 403;
    and loss of old culture, **18** 1689;
    "loving and terrible mother" in, **9i** 158;
    mandala in, **13** 32;
    "mountain of Adam," **5** 288*n*;
    mythology, **5** 176, 659; **11** 950;
    as part of Asia, **10** 989;
    performance of rites in, **18** 626;
    philosophy, *see* philosophy *s.v.*;
    psychology, **7** 240*n*; **11** 956;
    "Quicksilver System," **13** 254;
    religious philosophy of, *see* philosophy *s.v.* Indian;
    sacred tree in, **5** 545; **13** 461;
    spirituality, **11** 933;
    stones in, **13** 129;
    sun-wheels, **11** 484;
    symbols, **9ii** 271;
    temple sculptures in, **9ii** 339*n*;
    theosophy, **13** 342, 345;
    thought, **9ii** 271; **10** 1007, 1012;
    and Western culture, **10** 404;
    wholeness of life in, **10** 988;
    Yama, **5** 421;
    see also Brahma; Brahmans; Hinduism; Indra; purusha; yoga
Indian corn, *see* maize
Indian Journal of Psychotherapy, J.'s foreword, **18** 1790–1
Indian Ocean (alchemical), **14** 7, 8
Indian Science Congress, **10** 993
indicium(-a), **16** 79–80;
    age as, **16** 75;
    attitude, extravert/introvert, **16** 77;
    resistance as, **16** 75
Indies, in quaternity, **9ii** 206
indifference: emotional, **3** 145;
    of hallucinated patient, **3** 483,

487;

moral, **11** 825;

see also hysterical subjects *s.v.*
belle indifférence

indigestion, **8** 516

indignation, misplaced, **4** 229

indirect associations, *see* associa-
tion(s), classification of *s.v.*

indistinguishability, of self and
God-image, **11** 289

individual, **6** 755 (Def.); **7** 235/455,
240, 242/463, 311, 404, 461; **11**
88, 140, 452; **14** 194; **16** 11, 103,
354; **17** 289, 343, 345;

TITLES: "The Individual's Understanding of Himself," **10**
525–48; "The Plight of the Individual in Modern Society,"
10 488–504; "The Significance
of the Father in the Destiny of
the Individual," **4** 693–744;
"The Significance of the Unconscious in Individual Education," **17** 253–83;

and collective, **7** 237–40,
484–6, 489, 490, 503–4, 507,
513, 515; **8** 494; as opposites,
12 557;

collectivization of, **18** 495;

diminishing importance of, **10**
501–2;

and disposable energies, **7** 74;

doctor and, **14** 125;

egocentric interests of, **7** 455;

as element of differentiation, **7**
240;

freedom of, *see* freedom *s.v.*;

and goodness, **18** 1378–80; and
group formation, **18** 1314;

idiosyncrasy of, **7** 267;

importance of, in psychiatry, **3**
72;

and individuation, **7** 266;

inner consolidation of, **16** 444;

and mass, **7** 35;

and nation, **7** (*p*4), 150; **10** 45;

need for change in, **18** 599;

needs of, **7** 288; **10** 893;

a new experiment of life, **17**
173;

normalization of, **11** 539;

nucleus, **6** 174–5, 183*n*;

outstanding, **7** 237;

and persona, **7** 245–6/465–6,
485;

Protestantism and, **11** 862;

psychology, **3** 406; **7** (*p*4),
484–6 (*see also* Adler, A. *s.v.*);

as resultant, **10** 142;

revaluation of, **10** 719;

salvation of, **10** 536;

and social function in conflict,
6 120;

and society, *see* society *s.v.*;

and species, **11** 146; **17** 105,
329;

as twig from the mother, **5** 296;

understanding the, **10** 496–7;

and universal, **16** 1–5;

variability of, **4** 679;

see also child(ren)

individualism, **6** 168&*n*, 376, 433,
761; **7** 267; **16** 42; **17** 292–3, 298;

extreme, **16** 227;

neurotic, **12** 557

individuality, **5** 258; **6** 756 (Def.); **7**
246–7, 266, 305, 501; **10** 500–1,
894; **11** 390; **16** 1, 5, 11; **17** 181;
18 1102, 1172;

TITLES: "Attempts to Free the
Individuality from the Collective Psyche," **7** 471–9; "Negative Attempts to Free the
Individuality from the Collective Psyche," **7** 254–65;

of child, **17** 93, 223;

concept of, **7** 503–5, 507;

conscious, achievement of, **16**
227;

consciousness of, **7** 248;

definition of, **6** 756; **7** 514, 519;

destruction of, **7** 240;

dissolution/obliteration of, **6**
174–6, 227;

and ego, **9ii** 10;

and family, **16** 223;

351

individuality (*cont.*):
    and functions, **6** 111;
    independence of, **7** 265;
    as masculine, feminine or her-
    maphroditic figure, **7** 520;
    mental, **7** 504;
    of observer, **6** 11;
    overestimation of, **16** 5;
    and persona, **7** 245/465, 504;
    psychological development of,
    6 184; **8** 110, 112;
    and self, *see* self *s.v.*;
    spiritual, **13** 41;
    suppression of, **6** 123;
    synthesis of, **6** 472;
    true, **7** 393, 478;
    uniqueness of, **16** 1, 6;
    violated in Christianity, **6** 110
individualization: of treatment, **16**
42–3;
    urge to, **4** 658
individuation, **5** 459, 624*n*, 672; **6**
168*n*, 757–62 (Def.), 876; **7**
(*p*125), 241&*n*/462, 242/463, 310,
372–3, 505; **8** 75, 111, 400,
430–2, 557; **9i** 83, 194, 254, 256,
258, 289, 355, 520, 616–17, 620,
624, 626, 679; **9ii** 73, 79, 312; **10**
714, 718, 722, 809; **11** 233, 390,
400, 448, 739, 746, 755–6, 849,
906; **12** 116, 150, 163, 253, 291,
324, 330, 564; **13** 44, 247, 287–8,
344, 433, 437, 459; **14** 354*n*, 645,
669, 670, 680 *et passim;* **16** 11, 12,
25, 219, 227, 352, 419, 441–2,
454*n*, 469, 474; **17** 307; **18** 271,
377, 830, 1412, 1526, 1554, 1582,
1588;
    TITLES: "Adaptation, Indi-
    viduation, Collectivity," **18**
    1084–1106;
    "Conscious, Unconscious and
    Individuation," **9i** 489–524;
    "Individuation," **7** 266–406;
    "The Mass and the Individua-
    tion Process," **11** 414–48;
    "Melusina and the Process of
    Individuation," **13** 215–22;

"A Study in the Process of Individuation," **9i** 525–626;
and adaptation, **18** 1094–7;
of the adept, **13** 435;
and alchemy, *see* alchemy *s.v.*;
apocatastasis in, **9ii** 260;
and archetypes, *see* archetypes
s.v.;
Ares and, **13** 176–7;
beginning of, **14** 753;
and child motif, **9i** 270, 278;
Christianity and, **9ii** 125; **10**
529; **14** 650;
and collectivity, **18** 1099–1106;
dangers of, **14** 49;
definition, **6** 757–62; **9i** 489–
90, 523;
devil and, **11** 471;
a dialectical process, **18** 1505;
dream-series and, **8** 550–3; **9i**
235;
goal of, **7** 241*n*, 266–9, 405; **9i**
278; **13** 242, 307; **16** 442;
guilt in, **18** 1094–5;
hero and, **9i** 281;
and *hierosgamos,* **11** 743;
Iliaster and, **13** 171;
and individualism, **7** 267;
inescapable, **18** 1641;
and integration of collective
unconscious, **9ii** 72;
involves suffering, **11** 411;
as life in God, **18** 1624;
mandala symbol of, **9i** 73; **10**
693;
Mass and, **11** 414;
matter and, **11** 252;
Mercurius and, **13** 277, 284;
moon prototype of, **14** 217;
motifs in, **16** 18;
as *mysterium coniunctionis,* **9ii**
117;
natural process of, **7** 186–7; **9i**
234;
numinous experience of, **11**
448;
and opposites, problem of, **18**
1171;

opus and, *see* opus, alchemical
s.v.;
principle of, **7** 478;
psyche and, **9i** 256;
psychopathology of, **9i** 290;
regulating process of, **8** 96;
repressed, **9ii** 125;
as salvation/redemption, **18**
1664;
self and, **9ii** 257; **13** 241; **16**
442;
shadow and, **11** 292;
and shamanistic symbolism, **13**
462;
source of all evil, **13** 244;
spirit of darkness and, **9i** 453;
stone compared with, **9ii** 264;
symbol(s) of, **7** 367; **10** 621,
762; **11** 460; **13** *fig.* 24;
symbolism of, **9i** 523; **11** 447*n*;
12 44–5; **13** 393; **14** 297; **18**
595; and alchemy, **12** 40, 555;
symbolized in dreams, **9i** 235;
12 44; **14** 645;
in Theseus myth, **5** 449*n*;
transference and, **16** 539;
two aspects of, **16** 448;
unconscious, **11** 756;
union of conscious and unconscious in, **18** 1419;
urge to, **11** 401; **16** 447; **18**
1198;
see also transcendent function;
wholeness
indolence, **3** 184; **4** 470, 667; **13** 17;
17 194; *see also* laziness
Indomalaysia, **18** 1253
Indonesia, **8** 441; *see also* Bataks
Indra, **5** 306, 408, 658; **18** 1077;
as psychopomp, **5** 659;
as Shyena (falcon), **5** 450*n*
induction, psychological, **16** 399,
401
industrialization/industry, **7** 428; **9i**
335; **10** 453
ineducability, **17** 257; *see also* education
ineptia mysterii, **12** 24

inertia, **4** 470, 571; **8** 764, 825; **17**
194;
La Rochefoucauld on, *see* La
Rochefoucauld;
of libido, **5** 449;
psychic, **6** 313; **10** 287;
and regression, **5** 345;
slothful, **5** 540;
of unconscious identity, **7** 172
infancy, **7** 118;
everlasting, **5** 619;
paradise of, **5** 448;
presexual stage of, **5** 654;
see also childhood
infans: Mercurialis, **18** 1360; *noster,*
Mercurius as, **9i** 268
infant(s)/babe/baby, **16** 212;
gesture of hands before
mouth, **5** 228–9;
lamia and, **5** 368–9, pl.
XXXVIIIa;
libido in, **5** 206;
threatened by snakes, **5** 396;
unbaptised, **9i** 55;
see also child(ren)
infantile:
TITLE: "Reversion to the Infantile Level," **4** 382–90;
attitude, *see* attitude *s.v.*;
bond with mother, **7** 171; **17**
270;
complex, *see* complex *s.v.*;
contents of personal unconscious, **12** 81;
demands, **7** 189;
fantasies, *see* fantasy(-ies) *s.v.*;
fixations, **6** 90; **7** 261/477; **16** 9;
Freud on, *see* Freud *s.v.*;
forces, **12** 302;
illusions, **7** 88, 91;
image, **7** 217;
innocence, **12** 152;
instinctual impulses/drives, **3**
389; **7** 21/434;
interest, anal, **5** 276;
memories/reminiscences, *see*
memory *s.v.* infantile;
mentality/disposition, **4** 312–

infantile (*cont.*):
   13; **5** 431;
   perversions, *see* perversions *s.v.*;
   relationships, **7** 134;
   sexuality, *see* Freud *s.v.*;
   symptoms, **5** 204–5;
   tendencies, **7** 202–3/443–4;
   thinking, **5** 26;
   transference, **7** 96, 105;
   types, **4** 659;
   wish(es)/craving/desires, **3** 411;
   4 540; **5** 277; **6** 89; **7** 21/434,
   27, 128, 133, 236; **13** 463;
   world, **7** 248, 284
infantilism/childishness, **5** 278, 507;
  6 550; **7** 171, 182, 257, 263; **9i**
  303–4; **10** 867; **12** 74, 171, 173–4;
  16 55; **17** 270, 281, 284;
   and the artist, **15** 158;
   and the early Christians, **15**
   176;
   and neurosis, **10** 343, 345–8;
   Western, **18** 563
infantium dii, **5** 547
infatuation, **9i** 141
infection, psychic, **7** 152; **9ii** 390*n*;
  10 493, 519, 520; **16** 365, 545;
   moral and mental, **18** 562;
   racial, **10** 966
inference(s): on the nature of matter, **8** 747;
   rational, **11** 469
inferior: function, *see* function(s)
  s.v.; Logos, animus as, **13** 60;
   man, **11** 134, 136
inferiority(-ies), **7** 72, 84–5, 218/
  450; **8** 762; **9i** 304; **9ii** 15, 34; **11**
  131, 457;
   cause of, **16** 280;
   complex, *see* complex(es) *s.v.*;
   in doctor, **16** 170;
   feelings, **10** 416, 977, 998; **13**
   164, 454; **16** 231, 546; **17** 215,
   226; of introverts, **6** 144, 306;
   of J., **7** 306;
   intellectual and emotional, **1** 5;
   moral, **7** 218/450; **16** 234; **17**
   226, 244;

neurasthenic, diagnostic difficulty, **1** 31;
psychopathic, **1** 1–5; **6** 461–2;
  10 419, 423, 466, 479; (Gross),
  6 461, 879; borderline between
  clinical pictures of, **1** 191;
  character of affects, **1** 357; classification of cases, **1** 5, 29; and
  hysteria and epilepsy, **1** 5; influence of affects on, **1** 319;
  phenomena related to other
  clinical pictures, **1** 34;
  sense of, **7** 225, 237/458; **16** 67;
  spiritual, **11** 778
infinite/infinity, **7** 250, 288; **8** 696;
  hungering for, **10** 423
inflation, **7** 110, 243, 250, 259–60,
  265, 378; **9i** 254, 393, 621; **9ii** 47;
  10 671, 675, 721, 1003; **11** 142,
  144, 156, 267, 758; **12** 320, 411,
  559, 562–3; **13** 332, 434*n*; **14** 184,
  522; **16** 472, 500, 503, 522; **17**
  246; **18** 1320;
   in *Acts of John*, **11** 438–9, 446;
   before the Deluge, **11** 669;
   of consciousness, *see* consciousness *s.v.*;
   of ego, **9ii** 44; **10** 431, 500,
   721;
   ego-subjective, **8** 176, 426;
   in Hegel, **8** 359;
   and integration of archetype,
   11 472–3;
   negative, **9i** 304; **9ii** 114;
   peril of, **9ii** 44;
   psychic, **7** 227, 233;
   psychotherapist and, **18** 356;
   religious, **9ii** 140;
   social/national, **8** 426;
   spiritual, **10** 673;
   theosophical, **11** 840
influence(s), **11** 240;
   magnetic, **1** 68;
   maternal, **5** 272;
   parental, on children, **4** 307–
   11; **5** 263
influxus divinus, **18** 1662
informatio, **12** 214, 366*n*

information, "supernatural," **7** 295
Ingram, J. H.: *Haunted Homes and Family Traditions of Great Britain*, **9i** 268*n*
inherence, principle of, **6** 45, 50, 52–5
inheritance, **11** 491;
    child's psychic, **8** 99;
    of ideas, *see* idea(s) *s.v.*;
    see also heredity
inhibition(s), **2** 640, 1111, 1122; **3** 12, 108–9, 137, 174, 184; **7** 89, 273; **10** 753*n*; **15** 64;
    of association, **1** 312;
    of attention, **3** 135;
    by conscious of incompatible material, **1** 172; **8** 132;
    emotional, **3** 90, 93;
    mental, **4** 87;
    and repetition of affect, **3** 182;
    from repressed complex, **3** 109;
    of unconscious, **8** 62, 249, 702
In hoc signo vinces, in dream, **5** 9
inimicitia elementorum, **16** 383
initiate/initiation, **7** 393; **8** 521; **12** 171, 177*n*, 527; **13** (*p*63*n*), 106, 121;
    in America, *see* America *s.v.*;
    and baptism, **4** 330; **7** 384, 393; **18** 256, 361;
    ceremonies, *see below* rites;
    doctrines taught at, **18** 536, 538;
    illumination of, **5** 553*n*; **12** 83;
    into manhood, **7** 172, 176, 179, 314; **10** 71; **16** 223; **17** 271, 276; at puberty, **16** 214;
    Mithraic, *see* Mithras *s.v.* mysteries
    into mysteries, **9ii** 414;
    process: analysis as, **11** 842, 854; *Bardo Thödol* as, **11** 841–2;
    rites of, **4** 330, 777, 782–3; **5** 530; **7** 176, 314, 384; **8** 558, 688; **9i** 208; **10** 71; **11** 197, 287; **12** 66; **13** 86*n*; **15** 150; **16** 124, 133–4, 214; **17** 158; **18**

363; in Christianity, **7** 384, 393; among primitives, *see* primitive(s) *s.v.*; and rebirth, **11** 828, 841; snake and, **5** 530; and transformation into spirits, **11** 245 (*see also under* circumcision; primordial image);
    self-restraint in, **16** 130;
    and shamanism, **11**, 346*n*, 410;
    symbolism in, **5** 644*n*; **7** 385;
    see also Tewekkul-Beg
initiative, lacking in unconscious, **7** 290
injuries: brain, *see* brain *s.v.*;
    idea of, as compensation, **3** 276, 309;
    psychic, *see* psychic injury
Inman, T.: *Ancient Pagan and Modern Christian Symbolism*, **12** *fig.* 87
inner: *homo maximus*, **13** 203;
    life, of child, **17** 107; of neurotic, **17** 315;
    light, *see* light *s.v.*;
    man, *see* man *s.v.*;
    things, **13** 63;
    voice, *see* voice *s.v.*;
    world, *see* world *s.v.*
innervation (yoga), **11** 866
innocence: infantile, **12** 152;
    personal, defence of, **5** 69;
    sexual, **3** 104
Innocent III, Pope, **9i** 458; **9ii** 138, 156
Innocents, massacre of, at Bethlehem, **9ii** 163; **17** 321; **18** 626;
    Herod and, **5** 316*n*; **11** 649
Innocents' Day, children's bishop at/*episcopus puerorum*, **9i** 458, 460
innovations, **13** 81
inorganic, **13** 286;
    realm, **13** 242;
    stone, symbol of the, **13** 286
Inouye, Tetsujiro: "Die japanische Philosophie," **6** 370*n*
Inquisition, **6** 400
inquisitiveness, holy, **7** 325
insane, the/madmen, **15** 173;

355

insane (*cont.*):
    and *abaissement du niveau mental*, **15** 166*n*;
    delusions of, **9i** 309; **13** 298; **15** 152 (*see also* delusion(s);
    unconscious in the, **10** 2;
    and visionary experience, **15** 149;
    see also patients *s.v.* mental; voice(s) *s.v.* hallucinatory

insanity, **3** 339; **7** 470; **9i** 83, 496; **10** 642; **11** 765, 899; **13** 24, 53, 434; **17** 181, 207, 253; **18** 795, 900;
    TITLES: "A Medical Opinion on a Case of Simulated Insanity," **1** 356–429; "On Simulated Insanity," **1** 301–55;
    complexes in, **1** 478; **8** 593;
    contamination of images in, **11** 783;
    cyclic, **1** 112;
    deciphering of products of, **18** 827;
    dreaming as, **3** 523;
    epidemic, **10** 432, 490;
    epileptic, **3** 472;
    fantasies in, **8** 719;
    fear of, **12** 38, 60; **16** 374;
    idea of solid sunbeam in, **5** 638;
    legal definition(s) of, **1** 426, 477; **18** 899;
    logical mechanism in, **3** 5;
    moral, *see* moral insanity;
    and mythological ideas/symbols, **8** 589;
    and possession by evil spirits, **8** 576;
    precursors of, **3** 333;
    primitive view, **3** 528;
    simulated, case of, **1** 301–55; anamnesis in, **1** 330, 338; and false accusation, **1** 348; medical opinion on, **1** 356–429; response to instructions, **1** 326*ff*;
    unconscious and, **11** 774;
    see also mental illness; psychosis

insects, *see* ANIMALS *s.v.*
insecurity, and social security, **17** 343
inside, **13** 18, 24;
    and outside, **14** 8; —, and life process, **7** 311
insight(s), **7** 165, 248, 391, 440; **11** 452, 541, 876; **13** 20, 45; **16** 149–50, 237;
    and anima, **11** 240;
    of defendant as to her swindling, **1** 474;
    destructive, **13** 152;
    during psychic disturbance, **1** 306;
    and emotions, **4** 312;
    flashes of, **17** 94;
    gained in analysis, use of, **4** 647; **7** 224;
    increased, into question of simulation, **1** 301;
    intellectual, insufficiency of, **9ii** 61;
    into one's mistakes, **16** 503;
    limitations of, **16** 150;
    patient's, as to illness, **1** 194, 203, 209, 214; **3** 309, 342, 490; **16** 359;
    scientific, **18** 1277;
    secret, **13** 55;
    superior, **13** 467, 469
insomnia, **2** 666; **3** 87, 137; **8** 516;
    Jung's own, **18** 769, 772
inspiration(s), **3** 176; **7** 106, 470; **8** 574, 668; **9i** 393; **11** 272; **14** 445, 786;
    creative, **7** 270;
    divine, **12** 356*n*, 423, 450, 462;
    fantasies as, **17** 193;
    "in-spiration," **11** 240;
    Nietzsche on, **1** 139*n*, 184;
    pathological, **3** 10, 180;
    prophetic, **7** 260, 476
instability: and inner unrest, **1** 414;
    psychopathic, **1** 192–5;
    social, in manic mood disorder, **1** 205–10
instinct(s), **5** 38, 185, 524, 631; **6**

357

instinct (*cont.*):
and love, **10** 200;
maternal, **9i** 167; over-development of, **9i** 172;
migratory, **4** 728; **10** 849;
modern art and, **10** 755;
modified, **8** 234;
and morality, **11** 390*n*;
multiplicity/plurality of, **4** 287, 371;
natural, and *prima materia*, **5** 631; and spiritual love, **5** 615;
natural power of, **5** 89;
nature of, **11** 419;
and neurosis, **7** 29, 91; **11** 450; **16** 208;
neurotic perversion of, **5** 199;
non-personal, **11** 419;
nutritive, **4** 251, 283, 568;
objectification of, **14** 672;
origin of, **8** 268 (*see also above* intuition);
overvaluation of, **17** 157;
paradoxical character of, **16** 362;
pathological, **1** 466;
as phenomenon of energy, **5** 196;
and philosophy of life, **16** 185;
physiological, psychological aspects of, **8** 374; **9i** 112;
play, **6** 171–4, 185, 196; **8** 240;
power, **5** 102; **6** 150, 373; **7** 50; **8** 708; **10** 653, 654; **16** 151; **17** 156; Nietzsche and, **7** 37–9, 43; **10** 658; and sex-, constellation of, **5** 102;
power of, **5** 89; **8** 657;
preformation of, **4** 728; **8** 589;
for preservation of self vs. preservation of species, **4** 49*n*, 234, 237, 280; **5** 195; **7** 38; **8** 237, 238; **10** 413, 555; **17** 156;
primary, **4** 757; and endogamous/exogamous tendencies, **5** 226;
in primitives, see primitive(s) *s.v.*;

primordial, **6** 571; **7** 256;
and psyche, **10** 7, 646; **11** 491;
relation to, **8** 234–5, 375; **11** 769, 798;
psychoanalysis and, **7** 28;
and psychoneuroses, **11** 491;
psychosomatic, **13** 475;
rationalization of, **8** 272;
and reason, **16** 178;
reduction to, **16** 41;
reflective, **8** 241–3;
release of, and unity of individual, **10** 661;
religious, **10** 659; **17** 157; and wholeness, **10** 653 (*see also* religion *s.v.* instinct);
repressed/repression of, **5** 223, 263; **8** 36; **13** 69; **16** 178; **17** 17*n*, 194; and dreams, **9i** 101;
reproductive, **4** 279; **5** 194, 219;
restrictions on, **17** 156;
self-preservation, *see above* preservation;
sensuous (Schiller), **6** 152–5;
sexual, **4** 237, 251; **5** 102, 219, 338; **8** 107, 238, 762; **9i** 91; **11** 492; and "bundle of" hypothesis, **5** 190; and psyche, definition of, **10** 278, 312;
sexuality as, **5** 199, 261, 652; **8** 108; **10** 5;
social, **7** 235/455;
and spirit, **4** 776; **5** 338; **7** 32; **8** 379; **16** 363; antithesis of, **8** 407–8; transformation into, **17** 335;
and symbol(s), **5** 338; **10** 652; **16** 361; choice of, **10** 637, 652; colour(red), **8** 384, 414; dream, **10** 679; theriomorphic, **5** 261, 615; **9ii** 385;
theory of, **5** 190; **8** 232; **16** 206;
two aspects of, **8** 414; **10** 556;
as typical modes of action, **8** 273, 398–9;
and unconscious, **8** 270, 339, 750; **11** 774; forces of, **5** 463; **10** 25;

unconsciousness of, **8** 265;
variability of, **8** 235;
vital, **7** 520(6);
weakness of, **7** 206;
for wholeness, **10** 653, 661; **11** 745; **16** 471;
world of, **12** 157, 163, 203; **14** 602

instinctive: attitude, religion as, **10** 512;
demands, **13** 6;
dispositions, **13** 355;
forces of unconscious, **9i** 660;
impulse, **17** 194, 211

instinctual: drives, excess of, **1** 220;
transformation of, **5** 91;
forces, *see* force *s.v.*;
impulses, **5** 106, 683; and sublimation, **7** 71; in the unconscious, **7** 21;
nature, **8** 693;
"pattern," **8** 856;
processes, **5** 185, 199; **7** 122;
sphere, disturbances of, **11** 517

instinctuality, **11** 56; **13** 7, 13, 244, 448;
father as spirit opposed to, **5** 396;
and imagos, **5** 505;
and psychic systems, **5** 337;
renunciation of, **5** 398;
repressive, and hunger, **5** 526*n*;
symbolical sacrifice of, **5** 299, 665;
theriomorphic symbol, **5** 673

Institute of Medical Psychology (The Tavistock Clinic), J.'s lecture to, **18** (*pp*3, 566*n*)

"Instructio de arbore solari," *see* AL-CHEMICAL COLLECTIONS: *Theatr. chem. s.v.* Espagnet

"Instruction of Cleopatra by the Archpriest Komarios," *see* AL-CHEMICAL WRITERS: Comarius

instructions, response to, in case of simulated insanity, **1** 326*ff*

insulin shocks, **14** 680

insurance money, and hysteria, **4** 11

integration, **9i** 64*n*; **9ii** 58, 73, 312; **12** 188; **16** 19, 357, 386;
of anima, *see* anima *s.v.*;
of collective unconscious, **9ii** 43, 72;
of consciousness, *see* consciousness *s.v.*;
ethical aspect of, **18** 1417;
inner, **17** 334;
of mandala, **9ii** 60;
new, **13** 71;
of numen, **11** 472;
of parental images, **16** 218;
pathological attempts at, **8** 430;
of personality, **18** 1412;
of projections, **16** 472;
of psyche, **16** 266;
of the self, *see* self *s.v.*;
of shadow, *see* shadow *s.v.*;
of the unconscious, **5** 459, 672; **9i** 563; **9ii** 282; **14** 348; **18** 1572; **9ii** 44; **10** 451, 473; **11** 233, 280, 292; **12** 171, 496; **13** 433, 477; **14** 779; **16** 408; **18** 1388, 1402, 1413; alchemical symbols for, **16** 408;
of unconscious tendencies in conscious mind, **5** 683

integrity of personality, *see* personality *s.v.*

intellect/intellectual(-ism), **6** 242, 766 (Def.); **7** 344, 483, 507; **9ii** 141; **10** 701; **11** 27, 417, 905; **12** 60, 81, 84, 87–8, 112, 119, 121, 137, 149–50, 168–9, 178, 188, 350, 366, 376, 423*n*, 442, 462; **13** 1, 7, 75, 248, 286, 296–7, 299, 343, 413, 438; **16** 487–9; **17** 198, 303; **18** 784;
and action, **1** 221;
activity, loss of, **3** 15;
cannot grasp: psyche, **7** 201;
ritual, **18** 617;
concretizations of, **7** 361;
demand for autonomy, **11** 444;
deposition of, **12** 88, 92;
devilish aspect of, **12** 88, 119,

intellect (*cont.*):
  fig. 36;
  differentiation of, **12** 112;
  and emotions, **1** 219;
  as employee, **12** 87, 137;
  eternalistic, **13** 9;
  exaltation of, in ecstasy, **1** 148;
  and feeling, discrepancy, **10** 569, 657, 774;
  and feeling-values, **17** 183;
  helpful, **12** 169;
  not independent, **11** 766;
  insight, insufficiency of, **9ii** 61;
  in James's theory, **6** 507, 523;
  limits of, **16** 532;
  as Logos, **5** 198;
  Mercurius as, **12** 90;
  murderous, **18** 635;
  and neurosis, **18** 665;
  one-sided, **7** 350;
  and perceiving subject, **11** 892;
  philosophic, **11** 766;
  precocious, **17** 238;
  and primordial images, **8** 794;
  rationalist(ic), **13** 456; **18** 601;
  in Schiller, **6** 132, 135–6, 185;
  and science, **6** 84–6;
  not self-sufficient, **8** 600;
  speech and, **5** 14;
  and spirit, **9i** 31, 391; **12** 178;
  symbolism of: Mercurius, **12** 90; pointed instrument, **5** 261;
  thinking and, **8** 794;
  and values, **9ii** 60;
  Western, **13** 71;
  and will, **1** 220–1;
  and wisdom, **11** 221;
  in women, *see* woman *s.v.*;
  world of, **7** 347
intelligence, **7** 198; **8** 673; **12** 372–4;
  -complex, **2** 985–6;
  flashes of, **8** 668;
  in manic mood disorder, **1** 206, 212, 220;
  patient's, and prognosis, **3** 574–5;
  suspicion of, **17** 233;

temporary loss of, in hysteria, **1** 280;
  tests, **4** 622, 633; **17** 213, 224; **18** 913
intensity(-ies), **13** 37;
  of conflicts, *see* conflict(s) *s.v.*;
  emotional, **13** 341;
  of idea, **9ii** 53;
  psychic, *see* psychic *s.v.*
intention(s), **8** 264, 697; **10** 646;
  conscious, **7** 187, 505;
  good, **8** 683; **17** 228;
  real, **17** 185;
  unconscious, **4** 364
intentionality, **5** 197
intercessio: divina, **18** 362;
  sacerdotis, **18** 362
intercourse, *see* cohabitation; coitus
interdependence of events, *see* synchronicity
interdiction: in association experiments, **3** 177;
  as automatism, **8** 22
interest(s), **3** 418; **4** 273, 530, 663;
  abnormal, **17** 237;
  aesthetic, **17** 194, 281;
  erotic, **4** 274–5, 277;
  failure of, **11** 784;
  Freud on libido as, **5** 190–1;
  intellectual, **17** 281;
  and object, **1** 139;
  objective, and libidinal condition, **5** 192;
  object of, **17** 199a;
  religious, **17** 281;
  shifting of, from inner to outer world, **5** 113;
  symptomatic, **3** 104;
  and telepathic phenomena, **8** 830
"interest-draughts," *see* association-chain(s) *s.v.*
interjections as responses, **2** 75
internalization through sacrifice, **16** 438
International Congress of Education, **17** 98*n*, (*p*63), 253*n*

International Congress for Psychiatry, Amsterdam, 1907, J.'s report, **18** 956

International General Medical Society for Psychotherapy, *see* Psychotherapy, (International) General Medical Society for

International Institute of Intellectual Cooperation, **10** 943*n*

internationalism, **10** 195

International Journal of Parapsychology, **18** (*p*510)

International Psychoanalytic Association, *see* Psychoanalytic Association, International

internment: in case of fraud, **1** 455; and simulation, **1** 344; *see also* detention

interplanetary travel, **10** 614

"Interpretatio cuiusdam epistolae Alexandri Macedonum regis," *see* ALCHEMICAL COLLECTIONS: *Art. aurif. s.v.*

interpretations/interpretative, **9i** 267; **11** 957; **17** 17*n*;
anagogic, **16** 9;
analytical-reductive, **16** 9, 12;
of anima, **9i** 66;
anthropomorphic, **7** 162; **13** 89;
at beginning of treatment, **7** 129;
causal-reductive, **7** 128–31;
complete, sometimes unwise, **4** 537;
of dreams, *see* dream(s), analysis/interpretation of;
and emotional value, **18** 596;
of fear symbols, **5** 681;
Freudian, **4** 40; **17** (*p*3), 195; alleged arbitrary character, **4** 14, 526;
"low down," **10** 356;
method, **16** 143;
"monotony" of, **5** 9;
need of patient's assent to, **16** 316;

objective, **7** 130, 139, 141;
only for the uncomprehending, **9i** 65;
of patient's painting, **16** 111;
psychoanalytic, **16** 9;
regressive and progressive, **16** 9;
rules of, **16** 334;
semiotic constructive, **7** 132–40;
and settlement with the unconscious, **7** 342;
sexual, **16** 277; **17** 196;
subjective, **7** 129–31;
as symbols in later dreams, **4** 649;
synthetic/constructive, **7** 132–40;
synthetic/hermeneutic, **7** 493; **16** 9, 25;
of transference, **7** 95–6;
of unconscious, **8** 832; **13** 463–82;
of unconscious material, **11** 541

"Interrogationes magnae (Mariae)" and "Interrogationes parvae," **9ii** 314; **12** 209

intervention, active, in confession, **11** 544

intestinal canal, **4** 513

intolerance, **8** 773

intonation, *see* America *s.v.* speech

intoxicants/intoxication(s), **3** 569; **11** 384, 387; **12** 171, 182; **16** 501*n*;
chronic, **3** 471;
and Dionysian impulse, *see* Dionysus;
as libido symbol, **5** 315;
mass, **9i** 226

intra-uterine period, **4** 237; **11** 842

"Introitus apertus," *see* ALCHEMICAL COLLECTIONS: *Mus. herm. s.v.* Philalethes

introitus solis, **5** 496

introjection, **5** 195&*n*; **6** 767–8

introjection (*cont.*):
(Def.); **7** 110; **18** 1638;
of anima, **16** 438;
see also Ferenczi
introspection, **11** 784, 823, 961; **13**
58; **16** 64;
in aging process, **5** 553;
intuitive, **13** 208;
lack of, **11** 28; **13** 455; in modern man, **18** 555
introversion/introvert, **3** 418, 429n,
435; **4** 405; **5** 19n, 40, 58–9, 259;
6 4, 459, 478–9, 769 (Def.), 873,
940, 943, 976–81; **7** 62, 82, 87,
356, 373; **9i** 431; **10** 658, 754,
890; **11** 770, 773, 803; **13** 415; **14**
262; **16** 59; **17** 18; **18** 496, 1157,
1259;
and aesthetic standpoint, **6**
239;
affectivity of, *see* affectivity *s.v.*;
Apollinian, **6** 236, 239;
artificial, **6** 47; **11** 873;
in children, **6** 897; **17** 13;
of conscious mind into unconscious, **18** 80;
and creative spiritual activity/
self-liberation, **5** 588, 590, 592;
11 773;
and empathy, *see* empathy *s.v.*;
extraversion and, *see* extraversion *s.v.*;
and feeling, **6** 638–9;
Freud on, *see* Freud *s.v.*;
and "godlikeness," **6** 140;
and hypnagogic vision, **5** 255;
and intuition, **6** 655–60;
of libido, *see* libido *s.v.*;
and monism, **6** 536;
neglected, of Western culture,
7 303;
and neurosis, **5** 19n, 193;
Promethean, *see* introverted
type *s.v.*;
and regression, **5** 40, 64, 587,
625; **6** 860; **8** 77;
and relation to ideas, **6** 238;
in schizophrenia/dementia

praecox, **18** 1008–10;
and sensation, **6** 647–9;
and *tapas*, **5** 588–9; **6** 189;
thinking and, *see* thinking
s.v.;
unconscious contents in, **7** 373;
into unconsciousness, **6** 186;
yoga as, **11** 873;
see also attitude, introverted
introverted type, **3** 418–21; **4** 763; **6**
142, 149, 214; **7** 80–4, 482; **16**
241–2;
TITLE: "The Introverted Type,"
6 620–71;
abstracting attitude of consciousness in, *see* abstracting
s.v.;
and Adler's psychology, **6** 91;
affectivity of, *see* affectivity *s.v.*;
anima in, **7** 356;
and classic type (Ostwald), **6**
542–57;
and ego, **6** 138, 141; **7** 462n;
and empathy, *see* empathy *s.v.*;
Epimetheus as (Goethe), **6** 306;
and functions, **6** 103, 248, 472,
913;
and Gross's typology, **6** 467–8,
473–6, 483, 879;
inferiority feelings in, **6** 144,
306;
irrational, **6** 664–5;
and Jordan's typology, **6** 244–
52, 255, 269–72, 470;
Kant as, **6** 526, 532;
and object, **6** 63–4, 535, 626–7,
650, 897–8; **7** 62, 81–4 (*see also*
abstraction); identity with, **6**
164; negative relation to, **6**
633, 937–8;
Plato as, **6** 55;
poet as, **6** 213, 218;
Prometheus as, in Spitteler, **6**
276–7, 282, 289; **7** 82;
psychoanalysis and, **6** 92;
rational, **6** 644–6;
Schiller as, **6** 103–4, 163–4;
Scotus as, **6** 39;

Spitteler as, **6** 288;
and thinking, **6** 38; **7** 462*n*, 482
(*see also* thinking);
unconscious contents/fantasy,
in, **6** 171;
woman, **6** 256–9
intuition(s), **3** 539; **4** 490; **6** 540,
770–3 (Def.), 951, 953–4; **8** 594,
863; **9i** 541; **11** 69, 446, 784; **12**
148–9, 153, 175, 517; **13** 1–2, 7;
15 148; **16** 194, 345, 486; **18**
24–6, 89, 110;
archetypes and, **8** 270; **12** 175;
creative, **7** 270;
Eastern, **11** 804, 818;
in extraverted attitude, **6** 610–
12;
as fourth dimension, **18** 53, 54;
as function, *see* function *s.v.*;
highest/loftiest, **13** 44–5;
and instinct, **8** 269, 277;
and interpretation of symbols,
18 577;
in introverted attitude, **6** 655–
60;
irrational, **18** 502;
lack of, in Swiss, **10** 916;
and nose/world of smells, link,
18 779, 780;
and object, **6** 219;
as "perception via the uncon-
scious," **9i** 504; **11** 245; **18** 26,
502;
in physics, **18** 576;
among primitives, **8** 278;
retrospective, **8** 98;
in Schiller, **6** 104, 117–18;
of the self, **13** 36;
subliminal, **18** 780;
about the unconscious, **12** 517;
of/arising from the uncon-
scious, **5** 546; **10** 25, 574; **12**
153, 175;
in woman, **7** 296;
intuitive: ideas, *see* idea *s.v.*;
introspection, **13** 208;
thinking, *see* thinking *s.v.*;
type, *see* type *s.v.*

"In Turbam philosophorum exercitationes," *see* ALCHEMICAL COL-
LECTIONS: *Art. aurif. s.v.*
invasion(s), **18** 90;
and affects, **18** 64, 65, 68;
and artistic inspiration, **18** 71,
72;
as endopsychic factor, **18** 43;
extra-terrestrial, Ufo(s) as, **10**
600
inventions/inventiveness/inventing,
4 412;
etymology of, **18** 549;
misuse of, **10** 1009–10;
mythological anticipation of, **18**
81;
see also paranoia, "inventor's";
primitive(s)
inversion, **7** 162; **17** 282;
of types, **7** 82
invertebrates, *see* ANIMALS *s.v.*
investment, libidinal, of analyst, **4**
661
invisible(s)/invisibility: *cucullatus,*
hooded one, **9i** 298 (*see also* veil);
homo maximus, **13** 208;
and mediums, **18** 746, 751,
752, 753, 755;
staff of, **9i** 404*n*
invocation, **11** 7;
as expression of introversion, **5**
260;
see also prayer
involution, **5** 366; **8** 69, 70
invulnerability of Mercurius, **13**
295
Io, **9i** 195
Ion (in Zosimos), **11** 345; **13** 86&*n*,
106, 111; **16** 472*n*;
Ionians, **13** 86*n*
ionosphere, **8** 875
ions/ionization, and mediums, **18**
1498
iosis, see COLOURS
iota, **8** 395; *see also* point
Iran, *see* Persia
'Iraqi, al-, *see* ALCHEMICAL WRITERS:
Abu'l Qasim

irascibility, *see* irritability
Irenaeus, **9i** 5; **11** 133, 207*n*; **14**
288; **18** 1617;
and Gnostic philosophy, **8**
388*n*; **9ii** 80, 118*n*, 233*n*, 307;
11 216; **13** 419, 451, 459; **14**
327, 574, 576, 648*n*; shadow/
umbra in, **9i** 469*n*; **9ii** 75*n*;
Adversus/Contra Haereses in *Writings of Irenaeus,* tr. A. Roberts
and W. H. Rambaut, **5** 515*n*; **8**
388*n*; **9i** 5*n*, 120*n*, 131*n*, 142*n*;
9ii 80*n*, 99, 120*n*, 171*n*, 307*n*,
340*n*, 344*n*; **10** 75*n*; **11** 60*n*,
126*n*, 133*n*, 216*n*; **12** 139*n*; **13**
419*n*, 451*n*, 459*n*; **14** 42*n*, 50*n*,
288*n*, 327*n*, 476*n*, 483*n*, 574*n*,
576*n*, 585*n*, 589*n*, 602*n*, 701*n*;
16 378*n*; **18** 1617*n*
iridodiagnosis, **15** 20
Irira, A. Cohen/Hacohen Herrera,
14 619
Iris, **9i** 580*n*; **14** 389, 392, 397;
Junonia, **14** 398
"Irma's injection," dream of
(Freud), **10** 351
Irminger, H., **18** (*p*645*n*)
iron, **13** 176*n*, 239;
Age, Fourth, **9ii** 169;
alchemical: -smith, **13** 252;
-stone, magnetic, **9ii** 241*n*; and
tree, **12** 425; **13** 119, 267, 357,
446;
man, in fairytale, **9i** 407
Iron Curtain, **10** 488, 517, 544; **18**
561
Iroquois, *see* American Indians:
NORTH *s.v.*
irrational, **7** 110–11, 150–1, 486;
Christianity and the, **11** 444;
definition, **6** 774–7, 953;
type, *see* type;
values, **17** 81
irrationalism, **10** 375*n*
irrationality, **7** 72; **9ii** 34–5; **10** 490;
13 23, 325;
of dogma, **12** 19;
return of, **14** 343

irrealism, Gnostic, **11** 438
irreality, **7** 351, 353
irregularity, and absolute reality, **10**
494
irrelevant answers, **3** 554
irreparabile damnum, **1** 130
irresolution, in obsessed persons, **3**
184
irresponsibility: infantile, **4** 667;
legal, *see* responsibility
irritability, **1** 187, 208, 212, 214,
215, 222, 320*n*; **4** 249;
in chronic mania, **1** 189–91;
of schizophrenics, *see* schizophrenia *s.v.*
irritation, **3** 80; **8** 516; **13** 108
Isaac: burial place of, **14** 556;
sacrifice of, *see* Abraham *s.v.*
Isaiah/Isaias, *see* BIBLE: O.T. *s.v.*
Ischys, **14** 144*n*
Isha Upanishad, see Upanishads
Isherwood, C., see under *Bhagavad
Gita*
Ishmael, Rabbi, **9ii** 110
Ishtar/Istar, **5** 577*n*; **9ii** 174; **11**
612; **13** 278; **14** 24*n*, 161, 415*n*,
609, 622*n*, 646;
and Gilgamesh, *see* Gilgamesh
Epic;
journey to hell, **11** 176;
love-goddess, **14** 364*n*;
palm of, **14** 75*n*, 364*n*;
veiled, **14** 75*n*
Ishvara, *see* Shiva
Isidore of Seville, St.: *De natura rerum,* **14** 553*n*;
Liber etymologiarum, **8** 866*n*; **9ii**
239*n*; **12** 522*n*, 524&*n*; **14**
173*n*, 245&*n*, 281*n*, 641*n*; **16**
496&*n*
Isidorus/Isidore (son of Basilides),
11 62*n*, 245*n*; **14** 75*n*, 374*n*
Isis, **4** 106; **5** 102*n*, 133*n*, 452–3,
455; **8** 307; **11** 348; **13** 399*n*; **14**
351, 365*n*, 395, 607, 609, 726,
727; **18** 1287;
in alchemy, **12** 209*n*, 435*n*,
487; **14** 14, 6, 64*n*, 317, 734;

"Isis to Horus," *see* ALCHEMICAL WRITERS: Berthelot, *Coll. alch. grecs s.v.*; visions of, **13** 107;
basket, **5** pl. LIII; **6** 396;
cow-headed, **5** 374, pl. XXX*b* (*see also* Hathor);
and Echidna, **5** 265*n*;
as evil mother, **5** 374;
as feminine intercession, **18** 1660;
festival/mysteries of (at Bubastis/Busiris), **5** 390; **12** 105; **18** 264;
and Horus, *see* Horus *s.v.*;
and Melusine, **13** 418;
as mother-image, **5** 415;
Mother of God, prefiguration of, **9i** 195;
mysteries of, **5** 130&*n*; **9i** 84, 107, 619; **13** 106; **18** 264 (*see also* Apuleius; *see above* festival);
and Osiris, *see* Osiris *s.v.*;
and Ra, **5** 274, 452–5; **18** 230&*n*
Islam, **8** 683; **9ii** 99*n*, 130, 151*n*, 156, 272; **10** 507; **11** 10; **12** 22, 155; **18** 1389, 1507;
conception of God in, **11** 226;
and Elijah (Ilyās), **18** 1527;
in India, **10** 990;
Khidr legend in, *see* Khidr;
new, **18** 638;
rise of, **10** 938; **11** 223, 860;
see also Arab(s)
island(s)/isles, **12** 56, 438; **13** 348, *figs.* 1, 23;
of the Blessed, **6** 60, 62; **13** 406–7;
motif, in dream, **9i** 344;
"neurosis," **16** 374;
tree of life on, *see* tree(s) *s.v.*;
tree of planets and, **13** 406–7
"isms," **8** 366, 405, 425, 427; **9i** 125, 617; **10** 103, 469; **11** 144, 772; **16** 3
isolation/aloofness, **3** 455, 457, 459; **7** 320; **12** 174; **13** 395;
auto-erotic, **13** 307;

feeling of, in psychosis, **5** 683;
individual, state and, **10** 577–80;
moral, **4** 432;
national, Germany's, **10** 484–5;
of psychic processes, **8** 197;
result of will of God, **11** 525;
by a secret, **12** 57, 61, 63, 118
isopsephia, **14** 329*n*, 636
Israel, **13** 182; **14** 25*n*;
children/people of, **11** 618, 619, 631, 637;
and Yahweh, *see* Yahweh
Israïlovitch, D., *see under* Claparède
Isserlin, M., **2** 918; **4** 156*n*;
"Die diagnostische Bedeutung der Assoziationsversuche," **18** 950;
"Über Jungs 'Psychologie der Dementia praecox' etc.," **2** 918*n*
Istar, *see* Ishtar
Istria, **13** 392*n*
Italy/Italian, **10** 396–7, 420, 476, 601, 908, 975; **17** 29, 284; **18** 369, 1311;
ancient, slavery in, **10** 249–50 (*see also* Rome);
conquest of Ethiopia, **18** 1327*n*;
tiled roofs, **18** 261
I-Thou/You relationship, **9i** 11; **11** 549; **12** 5
ithyphallic: Mercurius as, *see* Mercurius *s.v.*;
old man, **13** 278
Itten, W., **3** 390;
"Beiträge zur Psychologie der Dementia praecox," **3** 390*n*
Ivan, Czarevitch, **9i** 435
Ivenes (S. W.'s somnambulistic ego), **1** 58, 62;
character and reincarnations of, **1** 62–3;
deterioration of, **1** 134;
improvement over normal personality of S. W., **1** 116;
mental products grouped

Ivenes (*cont.*):
  around grandfather, **1** 127;
  study of, **1** 114–16;
  subconscious   personalities'
    knowledge of, **1** 127
ivory figure, Japanese, **7** 177; **17**
  275, 277
ivy, **5** 636
Ixion, **14** 144*n*; **18** 82;

wheel of, **5** 154, 460*n*, pl.
  XLVI*b*; **9i** 705; **18** 203
I-You relationship, *see* I-Thou
Izanagi legend (Orpheus parallel),
  5 528*n*
Izquierdo, S., **12** *fig.* 151; **14** 255;
  Praxis exercitiorum spiritualium P.
  N. S. Ignatii/ Pratica di alcuni
  Esercitij Spirituali di S. Ignatio, **9i**
  236*n*; **12** *fig.* 151; **14** 255*n*

J

J. S., J.'s memorial to, **18** 1705–10
Jabir ibn-Ḥayyan, *see* ALCHEMICAL
  WRITERS: Geber
jackal, *see* ANIMALS *s.v.*
jack-in-the-box, **4** 511
Jacob, **9ii** 336; **13** 182; **14** 556; and
  the angel, **5** 524; **10** 869; **11**
  233*n*; **18** 1588; and Esau, **11** 629;
  his ladder, in dream, **12** 66&*n*, *fig.*
  14; **14** 568*n*; his well, **16** 485
Jacob, St., lazar-house, and battle of
  1444, **18** 183, 191, 229
Jacobi,—, **1** 346
Jacobi, Jolande, **13** (*p*vi); **18** 1107,
  1108, 1134, (*pp*606*n*, 811*n*);
  Complex/Archetype/Symbol, **6**
  684*n*; **9i** 623*n*; **18** 205*n*, 525*n*,
  1134*n*; J.'s foreword, **18**
  1256–8;
  ed., Paracelsus, *Selected Writ-*
  ings, **11** 113*n*; **15** 6*n*; **17** 203*n*;
  J.'s foreword, **18** 1755–9;
  The Psychology of C. G. Jung, **9ii**
  398*n*; **12** *fig.* 49; **16** 405*n*; **18**
  1108, 1134*n*, 1402*n*; J.'s
  forewords, **18** 1121–4
Jacobi, K.G.J., **8** 942; **10** 777
Jacobi-Jenssen,—, **1** 306
Jacobsohn, H., **11** 177;
  "Die dogmatische Stellung des
  Königs in der Theologie der
  alten Aegypter," **9i** 438*n*; **11**
  177*n*, 209*n*; **13** 97*n*, 458*n*; **14**
  350*n*, 351*nn*, 352*n*, 358*n*, 726*n*;
  "Das Gespräch eines Lebens-
  müden mit seinem Ba," **11**
  441*n*
Jacobsohn, S., **1** 186&*n*
jade, **11** 993
Ja'far ibn Muhammad, *see* Al-
  bumasar
Jaffé, A., **9i** 60; **18** 782, 1825*n*;
  Apparitions and Precognition, **10**
  700*n*; J.'s foreword, **18** 782–9;
  "Bilder und Symbole aus

E.T.A. Hoffmanns Märchen
  'Der goldene Topf,' " **5** 615*n*; **8**
  931*n*; **9i** 60*n*; **13** 416*n*; **14** 41*n*;
  15 142*n*; **18** 782*n*, 1247&*n*
Jagaddeva, dream-book of, **5**
  542
Jagatimetrum, **5** 210
Jähns, M., **5** 421;
  Ross und Reiter, **5** 421*nn*
Jahrbuch für psychoanalytische und
psychopathologische Forschungen, ed.
  C. G. Jung, **3** (*p*197*n*); **4** (*p*56*n*),
  (*p*74*n*), (*p*83*n*); **5** (*p*v); **18** 274*n*,
  282, 925&*n*, (*p*398*n*), 1063,
  (*p*551*n*)
Jains/Jainism, **14** 46;
  tree of knowledge of, **5** 403
Jakoby, E., **10** 736, pl. II
Jalal-ud-din Rumi, **14** 552
Jambu-tree, *see* TREES *s.v.*
James, Epistle of, *see* BIBLE: N.T. *s.v.*
James of Sarug, **9ii** 128
James, M. R., *Apocryphal New Testa-*
  ment, *see* BIBLE: N.T.: Apoc-
  rypha/etc.
James, W., **4** (*p*86); **5** 18–19; **6** 580,
  967; **7** 483; **8** 262, 413; **10** 928,
  941; **11** 8; **13** 60*n*; **18** 46&*n*, 465,
  474;
  on case of psychopath with
  amnesia, **1** 20;
  on "fringe of consciousness," **3**
  569*n*; **8** 210, 382;
  on instinct, **8** 267, 271;
  on "nothing but," **3** 423; **12**
  11*n*; **16** 98*n*;
  on "subliminal consciousness,"
  8 356*n*, 382*n*;
  on two types, **3** 419; **4** 676;
  empiricist/extraverted/tough-
  minded, **6** 506–9, 514, 517,
  525, 527–33, 864, 867–8; **7** 80;
  rationalist/introverted/tender-
  minded, **6** 506–9, 517, 864–6;
  7 80;

James, W. (*cont.*):
on unconscious psyche, **18**
1144;
WORKS:
"Frederic Myers' Service to
Psychology," **8** 382*n*;
Pragmatism, **3** 419; **4** (*p*86*n*);
6 505*n*, 527&*n*, 528*n*, 864*n*–
869*n*; **7** 80*n*; **11** 8*n*; **12** 11*n*;
Principles of Psychology, **1** 20*n*,
107*n*; **5** 11*n*, 18*n*, 20*n*; **6**
831*n*; **8** 267*n*;
*Varieties of Religious Experi-
ence,* **7** 270; **8** 356*n*, 366*n*,
382*n*; **9i** 113, 388; **16** 98*n*; **18**
1331
James-Lange theory of affect, *see* affect
Jamsthaler, Herbrandt, *see* ALCHEM-
ICAL WRITERS *s.v.*
Janet, P., **3** 28*n*, 137*n*, 155*n*, 170,
496; **4** 28, 155&*n*, 254*n*; **6** 966; **7**
2, 4; **8** 371&*n*, 383; **9i** 490, 493;
10 2, 3, 366, 1034*n*; **16** 294; **17**
128–9; **18** 139, 154, 421, 511,
560, 798, 922, 1070, 1130, 1145,
1223, 1737;
and *abaissement du niveau mental,* see *abaissement;*
and automatism/automatiza-
tion, **1** 339–40; **4** 28; **6** 712;
on consciousness: dissociability
of, **8** 202; double, **8** 351; withdrawal of, **16** 231;
and *fonction du réel,* **2** 1066; **3**
19, 186, 195, 233, 298, 491; **4**
274; **5** 192; **18** 21, 1232;
on hysteria/hysterical subjects:
affects, influence of, **1** 318–19,
340; **2** 1354; **3** 147; automatism and, **1** 319; **4** 28; behaviour of, **3** 159; disturbances
of attention in, **1** 73; **3** 162; disturbances of memory in, **3**
175*n*, 176*n*; epileptic attacks in,
1 130; lying of, **1** 119*n*;
symptoms of, **3** 506; **16** 231;
on "idées fixes," **18** 1145;

and "mental eclipse," **3** 175*n*;
on neuroses, **4** 296, 574; **9i** 113;
on obsessions, **3** 29, 184, 192;
15 62; **18** 1145; and "rêverie
forcée," **3** 176*n*;
on partial hypnosis, **1** 122;
parties supérieures et inférieures, **4**
569; **5** 26*n*; **7** 235/456, 344; **8**
39, 374–6; **15** 123; **18** 1145;
and *sentiment de perception
incomplète/d'incomplétude,* **2** 949;
3 171, 172;
on sleep, **3** 177*mn*, 181;
suggestions, whispered, **1** 86*n*,
122;
and unconscious, nature of, **9i**
492;
CASES:
(1) hystero-epileptic male
whose attacks were as-
sociated with visions of fire, **1**
130;
(2) Léonie, **1** 110, 116;
(3) Lucie: unconscious personality of, **1** 92–3&*n*; use of
double hypnosis in, **1** 294;
WORKS:
"L'Anesthésie hystérique," **1**
73*n*, 130*n*;
L'Automatisme psychologique, **1**
86*n*, 92*n*, 93*n*, 110*n*, 122*n*,
294*n*, 318*n*, 339*n*; **3** 12*n*; **7**
2*n*; **8** 351*n*; **9i** 113*n*;
The Mental State of Hystericals,
1 119*n*; **9i** 113*n*;
Les Névroses, **5** 26*n*; **7** 235*n*; **8**
374*n*, 375*n*; **9i** 213*n*;
Névroses et idées fixes, **1** 319*n*;
3 12*n*; **7** 2*n*; **9i** 113*n*; **15** 62;
*Les Obsessions et la psychas-
thénie,* **1** 319*n*; **2** 1067*n*; **3**
12*n*, 19*n*, 28*n*, 29*n*, 55*n*,
137*n*, 147*n*, 155*n*, 159*n*,
170*nn*, 171*n*, 175*n*, 176*n*,
184*n*, 192*n*;
"Le Renversement d'orientation ou l'allochirie des représentations," **18** (*p*421)

Jesuit(s), **8** 917; **9ii** 104; **10** 610; **11** 506; **12** 24*n*, 36; **13** 28; **14** 255; exercises, *see* Ignatius Loyola; and psychotherapy, **18** 613, 614, 680; theologian, **18** 1645, 1678
Jesus Christ, *see* Christ
Jesus ben Pandira, **5** 594
Jesus ben Stada, **5** 594
Jesus, son of Sirach, **11** 610; *see also* BIBLE: Apocrypha/etc. (O.T.) *s.v.* Ecclesiasticus
Jethro/Jothor, **9ii** 328&*n*, 329, 361–2, 383
jeux de paume, **12** 182
jewel(s), **9i** 270; **11** 230; **12** 438; Spitteler's, **12** 103, 160, 514; symbol/motif, **6** 297*n*, 299–300, 304, 310, 318*n*, 434–7, 450–5; **13** 80; *see also* stone, alchemical *s.v.* precious
Jewess, dream of, **4** 164–5
Jewish Encyclopaedia, **11** 368*n*; **14** 552*n*, 553*n*, 555*n*, 571*n*, 572*n*, 585*n*, 588*n*, 592*n*
Jews/Jewish tradition/Judaism, **2** 616, 739; **6** 313; **8** 338; **9i** 253, 324; **9ii** 174; **10** 478, 507; **11** 509; **12** 118; **13** 292; **14** 646; **15** 176; **18** 370, 565, 1505;
Adam, *see* Adam *s.v.* legends/traditions;
Behemoth, *see* ANIMALS *s.v.*;
cabalism, *see* Cabala; cabalism;
and Christ, **5** 287, 396; **11** 647, 688;
Christ-complex of, **10** 963;
and Christians, difference, **10** 1029, 1032;
and circumcision, *see* circumcision;
as complex, in Germany, **10** 1024;
complexes of, and loss of tradition, **16** 218;
concept of God, **9i** 189; **9ii** 105; **18** 1584; "chosen people"

and, **11** 577; as demiurge, **13** 271*n*;
and consultation of Rabbi for psychological troubles, **18** 610;
culture(s) of, **10** 353; two, **10** 18–19, 1034*n*;
in Germany, **18** 1322, 1375, 1385;
Leviathan, *see* ANIMALS *s.v.*;
and membership of International Society for Psychotherapy, **10** 1035*n*, 1060;
Messianism and, **9ii** 168; **17** 309; **18** 527;
Moses, Mosaic law, *see* prophets;
neurotic fear in, **4** 738*n*;
Passover, **9ii** 181;
persecutions of, **6** 454; **9i** 98 (*see also* anti-Semitism);
projection on, **10** 374, 610;
ritual murder as, **6** 454;
psychological consciousness of, **10** 353–4, 1034*n* (*see also* psychology *s.v.* Jewish);
and race theories, **10** 353–4, 416;
resentment in, **10** 915;
snake in, **13** 460;
teraphim, **11** 368;
Wandering/eternal, *see* Ahasuerus
Jezebel, **11** 703, 730
Jimson weed (datura), **16** 501*n*
jinn, **8** 335; **12** 537; **14** 78
Joachim of Flora, **9ii** 137–9, 140, 142, 232, 397*n*, 399, pl. II; **14** 22; **18** 1530, 1552&*n*;
"everlasting gospel" of, **9ii** 137, 140, 144;
and Holy Ghost Movement, **9ii** 137–41, 143, 144, 235;
and "third kingdom," of Holy Ghost, **14** 22
Joannes de Garlandia, **16** 498*n*
Joannes de Rupescissa, *see* ALCHEMICAL WRITERS *s.v.* Rupescissa
Joannes Lydus, *see* Lydus

Jonah/Jonas (prophet), **7** 160; **9ii** 180; **13** 180; **16** 510;
    sign of, **9ii** 173, 180*n*;
    story, as motif, **4** 477;
    and the whale, **5** 509, 576*n*, 631, 654; **12** *figs.* 170, 172, 174, 176, 177; **18** 1362, 1523
Jonah, Book of, *see* BIBLE: O.T. *s.v.*
Jonathan, Rabbi, **9ii** 110
Jones, E., **4** 478; **18** (*p*398*n*), 1160;
    Freud: Life and Work, **4** 1*n*, (*pp*10*n*, 56*n*), 155*n*, 695*n*;
    "Freud's Theory of Dreams," **4** 154;
    On the Nightmare, **4** 169; **5** 2&*n*, 370*n*;
    "Remarks on Dr. Morton Prince's Article," **4** 193*n*
Jones, H. S.: ed., *Catalogue of Ancient Sculptures,* **5** pl. LVIII
Jones, W.H.S., *see under* Pausanias
Jordan, F., **6** 243–74, 466, 471*n*, 547, 848;
    Character as Seen in Body and Parentage, **6** 243, 286*n*
Jordan, P., **18** 1133;
    Anschauliche Quantentheorie, **17** 164*n*;
    Die Physik und das Geheimnis des organischen Lebens, **17** 164*n*;
    Die Physik des 20. Jahrhunderts, **17** 164*n*;
    "Positivistische Bemerkungen über die parapsychischen Erscheinungen," **8** 440*n*, 862*n*; **17** 164*n*;
    Verdrängung und Komplementarität, **8** 862*n*
Jordan river, **9ii** 330; **12** 540, 550; **13** 98*n*;
    baptism in, **9i** 93
Jörger, J.: "Die Familie Zero," **4** 695*n*
Joseph, St., father of Jesus, **5** 4, 515; **9ii** 131
Joseph [Genesis], **12** 456*n*, *fig.* 170;
    cup of, **12** 550&*n*

Joseph/Josef bin Gorion, *see* Bin Gorion
Josephus, Flavius, **9ii** 129; **10** 414; **17** 262; **18** 240, 1744;
    Antiquitates Judaicae, **12** 456*n*;
    Contra Apionem/Against Apion, **5** 622*n*; **9ii** 129*n*;
    De bello Judaico/The Jewish War, **18** 240*n*, 1568*n*, 1744*n*
Joshua, Palestinian god, **5** 330*n*
Joshua (son of Nun/ben-Nun), **5** 671*n*; **9ii** 173; **13** 428; *see also* Moses *s.v.*
Joshua, Book of, *see* BIBLE: O.T. *s.v.*
jot, **9ii** 340; **14** 38
Jothor, *see* Jethro
journalists, **13** 54
Journal of Abnormal Psychology, **4** 155
journey(s), **8** 809;
    to the East, **5** 635; **12** 262;
    ecstatic, **13** 462;
    to four quarters, **12** 416*n*, 457&*n*;
    to Hades/Hell/underworld, **5** 374, 449, 484, 571–3, 654, 682*n*; **12** 61*n*, 438–9, 441, 451, 457*n*, *fig.* 69; of Zarathustra, **1** 140–1, 180–3;
    heavenly, **5** 141*n*; of the shaman, **13** 399, 407;
    of Moses, **5** 291;
    as symbolic separation from family ties, **5** 461;
    trance, **1** 42, 48, 51, 59;
    to the Western land (Hiawatha's), **5** 552;
    see also night sea journey; *peregrinatio*
Joyce, J., **15** 52, 208*n*;
    TITLE: " 'Ulysses': A Monologue," **15** 163–(*p*134);
    and Catholicism/Church, **15** 180–3, 195;
    influence on contemporaries, **10** 430; **15** 171, 174, 181;
    and J., **15** (*pp*132–4);
    language/style/themes, **15** 165–6, 169, 194;

and symbolism, **15** 185;
James Joyce, R. Ellmann, **15** 196*n*, (*p*133);
James Joyce's World, P. Hutchins, **15** (*p*133);
WORKS:
  Finnegans Wake, **15** 164*n*;
  Portrait of the Artist as a Young Man, **15** 188*n*, 197;
  Ulysses, **10** 430; **11** 402*n*; **14** 454; **15** 143*n*, 171–2, 183, 188, 198, (*pp*132–4); analogies with schizophrenia, **15** 173–4; and symbolism, **15** 185, 186; Bloom, Leopold and Molly, **15** 169, 185–6, 191, 196–8, 200; Dedalus, Stephen, **15** 169, 185–7, 196–8; Ulysses as demiurge, **15** 192
  Work in Progress, **15** 164*n*, 165*n*
Jubinal, M.L.A.: *Mystères inédits du XV. siècle,* **5** 368*n*
Jud, G., **11** 296*n*, 306*n*
Judaea: fountain in, **14** 341, 344; secret, **14** 344
Judaeus (son of Set), **9ii** 129*n*
Judah, lion of the tribe of, **13** 275, 390*n*
Judaism, *see* Jews/etc.
Judas, **5** 41–5; **11** 649; **18** 1744, 1747;
  death of, **18** 1561
Jude, Epistle of, *see* BIBLE: N.T. *s.v.*
Judex mundi, Christ as, **11** 229
Judges, *see* BIBLE: O.T. *s.v.*
judging types, *see* type(s) *s.v.* rational
Judgment/judgment(s), **11** 519;
  acts of, and consciousness, **11** 238;

of animus, **7** 332;
clouding of, **3** 578;
conscious, **13** 23;
day of, **13** 392;
of the Dead (Tibetan), **11** 846;
and directedness of consciousness, **8** 136;
false/falsification of, **3** 90, 169;
good/evil as, **9ii** 97;
individual, **17** 255;
intuitive, **7** 149;
Last, **9i** 257; **12** 436*n*, 462; **13** 392 (*see also* Rubens, Peter Paul);
moral, **9ii** 84; **11** 247;
personal and social, **5** 15;
projections of, **7** 513;
quaternity as basis of, **11** 246;
rational, **13** 12;
senseless, **7** 469;
in unconscious, **8** 362
Julian, the Apostate, Emperor, **5** 118*n*, 528;
  and Helios, **6** 114; **12** 99; **14** 501;
  "Hymn to King Helios," **6** 114&*n*;
  "Hymn to the Mother of the Gods," **6** 141*n*;
  Oratio V, tr. W. C. Wright, **5** 528*n*
Julius Caesar, **5** 421; **7** 279, 352;
  and Brutus, **5** 42;
  Cicero on, **14** 324;
  and mothers, **5** 371;
  The Gallic War, tr. H. J. Edwards, **5** 371*n*
Julius Caesar, see Shakespeare
Jûnân ben Merqûlius/Marqûlius, **13** (*p*60*n*); **16** 472*n*

*   *

JUNG, C. G.

(Headings: AUTOBIOGRAPHICAL ITEMS; DREAMS; PAINTINGS; JOURNEYS; CASES IN SUMMARY. J.'s WORKS are indexed in each CW volume, and these entries have not been repeated in the General Index. But see Freud: WORKS *s.v.* Freud/Jung Letters; and see *Psychologische Abhandlungen.*)

AUTOBIOGRAPHICAL ITEMS

his school teacher, **17** 232–3, 246;
confirmation lessons with his father, **9i** 30;
early professional career, **1** (*p*vi);

1900	dissertation for medical degree, **1** (*p*vi), 3*n*, 478; **3** 554–5;
1900–9	at Burghölzli Mental Hospital, **1** (*p*3*n*); **2** (*p*vi); **3** 554, 558; **18** (*p*361*n*);
1908	International Psychoanalytic Association, president of, **4** (*p*v); **18** (*p*423&*n*);
1913–17	"fallow period," **6** (*p*v);
1914	Bedford College, London, symposium, **8** 660;
1923–7	Bollingen "Tower," **18** 1782*n*;
1933–8	International General Medical Society for Psychotherapy, president of, **10** (*p*vi), 1014, 1016&*n*;
?	Pope's private blessing, **18** 618, 619;
1955	80th birthday celebrations, **18** 1212

Other items
daughters, *see* Niehus-Jung, Marianne; *see also* Jung CASES: **17** (1)
father-complex of, **10** 1026;
and Freud, personal relationship:
analysis by Freud of Jung's dream, **18** 483–91;
collaboration, **1** (*p*vi); **4** (*p*pv–vi); **10** 1034*n*; **17** 128; **18** 274, 832, (*p*374*n*);
parting of ways, **4** (*p*pv–vi); **5** (*p*xxvi); **6** (*p*499*n*); **17** 180; **18**

274, 487, 1156;
in haunted house, **18** 769;
and James Joyce:
dealings with, **15** (*p*p132–4);
letter from, **15** (*p*133);
and Jewish problem, **10** 1024–34&*n*;
and Nazis, **10** (*p*vi), 464, 1023;
son, in childhood, **5** 13*n*;
Swiss character traits, **10** 911, 1026;
wife, *see* Jung, Emma

DREAMS
(in order of presentation)

horse dropped from height, **3** 123–33;
woman in castle tower, **7** 189–90, 281; **16** 549–51; **18** 336;
mountain plateau with two paths, **9i** 334–8;
magnolia tree in Liverpool, **9i** 654;
Mr. X. tries to jump on dreamer's back, **18** 463;
discovery of wing of own house, or guest house containing old library, **18** 478–9;
house with historical layers and prehistoric tomb beneath lowest, **18** 484–91;
pretty girl with father-complex, **18** 635;
dreamer as small man with beard and no glasses, **18** 1077

PAINTINGS
9i frontispiece, *figs.* 6, 28, 29, 36; **13** *figs.* A3, A6, A10

JOURNEYS
America:
TITLES: "Press Communiqué on Visiting the United States," **18** 1300–4; "Report on America,"

CASES IN SUMMARY

(in order of presentation, volume by volume; numbering starts afresh for each volume; cross references herein pertain to this section. Cases are those discussed by Jung, but not necessarily treated by him.)

volume 1

to her children and later had a psychosis in which she acted like an animal, and thus became symbol of the all-devouring mother. — 504; *see also* **17** case 4, 107

(21) Schizophrenic whose dream of sun and moon illustrates weakening of parent archetypes by apotropaic means. — 576

(22) Male patient who dreamed of snake-bite when beginning to free himself from the mother. — 585

(23) Female patient who dreamed of snake after relapse into neurosis. — 585

(24) Patient who complained of a snake stuck in her throat. — 585

(25) Male schizophrenic whose first symptom was feeling of relation to stars. — 624n

(26) Patient who understood the language of birds. — 624n

(27) Female patient who had fantasy of being a snake crawling into her mother. — 676

(28) Female patient who said that snake crawled into her mouth. — 677 (*same patient as case 19 above*) (*see also* **3** case 18, 283–5)

volume 6

(1) Negro psychotics with classical dream-motifs. — 747&n, 851 (*see also* **5** 154; Negro(es) *s.v.* American)

(2) Printer, whose business was ruined. — 572

(3) Swiss clerk, with vision of solar phallus. — 746n, 851&n; *see also* **5** case 2, 151–3, 223; **8** case 6, 228, 317–20; **9i** case 1b, 105–9; **18** case 1a, 85

volume 7

(1) Young woman whose hysterical neurosis arose following a trauma. Case leads to problem of predisposition as a cause of the neurosis. — 8–15, 417–22 (*see also* **4** case 2, 218–21, 297–301, 355–64)

(2) Young married woman with anxiety attacks and hysterical asthma, and background of father fixation; case used to illustrate Adlerian system. — 44–55

(3) American business man, aged 45, who became hypochondriacal upon retiring from business; case illustrates factors of disposable energy in relation to energy gradients. — 75, 111, 117

(4) Woman with homosexual attachment whose dream of crossing a ford and encountering crab is analysed to show critical nature of transition from personal to collective unconscious. — 123–40, 157–66 (*see also* **5** case 18a, 365)

(5) Homosexual youth: religious dreams compensate the negative view of his condition. — 167–83 (*see also* **17** case 28, 266–81, *where discussed more fully*)

(6) Woman, treatment of whom does not succeed until doctor's dream of her. — 189–90, 281 (*see also* **18** case 10, *and refs. listed there*)

(7) Young girl, a somnambulistic medium; here only referred to (J.'s first published case). — 199, (*p*123) (*see also* **1** case 2, *and refs. listed there*)

(8) Young woman philosophy student with father fixation, in which the father image deepened into the image of God, through it the transference being resolved. — 206–17, 243, 247–8, 255–7 (*see also* **18** case 23, 634)

(9) Youth with sentimental lovefantasy who intends suicide, has hallucination of stars, commits crime. — 231–2, 252

379

cer. — 190 (*see also* **18** case 15, 467, 556)

(4) Woman with fantasy of primitive mother-figure. — 311*n*

(5) "Case X," spontaneous visual impressions of Kore archetype. — 321–39

(6) "Case Y," dreams of same. — 340–55

(7) "Case Z," dreams with animal affinities. — 358–83

(8) American lady in psychic impasse: active imagination expressed in paintings. — 526–621; Pictures 1–24 (*see also* **13** case 3, *fig.* A4, (*p*56&*n*))

(9) Woman of artistic gifts fond of playing with forms. — *fig.* 5, (*p*347)

(10) Woman born in Dutch East Indies. — 656–9, *figs.* 7, 8, 9 (*see also* **18** case 10, *and refs. listed there*)

(11) Seven-year old son of a problem marriage who hung pictures of circles round his bed. — 687, *fig.* 33 (*see also* **18** case 31); *see also* many mandalas from cases, 647–98, *figs.* 4–43; cf. volume **13**, first entry

volume 9ii

(1) Young woman with intense inner life who dreamed of fishes. — 236–8

volume 11

(1) Hysterical fever cured by confession of psychological cause. — 15

(2) Psoriasis, cured by analysis. — 15

(3) Distended colon. — 15

(4) Intellectual with series of 400 dreams. — 38–63 (*see also* **12** case 1, *and refs. listed there*)

(5) Young woman, who dreamed of baptism and planetarium, — 162–5

(6) Of adherent of doctrine of *privatio boni.* — 457

volume 12

(1) Scientist who recorded his own dream-series illustrating mandala symbolism. — 45–331; *see also* **11** case 4, 38–63; **18** case 13, 402–6, 673&*nn*, 1265

volume 13

For mandalas drawn by various patients, see above **9i** *last entry; they also appear, with comments, in* "Concerning Mandala Symbolism" (refs. in parens., and para. numbers are to **9i**). — A1 (*fig.* 9) 659; A3 (*fig.* 6) 654; A5 (*fig.* 25) 679; A6 (*fig.* 28) 682; A7 (*fig.* 38) 693; A8 (*fig.* 37) 692; A9 (*fig.* 26) 680; A10 (*fig.* 36) 691

(1) Woman whose letter showed that she had learned to accept her own nature fully. — 70

(2) Somnambulistic girl, 15½, who drew mandala. — 31*n*, 37 (*see also* **1** case 2, *and refs. listed there*)

(3) Patient (Miss X) who drew mandala. — *fig.* A4, (*p*56&*n*) (*see also* **9i** case 8, picture 9, and 596–603)

(4) Patient, woman, who drew *figs.* 2, 30, 31. — 307, 343–4, 345–6

(5) Patient, woman, who drew *figs.* 26, 28, 29. — 334–5, 337–8, 339–42

volume 16

(1) Man who experienced dream series including water motif, unknown woman motif, etc., illustrating continuity of unconscious themes. — 14, 15

(2) Man whose initial dream criticized his interest in occult subjects. — 93–6

(3) Man with symptoms resembling mountain sickness, and archetypal dreams indicating need for check on his ambitious plans. — 297–305 (*see also* **18** case 2, 161–70, 180–201, 206, 207)

CASES (cont.):

(4) Woman aged 25, with dreams of crossing frontier, indicating course her three attempts at analysis would take. J.'s own dream about her led to a change in approach; symptoms linked with her childhood in Java then appeared and were analysed. — 307–11, 546–64 (see also 18 case 10 and list of refs. there)

(5) Mountain climber with dreams presaging fatal climbing expedition. — 323–5 (see also 8 164; 17 case 5, 117–22; 18 case 16, 471)

(6) Young man with derogatory dreams of father compensating his "too good" relationship with parent. — 335–7

(7) Girl, 17, whose dreams, studied to establish diagnosis between hysteria and progressive muscular atrophy, pointed to grave organic disease, death. — 343–51

(8) Woman over 60, whose dreams and pictures (notably of divine child) illustrate onset of transference. — 377–81

(9) Woman whose attempt to overcome phobia of Paris by visit there, resulted in death. — 463

(10) Man with phobia of flights of steps, who dies in an accident on steps. — 463

volume 17

(1) Anna, aged 3, subject of "Psychic Conflicts in a Child." [identified as J.'s daughter Agathe in *Freud/Jung Letters*] — 3–74 (see also 5 case 15, 277)

(2) Girl, aged 15, who harboured an unconscious fantasy of mother's death. — 7–8

(3) Boy, who dreamed the erotic and religious problems of father. — 106

(4) Three sisters, who dreamed of "devoted" mother as dangerous animal; she later went insane and acted like an animal. — 107 (see also 5 case 20, 504)

(5) Mountain-climber, man of 50, whose dreams presaged a fatal climbing expedition. — 117–24 (see also 8 164; 16 case 5, 323–5; 18 case 16, 471)

(6) Boy, aged 6, imbecile, whose fits of rage were caused by his mother's ambition. — 133

(7) Boy, aged 14, who killed his stepfather. — 133

(8) Boy, who at 5 violated his sister, later tried to kill father, and grew up to be normal. — 136

(9) Epileptic boy who had stabbed his sister following hallucination of a little man with a beard. — 137 (see also 18 case 26, 802–15)

(10) Boy, aged 14, schizophrenic, whose first symptom was a sexual conflict. — 140

(11) Girl, aged 4, whose psychogenic constipation was caused by her mother. — 141

(12) Four abnormal siblings, all infected by unlived erotic life of mother, who subsequently became melancholic. — 147–53

(13) Recruit, aged 19, hysterical, cured by anamnestic analysis. — 177

(14) Recruit, neurotic, cured by anamnestic analysis. — 178

(15) Man, aged 30, who was "kept" by older woman, and whose "psychoanalytical autobiography" omitted essential moral element. — 182–3 (see also 8 case 10, 685; 18 case 6, 282, 284)

(16) Widow, aged 54, whose "snapshot" dreams contained her real intentions. — 185–6

(17) Crusty old general, whose dream showed an undeveloped interest in art. — 187–8

K

ka, **7** 295; **9i** 702; **10** 84; **11** 198; **12**
66; **14** 355–6;
Christ and, **5** 318*n*; **11** 177;
and Holy Ghost, **11** 177, 197;
of kings, **11** 197*n*; **13** 132; **14**
350–2
Ka'ba, **14** 570
Kabasilas, N., *see* Cabasilas
Kabbala/kabbalism, *see* Cabala;
cabalism
Kabbala Denudata, see Knorr von
Rosenroth *s.v.*
Kabras forest, **10** 126
Kaegi, W., **15** 211*n*
Kagarow, E., **13** 462;
"Der umgekehrte Schamaner-
baum," **13** 462*n*
Kaineus, **5** 378*n*, 439, 460, 480, 638
Kainis, **5** 439
kairos/καιρός, **10** 398, 585
Kaiser, O.: "Beiträge zur Differen-
tialdiagnose der Hysterie und
Katatonie," **3** 12*n*
Kalevala, Finnish epic, **5** 474*n*
Kali, **9i** 158, 186, 189; **10** 989; **16**
518;
-Durga, **10** 880
Kalid/Kallid, *see* ALCHEMICAL
WRITERS *s.v.*
Kalighat (Calcutta), **13** 128*n*
kalit, **8** 125
Kallisthenes, pseudo-, **9i** 604
Kalthoff, A., **5** 113;
The Rise of Christianity, **5** 42*n*,
113*n*
Kama, **5** 198, 590*n*
Kamea, **14** 636
kamma, see *karma*
Kammerer, P., **8** 825, 827;
Das Gesetz der Serie, **8** 825*n*,
840*n*
Ka-Mutef, **9i** 438; **9ii** 322; **11** 177,
197, 222, 235, 237; **14** 350*n*, 351,
355
k'an (hexagram), see *I Ching s.v.*

Kanathos, fountain of, **5** 363
Kankeleit, O.: *Das Unbewusste als
Keimstätte des Schöpferischen,* J.'s
foreword and contribution, **18**
1760–8
Kant, I., **2** 46; **4** 688, 690; **5** 14*n*; **6**
61, 63–6, 193, 512, 519, 659, 680,
733; **8** 212, 276, 352, 358; **9i** 160,
259; **9ii** 11; **10** 779, 871; **11** 375;
15 31; **16** 294; **18** 8, 124, 485,
714, 758, 1734;
anthropology of, **18** 1223;
on *a priori* categories, **3** 527; **8**
840; **9i** 136*n*, 150;
on categorical imperative, **15**
31;
and categories, **10** 14;
and comprehension, **3** 393; **8**
454;
on *Ding an sich* (Thing-in-
itself), **4** 317; **11** 399*n*, 819; **12**
247; **13** 82;
on idea, **6** 519, 733, 753;
on instinct, **8** 265;
as introverted type, **6** 526, 632;
psychology of, **18** 900;
on "shadowy representations/
thoughts," **3** 440; **9i** 160;
on Swedenborg, **18** 706–9;
theory of knowledge, **9i** 120*n*;
threefold postulate of, **6** 534;.
on *Urbild,* **6** 519, 733; **8** 276;
WORKS:
*Anthropologie in pragmatischer
Hinsicht,* **8** 265*n*; **18** 8*n*;
Critique of Practical Reason, **3**
18*n*; **6** 66&*n*;
Critique of Pure Reason, **2** 46*n*;
6 63*n*, 64*n*, 65*n*, 733*n*, 753*n*;
8 654; **9i** 150; **11** 819*n*, 967;
18 1589;
*Kant's Cosmogony as in his "Es-
say on the Retardation of the Rotation of the Earth" . . . . ,* ed.
and tr. W. Hastie, **1** 66*n*

king (*cont.*):
divine right/divinity of, **9ii** 274; **14** 349–50, 516;
in dreams, **9i** 71–2;
in Egypt/Egyptian: birth of, **5** 401*n*; and sun-disc, **5** pl. VII; and sun-god, **5** pl. XI*a* (see also *ka*; kingship);
as filius philosophorum, **12** *fig.* 155;
of forest, *see* TREES *s.v.* oak;
four, **13** 365;
of Glory/*rex gloriae*, **9i** 577, 603*n*; **9ii** 304, 318; **11** 281; **13** 182; Christ as, **11** 229; in mandala, **11** 113, 229, 946;
as God's sun, **12** 497;
as gold, **14** 354, 355, 720, 724–5, 736;
as hermaphrodite, **12** 142, *fig.* 54; **13** *fig.* B2;
individuality and, **16** 223;
ka of, see *ka s.v.*;
killing/*mortificatio* of, **13** 106, 107*n*;
and land, marriage with, **5** 306;
as lapis, *see* lapis *s.v.*;
and Leo/lion, **14** 467;
Mercurius as, **13** 282;
patria potestatis of, **16** 227;
with planets, **12** *figs.* 79, 149, 154, 155;
plumed, **12** *fig.* 228;
as *prima materia*, **12** 491, *figs.* 149, 168;
projection of, **14** 520;
and queen/Rex and Regina, **12** 315, 322, 334, 500, *figs.* 142a, 183; **14** 349–543, 570, 592*n*, 725, 731; **16** 437; in bath, **14** 537; **16** 453–6; as *coincidentia oppositorum*, **14** 540; *coniunctio* of, **16** 410–11; countercrossing, **16** 421–2; death of, **16** 467; as dragon's tail, **14** 491*n*; as hermaphrodite, **12** *fig.* 116; as opposites, personification of, **14** 2, 109, 337 (see also

above *coincidentia oppositorum*); reunion of, **14** 18; rose symbolism of, **13** 387; as spirit and soul, **14** 536; as symbols of self, **9i** 315; transformation of, **16** 473;
rebirth/renewal of, **12** 210*n*, 491–3, 496, *fig.* 175; **14** 75, 262*n*, 357, 425, 432, 443, 450, 465, 472, 498, 504, 507, 519, 522; religious problem of, **14** 514–31;
redeemer, **12** 491, 501;
and redemption, his need/capacity for, **13** 183;
regicide, **6** 322 (*see also below* sacrifice);
as *Rex marinus*/of the sea, **12** 193*n*, 435, 449, *fig.* 166; **13** 183; **14** 104, 105, 465; **16** 455; brain children of, **12** 435; in Ripley's *Cantilena*, **12** 491–501; and queen in, **14** 368–463; sick, **12** 496, *fig.* 149;
sacrifice of, **14** 357–8, 525; Jesus as, **11** 339, 406; ritual, **11** 407, 409;
sick, **12** 496, *fig.* 149; **14** 375;
as Sol/sun, **12** 210*n*, *figs.* 79, 268; **13** 107*n*, 398; **14** 168, 180*n*, 349, 353, 424, 465, 498, 501–5, 519, 520, 725;
son of, **12** 434–6, 439*n*, 440*n*, 446, 451, 454, 496, *fig.* 179; **13** *fig.* B6; death of, **12** 436, 437; devoured by king, **12** *fig.* 168; rebirth of, **12** 449*n*, 498 (see also *filius regis; filius regius*);
sterile, **12** 435, 491, 496; **14** 465;
stone as, **14** 521;
submerged/concealed in sea, **11** 160*n*;
-symbol, and consciousness, **14** 498–513;
theriomorphic form of, **14** 405;
tomb of, **14** 65;
transfixed, **11** 357;

transformation of, **14** 356–67, 368, 381, 406;
in *Visio Arislei*, **12** 435, 437, 496;
wholeness of, **14** 373, 506;
wounded, *see* Grail;
see also under Anthropos
Kingdom of God/Heaven, **4** 640; **9i** 156, 405; **9ii** 224, 310; **12** 8, 24, 550; **13** 96, 116*n*, 250, 321;
on earth, **18** 563;
two, **9ii** 100;
"within us," **7** 373; **9ii** 69&*n*; **12** 176; **13** 141
kingfisher, *see* ANIMALS *s.v.*
"kingless race," **9ii** 410
Kings, First/Second books of, *see* BIBLE: O.T. *s.v.*
Kingsford, A., **9i** 133; **11** 47; **13** 40; **14** 220
kingship: dual, **16** 433;
in Egypt, **11** 197; **14** 350–2;
and self, **9ii** 310;
theology of, **14** 349–50
kinship: libido, see libido *s.v.*;
psychological, in family, **17** 107*n*;
sections, **16** 435 (*see also* marriage classes)
Kircher, Athanasius, *see* ALCHEMICAL WRITERS *s.v.*
Kirchmaier, G. C.: *Disputationes Zoologicae*, **9ii** 178*n*
Kiriath Arba', **14** 556
Kirsch, J., **18** (*p*692*n*)
kiss/kissing, **3** 285;
derivation of, **5** 652;
of the Lord (Mechthild of Magdeburg), **9ii** 320; **13** 389*n*;
see also fondling
Kiswahili, **9i** 250*n*; *see also* Swahili
Kitâb el Foçul, **13** 407
kitchen(s): god of, **5** 663;
symbol of unconscious, **16** 378
Kitchin, Derek, **18** (*p*265), 685
Kitoshi, **10** 126
Klagenfurt, Mithras monument, **5** 288, pl. XXIV*a*
Klages, L., **9i** 32; **10** 375&*n*; **15** 72;

Der Geist als Widersacher der Seele, **9i** 32*n*, 391*n*; **10** 657; **15** 72*n*;
Vom kosmogonischen Eros, **10** 375*n*;
ed., *Psyche,* **15** 157*n*
Klaus, Brother, *see* Brother Klaus
Klein, J., *see under* Wertheimer
Kleinpaul, R.: *Das Leben der Sprache,* **5** 12*n*
Kleist, K.: *Untersuchungen zur Kenntnis der psychomotorischen Bewegungsstörungen bei Geisteskranken,* J.'s review, **18** 908
kleshas, see yoga
Klettenberg, Fräulein von, **12** 85
Klingsor, *see* Wagner: *Parsifal*
Klinke, O.: "Über das Symptom des Gedankenlautwerdens," **3** 175*n*
Klinz, A.: Ἱερὸς γάμος, **16** 355*n*
klippoth, **9i** 576
Kloeckler, H. von: *Astrologie als Erfahrungswissenschaft,* **8** 868*n*
Klopstock, G., **11** 468
Klug, I.: article in *Theologie und Glaube,* **11** 324*n*
Kluge, F.: *Etymologisches Wörterbuch der deutschen Sprache,* **5** 579, 682*n*; **8** 627
Kluger, H. Y., **10** 704*n*
Knapp, A., **18** 891;
Die polyneuritischen Psychosen, J.'s review, **18** 895
Knapp, M. J.: *Antiskia,* **9ii** 136*n*
Kneeler, the, **14** 176&*n*
Kneph, **5** 401*n*
knife, sacrificial, **11** 324; **13** 110
Knife Prince, **9i** 416
knights, combat of, **5** 395*n*
Knights of Columbus, **10** 977
Knoll, M., **8** 987; **10** 591;
"Transformations of Science in Our Age," **8** 875*n*, 987*n*
Knorr von Rosenroth, Christian, **12** 313; **13** 411; **14** 592–3;
Kabbala Denudata, **9i** 557*n*, 576*n*, 596*n*; **12** 313*n*; **13** 411*n*; **14** 14*n*, 18*nn*, 19*n*, 557*n*, 568*n*,

L

labial keys, **2** 563&*n*, 593
labile/lability, emotional, **1** 190,
198, 199, 203, 204, 209, 210, 223;
4 411*n*
laboratory and oratory, **12** *fig.* 145;
13 482
labor Sophiae, **13** 209
labour camps, **10** 615;
in Russia, **18** 1505;
see also concentration camps
Labour Party, **18** 1335
labours, twelve, **9i** 433&*n*;
of alchemists, *see* opus, alchemical, stages in;
of Heracles, *see* Heracles *s.v.*
labours
Labrunie de Nerval, G., *see* Nerval
labuni (New Guinea), **8** 129*n*
labyrinths, **13** 433
Labyrinthus medicorum, see Paracelsus
s.v.
Lachat, Père W.: J.'s letter to, **18**
1532–57; *La Réception et l'action du
Saint-Esprit dans la vie personnelle et
communautaire*, **18** 1532*n*
Lacinius, Janus, *see* ALCHEMICAL
WRITERS: Bonus
Laconia, magic stone in, **13** 129
Lactantius, F., **12** 370*n*;
Divinae Institutiones, **5** 668*n*;
Opera/Works, tr. W. Fletcher, **9i**
533*n*; **12** 185*n*
lac virginis, see virgin(s) *s.v.* milk of
Ladame,—:"L'Association des idées
et son utilisation comme méthode
d'examen dans les maladies men-
tales," **18** 983
ladanum, see *laudanum*
Ladd, C. T., **1** 101;
"Psychology of Visual Dreams,"
1 101*n*
ladder, **12** 66, 78, *figs.* 15, 215; **13**
40;
Jacob's, *see* Jacob *s.v.*;
of the twin gods (Egyptian), **9ii**
187

Ladislaus II (of Hungary), **12**
480&*n*; **13** 195
"Lady Soul" (Spitteler), **9ii** 25; **13**
460
lady, white, **9i** 352;
anima-figure as, **10** 713;
see also woman
Laforgue, R., **18** 1518*n*
Lagarde, P. A. de: *Clementina*, **9ii**
100*n*
Lagerlöf, S.: *Gösta Berlings Saga*, **17**
339*n*
Lagneus, David, *see* ALCHEMICAL
COLLECTIONS: *Theatr. chem. s.v.*
Laiblin, W.: "Vom mythischen
Gehalt unserer Märchen," **9ii**
232*n*
Laignel-Lavastine, M.: *Histoire générale de la médecine*, **12** *fig.* 61
Laistner, L., **5** 370;
Das Rätsel der Sphinx, **5** 370*n*
Lajard, J. B. F., **5** 297;
"Mémoire sur une représenta-
tion figurée de la Vénus orien-
tale androgyne," **5** *fig.* 19; **12**
fig. 183; **14** 416*n*;
Recherches sur le culte de Vénus, **5**
298; **14** 416*n*
Lake, K.: *Apostolic Fathers*, **13** 115*n*
lake: dream of, **4** 96–128;
as symbol of self, **9ii** 356;
of Vourukasha, **5** 306*n*, 367*n*,
428; **13** 406, 461
Lalita-Vistara, **6** 297;
tr. R. Mitra, **6** 297*n*
Lamaism, **12** 122;
rimpoche, **12** 123;
see also mandala, Lamaic
lamb/Lamb, *see* ANIMALS *s.v.*
Lambarene, **10** 783
Lambert, G.: *The Slide Area*, **3** 150*n*
Lambspringk, *see* ALCHEMICAL
COLLECTIONS: *Mus. herm. s.v.*
Lamentations, *see* BIBLE: O.T. *s.v.*
Lamia/lamia, **5** 369, 370, 577, pl.
XXXVIIIa; **9i** 53; **12** 61;

Hera as, **5** 451*n*;
mother-imago as, **5** 457, pls.
XXXVIIIa, XLVIII;
myth of, **5** 369
lamp, **9ii** 174; **11** 427
Lamprecht, K., **11** 576
lance, **5** 638, pl. XLV;
    piercing by, **5** 445;
    significance of, **5** 439
land(s): ancestral, **12** 170;
    beyond, *see* other world;
    children's, **12** 74;
    fertile, **5** 306;
    of sheep, **12** 71, 73;
    two (Egyptian), **9i** 702
Landgraf, K., **1** 344;
    "Ein Simulant vor Gericht," **1** 344*n*
landing: on shore, in myths, **5** 309, 310;
    from Ufos, *see* Ufo(s)
Landmann, S.: *Die Mehrheit geistiger Persönlichkeiten in einem Individuum*, **6** 797*n*
Lang, J. B., **18** 1825*n*; *Hat ein Gott die Welt erschaffen?*, **12** 26*n*
Lange, C. G., **18** 46*n*; *see also* affect *s.v.* James-Lange theory of
Lange, Wilhelm, **18** 795; *Hölderlin, eine Pathographie*, **18** 795*n*
Langmann, Dr. (clergyman), **10** 397*n*
language, **1** 179; **5** 11–16;
    affected, **3** 154;
    affective results of, **10** 965;
    alchemical, *see* alchemy *s.v.*;
    allegorical, **13** 126;
    conceptual, causalistic colouring of, **8** 965;
    of conscious mind, **13** 44, 395;
    of dreams, *see* dream(s) *s.v.*;
    exaggerated: in hysteria, **5** 654;
    in manic mood, **1** 199;
    French, *see* France *s.v.*;
    German: in Germany, *see* Germany *s.v.*; in Switzerland, **2** 10–11;
    Greek, **1** 144, 183;

"heavenly," **3** 157;
Hebrew, **1** 183;
history of, **5** 12; **9i** 67; **18** 1077;
idiom used by S. W., **1** 40, 50, 60;
innovations in, **3** 303 (*see also* neologisms);
Latin, **1** 144; **10** 905;
loftiness of, **1** 214;
Martian, **1** 144;
of myths, **11** 441;
mythological, of infancy, **7** 374;
of nature, **5** 568, 624*n*;
neutral, **8** 960;
official, **3** 269;
and opposites, **5** 581;
primitive, **7** 132, 447; **11** 339, 389;
of psychology, **8** 224;
secret, **13** 199;
of the spirits, **1** 59;
structure, **6** 878 (*see also* Finck);
Swiss dialect, **1** 38, 152–6; **2** 10–11; **18** 41;
of theologian and empiricist, **11** 454;
thought and, **5** 12–16;
of unconscious, *see* unconscious, the *s.v.*;
unconscious contaminations in, **6** 180;
of universal validity, **7** 229/447;
see also glossolalia; linguistic; speech; terminology
"Languedoc," **3** 303
Lankavatāra Sutra, *see* Sutras *s.v.*
Lanzone, R. V.: *Dizionario di mitologia egizia*, **5** *fig.* 11
Laodicea, **11** 705
Laodonia, cattle of, **5** 212
Lao Nai-hsüan, **11** 965
Lao-tzu, **6** 95, 188, 192, 358–61, 369; **7** 365, 388; **8** 918–20; **11** 954, 976, 1001; **14** 200;
    "high stands on low," **7** 308; **9i** 603; **11** 791; **17** 249; **18** 536;
    Tao Te Ching, **6** 359&*n*, 360–4; **8** 918–22; **9i** (*p*290); **11** 791,

Lao-tzu (*cont.*):
    954; **14** 164*n*; **18** 1267*n*;
    tr. A. Waley, *The Way and Its Power: A Study of the Tao Tê Ching*, **6** 359*n*; **8** 918*n*; **14** 164*n*
lap, as symbol: in initiation ceremonies, **5** 530;
    procreative, **5** 583
"Lapidis philosophorum nomina," *see* ALCHEMICAL WRITERS *s.v.*
lapis/*lapis philosophorum*, **8** 931; **9i** 117, 541, 549*n*, 555, 580*n*, 601*n*; **9ii** 194, 216, 220, 239, 244, 417; **11** 278*n*; **12** 94, 99, 103, 165, 247, 402; **13** 89, 112, 115, 123, 127, 134, 175, 177, 207*n*, 214*n*, 222, 299, 359, 371; **14** 2*n*, 36&*n*, 47, 120, 181*n*, 284, 286*n*, 364, 666, 697, 715, 749*n*; **16** 383, 454, 458, 533;
    TITLE: "The Lapis-Christ Parallel," **12** 447–515 (*see also* Christ/Jesus Christ *s.v.* lapis);
    Adam as, *see* Adam *s.v.*;
    aerial aspects of, **13** 261;
    as *alexipharmacum*, **18** 1631;
    as Andalusian prince, **13** 424–5, 428, 436;
    androgyny of, **14** 524;
    Anthropos as, *see* Anthropos *s.v.*;
    anticipation of (fourth stage of process), **16** 492;
    aqua permanens as, **12** 159*n*, 336&*n*;
    as arcane substance, **9ii** 374; **13** 177; **14** 36, 38, 321, 354*n*, 674, 758;
    and artifex, **18** 1631&*n*;
    as *aurum non vulgi*, **12** 343; **13** 203;
    birth of, **13** 392; **14** 186*n*;
    bitterness of, **14** 245–55;
    body/soul/spirit, **12** 243, 420; **14** 525; **16** 454, 468;
    in Cabala, **14** 45*n*, 568, 640–3;
    carbuncle as, **9i** 580*n*; **12** 552&*n*; **14** 608;

and centre, **12** 125, 155;
as *cervus fugitivus*, **14** 188;
chaos and, **12** 433;
as child of Sol and Luna, **14** 524;
-Christ parallel, *see* Christ/Jesus Christ *s.v.*;
as *cibus immortalis*, **14** 525;
colours in (*cauda pavonis*), **12** 220; **14** 397–9;
coniunctio of, **12** 140&*n*, *fig.* 13;
and consciousness, **13** 287;
as *creatum/increatum*, **16** 527;
crystal, **12** 221–2;
Dorn on, **11** 262;
in dunghill/filth, **12** 103, 421, 454, 514;
as egg, **13** 115;
and (four) elements, **12** 209, 220, 449, 457; **13** 357*n*; as quintessence of, **13** 207*n*; **16** 404;
and elixir, *see* elixir *s.v.*;
in Ezekiel's vision, **12** 471;
feminine aspect of, **14** 185;
as *filius macrocosmi/philosophorum/unius diei*, see *filius s.v.*;
as fire, **12** 157*n*;
as First Man, **16** 527;
as fish, **9ii** 193–4;
from flesh and blood, **12** 243;
as *flos*/flower, **12** 99&*n*; Sapphirine, **13** 322, 346;
as fountain and garden, **12** 155;
as *frumentum nostrum*, **13** 408;
as God, *see* God *s.v.*;
as gold (philosophical), **9i** 543; **12** 335, 343; tincture of, **12** 462, 505;
heavenly origin of, **9ii** 262;
as helper, **12** 155;
hermaphrodite, **12** 142, 305, 335; **16** 468;
as *homo totus*, see *homo totus s.v.*;
as homunculus, *see* homunculus *s.v.*;
hydrolith/water-stone, **12** 487;

13 87; **16** 398;
ideal for hermits, **14** 525;
and immortality, **13** 133;
incorruptibility of, **14** 87, 770;
and individuation process, **13** 242;
as inner man, **13** 126, 134;
and king, **12** 142, 552*n*; **13** 203;
as light, **13** 203, 299;
light and darkness, **12** 99, 140;
"light-nature" of, **14** 179;
living, **12** 155, 243, 426*n*; **13** 134; man as, **9ii** 390–1; **12** 187, 378; **16** 383;
as master, **12** 142;
meaning of, in alchemy, **14** 677, 716;
as mediator, **9i** 293*n*;
Mercurius as, *see* Mercurius *s.v.*;
minera of, **9i** 555;
and Monad, **12** 427*n*;
numinosity of, **14** 758;
as old man, **14** 7;
and opposites, union of, **9ii** 390–1; **14** 141;
and *opus*, **9ii** 375; **12** 243, 335, 427*n*, 431; goal of, **14** 6*n*, 525, 759, 763, 773;
as "orphan," **12** 426; **14** 13, 31, 35; "one stone," **14** 45;
as panacea, **14** 443, 680, 758;
paradoxical, **12** 420; **14** 36–41, 646;
as pelican, **12** *fig.* 256;
philosophical tree as, **13** 421–8;
philosophy of, **13** 126–7;
as *prima materia*, see *prima materia s.v.*;
production of, **12** 94, 142, 157, 167, 218, 220&*n*, 356;
quaternary form/*quaternio*, **9i** 651; **9ii** 374–7, 392; **11** 262, 727; **13** 272; of elements, **14** 238, 607;
as *radix ipsius*, **16** 527;
red tincture/medicine, **14** 690;

as redeemer, **12** 462–3; **14** 146, 375, 443 (*see also below* salvator);
as rock, **9ii** 143;
roundness of, **12** 167, 220, 433, 486;
salvator/saviour, redeemer, **12** 335, 512; **14** 33, 676;
sanctuary, **12** *fig.* 51;
sand (*arena*) as, **14** 263;
as self, *see* self *s.v.*;
semel factus, **18** 1631;
as serpent, **9ii** 387, 390, 391; Uroboros, **16** 527;
simplicity of, **12** 220, 427*n*;
as "son of man," **14** 295;
and soul, extraction of, **13** 89; **14** 372;
spirit in, **12** 512 (*see also above* body/soul/spirit);
as *spiritus humidus et aereus*, **13** 137*n*;
symbolism of, **14** 286*n*, 525, 649; **18** 1704;
synonyms for, **9i** 289, 543; **9ii** 194; **14** 2*n*, 142, 354, 396, 524, 661;
tetrameria of, **11** 727;
"theology" of, **12** 512;
"thousand names of," **9ii** 284, 296; **12** 431; **13** 209;
and time, **12** *fig.* 99;
torment of, **13** 439;
touchstone/*lapis Lydius*, **13** 94;
as "treasure hard to attain," **12** 222;
trinus, **12** 508; *et unus*, **12** 449;
triunity of, **14** 355;
ubiquity of, **12** 103, 433;
as *ultima materia*, **13** 421;
uncomely, **12** 103 (see also *lapis exilis*);
unity of, **14** 86, 294, 483*n*;
as universal medicine, **13** 133;
unum/unus mundus, **14** 661;
as Uroboros, *see above* serpent;
as *vas*, **12** 245*n*, 338;
volatile, **12** 390; **14** 727;
water and, *see* water;

ages of, **7** 151;
of the earth, **13** 6;
eternal, **7** 389;
of frequency, **2** 21, 382–6,
475–7, 587;
general, **7** (*p*4);
governing structure of dreams,
7 434*n*;
of inner, future man, **13** 221;
of least resistance, *see* least resistance;
of life, **13** 24;
mathematical, **13** 195;
of matter, **13** 286;
mechanistic, substrate of, **8**
964;
moral, **7** 218, 450; validity of, **7**
30;
natural, **7** 87; **8** 818–19; **11**
967; merely statistical, **8** 828;
no "absolute," **8** 821;
of our being, **13** 4, 30;
outward, **13** 81;
Pauline overcoming of, **7** 401;
plenitude of life governed by, **7**
72;
psychic, **7** 365; **13** 285, 357;
psychological, **7** 111, 389;
of reason, **13** 294;
Roman, **10** 517;
social, **7** 455*n*;
of the species, **5** 673;
tables of, **14** 571;
transgression, **13** 292;
unconscious, **7** 248; **13** 286
lawlessness, man of, **9ii** 68*n*
Laws of Manu, see Manu
lawyers, **8** 511–13
lay analyst, *see* analyst *s.v.*
Layard, J. W., **16** 433*n*, 438;
"The Incest Taboo and the
Virgin Archetype," **5** 497*n*,
652*n*; **9ii** 381*n*; **16** 433, 436*n*,
438*nn*;
Stone Men of Malekula, **9ii** 381*n*;
16 433*n*, 435*n*
layers, circular, *see* Böhme *s.v.*
Lazarello, Ludovicus, *see* ALCHEM-

ICAL WRITERS *s.v.*
laziness, **4** 470, 474, 516, 633, 641;
17 90, 248;
mental, **7** 263;
see also indolence
lead(-en), **9i** 581*n*; **9ii** 215; **11** 344*n*;
12 425, 440*n*, 518*n*; **13** 35, 119,
139*n*, 251, 267, 357, 433; **14** 303,
472*n*, 493, 616;
of the air, **12** 443;
as arcane substance, *see* arcane
substance *s.v.*;
demonic attacks on, **13** 430;
homunculus, **13** 93;
man of, *see* man *s.v.*;
nature of, **9ii** 215; **14** 545;
Osiris and, **13** 97&*n*;
philosophic, **13** 274;
as *prima materia*, see *prima
materia s.v.*;
Saturn and, **12** 440*n*; **13**
164*n*, 274, 445; **14** 299;
and water, **13** 97;
white, **13** 87;
see also *lato*
Leade, J., *see* ALCHEMICAL WRITERS:
Pordage *s.v.*
leader(s)/leadership, **10** 326, 462,
500; **17** 248, 284, 306, 323; *see
also* masses
leafless tree, *see* tree(s) *s.v.*
League of Nations, **10** 395, 943*n*;
18 1333;
and internationalism, **10** 195
Leah, **14** 556
leap-year, **14** 571
learning and instinct, **5** 673; **8** 268,
269; **10** 556, 557
"least of your brethren," **18** 638
least resistance, law of, **4** 516, 633,
634, 641, 642, 652
Lebhûdhâ, **14** 555
Le Blant, E.: *Sarcophages de la Gaule*,
5 163*n*
Le Bon, G., **10** 477;
The Crowd, **9i** 225*n*; **10** 477*n*;
18 318, 1474
Leclercq, H., *see under* F. Cabrol

libido (*cont.*):

and instinct, **4** 280, 283;
introversion of, **4** 276&*n*, 277, 304&*n*, 420; **5** 134, 193, 253, 260, 299, 448–50, 517–19, 580, 591; **6** 183, 189–90, 310, 314, 343, 423–4; **8** 169; **17** 13*n*; *manas* and, **6** 343;
and introverted type, **3** 418–19;
intuitive faculty of, **5** 182;
investment of, **4** 50, 661; in functions, **8** 91; in unconscious, **6** 446;
kinship, **9ii** 381; **16** 431, 445, 469;
liberation of, **6** 350&*n*, 371;
life-energy as, **8** 32;
localization of, **4** 268; **6** 869;
loss of, **8** 598; **16** 87;
and mana, **8** 441;
in meditation, **6** 189;
Mercurius as, **16** 455;
metaphysical aspect, **8** 56;
migration(s) of, **4** 291–2; **5** 206;
mother-, **5** 658;
and mother: subterranean, **5** 627, 669; withdrawn from, **5** 379, 473 (*see also above s.v.* canalization; *below s.v.* regression);
movement of, **7** 514;
myth, typical elements of, **5** 441;
natural flow of, **6** 355–6;
neurosis and, *see* neurosis *s.v.*;
nutritional/alimentary, **4** 269, 290; **5** 206;
object of: concrete vs. psychic, **5** 128; internal vs. external, **5** 253–4;
personifications of, **5** 388;
phallus as source of, **5** 146;
primitives and, *see* primitives *s.v.*;
progression of, **5** 459; **8** 60–1;
and projections, **8** 507;
psychic energy as, *see above*

energic theory of;
in puberty, *see* puberty *s.v.*;
regression of/regressive, **4** 277, 365–9, 420, 516, 568–9; **5** 193, 207, 217–18, 248, 299, 450, 518, 580, 631, 659; **6** 314; **8** 60–2; **16** 368; and activation of archetypal images, **5** 466, 655; and canalization into the god, **5** 390; desexualized, **5** 654; of father, **17** 219; and infantile kicking, **5** 481; to mother-imago, **5** 329–30, 450*n*; to the primordial, **5** 450; **6** 202; and reactivation of infantile stage, **5** 134, 226–7, 299, 313; and snake symbol, **5** 530; and water symbol, **5** 503*n*;
and religion, **5** 669; **7** 150;
repressed, **4** 275, 515;
retention of, and spiritualization, **6** 401;
sacrifice of, **5** 379, 398, 638, 646, 659, 668*n*, 671;
self-perceptions of, **5** 255;
self-realization of, **5** 332;
sexual, recession of, in paranoia, **5** 191;
not sexual, **4** 268–70; **5** 185; **8** 56&*n*;
and sexuality, **4** 283–4, 286; **6** 401;
as sexuality (Freud), **5** 190;
sexuality a symbol of, **5** 298;
spiritualization of, **5** 332, 398;
splitting of, **4** 381; **6** 30, 326, 337, 347;
stagnant pools of, **5** 254;
symbols, *see below*;
tejas and, **5** 238;
theriomorphic representations of, **5** 24, 149, 261;
transferred to the earth, **8** 85–6;
transformation(s) of, **5** 216, 425; through culture, **8** 81, 87; through faith, **5** 339, 342; and investment of analogous ob-

ject, **5** 226, 337; **8** 38–9; and symbol-formation, **8** 93;
unchained, **5** 104;
and unconscious: attraction of, **5** 253; directed into, **5** 257, 450; **6** 310; immersion in, **5** 655; investment in, **6** 446; sinking/withdrawal into, **4** 257; **5** 448–50; **6** 183, 201, 296, 401, 423–4, 427; as source, **7** 258/473; withdrawal from, **6** 83; undifferentiated, **5** 332*n*, 505; unity of, **5** 659;
untamed, **5** 505; **6** 33*n*; **7** 133, 138;
winding path of, **5** 84
libido-symbol(s)/symbolism, **5** 143, 146–7, 255, 322, 324, 329, 388, 481, 638, 669; **6** 330, 336–7
as analogues, **8** 91–3;
animals as, **5** 261, 659 (*see also below* horse; lion; snake);
as opposites, **6** 337;
and relation to unconscious, **6** 401, 435, 445–6;
and time and fate, **5** 423;
INSTANCES: **6** 353–4;
arrow, **5** 447;
fire, **5** 145–6, 227, 237, 246, 324, 388; **9ii** 203*n*;
fire-maker, **5** 481;
gods and goddesses, **5** 324, 481;
heroes, **5** 283*n*, 297;
horse, **5** 421–2;
human figure, **5** 251;
intoxicating drink, **5** 315;
light, **5** 145, 171*n*, 322, 324, 388;
lion, **18** 1078;
mother-imago, **5** 421;
rta, **6** 355;
sexuality, **5** 298;
snake, **18** 1078;
sun, **5** 145–6, 297–8, 388; **6** 355;
sun-heroes, **5** 297;
tree, **5** 326, 329;

wind, **5** 422; **6** 355;
worm, **5** 455
Libitina, goddess of the dead, **5** 188*n*
Libra, *see* zodiac, twelve signs of,
Libya, **5** 460*n*; **9ii** 213
licentiousness, **4** 200, 667
Licetus, Fortunius: *Allegoria peripatetica de generatione amicitia*, **14** 95&*n*
Li Chi (Book of Rites), **5** 663; **12** 548
Liddell, H. G., and R. Scott: *Greek-English Lexicon*, **11** 113*n*
Lidzbarski, M.: *Ginza der Schatz*, **14** 701*n*, 727*n*;
Das Johannesbuch der Mandäer, **14** 589*n*, 590*n*
lie(s), *see* lying
Liébeault, A. A., **4** 748; **10** 366; **17** 128; **18** 797&*n*; with H. Bernheim, suggestion therapy, **16** 1, 231;
Du Sommeil et des états analogues considérés au point de vue de l'action du moral sur le physique, **7** 2*n*
Liebig, Justus von, **6** 548
Liepmann, H. K., **2** 387–8; **3** 21, 37; **18** 891;
Über Ideenflucht, Begriffsbestimmung und psychologische Analyse, **2** 387*n*; **3** 21*n*; **5** 11*n*
life, **7** 303; **8** 775; **12** 105; **13** 76, 370;
TITLES: "Experience of the Transcendence of Life," **9i** 208–11; "The Renewal of Life," **12** 447–52; "Return to the Simple Life," **18** 1343–56; "The Rules of Life," **18** 1428–30; "Spirit and Life," **8** 601–48;
"aerial," **13** 200–1;
aim of, **8** 792, 803;
anima as archetype of, *see* anima *s.v.* archetype;
art of, **8** 789;
banal, **18** 627;
bread of, **13** 403;
-breath, **8** 662;

life (*cont.*):

climax of, **9i** 548, 549;

and conflict of opposites, **7** 78–80;

consciousness and, *see* consciousness *s.v.*;

contraction of, **8** 785;

curve of, **8** 798–9;

and death, **5** 417, 432, 531, 577, 681; **8** 803–4; **13** 68, 76*n*;

as opposites, **9ii** 187; **13** 76*n*; **14** 4;

after death, **8** 790, 793; **13** 76*n*; **18** 683–6, 700 (*see also* death *s.v.* rebirth; immortality);

demands of, **7** 161, 208;

devotion to, **13** 36;

a disease with bad prognosis, **11** 167, 842;

divine drama of, **18** 628, 630;

double, **7** 352;

duty to, **7** 113;

elixir of, *see* elixir *s.v.*;

energy and, *see* energy *s.v.*;

everlasting, **13** 193;

"ever-living fire," **12** 297;

fantasy-, **7** 161;

fear of, **5** 456–7, 681; **8** 796–9;

-feeling, **7** 240/460, 260/476;

flight from, **5** 617, 629;

flirtations with, **13** 25;

-force, **4** 282; **7** 79; **8** 32, 662–3; **12** 157, 209; **13** 263; daemonic, **13** 55; psychic, **5** 323; renewal of, **5** 392, 671; sun as symbol of, **5** 297; tree as symbol of, **5** 392; **13** 350;

fountain of, **5** pl. XXVI; **13** 112, 137*n*;

fulness of, **12** 18, 293, 296–7;

as function of matter, **8** 529;

goal of, *see* goal(s) *s.v.*;

half-, **8** 959;

-history, **17** 259–60;

Holy Ghost as, **11** 197;

human nature and, **13** 27–8, 34;

inner, *see* inner *s.v.*;

-instinct, **4** 237; **10** 312;

ka as, **11** 197, 241;

law of, **13** 24;

length of, **13** 171;

-line, **7** 497, 500–1, 515;

-mass, shapeless/gelatinous, **12** 183–6, 242, 244;

meaningful, **18** 630, 631;

meaning of, **7** 113–14, 327; **8** 686, 731, 796; **11** 514, 517; **18** 565, 604;

mystery of, **13** 287;

natural/unconscious, **7** 504;

negation of, **10** 375*n*;

"ordinary" and "heroic," **7** 72;

Paracelsus' definition of, **13** 170;

philosophy of, *see* philosophy *s.v.*;

plan of, **7** 205/446;

principle, **13** 171, 243, 262;

private, **7** 305–7, 310, 317–18;

problems of, **13** 18;

-process, **4** 237, 282; **7** 210, 311, 486; **8** 31–2, 529, 792; **9ii** 3;

prolongation/continuation of, **9i** 241; **13** 76&*n*;

provisional, **16** 336;

and psyche, **11** 769;

psychic, **7** 399; **12** 93, 104; **13** 200;

-relationship, **7** 356;

renewal of, **7** 260/476; **11** 56; **12** 447–52;

rules of, **18** 1428–9;

science and riddle of, **8** 620;

"simple," **7** 258;

situations, typical, **5** 450;

-soul, mercurial, **13** 263;

source of, **12** 157; sister as, **12** 92; soul as, **8** 662–3, 668; sun as, **5** 176; tree as, **13** 350;

and spirit, **5** 615; **8** 601–48;

"spiritual" or "symbolic," **5** 510; **8** 633, 686–7;

stages of, *see below;*

stasis of, **7** 206;

stone as, **9i** 238*n*;
stream of, **13** 23;
-style, **4** 310; **14** 514*n*; masculine, **8** 783;
symbolic, **5** 510; **18** 649;
too rational, **18** 628;
tree of, *see* tree(s) *s.v.*;
-urge, **4** 280; **5** 195; **7** 88, 488; **13** 17;
as vehicle of perfection, **11** 856;
water of, *see* water *s.v.*;
way of, **13** 15;
wood of, **13** 459;
-wound, **3** 428, 430
life, stages of:
　TITLE: "The Stages of Life," **8** 749–95;
　three phases of, **4** 263–6;
　first half of, **5** 680; **8** 113, 782; **13** 69;
　noonday of, **8** 778, 780–1;
　around forty, **8** 773, 783;
　middle, **8** 555–6; **13** 16, 68; **17** 331a, 333, 335, 337; collective unconscious in, **17** 211; marriage in, **17** 337;
　afternoon/second half of, **5** (*p*xxvi), 458–9, 680; **8** 113, 768–95; **9i** 184, 355; **16** 83; **18** 754, 1161; and changes in physique, **8** 780–3; and integration of self, **16** 110, 474; meaning and purpose of, **7** 114–15; **8** 792, 800; **17** 331a–b; preparation for, **8** 784, 787; and problem of opposites, **7** 91, 116; psychology of, **4** 762; **16** 75; and religious outlook, **8** 786; **11** 509;
　evening of, **8** 780 (*see also* climacteric)
lift, in dream, **12** 200, 201
ligamentum spiritus/mentis/animae et corporis, **8** 931; **9i** 386, 555; **9ii** 118
light/Light, **9ii** 115*n*; **12** 258–62, 270–1, 436; **13** 102, 112, 141,

198, 328, 341, 393, 462; **14** 41, 164;
　TITLES: "The Light of Nature and the Light of Revelation," **13** 145–68; "The Light of the Darkness," **13** 197–9;
　from above, **13** 197;
　in Adam's nature, **14** 585;
　archetypal, God as, **9i** 5, 149;
　of the body, **13** 141;
　in Böhme, **9i** 535–6, 717;
　-bringer, **9i** 288; **13** 163, 273;
　Christ as, **18** 1515, 1827;
　Lucifer as, *see* Lucifer *s.v.*; Mercurius as, *see* Mercurius *s.v.*;
　primordial, **13** 300;
　central white, **13** 37;
　children of, **7** 395; **13** 299;
　Christ and, **11** 228; **14** 476&*n*;
　circulation of, **12** 229, 259; **13** 20;
　clarifying, **13** 60;
　clear, **11** 796;
　coming of, **13** 273;
　consciousness and, **8** 396; **12** 259; **13** 28–9, 50, 59, 120, 294, 298; **14** 117;
　creation of, **5** (*p*453);
　cross of, **13** 334;
　crown of, **14** 6;
　dark, **12** 140;
　and darkness/dark, **12** 22, 140; **13** 38, 197, 199, 290–3, 391, 456; **14** 476; **16** 510–11;
　daemons of, **13** 291; fifteen steps of, **12** 80; **13** 86; hierosgamos of, **13** 198; as opposites, **8** 401; **9i** 563; **9ii** 187; **12** 22, 192; **15** 213;
　divine, **13** 141, 443; epiphany and, **10** 622;
　and divine hero, **5** 274*n*;
　emission by fish and insects, **10** 636;
　entoptic perceptions of, **1** 100;
　eternal, **9i** 257, 536;
　"everything must be ruled by," **12** 117, 120, 181, 246;

light *(cont.)*:
figure of, **13** 334;
as *filius,* **13** 161–3;
flower of, **13** *fig.* 32;
gathering the, **13** (*p*30);
globes of, **13** *fig.* 25;
of God/aspect of God, **11** 651, 694; **13** 377;
god (of), **5** 128, 173; **9i** 189;
great, in mysticism, **11** 828;
of heaven/heavenly, **13** 28; between the eyes, **13** 28&*n*, 31*n*;
symbol, **8** 396; is Tao, **13** 28, 33;
of Holy Spirit, **13** 149;
of human nature, and alchemy, **13** 46, 161;
as image of God, **14** 41;
inaccessible, **13** 98*n*;
inner, **12** 381, 431; **13** 64, 141;
of justice, **13** 301*n*;
kept from those behind, **12** 55;
lapis as, see *lapis philosophorum s.v.;*
of man, **13** 141, 163, 301, 302;
man of, **11** 380; **12** 456, 458; **13** 138*n*, 168&*n*; **16** 458;
Mercurius as, *see* Mercurius *s.v.;*
of moon and stars, **13** 300;
natural, **13** 286;
nature of, **13** 188;
of nature, in alchemy, **12** 381, 431; **13** 148–50, 161, 184, 197, 229, 300, 377; **14** 41; Mercurius and, *see* Mercurius *s.v.* light;
new, **13** 161, 300;
obfuscation of, **16** 399;
physical fact and psychic image, **8** 623, 745;
of Pleroma, **13** 451;
pneumatic realm of, **13** 452;
powers of, **1** 67, 69;
primordial, **8** 854;
rays of, **13** 86*n*;
of revelation, **13** (*p*111), 148;
seeds of, **8** 388*n* (see also

scintilla(-ae)));
of self, **13** 301;
and shadow, as opposites, **16** 146;
simulacrum Dei, **13** 188;
and sound, etymological connections, **5** 235–7;
spark of, **12** 138–9;
spiritual, **9i** 133*n*;
and spiritual man, **12** 458; **13** 126;
substances, **5** 171*nn*;
supernatural, **13** 148;
surpassing all lights, **13** 299;
symbolism, **5** 158, 180*n*, 322; **13** 37;
symbols, **5** 423, 481; **13** 187*n*, 329–31;
theory of, **4** 282; **18** 69&*n*;
tree of, **13** 308;
unconscious as nocturnal, **16** 469;
virgin of, **12** 506;
vision(s) of, *see* vision(s) *s.v.;*
wavelengths of, **8** 367, 680;
white: of *Dharmakaya,* **13** 50; in firmament, **13** *fig.* A6;
world of, **13** 456;
yellow, **12** 270; **13** 161*n*;
see also *lumen; lux moderna*
Lightfoot, J. B.: *Notes on the Epistles of Saint Paul,* **9ii** 333*n*
lightning, **9i** 532–6, 538–41, 543, 558, 564, picture 2; **13** 198;
in alchemy, **9i** 533, 575; **13** 190&*n*, 417;
ball/bead, **18** 1437;
flash, symbol of liberation, **9i** 532–3; Böhme's, *see* Böhme *s.v.* fire;
phallic symbol, **16** 340;
theriomorphic symbols: horse, **5** 421; snake, **13** 270*n*
"Lignum vitae," *see* ALCHEMICAL COLLECTIONS: *Bibl. chem. cur. s.v.* Braceschus
"like," word, **5** 203
like with like, mating of, **12** 435, 496

literature (*cont.*):
109, 174;
and psychology, 15 (*p*85);
syzygy motif in, **9i** 115
literature, psychoanalytic: confusion in, **4** 638;
need of knowledge of, **4** 632;
see also psychoanalysis
Litigius, **13** 176*n*
"Little Hans," *see* Freud: CASES *s.v.*
Little Red Riding-Hood, *see* fairytales: INSTANCES *s.v.* German
liturgy: Byzantine, **11** 331;
Gallican, **11** 321;
of the Mass, **11** 406;
Mithraic, *see* Mithras *s.v.*;
Mozarabic, **11** 317&*n*, 321, 332;
Protestantism's loss of, **11** 33;
Uniate, **11** 311*n*
liver, animus housed in, **13** 57
liver/Liverpool, **9i** 654*n*
"living being," **8** 605–6, 620–1; *see also* spirit(s)
living standard, *see* America(n) *s.v.* way of life
"Livre des ansienes estoires," **13** *fig.* B1
"Livré des Balances," **14** 584*n*
Livre des Secrez de Nature, **14** 188*n*
Livre d'Heures du Duc de Berry, **13** 405*n*
lizard(s), *see* ANIMALS *s.v.*
Ljubljana earthquake, **1** 319
Llewellyn, R. T., **13** 141*n*, 146*n*, 167*n*
loathsome sponge, **13** 380&*n*
locality, changes of, **8** 809
localization, **3** 582, 583;
of symbol, **3** 286
Locke, J., **18** 14*n*
Lockheed Aircraft Corporation, **10** 791
locksmith, apprentice, *see* CASES IN SUMMARY: Maeder *s.v.*
locomotive, function/meaning of, **4** 688

Loco Tenente Gobernador (Taos), **9i** 48
locustae, see TREES *s.v.*
lodestone, **9ii** 295*n*; *see also* magnet
Lodge, Sir Oliver, **18** 750
Loewenfeld, *see* Löwenfeld
Löffler, K.: *Schwäbische Buchmalerei,* **12** *fig.* 62
log, in dream, **3** 123, 128, 130
logical contradictions, **13** 295
logos/Logos, **5** 99, 102, 104*n*, 272; **6** 347; **9i** 178; **9ii** 230, 293, 313, 397; **11** 359, 422, 432, 610, 619, 655; **12** 356*n*, 412, 436, 440, 551, *fig.* 104; **13** 59, 110, 278, 366; **14** 124, 224, 226; **16** 458;
ancients on, **5** 22;
animus as, *see* animus *s.v.*;
Archanthropos as, **9ii** 327;
Christ as, *see* Christ/Jesus *s.v.*;
compensatory, **13** 391;
cosmogonic, **9ii** 330;
dog/*canis* as, **13** 278*n*; **14** 174*n*, 176;
and fire-spirit, **5** 663;
Gnostic, **9ii** 314;
ibis and, **14** 250;
image of, in the sun, **5** 158;
incarnation of, **11** 336;
Johannine, **13** 271;
as magnetic agent, **9ii** 293;
man's advance towards, **11** 442;
masculine, unconscious as consort of, **18** 1653;
as mediator, **6** 94;
Melchisedec as, **11** 306;
Mercurius, become world, **13** 271;
Mercury/Hermes as, **9ii** 313; **11** 421;
modern spirit and, **5** 113;
principle, **5** 458; **13** 59; **18** 265;
male, **10** 255–6;
as projected idea, **5** 102;
in scholasticism, **5** 22;
serpent as, **9ii** 293, 367;
and Sophia, **11** 193, 240, 610;

spermatikos/λόγος
σπερματικός/spermatic word,
5 492, 557; 7 336; 9ii 323; 13
59;
supremacy of, 10 554;
and sword, 11 357;
and Thoth, 5 401n;
transformation into mother, 5
558;
universals and, 6 59;
wisdom identified with, 11 221,
611;
and world-soul, 5 198
Lohengrin (Wagner), Wedding
March, 3 113
Lohmeyer, E.: "Vom göttlichen
Wohlgeruch," 14 701n
Loki, 5 421; 9i 682;
in Wagner, *see* R. Wagner *s.v.*
Fire Music
Lolium tremulentum, 13 377n
Lombard, E.: "Essai d'une classification des phénomènes de glos-
solalie," 18 (p420)
Lombard, Peter, *see* Peter Lombard
Lombroso, C.: on genius, 1 175;
"graphomaniacs," 1 219; 5 277;
Genio e Follia, 5 277n
Lomer, G.: *Liebe und Psychose*, J.'s
review, 18 904
London, 18 145;
slums of, 8 706
loneliness, 4 177, 179; 7 243n, 259,
320; 9i 288; 11 525, 532, 905;
fear of, 18 632;
see also alchemy *s.v.* solitary life
Long, Constance, 4 670n, 684; 6
243
longevity, 8 787; 13 170, 172, 185,
190n, 193, 204, 214, 434;
and civilization, 8 802
Longfellow, H. W.: *The Song of
Hiawatha*, 5 474–554, 614,
(p461); 7 160; 9i 248n
longing: for infantile security, 5
351;
of moth for star, 5 (p456);
regressive, "for the mother," 7

260/476; sacrifice of, 5 650;
to return to mother, 5 352;
spiritual, 5 615;
unappeasable, 8 711;
unfulfilled, hanging as symbol
of, 5 594;
wandering as symbol of, 5
299;
see also desire
Longinus, spear/lance of, 5 671n;
13 *fig.* B4
"Long-lived one," *see* Khidr *s.v.*
looking back, 5 631;
and regression, 5 625;
and world as mother, 5 646
lop-sidedness, 12 227
Lord: kiss of, *see* Mechthild von
Magdeburg *s.v.*
of spirits, 13 294;
of trees, 13 457n;
"of this world"/"Prince of this
world," devil as, 11 250, 255,
263, 290, 697, 754; 12 547
Lord's Prayer, 9i 394; 11 416, 651,
659, 779
Lord's Supper, *see* Communion
"Lorelei," association-chain, 3 225–
7, 373
Loreto, Litany of, see *Litany*
Lorichius, J.: *Aenigmatum Libri III*,
14 66n, 89n
Lorind, 15 25
Los Angeles, 10 1020
loss: of hearing, 7 413;
sense of, and repression of
complex, 8 590;
of soul, *see* primitive(s) *s.v.* soul,
loss of; soul *s.v.*;
of speech, *see* aphasia
lost: and found, motif of, 5 531;
objects, return of, 8 831
Lot's wife, 14 91n
lottery tickets, case involving, 1
430–77
lotus/*padma*, 5 405; 9i 315; 12 *figs.*
52, 102; 13 360, 389, *fig.* 31; 16
560; 18 1331;
birthplace, seat: of Buddha, 9i

M

Maack, F., **16** 416n
Maag, V.: "Jahwäs Heerscharen," **9ii** 284n
Mabbott, J. D., **18** 1689n
Mabinogion, **14** 626n
Macario, M.M.A., **1** 106;
"Des Hallucinations," **1** 106n
Macarius, J.: *Abraxas,* **5** *fig.* 37
McCarthyism, **18** 1443
McClure, M. L., *see under* Duchesne
McConnell, R. A.: "ESP—Fact or Fancy?," **8** 839
McCormick, E. R., **4** 692
McCormick, F., **10** (*p*245)
McCrindle, J. W., *see under* Ctesias; Kosmas
MacCulloch, J. A., *see under* Gray, L. H.
MacDonald, Ramsay, **18** 1335&n
Macdonell, A. A.: *Sanskrit Dictionary,* **5** 237n; **8** 966n; **14** 159n, 735n
McDougall, W., **3** 504; **16** 263, 266, 272; **18** 142&n;
review of W. Brown, "The Revival of Emotional Memories and Its Therapeutic Value," **16** 255
Mace, C. A., **2** (*pvn*)
Macedonia, phalanx of, **5** 321
McGee, W. J., **8** 115;
"The Siouan Indians—A Preliminary Sketch," **8** 115n
McGlashan, A.: "Daily Paper Pantheon," **9i** 465n
Machaon, **14** 144n
machinations, delusions of, **3** 169
machine: life and use of, **8** 81;
man and the, **10** 524
Machpelah, cave of, **14** 556
MacIntyre, A., **18** 1689n
MacKenna, S., *see under* Porphyry
Mackenzie, M., **18** 294
McNab, J. S., *see under* Barth
MacNeice, Louis, *see under* Goethe: *Faust*

Macnish, R., **1** 24, 280;
The Philosophy of Sleep, **1** 24n, 280n
Macrembolites, Eustathius, *see* Eustathius
Macrobius, A., **5** 425; **9i** 119; **14** 154, 173;
Commentarium in Somnium Scipionis/Commentary on the Dream of Scipio, **9i** 119n; **9ii** 344n; **10** 766n; **11** 180n; **14** 42n, 154nn, 155n, 173nn, 630n;
Saturnalia, **5** 425n; **14** 154n, 155n, 173n, 701n
macrocosm/Macrocosm, **8** 929; **9i** 557; **9ii** 335; **11** 92, 390, 440; **12** 472, *fig.* 195; **13** 125, 162, 188, 203, 268, 283, 321, 372; **14** 412, 770;
Adam as, **14** 590;
hermaphroditic seed of, **13** 268;
lapis as saviour/preserver of, **14** 33, 355, 676;
and microcosm, **10** 635; **14** 355; **15** 25;
Preserver of, **13** 162;
son of, *see filius macrocosmi*
Macroprosopus, **14** 643&n
mactatio/mactation, **11** 324&n, 403; **12** 417
macula peccati, **18** 1550, 1620, 1633, 1645
Madathanus, *see* ALCHEMICAL COLLECTIONS: *Mus. herm. s.v.*
Madeleine, Mme., **18** 893
madness, **9i** 162; **11** 344; **13** 251, 325;
and alchemy (*afflictio animae*), **16** 408n;
Caesarean, **13** 14;
fear of, **16** 374;
"of magic," **7** 258/475;
sent by spirit-mother, **5** 577;
see also insanity; mental illness
Madonna, **9i** 189;

mahatmas, **9i** 398*n*; **10** 190; **18** 353
Mahāyāna, *see* Buddhism/Buddhists *s.v.*
Maheshvarapurana, see Puranas *s.v.*
Maheswar, **5** 545
Mahomet/Mohammed, **9i** 580*n*; **9ii** 130*n*, 153, 159; **11** 10, 778*n*; **12** 390*n*; **14** 11*n*, 188*n*; **18** 690;
Mahrya, **13** 458*n*
maid/Maid: crowned, **14** 450;
of Orleans, *see* Joan of Arc;
as quintessence/quinta essentia, **14** 450–2
maiden(s), **9i** 309–13, 324, 351, 355;
sacrificed to dragon, **5** 671;
as snake or dragon, **5** 567*n*;
see also Kore
Maidenek concentration camp, **10** 403; **18** 1374&*n*
Maier, Michael, *see* ALCHEMICAL WRITERS *s.v.*
maieutics, *see* Socrates *s.v.*
Maimonides, Moses, **14** 571;
Guide for the Perplexed, **9ii** 178*n*, 183*n*
Main, River, **10** 375
Mainyo-i-Khard, **5** 367*n*, 664; **9ii** 389*n*;
tr. E. W. West, *Book of the Mainyo-i-Khard,* **5** 664*n*
maior homo, see homo *s.v.*
Mairet, P., **7** 442*n*
Maitland, E., **9i** 133; **11** 47; **13** 40;
vision of, **9i** 133; **13** 40, 42; **14** 220;
Anna Kingsford: Her Life, Letters, Diary, and Work, **9i** 133*n*; **11** 47*n*; **13** 40*n*; **14** 220*n*
Maitrayana-Brahmana Upanishad, see Upanishads
Maiuri, A.: *La Villa dei Misteri,* **12** 177*n*
maize (Indian corn), **9i** 248&*n*, 288; god who is eaten, **5** 522
majesty, **10** 685
Majjhima Nikaya, ed. and tr. B. Silacara, *The First Fifty Discourses*

from . . . the Majjhima Nikaya of Gotama the Buddha, **9i** 596*n*;
see also Buddhism *s.v.* Pali Canon
Majui/Majuj, *see* Gog and Magog
Makara, **13** 334; **16** 560
Malachi/Malachias, *see* BIBLE: O.T. *s.v.*
maladaptation, **9ii** 50; **13** 12
malade imaginaire, neurotic as, **11** 12
maladjustment, **7** 236; **17** 258;
pathological, **5** 199
Malagasy, **8** 125
malaise, spiritual, after first World War, **11** 83
Malalas, J., **8** 854
Malaya, *badi,* **8** 120
Malchamech, **14** 181*n*
Malchuth/Malkhuth, **9i** 576*n*; **9ii** 425; **13** 411; **14** 14*n*, 18–19, 25*n*, 45*n*, 327, 568–9, 592, 604*n*, 607, 635, 643*n*, 652; **16** 497*n*, 498*n*
Mâle, E.: *L'Art religieux du XIIème siècle en France,* **14** 267*n*
male, *see* masculine
Malebranche, N., **8** 276
male organ, *see* penis; phallic symbolism; phallus
Male Shooting Chant, **9i** 701,*fig.* 46
malignity, of collective man, **14** 232
malingerer(-ing): character of, **1** 303–5;
difficulty of unmasking, **1** 301–2;
passage into subconscious, **1** 340;
use of feeble-minded behaviour, **1** 320;
see also shamming; simulation
Malinine, H. M., with C. Puech and G. Quispel, ed., *Evangelium Veritatis,* **18** 1515*n*
Malinowski, B., **17** 79*n*; **18** (*p*561*n*)
Malkhuth, *see* Malchuth
Malta, caves of, **5** 536
Malthusianism, **4** 286
Malus (Philosophus), *see* ALCHEMICAL WRITERS *s.v.* Magus

Malvasius, Caesar, *see* ALCHEMICAL
WRITERS *s.v.*
mamba (snake), *see* ANIMALS:
serpent/snake *s.v.*
Mamba clan, in Africa, **5** 594&*n*
"mamma"/ma-ma, **4** 346; **5** 373,
418
Mammaea, **6** 22
mammon of unrighteousness, **7** 395
Mamun, Caliph, **11** 365
man/Man, **9i** 146; **13** 83;
    TITLES: "Archaic Man," **10**
    104–47; "The Hierosgamos of
    the Everlasting Man," **13**
    223–7; "The Meaning of
    Psychology for Modern Man,"
    10 276–332; *The Spirit in Man,
    Art and Literature,* **15**; "The
    Spiritual Problem of Modern
    Man," **10** 148–96; "The Union
    of Man's Two Natures," **13**
    200–5;
    accursed, **13** 173;
    alliance with world and nature,
    5 113;
    angelic qualities of, **13** 167*n*;
    animal ancestry/instinct/na-
    ture/soul of, *see* animal(s) *s.vv*;
    and animals, distinguished, *see*
    animal(s) *s.v.* man;
    archaic, **10** 104–47; **12** 169; **18**
    522;
    "as he really is," **4** 442; **12** 105;
    astral, **13** 168, 190, 203, 207*n*;
    average, **7** 305;
    begetting of, **13** 97*n*;
    biological vs. cultural view of, **5**
    259;
    black, **14** 731;
    blindfolded, **12** *figs.* 16, 93;
    brazen, **11** 347; **13** 86–7;
    bridge between world and
    Trinity, **11** 263, 267;
    brown, dream of, **8** 945;
    in Buddhism, **14** 520;
    celestial, **13** 168;
    centre of events, **8** 928;
    as child of nature, **5** 624;

Christ as, *see* Christ *s.v.*;
circle as symbol of, **11** 153; **18**
638;
civilized, **5** 104, 221, 248, 500;
8 750; **13** 66;
collective/collective element in,
4 728; **6** 122, 159, 356; **7** 390;
10 460, 462–3; **11** 23; **14** 232;
16 4–5, 11, 18, 443;
complete, **8** 739; **9i** 549; **9ii**
312; **11** 742;
consciousness of himself as a
personality, **5** 388;
contemporary, *see* modern
man;
cosmic, **8** 395; **11** 276;
creation of, **13** 113;
as creature, **11** 391;
daemonization of/governed by
demon, **13** 365; **18** 1365;
dangers of success to, **5** 457;
dehumanization of, **18** 1363;
demasculinization of, **10** 932;
Dionysian nature of, **5** 623;
divine, **16** 517;
in divine process, **11** 290;
domestication of, **5** 103;
and dragon, as brothers, **5** 575;
earthly and heavenly, **14** 592;
effeminate, **8** 783;
as ego and self, **5** 596*n*;
empirical, **14** 601, 647, 765;
in Esdras II, **9ii** 185;
eternal, **13** 403*n*; **16** 502;
in Ezekiel's vision, **9i** 588*n*;
fall of, *see* fall *s.v.*;
as father, **17** 330;
femininity/(unconscious) feminine nature of, **5** 458–9,
484, 678; **7** 297–8, 336; **9i** 223;
9ii 41*n*; **12** 26, 61, 145, 192,
320; **13** 14, 58, 131, 433, 458;
14 124*n*, 221, 498 (*see also*
anima);
fire as divine element in, **5**
297*n*;
First/Original/Primordial, *see*
Anthropos etc.;

fleshly, **13** 126;

flint, **13** 132;

freed from family fixations, **5** 644;

Freud's idea of, **15** 47;

Germanic, *see* Germanic *s.v.*;

and God, *see* God; godlikeness; God-man;

golden, **13** 87;

guilt of, **12** 152;

half-, half-fish motif, **13** 218;

and heaven, affinity, **8** 925–6, 932–3;

and hero, **5** 516;

high, **13** 268 (see also *homo altus*);

higher, **11** 446, 742; **13** 81; and lower/spiritual and carnal, **9i** 243*n*; **10** 843; **11** 153; **12** 148; **13** 126; in Moses quaternio, **9ii** 360; in Nietzsche, **8** 162;

of honour, **7** 319–20;

hooded, **9i** 408;

hylical, *see* hylikoi;

ice-, **9i** 407;

idea of God, *see* God;

immortality within, **5** 296, 596*n*, 657;

individuality of, **5** 258–9;

inferior, **11** 134, 136;

inner, **8** 390; **9ii** 326, 360; **10** 843; **11** 962; **13** 116*n*, 118–20, 141, 190, 194, 221, 301*n*; **14** 547–8, 627; **16** 482; of Adam, **12** 458; as Anthropos, **12** 476; Christ as, *see* Christ *s.v.* man; and Christianity, **12** 7–8, 12; eternal, **13** 187; future, **13** 221; imaginary, **13** 201*n*; invisible, **14** 547; lapis/stone signifies, **9ii** 326; **13** 126, 134; and outer, **12** 7–8, 459; secret of, **13** 199; spiritual, **13** 119, 185; **14** 487–8, 490 (*see also below* spiritual);

interior, **13** 168*n*;

isolated in cosmos, **18** 585;

"is what he eats," **18** 1372;

knowledge of, **13** 301;

leaden, **9i** 408; **13** (*p*62);

of light/light of, *see* light *s.v.*;

little, in hallucination of boy who stabbed his sister, **17** 137; **18** 810–14;

and Logos principle, **5** 458;

and love for fellow men, **5** 97, 101;

and mana-personality, **7** 393;

mass, *see* mass *s.v.*;

in the Mass, **11** 379;

medieval, *see* Middle Ages;

metal/metallic, *see* metal *s.v.*;

microcosm, *see* microcosm *s.v.*;

modern, *see* modern man;

as monad, *see* Monad *s.v.* Gnostic: Anthropos/etc.;

most pure, **13** 381;

myths of origin of, **5** 201*n*, 279, 321, 367, 439, 487;

natural, **12** 104; **13** 177, 208, 229, 323; **17** 159–60; or cultural, **17** 160; sacrifice of, **5** 673–4; of supernatural, **16** 473;

and Nature, *see* Nature *s.v.*;

nature of, **4** 728 (*see also above* collective; *and see* human *s.v.* nature);

new, **8** 766; **14** 11;

normal, **4** 442;

old: in dream-series, **11** 63; in fairytales, **9i** 412–13; one-sided, **9i** 413; rejuvenation legend, **5** 549; wise, *see* wise old man;

One, **9ii** 320; **13** 168, 227; in all men, **11** 419;

in opposition to himself, **6** 173;

original, *see* Anthropos etc;

outer, mortal, **13** 187;

perfect, **9i** 529, 549; **9ii** 312, 333; **14** 80*n*;

philosophic(al), *see* philosophic man;

physical, **14** 775; five as, **12** 287*n*;

man (*cont.*):
planets in, **13** 160&*n;*
pneumatic, see *pneumatikoi/*
pneumatic man;
predominantly unconscious, **11** 400;
and *prima materia,* see *prima materia s.v.;*
primitive, *see* primitive(s);
Primordial, *see* Anthropos/etc.;
prisoner of mandala, **11** 157;
psychic and spiritual, **9i** 55;
quadripartite, **13** 207;
rational or eternal, **16** 502;
rebirth of, **5** 335; **13** 41;
red, **13** 123&*n;*
as redeemer, **12** 414, 417;
redemption of, **11** 697; **12** 26, 414–15, 453;
red-haired, **12** 200, 211, 365;
and religious myth, **5** 343;
sacrificer and sacrificed, **5** 89;
scientific and inventive mind of, **18** 597;
and his shadow, **13** 296;
silver, **13** 87;
somatic, **11** 133;
as son: of God, **14** 447&*n;* of Heavenly Father and Mother, **11** 486;
and his soul, **13** 196;
spiritual, **13** 126, 168*n,* 194 (*see also above* inner; psychic);
star/firmament in, **13** 163, 188;
stone as, **9i** 238*n;* **13** 125, 394; **9ii** 257; as total man, **11** 471 (*see also above* inner man *s.v.* lapis);
strong, *see* "strong man";
synthesis of three worlds, **8** 928;
taking place of intellect, **12** 84;
totality of, *see below* wholeness;
transformation of, and opus, **12** 366, 378;
tree signifies, **13** 411–12, 458&*n,* 459–62;
true/complete, **13** 168, 390,

432; **14** 490–1 (see also *chên-yên*);
true spirit in, **13** 171*n;*
of twentieth century, **11** 463, 465–6; (*see also* modern man);
two halves of, **6** 314;
unitary, **14** 493;
universal and individual, **8** 738;
unknown, **12** 121, 413;
Western, *see* Western man;
"white," **11** 153; **13** 124;
wholeness/totality of, **5** 460; **11** 139–40; **12** 6, 20, 36, 112, 210; **13** 173, 390, 433; **14** 63, 152, 239, 613, 679–80, 760, 765, 770, 779; **16** 416; **17** 198, 248; **18** 268, 269, 757;
wise old, *see* wise old man;
and woman, *see* woman *s.v.;*
as work of art, **6** 227;
yellow, **13** 123;
see also *homo;* initiation, into manhood; men's house
mana, **3** 424*n;* **7** 108*n,* 375–82; **8** 52*n,* 123–4, 127–9, 278*n,* 335, 341, 411; **9i** 26, 68; **9ii** 394*n;* **10** 128, 137, 139–40, 146, 583, 845; **11** 89*n,* 198, 371, 385, 558; **12** 537; **13** 341; **14** 336*n;* **16** 4, 340; **18** 551, 554, 1612;
anima and, *see* anima *s.v.;*
-concept, **8** 441; **14** 114*n;* in Rudra, **5** 323;
of dead, **13** 128;
mana-personality, **5** 612; **8** 336; **10** 139, 142; **12** 121;
TITLE: "The Mana-Personality," **7** 374–406;
as archetype, *see* archetype(s) *s.v.;*
and collective unconscious, **7** 377, 388;
definition of, **7** 388;
dissolution of, **7** 398;
ego as, **7** 377, 389;
identifying with, **7** 394;
see also Lehmann, F. R.

manas, **6** 340–1, 343–4, 347; **14**
159*n*, 251
Manda d'Hayya, *see* Mandaeans *s.v.*
Mandaeans/Mandaeism, **9ii** 190; **13**
278; **14** 80*n*, 326, 566, 590, 727*n*;
and Manda d'Hayya/Hibil Ziwa
(Saviour), **11** 173, 841; **14** 566
mandala(s), **3** 582; **8** 396, 417, 436;
9i 156, 542, 549*n*, 569, 570,
574*nn*, *frontispiece;* **9ii** 237; **11**
123, 418, 850; **12** 46*n*, *fig.* 246; **13**
31–2, 301*n*, 304, 346, *fig.* 31; **14**
286*n*, 523, 555, 574, 576; **16** 400,
535; **18** 409–11, 1265–6, 1331–2;
TITLES: "Concerning Mandala
Symbolism," **9i** 627–712, *figs.*
1–54; "Mandalas," **9i** 713–8;
"The Symbolism of the Mandala," **12** 122–331;
in alchemy, **9i** 564*n*, 714; **10**
619; **13** 346; uroboros as, **9ii**
410; **12** 165;
animals in, *see* animal(s) *s.v.*;
a priori presence of, **9i** 541*n*;
as archetype, **9ii** 73; **11** 230; **12**
50, 329–30;
astrology and, **12** 314;
as atomic nucleus, **12** 249;
and attitude, expression of, **12**
247;
Böhme and, *see* Böhme *s.v.*;
in Brother Klaus's vision, **9i** 12,
16;
Buddha and, *see* Buddha *s.v.*;
Buddhist, *see* Buddhism *s.v.*
mandala;
as building, **12** 166;
centre of, **12** 46*n*, 237, 249; **13**
346, *fig.* 31; **14** 661, 757; deity
in, **12** 125, 139&*n*, 246*n*, *figs.*
42, 62;
child(ren) in, **9i** 270, 714;
Christ in/Christian, **9i** 73; **9ii**
69; **11** 229, 484, 948, 949; **12**
fig. 62; **13** 31; cross as, **10** 761;
11 433–5 (*see also* cross);
medieval, **11** 128; as *Rex
gloriae,* **11** 229;

coronation of Virgin as, **12** 500,
fig. 232;
cortices in, **9i** 576, 590, 596;
dance *(nrithya),* **13** 32;
disturbed, **12** 287&*n*, 320;
division into four, **9i** 565; **13**
334;
in dream(s), *see* dream(s) *s.v.*;
Eastern, **13** (*p*56);
ecclesiastical, **12** 314;
Enoch's vision and, **11** 671–3;
European, **13** (*p*2), 31*n*, 34,
(*p*56), pictures A1–10;
as eye, *see* eye *s.v.*;
Ezekiel's vision as, **9ii** 379; **11**
100;
five-rayed, **12** 327;
four-dimensional, **12** 312;
functional significance of, **9i**
710–11, (*p*387);
golden, **12** 321; flower, *see*
flower *s.v.*;
hat as, **12** 53, 254–5, 329;
healing purpose of, **18** 271;
horoscope as, **12** 314, *fig.* 100;
in India, **13** 32;
and individuation, **9i** 73; **10**
621; **18** 1624;
khilkor, **9i** 689; **12** 123;
Lamaic/Lamaistic, **9i** 635–7; **11**
851; **12** 123, 139, 166, 247, *fig.*
43; **13** *fig.* A2; **18** 413, 1225,
1332;
Mahayana, **18** 1617;
mathematical structure of, **10**
777, 805;
in medieval Western specula-
tion, **11** 128, 158; **12** 169, *fig.*
62;
"metaphysical" nature of, **12**
126&*n*, 135;
as model of space-time, **12** 312;
modern, **11** 139, 156–7; **14**
757–8;
moon in, *see* moon *s.v.*;
motif, **18** 139*n*;
ogdoad and, **11** 424;
in patients' pictures, **9i** 588–9;

mandala (*cont.*):
9ii 399; **14** 12, 296*n*;
pentadic, **9i** (*p*347), *fig.* 5;
as *perpetuum mobile*, **12** 135,
246, 329;
and personality, non-ego
centre of, **12** 126, 135;
as philosophical garden, **12**
235, *figs.* 26, 84;
in Plato, *see* Plato *s.v.*;
as protective circle, **9i** 16;
quaternity of, **12** 201; **14** 12,
329, 555;
of Rhodesia, prehistoric(?)
sun-wheel rock drawings, **11**
484&*n*; **13** 45; **15** 150; **18** 1225;
ring as, **12** 301, 305;
ritual use of, **9i** 635;
as rose, **12** 235-7; **13** 389;
rotation of, **9ii** 410; **14** 704&*n*;
18 1332;
as self, symbol of, **5** 302*n*; **8**
870; **9i** 542, 634, 717; **9ii** 117,
208, 378; **10** 621, 805; **11** 230;
12 247; **13** 304; **14** 717, 776; **16**
442;
of somnambulist (J.'s case), **13**
31*n*, 37;
space-ship as, **10** 635;
spontaneous, **11** 158, 947-8;
square, **12** 46*n*, 123, 169, *fig.*
62;
sun-wheel as, *see above*
Rhodesia;
swastika as, **18** 1332;
symbolism, **5** 460*n*, 619*n*; **9i**
156, 234, 535*n*, 645-6; **9ii** 59,
343; **10** 450; **11** 136, 138, 158,
166, 167, 672, 945; **12** 22, 45,
46&*n*, 126, 216, 247, 314, 331;
13 32; **14** 660, 776; **18** 410,
1225; Christian, **9i** 73; formal
elements of, **9i** 646; and God-
image, **18** 1495; of order, **9ii**
60, 209; pagan sources of, **11**
160;
Tantric, **9i** 643; **12** 247; **18**
1332;

tetradic, **9i** 646;
three-dimensional, **12** 308,
320;
Tibetan, **9i** 597*n*; **11** 136*n* (see
also *sidpe-korlo*);
totality, images of, **9ii** 73, 426;
10 619; **13** 127; **14** 262, 757;
and unity, **9ii** 59; **14** 294;
triadic, **9i** (*p*347), 646; **18**
1617; and Germans, **10** 775; **18**
1606;
Ufos as, **10** 731, 803;
and unconscious personality,
9ii 318;
and union of opposites, **11** 150,
152;
of unity, **12** 32; **14** 294, 717,
757;
"unused," **12** 261;
wheel in, *see* wheel(s);
as wholeness, **12** 216;
world-clock as, **12** 308, 314;
world-wheel, **9i** 644, 689; **12**
123
see also mandorla; Vajramandala
mandapam, **9i** 629
mandorla, Christ in, **12** *fig.* 101; *see
also* mandala
mandrake/mandragora, **13** 380*n*,
382, 410; **14** 158
Manes (spirits), **14** 216, 316
Manes (vessel), **14** 31
Manget, J. J./Mangetus, *see* ALCHEM-
ICAL COLLECTIONS: *Bibl. chem. cur.*
Manheim, R., **11** 415*n*
manhood, initiation into, *see* initia-
tion(s)
Mani, **5** 516, 594; **11** 173; **13** 92; **14**
14*n*, 31;
Kephalaia, **14** 567;
renamed Manes, **14** 31;
system of, *see* Manichaean
mania, **1** 154; **3** 329; **11** 474; **13** 55;
animal noises in, **1** 216
associations in, **2** 731, 882;
chronic, **1** 189-91;
flight of ideas in, **2** 116*n*, 388;

motor excitation in, **2** 116;
periodic, diagnosis of, **1** 214
maniac, homicidal, **17** 292
manic:
  TITLE: "On Manic Mood Disorder," **1** 187–225;
  element, **3** 435;
  excitation, **2** 132;
  ideas, **16** 254; **17** 162;
  mood disorder: periodic
exacerbations of, **1** 216, 217,
224; symptoms of, **1** 191;
  reaction, **2** 387;
  stupor; **2** 116;
  see also hypomanic
manic depression/-depressive insanity, **3** 329; **6** 879; **18** 60, 61, 829,
889, 916;
Manichaean(s)/Manichees/Manich-
aeism/system of Mani, **9ii** 85,
103n, 112n, 156; **11** 10, 161, 470,
(p357); **12** 458, 462n, 469, 470n;
14 14, 21n, 28n, 33, 34, 46, 68n,
567;
  Anthropos/first/original man,
11 173, 380; **14** 21n, 33, 450;
  "children of the widow," **14** 14;
  connections with alchemy, **12**
469n, 470n;
  dualism, see dualism s.v.;
  and fire-substance, **5** 149n;
  and light particles, **8** 388n;
  and "light-ships," **14** 28n;
  and light-substance, **11** 400;
  and metempsychosis, **14** 31n;
  and snake, **5** 163n;
  and sun-worship, **5** 163;
  see also Hegemonius; Mani
Manichaeus, **12** 456n
manie sans délire, **1** 188
manifest, occultation of the, **13**
187n
manikin(s) **11** 345; **17** 277;
  (male organ), **7** 177;
  wax, **13** 156&n;
  see also homunculus
manipūra-chakra, see Tantra/etc. s.v.
chakra

manitu, **8** 116, 117
Manmatha Nath Dutt, see under
Ramayana
Mann, T., **18** (p697n)
manna, **13** 403;
  fat or oil of/pinguedo, **13** 190n
mannerisms, **3** 154, 211
Mannhardt, W., **5** 662;
  Wald- und Feldkulte, **5** 214n; **8**
86n
"manning," **10** 698, 703
Mantell, Capt., **10** 628n
manthāmi or mathnāmi, etymology, **5**
248
mantic methods/procedures, **8** 863,
865, 866, 870, 900, 911, 916, 940,
944, 994
manticism, **8** 986; **13** 154
mantle: scarlet, **5** 156n;
  symbol of invisibility, **5** 291&n,
536
Manu, **5** 211n; **6** 327–8&n; **12**
533&nn;
  fish of, **5** 290n; **9ii** 127, 176; **12**
533; **13** 334;
  Laws of Manu, tr. J. G. Bühler,
6 328n; **12** 533n
manuscripts, see CODICES AND MSS.
many, see NUMBERS: one s.v.
Maoris, **8** 125;
  Maui, myth of, **5** 392n, 538n;
12 416n; **17** 219n
Maqrîzi, Al-, **16** 472n
mar, **9i** 439;
  etymology, **5** 370–3
Mara, **5** 370, 374n, 392; **17** 319
Marais, E. N.: The Soul of the White
Ant, **8** 374n
Marandon de Montyel, E., **1** 345;
  "Folie simulée par une aliénée
inculpée de tentative d'assas-
sinat," **1** 345n
Marbe, K., see under Thumb, A.
marble, **13** 87; **14** 80&n
Marcasita, **13** 375&n
Marcellinus, Ammianus, **18** 703
Marchos, **14** 77&n, 386, 409, 412n
Marcion the Gnostic, **12** 126, 436n

Marcionites, **9ii** 89; **11** 408
Marcus (in *Ars chemica*), **14** 34*n*
Marcus (Gnostic), **11** 62*n*; **14** 220*n*
Marcus Aurelius, **5** 158
Marcus Graecus: "Book of Fire," **14** 77*n*
Marduk (Babylonian), **9ii** 185, 189; **11** 174, 176&*n*;
 god of spring, and Tiamat, **5** 376–9, *fig.* 41; **18** 234;
 as redeemer, **11** 173;
 as sun-god, **5** 376
mare, *see* ANIMALS *s.v.*
mare: nostrum, see sea, "our";
 tenebrositatis, **9i** 246; **16** 402, 459
mare's-tails, forest of, **13** *fig.* 27
Marez, **14** 591&*n*, 608
Marguliès, A.: "Die primäre Bedeutung der Affecte im ersten Stadium der Paranoia," **3** 169*n*
Maria, Axiom of, *see* ALCHEMICAL WRITERS: Maria Prophetissa
Maria Aegyptiaca, **9i** 190
Maria the Jewess/Coptic, *see* ALCHEMICAL WRITERS: Maria Prophetissa
Mariam/Mariamne (sister of Moses), *see* Miriam
"Maria Morevna," fairytale, **9i** 435
Marianus, alchemist, *see* ALCHEMICAL WRITERS *s.v.* Morienus Romanus
Marianus, Doctor, *see* Goethe: *Faust s.v.* Characters
Maria Prophetissa, *see* ALCHEMICAL WRITERS *s.v.*
"Maria Theresa," *see* association-chains
Marie, A.: "Sur quelques troubles fonctionnels de l'audition chez certains débiles mentaux," **18** (*p*421)
Mariette, F.A.F.: *Dendérah,* **9ii** 129*n*
marination (alchemical), **14** 240, 320, 366;
 as *dealbatio,* **14** 240, 320
Marinus, **9ii** 99; **14** 32*n*

Marius Victorinus, **12** 457*n*
Mariyah, **14** 77&*n*
Marjoram, **13** 409
Mark, St., Gospel of, *see* BIBLE: N.T. *s.v.*
Mark Antony, **9ii** 223
Marmara, **13** 87*n*
Mar Mummi, **11** 176
Marolles, M. de: *Tableaux du temple des muses,* **12** *fig.* 162
Marqûlius, *see* ALCHEMICAL WRITERS: Merlinus
Marqûš, **14** 77*n*, 409*n*
marriage, **6** 898; **7** 22/434, 47, 88, 113, 181, 428; **17** 279–80, 324;
 TITLE: "Marriage as a Psychological Relationship," **17** 324–45;
 Apocalyptic, of lamb, *see* ANIMALS: lamb *s.v.* in Apocalypse;
 arranged, **17** 330;
 biological aim of, **17** 343;
 brother-sister, **5** 350, 458, 676;
 of Cana, *see* Cana;
 catastrophes in, **8** 783;
 ceremonies/rites, **11** 287: **16** 214; in Catholic Church, **18** 362;
 choice, **17** 330;
 of Christ and Church, *see* Christ *s.v.* Church;
 Christian, **18** 1799, 1800;
 classes, **5** 332, 652; **9ii** 42, 381*n*; **14** 613; **16** 435–8; in China, **16** 438*n*;
 compensatory character of, **18** 1139;
 connections, **8** 868;
 consanguineous, **5** 350;
 as conscious relationship, **9ii** 381;
 constellation of unconscious in, **9ii** 381;
 conventional, **17** 329;
 cross-cousin, **5** 217, 415*n*, 652; **9ii** 42, 328*n*, 363, 381; **10** 762; **13** 358; **14** 664*n*; **16** 433; **18** 1133;

customs, modern, **5** 34;
daughter-father, **5** 496;
difficulties, **4** 531;
disorder in, **17** 343;
divine, **9i** 295;
dream anticipating, **16** 311;
effect of break-up of, on patient, **1** 197;
in first half of life, **17** 337;
game of illusion, **7** 309;
heavenly, **13** 199; **14** 2*n*, 458, 525; **18** 713;
horoscopes, **8** 872–910, 988–94; **18** 1176–8, 1194, 1197;
ideal of, **7** 316;
ill advised, **17** 109;
infantile projections in, **16** 420;
insecurity of, **9i** 61;
medieval, **10** 260;
metaphorical use of term, **17** 144;
mingling of subtle with dense, **9ii** 256*n*;
and mother archetype, **10** 64;
mystic(al), **14** 106, 356, 664; **16** 353, 355, 538;
nefarious character of, **14** 523*n*;
and new moon, **14** 154;
pair, **13** 110;
perfect, **10** 248, 261;
problems, **10** 263; **13** 5;
psychology of, **18** 158;
quaternio, *see* quaternity/quaternio *s.v.*;
royal/kingly, **12** 496; **13** 358, 434; **14** 80, 200, 410, 541; **16** 381, 398, 500; love-play of the, **13** 441*n*;
settlements, **9ii** 381*n*;
sister-exchange, **16** 433;
son-mother, **5** 357; **9ii** 22;
spagyric, **14** 364;
spiritual, **16** 442;
and the student, **10** 209, 215;
transitions in relationship, **17** 342;
trial, **10** 231–5;

types in, **7** 80;
typical, **17** 222;
unhappy, **1** 362–3;
women and, **10** 248;
wrecking of, **9i** 176;
young people and, **17** 327;
see also chymical wedding; *coniunctio; hierosgamos; unio mystica*
Mars (god), *see* Ares
Mars (in alchemy/astrology/mythology/planet/ ♂), **5** 294; **8** 878; **9i** 588*n*; **12** 484; **14** 217, 287;
aspects of, **8** 897;
as Daemogorgon, **13** 176*n*;
as fire/fiery, **14** 6*n*; **16** 518;
inhabitants of/Martians, **8** 791; **10** 599, 611, 614;
as instinctive nature of man, **9ii** 130; **13** 176*n*;
and Jupiter, in conjunction/opposition, **9ii** 130, 151*n*;
malefic, **11** 690*n*; **13** 358; **14** 6;
in Paracelsus, **13** 171*n*;
regimen of, **14** 393&*n*;
as ruler of Aries, **13** 193, 409*n*; **14** 6, 49*n*;
as sulphur, **13** 176*n*;
S. W.'s description of, **1** 59;
and tree, **13** 355, 409;
and Venus, **13** 125; caught in net, **12** 484*n*; cohabitation/*hierosgamos*, **13** 228, 234; **16** 508–9; in conjunction, **8** 869, 989; son of, **13** 234;
visions of (Flournoy's case), **1** 105;
wolf as animal of, **12** 440*n*; **13** 176*n*
Marseilles, **18** 252*n*
Marsen, M., **7** 442*n*
Marsilio Ficino, *see* ALCHEMICAL WRITERS *s.v.* Ficino
Marsyas, **5** 349, 595; **11** 348; **13** 92
Marti, F., **18** 1040&*n*
Martial, **13** 270; **14** 98
　　Epigrammata, **13** 270*n*; **14** 98*n*
Martians, *see* Mars
Martianus Capella, **9i** 538

142*n*; **11** 81, 126*n*, 469, 626, 690*n*; **13** 127; **14** 237, 744*n*; **18** 1607, 1674;
laurel as, **9i** 582&*n*;
as "leader of hosts," **9i** 435;
and Marianic movement, **18** 1607;
as mediatrix, **11** 469, 625, 748, 754; **14** 218*n*, 237; **18** 1552;
Mercurius as, *see* Mercurius *s.v.* virgo/Virgin Mary;
miracles of, **11** 469;
as moon, **11** 176*n*; **14** 499; **16** 496;
as mother-archetype, **9i** 156, 158;
Mother of Christ/Christ-bearer/God-bearer/Theotokos, **5** 76, pl. III; **6** 34, 377–80, 392, 438; **9i** 156, 195, 374, 661; **11** 107, 175*n*, 194, 240, 252, 469, 625, 626, 628, 646, 748; **12** *fig.* 107; **14** 237, 744*n*; Immaculate, **5** 76; Queen of motherhood, **13** 228*n*;
obumbratio/overshadowing of, **5** pl. VIII; **11** 744*n*; **13** 263;
patron saint of Swiss, **10** 914;
pierced heart of, **5** 435*n*;
Protestant view of, **18** 1550;
Sapientia as, **16** 361;
Sophia as, **11** 625, 628, 646, 714, 743; **14** 744;
as starry heaven, **12** *fig.* 105;
as *stella maris*, **13** 313;
as sun, **6** 395;
symbolism/allegories of, **6** 379, 390–6, 406; **11** 711*n*; **12** *fig.* 26; **13** 389; alchemical, **9i** 238*n*; **13** 279 (*see also individual subheadings above*);
as tower, **6** 406; **12** *fig.* 26;
transfiguration of, **12** 500, *figs.* 224, 232;
and Trinity, *see* Trinity *s.v.*;
and unicorn, **11** 408; **12** 498*n*, 519, 522&*n*, 523, *figs.* 241, 242, 245, 247;

as *vas*/vessel, see *vas s.v.* Virgin Mary;
as virgo terra, **18** 1552;
visions of (Pope Pius XIII), **11** 748;
as water, **5** 373; **16** 496;
worship of, **8** 336;
writing inspired by: *Dispute between Mary and the Cross*, **5** 412–5&*n*;
   Hymn to, attr. to Albertus Magnus, **12** 481–4;
   Litany of Loreto, **6** 379–80, 390–2, 399, 406; **9i** 652; **11** 126*n*; **12** 246*n*, 257; **13** 389*n*;
   Melk *Hymn to Mary*, **5** 577*n*
see also Madonna; Maria Aegyptiaca
Mary Magdalene, **18** 1560
Mary Reynolds, *see* Reynolds
Masai, **8** 125
masculine/male, **7** 471; **13** 14, 57; consciousness, *see* consciousness *s.v.*;
-feminine/female, **9ii** 100; man, **12** 550; Mercurius as, **13** 420 (*see also* Mercurius *s.v.* androgyny); numbers, *see* numbers *s.v.*; opposites, *see* opposites *s.v.*; powers of, **13** 267; principle, **11** 620, 627; **12** 26; **18** 261–2, 264, 266; symbols of, **11** 727;
ideal, **5** 273;
mind, **7** 330; **13** 455; **14** 331; differentiated, **13** 60;
principle: animus as, **13** 342; of Mercurius, **13** 276;
protest, *see* Adler, A.;
psychology, **7** 328; **13** 108, 344; **14** 222–5;
soul, **13** *fig.* A6;
thinking, **13** 339;
traits in woman, *see* woman *s.v.* masculinity of;
Trinity, *see* Trinity *s.v.*
masculinity, **8** 248;
   premature, **4** 736;

masculinity (*cont.*):
    prestige of, **7** 316;
    step towards, **7** 180;
    woman's, *see* woman *s.v.*
Masculinus, **12** 439n
Masenius, J., *see* ALCHEMICAL
    WRITERS *s.v.*
Mashya and Mashyoi, **5** 367
mask(s), **7** 237, 245/465, 305, 390,
    504;
    of collective psyche, persona as,
    7 246
Maspero, Sir G., **12** 84;
    Études de mythologie, **12** 84n
Mass, **8** 314; **10** 674; **11** 448; **12**
    417;
    TITLE: "Transformation Sym-
    bolism in the Mass," **11** 296–
    448;
    accounts of institution of, **11**
    296–308;
    in alchemy: *opus alchymicum*
    and, **11** 374; **12** 420, 450–1,
    453, 474, 490; **13** 158, 196; **14**
    401n; paraphrase of, **12** 480–9;
    16 454 (see also *opus divinum*);
    Black, **9i** 324; **12** 191;
    Canon of, **11** 321, 323;
    and Christ, *see* Christ *s.v.*;
    commixtio in, **11** 334–5; **16** 454;
    for dead, **9i** 535n; **11** 855;
    duality in, **11** 378–80;
    edict against translation of, **11**
    322n;
    elevation in, **11** 325, 326;
    ethnological prefigurations of,
    11 339;
    Fractio in, **11** 331–2, 336;
    Host in, *see* Host;
    and individuation, **11** 414;
    liturgy of, **11** 300, 405;
    as living mystery, **18** 615, 616;
    and magic, **11** 323;
    miracle of, **18** 632;
    Offertory in, *see* Offertory;
    parody of, **9i** 463;
    psychological efficacy of, **11**
    296;

rite/ritual of, **11** 307; Protes-
    tant loss of, **11** 33; spirit(s) in,
    11 317, 319;
sacrifice in, **11** 302, 307, 399,
    406, 413; *deipnon/thysia* in, **11**
    302–4, 307, 346, 347;
Sanctus in, **11** 321;
"sicut" in, **8** 314;
sublimation and, **4** 738n;
symbolism of, **11** 308, 339;
    bread, *see* bread *s.v.*; candles,
    11 60n;
transformation and, **9i** 205,
    209; **11** 390, 399, 413; of God,
    as core of, **11** 338, 399; as
    mysterium/-fidei, **11** 307, 379;
    and Zosimos, comparisons, **11**
    403–6, 413;
    see also Incarnation; Missal; Of-
    fertory; transubstantiation
mass(es)/mob, **7** 35, 237; **9i** 618; **10**
    535–40; **11** 43, 508;
    anonymity of, **10** 326, 462;
    churches and, **10** 536–7;
    conversions, **18** 1380;
    danger of, **18** 1347;
    degeneration, **16** 502;
    destruction, **8** 428;
    and the educated, **11** 513;
    emotions, **9i** 97;
    energy and, **8** 37n;
    evil and, **18** 1378;
    formation of, **10** 449; **11** 23;
    hypnotism, **18** 1377;
    identity with, **9i** 293;
    individual in, **18** 1139;
    industrialized, **10** 413; **11** 443;
    intoxicants, **9i** 226;
    leaders and, **10** 326, 462, 500,
    535;
    loss of images and, **14** 510;
    -man, **8** 410, 425–6; **11** 23, 443,
    508; **16** 103, 443, 539; and evil,
    9ii 255 (*see also* man *s.v.* collec-
    tive);
    and manifestation of arche-
    types, **10** 461;
    -meeting, numinous experi-

ence in, **10** 567;
-mindedness, **10** 719, 723; **14**
9*n*, 346; **18** 1387;
movements, psychic, **11** 275;
-murder, **7** 150&*n*;
-organizations, **7** 463; **10** 535;
phenomenon, demonic fea-
tures in, **18** 1377;
politics and, **18** 1301;
power and, **14** 470;
psyche, *see* psyche *s.v.*;
psychology, *see* psychology *s.v.*
mob/mass;
psychoses, **9ii** 390*n*; **13** 52; **18**
1389;
resistance to, **10** 540;
shadow and, **9i** 478;
state totalitarian, **9i** 393;
suggestions, **7** 326; **10** 469,
503, 536–7; **17** 159; **18** 1378,
1379, 1393;
"telluric," **10** 939;
therapy and psychanalysis, **4**
45;
see also herd; intoxication,
mass; psyche, mass; psychology
s.v. mob/mass
massa: confusa, **9i** 538; **9ii** 230, 240,
371, 375; **11** 160*nn*; **12** 185, 334,
370, 426*n*, 433, 442, *fig.* 256; **13**
111, 433; **14** 381, 388, 422, 552,
696, 718; **16** 387, 457, 462; as
prima materia, **12** 244, 433;
informis, **12** 185, 244, 366*n*
Masselon, R., **3** 14–20, 74, 76;
La Démence précoce, **3** 14*n*;
Psychologie des déments précoces, **3**
14*n*, 17*n*
Master, vision of, **8** 632
"master-key," *see* association-chains
s.v.
mastery, idea of, **7** 397
mastodon, *see* ANIMALS *s.v.*
masturbation, **2** 678, 689, 698, 713,
716; **4** 58, 225, 291, 487, 599,
693*n*; **10** 216; **17** (*p*5), 221;
boring, analogy of, **5** 204–6,
227;

complex, **2** 816;
effects of, **10** 226;
infantile, **4** 54, 55, 240, 370; **5**
204, 206;
mutual, **4** 483; **10** 220;
-mysticism, **3** 141
Masudi, **14** 552
matador, as hero, **5** 421*n*
Matarisvan, **5** 208, 580
mater/Mater: *Alchimia, see* alchemy *s.v.*;
dea, **12** 431 (*see also* mother *s.v.*
-goddess);
Dei, **9i** 242*n* (*see also* Mary/
Mother of God);
dolorosa, **9i** 172;
Ecclesia, *see* Church *s.v.*;
Gloriosa, *see* Goethe: *Faust s.v.*
Characters;
Magna, **6** 398; **8** 336; **18** 1287;
magical figure, **17** 97 (*see also*
Mother, Great);
natura, see nature *s.v.* Mother;
spiritualis, **9i** 172
materia: confusa, **12** 433*n*;
globosa, **12** 116;
hypostatica, **12** 354;
medica, **13** 158; torturing of, **13**
139*n*
prima, see prima materia
material, subliminal, **7** 203–4,
444–5
materialism, **3** 318, 324, 496; **6** 582,
594, 961, 965; **7** 80; **8** 529, 707,
712, 960; **9i** 196, 391–3; **9ii** 170,
235, 274, 282, 410; **10** 142, 454,
510, 653, 975; **11** 142; **15** 149; **16**
79, 240, 440, 442; **17** 127; **18**
1383*n*, 1658, 1660;
and empirical psychology, **17**
127–8;
and James's typology, **6** 524–5;
and metaphysics, **11** 765;
and mysticism, as opposites, **8**
712;
philosophical, **12** 432;
and psyche, **10** 780;
and psychology, **3** 467; **4** 675;

materialism (*cont.*):

18 1239; Freud and, *see* Freud *s.v.*;

scientific, 4 675; 8 649; 9ii 368, 406; 11 452, 547, 762; 15 12, 45; 18 750, 1115, 1659; of medicine, 11 490;

and spiritual devastation, 18 1345;

and spiritualism/belief in spirits, 6 61, 279; 8 571-2; 14 765

materialistic mentality, 6 582

materiality of cosmos, 13 286

materialization, 10 788;

as origin of Adam, 1 64;

of soul, 13 316;

trance, 1 51, 70

maternal, *see* mother

mathematics, 7 121*n*; 8 870, 927, 942-3; 9ii 413; 17 239;

incapacity for, 17 257

Mathieu de Vendôme, 14 89, 103

mathnāmi, see *manthāmi*

mating: in the mother, 5 620;

sacramental, between spear and hole in the earth, 5 213-14

matriarchy/matriarchal society, 9i 383;

in America, 10 790;

man in, 13 131;

primitive, 9i 176;

see also mother

matrimonium, 12 334;

alchymicum, 12 209;

see also *coniunctio; hierosgamos*

matrix, 16 402*n*;

instinctual, 11 798, 800;

mother as, *see* mother *s.v.*;

unconscious as, *see* unconscious, the *s.v.*;

vas as, 12 338*n*

Matsya, 9ii 272

Matter, Jacques: *Histoire critique du gnosticisme,* 6 396*n*

matter, 9i 156, 195, 392; 10 681; 11 95, 290, 375; 13 89, 117, 127-8, 138, 160, 163, 165, 173, 183, 198,

210, 229, 286, 372, 395;

in alchemy, *see* alchemy *s.v.*;

Assumption and, 9i 197;

autonomy of, 13 286;

chemistry of, 12 40;

descent of spirit (nous/ pneuma) into matter/physis, 12 410, 413, 436, 438, 440, 447, 513;

and evil, 12 413;

and form, union, 14 654;

formed by illusion, 12 355;

God and, *see* God *s.v.*;

hermaphroditic, 13 268;

and individuation, 11 252;

inert, 13 89;

inertia of, 14 673;

inscrutable, 8 657;

latent psyche in, 8 441;

laws of, 13 286, 393;

and mind, 8 650; 12 332, 366, 377, 410; intermediate realm between, 12 394, 400;

modern view of, 14 715;

mother as, 9i 170;

mystery of cosmic, 13 127;

myth of, 16 353;

nature of, 8 623, 747;

numinosity of, 9ii 120, 410;

One Substance as, 9i 391;

Paracelsist view of, 14 766;

philosophic, 13 380;

physical, 18 584;

physicist and, 10 311;

as principle of existence, 11 763;

projection into, *see* projection *s.v.*;

and psyche, 10 780; 12 332, 394, 410; 14 147, 699; 18 750; identity of, 12 375-6, 377-8, 410; 14 766; as opposites, 16 499; relation, 8 417, 418, 441, 653; 9i 195;

as psychic category, 8 251;

"psychization" of, 9i 197;

redemption of divine soul/ spirit from, 12 414, 420, 452,

God *s.v.*;
Mercurius as, *see* Mercurius
s.v.;
moon as, **14** 19, 154;
number as, **10** 779;
stone as, **11** 150; **13** 131;
sun woman's child as, **11** 716;
unconscious as, **11** 419;
Wisdom (Sophia) as, **11** 625,
640
mediatory: condition, **6** 206–7, 211;
function, *see* function *s.v.*
mediatory;
meaning, **7** 311
medical: psychology, *see* psychology
s.v.;
schools, **13** 149
medicament, incorrupt, **9ii** 262; **12**
377, 511
medicina, **12** 489; **14** 148;
catholica, **11** 160n; **12** 420; **13**
353n; **14** 304, 344; **16** 375, 408;
18 1578; lapis as, **18** 1631;
Mercurius as, **13** 283;
transformed bread as, **12** 418
medicine, **13** 145; **15** 16; **18** 839,
840;
TITLE: "Medicine and Psychotherapy," **16** 192–211;
academic, **15** 19–20, 27;
ancient, **15** 65;
bags, **13** 66;
chemical, **13** 158;
Egyptian, *see* Egypt *s.v.*;
fiery, **13** 103n;
folk, **15** 13;
Germanization of, **13** 180n;
Greek, *see* Greece *s.v.*;
of immortality, **8** 794;
and politics, **10** 1022;
primitive, **16** 4;
and psychiatry, **3** 320, 467;
and psychoanalysis, **4** 524;
and psychological understanding, **18** 834;
and psychology, **3** 541;
psychosomatic, **16** 232;
and psychotherapy, **16** 192–211;

scientific materialism of, **11**
490;
sixteenth century, **8** 688;
"spagyric," **14** 663, 677–8;
study of, **8** 526;
and treatment, **8** 684;
see also *medicina*
medicine-man, **4** 578; **6** 414; **7**
154&n, 237, 276; **8** 411, 573,
575n; **9i** 77, 213, 414, 457; **10**
122, 132, 137, 939; **11** 30, 346n,
448, 531; **16** 4, 73; **17** 300, 315;
18 674, 1313;
ability to "smell," **18** 779;
on dreams, **18** 1291;
fallible, punishment of, **14**
607n;
as mana-personality, **7** 377; **8**
336
medicine-woman, **5** 452n
medieval/medievalism, *see* Middle
Ages
mediocrity, **7** 240
meditatio, **12** 390; **13** 20n;
in alchemy, **9i** 85, 236; **14** 313
meditation(s), **6** 189; **7** 303; **9i**
130n, 562; **11** 7, 63, 827; **12** 187,
388, 390–1, 420, 441, *fig.* 137; **13**
(*p*30), 172, 442, 477; **14** 283; **16**
134;
TITLE: "The Psychology of
Eastern Meditation," **11** 908–
49;
of alchemy, **11** 344, 793; **14**
707;
Eastern and Western, **11** 939;
imaginative, **11** 344;
interminable, **13** 286;
"sinking into," **11** 911;
on sun and water, **11** 935;
unknown to New Testament,
11 421
medium: of conjunction, **14** 658;
spiritualistic, *see* spiritualistic
mediums
medulla, **3** 582n; **9ii** 320, 369
medusa, **9ii** 193–212
Meerpohl, F.: "Meister Eckhardts

Meerpohl (*cont.*):
Lehre vom Seelenfünklein," **9ii** 344*n*; **14** 42*n*
megalithic culture, **13** 132
megalomania, **1** 190, 212–14, 218; **4** 404; **5** 530*n*; **7** 228, 237/458, 260/476; **8** 317; **9i** 107, 138, 304; **9ii** 34; **10** 185, 727; **11** 791; **16** 472; **18** 332;
and inferiority, as opposites, **7** 237/458;
Keyserling's, **10** 906;
Maeder's case of, *see* Maeder *s.v.*;
Nebuchadnezzar's, **8** 163, 485;
of schizophrenia, **8** 360;
stage of, in paranoid patient, **5** 154*n*;
see also egotism
megaphone oratory, **18** 1377
Megara/Megarian school of philosophy, **6** 42–4, 48, 52, 55, 473; **7** 80;
envy characteristic of, **6** 43
Meggendorfer picture-book, **1** 333
Mehlich, R.: *J. H. Fichtes Seelenlehre und ihre Beziehung zur Gegenwart*, J.'s foreword, **18** 1730–6
Mehnit, **5** 408; **14** 25*n*
Mehung, *see* ALCHEMICAL COLLECTIONS: *Mus. herm. s.v.* Jean de Meung
Meier, C. A., **2** vii, 563*n*, (*p*379*n*); **10** 1036; **12** *fig.* 112; **14** 82*n*; **18** 1133, 1826–7, (*p*826*n*);
Antike Inkubation und moderne Psychotherapie/Ancient Incubation and Modern Psychotherapy, tr. M. Curtis, **8** 549*n*; **9i** 553*n*; **14** 304*n*; **18** (*p*487*n*);
"Moderne Physik—Moderne Psychologie," **8** 385*n*, 440&*n*; **16** 468*n*; **17** 164*n*;
"Spontanmanifestationen des kollektiven Unbewussten," **8** 589*n*; **9i** 622*n*; **11** 781*n*; **16** 477*n*;
Zeitgemässe Probleme der Traum-

forschung, **8** 938*n*
Meige, H., and E. Feindel: *Les Tics et leur traitement*, **2** 794*n*; **3** 187*n*
Meir ben Isaac, **9ii** 181
Meir, Rabbi, **14** 552; **18** 1525
Meister Eckhart, *see* Eckhart
Meisterlieder der Kolmarer Handschrift, ed. K. Bartsch, **6** 394&*n*
Melampus (Blackfoot), **5** 183; **14** 85*n*, 726*n*
melancholia(-y), **1** 187; **3** 181, 329, 358; **6** 470; **7** 344; **13** 133, 190; **16** 197; **17** 152; **18** 62–3;
in alchemy, **12** 41; **13** 209, 445;
depressive, **1** 343;
nigredo as, *see* COLOURS: *nigredo s.v.*;
Saturnine, **13** 190
melancholic temperament, **1** 191; **6** 546, 547, 883, 960
Melanesia(ns), **8** 123, 441; **11** 372; **13** 128, 129;
bariaua, **8** 123*n*;
see also Codrington; Seligmann
melanosis, see COLOURS *s.v.*
Melchior, Cardinal Bishop of Brixen, *see* ALCHEMICAL COLLECTIONS: *Aureum vellus*
Melchior Cibinensis, Nicholas, of Hermannstadt, *see* ALCHEMICAL WRITERS: Melchior
Melchisedec, **11** 306–7; **13** 172*n*; **14** 350*n*, 556
Melicertes, **5** 369*n*
Melissa (Paracelsus), **13** 190&*n*, 193
Melito of Sardis, **5** 158;
De baptismo, **12** 314*n*;
Fragmentum V, **5** 668*n*
Melkarth, **5** 369*n*
Mellon, Paul: alchemical collection, **13** (*p*vi); **18** 1691*n*
melody: and complex constellation, **3** 109;
infectiveness of, **10** 965
melons, **8** 388*n*
melothesia(e), **9i** 605; **11** 113&*n*; **13** 122*n*; **18** 17*n*
melting-pot, *see* athanor

memory-image (*cont.*):
of mother, **17** 218;
obscuration of, **3** 16;
of personal unconscious, **7** 118;
of primitives, **6** 46;
in transference, **16** 283;
and unconscious perception, **1** 166–7
Men (Phrygian god), **5** 299;
birth of, **5** 396;
and Caesar, **5** 421;
on the cock, **5** pl. XXIa
Mendel, E., **1** 188;
Die Manie, **1** 188*n;*
Leitfaden der Psychologie, **3** 175*n*
Mendel, K., **4** (*pp*76–7)
Mendes, ram of, *see* ANIMALS: ram
mendicant orders, **9ii** 137–8; *see also* monk(s)
menhirs, **13** 132
Men-kau-Re (Mykerinos), **5** 682*n*
Mennens, Gulielmus, *see* ALCHEMICAL WRITERS *s.v.*
Menninger, K., **18** (*p*634*n*)
menopause, **7** 114; *see also* climacteric
mens, **12** 360, 368, 377, 381; *see also* mind
"men's house," **7** 172
menstruation, **2** 850; **4** 228; **8** 842; **14** 215;
and abnormal emotional state, **1** 209–10;
in case of spontaneous somnambulism, **1** 6, 8;
disturbances of, **9i** 170;
menstrual blood/fluid, **9i** 311; **16** 340
mental: activity, and simulation, **1** 422;
contagion, **7** 242/463;
corrective, **7** 170;
defectives, *see sep. entry below;*
function, **7** 235/455–6;
healing/healers, **4** 526, 578, 588; **16** 3;
illness, *see sep. entry below;*
patients, *see* patients *s.v.*;

phenomena, in automatic table turning, **1** 85–7;
processes, unconscious, **13** (*p*56);
productivity, and chronic mania, **1** 189–90
mental defectives/feebleminded/feeblemindedness, **1** 190; **3** 325; **17** 131–4, 234–5, 257;
adaptability of, **1** 317;
and compulsive talking, **1** 184;
and critical faculty, **1** 219;
and emotional changes/adaptability, **1** 317, 357;
moral, *see* moral insanity/defect;
simulation of insanity among, **1** 308–12;
and social incapacity, **1** 220;
see also idiots; imbeciles
mental illness/disease/disorder/derangement, **1** 29; **2** 1067; **7** 2, 252, 270, 469–70; **11** 489; **13** 47, 49, 429, 431; **15** 27, 122; **18** 832;
TITLES: "Mental Disease and the Psyche," **3** 496–503; "On the Problem of Psychogenesis in Mental Disease," **3** 466–95; *The Psychogenesis of Mental Disease,* **3**;
alchemical treatment, **15** 27;
association in, *see* association(s) *s.v.* in dementia praecox;
brain and, *see* brain *s.v.*;
functional and organic, **3** 318;
irruption of complexes and, **8** 590;
social definition of, **18** 72;
see also dementia: insanity; madness; mania; manic depression; neurosis; paranoia; psychosis; schizophrenia
mentality, **11** 768;
Aryan/Hamitic/Mongolian/Semitic, **7** 240*n;*
collective, *see* collective *s.v.*;
infantile, **4** 312–13;
neurotic, **7** 256

mentula, **5** 208n

Mentz, P., **2** 1058, 1059, 1187; "Die Wirkung akustischer Sinnesreize auf Puls und Atmung," **2** 1058n, (p580);

Menzel, D. H., **10** 701, 782; reflection theory, **18** 1435; *Flying Saucers*, **10** 701n

Mephistopheles, *see* Goethe: *Faust s.v.* Characters

Merculinus, see ALCHEMICAL WRITERS: Merlinus

Mercurialis, *see* mercury (plant)

Mercurius/Hermes/Mercury: *A distinction is made between separate senses, but see* **12** 31n, 84 *for problems involved. The following groupings have been used:*

(1) *Mercurius/Hermes/Mercury, in alchemists' writings, and J.'s interpretation of these;*

(2) *Mercury/Hermes, Greek/Roman god, classical and postclassical;*

(3) *mercury/mercurial, liquid metal/chemical element, used in alchemy;*

(4) *Mercury, planet/in astrology;*

(5) *mercury (plant) dog's mercury*

Mercurius/Hermes/Mercury (1) *(in alchemists' writings, and J.'s interpretation of these),* **8** 388n; **9i** 238, 268, 456, 554, 689; **9ii** 41, 200, 240, 367, 386, 393, 396; **10** 628, 629; **11** 160, 356, 423, 656; **12** 31n, *figs.* 24, 80, 127, 164, 165, 192, 257; **13** 86n, 88n, 101, 103n, 105n, 110, 113, 127, 157, 161, 162n, 168n, 171nn, 180n, 184, 218, 234n, (p192), 239n, 243, 245, 250–1, 255–303, 267, 273n, 344, 355, 357, 370, 371, 381, 408, 439, 444, *fig.* B6; **14** 6, 14, 33, 50, 117, 155, 166, 282, 295, 298, 313, 360n, 372, 416, 473, 477, 478–80, 570, 688, 713–14, 726; **15** 159n; **16** 384, 386, 398, 453, 458n,

472n, 478, 483, 484, 500n, 510, 513, 515;

TITLE: "The Spirit Mercurius," **13** 239–303;
and Adam, **13** 273n, 282; **14** 545, 565, 587, 589;
Adamic, and Eve, **13** 282n;
and Adam Kadmon, **13** 268;
as Agathodaimon, **14** 6&n;
as *alexipharmakon/medicina catholica*, **13** 283;
ambiguity/ambivalence/paradox of, **13** 295; **14** 19, 38, 113, 139, 534, 656, 717; **16** 384;
androgyny/hermaphroditism of, **9i** 268; **10** 727, 772; **11** 47n; **12** 84, 209, 336, 404, 410, 447, 460, 470, 517, *fig.* 125; **13** 268, 283, 315, 420; **14** 12, 22, 235, 416, 565, 634, 655n, 712n, 726; **16** 454 (*see also* Edem);
as anima/*anima mundi*/world soul, **8** 393; **9i** 391n, 554; **9ii** 212; **11** 161n; **12** 172, 265, 499, 506, 528, *figs.* 91, 157, 208; **13** 262, 263; **14** 168, 318, 450, 658, 699, 748, 749; (soul), **13** 262–3, 266, 384; in chains, **18** 1701; *media natura*, **13** 261, 263; *nostra*, **13** 262;
as Anthropos, **9i** 541; **9ii** 366; **12** *figs.* 16, 215; **14** 12, 238, 285; **16** 402; **18** 1701;
and *aqua: alba*, **13** 255; *aurea*, **13** 255; *divina*/divine water, **12** 528, 531; *mercurialis*, **12** 209, 210n, 336, *fig.* 152; **13** 176n, 256; *nostra*, **12** 531; *permanens*, **10** 629; **11** 357, 420; **12** 90, 338&n; **13** 103n; **14** 401n, 655n, 658, 688, 701, 717; **16** 454, 483; *sicca*, **13** 255 (*see also below* water);
as arcane substance, **5** 465n; **9ii** 237; **11** 151, 420; **13** 255, 266, 282, 359; **14** 9, 38, 243, 311, 663; **16** 454;
as archer, *see below* Cupid;

Mercurius (*cont.*):

as archetype of the unconscious, **13** 299;

as *argentum vivum,* see *argentum vivum s.v.;*

as artifex, **13** 284; **14** 401*n*;

ascent and descent of, **13** 267, 280; **14** 303, 478–80&*n*;

aspects of, **13** 284;

associations of, **13** 250;

astrology/astrological/planet, *see sep. entry below* Mercury, planet;

attributes of Aphrodite, *see below* Venus;

avis Hermetis, see ANIMALS: bird *s.v.* of Hermes;

Azoth/Azoch, alpha and omega, **8** 388*n*; **13** 271, 383&*n*; **14** 545*n*; **16** 484&*n*;

as begetter of his parents, **13** 273; **16** 402;

as beginning, middle, end of *opus,* **13** 283;

as bird, **14** 637 (*see also below* dove; eagle; goose; ibis; phoenix; raven; swan; vulture);

bird of/*avis Hermetis, see* ANIMALS: bird *s.v.* of Hermes;

as blood, **10** 629;

body/soul/spirit, **12** 426*n*; **13** 261;

in Böhme's writing, **9i** 534, 535*n*, 537;

as boy/*puer,* **13** 269; **14** 298; *leprosus,* **13** 273*n*;

as bridegroom and bride, **13** 268;

bronze of, **14** 404*n*;

and caduceus/wand, **12** *figs.* 148, 165; **14** 305&*n*, 408; golden, **9ii** 326; as magic wand, **9i** 553; water as, **13** 255;

as *caput corvi,* **12** 404;

carbuncle as, **13** 282;

as *cauda pavonis,* **12** 404;

as *cervus fugitivus, see* ANIMALS

s.v. deer;

as chaos, **13** 282; **18** 1701; *see also below* child;

as child, **12** *fig.* 216; of chaos, **13** 275; of Saturn, **13** 101*n*, 274; of sun and moon, **13** 101*n*, 273;

Christ and, **10** 767; **12** 519; **13** 271, 282, 283, 295, 299; **14** 11, 147, 285;

chthonic, **12** 84; **13** 271, 299; **16** 455, 494;

as *coelum,* **13** 268;

common, **13** 355; and philosophic, **13** 267;

as *complexio oppositorum,* **10** 727;

concoction of, **14** 683;

and *coniunctio,* **12** 404, 484*n*; as "matrimonium," **14** 12; of Sol and, **14** 121;

as cup bearer, **14** 415;

as Cupid/archer, **13** 278, 299; **14** 416, 426*n* (*see also* arrow *s.v. telum passionis*);

dark, **13** 279, 289; and Lucifer, **11** 470;

deus absconditus, **9ii** 209; **13** 289;

deus terrenus/terrestris, **13** 282, 289; **14** 699; **16** 480 (*see also below* God);

as devil, **12** 84, 173; **13** 110, 284, 300; **14** 22, 235, 687, 727; and Mephistopheles, **9ii** 371;

as *divinus ternarius,* **13** 278;

as *donum Spiritus sancti,* **16** 389;

as dove, **12** 518&*n,fig.* 134; **16** 453;

as dragon, *see* ANIMALS *s.v.*;

dual, double nature of/*duplex,* duplicity of/twofold, **9i** 553, 555, 556, 567*n*, 689; **9ii** 234, 397, 401; **10** 727; **11** 400, 470; **12** 84, 409, 460, 518, 547,*figs.* 22, 86, 142K; **13** 105*n*, 180, 266, 267–9, 270, 278*n*, 284, 295, 303, 315, 316, 343, 384, 408, 420, 422, 481; **14** 34, 80*n*,

86, 110, 117, 121, 238, 404, 416, 480, 565, 635, 699, 720, 726, 757; **16** 389, 403, 454, 494; *duplicatus,* **12** 508; as physician of soul, **13** 384; as eagle, **12** 84, 518; **13** 246; **14** 637; as earth, **13** 267; spirit, **12** 447; **16** 453, 480; and Echidna, **13** 180*n*; as egg, in alchemy, **13** 267; and Elijah legend, **18** 1528, 1529; elusive/evasive, **13** 241*n*; **14** 742; essence, mercurial, **13** 244; *familiaris/paredros,* **12** 84; **14** 707; feminine aspect of, **13** 262, 427; **14** 22, 168, 634, 659; **16** 402; *femina,* **13** 262; as wisdom, **13** 420 (*see also below* moon/ Luna); as *filius/*son, **9i** 268; **12** *fig.* 22; **13** 271; **14** 473; of God, **13** 271; *hermaphroditus,* **12** *fig.* 23; *macrocosmi,* **11** 357; **13** 280; "of one day," **14** 718; *philoso- phorum,* **13** 157; of Tiamat, **13** 283; as fire, **12** 265, 338, 404&*n*, 473, *fig.* 130; **13** 256–8, 282*n*, 408; **16** 455*n*; and water, **13** 408 (see also *ignis mercurialis*); as *foetus spagyricus,* **12** *fig.* 210; food of, **16** 510; fountain, mercurial/*fons mer- curialis,* **9i** 246*n*; **12** 355, *fig.* 25; **14** 9, 23; **16** 402–3, 408–9, 411, 416, 453, 455*n*; and four elements, **12** 529; **13** 267; four forms of, **13** 360 (see also below *quadratus;* quadripartite; quaternity; *and see* Mercury (god) *s.v.* fourfold); *fugax/*fleeing, **16** 396, 478; giver of life, **11** 357;

goblin, **12** 84; as God: chthonic, **9ii** 367; -Man, **14** 22; in physical na- ture, **13** 284; gold of, **13** 250, 278, 282; **14** 713; *aurum non vulgi* as, **12** 518; golden wand of, *see above* caduceus; as gold-solvent, **14** 416; as goose, **14** 637; heart of, at North Pole, **9ii** 206, 209, 212; **12** 265; **13** 256&*n*; herb of ablution, **14** 401*n*; hermaphroditism of, *see above* androgyny; as hermeneut/interpreter, **13** 278; as Hermes Kyllenios, iden- tified, **9ii** 367; as Hermes Trismegistus, *see* ALCHEMICAL WRITERS *s.v.*; as Hermes Trisomatos, **14** 303; "Hermes the vintager," **13** 359*n*; as "high man," *homo altus,* **9i** 550*n*; **9ii** 367; **13** 268; as Holy Ghost, **8** 393; **11** 160*n*; **12** 518; **14** 12, 22; as *homo philosophicus,* **12** *fig.* 214; philosophic man, **13** 268, 282; **14** 476 (see also below *philosophicus*); as husband and wife, **13** 268; and ibis, **12** 530; **13** 359; incorruptibility of, **13** 264, 295; as individuation process, **13** 277, 284; as *infans noster,* **9i** 268; as intellect, **12** 90; as Jehovah, **13** 270; J.'s patient on, **9i** 545; *juvenis,* **13** 301; *katachthonios/*subterranean, **10** 727; **13** 278; as king, **13** 282; krater of, see *krater s.v.* of Hermes; and *lac virginis,* **12** *fig.* 152; **16**

443

poisonous nature of, **12** 459; **13** 267; **14** 110, 235, 688; **16** 510, 515;

positive aspect of, **13** 289;

as *prima materia*, **12** 84, 404, 517, 530, *fig.* 142F; **13** 282, 408; **14** 12, 565, 636, 714, 715; **18** 1701;

psychic nature of, **13** 266;

psychologem of, **13** 266;

as psychopomp/*psychopompos*, **9i** 238, 689; **11** 160*n*; **12** 84, 404, 409, *figs.* 9, 23; **13** 106, 270, 284, 303;

puer, see above boy;

quadratus, **10** 767; **11** 672; **12** 31; **13** 359, 360; **14** 719;

quadripartite, **12** 173 (*see also above* four forms of);

quaternity as, **12** *fig.* 192; **13** frontispiece; **14** 719;

as queen, **14** 534;

and quicksilver, **12** 84, 90, 172, 404*n*, 473; **13** 97&*n*, 157, 255&*n*, 258, 259, 273, 274, 371; **14** 699, 712, 717; **16** 408 (see also *argentum vivum;* mercury (metal); quicksilver);

raven as, **12** 84, 404; **13** 246;

as redeemer/Salvator/Saviour, **9i** 456; **10** 629; **11** 160*n*, 357; **12** 460, 529; **13** 283, 303; **14** 688;

redemption of, **11** 420;

rotundum as, **9i** 549; **14** 167;

round and square, **9i** 541, 549&*n*;

as salamander, **12** 537*n*, *fig.* 138; **13** 258; **14** 632;

and salt, **14** 318, 322;

as Sapientia, **13** 277; **14** 22; **16** 484;

and Saturn, **13** 88*n*, 110; child of, **13** 101*n*, 274; relation to, **13** 274, 301; **14** 476;

scarab and, **12** 530;

as self, **13** 284, 289, 296;

senex, **11** 400; **12** *figs.* 134, 232;

13 218, 269, 274, 301, 420;

as servant/*servator*, **9i** 289*n*; **10** 629; **13** 283, 303;

as *servus fugitivus*, **12** 84, 187; **13** 218, 259; **16** 478;

as snake/*serpens Mercurii*/*mercurialis*/mercurial serpent, **9i** 553–4, 556, 560*n*, 686; **9ii** 246, 367, 371–2, 386; **11** 160*n*, 356, 359; **12** 26, 31, 215, 355, 469, 517, *fig.* 130; **13** 89, 102, 109–10, 180, 188, 246, 316–17, 319, 416; **14** 68, 236, 251, 261, 270, 273, 341*n*, 348, 472–3, 480, 626*n*, 632; **16** 403, 409, 533; **18** 533, 1631; as serpent-daemon, **13** 288; as *spiritus Mercurius*, **9i** 561; **12** 537*n*; and stone, **9ii** 386; three-headed, **12** 31; **13** *fig.* 32; **14** 122*n*, 643; **16** 403; as transformation symbol, **5** *fig.* 6; and Sol/sun, **12** 84, 355, 436; **13** 273*n*, 357; **14** 87, 113, 117, 120–1, 167, 235; and moon, **12** *figs.* 22, 125, 192; **13** 101*n*, 273, 357;

son of, *see* Jûnân ben Merqûlius;

as son of God, **13** 271;

as souls, *see above* as anima;

as spirit/*spiritus mercurialis*/*mercurii*, **9i** 541, 554, 561; **10** 629, 767; **11** 160, 356; **12** 84, 90, 404, 406, 433*n*, 447, 518, 519, 537*n*, *figs.* 134, 138, 179; **13** 105*n*, 164*n*, 168*n*, 171, 187*n*, 250, 261, 263, 264, 287, 321, 384, frontispiece; **14** 9–10, 41, 117, 251, 318, 493*n*, 494, 658, 659, 700; **16** 416; aerial/*aereus*, **13** 261; "animal," **9i** 534; and body, **13** 261; evil, as serpent-daemon, **13** 288; helpful/*paredros*, **12** 84; matter and, **12** 404; *Phytonis*/procreator, **13** 263; seminalis, **13** 263; and soul, **13** 259–66; "spiritual blood," **14** 11; *veg-*

Mercurius (*cont.*):

etativus, **13** 250, 263, 408, 459; **14** 33, 117, 298, 634, 636; —, chthonic, **13** 416;

as square, **9i** 554 (*see also above* round and square);

stag as, *see* ANIMALS *s.v.* deer/ stag;

statue(s) of, in alchemical writings, **13** 278; **14** 276, 287, 560, 564;

storm-daemon, **13** 250;

as subtle thing, **14** 493;

and sulphur, **12** 470; **13** 276&*n*, 357; **14** 32, 135, 144, 415, 478;

as swan, **14** 637;

sword of, **9ii** 292; **14** 58&*n*;

symbols of, **9i** 396; **13** 315–16;

synonyms for, **9ii** 379; **10** 629;

as *terminus ani,* **13** 269;

as Thoth, *see* Thoth *s.v.*;

threefold: *ternarius,* **13** 270; three-headed/*tricephalus,* **12** 31, 539,*fig.* 16; **16** 403; three manifestations of, **16** 404; triadic/in triad, **9ii** 200; **13** 270, 271, 289, 357; **14** 235, 303; **16** 403; as Trinity, **13** 271, 283, 289; **16** 403, 416; *trinus et unus,* **13** 243; *triplex nomine,* **16** 403, 411, 416; triunity/*triunus,* **12** 31; **13** 270–2; **14** 235; **16** 403 (*see also* Mercury (god) *s.v.*);

as tincture, **13** 282; golden, **13** 255;

tomb of, **12** 457; **14** 65;

totality/wholeness of, **13** 295; **14** 12;

transformations of, **13** 275, 283, 449; **14** 404, 565, 757; as goal of his own, **13** 277, 282;

as transforming substance, **12** 31*n*, 172, 173, 187, 459, 517, 529; **13** 259; **18** 1693;

in/as tree, **14** 636; of metals/ *arbor metallorum,* **13** 408, 409*n*; -numen, **9ii** 372; **13** 287, 420,

459; **14** 75; of paradise, **13** 247*n*, 288; as "personal atman" of, **13** 287; philosophical, **12** *fig.* 231; **13** 278, 288;

triadic, *see above* threefold;

as trickster, **9i** 456, 682, 689; **9ii** 315*n*; **13** 251, 284; **14** 332;

as trinity, *see above* threefold;

Trismegistus, *see* ALCHEMICAL WRITERS: Hermes Trismegistus;

twofold aspect of, *see above* dual;

as *ultima materia,* **13** 282;

and unconscious, **11** 419; archetype of, **13** 280, 299; personification of, **13** 449; **14** 117, 534, 660, 700, 749; **16** 453;

and unconscious, collective, **13** 271, 277, 284; **14** 660;

as unicorn, **9ii** 234; **12** 518, 529, 530, 547; **14** 712*n*;

unigenitus, **13** 283;

as unity/uniting symbol, **12** 404,*figs.* 146, 148; **13** 270, 284, 408; **14** 12, 635, 660, 720 (*see also above* One; threefold *s.v.* triunity);

as uroboros, **11** 420; **12** 404, 447,*fig.* 20;

"utriusque capax" (capable of anything), **13** 481; **14** 688 (*see also* Mercury (god) *s.v.*);

in vein swollen with blood, **13** 299;

and Venus, **13** 273&*n*, 301; **14** 415;

as *veritas,* **11** 421;

versipellis, **12** 538; **13** 267;

in vessel, **12** 338&*n*, *figs.* 120, 121;

as vine of the wise, **13** 414;

vinum ardens, **10** 629;

as virgo/Virgin (Mary), **9ii** 194; **12** 470, 505, 506, 519,*figs.* 38, 231; **13** 262, 273; *lac virginis,* **13** 255*n*; of light (Gnostic), **12** 505, 506; -serpent/Edem (Gnostic), **9i** 552, 560; **12** 413*n*,*figs.* 157,

257; virgin's milk, **14** 401*n*;
Virgin Mary and, **14** 121;
vis Mercurii, **13** 171*n*;
"volatile"/winged, **11** 160*n*; **14**
637;
vulgi/vulgaris/crudus, **9i** 554,
561, 609;
as vulture, **14** 637;
as water, **9ii** 281; **12** 90, 338,
fig. 142XX; **13** 255, 408; **14**
401*n*, 545, 717; vapour from,
13 255 (see also above *aqua*);
as wheel, **12** 215;
white and red in, **14** 12, 401*n*;
wings of/winged, **9i** 549, 569,
574, 588; **12** 305, 404; **13** 261;
as world soul, *see above* as
anima;
Yesod and, **14** 634–7
Mercury/Hermes (2) *(Greek/Roman
god, classical and post-classical)*,
9i 193, 456; **9ii** 327; **12** *fig.* 139;
13 278;
Adamas and, **14** 589;
all-encompassing, **13** 360;
ambiguous, **9ii** 240;
bats of, **9ii** 327;
as begetter of gods and men,
9ii 327;
as Dactyls, **9i** 298;
in Egyptian Hellenism, **13** 360;
fourfold, **9i** 538; **13** 360; quadrangular, **12** 172; *tetracephalus/*
four-headed, **12** 172; **13** 272
(*see also* Mercurius (in alchemists' writings etc.) *s.v.* four
forms of);
in Gaul, **13** 270;
Gnostics and, **9ii** 325; **14** 6*n*,
589;
god of illusion and delusion, **13**
299;
god of revelation, **9i** 193; **9ii**
386; **10** 394; **11** 160, 356; **12**
84, 172, 404, 446; **13** 256, 278,
281;
god of thieves and cheats, **13**
281;

guide of dreams, **9i** 538;
ithyphallic, **5** 183; **9i** 193, 556;
9ii 313, 366; **11** 420; **12** 172,
fig. 63; **13** 273, 278; **14** 85, 589,
688;
Kadmilos, **14** 85*n*;
as Korybas, **9ii** 332; **13** 278; **14**
627;
as Kriophoros (ram-bearer), **9ii**
162; **14** 305;
Kyllenic/Kyllenios, **9i** 533*n*,
538; **9ii** 313, 331, 332, 367; **11**
420; **12** 550*n*; **13** 278, 299; **14**
140, 416, 627, 634, 688; and
Mercurius, identified, **9ii** 367;
18 1696; and Osiris, parallel,
14 627*n*;
as Logos, **9ii** 313; **11** 421;
magician and god of magicians,
9i 553;
many-faced, **5** 515;
mediator, **13** 283;
as Nous, **11** 421;
originator of souls, **9i** 538;
prayers/invocation to, in Greek
Papyri, **5** 274*n*, 530*n*; **9i** 549*n*;
13 (*p*192), 359; **14** 39, 46, 251;
Psychopompos/ΨυΧοπομπός,
9ii 325; **12** *figs.* 45, 139;
quadrangular, *see above* fourfold;
round and square (Greek
Magic Papyri), **12** 172; **13**
(*p*192);
"skilled in both" (life and
death)/*ad utriumque peritus,* **9i**
413;
and snake, **14** 483;
statues of, **14** 560, 564–5 (*see
also* Mercurius (in alchemists'
writings etc.) *s.v.*);
ter unus, see below threefold;
tetracephalus/four-headed, *see
above* fourfold;
threefold: *ter unus,* **9ii** 274; "All
and Thrice One"/*Omnia solus et
ter unus,* **4** 106; **13** 270;
threeheaded/*tricephalus,* **13** 270,

447

Messenger, E. C., *see under* Palanque
messenger: of the Grail, see Grail
  s.v.;
    Khidr as, **9i** 251
Messiah(s), **6** 326; **9i** 533*n*, 576*n*; **9ii**
  166–9, 185; **10** 90, 622; **11** 643,
  743; **12** 416; **14** 18, 593, 595*n*; **16**
  472*n*; **17** 309;
    birth of, **9ii** 166, 232;
    coming of, **9ii** 128, 181; sec-
    ond, **11** 713; **14** 443;
    "of the Lie," **13** 278;
    self as, in delusion, **1** 214;
    two, **9ii** 168–9;
    in Zohar, **9ii** 335
Messianic: mission, **17** 309;
    prophecies, **6** 438
Messias, *see* Spitteler *s.v.*
Messina earthquake, **17** 19; **18**
  197&*n*
Mestha, **9ii** 188; **13** 360
metabolism, change in, **3** 75, (*p*272)
metal(s)/metallic/minerals, **13** 95,
  119, 267, 274*n*, 375, 381&*n*, 444;
    alchemical, **9i** 268; as symbols
    of spiritual growth, **13** 119;
    base, **13** 133;
    child-figure and, **9i** 288;
    diseases of, **15** 25–7;
    earth, **13** 409;
    four, **14** 136*n*;
    impure, **13** 381*n*;
    leprositas/leprous, **12** 207; **13**
    381&*n*;
    man, **8** 945*n*; **9i** 268, 407–8; **13**
    119, 124, 246;
    Mercurius as, *see* Mercurius
    s.v.;
    molten, **12** 353;
    moon and, **14** 217;
    of philosophers, **13** 268*n*; un-
    ripe, **12** *fig.* 142K;
    seven, **12** 84, 348, 410, 468,
    490, *figs.* 154–5; **13** 376, 458*n*;
    14 14, 218, 563; **16** 402; con-
    nection of tree with, **13** 380,
    409;
    sick, **12** 420;

-spirit, **13** 392;
spirits of/*spiritus metallorum*, **11**
  347; **12** 40; **13** 121; **14** 217;
transmutation of, **13** 158; **16**
  499*n*;
tree of, *see* tree(s) *s.v.*;
see also antimony; brass;
  bronze; copper; gold; iron;
  lead; mercury; quicksilver;
  silver; steel; tin
"Metallorum metamorphosis," *see*
  ALCHEMICAL COLLECTIONS: *Mus.*
  herm. s.v. Philalethes
metamorphosis, **9i** 268; **13** 326;
    of the gods, **9i** 267; **10** 585
metanoia/μετάνοια, **9ii** 299; **10** 536,
  719;
    in J.'s life, **5** (*p*xxvi)
metaphors, **9i** 267; **10** 637;
    in dreams, **3** 218, 298; **8** 506;
    17 269;
    outworn, **8** 204;
    sexual/erotic, **5** 7, 192; **8** 506;
    17 144
metaphysical/metaphysics, **8** 568,
  649, 662, 814, 960; **9i** 59, 149; **10**
  438, 845; **13** 74, 82; **14** 630, 651,
  781;
    and archetypes, **18** 1229;
    assertions, **12** 15, 35; **13** 75; **14**
    667, 782; **18** 1670;
    Christian, **10** 738;
    definition of, **12** 126*n*, 135;
    entities, **11** 459;
    factors, and psychic factors, **11**
    273*n*;
    fear of, **10** 387; **15** 149;
    figures, psychic quality of, **11**
    463;
    ideas, **9ii** 65–7; projected into
    nature, **16** 440;
    Indian, **11** 933;
    Jung and, **9ii** 304*n*; **10** 623&*n*,
    624;
    and language, **5** 14*n*;
    materialism and, **11** 762, 765;
    metaphysicians, **13** 356;
    of mind and of matter, **8** 651;

metaphysical (*cont.*):
  mountains, **13** 329;
  need, man's metaphysical, **4** 554;
  of Paul's conversion, **8** 583;
  presumption, **13** 75;
  principle, amorality of, **18** 1656;
  "psychologizing," **10** 623*n*;
  psychology/psyche and, **9ii** 98, 112, 122, 304, 308; **11** 759, 760; **13** 73, 82; **14** 558, 630, 651, 667;
  and science, **18** 1591;
  spirit and, **13** 395;
  split, **13** 291;
  statements, of the psyche, **11** 835; and psychological explanation, **11** 376; unprovable, **11** 238;
  status of Satan, **11** 471;
  "unconscious," **16** 90, 94;
  world, **13** 293
metasomatosis, **13** 101
Metatron, **9ii** 335;
  Anthropos as, **13** 168
metempsychosis/transmigration of souls, **7** 108; **9i** 200; **14** 31*n*
meteor(s)/meteorites, **5** 275; **10** 603, 608; **18** 740&*n*;
  Indian name for, **5** 275, 481
method(s), **11** 501; **13** 4, 19, 30, (*pp*63, 65), 437; **16** 290;
  analytical, *see* analytical *s.v.*;
  cathartic, *see* cathartic *s.v.*;
  choice of, in therapy, **4** 604–5; **16** 1, 11, 541–4; and therapist, **16** 198;
  comparative, **18** 7;
  constructive, **3** 391, 404–15; **6** 701–4 (Def.); **17** 194–5;
  educational, **17** 253–7, 282, 284;
  empirical, **17** 127–8;
  explanatory, **16** 150;
  "false," **13** 433;
  Freudian, psych(o)analytic, **4** 38–42; as autosuggestion, **4**

17–20; and hysteria, **4** 9–12; interpretative, **16** 143–6;
  individualization of, **16** 42;
  psychoanalysis as, **4** 622–3; **16** 292;
  psychoanalytic, **4** 79–82, 523–5; purely empirical, **4** 195;
  psychobiological, **17** (*pp*3–4);
  rational, **16** 20;
  reductive, *see* Adler; Freud; reductive;
  "right," **13** 4;
  scientific, **17** 262; **18** 742; and religious, **11** 865–6;
  statistical, **18** 761;
  teaching of, **18** 575, 1380;
  technical, **16** 3;
  see also abreactive; anamnestic; association; unconscious, the, *s.v.* analysis of
methodology, **11** 4
Metra, **9i** 564
Métral, M.: "Expériences scolaires sur la mémoire de l'orthographe," **18** (*p*420)
metropolis, **12** 139; **13** 212
Meumann, E., **7** 408; *see also under* Zoneff
Meung, Jean de, *see* ALCHEMICAL COLLECTIONS: *Mus. herm. s.v.* Jean de Meung
Mexican/Mexico, **8** 121, 333;
  ancient, **11** 348, 484; **13** 107*n*;
  Cross of Palenque, **5** 400, pl. XLIa;
  hieroglyphic, **5** 400;
  rite of Teoqualo, **5** 526*n*; **11** 340;
  sacrificial rite, **5** 402*n*;
  world tree, **13** *fig.* 8;
  see also American Indians: NORTH *s.vv.* Aztecs; Huichols; Mayas
Meyer, Adolf, **4** 154&*n*;
  report in *Psychological Bulletin,* **2** 1020*n*
Meyer, E.: *Beitrag zur Kenntnis der acut entstandenen Psychosen,* **3** 5*n*,

Middle Ages (*cont.*):
TITLE: "The Problem of Types
in the History of Classical and
Medieval Thought," **6** 8–100;
adultery in, **10** 248;
alchemy in, *see* alchemy *s.v.*;
art in, **5** 368; **18** 401;
Christianity in, **13** 25, 399;
Church and family in, **17** 158;
dreams in, **18** 136, 250, 544;
and *jus primae noctis*, **18** 365;
magic, **13** 295;
man in, **8** 426;
medievalism, **6** 8, 315;
mind, **11** 191;
modern man and, **15** 179–81,
184;
mysteries celebrated in, **18**
254;
mythological world of, **18**
1363;
"possession" in, **8** 204;
"psychic" in, **14** 630;
psychology, **11** 284; **18** 370;
religious ideas of, **10** 79; **15** 45;
secret traditions in, **18** 254,
264;
tree in, **5** 368;
Weltanschauung/world view of,
10 623; **14** 507; **18** 253a
Middle East, Cybele cults of, *see*
Rhea/Cybele
middle life, *see* life, stages in *s.v.*
Middle Path/Way, **6** 326, 356–8; **7**
116, 365; **11** 797;
and opposites, **6** 192, 326; **7**
327
Midgard Serpent, *see* ANIMALS:
serpent/snake *s.v.*
midpoint, universal, **13** 349; *see also*
centre; circle; personality *s.v.*
Midrashim, **9ii** 107–8; **12** 456*n*; **18**
1551;
Midrash Rabbah, **9ii** 108*n*; **14**
587;
Midrash tanchuma (Shemoth), **9ii**
107*n*, 181*n*;
Midrash Tehillim, ed. S. Buber,

12 545&*n*;
Midrash of Ten Kings, **14**
640*n*; *see also* Eliezer ben
Hyrcanus (midrash collection)
Midwich Cuckoos, The, see Wyndham
Mieg, Joannes Fridericus: *De raptu
Eliae*, **18** 1521
Migne, J. P.: *Dictionnaire des sciences
occultes*, **12** 550&*n*; *Patrologiae, see
names of individual authors*
migraine, **8** 709
migration(s): European, **10** 1001;
and motifs/symbols, archetypal, **11** 88, 845;
myth-, **8** 228; **9i** 259, 262; **18**
1286
migratory instinct, **4** 728; **10** 849
Milan, **4** 109, 119; **11** 211; **14** 67
Miles, degree of (Mithraism), **5** 288
milk/milky, **11** 359; **13** 381;
drying up, **10** 700;
fermented, in dream, **8** 478–9;
ocean, churning of, **5** pl. XV;
virgin's, *see* virgin(s) *s.v.*;
vomiting of, **3** 149*n*
Milky Way, **12** 246
Mill, J., **2** 21
millennium, **10** 162;
first, end of, **10** 488, 617;
see also world *s.v.* end of
Miller, E., **18** 228
Miller, Miss F., **5** 46; **9i** 319, 518*n*;
TITLE: "The Miller Fantasies:
Anamnesis," **5** 47–55;
"The Miller Fantasies," **5**
(*pp*447–62);
capacity for identification, **5** 47,
52, 72, 84, 87;
dependence on family ties, **5**
461;
fantasies, **5** (*p*xxviii), 46 (*see also*
association-chain); inner neces-
sity in, **5** 675; symbols of sacrifice in, **5** 645;
first publications by Flournoy,
5 (*p*xxviii), 46;
ideal figure of, **5** 432;
lack of understanding of sym-

bols, **5** 683;

name associations, **5** 280–1;

as object of hero's longing, **5** 614;

participation in hero's sacrificial act, **5** 675;

personal influence over artist, **5** 53–4;

sea-voyages of, **5** 51, (*pp*448, 450);

and ship's officer, **5** 81, 124–5, 127, 168, 273, (*p*450);

significance of Sphinx symbol, **5** 266;

spirituality personified as Aztec, **5** 273;

"Chiwantopel, hypnagogic drama," **5** 251, 613, (*pp*457–62);

Ahamarama, **5** 280, (*p*460); Chiwantopel: animus figure, **5** 267, 462, 465; apparition of, **5** 266, (*p*458); death threat to, **5** 420; horse and snake symbolism and, **5** 678–9; meaning of role of, **5** 272, 468; name, **5** 274, (*pp*458, 460); —, Biblical parallels of, **5** 280–1; as personification of regressive reverie, **5** 644; prophecy of, **5** 613–14; significance of birth from Popocatepetl, **5** 279;

"Glory to God," **5** 56, 61, 105, (*pp*450–4);

"The Moth and (to) the Sun," **5** 116, 123, 165, 171, 176, (*pp*455–7);

"Phenomena of Transitory Suggestion or of Instantaneous Autosuggestion," **5** 47, (*pp*447–9)

Mill of the Host, **12** *fig.* 158

Milton, John: and devil, **11** 470, 471;

Paradise Lost, **5** 60, 68–9, 72, 83, 84, (*pp*451, 453); **11** 468, 473

Milvescindus, **14** 7*n*

Mimallones, in Dionysian train, **4** 106

Mimaut Papyrus, *see* ALCHEMICAL WRITERS: Magic Papyri *s.v.*

Mime/Mimir (dwarf), **10** 399, 400; **11** 44*n*;

chthonic god, **5** 566–8;

fountain of, **5** 371*n*, 566*n*; **9i** 413

mimicry, **4** 652

Mimir, *see* Mime

mind, **9i** 555; **12** 359, 366, 377, 456(4); **13** 60, 82, 137*n*;

archetypal, **18** 92;

basic conformity of, **18** 87;

between death and birth, **18** 204;

as biochemical phenomenon, **8** 650;

biological structure of, **17** 101;

and body, *see* body *s.v.*;

causal concept of, **10** 49;

collective, **4** 520; **7** 455;

conscious, *see* conscious mind;

differentiated masculine, **13** 60;

Eastern, *see* East/Eastern *s.v.*;

as epiphenomenon of matter, **8** 653;

eyes of, see eye(s) *s.v.*;

growth of, and widening consciousness, **17** 143; **18** 553;

history of the, **11** 56; **18** 837;

horrible darkness of, **13** 302;

human, **7** 455; **13** 82; suprapersonal, **16** 157;

image creating, **11** 781;

individualized, **11** 766;

influence of country on, **10** 971;

and instinct, **16** 185;

instinctive, archaic basis, **5** 38;

and intuition, **11** 804;

latent archetypal symbolization, **5** 554;

man cannot escape from his, **11** 765;

masculine, *see* masculine *s.v.*;

Mithras (*cont.*):
XXIV*a*; Osterburken, **5** 288;
13 404; Ostian head, **5** *frontispiece;*
moral values of, **5** 102, 104&*n*;
mysteries, **5** 288, 425, 526; **14**
578; initiation into, **5** 674*n*; **8**
929; **11** 828*n*; **14** 168;
Orphos, son of, **9ii** 186;
phallic sun-tube, vision of, **5**
149–53; **8** 318; **9i** 105; breath
of spirit and, **5** 486*n*; parallel in
patient's vision, **5** 151, 154; **8**
317–18; **9i** 105;
raven in, **5** 89*n*, 369*n*;
Roman army and, **18** 1287;
snake in, **5** 288*n*, 396, 421, 425,
671, pl. LXIIIb;
sun-disc in, **5** 138;
sun-god and, **5** 368, 664; **9i**
235; eyes of, **5** 177*n*; Helios
and, **5** 155, 288, 289, 596*n*, pl.
XXIV*a*; and Sol, **5** 155, 354,
398, 596*n*; **18** 1528; triadic/
threefold, **5** 294&*n*;
sword and torch in, **5** 156*n*, *fig.*
9;
symbolism, **5** 155, 671;
and water/springs, **5** 319, 368,
439*n*; **18** 259, 616
μίτος, **5** 184
Mitra (sun-god), in Vedic Hymns, **6**
349
mixing-bowl, see *krater*
Mjollnir, **8** 966*n*
mneme, phylogenetic (Semon), **6**
624; **7** 159*n*
mob, *see* mass(es)
Möbius, P. J., **2** 661; **5** 190*n*; **18**
795&*n*;
on hysterical symptom, **18** 885,
922;
on Nietzsche, **7** 66
Moby Dick, see Melville
Moctezuma, **11** 340
modalities of psychic functioning, **8**
248
model(s), **11** 460

modelling, **8** 180, 400
modern/contemporary man, **5** 113;
11 84, 523–4, 570, 738, 962; **13**
81; **15** 210; **18** 466, 587;
TITLES: "The Meaning of
Psychology for Modern Man,"
10 276–332; "The Spiritual
Problem of Modern Man," **10**
148–96;
dreams of, **11** 738;
and the mystical, **11** 274;
and power instinct, **10** 653;
pseudo-, **10** 154;
and psyche, **17** 302;
"restratification of," **15** 179–81;
spiritual outlook of, **11** 537;
and tradition, **11** 516, 528;
and unconscious, **10** 678;
see also man *s.v.* of twentieth
century
modesty, **9ii** 47
Moebius, *see* Möbius
Moguls/Mogul Empire, **10** 984,
990–1; **13** 278
Mohács, defeat of (1526), **12** 480*n*
Mohammed, *see* Mahomet
Mohammed ibn Umail, *see* ALCHEMICAL WRITERS: Senior
moieties, marriage and, **16** 433,
435, 436
Moira, **9i** 157; **11** 606
moist/dry, **13** 359; **14** 1, 7, 31, 330,
607
moisture, **13** 114*n*;
of Mercurius, *see* Mercurius
s.v.;
radical/*humidum radicale*, **14** 6,
41, 50, 337;
Moknine, **9i** 699
mole, *see* ANIMALS *s.v.*
molecular movement, **9ii** 394
molecules, **4** 764;
psychic, **3** 78–80, 82, 135
Moleschott, J., **4** 687; **6** 593, 699; **18**
1372
Moll, A., **18** 798&*n*
"Die Bewusstseinsspaltung in
Paul Lindau's neuem Schau-

monograph, patient's, on his own neurosis, **8** 685

Monoïmos, **9ii** 347, 350; **11** 400; **14** 38–9, 50;
    and monad, **8** 395; **9ii** 340–1; **14** 38; **16** 525*n*

monolith, **13** 113

monomania, **7** 111

Monophysites, **6** 31; **9ii** 171; **11** 312

"monopoly," *see* association-chains *s.v.*

monotheism, **9i** 189; **9ii** 427; **10** 634; **11** (*p*358); **15** 176;
    of consciousness, **13** 51;
    polytheistic tendency in, **5** 149;
    psychological, **7** 482

monotony, **3** 184

Mons, battle of, **10** 597

monsters, *see* ANIMALS *s.v.*

Montanus/Montanism, **6** 19; **8** 645

Montelius, O.: *Opuscula,* **5** pl. XI*b*

Montessori, M., **4** 643&*n*

months, Platonic, **9i** 551; **10** 589

Montpellier school, **15** 27

Mont Ventoux, **16** 412

mood(s), **7** 273, 307, 355–6, 370, 375; **8** 167, 667; **9ii** 34; **13** 48, 55, 58; **17** 189;
    actions affected by, **1** 475;
    of affection and remorse, **17** 213;
    anima and, **7** 331;
    bad, **13** 108
    born of life's meaninglessness, **11** 517;
    changes of, **8** 639; **10** 287;
    children's, **17** 13;
    compensation of, **17** 269;
    disguise of complex by, **3** 105, 145;
    and dreams, **7** 168; **8** 444;
    elegiac, **17** 12, 13;
    and ESP experiments, **8** 980;
    hysterical, **7** 27, 438;
    of man, **7** 331;
    peaceful, **8** 693;
    peculiarities of, **3** 105;
    personal, **13** 59;

poetic, **17** 268;

receptivity of, and libido, **5** 251;

as smoke-screen, **5** 458;

succumbing to, **7** 348;

sudden, **8** 266;

unstable, **1** 234;

venomous, **7** 45;

in woman, **10** 244

moon (☽), **3** 571; **8** 330, 842; **9i** 311; **9ii** 130&*n*, 240, 393; **10** 611, 614, 766; **12** 179, 486, 524*n,figs.* 106, 220; **13** 64, 114, 198, 273, 334, 355, 406, 409, 459, *fig.* 32; **14** 6, 19, 29, 171, 499;
TITLE: "The Significance of the Moon," **14** 154–73;
in alchemy, **11** 176; **12** 334, 486–7; *albedo* and, *see* COLOURS;
as Shulamite, **14** 625; as tincture, **16** 514;
as archetype of parent, **5** 576;
in astrology, conjunction, in marriage horoscopes, **8** 869&*n*, 988; **14** 222; **18** 1178, 1180, 1184–5, 1194, 1197–8, 1200, 1203, 1207;
as bitch/canicula, **14** 24, 172*n*, 174, 181; **16** 458 (*see also* Hecate *s.v.* animal attributes);
and brain, **14** 626;
celestial horn of, **9ii** 330;
changefulness of, **14** 19, 20, 21, 28&*n*–30;
circle of, **9i** 541; **13** (*p*192), 273*n*; **14** 157, 167, 211;
corruptibility of, **14** 21;
course of, **5** 163*n*;
day of (Monday), **14** 238;
dog and, **14** 183;
in dreams: -bowl, **9i** 342, 343, 557; -goddess, **9i** 344; lady, **9i** 345–7;
and eagle, **14** 183;
and earth, **14** 154, 171, 173, 630; moon as funnel of the earth, **14** 154; -mother, **9i** 312; united, **14** 154&*n*, 630&*n*;

eclipse of, **12** *fig.* 142, YY, ZZ;
as female consciousness, **14** 159, 227, 331;
and fertility, **14** 630*n*, 646;
in folklore, **14** 214;
full, **14** 21, 28*n*, 154;
further side of, **10** 612;
-goddess, **5** 488; **9i** 344; **11** 348; **13** 398; link with Hecate, **5** 355 (*see also* Artemis);
heavenly horn of, **12** 529, 550–1; **13** 193*n*;
and individuation process, **14** 217;
Isis as, **14** 14;
in mandalas, **9i** 604, 609–11, 685;
as masculine unconscious, *see below* unconscious;
as mediatrix, **14** 19, 155;
Mercurius and, *see* Mercurius *s.vv.* moon; Sol/sun;
moisture of, **14** 154, 155&*n*, 173;
as mother-symbol, **9i** 156; **10** 808; **14** 43, 499 (*see also* Mary/Mother of God *s.v.* moon);
nature of, **14** 214–33;
new, **14** 21, 25, 154, 173, 214, 437 (*see also* novilunium);
as nymph, *see* Luna;
orbit of, serpent as, **5** *fig.* 10;
-plant, **14** 157; **16** 408 (*see also* adept);
prayer to, **5** 148;
as prefiguration of self, **14** 217;
as *prima materia*, **12** 425, 487; **14** 15;
primitive idea of, **5** 487;
and quicksilver, **13** 273;
as rotundum, **14** 498–9;
and Saturn, **14** 216*n*, 217;
and sea, **14** 157, 244;
sickle-, **13** 193*n*; **14** 214;
significance of, **14** 154–73;
son of, **16** 495;
and soul, *see* soul;

and stars, light of, **13** 300;
and sun, *see* sun and moon;
three and, **14** 563;
as type of man, **14** 568*n*;
as unconscious in man, **14** 159, 172, 223; **18** 412;
unfavourable/dangerous aspect, **14** 19–22, 25, 144*n*, 171–3, 183, 203, 210, 214, 216, 437;
as uterus, **5** 298;
and Venus, **14** 6, 171;
as vessel, see *vas*/vessel *s.v.* sun/moon;
visionary, **10** 597;
waning, **14** 157, 214;
and water, *see* water *s.v.*;
waxing of, and departed souls, **10** 699 (*see also above* full);
-wolf, **14** 214;
woman in, **5** *fig.* 32;
see also *coniunctio;* eclipse; Luna; Sol/Luna; sun and moon; TREES *s.v.* lunatica
moon-bowl, in dream, **9i** 342–3, 557
moonlight, **14** 498
moon-sickness, **5** 577; **14** 183*n*, 214
Moor, the, **14** 731
Moors: King of the, **14** 418; kingdom of, **18** 253a
moral: authority, **7** 332;
balance, and dreams, **4** 576;
code, **10** 831, 833–8, 840; **12** 36; **13** 229; and religion, **10** 870;
conflict, *see* conflict *s.v.*;
consciousness, *see* consciousness *s.v.*;
contradictions, **13** 295;
decision, **17** 296, 299;
defect, *see below* moral insanity;
development, **17** 136;
distinctions, **11** 459;
factor, **7** 499;
freedom, *see* freedom *s.v.*;
function, **7** 498, 501*n*;
guilt, **7** 427;

Moroney, M. J., **18** 1206*n*
Morpheus, **12** 305
morphogenesis, biological, **8** 959
morphomata, **9ii** 136
Morris, R.: *Legends of the Holy Rood*,
    5 412*n*; **14** 26*n*
mortal and immortal, **5** 296;
    motif of the Dioscuri, **5** 294
mortality, **13** 169*n*, 207–8;
    child and female, **7** 429;
    curve/rate, **8** 875, 987
mortification, **10** 650;
    in alchemy/*mortificatio, see* opus,
    alchemical, stages in *s.v.*
Mosaic Law, **4** 738*n*
Moser, F.: *Okkultismus: Täuschungen
    und Tatsachen,* **18** 757*n*;
    *Spuk: Irrglaube oder Wahr-
    glaube?,* **18** (*p*317); J.'s fore-
    word, **18** 757–81
Moses, **5** 34, 286; **6** 392; **7** 108; **9i**
    533*n*, 579&*n*; **9ii** 128, 168, 187*n*,
    328&*n*–9; **10** 641, 643; **12** 347,
    349, 475*n*, 520, 545, *fig.* 213; **13**
    148*n*, 167; **15** 165*n*, 168, 182; **18**
    466;
    in alchemy, **13** 381*n*, 393; **14**
    372; sister of, *see* ALCHEMICAL
    WRITERS: Maria Prophetissa
    s.v.;
    and Elijah parallels, **18** 1524;
    Freud and, **15** 67
    horned, **14** 573*n*;
    and Joshua, **5** 282, 289, 291,
    531; **9i** 243–5, 248; **13** 428;
    and Khidr, *see* Khidr *s.v.*;
    Mosaic law, **4** 738*n*;
    quaternio, *see* quaternity;
    serpent of, **11** 349; **12** *figs.* 217,
    238; **13** 137;
    sister of, *see* Miriam (*see also
    above* in alchemy);
    staff of, **9i** 533;
    striking water from rock, **14**
    372
Moses ben Leon, **18** 1526
Moses Cordovero, **18** 1526
Moses ha-Darshan, **9ii** 167

Moses of Chorene, **5** 528
Mosley, Sir Oswald, **18** 1327&*n*
mosque, **10** 372; **12** 155, 176, 181
Mosso, A., **2** 1058, 1187&*n*;
    *Über den Kreislauf des Blutes im
    menschlichen Gehirn,* **2** (*p*580)
moth, *see* ANIMALS *s.v.*
"Moth, Song of the," *see* Miller, Miss
    F. *s.v.*
mother, **9ii** 240; **10** 67; **12** 18, 91,
    141, 151–2, *fig.* 6; **13** 116, 228*n*;
    14 424; **17** 289–90;
    TITLES: "The Battle for De-
    liverance from the Mother," **5**
    419–63; "The Dual Mother," **5**
    464–612; "Psychological As-
    pects of the Mother Ar-
    chetype," **9i** 148–98; "Symbols
    of the Mother and of Rebirth,"
    5 300–418;
    aetiological significance of, **9i**
    159; **18** 796;
    ambition/will to power of, **17**
    133, 221–3;
    Aniadic, **13** 204;
    anima and, *see* anima *s.v.*;
    animals and, *see* animal(s) *s.v.*;
    archetype, **5** 351, 459; **7** 185; **8**
    722–3, 728; **9i** 148–98; **10**
    64–5; **16** 344, 347; **17** 219*n*; at-
    tributes, **9i** 157–8; carrier of
    archetype, **9i** 188; and
    mother-complex, **9i** 161–2;
    in association, **2** 717, 816,
    (*pp*372, 380);
    assault on, **5** 487;
    assimilation of, **9i** 141;
    and birth fantasies, **4** 477; **13**
    132;
    in Breuer's case (Anna), **7**
    6/415;
    -bride, **5** 318;
    burial and resurrection/re-
    newal in, **5** 332, 349, 354, 398,
    408, 441, 460, 577, 671, 682*n*
    (*see also* rebirth *s.v.*);
    call for help to, **5** 602, 628;
    in *Cantilena,* **14** 371, 373,

mother (*cont.*):
    386–7, 399–400, 424, 434–6;
    chaos as, **14** 415;
    child-giving, **17** 42;
    -child relationship, **4** 693–4; **5** 313&*n*, 465, 504, 518; **7** 58, 75, 88, 171; **8** 723; **15** 50; **17** 133, 141, 331a; and choice of wife, **5** 502; **17** 328;
    Christ's conquest of, **11** 229;
    Church as, *see* Church *s.v.*;
    clings to child, **7** 114;
    complex, *see* complex *s.v.*;
    and conception in sin, **11** 626;
    conquest of, **5** 375, 450*n*, 459, 599;
    and consort, **5** 330*n*;
    as content and container, **14** 439;
    danger of erotic aspect, **5** 662;
    dark, **7** 396;
    and daughter, **9i** 316; **12** 26; **17** 223&*n*; as predicate types, **2** 1006; relationship, in analysis, **2** 717–18, 835, 848; rivals, **7** 47, 248; unconscious death wish, **7** 21–2/434; **17** 54&*n*, 223;
    deadly/as source of death, **5** 571, 577;
    death of, **17** 8–11, 223;
    devouring, **5** 264, 396, 548, 577, 658, 671, pl. XXXVIII*b*; **17** 219*n*; and birthgiving, **5** 658;
    differentiation from, **5** 624*n*;
    divine, **5** 371; **13** 448; **14** 352;
    divinities, birth of, **6** 201;
    doctor as, **7** 97–8;
    doctrine replaces, **17** 158;
    -dragon, **5** 379, 646; **6** 445; **18** 193, 234 (*see also* Tiamat);
    dragon: as evil symbol of, **9i** 157; as negative mother-imago, **5** 395;
    in dreams, **2** 838–9;
    dual/two, **5** 450*n*, 464–612; **7** 100; **9i** 93–7, 158; **13** 148, 153, 238; **15** 55; **16** 246; **18** 1492;

    of dying god, **11** 646;
    eighth as, **14** 579;
    of elements, **12** 430;
    embracing, **5** 682;
    entry into, **5** 441, 459, 549*n*;
    "of fair love," **11** 727;
    fantasy of oral impregnation, **4** 477;
    -father, Mercurius as, **13** 269*n*;
    and feeling function, **18** 186;
    feminine aspect of father-son, **14** 402;
    fertilization of, in act of sacrifice, **5** 332, 671;
    figurative, **9i** 156;
    figures, three, **18** 1653;
    first bearer of anima-image, *see* anima *s.v.* -image;
    fixation, **18** 633;
    foster-, and animals, *see* animal(s) *s.v.* mother;
    four, **13** 186;
    -friend, **7** 127, 129, 179–81;
    God as, **9i** 131; **11** 486; **13** 40;
    -goddess, **5** 303, 330*n*; **9i** 148, 297*n*; **11** 612; **13** 228*n*; **14** 744; boar-headed, **5** pl. IV*a*; cow-headed, **5** 351, pl. XXX*b*; Hittite, **14** 185*n*; son-lover of, **5** 466 (*see also* Mater *s.v. dea*);
    of the gods, **6** 141&*n*;
    helpful, **5** 546;
    hierosgamos with, **5** 411;
    higher, in Moses quaternio, **9ii** 360;
    and homosexuality, *see* homosexuality *s.v.*;
    -hood, sanctity of, **17** 292;
    idealization of, man's, **9i** 192&*n*;
    identification with, **5** 351, 431; **9i** 169;
    -image, **5** 271, 404, 646; **8** 720–1, 723; **9i** 155, 158, 191–3; **10** 64;
    -imago, *see* imago *s.v.*;
    incestuous longing for, figurative, **17** 144;

in India, **10** 997;
and infant's kicking, **5** 481;
instinct, *see below* maternal instinct
liberation from, **7** 393;
-libido, **5** 658;
longing for, **5** 312; **7** 260/476;
-love, **9i** 172; **18** 796;
loving and terrible, **9i** 158 (*see also sep. entry* Mother, Terrible);
lower and upper half, **5** 316;
masculine principle in, **5** 543;
maternal instinct, **9i** 167; hypertrophy of, **9i** 167–9, 172;
mating in, **5** 349, 620;
as matrix, **9i** 187; **16** 344;
"mother's son," **5** 392;
as murderess, **5** 369;
nature as, **5** 500, 568 (*see also* Mother *below s.v.* Nature);
negative aspects of, *see above* dark; deadly; devouring; dragon; murderess; *and below* pursuing; *and sep. entry below* Mother, Terrible;
nourishing, **4** 345–6; **5** 519, 522, 526n, 530n;
numen of, **5** 452;
Oedipus complex and, **4** 344–5;
oneness with, **5** 500, 640;
pampering, **8** 306;
personal, **9i** 156, 159, 188, 356;
as *prima materia*, **12** 425; **14** 15, 422;
primordial image of, **5** 373; **10** 64; **12** 26; **13** 147;
prototype of, **9i** 149;
pursuing, **5** 540;
of Quetzalcoatl, **13** 132;
racial, **5** 75;
re-entry into, **5** 351, 654 (*see also above* burial; entry);
regeneration in, **5** pl. XLII;
regression to, **5** 519; **7** 325; **9ii** 21; **17** 218, 280;
renewal through, **14** 399, 400;
resistance to, **9i** 170–1;

-sacrifice, **5** 659;
self expressed by, **9i** 315;
separation from, need for, **5** 351, 415, 461, 465, 473, 624n; **7** 314;
-ships, **10** 761, 793;
-sister-wife, **5** 607;
and son, *see separate entry below;*
-substitute, **7** 171; **17** 270;
of sulphur, **14** 140;
sun-woman as, **11** 711, 713, 743;
symbols, *see below;*
tie with, **5** 449n, 465, 522; **7** 171, 280;
and tree, *see* tree(s) *s.v.;*
of twin gods, **13** 130;
as the unconscious, **5** 508, 536, 580; **12** 94; **14** 500; **16** 344; collective, **5** 393; **12** 92;
union with, in death, **5** 398, 659;
unmarried, **4** 666; **9i** 311;
very old, **9i** 328;
violation of, **4** 478;
virgin as, **14** 57;
wife as substitute for, **7** 89–90, 316; **10** 64;
woman as, **17** 330;
-world, **12** 26–7; **14** 16;
world-, **5** 550; womb of, **5** *fig.* 40;
world created from, **5** 379, 658;
see also Mater; matriarchy; mère Lusine
mother, and son, **5** 272, 394, 569, 599; **9ii** 20–4; **12** 26; **14** 439, 609;
danger of mother's erotic aspect, **5** 662;
hierosgamos of, **14** 178, 412;
incest, **5** 332, 392, 450, 652; **12** 171, 435n, 436&n, 496; **13** 278; **14** 14, 402, 610; **16** 419, 529;
libido of son possessed by mother, **5** 329, 569;
marriage, **5** 357; **9ii** 22;
mother's betrayal of, **5** 375;

Characters/Themes
motif(s), **9i** 89, 260, 309; **16** 13–18;
of ascent/descent, *see* ascent;
betrayal of the hero, **5** 42;
biting, by animals, **12** 183, 186,
272, 273, *fig.* 118;
of boy, **12** 197, *fig.* 95;
of brothers, hostile, *see* brothers
s.v.;
of castration, **5** 681;
containment, **5** 351;
cross, *see* cross *s.v.* mandala;
Dioscuri, *see* Dioscuri *s.v.* dual
motif;
double quaternity, *see* quaternity;
drowning, **14** 360;
dual, **16** 16;
duplication, **9i** 608;
early Christian, *see* Christian;
of god's renewal, *see* god(s) *s.v.*
dying (*see also* rebirth);
harlequin, *see* Picasso
incorporation, **12** 440*n*;
investigation of, **16** 254;
kicking and stamping, **5** 538;
Loki, *see* Wagner;
lost and found/dying, rising
again, **5** 531 (*see also* rebirth);
"manning," **10** 698, 703;
of mother dragon, *see* mother;
murder of king, **14** 358;
mutilation, *see* mutilation;
mythological/myth-, *see* myth
s.v. motifs;
prostitute, *see* Picasso;
putting together, **12** 242*n*;
quaternity, *see* quaternity;
religious, **7** 250;
repetition of, **16** 13;
rotation, **12** 283;
spellbound spirit, *see* spirit;
365 steps, **5** 572, 577;
torture (alchemical), **12** 438*n*;
13 93, 439–49;
two hostile brothers, *see* devil
s.v. Christ;
union of opposites, **15** 213;

of violation, **13** 99;
wounding, **14** 24;
see also ANIMALS *passim*; archetype; assault; bath; child;
conflict; devouring; dismemberment; dream-; dwarf;
entwining; fairy; fairytales;
flaying; folklore; Frobenius, L.;
frontier; hero; hierosgamos;
incest; island; katabasis; mountain; myth(s); night sea
journey; rejection; rejuvenation; roundness; running
away; swallowing; sweating;
treasure; trinity; water; witch;
woman unknown
motility, **2** 26, 136;
speech, **2** 176
motion, *see* movement
motive(s)/motivation, **8** 697; **17**
214;
in case of simulated insanity, **1**
338;
characterological, **1** 220;
conscience and, **11** 86;
conscious, **7** 275; **17** 17*n*;
feeling-toned, and subconscious mechanisms, **1** 305;
psychological, **1** 320;
and psychotherapy, **18** 1391,
1396, 1402;
unconscious, **5** 37; **7** 12/421,
51, 94*n*; **17** 327, 331
motor: automatism, **1** 129, 146;
centres, hypnosis of, **1** 96;
excitation, **1** 126; **2** 116–17,
132, 136*n*, 176, 388, 882;
hyperactivity, **1** 219;
impulses, barring of perception
of, **1** 86;
perception, **2** 136;
phenomena: automatic, **1** 85;
in automatic writing, **1** 96;
suggestion and, **1** 82
mountain(s), **5** 634; **13** 17; **14** 621;
in alchemy, **12** *fig.* 142L,M; **13**
fig. B6; of adepts, **12** *fig.* 93; **13**
241*n*; burning, **12** 293, 298, *fig.*

465

mountain(s) (*cont.*):
94; *coniunctio* on, **12** 209; of knowledge/no differences, **12** 516&*n*; **14** 660*n*; Saturn and/Saturnine, **13** 274, 383; stone and, **9ii** 326&*n*; **13** 381*n*, 392; and tree, **13** 407;
as ascent, mystical/spiritual, **9i** 403&*n*; **9ii** 317;
association-chain, **3** 245–6;
Christ as, **9ii** 326; **13** 407;
Christ on, in *Interrogationes*, **9ii** 314; **12** 209;
-climber(s): example of, **4** 378; vision of hooded man after accident, **9i** 408;
in dreams: associations with, **3** 124–5; climbing motif in, **7** 366–7; **8** 164; **9i** 40, 334; **16** 303, 323–4; **17** 117–22; **18** 471;
five, **13** 311;
four, **12** 217; **13** 311, *fig.* 24;
heavenly, **13** 329;
and Golden Flower, **13** 33;
in midrash, **12** 545;
sickness, **18** 161, 164, 184, 186, 208; in neurosis, **16** 297, 303;
as symbol of self, **9i** 403*n*; **9ii** 356; **13** 407;
and tree, **13** 325, 407, 412;
Two, in Khidr legend, **9i** 252, 256;
world- (Meru), **9i** 691; **12** 139; **13** 381*n*
Mountain Chant Rite, **9i** 700
Mountain Lake (Pueblo Indian), **10** 138 (*cf.* also) 184; **11** 474
mourning, **8** 456
moustaches, on older women, **8** 780
mouth, **17** 217, 219;
etymological connections with fire and speech, **5** 233;
Freudian symbolism of, **2** 839;
re-entry into mother through, **5** 654;
significance of, in infancy and early childhood, **5** 228–9;
snake in, **5** 585–6, 677

movement(s)/motion:
TITLE: "The Circular Movement and the Centre," **13** 31–45;
in Americans, **10** 956;
automatic, *see* automatism *s.v.* motor;
circular, **13** 38–9, 102;
and energy, **8** 4;
as expressing unconscious, **8** 171;
forces of, **1** 67;
leftward and rightward, **9i** 564;
perpetual, see *perpetuum mobile*
Moyses, **13** 429
Mozarabic liturgy, *see* liturgy *s.v.*
Mozart, W. A., **17** 206
M'tu-ya-kitabu, **9i** 250
mudrā, **13** 334&*n*
Mueller, *see* Müller
Muenter, F., **9ii** 128;
Sinnbilder und Kunstvorstellungen der alten Christen, **9ii** 128*n*;
Der Stern der Weisen, **9ii** 128*n*
Muḥammad ibn Ishak al-Nadim, *see* ALCHEMICAL WRITERS: Nadim
Muḥammad ibn Jarir Abu-Jafar al-Tabari, *see* Tabari
Muḥammad ibn Umail, *see* ALCHEMICAL WRITERS: Senior
Muḥammed, *see* Mahomet
Muirhead, J. F., **13** 460*n*
mukti, **11** 958; **16** 219
mūladhāra, **9i** 679; **16** 560
mulier taceat in ecclesia, **18** 1684
Müller, Erdmann: "Über Moral Insanity," **1** 223*n*
Müller, Ernst: *Der Sohar und seine Lehre*, **14** 2*n*, 592*n*
Müller, E. K.: "The Influence of Psychic and Physiological Phenomena upon the Electrical Conductivity of the Human Body," **2** 1042
Müller, F. M., *see* Max-Müller
Müller, G. E. and A. Pilzecker, **3** 12;

467

music (*cont.*):
American, **10** 964;
atonal, **10** 430;
as compensation, **3** 344, 347;
in dream, **17** 275, 280;
"etheric," in Ufo, **10** 796, 799;
as gift, **17** 239;
and individuation, **14** 754;
organ, **7** 175, 181;
of the spheres, **5** 235;
Wagnerian, **3** 80*n*; **14** 754
musicality, **13** 143
musk, **13** 193, 215
mussel-shell, **9ii** 196
Mussolini, Arnaldo, **10** 420
Mussolini, Benito/the Duce, **10** 420;
17 284; **18** 279, 373, 1328, 1333,
1334
mustard seed, **13** 321
Mut, **9ii** 322
Muther, R.: *Geschichte der Malerei,* **5**
332*n*
Mutianus Rufus, **5** 148*n*
mutilation: motif, **5** 356*n*, 367*n*; **13**
401*n*;
numinous, **18** 823;
of the soul, evil as, **9ii** 85
mutism, simulated, **1** 342
Mutus liber, see ALCHEMICAL
WRITERS: Altus *s.v.*
Muyscas Indians, *see* American In-
dians: SOUTH *s.v.*
Myers, F.W.H., **1** 88, 100; **8** 371*n*,
382*n*, 571, 830*n*, 862; **18** 1144;
"Automatic Writing," **1** 91*n*;
"The Subliminal Conscious-
ness," **8** 356*n*
Mykerinos, *see* Men-kau-Re
Mylius, J. D., *see* ALCHEMICAL
WRITERS *s.v.*
myrtle, *see* TREES *s.v.*
mystagogue, **13** 106;
anima and animus as, **11** 48*n*;
Mercurius as, *see* Mercurius *s.v.*
The Mysteries, see Eranos Yearbooks
s.v.
"Mysteries of Saint John and the
Holy Virgin, **5** 479

mysterium, **12** 416;
alchemical, **13** 450;
altaris, **12** 490;
of *coniunctio/coniunctionis, see*
coniunctio s.v.;
fidei, see Mass *s.v.* transformation;
increatum, **12** 430*n*;
iniquitatis, **9i** 189, 295; **9ii** 78,
141; **12** 216, 470*n*; **18** 1555;
et magnale Dei, **13** 155;
magnum, **7** 369; **12** 13, 40*n*,
430*n*, 468, 516;
paschale, **16** 397;
tremendum, **18** 615
mystery(-ies), **5** 596; **9ii** 414; **11**
448; **13** (*p*63), 287; **14** 312;
ancient/antique, **9i** 21; **10** 13;
12 177*n*; **18** 246, 267;
Christian, **5** 656; **11** 448; **13**
194, 236; **16** 124; **18** 254; alchemical parallel to, **13** 137*n*,
236, 356;
cults, **9ii** 162; **16** 124, 133;
deification through, **5** 130;
divine, **13** 236;
Egyptian, *see* Egypt *s.v.*;
Gnostic, **10** 21; of Naassenes,
see Naassenes *s.v.*;
Greek, **6** 124*n*; **7** 384; **11** 448;
16 133; Roman, **15** 150 (*see also*
Dionysus; Eleusinian; Orphic;
Pythagorian; Samothrace);
of Isis, *see* Isis (*see also* Egyptian
s.v. mysteries);
Mithraic, *see* Mithraism;
nature, **13** 195;
neophytes veiled in, **5** 291*n*, pl.
IV*b*;
new forms of, **11** 206;
purpose of, **5** 644*n*; **18** 617;
of rebirth (alchemical), **13** 459;
religions, **5** 644*n*; **7** 172, 384,
393; **10** 22, 192; **11** 448; divine
hero in, **5** 274*n*; modern coun-
terparts of, **10** 977;
Sabazius, **5** 530; **12** 184;
serpent in, **5** pl. LXI*a* (*see also*

myth(s) *(cont.)*:

as collective dreams, **5** 28–9;
and collective unconscious, **7** 284; **8** 325; **15** 125; **18** 1 164;
comparative, **9i** 110; **9ii** 64; **12** 38; **16** 351;
concordance of, **8** 228;
Coptic, of Father-Creator, **5** 479;
of creation, *see* creation *s.v.*;
and creative force, **5** 198;
creative phallus in, **5** 183;
divine, **13** 331–2;
and dogma, **9ii** 278;
dragon in, *see* ANIMALS *s.v.*;
and dreams, *see* dream(s) *s.v.*;
Egyptian, *see* Egypt *s.v.*;
experienced, **9i** 261;
as explanations, **8** 71, 327; **9i** 7;
and fantasies, **13** 319;
fertility, **4** 494;
fire, **5** 247;
fire-making, **5** 248;
-formations, **7** 152;
gods in, **9ii** 274;
Great Mother in, **9i** 193;
Greek, *see* Greek mythology;
hero, *see* hero;
horse in, *see* ANIMALS: horse *s.v.*;
incest in, *see* incest *s.v.*;
Indian, *see* India *s.v.*;
-interpretation, **5** 611; **14** 170;
scientific, **6** 428;
king as carrier of, **14** 349;
language of, *see* language *s.v.*;
as libido transformation, **6** 355;
living and lived, **9i** 302;
lunar, **6** 325; **8** 330; **9i** 356;
matrix of, **5** 611; **11** 899;
as mental therapy, **18** 548;
modern, **10** 699; **15** 152;
as mother archetype, **9i** 187;
motifs, **3** 549, 563–5; **5** 42, 611;
6 281, 629, 746–7, 851; **7** 100–11; **8** 254, 325, 474, 554, 558, 589&*n*; **9i** 89, 260; **11** 557, 781, 945; **13** 11, 351–2, 393; **16** 17–18; **18** 80, 81, 522, 523;

universal, **13** 11, 352, 478;
and mythologizing factor, **18** 1 362;
nature-, **14** 170;
necessity and meaning of, **5** (*p*xxiv), 466, 659;
Negro, **18** 262;
night sea journey, *see* night sea journey;
Nordic, *see* Nordic myths;
and numinous experiences, **5** 223;
opposites in, **5** 581; **18** 1077;
of phoenix, *see* ANIMALS: phoenix;
Polynesian, *see* Polynesia;
and primitive consciousness, **9i** 264;
primordial images and, **11** 944; **12** 28;
as psychic phenomena, **9i** 7–8; **18** 783;
psychoanalysis and, **4** 457;
psychotherapeutic, **11** 287, 291, 292;
psychotherapist and, **3** 576;
and racial and national complexes, **5** 45;
rape theme, **5** 34&*n*;
rationalized substitutes for, **9i** 287;
rebirth, **5** 362, 374*n*;
reinterpretation of, **18** 1 665;
religious, **5** 343;
sacred, **13** 393;
sacrifice in, **5** 671;
Scandinavian, **18** 195;
and schizophrenia, *see* schizophrenia *s.v.*;
seasonal, **6** 325;
serpent in, *see* ANIMALS: serpent;
sexual symbolism in, **4** 63;
solar, *see* sun *s.v.*;
South African, **5** 367*n*;
steeds of, **5** 421;
symbols in, **5** 329;
as symbols that happened, **18**

N

Naaman, **14** 360&*n*

Naas/Naassene(s), **9ii** 117, 144, 310, 334; **12** 314, 550&*n*; **13** 278*n*; **14** 510*n*, 566, 570*n*, 626*n*, 726; **18** 1515, 1827;
   and Adam, *see* Adam *s.v.* Anthropos;
   demiurge, *see* demiurge *s.v.* Gnostic;
   and First Cause, **13** 278*n*;
   gnosis, **9i** 665;
   Jothor, **9ii** 328–9;
   mysteries, **13** 182; **14** 146;
   quaternity, **9ii** 42*n*, 361, 386;
   serpent, *see* ANIMALS: serpent *s.v.*;
   symbolism, **9i** 571; **9ii** 288–9; **11** 440; of creation, **9ii** 313, 326–8; paradise, four rivers of, *see* Paradise *s.v.* four rivers, Gnostic; of self, **9ii** 358;
   Trinity, *see* Trinity *s.v.*

Nabu, **13** 278

Näcke, P.: *Ueber Familienmord durch Geisteskranke,* J.'s review, **18** 918

Nadim, Ibn al-, *see* ALCHEMICAL WRITERS

nadir, **10** 771

Naef, M., **1** 17–18, 295;
   "Ein Fall von temporärer, totaler, teilweise retrograder Amnesie," **1** 295*n*

Näf, Hans, evidence experiment in trial of, **2** 1357–88

Nagaga-uer, **5** 389

naga stones, **13** 461

Nagel, A.: "Der chinesische Küchengott (Tsau-kyun)," **5** 663*n*

Nagel, Hildegard, **13** (*p*191); **18** (*p*645*n*, *p*654*n*)

Nägeli, Prof. (Freiburg i. B.), **18** 702

Nag Hamadi, Upper Egypt, **18** (*p*671*n*)

Nagy, P.: tr. into Hungarian of J.'s *On the Psychology of the Unconscious,*

J.'s foreword, **18** 1107–9

Nahlowsky, J. W., **6** 678;
   Das Gefühlsleben in seinen wesentlichsten Erscheinungen und Beziehungen, **6** 678*n*, 723*n*

nailing to the cross, **5** 398, 400

naïve poetry, *see* Schiller *s.v.*

Nakassä (inverted tree), **13** 462

naked(ness), **13** 81;
   Freud's patient and, **3** 64;
   snake, *see* ANIMALS: serpent *s.v.*

Namaquas (South Africa), **5** 530*n*

namazu, **18** 67*n*

name(s): compulsion of the, **8** 827*n*;
   and facts, **8** 223;
   of God, four letter, **16** 497*n*, 533*n* (*see also* tetragrammaton);
   and magical compulsion, **10** 809;
   magical power of, **5** 201, 274;
   multiplicity of, **11** 806;
   new, **9i** 231;
   pagan, of days of week, **13** 301;
   and profession, **8** 827*n*;
   "right" and "true," **8** 735;
   secret, **5** 599; **7** 393; **13** 436;
   and soul, **8** 665; **11** 153;
   spellbinding, **13** 438;
   spirit has no proper, **11** 276*n*;
   and thing, **9ii** 60;
   of tribes, **10** 280;
   true, libido-symbol, **5** 455

naming: act of, **5** 274;
   and touching, symptom of, **3** 3*n*, 54

Nancy school, **3** 496; **7** 2, 4, 413; *see also* Bernheim

Nandi Tribe (Kenya), **5** 536; **11** 371

Nanni, G., **9ii** 159*n*

naphtha, **9ii** 290&*n*

Naples, **5** 60, (*p*451); *see also* Farnese

Napoleon I, Bonaparte, **3** 267; **6** 116; **7** 279, 388; **8** 707; **10** 907; **17** 301; **18** 509

Napoleon III, **18** 715

narcissism, **10** 204, 340; **11** 770; **15** 102;
> pathological, **14** 709

narcolepsy, **1** 1, 121
narcotics, **6** 573; **14** 680
narrow-mindedness, **3** 158
narwhal, *see* ANIMALS *s.v.*
nasal feeding, **7** 270
Natal: medicine woman, **5** 452*n*
natalitia, **8** 934&*n*
Natchez Indians, *see* American Indians: NORTH
Nathan, Rabbi: *Abot de Rabbi Nathan,* **9ii** 175*n*
nation(s): "aunt of," **10** 931;
> changes in life of, **8** 594;
> in collective misery, **18** 1330;
> comity of, **7** 237;
> fate of, and individual psyche, **9i** 97;
> as functions of mankind, **10** 905, 922;
> identification with, **10** 910, 923;
> and individual, **7** (*p*4), 150; **10** 45;
> as man's world, **7** 338;
> personified, **10** 921;
> psychology of, **7** (*p*4); **18** 1316

National Industrial Recovery Act (U.S.A.), **18** 1327*n*
National Investigations Committee on Aerial Phenomena (NICAP), **18** (*p*626*n*);
> J.'s statement to, **18** 1445–6

nationalism, **18** 1306;
> fear of, **10** 517

National Recovery Administration (U.S.A.), **18** 1327
National Socialism/Nazism, **10** 354, 474, 476, 478, 559, 818, 1019, 1021, 1023, 1034; **11** 275, 770, 778; **16** 20; **18** 373, 689, 1324, 1366, 1610;
> Jews and, **10** 478;
> and Luther, **9ii** 159;
> Wotan and, **9i** 453; **10** 385, 399;

see also swastika
Nativity, *see* Christ *s.v.* birth
Natorp, P.: *Einleitung in die Psychologie nach kritischer Methode,* **6** 700*n*
natura abscondita, **11** 152*n*; **12** 447; **13** 126; **14** 114
natural: consciousness, **13** 299;
> elixir, **13** 170;
> laws, *see* law(s) *s.v.*;
> light, *see* *lumen naturae;*
> man, *see* man *s.v.*;
> phenomena, source of names for, **5** 275;
> philosophy, *see* philosophy *s.v.*;
> psyche, **13** 286;
> science, *see* science *s.v.*;
> secrets, **13** 395;
> selection, **4** 234;
> spirit, *see* spirit (1) *s.v.*;
> and spiritual, **8** 98;
> transformation mystery, **13** 194;
> wisdom, *see* wisdom *s.v.*

naturalism, **6** 356–7
naturalness, **13** 229
nature/Nature (1) (phenomena of the external world; these personified; vital force etc.), **7** 32, 50, 114, 162, (*p*124), 206, 209, 257, 273, 428–9; **11** 531; **12** 374, 547; **13** 87, 196, 229, 245; **16** 411–16; **18** 361, 597;
> ambivalent forces of, **5** 165;
> aristocratic, **7** 198, 236; **11** 537; **17** 343, 345;
> in Böhme, **9i** 534;
> changing of the, **9ii** 256;
> Christianity and, **5** 111–12; **9ii** 267, 270; **11** 261;
> classical feeling for, **5** 109–10; **12** 40;
> composite/discriminated, **12** 374;
> conquers nature, **12** 472 (*see also* ALCHEMICAL WRITERS: Democritus *s.v.* axiom on nature);

nature (*cont.*):
conquest of, **18** 598;
and conscious values, **7** 347;
converges in man, **13** 125;
and culture, *see* culture *s.v.*;
-daemon, **7** 217;
darkness of, **13** 197;
de-deification of, **18** 1364, 1380;
deity, **13** 247; dark, **13** 299;
Dea Natura, **13** 130 (*see also* god(s) *s.v.* nature);
Deity garbed as, **9i** 210;
demands death, **18** 631;
Democritus (pseudo-) on, *see* ALCHEMICAL WRITERS *s.v.*;
demonism of, **18** 1365;
de-psychization of, **18** 1360, 1364, 1366, 1368;
and differentiation, **7** 198;
egg of, **13** 267;
esoteric, **11** 537; **17** 345;
eternal, **12** 214;
European man and, **11** 868;
fire of, **9i** 536;
forces of, **13** 163;
formal factor in, **8** 946;
four, **13** 101, 125 (*see also* elements, four, in alchemy);
gods, *see* god(s) *s.v.; and see above* deity;
as guide in psychotherapy, **16** 81;
hermaphrodite of, **14** 472, 476;
hero's closeness to, **5** 500;
hidden, **11** 152*n*, 154, 161*n*;
improvement of, **9ii** 220;
instinct and, **8** 750;
invisible body of, **13** 148;
language of, **5** 568, 624*n*;
laws of, **7** 95;
of light/light of, *see* light *s.v.; lumen naturae;*
man and, **5** 113; **10** 134; **18** 597; his communication with, **18** 585; his identity with, **11** 375&*n*;
maternal significance, **5** 568,

624*n*;
of Mercurius, *see* Mercurius *s.v.*;
metaphysical explanation of, **3** 466;
mind and, **16** 120;
monarchy of, **13** 200;
Mother Nature/Mater Natura, **5** 500; **7** 428; **9i** 172, 595*n*; **12** 214; **13** 148, 153, 184;
mystery, **13** 195;
nymphididic, **13** 214;
observation of, in primitives, **11** 800;
oneness with, **11** 201;
perfected by the art, **11** 310;
philosophy, Hellenistic, *see* philosophy *s.v.* nature;
Platonic, **13** 382;
poet and, **6** 213, 215–17;
principle of, **12** 141, 163*n*;
processes of, as symbols of Psyche, **9i** 7;
qualities of, **16** 510, 515;
and reason, **8** 739;
reflection of contents of unconscious, **5** 170*n*;
rejoices in nature, *see* ALCHEMICAL WRITERS: Democritus *s.v.* axiom on nature);
religious attitudes to, **5** 110–13;
roots of eternal, **11** 246;
separation of, **13** 198;
signs of, **7** 162;
-spirit, **18** 1475;
spirit and, **8** 678; **9i** 385, 389; **11** 261; **12** 547; conflict of, **8** 680; East and West and, **8** 682; as opposites, **8** 96;
spiritual *vs.* physical, **5** 104;
symbolism of, in antiquity, **5** 24;
terror of, **8** 331;
transference of libido to, **5** 518;
two, **13** 370;
two powers of, **9ii** 187;
unchained power of, **5** 89&*n*;

and unconscious, **10** 34;
union of, in alchemy, **13** 198;
14 654, 664*n*;
unity of, **8** 865;
the West and, **8** 682;
wisdom of, **13** 155;
womb of, as maternal womb, **3** 619;
workings of, **8** 864;
worship of, **5** 109–11, 118; **13** 198 (see also *lumen naturae; natura abscondita; sensus naturae*)
nature (2) (essential quality of an object): Divine, **11** 154; and Trinity, **11** 289;
feminine/maternal, of tree, **13** 419;
individual, of Christ's disciples, **9ii** 331
nature (3) (human/man's): collective, man's, *see* man *s.v.* collective;
collective, of self, **13** 287;
human, *see* human *s.v.*;
of man, *see* man *s.v.*;
man's instinctual, *see* animal(s), instinct/nature *s.v.* man;
one's own, **13** 70; reversal of, **13** 24;
other side of our, *see* other *s.v.* side
Naumann, H. and I.: *Isländische Volksmärchen,* **16** 425*n*
Naumburg, **7** 37
Naunet, goddess, **5** 359
nausea, **4** 461, 462, 464, 513
Navahos/Navajos, *see* American Indians: NORTH
navel: point of cleavage, **5** 449;
of Vishnu, **5** 449, pl. XLVI*a*
Nazareth, **12** 126
Nazari, G. B., *see* ALCHEMICAL WRITERS *s.v.*
Nazari, O., **5** 188*n*
Nazis, *see* National Socialism
Neale, J. M.: *Collected Hymns, Sequences and Carols,* **13** 384*n*, 391*n*
Neanderthalensis, **18** 486
Near East: Cybele cults, *see* Rhea *s.v.*;

sun-worship in, **5** 165;
symbolism of dying god in, **18** 550
Nebit Hotpet (Jusas), **5** 408
Nebo, **14** 384&*n*
Nebuchadnezzar, **11** 173; **13** 14;
dream/vision of, **3** 450; **5** 4; **8** 163, 484, 495, 496, 559, *frontispiece;* **12** 449; **13** 350*n*, 458; **14** 626*n*; **18** 245–6; tree in, **3** 450; **8** 484, 559, *frontispiece;* **13** 350*n*, 408, 458
nebulae, **9i** 31
necessity, **7** 28/439, 80, 240, 258, 429, 438;
causal, **17** 293;
in Church Fathers, **11** 271;
inner, **7** 369, 401; instinct as, **8** 265;
and moral decision, **17** 299;
psychological, **7** 241/462;
therapeutic, **7** 373;
vital, **4** 679
necrocomic/*necrocomica* (Paracelsus), **13** 174&*n*
necrolica (Paracelsus), **13** 211*n*
Necrolii (Paracelsus), **13** 211&*n*
necromancy, **9ii** 415; **13** 154; *see also* magic
nectar, **5** 198
Needham, J., **9i** 120*n*;
Science and Civilization in China, **9i** 120*n*
needlepricks, *see* pricks
needs, of dreamer, **7** 169
nefesh (Cabbalist), **14** 592&*n*
negation, world- (Schopenhauer), **6** 322
negative: aspect of parental imagos, **7** 296;
attitude, **7** 195;
side, *see* other *s.v.* side;
values, **7** 71–2
negativism, **1** 346; **3** 16–17; **18** 874;
catatonic/schizophrenic, **1** 279; **3** 157, 179, 425, 427; Bleuler's theory of, *see* Bleuler *s.v.*;
causes/origin of, **3** 17, 428;

Nerval, Gérard de (pseudonym of Labrunie): *Aurelia,* **5** 83*n*; **7** 121; **18** 1279;
  J.'s lecture on, **18** 1748
nerve-endings: and conscious image, **8** 745;
  stimulation of, **8** 607
nerve system of yoga, **9i** 81
nervous disorders/breakdown, **7** 1/409, 425;
  TITLE: "On the Psychoanalytic Treatment of Nervous Disorders," **18** 1041–54;
  child's, **17** 107;
  in the forties, **8** 783;
  hysterical and psychasthenic, **3** 418;
  sexual origin of, **17** 99;
  see also neurasthenia; neurosis
nervousness, **13** 15, 55;
  psychic origin of, **7** 1/409, 11/420
nervous shock, theory of, **7** 8/417
nervous system: of analyst, **18** 356;
  ego's ignorance of, **8** 613;
  emotional processes and, **8** 642;
  and psyche, **8** 234, 607, 729;
  psychopathic disposition of, **1** 136
nervous temperament, **5** (*p*449)
Nessus shirt, **9i** 221
nest, **4** 280, 665, 728
Nestle, E.: "Der süsse Geruch als Erweis des Geistes," **14** 701*n*
Nestorius/Nestorian Church, **6** 34; **14** 237
net of Hephaestus, **5** 364*n*
Netherlands/Holland, **10** 908, 975; **15** 90; **18** 1276;
  Society for Psychotherapy, **10** 1048, 1055
neti neti, **9i** 597
nettles, in Paracelsan medicine, **13** 193, 194, 216
Neue Preussische Zeitung, **18** 702
Neue Zürcher Zeitung, **4** 197&*n*; J.'s

letters in, **18** (*p*427*n*)
Neumann, Erich, **5** 3; **18** 1134, 1160, 1250;
  Amor and Psyche, commentary on Apuleius, **13** 453; **18** 1510;
  The Great Mother, **5** 3*n*; **9i** 312*n*; **9ii** 178*n*;
  The Origins and History of Consciousness, **5** 3; **6** 445*n*; **9i** 487*n*; **9ii** 230*n*, 286*n*; **11** 448*n*; **14** 129*n*, 359*n*; **18** 1134*n*; J.'s foreword, **18** 1234–7;
  Tiefenpsychologie und Neue Ethik/Depth Psychology and a New Ethic, **9i** 595*n*; J.'s foreword, **18** 1408–20;
  Umkreisung der Mitte, **5** 3*n*
Neumann, Karl Eugen: *Die Reden Gotamo Buddhos,* J.'s comment on, **18** (*p*697*n*), 1576
Neumann, T., *see* Therese of Konnersreuth
neuralgia, **18** 884
neurasthenia, **1** 1–2, 5, 29, 31, 33; **3** 433, 471; **10** 248; *see also* nervous disorders; neurosis
neurology(-ists), and psychology/psychotherapy, **3** 470; **10** 1056; **11** 489–90; **18** 799, 922
  TITLE: "The Significance of Freud's Theory for Neurology and Psychiatry," **18** 922
neuropathy, **1** 29
neurosis/psychoneurosis(-es), **6** 970; **7** 41, 72, 192, 199, 218/450, 252, 348, 397, 431; **8** 208, 372, 480–1, 526, 685, 702, 712, 763, 808; **9i** 83, 97–8, 139, 190, 259, 267, 493, 495, 521; **9ii** 40, 282; **10** 72, 285, 337–8; **11** 26, 79, 542, 784; **12** 40; **13** 5, 12, 14, 16, 51, 66, 463; **14** 308, 705, 750; **15** 56–7, 61, 106; **16** 46, 131, 134, 208; **17** 130, 172, 181, 191, 200, 316, 343; **18** 43, 797;
  TITLES: "The Aetiology of Neurosis," **4** 353–406; "A Case of Neurosis in a Child," **4**

neurosis (*cont.*):

458–522; "Neurosis and Aetiological Factors in Childhood," **4** 294–313; "Psychoanalysis and Neurosis," **4** 557–75; and *abaissement*, **3** 509, 511, 515–17; **17** 204;

acceptance of, **16** 11, 392;

adaptation and, *see* adaptation *s.v.*;

Adler's theory of, *see* Adler, A. *s.v.*;

aetiology of, **9i** 159; **16** 53, 306; in childhood, **2** 1008; **4** 303, 354; **17** 25, 201; **18** 1024–5 (*see also below* childhood trauma); false, **17** 97; psychogenic, **3** 496, 505–6; **11** 15, 489–91; **16** 49, 66; **18** 903 (*see also below* causes);

analysis and, *see below* psychoanalysis;

and anima concept, **9i** 115;

anxiety, *see* anxiety *s.v.*;

archetypes in, **9i** 98;

artistic creation and, **15** 100, 155–6, 208*n*; **17** 206;

association experiment and, *see* association experiment *s.v.*;

and attitude to instinct, **5** 199;

autoeroticism and, **5** 37;

and Catholic Church, *see* Church, Catholic *s.v.*;

causes of, **5** (*p*xxvii); **8** 255; in the present, **10** 363; **11** 517 (*see also above* aetiology);

of childhood/infantile, **4** 259, 354; **9i** 159, 161; **10** 62; **17** (*p*5), 141, 212, 228; and parents, **16** 420*n*; **17** 80&*n*, 84, 99, 106–7, 133, 179, 217–18, 258–9; **18** 296, 840; psychology of, **17** 201, 212, 215; therapy of, **17** 179;

and childhood trauma, **4** 205, 353, 559; **7** 10/419, 15/424; **16** 33; **17** 201 (*see also above* aetiology *s.v.* in childhood);

and childishness/infantilism, **4** 312; **7** 27/438, 117; **10** 343, 345–8;

"choice of," **6** 929–30;

and civilization, **7** 16;

classification/diagnosis of, **16** 195–7; **17** 203;

climacteric, **4** 703;

compensation in, **7** 187; disturbance of, **6** 695; **10** 448; **15** 152;

complex and, **2** 665, 1351–4; **7** 54; **8** 255, 590, 710; **11** 37; **16** 179; **18** 832;

compulsion, *see* compulsion *s.v.*;

as conflict, **3** 516; **7** 16; **18** 662, 664;

and conscious attitude, **16** 26, 53;

and conscious mind, **8** 134;

defence against inner voice, **17** 313;

definition, **18** 382;

and disintegration of ideas, **3** 546;

and dissociation, *see* dissociation *s.v.*;

and dreams: mythological parallels in, **9i** 136; at onset of neurosis, **5** 78, 585; **16** 296; therapy of, **9i** 299; **13** 90; **16** 294, 305–6;

dual mother in, **9i** 96;

and endocrine disorder, **10** 1063; **11** 14;

energic viewpoint, **4** 566;

and erotic conflict, **7** 14–15, 16/422–4, 27;

extraverted type, **6** 565–6, 573, 587;

falsification of reality in, **5** 200;

and family milieu, *see* family *s.v.* milieu and neurosis;

and fantasies, *see* fantasy *s.v.*;

Freud's theory of, *see* Freud *s.v.*;

and functions, **5** 26*n*;

a humiliating defeat, **11** 12;
and identification with social role, **7** 307;
individualistic nature of, **17** 203;
and inner disunity, **7** 206;
instinct and, *see* instinct *s.v.*;
in introverted woman, **6** 642–3;
Janet's view, **4** 296;
with latent psychosis, **3** 517–18, 520, 546, 558;
and libido: displacement, **4** 275; introversion, **4** 277, 377; **5** 193; theory, **4** 200, 254;
loss of, **10** 355;
masculine, **13** 455;
in maturity, **7** 88, 114; **16** 75;
moment of outbreak, **4** 563; **8** 207;
moral attitude and, **8** 685; **17** 182; **18** 1412;
moral suffering in, **11** 794;
and need for independence, **5** 461;
as negative aspect of relationship, **2** 1010, 1012;
as new name for devil, **10** 309, 311, 331;
no uniform direction of life in, **4** 623, 634;
obsessional, *see* obsession *s.v.* neurosis;
and parental influence, *see* parents *s.v.* influence of, and neurosis;
personal, **16** 248;
predisposition and environment, **4** 209, 213; **5** 199;
and problem of our time/as social phenomena, **7** 18/430, 438; **9i** 98; **15** 69; **16** 83;
projection and, **5** 507; **8** 517;
and prospective explanation, **4** 409;
and psychization of instinct, **8** 255;
psychoanalysis and, **4** 412–16,

527–8; **7** 499, 501; **16** 24, 282;
psychology of, **8** 383; **18** 799, 839, 840, 923;
in puberty, **12** 324;
reaction of whole man, **10** 1071; **11** 450; **16** 190; **18** 839;
reaction-times in, **2** 994;
reality of, **11** 17;
reason for, **18** 627;
and regression, **7** 497;
and religion, **11** 167, 514, 518; **16** 99, 249;
religious figures in, **5** 95*n*;
repression and, **10** 646; **11** 129; **17** 204;
and retardation of affective development, **4** 296;
and schizophrenia, compared, **3** 506, 559; **17** 207;
self-deception and, **11** 457;
as self-division/disunion, **7** 18/430; **8** 61; **11** 522;
seriousness of, **16** 37;
sexual theory of, **4** 2, 216; **7** 33, 422; **11** 784; **13** 467; **16** 48, 66; **18** 281, 922, 947, 1067–8;
shock, **1** 307; **7** 15*n* (*see also below* traumatic);
splitting of personality in, **5** 683; **7** 22; **8** 61; **11** 522;
as state of possession, **16** 196;
structure of, **18** 1504;
symbolic value of, **18** 1480;
teleologically oriented, **7** 54;
a *terra incognita*, **18** 833;
and toxins, **3** 496;
and transference, **7** 206; **14** 751; **16** 41, 357&*n*, 446, 471, 533; **18** 1151;
as transitory phase, **18** 667;
trauma theory of, *see* Freud *s.vv.* neurosis theory; sexual trauma theory;
traumatic, **1** 281, 320; **16** 255, 260–1; **17** 176;
treatment/therapy of, **7** 236/496–8; **8** 184; **9i** 270; **9ii** 297; **12** 4; and equivalence princi-

Nietzsche (*cont.*):

> *Sprach Zarathustra*," **3** 171*n*; and Kerner, parallel, **1** 140–2, 180–3; **18** 455–6; "higher" man in, **8** 162; and seven devils, **13** 163&*n*; and Superman, **7** 36; **8** 359; **12** 406–7, 559; **13** 163; **14** 330; **18** 1375; "ugliest man," **6** 208, 322, 706, 829; **8** 162; **9ii** 410; **10** 271; **12** 201; **14** 330; vision of rope-dancer/tight-rope walker, **7** 36; **9i** 217; **12** 184; —, buffoon in, **15** 214; vision of shepherd and snake, **5** 585; **12** 184, 201; **14** 483*n*; "To the Unknown God," **10** 379; **11** 44*n*; "The Use and Abuse of History," **6** 232*n*;

see also Bernoulli, C. A.; Förster-Nietzsche, E.

Nigeria (Yoruba myth), **5** 392*n*

night, **14** 219;
> club, **12** 227;
> day and, rhythm of, **13** 300;
> -fear, *see* fear *s.v.*;
> -heron, *see* ANIMALS *s.v.*;
> terrors of, **7** 325; **17** 213–14;
> world, **15** 149; of fantasy, **7** 325

nightmare(s), **7** 44; **8** 535; **9i** 157; **10** 62; **12** 38, 284; **13** 180; **15** 161;
> and the devil, **5** 421;
> of earthquake, **17** 35;
> etymology and "mare," **5** 370;
> Hecate and, **5** 577;
> lamia as, **5** 369–70;
> Nietzsche's, **10** 382;
> "Stempe" in, **5** 370*n*

The Night My Number Came Up (film), **8** 983*n*

night sea imprisonment, **5** 308, 374; "three days" as, **5** 512

night sea journey, **5** 308, 484, 541, 555, 577; **8** 326; **9ii** 173; **11** 348; **12** *figs.* 69, 170, 171, 172; **14** 262,

658;
> death as, **5** 319;
> as descent into unconscious/descensus ad inferos, **8** 68–9; **12** 436; **16** 455&*n*;
> in Egyptian mythology, **5** 349, 362;
> Frobenius on, *see* Frobenius *s.v.*;
> *see also* ANIMALS: whale *s.v.*; *nekyia*; night sea imprisonment

Nigidius Figulus, Publius, astronomer, **9ii** 212&*n*

nigredo, see COLOURS *s.v.*

Nikephorus Blemmides, *see* ALCHEMICAL WRITERS *s.v.*

Niklaus von der Flüe, *see* Brother Klaus

Nikotheos/Nikotheus, **12** 456*n*, 456(6), 458; **13** 101

Nile, **9i** 604*n*; **10** 629; **13** 132; **14** 287, 297, 309; **18** 264;
> water of, **13** 97; **14** 359, 717;
> *see also* ALCHEMICAL WRITERS: Ostanes *s.v.* Nile stone

Nilus, St., **12** 521;
> *Vita*, **12** 521*n*

nimbus, *see* halo

Nimrod, **11** 176*n*

Nina (Babylonian), fish offerings to, **9ii** 186

Ninck, M., **9i** 446*n*; **10** 392–4;
> *Götter und Jenseitsglauben der Germanen*, **13** 461*n*;
> *Wodan und germanischer Schicksalsglaube*, **9i** 446*n*; **10** 392*n*; **11** 29*n*, 44*n*

nine, *see* NUMBERS *s.v.*

Niobe, **14** 91–2

Nippur, **9ii** 190

nirdvandva, **6** 327, 371; **7** 367; **9i** 76, 597; **9ii** 298; **11** 435; **13** 15; **14** 66, 296, 711; **18** 1417;
> as self, **18** 1628

nirmānakāya, **11** 790

nirvāna, **11** 800, 879; **18** 1507

Nissl, F., **1** 226, 279;
> "Hysterische Symptome bei

einfachen Seelenstörungen," **1** 279*n*

Nit/Neith, **5** 358

nivis, **13** 255*n*

nixie(s), **8** 335; **9i** 52–4, 406, 677; **13** 215, 225; **16** 538*n*;
  and anima, *see* anima *s.v.*;
  and water-sprite, **9i** 311

njom, **8** 125

Noah, **11** 577, 671; **13** 414; **14** 392, 555, 571, 607;
  Ark, **5** *fig.* 21; **9i** 428*n*, 624*n*; **14** 264; dream of, **17** 32;
  and Deluge/Flood, **5** 311; **11** 653, 669; **14** 264, 555, 607; **16** 472*n*;
  Japhet, son of, **5** 171*n*;
  and Utnapishtim, **5** 293;
  see also ANIMALS: dove, raven; Deluge

nodes, **9i** 550; **9ii** 399

Nodfyr/Niedfyr, **5** 212&*n*

noises: animal, **1** 216, 217;
  hallucinatory, **1** 268;
  see also voices

Nola, Church of St. Felix, **11** 431*n*

nome, **13** 360*n*

nomenclature: antinomian, **13** 266;
  of egg, **13** 109*n*;
  symbolic, **13** 355

nominalism(-ists) (in medieval philosophy), **6** 40, 43, 73, 75;
  classical, **6** 40, 49–50;
  and extraversion, **6** 508;
  medieval, **6** 69–73;
  and object, **6** 75;
  and realism, **3** 419; **6** 40, 50, 54, 56–9, 68–72, 74, 76, 473, 540; **7** 80; **9i** 149; **13** 378; and extraversion, introversion, **6** 508–9; as opposites, **7** 80

non-action, **13** 20&*n*, 38

nonad (Egyptian), **9i** 242*n*

Nonconformists, **18** 656

non-differentiation, **7** 329, 372; **9i** 290; **13** 66; *see also* Lévy-Bruhl *s.v. participation mystique*

non-duality, **11** 881

non-ego, *see* ego *s.v.*

non-existence, yearning for, **5** 553

non-existing *(asat),* **13** 267*n*

non-identification, **16** 469

non-recognition, **9i** 290

non-resistance, **7** 395

nonsense, meaning of and attitude to, **11** 26

non-values, **7** 395

noonday, **8** 665;
  of life, *see* life, stages of *s.v.*

noöpsyche, **3** 33, 35

Nootka Indians, *see* American Indians: NORTH

Nordau, M. S., **2** 132*n*;
  on genius, **1** 175&*n*;
  WORKS:
    Conventional Lies of Civilization, **1** 175*n*;
    Degeneration, **1** 175*n*

Norden, E.: *Die Geburt des Kindes,* **5** 119*n*; **11** 178*n*

Nordic myth(s), **15** 151;
  of creation, **5** 367;
  of hero, **17** 298;
  see also Odin

normal(ity), **7** 236, 369, 464*n*;
  of analyst, **16** 544–5;
  consciousness, **17** 102;
  definition/concept of, **7** 80; **10** 477, 572; **16** 544–5;
  a fiction, **17** 343;
  and latent psychosis, **7** 192;
  and neurosis, closeness of, **18** 575;
  person/people, **7** 89, 206, 228, 508; **16** 161, 163; mental and moral conflicts of, **18** 1388;
  need for symbol, **5** 342;
  state, and dreaminess, *see* dreaminess *s.v.* pathological

normalization, **11** 539; **16** 152

Normans, **10** 1001

Norns, **5** 371; **9i** 157

North, the: significance of, **9ii** 156–7, 190–2;
  and south, as opposites, **12** 192

northern lights, **13** 256

North Star, **9ii** 206; **12** 265

Norton, Samuel, *see* ALCHEMICAL WRITERS *s.v.*

Norton, Thomas, *see* ALCHEMICAL WRITERS *s.v.*

Norwegian riddle, **5** 327

nose-rubbing, **5** 217

Nostoc/Nostoch (Paracelsus), **12** 244; **13** 190&*n*, 193

Nostradamus/Nostredame, Michel, **9ii** 151–7, 159, 160, 192, 193;
"The Prophecies of Nostradamus," **9ii** 150–61;
Vrayes Centuries et Prophéties de Maistre Michel Nostredame/The Complete Prophesies of Nostradamus, tr. and ed. H. C. Roberts, **9ii** 151*nn*; **10** (*p*179)

"Note factory," *see* association-chains *s.v.*

nothing (Lao-tzu), **8** 919, 920

"nothing-but," **7** 400; **8** 711; **9i** 290; **10** 35, 362; **11** 379, 777, 800, 857; **12** 11*n*, 120, 160, 327; **16** 98&*n*, 360; **17** 157, 302;
TITLE: "The 'Nothing but' Daughter," **9i** 182–3;
dream as, **10** 301;
Freud and, **10** 7, 347, 365, 658; **11** 843; **18** 633;
James on, **12** 11*n*;
neurosis and, **10** 357;
people as, **18** 627;
principle of, **3** 423;
psychology, **4** 668;
and reductive theory, **7** 67, 471;
and religion, **9ii** 279;
type of thinking, **6** 315, 593, 600, 867

nothingness, God as, **11** 893

Notker Balbulus, **12** 438*n*;
Hymnus in die Pentecostes, **16** 399*n*

not-knowing, dark abyss of, **13** 219

Notre Dame (Paris), **9i** 458; **10** 176;
Déesse Raison in, *see* Reason, Goddess of

nouns, **2** 475–80, 483–6, 585, 587–92, 594–8;
adjectives as reactions to, **2** 48–51;
as reactions, **2** 48, 56, 59–61, 594–8;
verb relationships, **2** 58–60, 64

nourishing: earth-mother, *see* Mother *s.v.* Earth;
fruits, **13** 350

Nous/nous/*νοῦς,* **6** 347; **9i** 193, 393, 545, 554, 560–61*nn*; **9ii** 41; **11** 358, 628; **12** 433, 456*nnn*; **13** 96, 137, 344; **14** 117, 161, 261, 311, 327, 348, 548, 717; **16** 456;
as Anthropos, **12** 410;
Christ as, *see* Christ *s.v.* Logos/Nous;
as daemon, **12** 410;
descent of, to Physis, **5** 113; **9ii** 368; **11** 160*n*, 312; **12** 410, 412–13, 436, 438, 440, 447;
female, **13** 427;
Gnostic, **11** 276, 380 (*see also* ANIMALS: serpent *s.v.* in Gnosticism, Nous as);
as hermaphrodite, **12** 436*n*, 447;
Hermes as, **11** 421;
krater filled with, **9ii** 299*n*; **12** 409;
liberation of, **12** 452;
and Mercurius, *see* Mercurius *s.v.*;
opposition with sex, **13** 344;
and physis, *coniunctio,* see *coniunctio s.v.*;
as redeemer, **11** 160*n*;
serpent as, *see* ANIMALS *s.v.*;
as tincture/dyestuff, **12** 409;
unconscious, **9ii** 315*n*;
as uroboros, **12** 447;
see also Logos; pneuma

novels, **15** 140, 142;
"psychological," **15** 136–7;
and sex, **10** 213

novelty, mania for, **17** 251

"Novi luminis chemici Tractatus"/

NUMBERS, SPECIFIC

294, 574; **16** 525&*nn*;
as allegory of Christ ("denarius"), **16** 525*n*;
Commandments, **10** 830; **11**
581, 599; **13** 230;
concentric circles, **14** 574&*n*;
perfect number, **12** *fig.* 117; **16**
525*n*;
as symbol of unity, **10** 692;
"denarius," **14** 294; **16** 525&*n*,
526
eleven, **10** 692
twelve, **12** 287*n*; **14** 158*n*;
and three, **9i** 552;
alchemical stages, **12** 340, *fig.*
122;
dorje, **12** 139*n*;
"fatherly, motherly" angels, *see*
angel(s) *s.v.*;
Monads, **12** 138, 139*n*;
in patient's pictures, **9i** 545,

546, 548, 588, Pictures 3, 8;
as time symbol, **9i** 433, 552;
and zodiac, *see* zodiac, twelve
signs of
thirteen, **18** 587–8
fourteen: *Kas*, **14** 351&*n*
fifteen: steps and ladders, **12** 80; **13**
86 (III, i, 2)
sixteen, **12** 313; **14** 634, pl. 3
twenty-two, **12** 313
twenty-four: eyes, **10** 766
thirty, **10** 766
thirty-two, **12** 307, 313;
symbolism of, **12** 313
forty: age of, **8** 773, 783 (*see also* life,
stages of);
in alchemy, **14** 77&*n*, 494, 729
sixty-four, **14** 636
one hundred: pulses, **13** 434
"ten thousand things," **13** 301

*　　*

Numbers, *see* BIBLE: O.T. *s.v.*
numen/*numen*, **8** 388, 441; **11** 746;
anima as, *see* anima *s.v.*;
of archetypes, *see* archetype(s)
s.v. numinosity;
divine, **13** 342; bread as symbol
of, **11** 387;
of the Gentiles, **11** 576;
of goddess, **16** 438;
integration of, **11** 472;
presence of, and dogma, **11**
222;
and snake, **5** 676;
transference of, **16** 440;
tree-, *see* tree(s) *s.v.*;
vegetation, **5** 615; **13** 268*n*;
wisdom, as feminine, **11** 612
numina, **12** 247;
flight of, **18** 598
numinal accent, **6** 982–5
numinosity, **8** 383, 388, 870; **10**
728, 731, 743, 784; **13** 396, 432;
of archetypes, *see* archetype(s)
s.v.
of Christ, **11** 663;

of the cross, **11** 433;
destruction of, **18** 581;
of fire-making, **5** 250;
of God-images, **11** 454, 558;
of Job's knowledge, **11** 584;
loss of, **18** 582;
of metaphysical statement, **11**
735;
of mystical experience, **11** 275;
of numbers, **8** 870;
of primordial images, **5** 223; **13**
396;
of self, **5** 612; **14** 776;
of series of chance happenings,
8 827*n*;
of sun, **5** 128;
of symbol, **11** 337*n*; **14** 514; **18**
579;
of words, **18** 590
numinosum, **8** 216; **10** 864;
creeds and, **11** 9;
defined, **11** 6;
effect of, produced by ritual,
11 7
numinous, **10** 647, 651, 720; **11**

numinous (*cont.*):
   982; **12** 247, 294, 448, 557, 564;
     character of changes of con-
     sciousness, **11** 274;
     complexes, **13** 437;
     experience, **14** 776, 781;
     "holy dread" of, **11** 222, 375;
     ideas; **13** 393;
     in individuation, **11** 448;
     religious idea/statement, **11**
     450; **13** 396
Nun: Babylonian, **9ii** 186;
     in Egyptian mythology, **5** 358,
     389;
     as fish, **5** 290*n*; **9i** 244; **9ii** 173,
     186;
     son of, Joshua, **5** 282, 290*n*; **9i**
     244; **9ii** 173
nun, vision of, **17** 137&*n*
nun, meaning of, **5** 359
Nunberg, H.: "On the Physical Ac-
   companiments of Association
   Processes," **6** 180*n*; **8** 23*n*
nuptiae chymicae, **5** 330; **16** 398;
   see also *coniunctio; hierosgamos;*
   marriage
Nuremberg, **10** 760; first German
   railway from, **18** 740*n*; *see also*

   Psychoanalytic Congresses
nurse, **9i** 156; **17** 12, 16–17;
   dream of, **8** 478–9
nursing, **7** 8/417;
   as displacement, **3** 105
Nut, sky-goddess, **5** 359;
   giving birth to the sun, **5** *fig.* 24
nut(s): four, cracked, **12** 299–300;
   hard, **12** 288–9
nutritive/nutritional: function, *see*
   function(s) *s.v.*;
     instinct, *see* instinct *s.v.*;
     zone, *see* zones *s.v.*
Nutt, A., **6** 401*n*
Nyagrodha, **13** 412*n*
nycticorax, see ANIMALS: night-heron
nymph(s), **9i** 311; **12** 114, 116, 118,
   329, *fig.* 33; **13** 178–80, 195, 278;
   14 70;
     tree, *see* tree(s) *s.v.*;
     water, **13** 179;
     wood, **9i** 53;
     see also Paracelsus: ARCANA *s.v.*
   Melusina
Nymphidida, nymphididic realm,
   see Paracelsus: ARCANA *s.v.*
   Melusina

O

oak, see TREES *s.v.*

Oannes, Babylonian fish-god, **5**
291–2, *fig.* 18; **9ii** 127, 174, 186,
313; **13** 268; **14** 566*n*, 570*n*;
-Ea, **5** 291

oath: modernist, **10** 1019;
Pythagorean, *see* Pythagoras

Obatala and Odudua (West African
myth), **6** 367

obedience: primordial instinct of,
18 1630;
as protection to gifted child, **17**
246

obfuscation of the light, **16** 399

object: and collective values, **6** 318;
conflict with, **6** 137;
cryptomnesic reproduction, **1**
139, 143;
and cultural ideals, **6** 110;
death of, **8** 522;
and dream interpretation, **7**
130, 141; **8** 508, 510;
dynamic animation of, **6** 495,
501&*n*;
ego as, *see* ego;
external, lack of, **5** 253;
and Freudian theory, **6** 90–1; **7**
58–61;
hysterical identification with, **1**
340;
and imago, **7** 223;
-imago, **7** 513, 518; **8** 521;
incorporation into psychic system, **5** 201, 203;
libido's choice of, **7** 77, 94–6,
105, 110;
light-symbols for, **5** 128;
Luther-Zwingli   controversy
and, **6** 98–9;
mischievousness of, **8** 202;
mood/affect as, **7** 348; **13** 17;
naïve or sentimental poets and,
6 213–21;
nominalism and, **6** 75;
overvaluation of, **7** 303; **8** 523;
projection and, **7** 520; **8** 519–

20; **18** 1511;
spell/magical   power   of,   **6**
383–4, 386, 496, 608, 626–7;
and subject, *see* subject *s.v.*;
subjection to, **6** 417;
symbolical,   displacement   of
libido on, **5** 83;
yoga and, **6** 191;
see also under empathy; extraverted   type;   introverted
type

objectivation: of assorted complexes, **1** 132*n*;
of dream, **1** 117;
of impersonal images, **18** 377,
378, 399, 401, 410;
of visual images, **1** 98

objective: causality, **7** 210;
level, **6** 779 (Def.); **7** 141, 143,
158,   223;   interpretations/
analysis on, **5** 175*n*; **7** 130, 139,
141, 158;
psyche, *see* psyche *s.v.*;
psychic, **11** 479;
psychology, *see* psychology *s.v.*;
and subjective, confused, **6** 46;
tendencies, **7** 210

objectivity, **7** 323, 348; **11** 786;
absolute/complete,   **11**   735,
785;
need of, **11** 519;
psychic/of psyche, *see* psyche
s.v.;
of psychology, **12** 17–20;
scientific, **13** 1, 378–9;
of the unconscious, **10** 562;
unprejudiced, **11** 521

oblatio/oblation: alchemical, **12** 485;
in the Mass, **12** 417;
see also Offertory

obliqueness, Indian, **10** 1000

oblong, in dream, **11** 128;   **12**
286–7, 289

obnubilation, **1** 106

obolus, sacrifice of, **5** 577

Obrycum, **14** 641*n*

obscene stories, **12** 105; *see also* scurrility; smutty talk

obscurantists, **13** 246

obscurity: in alchemy, *see* alchemy *s.v.*;
of dream, **16** 313

"obscurum per obscurius," *see* alchemy *s.v.*

observation: sources of error in, **18** 739;
uncertainty of, **9ii** 355

observatory, **7** 231

Observer (London), **18** 1339*n*

observer(s): and observed: identical in psychology, **11** 377; inseparable, **9ii** 355;
in physics, **8** 417, 438; **10** 498; **11** 465;
subjective states of, **11** 972

obsession(s)/obsessional, **3** 109; **8** 266, 702; **9i** 236; **9ii** 259; **10** 300, 308; **11** 22, 27, 35, 242; **13** 54, 298; **18** 467;
and conscience, **10** 843;
disturbances, **3** 184;
ideas, **3** 61, 148, 166; **6** 600; **7** 307; **8** 639;
neurosis, **3** 148, 451; **4** 32; **13** 48; **16** 540; Freud on, **3** 77; **18** 922; and psychoses, **3** 503, 539, 558;
personalities, **3** 29;
psychotherapy of, **18** 843;
states, **3** 17; and negativism, **3** 27;
thinking, *see* thinking *s.v.*;
transformations, gradual, **3** 192

obsidian, **9ii** 213*n*, 214*n*

obstacle, **7** 124–5, 140, 144, 163, 252–3;
and neurosis, **7** 52–3

obstetric methods, barbaric, **5** 487

obumbratio/overshadowing, *see* Mary *s.v.*

Ocampo, V., **6** (*p*xv)

Occam's razor, **6** 61, 855*n*; **8** 383; **18** 876*n*

occiput, **12** 517*n*;
as vessel of transformation, **12** 376;
see also skull

occult/occultism, **4** 749; **10** 1, 530, 623; **15** 86; **16** 93; **18** 893;
TITLE: "On the Psychology and Pathology of So-Called Occult Phenomena," **1** 1–150;
Eastern, **13** 3;
and heightened unconscious performance, **1** 137;
manifestation of the, **13** 187*n*;
and open, as opposites, **14** 1;
so-called, J.'s case of, see Jung: CASES, volume 1, Miss S. W.;
wisdom, **7** 412;
see also parapsychology; spiritualism;

"Occulta chemicorum philosophia," *see* ALCHEMICAL WRITERS: Valentinus *s.v. Triumphwagen*

occurrences, unusual, **10** 120, 608

ocean: "of divinity," **7** 476;
flows from centre of perfect man, **9ii** 333, 336;
world-encircling, **9i** 559*n*;
see also sea

Oceanus, *see* Okeanos

Och, **9i** 406

Ochwiabiano (Pueblo Indian), **11** 474; *see also* Mountain Lake

octagon, **11** 276, 932

octave, musical, **14** 579

octopus, *see* ANIMALS *s.v.*

Odin, **5** 528*n*; **8** 966*n*; **10** 391*n*; **11** 44*n*; **13** 448; **18** 1077;
hanging/sacrifice of, **5** 349, 399, 445, 671*n*, 672*n*;
horse of, **13** 461*n*;
riddle, **5** 421*n*;
see also Wotan

odor sepulchrorum, see graves *s.v.* stench

odour: of immortality, **13** 451; of sanctity, **14** 421; *see also* smell

Odysseus: as Cabiric dwarf, **5** *fig.* 13;

journey to Hades/descent *ad inferos*, **5** 634*n*; **18** 80;
see also Joyce *s.v. Ulysses*
Odyssey, see Homer *s.v.*
oedema, brain, **3** 537
Oedipus, **6** 43; **9i** 259*n*; **12** 401;
complex, *see sep. entry below;*
Greeks and, **5** 45&*n*;
name of, **5** 356; **14** 726*n*;
and sphinx, **5** 264–6; **10** 714
Oedipus complex, **4** 343–5, 347–9,
562, 565; **5** 654; **11** 842; **14** 107;
18 1150;
as archetype, **10** 658, 659;
and Electra-complex, **3** 564; **4**
347–9, 377, 562; **18** 1261;
Freud's theory, *see* Freud *s.v.*;
and neurosis, **4** 352, 377;
reactivation of, **4** 569
Oehler, F., *see* Epiphanius, St.:
Panarium
Oehler, Pastor, Nietzsche's grandfather, **1** 141
offences, criminal, source of, **1**
472–5
offerings, propitiatory, **5** 571
Offertory of the Mass, **11** 309; **12**
419, 450, 485; *see also* oblation
office, in society, **7** 227–8, 230–1,
310–11
offspring, protection of, **4** 234, 284
Og, King of Bashan, **12** 540–5;
and Sihon, **12** 543
ogdoad, **10** 740; **11** 942; **13** 187; **16**
411, 451;
and Adam, **14** 553;
of elements, **13** 359;
Gnostic, **9ii** 171, 307&*n*, 358;
14 574, 576; archon of, *see* archons *s.v.*;
and mandala, **11** 424;
motif of, **13** 402;
as totality symbol, **10** 692; **14** 8;
and transformation process,
symbol of, **13** 416
ogre, **12** 84
Ogyges/Ogygian, **5** 306
Ohazama, S.: *Zen: Der lebendige*

Buddhismus in Japan, **11** 877*m*,
881*n*
oil: in alchemy, **12** 336&*n*; **13** 375;
golden, **13** 274; from hearts of
statues, **12** 405*n*; **14** 561; Mercurius as, **12** 459*n*;
magic, **5** 541
Oka, **5** 321*n*
Okeanos/Oceanus, **5** 158*n*; **16** 525*n*;
and Anthropos, **16** 525*n*;
as origin of gods, **9ii** 327, 340;
13 101; **14** 38&*n*;
and Tethys, **14** 18*n*, 50;
see also ocean
oki, **8** 116
Olaus Magnus: *Historia*, **5** *fig.* 29
old: man, *see* man *s.v.*;
woman, *see* woman *s.v.*;
see also age
Oldenberg, H., **10** 189;
Die Religion des Veda, **6** 349*n*;
"Zur Religion und Mythologie
des Veda," **6** 349*n*
Old Kule, *see* Barlach, Ernst
Old Masters, **10** 944
Old Testament, *see* BIBLE *s.v.*
Oleg, Russian sun-hero, **5** 450*n*
"Oleum," *see* association-chains *s.v.*
olfactory: hallucinations, **18** 767,
780;
organ, degeneration of, in
man, **18** 779, 780
olive(-tree), *see* TREES *s.v.*
Oloron, **10** 668
Olympians, **13** 54
Olympian Spring, see Spitteler
Olympiodorus, *see* ALCHEMICAL
WRITERS *s.v.*
Olympus, **11** 347; **12** 84, 205, 210,
505; **13** 54;
Christian, **11** 471;
in Paracelsus, **9ii** 251
Omar, Mosque of, **12** 390*n*
omega: alpha and, **13** 271, 363;
element, *rotundum*/round, **9ii**
377; **13** 95, 101
omen(s), **8** 851; **10** 120, 608;
evil, averting, **9i** 47

169; **15** 8
Oppenheim, G.: *Fabula Josephi et Asenathae,* **12** 456*n*
Oppenheim, H.: **4** 31;
"Thatsächliches und Hypothetisches über das Wesen der Hysterie," **4** 31*n*
Oppenheimer, R. J., **10** 879
opportunism, **4** 599
opposites, **7** 504; **8** 518; **9i** 419; **11** 931; **12** 496; **13** 15, 39, 311, 446; **14** 199, 206; **16** 375, 384, 524, 527; **18** 564;
TITLES: "The Alchemical View of the Union of Opposites," **14** 654–58; "The Brahmanic Conception of the Problem of Opposites,"**6**327–30; "The Opposites," **14** 1–4; "The Personification of the Opposites," **14** 104–348;
alchemical, linked together in quaternities, **9ii** 383; **16** 425*n*;
annihilation of, **9ii** 124;
archetypes and,*see* archetype(s) *s.v.*;
assimilation of, **14** 513;
association of, **3** 426;
balance of, **13** 7; **14** 307; **18** 1417;
beauty and, **6** 127, 194;
cancellation of, **6** 187;
characterological, **14** 707;
in China, **12** 436*n*;
in Christianity, *see* Christian/ Christianity *s.v.*;
cinedian stone and, **9ii** 216;
clash of, **13** 15;
coincidence of, **9ii** 191; **13** 256; **14** 274; **16** 522; in Godhead, **9ii** 301 (see also *coincidentia*);
collision of, **9i** 285; **10** 814; **16** 381; **18** 1417; in St. John's visions, **11** 731;
compensation by, **7** 78, 80;
condition one another, **11** 791;
conflict of, **6** 357, 369; **7** 115; **13** 481; **14** 307, 493, 506; **18**

1551; and individuation, **18** 1641; in normal people, **18** 1388;
confrontation of, **11** 780; **18** 830;
conjunction of, see *coniunctio s.v.;*
conscious mind caught between, **9i** 287;
contamination of, **9i** 293; **14** 600–1;
conversion into, **7** 115–16;
cooperation of, **9i** 76; **18** 1625;
in deity, **12** 436*n*, 460;
deliverance/liberation from, **6** 189, 326–7, 330, 363; **14** 296;
detachment from, **6** 199;
differentiation of, **13** 291;
discrimination of, **9i** 178;
dissolution of individuality into, **6** 174; **7** 237;
dualism of, **14** 1;
equivalence of, **9i** 76; **9ii** 112;
experience of, **12** 23–4;
Father as without, **9ii** 298;
final severance of, **11** 728;
freedom from, **7** 367; **9i** 76; **11** 435, 438; **13** 15; **14** 66;
functions as, **18** 30;
fusion of, **14** 441; **16** 501;
in God, see God *s.v.* antinomies/opposites;
gods as, **11** 791;
gulf between, **14** 674;
harmony of, **5** 253;
identity of, **11** 437; **12** 398; **14** 601; **17** 209; and symbol, **9ii** 200;
integration of, **14** 86, 513;
irreconcilability of, **7** 237/458; **9i** 77, 608; **12** 192;
lapis a symbol of, **13** 289;
and libido, **8** 61–2; symbols, **6** 337;
in mania, **18** 830;
mediation between, **6** 184, 326, 370; cross as, **11** 739; man as, **6** 366–7; and symbol, **6** 178, 458,

opposites (*cont.*):

825 (*see also* transcendent function);

Mercurius and, *see* Mercurius *s.v.*;

metaphysical, **14** 86;

and middle way, **6** 192, 326; **7** 327;

moral accentuation of, **9ii** 126;

moral problem of: and conscience, **10** 843–4; and neurosis, **9ii** 281 (*see also below* problem); unconsciousness of, **14** 86;

natural combination of, **6** 447;

non-existence of, **11** 798;

in pagan unconscious, **6** 316;

pairs of, *see sep. entry below;*

personification of, **14** 2, 104*ff*;

play of, **4** 779; **13** 286;

in *prima materia,* **12** 435*n, fig.* 162;

principle of, **4** 758;

problem of, **7** 91, 116, 160*n*, 287; **8** 260; **11** 437; **12** 22, 43, 397; **13** 435; **16** 177–8; and Assumption of Mary, **18** 1607 (*see also above* moral problem);

psychic equilibration of, **14** 670;

Pythagorean, **6** 963–4;

quaternio of, **13** 358; **14** 1, 5, 237, 261, 274, 330 (*see also* quaternio);

reconciliation of, **6** 68, 228; **10** 706; **11** 133; **17** 250; Holy Ghost as, **11** 260 (*see also below* opposites, union of);

regulative function of, **7** 111;

relativization of, **9i** 76–7;

release of repression and, **6** 172;

renunciation of, **6** 372;

Schiller on, *see* Schiller *s.v.*;

in second half of life, **7** 91, 184;

self and, *see* self *s.v.*;

separation/splitting apart of, **3** 427*n*, 457; **5** 253; **6** 136, 434; **7**

113; **9i** 257; **11** 738; **12** 30; **14** 184, 252, 470; **15** 214; in Germans, **18** 1376;

before separation, **14** 252;

solution of conflict of, **7** 166; by creative act, **6** 541;

structure of, **18** 829;

suspension between, **18** 1553;

symbolism of, **18** 829;

synthesis of, **12** 193&*n*; **16** (*p* 165*n*);

tao and, **6** 192, 366, 369–70;

tension of, *see sep. entry below;*

theriomorphic/animal symbols of, **14** 2–3, 506*n*; **16** 494;

transconscious character of, **14** 4, 542;

unconscious consists of, **9i** 563; **12** 440; **14** 10*n*;

unconsciousness of, **14** 86;

union of, *see separate entry below;*

war of, **9i** 294; **12** 259;

Yahweh as totality of, **11** 567;

yogi and, **6** 336;

see also antinomy; *complexio oppositorum;* conflict; duality; enantiodromia; *hierosgamos;* syzygies

opposites, pairs of, **9i** 194;

contained in one word, **18** 1077;

moral, **7** 327;

psychic, **12** 496;

in Sanskrit (*dvandva*), **6** 327;

serpents as, **9ii** 181&*n*;

and symbol, **18** 520;

INSTANCES (many of the words listed here have entries in the main body of the index):

above/below, **10** 773, 912; **13** 457; **15** 213;

action/non-action, **13** 20*n*, 38;

active/passive, **13** 105; **14** 1, 655;

albedo/rubedo, **14** 7;

analysis/synthesis, **7** 122;

opposites, pairs of (*cont.*):
  of, **14** 43, 364, 527, 538, 630*n*, 656, 659;
  materialism / mysticism, **8** 712;
  matter/psyche, **16** 499;
  megalomania/inferiority, **7** 237/458;
  mercury/sulphur, **12** 436;
  moist/dry, *see above* dry/ damp;
  moral/immoral, **7** 18/430;
  morality/temptation, **11** 791;
  mother/son, **14** 655;
  nature/spirit, **8** 96;
  nominalism/realism, **7** 80;
  north/south, **12** 192; **18** 1625;
  occult (hidden)/open, **14** 1;
  odd/even numbers, **12** 436*n*;
  "one"/"other," **11** 180;
  organization/disorganization, **7** 111;
  Ormuzd/Ahriman, **11** 259;
  physical/spiritual, **8** 414; **12** 436; **13** 76*n*;
  precious, costly/cheap, **14** 1;
  Promethean/Epimethean, **7** 82;
  rational/irrational, **7** 72, 75, 110, 121;
  real/imaginary, **7** 121;
  red/white, **14** 655;
  red man/white woman, **14** 2, 154*n*, 655*n*;
  reflection/action, **7** 80;
  right/left, **8** 401; **13** 457; **18** 1662;
  right/wrong, **14** 31;
  round/square, **12** 436;
  same/different, **11** 188&*n*;
  samsara/nirvana, **11** 800;
  society/personality, **12** 557;
  Sol/Luna, *see* Sol and Luna *s.v.*;
  spirit/soul, *see* soul and spirit *s.v.*
  spirit or soul/body, *see* body

  s.v. spirit;
  spirituality / sensuality, **17** 336;
  subject/object, **7** 57–60, 82–6; **11** 849;
  suffering/non-existence, **11** 931;
  suffering/wellbeing, **18** 564;
  sun/moon, **12** 436;
  unconscious progressive-ness/conscious regressive-ness, **7** 182; **17** 281;
  unity/quaternity, **10** 774;
  upper/lower, **8** 401; **14** 7, 8;
  value/non-value, **7** 115;
  virtue/vice, **7** 237/458;
  visible/invisible, **12** 398;
  volatile/solid, **12** 436; **14** 1;
  yang/yin, see yang and *yin s.v.*;
  yea/nay, **13** 15;
  yellow/green, **14** 31;
  youth/age, **5** 184; **7** 114, 117; **14** 7

opposites, tension of, **5** 460, 581; **6** 330, 347, 370; **7** 34, 78, 115, 119; **8** 767; **9i** 196, 426, 446, 483; **9ii** 59, 390&*n*; **10** 779, 784; **11** 180, 291; **13** 147, 290; **16** 400; **17** 249;
  Antichrist and Christ as, *see* Antichrist *s.v.*;
  in child, **8** 99;
  Christian, **9ii** 147; **12** 26; **13** 291;
  cosmic, **6** 370;
  and culture, **8** 111;
  and dogma of Assumption, **11** 754;
  in dreams, **9ii** 390*n*;
  in God, **8** 103;
  Mercurius and, **12** 547;
  as source of energy; *see* energy *s.v.* opposites

opposites, union of, **5** 415, 576, 577, 671; **6** 115, 169, 174, 178, 185, 373, 441, 458–9; **7** 206, 224, 382; **8** 406; **9i** 20, 285, 292, 295, 637, 705; **9ii** 418; **10** 698, 789; **11**

803; **12** 6, 311, 334, 450, *figs.* 113, 167; **13** 199, 307, 310, 315, 456; **14** 35, 36, 66, 201, 258, 292, 542, 633; **16** 381, 460, 467, 493, 533; **18** 261–2, 266;

and alchemy, **9i** 198; **13** 187*n*, 462; **14** 104, 654–68, 676; **16** 537;

in arcane substance, **14** 291;

and archetypes, *see* archetypes *s.v.* opposites;

in astrology, **9ii** 130, 142;

Brahman is, **6** 330;

Christ is, **11** 690;

in *coniunctio*, **8** 899–900; **14** 200, 276; **16** 354, 410;

cross as, **10** 762; **11** 437;

Dorn on, **14** 681;

and enantiodromia, distinguished, **18** 1597;

and energy, **5** 671;

Father as, **11** 279;

in hermaphrodite, **12** 436*n*; **16** 454;

in *hierosgamos,* see *hierosgamos;*

and Holy Spirit, **11** 277; **18** 1553, 1556;

in human individual, **18** 1553, 1661;

in incest, **14** 106, 188, 664;

irrational, **6** 329, 362, 367; **9i** 603; **11** 755;

in lapis, **9ii** 390–1; **14** 141;

and mandala, **11** 150, 152;

in Mercurius, **13** 279, 408;

in Plato, **11** 184;

and rebirth symbolism, **11** 828;

and salvation, **9ii** 304;

self as, *see* self *s.v.* opposites, union of;

and son in St. John's vision, **11** 712, 739;

in stone, **9ii** 264; **13** 131, 385;

and symbol(s), **9i** 198, 278, 293; **9ii** 280–1; **11** 738, 746, 755, 756; **12** 404, 557; **13** 31; **14** 676, 718, 776; **18** 595;

in a third, **8** 401; **11** 438; **14** 705, 765;

and transcendent function, **6** 187; **7** 368; **8** 189; **9i** 524; **11** 803; **14** 261; **18** 1554;

and unconsciousness, **9ii** 301;

by worship, **6** 375

opposition(s), **7** 311;

absolute, **13** 256;

astrological, **8** 878–82;

between Nous and sex, **13** 344;

principle of, **7** 92;

in triad and Trinity, **11** 196;

of two types, **7** 80;

unconscious, **7** 187

opsianus, **9ii** 213&*n*

optic impression, and misreading, **1** 155

optimism: extraverted, and inversion of types, **7** 81–2;

of judgment, **7** 236;

of Negroes, **11** 200;

of patients, in manic disorders, **1** 199, 209, 214, 216, 219;

and pessimism, **6** 526–7; **7** 222/452, 225;

unjustified, in youth, **8** 761

opus(alchemical)/*opus (alchymicum),* **12** 187, 219, 451, *figs.* 4, 75, 132, 209; **13** 250, 284, 392; **14** 752; **16** 400, 402, 411, 460, 471, 490, 531, 538; **18** 1360;

ad album/ad rubeum, **14** 181;

amplificatio in, **12** 403;

as analogy of coitus, **16** 460;

as apocatastasis, **9ii** 260;

as *arbor philosophica,* **12** 499, *figs.* 188, 221 (*see also below* tree);

and artifex, **14** 294;

beginning of, in springtime, **13** 193;

chaos in, **14** 253;

children in, **12** 302;

and Christ as Redeemer, **13** 393;

and Christianity, **12** 40;

and circle/*circulatorium, see* circle *s.v.;*

499

opus (*cont.*):

colours in, **9i** 580;
completion/end of, **12** 478, *fig.* 215; **13** 190*n*; and homunculus, **9i** 529; paradoxical, **16** 532;
contra naturam, **13** 414; **16** 469;
as creation of world, recapitulation of, **9i** 550; **9ii** 230; **13** 286; **14** 478; **18** 1631;
dangers of, *see* alchemy *s.v.* art;
demands of, **16** 451;
dreams and visions during, **13** 88&*n*;
and ecclesiastical mystery/ sacrament, **11** 448; **13** 231–6;
effects of, **14** 446;
in *Faust,* **12** 42–3;
and *filius philosophorum,* **13** 163;
four aspects of, **12** 367;
four parts of, in Greek alchemy, **12** 478 (*see also* opus, alchemical, stages in)
goal/aim/purpose of, **11** 161; **12** 40; **13** 137, 190, 220, 355, 359, 393, 402, 404; **14** 62, 763;
lapis as, see *lapis philosophorum s.v.* opus;
God as product of, **13** 404;
as *hierosgamos,* **18** 1692;
and *imaginatio,* **12** 219, 400;
and individuation, **9i** 550, 570, 616; **9ii** 419; **16** 531;
and lapis, *see* lapis *s.v.*;
ad lunam/lunae et solis, **14** 181, 218;
magnum, **16** 449;
man's and woman's, **16** 519;
and the Mass, *see* Mass *s.v.* in alchemy; see also *opus divinum;*
mental attitude towards, **12** 357–89;
Mercurius and, *see* Mercurius *s.v.*;
microcosmic, **13** 244;
mistakes during, **13** 432;
moral character of, **16** 451;

nostrum, **18** 396;
and numbers, *see* NUMBERS: one, twelve;
as odyssey, **12** 457, *fig.* 97;
operatio in, **12** 401;
and Passion of Christ, *see* Christ *s.v.* Passion;
perfect and imperfect substance, **11** 310;
perfection of, **13** 117*n*;
as period of gestation, **16** 461;
philosophical, **11** 154; **12** 375;
practica and *theoria* in, *see below* two parts of;
and *prima materia,* **13** 209;
and projection, *see* projection *s.v.*;
and psyche, *see* psyche *s.v.*;
and psychic process, **12** 342, 375, 502; **13** 355; **16** 538*n*;
psychologicum, aim of, **16** 471;
as rebirth mystery, **13** 459;
as rite, **13** 158; **14** 509;
sacrament of, **13** 232;
secret of, *see* secret *s.v.*;
son brought to life by, **13** 184;
stages of, *see sep. entry below;*
supernaturale, **12** 417;
symbol (s) of, **12** *figs.* 3, 4, 122, 188;
synthetic character of, **12** 224;
tetrameria of, **9i** 564; **14** 261;
third part of, **16** 484;
three parts of, **12** 478*n*;
time sequence of phases, **16** 468*n*;
and transformation, **12** 403, 470*n*; **13** 176*n*; **14** 252, 509;
as transitus, **14** 288;
as tree, **13** 404, 409, 413, 414, 459; philosophical, **9i** 570; **16** 519 (see also above *arbor philosophica*);
two parts of (*practica, theoria*), **9ii** 278; **11** 160, 448; **12** 332, 342–3, 380, 403–4, 502; **13** 482; **16** 471, 488; *theoria,* **9ii** 219, 246, 264, 278, 281; **12**

see also Persia *s.v.* Ahura-Mazda
Oromazdes, *see* Persia *s.v.* Ahura-Mazda
Oropos, Amphiaraion, 5 571–2
Orosius, Paulus: "Ad aurelium Augustum commonitorium de errore Priscillianistarum et Origenistarum," 9ii 366*n*; 14 299*n*
orphan, *see* lapis *s.v.*
Orpheus, 9i 79, 573*n*; 9ii 162; 11 373; 12 416,*fig.* 211; 13 381*n*; 14 5*n*, 6*n*, 19*n*;
    frescoes, 5 163*n*;
    Japanese parallel, *see* Izanagi
Orphic/Orphism, 6 963; 8 854; 12 177&*n*; 14 160*n*; 18 259;
    Hecate in, 5 577;
    hymns, 5 528*n*, 530;
    and Iacchus, 5 528;
    mysteries, 6 963; 11 861; 14 5*n*;
    -Pythagorean doctrines, 11 861;
    Orphic Fragments, 14 154*n*
Orphos, son of Mithras, 9ii 186
Ortega y Gasset, J., 10 945
Orth, J., *see under* Mayer, A.
Orthelius, *see* ALCHEMICAL COLLECTIONS: *Bibl. chem. cur. s.v.; Theatr. chem. s.v.*
Orthodox Church, Eastern, 10 372
orthodoxy, Freudian, *see* Freud, S.
orthopedics, psychic, *see* Dubois *s.v.*
Orthos, as world, 18 753, 754
Orthrus, 5 265
Ortolano, *see* Benvenuti
Ortulanus, 14 460*n*
"Ortus," *see* ANIMALS *s.v.*
Ortygia, 5 316*n*
oryx, *see* ANIMALS *s.v.*
Osirification, 11 448
Osiris, 5 165, 330*n*; 8 333; 9i 229, 247; 9ii 188, 309, 310, 313; 10 645; 11 348*n*, 711; 12 416, 456*n*, 457, 529; 13 360; 14 34*n*, 65, 219, 350*n*, 356*n*, 395, 510*n*, 595, 653*n*, 726*n*; 18 1569*n*;
    in alchemy, 11 362; 14 14, 317, 365*n*, 627*n*, 734; as arcane sub-

stance, 13 97; black, and *caput mortuum* as head of, 11 366; 12 484*n*, 530; 14 727–30; and Mercurius, parallel, 14 726;
and Christianity, 11 178;
in coffer, 5 350–1, 361,*fig.* 23; 13 97; as winter solstice, 5 353;
death of, 5 321, 350, 392, 400; 13 97; dismemberment of, 5 356*n*, 361; 9i 208, 247, 435*n*; 9ii 187; 12 469; 14 351*n*, 365&*n*, 734; resurrection, 12 416*n*; 13 97; 18 1566;
eye of, 9i 413;
and goddess Mehnit, 5 408;
head of, 11 372; 12 530 (*see also above* in alchemy *s.v.* black)
and Horus, *see* Horus *s.v.*;
and Isis, 5 349–51, 354, 356, 400, 619, 662; 6 396; 14 609, 726;
as principle of moisture, 13 97*n*; 14 355;
sister-wives of: Isis, *see above*; Nephthys, 5 350, 400;
tree as, 11 612
Osnabrück Register of Santa Maria, 12 481
Osob, 9ii 227&*n*, 312
ossuary, Etruscan, 5 536
Ostanes/Astanus/Book of Ostanes, *see* ALCHEMICAL WRITERS *s.v.*
osteopathy, 15 20
Osterburken monument, 5 288; 13 404
Ostia, head from, 5 *frontispiece*
Ostwald, F. W., 6 323, 699; 7 72; 8 19*n*;
    on types: classic, 6 542–7, 554, 870; 7 80; —, and introvert, 6 548, 550–1, 552, 553, 555; romantic, 6 542, 546, 547, 554, 870; 7 80; —, and extravert, 6 548, 550–1, 555;
    WORKS:
        Grosse Männer, 6 542–5, 550, 551&*n*, 553, 555, 870; 7 80*n*;
        Die Philosophie der Werte, 7

Ostwald (*cont.*):
72*n*; **8** 5*n*
ed., *Annalen der Natur-philosophie*, **10** 214
"other," the, **11** 143, 890; **16** 470;
God as, **11** 201, 236, 772;
"in me," the, **11** 133;
"in us," **7** 43; **10** 321, 360, 918;
and the number two, **11** 180;
one and, **11** 180, 199;
principle, **7** 494;
self, **7** 43;
shore, **11** 810; **13** 254*n*;
side, **6** 630–1; **7** 124, 140, 170, 225, 315, 323, 326; **13** 133;
necessity of, **7** 35; of our nature, **7** 27/438; of soul's life, *see* anima; truths of, **7** 323; Western fear of, **7** 324 (*see also* onesidedness; shadow-side);
world, **5** 629;
see also Beyond, the; Hades; underworld
Otto, R., **8** 216; **10** 864; **11** 6, 881; *The Idea of the Holy*, **11** 6*n*, 772*n*
Oupnek'hat, *see* Upanishads
ourselves, split in, **13** 295
outer happening, **13** 18
"outflowing," **13** 36, 47
"outgrowing" of problem, **13** 17, 18
outlook(s): horizontal and vertical, **8** 649, 656;
religious, **11** 509; and scientific, **11** 516
outside and inside, *see* inside

oven, **9i** 156
over-activity, **1** 190, 199, 203–4
over-compensation, **17** 153
overdetermination, **3** 133; **4** 44
overpopulation, **10** 537
overvaluation, **7** 216; **9i** 141;
of conscious mind, **16** 51, 108;
of consciousness, **17** 343;
of instinct, **17** 157
overwork, **4** 474
Ovid: *Metamorphoses*, **5** 439&*n*, 526&*n*, 528*n*, 661&*n*; **14** 75*n*
owl, *see* ANIMALS *s.v.*
"owner of the world," *see* association-chains *s.v.*
ox(en), *see* ANIMALS *s.v.*
Oxford, **10** 1069
Oxford English Dictionary, **9ii** 48
Oxford Group (Buchman movement), **11** 34, 275; **16** 21; **17** 154; **18** 370, 620–2, 1676;
and Moral Rearmament Movement, **11** 275*n*;
see also confession *s.v.* public
Oxford Movement (Anglican), **11** 275*n*
oxides in alchemy, **11** 160; **13** 137*n*, 381*n*
oxyrhynchus (fish), *see* ANIMALS: fish *s.v.*
Oxyrhynchus, fish worship at, **9ii** 186
Oxyrhynchus fragment of sayings of Jesus, *see* Christ *s.v.* sayings of
oyster, *see* ANIMALS *s.v.*

P

Pachymeres, George: commentary on pseudo-Dionysius, *De coelesti hierarchia*, **14** 564*n*

Pacific culture, **13** 132;
Gilbert Islands, **13** 458*n*

Paderborn, **9i** 694

padma(s), see lotus

Padmanaba, **13** 278

Padmanabhapura, Temple of, **13** 278

paedogogics/pedagogics, *see* education

pagan(s), **13** 148, 149, 156, 238;
alchemists, *see* alchemy *s.v.*;
antiquity, **13** 194;
lore, **13** 157

paganism, **6** 313, 314, 316; **7** 97, 118; **9ii** 152; **12** 12, 182; **15** 9, 16; **16** 388;
in alchemy, *see* alchemy *s.v.*;
in eighteenth century, **11** 347;
images in, **11** 81;
relapse into, **7** 41;
return of, in Europe, **9ii** 273

paganum, see Pagoyum

Page, G. H., **18** 1826, (*p*826*n*)

Page, H. W., **4** 206&*n*;
"Shock from Fright," **4** 206*n*

pagodas, **13** 362*n*

Pagoyum(a)/*paganum* (Paracelsus), **13** 148&*n*, 150, 156&*n*, 195

Pahlavi Texts, tr. E. W. West, **9ii** 169*n*

Pai-chang Huai-hai (Hyakujo), **11** 877

pain, **17** 141;
aroused by complex, **3** 103;
avoidance of, **4** 634, 642;
and dreams, **8** 502;
hysterical, **4** 364;
perception of, **8** 607;
a psychic image, **8** 680;
self-inflicted, **1** 305, 353;
sensibility to, **1** 235, 327, 384, 395

pain-pleasure: affects, **1** 204;

reaction, **8** 256

painter, in dream, **9i** 349, 350

painting(s), **3** 562; **8** 168, 180, 400; **9i** 525–7; **15** 174; **16** 101–6;
medieval, **10** 770;
modern, pathological element in, **10** 430; and Ufos, **10** 724–56;
patient's, **1** 215;
rock, *see* rock-drawings/paintings;
sand, *see* American Indians: NORTH *s.vv.* Navajo; Pueblo;
see also mandala; picture(s)

pair(s): alchemical, **14** 181*n*, pl. 7; **16** 538*n*;
of angels, **16** 538*n*;
divine, **9i** 121 (*see also* syzygies);
parental, **9i** 135;
royal, **13** 446; **16** 496; in Moses quaternio, **9ii** 360;
transformation and union of, **13** 435;
see also antinomies; brother-sister pair; opposites

Palanque, J. R.: "The Church in the Christian Roman Empire," tr. E. C. Messenger, **11** 215*n*

Palatine: mock crucifixion on, **5** 421, 622, pl. XLIII; **9i** 463;

Palau, **8** 125

palaver, **3** 566

Palenque Cross, **5** 400, pl. XLI*a*
paleolithic age, **18** 81;
cult of soul-stones, **13** 132;
rock-drawings, *see* rock-drawings

paleontology, **17** 162; **18** 486

Palestine, **9ii** 128&*n*, 213; **18** 241

Pali Canon, *see* Buddhism *s.v.*

Palingenius, Marcellus, **12** 343*n*

palladium, **8** 92

Pallas, *see* Athene

pallor, in somnambulistic states, **1** 39, 46, 50–1, 125

palm, *see* TREES *s.v.*

palmistry, **6** 917
palolo worm, *see* ANIMALS *s.v.* worm
Pammeter, **18** 1769
Pamyles of Thebes, phallic daemon,
5 349
Pan, **5** 298; **9i** 35, 210; **9ii** 310; **11**
145; **13** 278; **14** 510&*n*
panacea, **9i** 289; **10** 629, 725, 727;
11 160*n*, 161; **12** 335, 420, 448,
460, 538, 557, 563–4; **13** 137,
187, 203, 218, 353*n*, 390, 403; **14**
663, 681; **16** 375, 389
Panarkes, riddle of, **14** 90*n*
Pañcavimsha   Brahmana,   *see*
Brahmanas
Panchatantra, **9i** 605; *Panchatantra
Reconstructed,* ed. F. Edgerton, **9i**
605n
Pandolfus, **9ii** 241
Pandora, in Prometheus myth:
Epimetheus and, **6** 315;
in Goethe, **6** 302–9, 315;
in Spitteler, **6** 294–303, 310,
434–5, 459
Pandora (alchemical), **12** 456(7); **13**
126; *see also* ALCHEMICAL WRITERS:
Reusner, H.: *Pandora*
panic(s), **3** 480; **7** 252; **9i** 49; **9ii** 62;
11 24, 76, 517; **12** 169; **16** 347; **17**
305–6
P'an Ku/Yüan-shi t'ien tsun, **14**
573&*nn*
pan-psychism, **8** 29
Pan Shan, **11** 884
panspermia, **9ii** 312; **11** 92*n*; **14** 643
pansy, mountain, *see* Paracelsus:
ARCANA *s.v. Cheyri*/etc.
Pantheus, Joannes, *see* ALCHEMICAL
WRITERS *s.v.*
Pantokrator, **9ii** 75*n*; **12** 173; **18**
1568
Pantophthalmos, *see* ANIMALS: dragon *s.v.* many-eyed; *see also* eye(s)
s.v. multiple
Papa, **8** 336; **9ii** 334; **14** 510*n*
papal, *see* Pope
Papers from the Eranos Yearbooks,
see Eranos Yearbooks

Paphnutia, **16** 505
Papremis, battle ceremony, **5** 390
Papuans, **10** 128
Papyri: Ani, **9ii** 129*n*; **11** 348*n*;
Berlin, **14** 6*n*;
British Museum Papyrus XLVI,
14 46*n*;
Gnostic Coptic (Jung Codex),
18 (*p*671&*n*), 1826;
Greek magic, *see* ALCHEMICAL
WRITERS: Magic Papyri;
Hunefer, **12** 314*n*;
Kerasher, **12** 314*n*;
Leiden, **5** 65; **9i** 105; **11** 160;
Mimaut and Paris, *see* ALCHEM-
ICAL WRITERS: Magic Papyri;
Nektu-Amen, **14** 482*n*;
Oxyrhynchus fragments, *see*
Christ *s.v.* sayings of
parable(s), **11** 344;
alchemical, **14** 189;
of house built on sand, **13** 421;
language of, **8** 474;
and symbols, **15** 105;
of talents, **9ii** 255;
of the unjust steward, **13** 292
"Parabola," *see* ALCHEMICAL COL-
LECTIONS: *Bibl. chem. cur. s.v.*
Sendivogius
parabolic figure, **13** 106
Paracelsist physicians, **3** 576
Paracelsus/Theophrastus Bombast
of Hohenheim, **3** 576; **4** 749; **5**
509; **8** 389, 930*n*; **9i** 533, 579; **9ii**
376; **10** 431; **11** 306*n*; **12** 85, 340,
356, 394*n*, 426, 468, 476, 478,
490, 513, 514, 516, *fig.* 261; **13**
(*p*110*n*), 195, 268; **14** 113*n*, 144,
687, 757; **15** 1–17, 18–43; **16** 22,
221, 222, 231, 401, 454; **17**
203&*n*; **18** 1700, 1755–9;
TITLES: "Paracelsus," **15** 1–17;
"Paracelsus the Physician," **15**
18–43;
"Paracelsus as a Spiritual
Phenomenon," **13** (*p*110)–238;
as alchemist/and alchemy, **9ii**
251, 281; **13** (*p*110), 151, 154,

157–9, 164, 166–7; **14** 116; on sulphur, **13** 357; **14** 135–6; **15** 32–3; thinking of, **13** 178; (*see also* alchemy *s.v.* Paracelsan);
arcana, see list below preceding WORKS;
arcane/secret doctrine, **13** 169–93; **15** 27–9; terminology, **13** 160; **15** 10, 18; and "onomastica," **13** 155 (*see also below* ARCANA);
on archons, gods as, **12** 468;
and astrology, *see* astrology *s.v.*;
and Bodenstein, *see* Bodenstein *s.v.*;
and Cabala/"Gabal," **13** 167; **15** 40;
chermes, **13** 184&*n*;
and Christianity/Church, **12** 41, 431; **13** 147–50, 197, 231, 236; **15** 9–10; **16** 20;
Hermetic philosophy and, **13** 158;
on *imaginatio,* **13** 173, 207, 215;
on leprosy of copper, **15** 25–6;
and magic, **13** 148, 151–6; **15** 21, 22, 40; *hapax legomenon,* **13** 155; witch-language, **13** 155–6;
and medicine: academic, **15** 19–22; alchemy, astrology, and, **15** 19–20, 26–30; disease, nature of, **15** 13–14, 17; nettles in, **13** 193, 194, 216; philosophy and, **15** 37–9; physician, art of, **15** 24–30; scientific, **18** 1115;
on Mercurius, **13** 171, 357; **14** 480*n*;
and Oporinus/Oporin pupil, *see* Oporinus;
philosophy of, **13** 158; **15** 37–40;
on spirits, **12** 508;
theoria/theorica of, **12** 403*n*; **14** 678; **15** 41; **16** 218;
thinking of, **13** 149, 178;
travels of, **15** 7–8;

triad, *see* triad *s.v.* in alchemy;
"vita cosmographica," **13** 205;
world/cosmogony of, **15** 9, 11–16;
ARCANA:
　Adech, **9ii** 334; **12** 150, 209*n*, 533*n*; **13** 168&*n*, 201–4, 209, 211–12, 214, 221, 226; **14** 43, 547 (see also *homo maior, homo maximus*);
　ambra, **13** 234;
　Anachmus, *see below* Aniada;
　Aniada/Aniadus/Anyadei, **13** 168*n*, 190–4, 200–4, 207&*n*, 214, 235; **14** 698; and Anachmus (-i), **13** 193&*n*, 207&*n*; Aniadin, year, **13** 214, 227, 232, 235; eternal spring, Paradise, **13** 193&*n*; exaltation, in May, **13** 193, 198;
　Anthera/Anthos/chelidonia, **13** 160, 171*n*; **14** 683*n*;
　Aquaster, **13** 172–5, 178, 179, 201, 204, 210; celestial, **13** 174, 175; derivation of, **13** 173*n*; "iliastric"/"scayolic," **13** 174;
　Archa, **13** 208;
　Arch(a)eus/"Archasius," **9ii** 205*n*, 334; **12** 508, 512&*n*; **13** 168, 176; **14** 49&*n*, 592*n*; **15** 39; hermaphrodite, **14** 43;
　Ares, **13** 173&*n*, 176–8, 216; **14** 49*n*; as formative principle, **13** 177, 202; and Mars, **13** 176*n*; Melusinian, **13** 173&*n*, 177–8;
　Astronomia, **8** 390;
　astrum(-a), **8** 390; **12** 394&*n*; **13** 148&*n*, 160, 167*n*, 173; **15** 22, 32–3, 38 (*see also* star *s.v.* in man);
　Cagastrum/cagastric, **13** 161*n*; **14** 41; Aquaster, **13** 174; magic, **13** 161&*n*; soul, **13** 201;

Paracelsus: WORKS (*cont.*):
468*n*, 516*n*; **13** 180*n*; **14** 32*n*;
"Philosophia sagax," **8** 388,
390*n*, 391*n*; **13** 149;
"Practica in scientiam divi-
nationis," **8** 391*n*;
"Scholia in poemata Macri,"
14 683*n*;
*Volumen Paramirum und Opus
Paramirum,* ed. F. Stranz, **9ii**
334*n*; "Paramirum," "De
quinque entibus morbor-
um," **13** 148; "Paramirum
primum," **13** 148*n*, 156*n*;
"Fragmenta ad Paramirum,"
15 31*n*;
"Von der Astronomey," **13**
168*n*;
"Von den dreyen ersten
essentiis"/"Von den dreyen
Principiis oder essentiis," **14**
43*n*;
"Von Erkantnus des Ges-
tirns," **13** 148*n*;
"Von dem Podagris," **15** 39*n*;
"Von den tartarischen
Krankheiten," **14** 683*n*
Paraclete, *see* Holy Ghost/Spirit *s.v.*
para-da, Indian "quicksilver" system, **9ii** 237; **13** 254*n*
Paradise/paradise, **7** 237/458; **8** 751,
754; **9i** 258; **10** 288; **11** 361; **12**
328*n*, 347, 456(7), 462; **13** 168*n*,
180, 193&*n*, 288, 392; **14** 276,
287, 630*n*;
angel at the gates of, **13** 110;
Christ in, **14** 475;
earth of (in alchemy), *see* earth;
earthly, **9ii** 402*n*; **11** 356; **13**
243;
four rivers of, **5** 368; **9i** 73,
552, 603*n*; **9ii** 311, 336, 353,
358, 372, 373; **11** 229, 727,
946; **12** *figs.* 62, 109, 197; **13**
186, 212, *fig.* 24; **14** 276;
Gnostic/Naassene symbolism
of, **9ii** 288, 311, 382; **13** 420*n*;
14 276, 389; —, Edem with, **9i**

665; **14** 626*n*; —, names of, **9ii**
311; —, as sensory functions,
9ii 311; **14** 389;
fruits and herbs of, **13** 403*n*;
honeycomb of, **12** 456(5)*n*;
as island in the sea, **13** 406*n*;
keys of, in dream, **7** 287; **9i**
71–2, 398;
Leviathan as eucharistic food
in, **9ii** 174, 185; **14** 338;
man implanted in, **13** 411;
Man of (in alchemy), **16** 517;
Mercurius and, **13** 278, 282;
quaternio, *see* quaternity;
serpent of, *see* ANIMALS: ser-
pent/snake *s.v.* paradise/
paradisal;
stone (alchemical) and, **14**
570&*n*;
symbolism of, **9i** 156; **9ii** 296;
14 276, 279;
tree of, *see* tree(s) *s.v.*;
see also Guillaume de Digulleville *s.v.* Paradise
Paradise Lost, see Milton
paradox(es), **9ii** 124; **12** 188, 190;
14 36–9, 715;
TITLE: "The Paradoxa," **14**
36–103;
of alchemy, *see* alchemy *s.v.*;
in Gnostic writings, **11** 417,
418;
in religion, **12** 11*n*, 18, 19;
self as, **12** 20, 22;
of unconscious, **16** 62–3;
of unimpaired virginity, **16**
529;
see also antinomy
paradoxicality of life, **13** 7
paraesthesia(s), **3** 308; **18** 922;
of head, **16** 554
parallel(s)/parallelism: mythological, **5** 282; **17** 210;
pre-established, **8** 938;
of psychic processes, **8** 503;
psychological, **13** 11;
psychophysical, **3** 7; **8** 33, 937,
948, 958; **10** 527, 780; **11** 881;

18 70, 136;
symbolic, **8** 845;
see also harmony *s.v.* pre-established

paralogia, **3** 185*n*;
metaphorical, **3** 135*n*

paralysis, **1** 154; **3** 193; **17** 141; **18** 728;
association chain, *see* association chain(s) *s.v.*;
emotional, **1** 123*n*, 307; **3** 147;
hysterical, **2** 911–13; **3** 503;
progressive, **3** 327, 497;
spastic, **7** 4, 6–7/413, 415–16;
of the will, **18** 787;
see also general paralysis of the insane

pārāmitās, **11** 919

paramnesia, **4** 499, 502; **8** 853; **17** 199a

paranoia/paranoid dementia, **2** 1072, 1263–9; **3** 471, 499; **6** 467, 865, 879; **7** 228, 254; **9i** 220; **18** 899;
of alcoholic, **3** 461;
delusions and, **3** 169;
Freud on, **3** 61;
Freud's cases of: Schreber, *see* Freud: CASES *s.v.*; of woman, **3** 61–72;
galvanometer and pneumograph experiments, **2** 1062, 1065, 1076;
Honegger's case, **5** 200;
induced, **16** 358*n*;
"inventor's," **1** 218, 219;
loss of reality in, **5** 192, 200;
megalomanic stage in, **5** 154*n*;
organic character, **3** 318;
originaria, **18** 889;
primary, **3** 73*n*;
stability of, **3** 72;
see also delusions *s.v.* paranoid

paraphasia, **3** 135;
dream, **3** 135*n*, 180

paraphysiological theory, Géley's, **13** 76*n*

parapraxes, **8** 210; **18** 1149

parapsychology/parapsychological/parapsychic phenomena, **8** 405*n*, 441, 600&*n*, 812, 856, 944; **9i** 457; **10** 169, 634, 780; **11** 443; **13** 60; **16** 254; **18** 757, 763, 781, 783, 1498, 1567*n*;
TITLE: "The Future of Parapsychology," **18** 1213–22;
of absolute knowledge, **10** 636;
future of, **18** 1213–22;
J.'s own experience, **18** 769;
and materialization, **10** 788;
and relativization of space/time, **10** 527, 849;
sources of, **18** 761;
truth of, **18** 788;
see also levitation; occult; spiritualism; telepathy

parasite(-ism), **7** 373;
intestinal, **8** 323;
psychic, **7** 188;
puer aeternus, **5** 393

paredroi/πάρεδροι, *see* familiar/*paredros*

parent(s), **7** 57, 296; **8** 774; **9i** 126; **11** 763; **15** 49, 100; **16** 212, 368; **17** 18, 217, 247, 259–60, 284–5;
archetype of, **10** 71; **16** 212*n*;
-child relationship, **4** 312, 662;
and child, unconscious identity of, **5** 351; **17** 106, 217a–20, 253 (*see also* Lévy-Bruhl *s.v. participation mystique*); unlived lives of, **6** 307;
in children's character development, **2** 1007–8, 1013–14;
complexes of, *see* complex(es) *s.v.*;
detachment/differentiation/liberation from, **4** 348; **5** 431; **7** 393; **8** 36, 725–6, 756; **12** 79; **17** 158–9; **18** 361–2;
and dreams, **17** 106;
excessive attachment to, **7** 172; **17** 107a, 146;
first, **13** 316, 427;
foster, **4** 377; **5** 34, 494, 566; **9i** 94; **17** 136; animal as, **5** 494,

ed. van Beek, *Passio SS Per-petuae et Felicitatis*, **14** 32*n*; *see also* M.-L. von Franz *s.v.* "Passio Perpetuae"

passivity, woman's, **10** 240; *see also* activity

Passover, **9ii** 181; **18** 1523

past: fascination of, **5** 631; and future, *see* future *s.v.*; idealization of, **9i** 471; reversion to, **4** 307; *see also* present

pastries, phallus-shaped, **5** 530

"pasture," etymology, **5** 214*n*

Patagonians, **13** 92

Patanjali, **6** 328*n*

Patarenes, **9ii** 139

pater mirabilis (synonym for *lapis*), **13** 203

paternalism, attribute of God, **5** 89

Pater noster, **11** 331

path, rocky (dream), **4** 170, 181, 183, 185, 186

Pathans, **10** 989

pathogenic: agent, **7** 13/422; conflict, *see* conflict *s.v.*; factor, **7** 70; significance, **7** 9/418

pathography, **18** 795

pathology, **4** 782; **9i** 465; **16** 192; and artistic creation, **15** 122, 144; primitive, **8** 587; sexual, **18** 904

patience, **9ii** 46

patient(s), **5** 683; **18** 338; age/type of, and aims of therapy, **16** 74–6; of alchemists, **16** 401; analyst's relation to, *see* analyst *s.v.*; attitude, *see* attitude *s.v.*; and catharsis, **16** 137–9, 142; confessions of, *see* confession (psychological) *s.v.*; doctor and, *see* doctor *s.v.*; doctor as, **4** 627 (*see also* analyst *s.v.* analysis of);

dreams of, **5** 62; **16** 92; face to face with therapist, **18** 319–21; information from, **5** 474; insight of, *see* insight *s.v.*; language of, **18** 518, 632; mental, with brain lesions, **3** 324; own need for knowledge, **18** 1128; pictures by, *see* pictures *s.v.*; rapport with doctor/therapist, *see* rapport *s.v.*; religion of, **11** 509; type of, and expediency, **4** 599; use of ideas gained from analysis, **4** 645

Patmos, island of, **11** 744*n*

"Patmos," *see* Hölderlin *s.v.*

patria/patris potestas, **4** 729; **16** 227

patriarch(s), *see* prophet(s)

patriarchal: order, **11** 223; **16** 215–16; in European civilization, **16** 217, 221–2; world, polytheism of, **11** 236

Patricius and Philarius, soothsayers, **18** 703

patristic: allegories, **11** 229; literature, **18** 655

Patrizi, Francesco, **12** 478; **13** 281; *Nova de universis philosophia*, **12** 478*n*

pattern(s): of behaviour, *see* archetype(s) *s.v.*; geometric, **13** 33; instinctual, **8** 856

Paul, St./Saul, **4** 780; **6** 816; **7** 104, 110, 243*n*, 365, 397, 401; **8** 767; **10** 265, 536, 783, 843; **11** 170, 289, 304, 549, 698, 890; **12** 165, 176; **13** 77; **14** 206, 232, 327; **18** 567, 638, 713, 1570,1574, 1642; allegory of, Indian dog as, **14** 174*n*; and Christ/Jesus, **11** 212, 222, 228; "inner Christ," **8** 584; **9i** 216; **13** 41; resurrection, **18** 1561, 1563;

perdition, son of, **9ii** 68*n*
Peredur Saga (Celtic), **6** 401*n*
peregrinatio, **5** 140*n*; **9ii** 206; **11** 105*n*, 676; **12** 457, 469, 515, *fig.* 97
Peregrinus: "Speculum virginum," **12** *fig.* 197
"peregrinus microcosmus," **13** 190
Pererius, Benedictus, S.J.: *De magia: De observatione somniorum et de divinatione astrologica libri tres,* **11** 32*n*
perfection, **7** 186, 303, 462*n*; **14** 348&*n*;
    accidental lack of, **11** 457;
    of Christ, **9ii** 72;
    and completeness, **9ii** 123;
    evil as lack of, **9ii** 74;
    idea of, **11** 144;
    as masculine, **11** 620;
    symbol of, **11** 727; **13** 346;
    and wholeness, **14** 616
perfectionism, **11** 620
perforation, **9ii** 185*n*
performance tests, **1** 333–5, 404&*n*, 410; *see also* unconscious (adj.) *s.v.* performance
perfume, autosuggestion and, **5** (*p*447)
Perga, coin from, **5** 298
Pergamum, **11** 702
"perils of the soul," *see* primitive(s) *s.v.* soul, perils of
perineum, **18** 17
peripeteia, **8** 563; **11** 642
permanence, **13** 322, 350;
    civilization and, **10** 923
Pernath, Athanasius *(The Golem),* **12** 53
Pernety, A. J., **9ii** 240, 247; **14** 87, 734;
    Dictionnaire mytho-hermétique, **9ii** 240*n*, 247*n*; **13** 176*n*; **14** 14*n*, 31*n*, 39*n*, 64*n*, 143*n*, 188*n*, 415*n*, 561*n*; **18** 1700;
    Les Fables égyptiennes et grècques, **13** 203*n*, 234*n*; **14** 87*n*, 144*n*, 486*n*, 724*n*, 734*n*

Peronelle, **14** 181*n*; **16** 505
"perpendicular cliff," **5** 418
Perpetua, St., **11** 714;
    Passion of, *see* "Passio Perpetuae"
perpetuum mobile, **18** 403; *see also* mandala *s.v.*
Perry, J. W.: *The Self in Psychotic Process,* J.'s foreword, **18** 832–8
persea tree, *see* TREES *s.v.*
persecution(s): of Christians, under Decius, **9i** 242*n*;
    ideas of, **8** 584; **10** 609;
    magical, **17** 207;
    mania, **3** 499, 506; **6** 469; **12** 57 (*see also* paranoia);
    motif of, **5** 559;
    and secret love, **18** 1375
Persephone/Proserpina, **5** 34, 148, 449*n*, 528; **9i** 169, 194, 313, 619; **9ii** 41, 339; **12** 26; **14** 24; **15** 152; **16** 518;
    Demeter and, *see* Demeter *s.v.*;
    Hecate and, **5** 577;
    Kore and, **5** 662;
    Luna as, **14** 24
Persepolis, **12** 532*n*
Perseus, **9i** 319
perseveration(s), **1** 312, 317*(tabs.)*; **2** 100–103, 397, 400, 419, 459, 750; **3** 12, 22, 25, 30, 37, 41, 53, 109, 182, 183, 544, 554, 578; **6** 463;
    of affect, **3** 87;
    in epilepsy, **2** 509;
    of feeling-tone, **2** 620, 645
Persia (Iran)/Persian, **7** 494; **13** 376; **14** 299;
    Ahriman, **3** 397; **5** 367*n*, 421*n*, 425, 528; **11** 256, 259, 470, 579*n*; **14** 34*n*;
    Ahura(-Mazda)/Ahuramazda/ Oromazdes, **5** 306*n*, 395, 421, 425, 560, 664; **11** 256, 262; **13** 119 (*see also* Ormuzd); and Angramainyu, **5** 421, 664;
    Buddhist monasteries in, **13** 278;
    disposal of dead in, **5** 354;

personalism (*cont.*):

Freud *s.v.*; and schizophrenia, **3** 544

personality(-ies), **1** 136; **3** 153; **4** 664; **5** 44-5, 274; **7** 28/439, 86, 171, 186, 218/450, 387, 400; **8** 631; **11** 1, 390; **13** 38, 41, 43, 58; TITLES: *The Development of Personality*, **17**; "The Development of Personality," **17** 284–323; of analyst, *see* analyst *s.v.*;

ancestral elements in, **9i** 224;

anima/animus as, *see* anima; animus *s.v.*;

archaic, in ourselves, **18** 36;

artificial, **7** 305, 307, 312;

automatic, **1** 125, 131;

autonomous, destiny as, **4** 727;

centre of, **7** 365; **9i** 304, 634; **9ii** 11; **11** 67; **12** 44, 126, 129, 135; **18** 410; self, not ego, as, **12** 44, 126, 129, 135, 137, 175, 310, 327; **13** 67; **16** 219;

change of, **1** 44; **5** 458; **7** 270; **8** 254-5, 809; **9i** 220, 223; **9ii** 10; **16** 373;

child's, **5** 457; **17** 284, 288;

of Christ, *see* Christ *s.v.*;

cleavage of, **7** 22;

collective, **7** 509;

complex/as complex, *see* complex(es) *s.v.*;

and compulsion neurosis, **7** 286;

conscious, **5** 459, 463, 467; **7** 128, (*p*124), 241/462, 251, 378, 512, 517; **9ii** 7-8; a segment of collective psyche, **7** 244/465;

includes conscious and unconscious, **9i** 315; **11** 66;

continuity of, **9i** 200-1;

creative, **17** 244;

cult of, **17** 311;

dark half of, **7** 152; **9i** 222; **12** 37 (*see also* shadow);

dependent, **17** 107a;

development, **7** 237/459, 239, 241*n*, 461; **13** 31;

of the devil, **11** 103;

differentiation, **7** 239; **17** 248;

diminution of, **7** 259; **8** 772; **9i** 213;

disintegration of, **3** 76, 142, 503, 509-10, 522, 578-80; **7** 233; **12** 439; **15** 174; and Joyce, **15** 169;

dissociation of, **1** 97, 117; **3** 105, 544; **4** 162, 295; **6** 503; **7** 63; **8** 61; **9ii** 280; **10** 417, 705; **13** 332; **14** 671; **16** 248, 329, 361; **17** 227; in neurotics, **7** 63; **8** 207;

dissolution of, *see* dissolution *s.v.*;

of doctor, *see* doctor *s.v.*;

double, *see below* second;

and dreams, **17** 123;

duplication of, **4** 106;

ego and, *see above* centre *s.v.*;

enlargement/extension/widening, **7** 218/450, 227, 235/457, 243/464, 255; **9i** 215, 219&*n*; **13** 24; **16** 472;

fictitious, **14** 753;

flattening of, **12** 291;

fragmentary, **11** 75; **15** 174; **18** 151, 153, 224;

fragmentation, **9i** 279 (*see also below* splitting);

in Freud's theory, **7** 203/444;

future, **18** 38;

greater/superior, **11** 902; **13** 17, 68, 120;

growth, *see below* transformation;

harmonious, **4** 623, 633;

ideal of, **17** 291, 311;

inferior, **5** 267; **9ii** 15 (*see also* shadow *s.v.* inferior side of personality);

inner, **5** 506;

innermost, **13** 36;

instinctual foundations of, **5** 660;

instinctual, reconstruction of, **11** 56;

phenomenon (*cont.*):
    collective psychic, **13** 51;
    psychic, **9i** 112;
    telepathic, **13** 174*n*
Pherecydes, **14** 630*n*;
    and oak-tree, winged, **14** 75*n*;
    and world-tree, **13** *fig.* 2; **14** 73
phial, spherical, **13** 109
Phidias, statue of Athene, **6** 44
Philadelphia, **11** 705
Philae, effigy of Osiris at, **5** 400
Philalethes, *see* ALCHEMICAL WRITERS
    s.v.
philanthropic work, **3** 105
Philebus, *see* Plato: WORKS
Philemon, Epistle of, *see* BIBLE: N.T.
    s.v.
Philemon and Baucis, *see* Goethe:
    Faust, Characters *s.v.*
Phileros, **6** 308
Philhellenism, **6** 314
Philip, Gospel of, *see* BIBLE:
    Apocrypha/etc. *s.v.*
Philippians, Epistle to, *see* BIBLE:
    N.T. *s.v.*
Philistines/Philistinism, **8** 776; **10**
    376
Philo Byblius, **11** 328
Philoctetes, **5** 450
Philo Judaeus, **5** 580; **9i** 106; **11**
    178, 619*n*; **12** 456*n*; **13** 168, 448;
    14 353, 586&*n*, 592, 643*n*; **18**
    1480&*n*;
        De opificio mundi/"On the Ac-
        count of the World's Crea-
        tion Given by Moses," tr. F.
        H. Colson and G. H.
        Whitaker, **8** 855, 925; **9i** 5,
        679; **13** 336*n*; **14** 586*n*,
        761&*n*;
        De somniis, tr. F. H. Colson
        and G. H. Whitaker, **5**
        158&*n*;
        In Genesim, tr. J. B. Aucher, **5**
        425; **14** 11*n*;
        "Who is the Heir of Divine
        Things?," **14** 73*n*
Philolaos, **12** 433

philology, **16** 351
philosopher(s), **7** 229/448; **11** 460,
    499–500; **13** 126;
    Adam as first, **14** 570;
    egg of, *see* egg *s.v.*;
    garden of, **13** 407;
    and meaning of life, **11** 514–
    15;
    metal of, **13** 268*n*;
    modern, **13** 155;
    neurotic, **7** 397;
    secrets of, **13** 101;
    son of, see *filius philosophorum;*
    stone of, *see* lapis; stone, philo-
    sophical;
    vinegar/water of, **13** 113, 359*n*
"Philosophia chemica," *see* ALCHEM-
    ICAL COLLECTIONS: *Theatr. chem.*
    s.v. Dorn: "Liber de naturae
    physica luce"
"Philosophia meditativa," *see* AL-
    CHEMICAL COLLECTIONS: *Theatr.*
    chem. s.v. Dorn
philosophic(al): dialectic, **13** 286;
    earth, **13** 380;
    egg, *see* egg *s.v.*;
    Eye, **13** 31;
    gold, *see* gold *s.v.*;
    heaven, **13** 271;
    lead, **13** 274;
    man, **12** 209; **13** 125, 282 (*see*
    also Anthropos *s.v. homo philo-*
    sophicus); Mercurius as, *see* Mer-
    curius *s.v. homo philosophicus;*
    matter, **13** 380;
    stone, *see* lapis; stone, philo-
    sophical;
    tree, *see* tree(s) *s.v.*
philosophy, **7** 80, 229, 302, 440; **8**
    683; **13** 145; **17** 127;
    TITLES: "Psychotherapy and a
    Philosophy of Life," **16** 175–
    91; "The Type Problem in
    Modern Philosophy," **6** 505–
    41;
    alchemical, *see* alchemy *s.v.*;
    Alexandrian, **11** 193;
    and archetypes, **8** 342;

Aristotelean, **13** 149;
Cartesian, **8** 845;
causal, **7** 72;
Chinese, *see* China/Chinese;
and the Church, **14** 325–6;
critical, **11** 759;
Eastern/Oriental, **7** (*p*124); **11**
759, 905, 961; **13** 1, (*p*56); **18**
144, 204, 532; introspective
character of, **8** 436; **13** 74;
German, *see* Germany *s.v.*;
Gnostic, *see* Gnostic(-ism) *s.v.*;
Greek/Hellenistic, **5** 113; **6** 23;
8 655; **11** 246; natural, **9i** 149;
13 104 (*see also* Cynics; Megarians; Plato; Sophism);
Hegel's, *see* Hegel;
Hermetic, *see* Hermetic philosophy;
Indian/Hindu, **5** 588, 590, 612,
646, 659; **7** 118*n*, 240*n*; **8** 436;
9i 76, 419, 506, 717; **10** 1006;
11 281, 397*n*, 713, 859, 933; **13**
178; **14** 90; **15** 189; religious, **6**
191–4; **9ii** 126; and supercon-
sciousness, **8** 369*n* (*see also* Sankhya; Upanishads; Vedas);
and instinct, **16** 185;
of life, **13** 75; **16** 84, 178–90,
218;
of materialism and, **3** 467;
and meaning of life, **11** 514–
15;
medieval, **18** 403;
and modern age, **10** 372; **13**
155;
mystical, **12** 332;
myths and, **8** 327;
nature/natural, **5** 113; **13** 134,
196, 353, 481; **15** 37; Greek/
Hellenistic, **9i** 149; **13** 104;
medieval, **11** (*p*358); **12** 40, 84;
13 353; **14** 326;
not one but many, **8** 659;
of Paracelsus, *see* Paracelsus
s.v.;
Platonic, *see* Platonic *s.v.* school
of philosophy;

and psychoanalysis, **4** 524,
554–5, 745; **7** 201;
psychology and, **2** 863–4; **7**
201, 407; **8** 525–6, 659; **11** 3;
16 232, 250–1; **17** 127, 128,
165; **18** 181, 557, 834, 1411,
1737–9;
psychopathology and, **10** 1040;
and psychotherapy, **16** 180;
and religion, *see* religion *s.v.*;
scholastic, *see* scholasticism;
and science, division, **11** 860;
and the soul, **8** 650;
speculative, **8** 678;
spiritualistic, **18** 753;
subjective, **11** 766;
Taoist, *see* Taoism;
true, **13** 377;
and *Weltanschauung*, **8** 689;
Western, **11** 759, 905;
see also Stoics; yoga
Philostratus: *The Life of Apollonius of
Tyana*, tr. F. C. Conybeare, **12**
526*n*
Philp, H. L.: *Jung and the Problem of
Evil*, J.'s letters in, **18** 1584–1624
Philyra, **5** 421*n*
Phlegians, **5** 208
phlegm/*phlegma*, **14** 691, 695, 703,
748
phlegmatic temperament, **6** 547,
883, 933, 960
phlegmone, **18** 544
Phlegyas, **14** 144*n*
Phleps, E., **1** 319;
  "Psychosen nach Erdbeben," **1**
  307*n*
phlogiston theory, **9ii** 394–5
phobia(s), **3** 539; **7** 307; **8** 266, 297,
702, 798; **9ii** 259; **13** 54, 298; **14**
225; **16** 13, 196, 463; **17** 30, 141,
185;
  of cats, **4** 183;
  infantile, **9i** 159
Phobos, **7** 78
Phocaeans, **18** 252&*n*
Phoebe, **14** 144*n*
Phoebus, **9ii** 367*n*

Piéron (*cont.*):
"L'Association médiate," 2 451*n*;
"La Théorie des émotions et les données actuelles de la physiologie," 18 (*p*421)
Pierre, Noel: "Soleil noir," 13 348&*n*
Pietà, 9i 312;
Etruscan, 5 pl. LIV;
and Terrible Mother, 5 662
pietism, 10 508
piety, 14 657;
and sexual impulse, 5 332*n*;
stork as allegory of, 13 417
pig, *see* ANIMALS *s.v.*
pigeon, *see* ANIMALS *s.v.*
Pignatelli, Jacobus: *Consultationes canonicae,* 12 40*n*
Pilcz, A.: *Lehrbuch der speziellen Psychiatrie für Studierende und Aerzte,* J.'s review, 18 914
pileus (Phrygian cap), 5 165*n*, 183, 299
Pilgrim, Spiritual, 10 764, pl. VII
"Pilgrim's Tract"/*Ein nutzlicher und loblicher Tractat von Bruder Claus und einem Bilger,* anon., 9i 16; 11 476&*n*
pill, golden, 12 247
pillar(s): fiery/solar/pneumatic, tree as, 13 408*n*;
of fire, *see* fire;
four, see *tetrapeza;*
of Hercules, 5 460*n*;
of Shu, *see* Shu
pilot (dream), 12 147, 148, 153
Pilzecker, A., *see under* Müller, G. E.
pince-nez, 3 335
Pindar, 5 439; 11 373
pine-cones/-tree, *see* TREES *s.v.*
Pinel, P., 1 188; 3 322;
A Treatise on Insanity, tr. D. D. Davis, 1 188*n*
pinguedo mannae, 13 190*n*
pinpricks, *see* pricks
pin-sticking, 10 700
pioneer work, 18 1234

Piper, L., 13 60&*n*
Pirkè de Rabbi Eliezer, *see* Eliezer Hyrcanus
Pisano, Antonio, medal by, 12 *fig.* 262
Pisces, *see* zodiac, twelve signs of; *see also* ANIMALS *s.v.* fish
pisciculi Christianorum, 9ii 162
piscina, see baptism *s.v.* font
Piscis Austrinus, *see* ANIMALS: fish *s.v.* in astrology
Pison river, 9ii 311, 353, 372; 14 389
pissing manikin, *see* homunculus
pistis (πίστις), 11 9, 74, 167; 14 147; 17 296
Pistis Sophia, tr. G.R.S. Mead, 5 318*n*; 9ii 128*n*, 131, 133*n*, 148*n*, 168*n*, 187*n*, 212*n*, 307*n*; 11 92*n*, 120*n*, 177*n*, 350*n*; 12 209*n*, 460*n*; 14 352*n*, 589*n*
Pitaval, *see* Gayot de Pitaval
"pitch-birds"/*Pechvögel,* 18 41
pith, 9i 535
Pithecanthropus, 14 279; 18 486
Pitra, J.-B.: *Analecta sacra,* 5 139*n*, 158*n*; 8 394*n*; 11 161*n*; 12 314*n*; 13 98*n*, 407*n*; 14 181*n*, 288*n*, 316*nn*, 701*n*;
Spicilegium solesmense, 12 522*n*
Pitys, 12 456*n*
Pius, brother of Hermas, 6 385
Pius IX, Pope, 9ii 142*n*; 14 744*n*
Pius X, Pope, 4 82
Pius XI, Pope, 18 1711*n*;
Encyclical *Casti Connubii,* 18 1711&*n*, 1799&*n*
Pius XII, Pope, 11 474*n*, 743&*n*, 748–9;
Apostolic Constitution "Munificentissimus Deus" (1950), 11 251*n*, 743*n*, 748; 14 201*n*, 207*n*, 237*n*; 18 1536*n*, 1683*n*;
Encyclical *Ad Caeli Reginam* (1954), 11 251*n*;
visions of, 11 748
Pius, Roman Bishop, 18 255
PK, *see* psychokinetic experiment

placenta, primitive idea of, **5** 356

plagiarism, and cryptomnesia, **1** 139, 179

plague balls, **13** 193*n*

"plan, great," **10** 420

planchette, **8** 171

planet(s), **8** 867; **9i** 588*n*; **12** 175, 220, *fig.* 100; **13** 176*n*, 357;
  fantasies about, **10** 611, 614;
  four, **9i** 588*n*;
  gods of, **9i** 242*n*, 246*n*, 682*n*; **12** 40, 84, *figs.* 21, 23; **14** 563;
  as spirits of metals, **12** 40 (*see also* demons *s.v.* planetary);
  influence of, **9ii** 230; **13** 160*n*; **14** 308, 757;
  and metals, **12** 348, 410; **13** 355;
  names, **13** 355;
  seven, **8** 394; **12** 66, 214, 348, 410, *figs.* 20, 29, 199; **13** 398, 416; **14** 287, 297, 472*n*, 574; 633; **16** 402; archons as, **14** 576; colours of, **14** 390, 577; spheres of, **12** 66, 410, *fig.* 51; **14** 288, 298, 576; stairway of, **12** 66; —, as "passage of soul," **14** 578; trees of, **13** 407, 409; six, **12** *figs.* 154, 155, 192; gods of, **12** *fig.* 23; sons of king Sol, **12** 210, *fig.* 79; as spirits of metals, **12** 40; **14** 217; united in seventh, **12** *fig.* 20;
  see also house(s) *s.vv.* astrological, planetary; Jupiter; Mars; Mercury (planet); Neptune; Saturn; Uranos; Venus; zodiac

planetarium (dream), **11** 162

planetary demons/spirits, *see* demon(s) *s.v.*

plant(s), **8** 605; **9i** 329; **13** 33, 66, 301, 392;
  asparagus, **13** 413;
  kingdom, and "blessed greenness," **13** 102;
  life forces of, **1** 67;
  love of, as compensation, **6** 468;

moon- (alchemical), **13** 406;
motif, in dreams, **12** 34, 198;
reivas (Iranian), **13** 458*n*;
seeds, in mandalas, **13** 34;
symbolism, **9i** 315; **13** 241, 304; in alchemy, **14** 687;
Paracelsan, **13** 193&*n*;
see also flowers; herbs; prickly poppy

plastic images, **2** 471&*n*, 473

Plataean cult of Hera Teleia, **5** 363

plateau, in dream, **9i** 334

Plato, **6** 42–4, 48–9, 52, 55–7, 733, 963; **8** 336, 942; **10** 408, 621; **11** 61*n*, 93, 196, 430; **12** 456(5), 462; **13** 393, 412; **14** 135*n*, 170*n*, 564, 732;
  "All-round" man of, **18** 638;
  and archetypes, **8** 275; **9i** 5;
  eidos / eide / eidola / εἶδος (form, species), **3** 527; **6** 57; **8** 942; **9i** 5, 68; **9ii** 64; **11** 845; **15** 12 (*see also below* on ideas);
  on Eros, *see* Eros/Cupid *s.v.* daemon;
  on ideas, **6** 40–60, 733; **8** 388, 943*n*; **9i** 149, 154; **10** 199, 621; **12** 368; **14** 181*n*; as *res simplex*, **14** 493*n*;
  on images, **6** 512;
  and laws of association, **2** 868;
  mandala structure in, **11** 190;
  Original/Primordial Man, **9i** 138*n*; **12** 109*n*; **13** 173; **14** 587;
  parables of, **8** 474; of black and white horses, **6** 963; **9i** 72; **10** 844; of cave, **5** 612; **8** 416*n*; **14** 768; **15** 105;
  on philosophy as preparation for death, **18** 753;
  pseudo-, *see* ALCHEMICAL COLLECTIONS: *Theatr. chem. s.v.* "Platonis liber quartorum";
  and quaternity, *see* quaternity *s.v.* in Greek thought;
  transcendentalism of, **6** 57;
  Trinitarian thinking of, *see* triad(s) *s.v.* Trinity;

Plato (*cont.*):
  unfinished tetralogies, **11** 192&*n*;
  and world-soul, *see* world-soul *s.v.* Plato;
  WORKS:
    Critias, **11** 190, 192*n*;
    Phaedrus, **6** 56*n*, 963*n*; **9ii** 118; **12** 456*n*;
    Philebus, **11** 186*n*; **12** 456*n*;
    Protagoras, **6** 289;
    Republic, **11** 192*n*; **14** 90*n*;
    Symposium, **5** 242; **9i** 138*n*, 557*n*; **11** 47*n*, 93*n*; tr. R. G. Bury, **14** 564*n*; tr. W. Hamilton, **5** 242*n*; **6** 56*n*; **14** 564*n*;
    Timaeus, **3** 582*n*; **5** 227*n*, 556; **9ii** 212; **11** 92, 99, 113, 120, 160*n*, 179, 180*n*, 181–92, 232, 290; **12** 109*n*, 456*n*; **13** 102, 263, 412*n*; **16** 531; "fourth" in, **8** 962; **9i** 425, 426&*n*, 436, 695, 715; **10** 738; **11** 119, 190–2, 243, 251, 280; **14** 278; tr. F. M. Cornford, **5** 404; **11** 179, 181*n*, 182*n*, 186*n*, 187*n*, 190*n*, 191; commentaries by Proclus, *see* Proclus; commentary by T. Taylor, **11** 190; numbers and creation in, **11** 181–5; *see also* Apelt
Platonic: demiurge, **11** 186;
  man, **13** 39;
  months, in astrology, **9i** 551;
  nature, **13** 382;
  school of philosophy/Platonists, **6** 57, 473; **7** 80; **8** 930
platonic relationships, *see* friendship *s.v.* platonic
Platonic Tetralogies, Book of, see AL-CHEMICAL COLLECTIONS: *Theatr. chem. s.v.* "Platonis liber quartorum"
"Platonis liber quartorum," *see* AL-CHEMICAL COLLECTIONS: *Theatr. chem. s.v.*
Plautus, **5** 279

play: in animals, **4** 235;
  creative activity as, **6** 198;
  fantasy and, **6** 93;
  of goats, **12** 105;
  instinct, *see* instinct *s.v.*;
  with numbers, **4** 145;
  and sport, **10** 977
playing cards, in experiment with hypnotized subject, **1** 130
pleasure, **4** 240, 634, 642;
  carnal, statue, **7** 437;
  craving for, **8** 764;
  infantile, **16** 66;
  and lust, **17** 145;
  and pain, *see* pain-pleasure;
  principle, *see* Freud *s.v.*;
  -seeking, **1** 220, 438;
  and sexuality, relation, **4** 241, 347;
  sources of, **5** 652
Pleiades, **9ii** 212; **14** 579
pleonasm, **2** 536, 733*n*
pleroma/pleromatic, **9i** 533*n*; **9ii** 75*n*, 80, 120*n*, 344*n*; **11** 620, 629, 675, 733, 748; **12** 138; **13** 116*n*, 451, 456; **14** 574; **18** 1513;
  Bardo State, **11** 620;
  Enoch as son of man in, **11** 686;
  hierosgamos in, **11** 624, 755;
  pre-existence of Yahweh and Sophia in, **11** 727
plethysmograph, **2** 1191
Pliny, **9i** 537; **9ii** 197, 214, 223, 241*n*, 274; **11** 89*n*; **12** 405, 456*n*; **14** 154, 474; **15** 27;
  Idaean dactyls, **5** 183*n*;
  The Natural History of Pliny, tr. J. Bostock and H. Riley, **5** 183*n*; tr. H. Rackham and W.H.S. Jones, **9i** 537*n*; **9ii** 197*n*, 214*n*; **12** 526*n*; **14** 87*n*, 474*n*, 731*n*
Plokker, J. H., **18** (*p*826*n*)
Plotinus, **6** 21; **9ii** 342;
  Porphyry's Life of, **12** 458;
  and *unus mundus*/unity of world, **14** 761;

Portmann, A., **10** 636;
   "Die Bedeutung der Bilder in
   der lebendigen Energie-
   wandlung," **10** 636*n*; **11** 447*n*
Portrait of the Artist as a Young Man,
   see Joyce
Portu, Bernardus à, *see* ALCHEMICAL
   COLLECTIONS: *Theatr. chem. s.v.*
   Penotus
Portugal, **18** 1287
Poseidon/Neptune, the god, **5** 316*n*,
   421*n*, 439, 457*n*; **9i** 328; **9ii** 338;
   12 203; **13** 398*n*; **14** 261;
   as animus, **12** *fig.* 132
positive values, **7** 70
positivism, **6** 621; **9i** 267
possession, **3** 321; **7** 111, 382, 388; **8**
   204; **9i** 82, 220, 277, 387, 455,
   501, 621; **10** 287, 309, 431, 435,
   721; **11** 20, 85, 143, 242*n*; **12** 182,
   563; **15** 62, 65, 71–2; **16** 196, 371;
   18 1374;
      anima, *see* anima *s.v.*;
      animus, *see* animus *s.v.*;
      by archetype(s), *see* archetype(s)
      s.v.;
      Church's view on, **9i** 220*n*;
      collective, **10** 490;
      by consciousness, **13** 51;
      criteria of, **11** 242*n*;
      demonic, **18** 522;
      by devils, *see* devil(s) *s.v.*;
      distinguished from disease, **11**
      242*n*;
      and hysteria, **8** 710;
      and insanity, **8** 576;
      power of, **7** 374;
      state(s) of, **7** 370; **13** 48; **18**
      884;
      symptoms of, **14** 225;
      by unconscious, **16** 397;
      see also *Ergreifer*/etc.
possibility: criterion of, **8** 821;
      psychological, and success of
      suggestion, **1** 93
postulates, metaphysical, **11** 460
potash, **14** 320
potential, difference of, **4** 779

potentiality(-ies): psychic, loss of, **8**
   770;
      of unconscious, **11** 805, 812
Potipherah, **12** 456*n*
Pototsky, —: "Die Verwertbarkeit
   des Assoziationsversuches für die
   Beurteilung der traumatischen
   Neurosen," J.'s abstract, **18** 996
Potter, Most High and Almighty,
   12 470
potter's wheel, *see* wheel *s.v.*
pounding, *see* hammering
"poures hommes evangelisans," **13**
   277*n*
poverty: Christianity and, **9i** 29, 30,
   33;
      spiritual, **9i** 29, 33
Powell, J. W., **6** 46;
      *Annual Reports of the Smithsonian
      Institution,* **11** 99*n*;
      "Sketch of the Mythology of
      the North American Indians,"
      6 46*n*
power(s), **5** 526*n*, 638;
      of anima, **7** 381, 389;
      Catholic Church and, **10** 654;
      complex, *see* complex *s.v.*;
      -concept, primitive, **7** 108; **8**
      95; **10** 134–5, 139;
      creative/destructive, **17** 244;
      fantasies/psychology, of intro-
      vert, **6** 535, 627;
      in human psyche, **7** 110–11; **10**
      312, 330;
      instinct/of instinct, *see* instinct
      s.v.;
      light and dark, **1** 66–9; **13** 291,
      450, 452;
      magical universal, **7** 108, 151,
      154&*n*, 375;
      mana as, **7** 388;
      personal, **7** (*p*5);
      principle/drive, *see* Adler, A.
      s.v.;
      psychotherapy and increase of,
      8 590;
      religion and, **11** 8;
      Roman worship of, **17** 309;

533

power(s) (*cont.*):
  striving for, *see* Adler *s.v.* power principle;
  supreme, **18** 1658–60;
  technical/material, dangers of, **11** 868–9; **13** 293;
  telluric, *see* Keyserling *s.v.*;
  trust in higher, **13** 82;
  of unconscious, **7** 258/474, 391; **13** 454;
  will to, *see* Adler, A. *s.v.* power principle;
  -word, **3** 155, 202, 208; **5** 201; **10** 102; **11** 442; **13** 73, 155
"powers," suprapersonal, subjection to, **8** 95
Prabhavananda, S., *see under* Bhagavad Gita
practica and *theoria*, *see* opus, alchemical *s.v.* two parts of
"Practica Mariae," *see* ALCHEMICAL COLLECTIONS: *Art. aurif. s.v.* Maria
practice, effects of, in association tests, **1** 316
pragmatism, **6** 540&*n*, 541; **10** 941
praise, of the Creator, **13** 299*n*
praising, formulae for, **11** 222
Prajāpati, **5** 589; **6** 338&*n*, 339–42, 347; **9ii** 322*n*; **11** 397*n*; **12** 533; **13** 168;
  with world-egg, **5** *fig.* 36;
  see also *tapas*
Prajna, **11** 879
Prakṛti/*prakriti*, **9i** 158; **11** 778, 798
pramantha, *see* fire-stick
Prampolini, G.: *La Mitologia nella vita dei populi*, **5** pl. XLVIII
prāna, **5** 659; **11** 866–7
prānayāma exercises, **11** 866
Prasiae, **5** 183*n*
Pratt, J. G., J. B. Rhine, C. E. Stuart, B. M. Smith and J. A. Greenwood: *Extra-Sensory Perception after Sixty Years*, **8** 833*n*
prayer, **6** 336–7; **8** 966; **9i** 44, 130*n*; **10** 666, 671, 679; **11** 740*n*; **14** 743; **18** 1536–7;
  common, **11** 543;

concentration of libido on the God-image, **5** 257;
  purpose of, **5** 261;
  -word, **5** 557;
  see also invocation
precession of equinoxes, **9i** 7; **9ii** 136, 148, 150
precinct, sacred, see *temenos*
precious/cheap, as opposites, **14** 1
precipitancy, **3** 41*n*
precipitation(s), in alchemy, **13** 444
precocity, **17** 238;
  abnormal, **17** 211, 238;
  sexual, **17** 145
precognition, *see* foreknowledge
preconscious, **5** 39*n*; **7** 218/449
predestination, **11** 646, 718, 739;
  individual, **7** 300
predicate(s): type, *see* type(s) *s.v.*;
  value, **8** 198
predication, principle of, **6** 45, 52, 54–5
predicative reactions, **2** 45–65, 396, 473
prediction, **15** 84;
  triple, of death, **14** 89
predisposition, **7** 8–10/417–19, 219;
  TITLE: "The Predisposition for the Trauma," **4** 218–23;
  to dementia praecox, *see* schizophrenia *s.v.*;
  to neurosis, *see* neurosis *s.v.*
Preemby, *see* Wells, H. G.: *Christina Alberta's Father*
Preface, of the Mass, **11** 321
prefiguration, **8** 829; **9ii** 414;
  doctrine of, **12** 253
preformation, **4** 728—9
pregnancy, **4** 234; **8** 662;
  abhorrence of, **9i** 170;
  -complex, *see* complex(es) *s.v.*;
  disturbances, **9i** 170;
  hysterical attitude towards, **2** 851;
  illness in, **17** 134;
  imitation of, **17** 39;
  primitive view of, **17** 79;
  psychic, **6** 806; **16** 465;

by swallowing fish etc., **17** 43–5
prehistory, neolithic, **9i** 21
pre-infantile period, **7** 118, 120
Preisendanz, K., *see* ALCHEMICAL
WRITERS *s.v.* Magic Papyri
Preisigke, F., **11** 177;
*Die Gotteskraft der frühchristlichen
Zeit,* **11** 177*n*;
*Vom göttlichen Fluidum nach
ägyptischer Anschauung,* **11** 177*n*
Preiswerk, S., **5** 534
prejudice(s), **3** 166; **7** 240; **13** 60,
66;
of analyst, **16** 8;
danger of, **16** 237;
moral, **17** 182;
positive or negative, **18** 579;
subjective, of Adler and Freud,
16 235, 243
Preller, L.: *Griechische Mythologie,* **5**
421*n*, 662*n*; **13** 91*n*, 275*n*
Prellwitz, W., **5** 579;
*Etymologisches Wörterbuch der
griechischen Sprache,* **5** 322*n*,
638*n*
prelogical: mind, **10** 106;
thought, *see* Lévy-Bruhl *s.v.*
l'état prélogique
premises, psychic, **13** 378
premonition(s), **1** 37;
of children, **17** 94;
and somnambulism, **1** 40, 44
prenatal: life, and neurosis, **16** 258;
stage, and regression, **5** 508,
654
preoccupation, and somnambulistic
attacks, **1** 77
prepubertal stage, **4** 264
Pre-Raphaelites, **15** 175
presence: collective, **11** 224;
psychic, **11** 224
present: aetiological significance of,
4 373–4;
consciousness of, **10** 149–54;
meaning of, **10** 239;
psychological, as result of the
past, **4** 44, 67
presentiments, **4** 453

preservation of species: instinct for,
see instinct *s.v.*;
and sexuality, **4** 235
presexual stage, **4** 263–6; **5** 206;
and libido, **4** 268–9, 291; **5** 227,
654
pre-Socratics, **15** 11
Press, the, in wartime, **8** 507
prestige, **7** 108, 200, 391;
dissolution of, **7** 239;
magical, **7** 237, 239;
personal, **7** 237, 238;
psychology, *see* Adler, A. *s.v.*
presuppositions, of primitive, **10** 112
Pretiosa margarita novella, see AL-
CHEMICAL WRITERS: Bonus *s.v.*
Preuschen, E.: *Antilegomena,* **13**
137*n*; **14** 525*n*
Preuss, K. T., **14** 114*n*;
"Der Ursprung der Religion
und Kunst," **5** 213*n*; **8** 83*n*,
128&*n*
Prevorst, seeress/Prophetess of, *see*
Kerner *s.v.*
Preyer, W. T., **1** 82*n*;
*Die Erklärung des Gedanken-
lesens,* **1** 84*n*
priapic animals, **5** 421
Priapus, **5** 198; **9i** 560; **9ii** 366&*n*;
Roman statues, **5** 321;
statue/stele with snake, at Verona, **5** 530*n*, 680, pl. LXI*b*; **18**
1078;
use of image *vs.* cattle-pest, **5**
212
Price, H., **18** 1326&*n*; *An Account of
Some Further Experiments with Willy
Schneider,* **18** 1326*n*; *The
Phenomena of Rudi Schneider,* **18**
1326*n*
prick(s) (pin-): on anaesthetic hand,
1 98, 138, 160;
insensibility to, **1** 230;
reaction to, **1** 235, 327
prickly poppy, **11** 340
pride, **7** 225, 226
priest(hood), **7** 325, 389; **11** 33,
505, 506;

lapis as, **9i** 289, 541; **9ii** 194, 375, 418; **12** 335, 425, 433, *fig.* 142F; **13** 421; **14** 714;
lead as, **12** 443; **13** 139*n*, 401*n*; **14** 183, 637, 703;
man and, **12** 426; **14** 513, 685;
massa confusa/informis as, **12** 244, 426*n*, 433; **14** 552;
Mercurius, *see* Mercurius *s.v.*;
meretrix, **11** 312;
of metals, **14** 40;
microcosm, **12** 425–6&*n*;
Monad as, **12** 427, 472;
monster as, **12** 426*n*, 517, 536;
moon as, **12** 425, 487;
mortificatio of, **13** (*p*60*n*); **14** 401*n*;
mother as, **12** 425;
"mumia" as, **14** 560&*n*;
nigredo, **12** 263, 334, 433;
opposites in, **12** 435*n*, *fig.* 162;
ore/iron, **12** 425;
poison, **12** 336, 425;
and principle of evil, **11** 107;
production of, **9ii** 240;
as psychic situation, **9ii** 240;
radix ipsius, **12** 429;
rebis, **12** 517;
res, **12** 427, 431;
return to, **14** 118;
salniter and, **9i** 535*n*;
as salt, **12** 425;
Saturn as, **12** *fig.* 161; **14** 637, 703;
sea as, *see* sea *s.v.*;
self-begetting, **12** 426*n*;
as shadow, **9ii** 240; **12** 425;
sky, **12** 425;
as spirit, **12** 425;
spirit in, **12** 444, 447, *figs.* 129, 229, 232;
sublimation of, **12** *fig.* 175;
sulphur as, **12** 425; **14** 134;
synonyms of, **9ii** 245; **13** 173;
thousand names of, **12** 165, 336, 431;
transformation process of, **14** 68;

ubiquity of, **12** 433;
and *ultima materia*, **11** 353;
= unconscious, **12** 516;
unknown substance, **12** 425;
Unum, **12** 427;
urine, **12** 336;
uroboros, **12** *fig.* 123;
vas, **12** 338;
Venus, **12** 425;
vinegar, **12** 336;
water of life, **12** 425;
wolf as, **12** *fig.* 175;
primal: being(s), **5** 648, 650–1;
hermaphroditic, **9i** 138*n*;
experience, **5** 500&*n*;
horde, Freud's myth, **5** 396; **9i** 126;
incest, **13** 396;
mother, sacrifice of containment in, **5** 652;
will, *see* will *s.v.* Schopenhauer's concept
Primary Force, **13** 37
Primas, *see* Gnostic(-ism) *s.v.* Saturn
Prime Cause, **12** 16
primitive(s)/savages, **4** 308, 369, 403, 564, 641; **5** 248; **6** 27, 402–3, 414–15, 422, 430, 962; **7** 132, 154&*n*, 173; **8** 217, 237; **10** 26, 214, 243, 625, 656, 969; **11** 198, 385, 800; **13** 76, 247, 475; **15** 149; **17** 79, 207, 315, 336;
and ancestors, **9i** 224; **16** 251;
anger in, **18** 42;
and archetypes, **8** 726; **9i** 5, 89, 271;
art, **6** 493;
associations, *see* associations *s.v.*;
and autonomous psychic contents, **8** 712; **10** 843;
and causality, **10** 106–7, 115–28, 138–9;
and chance, **10** 836;
children among, **4** 235; and incarnation of ancestral spirits, **17** 96;
and collective psyche, **7** 237/458, 239;

primitive(s) (*cont.*):

and collective representations, **16** 247, 251;

and concretism, **6** 697;

consciousness/unconsciousness, **4** 738; **6** 887; **8** 87, 158, 340, 695; **9i** 47, 213, 260, 264, 288, 290, 300; **10** 111, 280; **11** 28–9, 339, 442; **13** 66, 341; **14** 129*n*, 657; **17** 83, 104, 297; **18** 15;

and death, **10** 106;

and demons, belief in, **8** 578; **10** 26;

and dreams, **3** 566; **8** 92*n*, 574, 579; **10** 128, 320; **11** 32; **17** 208; **18** 176, 250, 436–7, 674, 1290–1;

and endogamy, **5** 217, 652;

"energetics," **7** 108;

fears of, **4** 474, 565; **5** 216–17, 221; **6** 383; **8** 94–5, 209, 586; **10** 14; of unknown, **5** 250; **7** 324; **10** 282; **13** 12; **17** 146;

and God, concept of, **7** 108;

hallucinations among, **6** 46, 254;

identity, *see* Lévy-Bruhl *s.v. participation mystique;*

and illness, causes of, **8** 587, 712, 941;

images among, **8** 278;

imago among, **6** 46; reality of, **6** 47;

and incest, **4** 349, 352, 470, 565;

initiation rites of, **5** 644*n*; **7** 172, 314–16, 384, 393; **8** 725; **16** 130; **17** 271; **18** 363;

instinct(s) among, **6** 230, 346–7, 422; **8** 272; **9i** 276; **10** 55; **17** 156;

instinctive sensuousness of, **6** 254;

intuition among, **8** 278; **18** 26;

"invention" and, **11** 339;

and libido, **4** 349; **5** 248, 250; **8** 86, 114–30;

and magic, **6** 425; **8** 89, 278,

340, 516, 668, 682, 712, 725; **9i** 271; **10** 106, 843; **15** 99, 150; **16** 374; and modern ideologies, **5** 221;

and mana-personality, **7** 388; **10** 139–40;

medicine, **16** 4;

mentality, **6** 313, 667; **13** 15, 66, 76*n*; **16** 393;

in modern man, **5** 411*n*; **7** 156, 240, 520; **10** 447–8, 1010;

and monotony, **18** 1404;

and morality, **6** 356; **8** 465; **10** 108, 958;

and myths, **5** 487; **8** 71, 327, 329–30; **9i** 7–8, 261;

and numinosity, loss of, **18** 582;

and object, relation to, **6** 495–6; and bushman incident, **6** 403–4;

old people among, **8** 86, 788, 802;

and pain, **18** 231;

palladium, **8** 92;

pathology, **8** 587;

politeness among, **11** 29; **18** 35;

power concept, *see* power *s.v.*;

presuppositions, **10** 112; **14** 336*n*;

and projections, **8** 516–17, 521; **9i** 187; **10** 44, 129, 131–2, 134, 137; **11** 140; into tree, **13** 248;

psyche unsynthesized in, **18** 440;

psychology, **3** 576; **6** 12, 529, 630; **7** 471; **8** 94–7; **9i** 213, 224; **10** 280; **12** 38, 394; **13** 341; **14** 349, 601; **15** 59, 66, 99, (*p*84), 150, 152; **16** 96; **18** 17, 87, 365, 434, 834, 1286, 1288–9, 1297–9; archaic, **13** 122;

rebirth and, *see* rite/ritual *s.vv.* rebirth, renewal;

religions, *see* religion *s.v.*;

and separation from parents, **8** 725, 726;

and sexual intercourse, **18** 281;
and sexuality, **8** 465; **10** 214;
and snake, *see* ANIMALS: serpent
s.v.;
and soul, **6** 419–20; **7** 108, 302;
8 521, 664–9; **9i** 55; **10** 136; **18**
43; bush-, **10** 132–3; **11** 198; **18**
440, 465; of child, **17** 96; loss
of, **5** 248; **6** 383; **8** 586, 587,
594; **9i** 213, 244; **11** 29; **12**
152; **13** 48; **16** 372, 477; "perils
of," **5** 248; **9i** 47, 254, 266, 501;
10 287, 367, 721; **11** 29; **12** 63,
437; plurality of, **7** 293; **8** 217,
365, 577, 587; **11** 198; **14** 502*n*;
wandering, **10** 128 (*see also*
soul(s) *s.v.* bird);
and spirit(s), **6** 46; **7** 108,
293–4, 323, 374; **8** 251, 278,
572–9, 586, 593, 628, 682, 712;
9i 388; **10** 14–15, 107; **11** 800;
13 62; dangerous, **7** 293; fear
of, **7** 293*n*; *revenants* and, **7**
293–4, 296; **8** 574; /
story-tellers, **18** 568;
superstitions of, *see* superstition
s.v.;
symbols, **4** 555; **5** 313; **6** 402; **7**
132; **8** 47, 309; **16** 340;
syzygy motif among, **9i** 115;
thought, **5** 32, 38; **6** 46; **7** 219;
8 589; **9i** 260; **10** 15, 1007; **11**
239–40, 469; **14** 336*n*; **18** 15,
465;
and unconscious, **6** 422; **11** 28;
and visions, *see* visions *s.v.*;
world-view, **8** 623, 840; **11** 761;
see also animism; Australian;
Elgonyi; Kenyan
primitivity: in dream-symbols, **10**
447, 449;
in the East, **11** 800;
in India, **10** 1011;
in inner world of man, **18** 587;
sexual, **10** 958
primordial: being, **5** 227*n*; **10** 772
(*see also* Anthropos/etc.);
creative principle, **5** 198;

experiences, **11** 535; **15** 141–2,
144, 146–8, 151;
father, *see* father *s.v.*;
ideas, *see* idea(s) *s.v.*;
instinct(s), *see* instinct(s) *s.v.*;
light-bringer, **13** 300;
man, *see* Anthropos/etc. *s.v.*;
monsters, **13** 130;
pass, **13** 33;
tree, **13** 458*n*;
waters, *see* water(s) *s.v.* primeval;
word, **5** 460;
world, **13** 291
primordial image(s), **5** 209, 316*n*,
467, 553, 640, 681; **6** 336, 371,
512–16, 529, 746–54 (Def.); **7**
100–4, 108, 110, 264, 284, 389; **8**
274, 278, 589, 794; **9i** 152; **10** 43;
11 441, 469; **12** 28, 565; **13**
12–13, 15; **15** 124–30; **16** 15, 456;
18 523;
activation of, **6** 534, 600;
and animus/anima, **7** 336, 507;
as archetypes, **5** 450; **6** 624,
747; **7** 102, 109, 219; **8** 229,
270*n*; **9i** 260; **15** 159;
and *brahman-atman*, **6** 188, 361;
and collective unconscious, **5**
631–2; **6** 373–4, 746; **7** 520; **8**
229;
divine harlot as, **6** 317;
Faust as, **5** 45*n*; **13** 154;
of goddess, **6** 383;
God-renewal as, **6** 325;
of hero's birth, **6** 806;
and idea, **6** 732–7; **9i** 68;
idealism and, **6** 516, 527;
and individuation, **7** 267, 269;
initiation rites as, **7** 172–3; **17**
271–2;
introverted type and, **6** 637,
639–40;
and inventions, **18** 81;
"irrepresentable," **6** 513;
and language, **9i** 136*n*;
of man as microcosm, **6** 367;
of mother, **5** 373; **7** 100, 293*n*;
10 64, 75; **13** 147;

primordial image(s) (*cont.*):
   numinous, **5** 223; **13** 396;
   and religion, **5** 259–60; **8** 278;
   16 251; **17** 276;
   as self-representations of
   libido, **7** 260*n*/476*n*;
   see also archetype(s); magic
primum mobile, **9ii** 201
Prince, M., **1** 110; **4** 154–93; **8** 202;
  9i 490;
   Journal of Abnormal Psychology
   (editor of), **4** 155;
   WORKS:
     The Dissociation of a Personal-
     ity, **4** 155; **6** 797*n*;
     "An Experimental Study of
     Visions," **1** 110*n*;
     "The Mechanism and In-
     terpretation of Dreams," J.'s
     review, **4** 154–93; "blinded,"
     theme in, **4** 185–6, 189
prince: Andalusian, **13** 425, 436;
   in dream, **12** 258;
   in story book, **4** 466;
   of this world, *see* Lord *s.v.* "of
   this world"
princess, black, **9i** 412
"principalities and powers," **7** 104
principium individuationis, **6** 88, 226;
  11 400; **13** 244;
   Christ as, **9ii** 118;
   devil as, **11** 470
principle(s), **10** 864, 883; **13** 31;
   animal, **13** 316;
   animating, **13** 287;
   of animus, **7** 332;
   archetypal explanatory, **13**
   378;
   of compensation, **13** 294;
   of conduct, **13** 433;
   cosmic, **13** *fig.* A6;
   demiurgic, **13** 278;
   eternal, **13** 208;
   feminine, and *tao*, **13** 433;
   formative, **13** 171, 202;
   fourth, feminine, **13** 127;
   guiding, **8** 642;
   hardening of, **8** 773;

of individuation, *see* individuation;
life, **13** 171, 262; of tree, Mercurius as, **13** 420;
masculine, **13** 342;
moral, **7** 439; **13** 433;
ordering, of consciousness, **13**
  433;
psychic, **13** 175;
spiritual, **13** 173–5; of tree,
  stork as, **13** 417;
of sufficient reason (Schopenhauer), **13** 111;
triad of, **8** 966;
vegetative, **13** 316
Prinz, H.: *Altorientalische Symbolik,*
  12 *fig.* 26
Priscillian, **9ii** 366*n*; **11** 259*n*; **12**
  521; **13** 134; **14** 299;
  Opera quae supersunt, **9ii** 143,
  212; **12** 521*n*;
  Tractatus I, **13** 134*n*
Priscus/Priscius, Lucius Agatho, **9i**
  223*n*; **14** 51, 68–9, 100
prism, **4** 610
prison: cell, **11** 90, 109;
  complexes, **1** 218;
  psychosis, **1** 283, 299, 302
prisoners:
  TITLE: "A Case of Hysterical
  Stupor in a Prisoner in Detention," **1** 226–300;
  characteristic states of, **1** 278–
  83;
  Ganser's complex, **1** 354
Pritchard, J. B., ed., *Ancient Near*
  Eastern Texts Relating to the Old Tes-
  tament, **5** 293*n*, 375*n*; **13** 458*n*
privatio boni/privation of good, **9i**
  603*n*; **9ii** 75, 79*n*, 80–3, 85, 89,
  94, 98, 104, 113–14, 115*n*, 171,
  428; **10** 640, 677, 879; **11** 247,
  456–9, 470, (*p*357), 600*n*, 685; **14**
  86; **18** 1537, 1553, 1593–4, 1600,
  1606, 1613, 1639;
  and devil, **11** 248;
  Origen on, *see* Origen *s.v.*
probabilism, **12** 24&*n*, 25, 36

probability, **8** 437, 825&*n*, 989;
calculus, **8** 830;
psychic, archetypes as, **8** 964;
statistical, **7** 72*n*
problem(s), **8** 751–4, 757, 760–5;
and consciousness, **8** 756;
insoluble, of life, **13** 18;
moral, **9ii** 48;
of opposites, **13** 435;
outgrowing of, **13** 17;
of parents, *see* parent(s) *s.v.*;
personal, **13** 396–7; attitude to,
10 157;
purpose of, **8** 771;
sexual, discussion of, **10** 254;
of woman, modern European,
10 238
procedure, reductive, **13** 480
process(-es): alchemical, *see* opus,
alchemical;
chemical, **13** 88;
cognitive, **13** 378;
of growth, self depicted as, **13**
304;
of individuation, *see* individuation;
instinctual, **7** 122; **8** 375;
psychic, *see* psychic *s.v.*;
of realization, **13** 482;
spagyric, **13** 187;
subliminal, **7** 270;
of transformation, *see* transformation;
unconscious mental, *see* unconscious processes
procession: of the devil, **11** 255;
of the Holy Ghost, **11** 197, 289
Proclus, **8** 278; **11** 190;
*Commentaries on the Timaeus of
Plato,* trs. T. Taylor, **14** 5*n*, 19*n*,
113*n*; **16** 525*n*
procreation, **13** 69, 263;
divine, **4** 783;
infantile theories, **4** 477;
of reborn, **5** 497
procreative urge, analogy of, **5** 87
Prodigal Son, **9i** 448
Prodromus Rhodostauroticus, see AL-

CHEMICAL WRITERS *s.v.*
product(s), unconscious, *see* unconscious (adj.) *s.v.*
productivity, unconscious, **7** 205/
446
professor, wise old man as, **9i** 398
"professorship," association-chain,
see association-chain(s) *s.v.*
proficiency, **10** 153
prognosis, **15** 32; **16** 195, 343;
and diagnosis, **16** 195–6;
dreams and, *see* dream(s) *s.v.*
progress, **9i** 276, 293;
age of, **18** 1345;
and culture, **17** 250;
impossible without mature
judgment, **17** 251;
mania for, and compensation,
5 653;
see also forward-striving
progression: and development, **8**
70;
educator's influence in favour
of, **17** 281;
energic view, **8** 72;
and extraversion, **8** 77;
hallmark of waking thought, **5**
25;
of libido, **8** 61;
origin of, **8** 72;
and regression, **7** 181; **8** 76
progressiveness: and differentiation, **7** 198;
unconscious, **7** 182
prohibition(s), **9i** 428;
and archetypal father, **5** 396;
see also incest *s.v.* barrier
Prohibition in U.S.A., **11** 291
projectile, **8** 799, 803
projectio (alchemical term), **12** 340,
406*n*
projection(s), **3** 175, 406, 522; **6**
421&*n*, 486, 491, 495, 783–4; **7**
142–4, 297, 373, 375, 513; **8** 407,
507, 517, 584, 712, 866; **9i** 7, 54,
120, 130, 134, 315; **10** 42–3,
131–2, 139, 608, 610, 1065; **11**
849; **12** 187, 396; **13** 52, 117, 121,

projection(s) (*cont.*):
141, 195, 209, 216, 259, 286, 374,
391; **14** 10*n*, 100, 129, 134, 263,
486, 507, 673, 696; **15** 37; **16** 239,
357, 359, 383, 397, 442, 499; **17**
339, 341; **18** 312–14;
  alchemical, **9i** 238; **11** 95; **13**
  88, 123, 143, 173, 286, 443; **14**
  446; **16** 440 (*see also below* into
  opus);
  in analysis, **6** 402;
  and analyst, *see* analyst *s.v.*;
  of anima, *see* anima *s.v.*;
  of animus, *see* animus *s.v.*;
  of Anthropos, **12** 411;
  appearance as physical facts, **10**
  635;
  of archaic personality, **18** 1330;
  of archetype(s), *see* archetype(s)
  s.v.;
  by artist into painting, **5** 445;
  ascetics and, **10** 649;
  basis of, **10** 624;
  carriers of, **9i** 121*n*; **10** 610; **11**
  389; **13** 286;
  by child, onto parents, **8** 99;
  and Christ, *see* Christ *s.v.*;
  Christian, **12** 413, 416;
  cognition a, **11** 765;
  and collective attitude, **6** 12;
  of collective unconscious, *see*
  below unconscious *s.v.*;
  of complexes, **5** 644;
  compulsion of, **16** 223;
  of conflict caused by repression, **5** 92;
  of coniunctio, **14** 106;
  consciousness and, *see* consciousness *s.v.*;
  cosmic, **13** 453;
  and counter projection, **8** 519;
  definition of, **12** 346;
  descent into matter, **16** 440;
  destruction of passion in, **5**
  170;
  detachment from doctor, **16**
  462;
  direct, **5** 170*n*;

  of dissociated tendencies, **13**
  55;
  dissolution of, **9ii** 37; **14** 696;
  in dream-analysis, **18** 506;
  in dreams, *see* dream(s) *s.v.*;
  effect of, **9ii** 17;
  of emotional contents, **18** 318;
  Enigma of Bologna and, **14** 52;
  of erotic fantasies in transference, **4** 663;
  explanatory, **10** 616;
  on external circumstances, **5**
  456;
  fantasy, **7** 98; **8** 507; **14** 673;
  of father-image, *see* father *s.v.*
  -image;
  and Faust drama, **12** 558;
  favourable and unfavourable,
  8 517;
  and fear, **10** 572, 616; **11** 85;
  on feminine partner/woman, **9i**
  297; **16** 454*n*;
  of femininity, **14** 222, 647;
  of God-image, **12** 12;
  of *hierosgamos*, **5** 672;
  imagination and, **12** 350, 394,
  399;
  impersonal, **18** 359, 368–9;
  withdrawal of, **9ii** 43;
  of incest tendency, **5** 450;
  and individual relationship, **17**
  341;
  of individuation process, **13**
  277;
  inductive effect of, **16** 364;
  infantile, in marriage, **16** 420;
  of inner Adam, **14** 593;
  instinctual and spiritual, **10**
  649;
  integration of, **16** 471; **18** 756;
  integration through, **16** 383;
  and interpretation of pain, **5**
  436;
  into man, **12** 413;
  mandala/circular symbols and,
  9ii 60; **10** 622; **12** 249;
  of man's unconscious on
  woman, **9i** 297;

in Mary, **9ii** 320;
upon masculine figure, **5** 462;
into matter, **11** 95, **12** 40, 43,
332, 345, 375, 376, 380, 394,
406, 410, 413, 472, 557; **13**
395; **14** 336, 697, 737, 776; of
God, **12** 432; of soul, **14** 147;
of menace to the power of God,
5 170;
metaphysical, **14** 86;
in modern life, **11** 140;
of mother imago, **9ii** 24; upon
water, **5** 320;
mutual, **11** 140; **18** 322;
mythological forms of, **18**
1330;
need to dissolve, **9i** 160;
negative, **8** 517;
and neurosis, **5** 507; **8** 517;
in neurotics, **8** 507;
never conscious, **9i** 122;
into object, *see* object *s.v.*;
object of, **16** 499;
of opposites, **12** 398;
into opus, alchemical, **12** 346,
350, 389, 399, 425; **13** 88 (*see
also above* alchemical);
of opus/transformation process, **14** 505, 775;
on outside world, **13** 49;
pagan, **12** 413, 416;
of parental imagos, **16** 212,
218;
of personal images, **18** 368;
of primitive psyche, **8** 253;
among primitives, *see* primi-
tive(s) *s.v.*;
of psyche, **14** 94; deities as, **11**
833;
of psychic actuality, **13** 285;
of psychic events, **13** 36;
of psychic life, **11** 140, 268;
and radar, **10** 782;
reality of projection-making
factor, **9ii** 44;
and reality of psyche, **9ii** 120*n*;
realization of, **17** 225;
of rebirth symbol, **5** 495;

of redeemer image, **12** 557;
reduction of, **16** 278;
religious, **12** 11;
return of, to origin, **10** 437;
of self, **5** 576;
of shadow, *see* shadow *s.v.*;
in solar mythology, **5** 296;
soul as, *see* soul *s.v.*;
therapeutic value of, **14** 446;
of torture, **13** 439;
transference and, **7** 94*n*, 110;
16 144, 285, 359, 366, 368,
445, 542; **17** 260; **18** 312, 314,
316, 351, 359; and impersonal
contents, **18** 359;
into tree, **13** 248;
Ufos and, **10** 607–8, 614, 706,
789;
and unconscious, **5** 507;
of the unconscious, **13** 253,
259; **14** 150, 252, 342, 509; collective, **10** 43; **13** 277; soul as,
9ii 219;
of unconscious contents, **5** 92;
6 212, 305; **12** 436, 448, 462*n*,
496, 555; **14** 410; **16** 357, 462,
486; **18** 756; into an object, **6**
399, 413–14; **10** 41–3; **13** 122;
in transference, **7** 94*n*;
of unconscious mechanism, **18**
315;
unconsciousness of, **14** 511;
of unity of personality, **14** 294;
of unrecognized evil, **10** 572;
of wholeness on family, **12** 152;
withdrawal of, **8** 515; **9i** 121&*n*;
10 577; **11** 143, 375; **12** 559; **13**
117; **14** 697; **16** 212, 218, 420,
504; **18** 1364, 1511
Prokonnesos, **13** 87&*n*
Proktophantasmist, *see* Goethe:
Faust s.v. Characters
proletarian inclinations of noble
families, **17** 90
proletarians, *see* Cynics *s.v.*
"prolific" type (Blake), **6** 460, 559
Prometheus/Promethean, **9i** 427;
11 471;

Prometheus (*cont.*):
  attitude, *see* attitude *s.v.*;
  chained, **5** 671*n*; **7** 224, 243*n*;
  13 13, 331;
  and Epimethean, **7** 82;
  and Epimetheus, **12** 456&*n*,
  459; **13** 126 (*see also* Spitteler);
  forethinker/"one who thinks
  ahead," **5** 208*n*, 209; **7** 82;
  freedom, **13** 13;
  in Goethe, **2** 315; **6** 288–95,
  302–3, 306–9, 311, 314;
  guilt, **7** 243*n*; **13** 238;
  introvert, *see* introverted type
  s.v.;
  in Plato's *Protagoras,* **6** 289;
  and *pramantha,* **5** 208–9;
  soul of, *see* soul *s.v.*;
  as symbol, **6** 314;
  and theft of fire, **5** 208, 250; **6**
  311, 314;
  see also extraverted type; godlikeness; Pandora
promiscuity, sexual, **10** 958
proof: demand for, **8** 790;
  difference of physical and psychological, **4** 194
προοίμιον, **13** 121
propaganda, **13** 303;
  political, **10** 609; **14** 342
propagation, **4** 664;
  change in principle of, **5** 194;
  and defecation, in mind of
  child, **5** 276–8
Propertius, Sextus, **9i** 605;
  Propertius, tr. H. E. Butler, **9i**
  605*n*
prophecy(-ies), **1** 37; **7** 254, 260/
  476; **18** 701, 705, 710;
  in dreams, **8** 493;
  and hallucinations, **18** 1113
prophet(s), **1** 34; **4** 738*n*; **7** 502; **12**
  41; **13** (*p*59*n*), 148&*n*; **15** 184;
  Christ as, *see* Christ *s.v.*;
  eight incarnations of, **14**
  573–4;
  frenzy of, **18** 1368;
  Hebrew/Old Testament, **11** 32,

  229, 962; **12** 416; **14** 646; **17**
  301, 316;
  role of, **5** 500*n*;
  true, **14** 673&*n*, 574;
  and visionary experience, **15**
  149;
  see also Elijah/Elias; Enoch/
  Enos; Hosea; Job; John, St.;
  Jonah; Joshua; Matthew, St.;
  Moses; Paul, St.
propitiation, **9i** 47; **11** 390;
  rites of, **10** 26; **15** 150
proportio sesquitertia, see NUMBERS:
  one, and three
Proserpina, *see* Persephone
"Proserpine's threshold," **7** 232
Prosper of Aquitaine: *Sententiae ex*
  Augustino delibatae, **8** 967*n*
prostitute: anima as, **10** 76;
  Picasso and, *see* Picasso *s.v.*
prostitution, **18** 912;
  houses of, **7** 430*n*;
  and love, **10** 208;
  and marriage, **10** 76, 248;
  tolerated, **10** 248;
  in Uganda, **10** 185
protagonist(s), in dream, **8** 561
Protanthropos, **9ii** 334; **11** 400; **14**
  43;
  and Korybas, **9ii** 332;
  Sophia and, **9ii** 307;
  see also Adam; Anthropos; Archanthropos
protective genies, **13** 363
protest, unspoken, **17** 154
Protestant/-ism, **3** 462; **4** 750; **6** 96;
  7 118, 325, 396; **9i** 29, 61, 77; **9ii**
  235, 276; **10** 516; **11** 43, 285,
  294*n*, 457, 509, 537; **12** 9, 419; **13**
  81, 107; **14** 286, 447, 475; **16** 218,
  392; **18** 528, 565, 603, 1595,
  1608;
  and analytical psychology, **11**
  544;
  and Assumption, dogma of, **11**
  749, 754;
  and Bible, *see* BIBLE *s.v.*;
  and Christ, *see* Christ *s.v.*;

psychasthenia (*cont.*):
 see also neurosis
Psyche, **18** (*p*347*n*)
psyche/ψυχη, **7** 27/438, 67, 209,
 216, 370, 480, 501*n*; **8** (*p*300),
 653; **9i** 518; **11** 533; **13** 7, 11, 36,
 51, 58, 63, 75, 84, 122, 163, 196,
 199, 287, 378, 475; **16** 71, 203–4,
 206;
  TITLES: "The Effect of Technology on the Human Psyche,"
  18 1403–7; "Mental Disease
  and the Psyche," **3** 496–503;
  "On the Nature of the Psyche,"
  8 343–442; *The Structure and
  Dynamics of the Psyche,* **8**; "The
  Structure of the Psyche," **8**
  283–342;
  abnormal affective states of, **1**
  357;
  abolishment of, **13** 395;
  affinity with cold, **9i** 387;
  ambiguity of, **16** 81;
  American, **18** 756;
  analogy with building, **10** 54–5;
  ancestral, **16** 61;
  ancestry of, **5** (*p*xxiv);
  animal, *see* animal(s) *s.v.*;
  animal part of man's, *see* ani-
  mal(s) *s.v.* instinct/nature in
  man;
  anthropoid, **5** 506;
  as arbitrary invention, **11** 5;
  archaic, **5** 258; **12** 12; **17** 209;
  archetypal world of, **13** 210;
  as arrangement of life-pro-
  cesses, **8** 606;
  attitude towards products of, **5**
  468;
  autonomous, **11** 555; **12** 51, 60,
  113, 186, 249; **16** 267; contents
  of, **11** 21;
  awakening to spontaneous activity, **11** 534;
  basic function of, **18** 378;
  biological aspect, **8** 688;
  and biological causality, **18**
  1119;

and body, *see* body *s.v.*;
border regions of, **13** 127;
brain and, *see* brain *s.v.*;
as breath, **11** 771;
broken off bits of, **7** 293;
as the Buddha, **11** 771, 931;
building up of, **10** 141;
and butterfly, **5** 372; **8** 663;
cannot be denied, **8** 671;
cannot know itself, **10** 779;
a category of existence, **11** 769;
causal and constructive views, **3**
 399, 404;
as causal factor in disease, **11**
 490;
in childhood/child's, **12** 3; **16**
 216; contents of, **17** 94; general
 picture of, **17** 108; and parents,
 10 61;
and Christ ideal, **12** 7;
Christian, *see* Christianity *s.v.*;
Church and, *see* Church *s.v.*;
collective, *see separate entry below*;
"comparative anatomy" of, **18**
 522;
complexity of, **4** 764; **10** 6,
 1046;
conflict between instinct and
 will, **8** 380;
conscious, *see* conscious *s.v.*;
and conscious mind, *see* conscious mind *s.v.*;
and consciousness, *see* consciousness *s.v.*;
as constellation, **14** 502;
constitutional defects, **3** 325;
creates reality, **6** 77;
creative capacity of, **12** 249;
current undervaluation of, **10**
 655;
dark side/powers of, **9i** 259; **13**
 62;
"dawn state," **5** 650;
definitions of, **12** 9*n*;
dependence on physiology, **8**
 220;
devaluation of, **14** 194;

differences in, **10** 285;
dimmer elements of, **13** 291;
discovery of, **11** 495;
dissociation of, *see* dissociation *s.v.*;
divine, **14** 601;
a divisible whole, **8** 582;
double aspect of, **14** 170;
and dream, **8** 300;
Eastern view of, **11** 770;
as ego-consciousness and unconscious, **16** 204;
elusiveness of, **3** 320;
energic aspect of, **8** 441;
as *ens per se*, **16** 202;
an epiphenomenon, **8** 657; **10** 527; **16** 202;
etymology, **8** 664;
European, **10** 1064;
evolutionary stratification of, **16** 351;
and external happenings, **8** 676;
falsifies reality, **8** 680;
fascination of, **10** 187, 191, 195;
fate of, **13** 482;
feeling of responsibility for, **11** 20;
feminine, **13** 58;
a fluid stream of events, **17** 156;
freeing of, from spirit, **14** 775;
genesis of collective, **8** 595*n*;
and geographical locality, **18** 1118;
German, **10** 389;
given immediately, **8** 283;
goal of, *see* goal(s) *s.v.*;
as god and demon, **7** 110;
God-image in, **12** 15;
growth and development of, **14** 424;
hinterland of, **7** 339;
as historical structure, **12** 74, 87; **18** 837;
hysteria has its roots in, **4** 5;
and "id" of Freud, **9i** 2*n*;

idea and thing in, **6** 77;
impersonal, **7** 235/456; **9i** 314;
importance of, **10** 561;
imprisoned in the elements, **14** 354;
indistinguishable from its manifestations, **11** 87;
individual, **17** 107; and archetype, **5** 97; differences of, **10** 279; and group, total, **9i** 225; infinite variety of, **5** 1;
and individuation, **9i** 256;
infantile, **8** 97; **17** 106;
inherited, **7** 235/457;
its inner life uncontrollable, **11** 144;
inside and outside, **10** 158;
instinctive/instinctual, **9i** 244, 282;
instincts and, see instinct(s) *s.v.*;
intellect dependent on, **11** 766;
interior world of, **13** 391;
irrationality of, **7** (*p*124); **17** 165;
knowledge of, **12** 5, 10, 15;
layers of, **12** 40, 175;
life of, **5** 296;
as light substance, **5** 171;
living, **13** 438;
and "living being," **8** 606;
localization of, **8** 670;
loss of, **9i** 244;
and loss of moral and spiritual values, **18** 583;
as machine, **8** 159;
man's greatest danger, **18** 763;
man's greatest instrument, **18** 605;
mass, **8** 426–7; **9i** 227; **16** 443;
materialist view of, **9i** 117; **11** 13–14;
materialized, **10** 788;
and matter, *see* matter *s.v.*;
meaning of its existence, **13** 476;
medical distrust of, **11** 13;
as metaphysical reality, **11** 836;
as microcosm, **16** 206;

shadow-side of, **7** 27/438;
and somatic illness, **4** 578;
and soul, **6** 797;
and space, *see* space and time
s.v. relativity of;
and spirit, **9i** 386;
split in, **8** 252, 253, 255; **14**
257, 332;
structure of, **5** 474; **9i** 432*n*;
not unipolar, **17** 156; and the
Trinity, **11** 221;
study of, **18** 1;
as subject and object, **11** 87; **18**
6, 277;
subjective, **7** 103*n*; **12** 48;
subjectively conditioned, **3** 397;
suprapersonal, **7** 235/456;
and sympathetic system, **18**
1116;
theological devaluation of, **18**
1649;
theories of, **17** (*p*7);
thymo-, **3** 33, 35;
and time and space, *see* space
and time *s.v.* relativity of;
total, **12** 88;
totality/wholeness of, **14** 181,
261, 558, 716, 759; **16** 212,
293; self, as, *see* self *s.v.* totality;
transcendental subject, **17** 169;
transformation of, **7** (*p*123); **14**
252;
trans-subjective, **17** 167;
"tumours" in, **11** 36;
two-sided, **10** 292;
unconscious, **7** 344; **9i** 518; **11**
375; **13** 11, 51; **14** 709; **15** 64;
16 232; **18** 8, 76, 438; activity
of, **8** 296–7; child's, **17** 95; clue
to historical problems, **5** 2; continuity of, **18** 162; uniformity
of, **8** 227; units of, **8** 210;
and the unconscious, **5** 296; **9i**
259; **11** 373; **12** 516; as collective psyche, **5** (*p*xxiv); as objective psyche, **5** (*p*xxiv); **12** 48,
51; as unknown psyche, **12**
247, 516;

underground processes mirrored in dreams, **11** 37;
undervaluation of, **11** 28, 771;
17 302; **18** 603;
unity of, **7** 323; **10** 306;
unknown, **12** 247, 516;
unpredictability of, **9i** 49;
upper and lower limits, **8** 379;
variability of, **8** 252; **16** 1;
various meanings of, **11** 769;
in waking and sleeping state, **8**
580;
as water, **12** 94;
weightlessness, **10** 667;
woman's, split in, **13** 344;
the world's pivot, **8** 423;
in youth and age, **16** 75;
see also mind; psychic; soul;
spirit
psyche, collective, **6** 123; **7** 150,
156, 235/456, 245/465, 251/468,
260, 476–9, 481, 500, 518; **9i**
225; **10** 160, 175; **12** 68, 104; **13**
478; **14** 313; **16** 65–6; **17** 93–4;
adaptation to, **11** 539;
assimilation of, **7** 237/458, 480;
composition of, **7** 513, 518;
and conscious psyche, **13** 478;
contents of, **7** 241/462;
historical, **7** 150;
outside the personal psyche, **7**
231;
and persona, *see* persona *s.v.*
collective psyche;
regressive libido and, **5** 654;
repression of, **7** 237/459;
segment of, **7** 472;
superstitious impulses of, **7**
495;
unconscious heritage of, **7**
235/456;
unconscious identity with, **7**
237/459;
universality of, **7** 240
Psyche and Symbol (de Laszlo), J.'s
preface to, **18** 1264–75
psychiatric cases, *see* CASES
IN SUMMARY

psychiatrist(s)/alienist(s), **3** 467–70; **10** 659; **13** 48; **18** 826–7, 831;
  and patient's psychology, **18** 837;
  and psychological aspect of his cases, **18** 838;
  school, **17** 249
psychiatry, **11** 489, 545; **17** 160; **18** 833, 834, 866–9, 879, 883–4, 889;
  TITLES: "On Pictures in Psychiatric Diagnosis," **18** 1792; *Psychiatric Studies,* **1**; "The Significance of Freud's Theory for Neurology and Psychiatry," **18** 922; "A Third and Final Opinion on Two Contradictory Psychiatric Diagnoses," **1** 430–77;
  and aetiology of psychosis, **7** 270;
  and anatomy, **3** 466–7;
  and causality, **8** 51;
  and documentary evidence, **18** 828;
  French, **3** 322;
  Freud's importance for, **18** 922;
  German, **3** 322; **18** 948;
  judicial, **18** 920;
  and latent psychosis, **7** 192;
  materialism of, **3** 324;
  and medicine, **3** 320, 467;
  as natural science, **3** 466;
  neglect of study of psychotic mind, **18** 835;
  prognoses from therapeutic hopelessness, **5** 58*n*;
  and psychoanalysis, **7** 3, 199;
  and psychology, **7** 409;
  and psychotherapy, **10** 1056, 1061;
  weakness of anatomical approach, **3** 333
psychic, **8** 376;
  TITLES: "On Psychic Energy," **8** 1–130; "Psychic Conflicts in a Child," **17** 1–79;
  actuality, projection of, **13** 285;

apparatus, regression as function of, **5** 25;
centre, **13** 189;
change, **15** 8;
collective phenomena, **13** 51;
complex(es), autonomous, *see* complex(es) *s.v.* autonomous;
complications, solution of, **13** 43;
contents, **13** 47, 122; autonomous, **13** 48, 54; division of, **7** 511, 516;
controls, **13** 60*n*;
crisis/disturbance, **14** 183, 294;
danger of alchemy, *see* alchemy *s.v.* art, dangers of;
definition of, **13** 76*n*;
development, *see* development;
disorders, **17** 128;
disposition, universal, **7** 234;
disturbances, **13** 464; causes of, **5** 1;
dynamism, **5** 670;
elements, combination of and originality, **1** 167; conscious and unconscious, **1** 171; disaggregation of, **1** 117;
energy, *see* energy *s.v.*;
epidemics, *see* epidemics;
equilibrium, *see* equilibrium *s.v.*;
events/happenings, **8** 661, 667; **13** 36, 43;
excitation, **1** 123;
existent, **5** 95;
experience(s), **13** 42*n*, 77;
factor: in alchemy, **13** 173; as combination of instincts, **11** 493; in psychoneuroses, **11** 490; subliminal, **17** 102;
facts, **13** 54;
figures, duplex, **9i** 310;
functions, *see* function(s) *s.v.*;
identity, **13** 122;
infection, **7** 152, 233;
inflation, **5** 612; **7** 227;
injury, **7** 257;
intensities, **7** 77*n*;
laws, **11** 778; **13** 285, 357;

psychology (*cont.*):
1499–1513; "The Significance of Constitution and Heredity in Psychology," **8** 220–31;
abstract approach of, **10** 531;
academic, **10** 531; **13** (*p*3); **18** 571, 1111, 1295;
Adlerian, *see* Adler, A.;
of the ages, **18** 297;
and alchemy, *see* alchemy *s.v.*;
American, **10** 927, 946–80;
and analysis, **7** 502;
analytical, *see* analytical psychology;
and ancient world, *see* ancient world *s.v.*;
anima and animus, **7** 328, 370;
arbitrariness of, **17** 166;
of art, *see* art *s.v.*;
and belief, **11** 376;
and biology, **8** 232; **17** 157;
brain, **8** 10, 29;
and causality, *see* causality *s.v.*;
chaos in, **18** 279;
child, *see* child *s.v.*;
Chinese, *see* China/Chinese *s.v.*;
and Christian doctrine, **14** 455*n*;
collective, **6** 322; **7** 241–2/462–3, 459, 514; **18** 371 (*see also below* mob/mass/herd);
collectivistic, **7** 462*n*;
comparative, **10** 647; **18** 1266;
compartment, **12** 6; **18** 558;
complex-, *see* complex(es) *s.v.*;
and complexes, **10** 456;
conscious, **7** 329;
of consciousness, *see* consciousness *s.v.*;
criminal, **10** 466;
danger of dogmatism in, **15** (*p*84–5);
depth, **18** 1142–62, 1803–17; *see also* Bleuler *s.v.*;
a "dirty joke," **10** 356;
discovery of, **10** 159;
divorce from other sciences, **16** 120;
and dogma, *see* dogma *s.v.*;

of dreams, *see* dream(s) *s.v.*;
in early and later life, **16** 75;
the East and, *see* East/Eastern *s.v.*;
in Egypt, ancient, **18** 230;
empirical, **9i** 11, 150; **11** 647, 947; **12** 15, 20, 394; **16** 175, 209; **18** 742, 1296, 1312, 1504, 1555; and Holy Spirit, **18** 1555; modern, **17** 128; origins of, **17** 127;
English, **18** 14;
enthusiasm for, **17** 302;
ethno-, **4** 457;
and evil, **10** 676;
exile, **18** 648;
experimental, **2** 863–4; **7** 2/407; **8** 701; **9i** 111; **16** 202; **17** 102, 128, 170; **18** 739; first use of term, **8** 345; and psyche, **11** 490;
and factor of value, **18** 596;
fear of, **12** 19;
and feeling, **18** 24;
feminine/female, *see* feminine *s.v.*;
a field of experience, **9i** 111;
four-dimensional, **18** 115;
French, *see* France/French *s.v.*;
Freudian, *see* Freud *s.v.*;
and the future, **8** 687;
general, **16** 232;
German, **18** 22 (*see also below* Jewish *s.v.* Germanic; mob/mass *s.v.* German);
Gestalt, **16** 245;
Hindu, **18** 17;
and historical material, **5** (*p*xxvii), 3;
of *homo religiosus*, **11** 11;
and the humane sciences, **5** (*p*xxvii); **17** 165–6;
and human soul, attitude towards, **5** 113;
idea of God and, **11** 242*n*;
Indian, **7** 240*n*; **11** 956;
of the individual, *see* individual *s.v.*;

interpretative methods, **11** 448;
introspective, **18** 139;
Jewish, **7** 240*n*; and Germanic, **10** 1014, 1025;
and knowledge of self, **11** 3;
layman's attitude to, **10** 276;
and literature, **15** (*p*85);
and man of twentieth century, **11** 465;
and Mary, dogma of Assumption, **11** 748;
masculine/male, **7** 328; **13** 108, 344; **14** 222–5;
meaning of colours in, **14** 390;
medical, **3** 541; **5** (*p*xxiv); **7** (*p*8), 199; **8** 347, 530; **13** (*p*3), 353; **15** 101; **16** 120, 232; **17** 102; **18** 5; absence of, **16** 52;
dilemma of, **16** 236; and dreams, **17** 262; and educational, meaning of, **17** 173; and personalistic attitude, **7** 122; psychotherapy as, **10** 1040; and whole man, **17** 160;
and medicine, **3** 541;
medieval, **11** 284; **18** 370;
and metaphysics, *see* metaphysics *s.v.*;
mob/mass/herd/crowd, **3** 513; **5** 104; **9i** 225, 228; **10** 453, 457, 460, 477, 536; **16** 4; **18** 369, 1315, 1351, 1386; German proneness to, **10** 448, 453 (*see also above* collective; *and see also* psychosis *s.v.* mass);
modern, **8** 688; **13** 122; **14** 694; **18** 1, 6, 754, 1374, 1394, 1409; and ancient world, **5** 1; rational, **18** 230;
multiplicity of, **8** 659; **16** 116–17; **18** 279;
must explain spiritual and psychological, **17** 160;
and myth, **14** 751;
national, **7** (*p*4); **10** 466; **18** 1302;
and national problems, **18** 1305–42;

and natural science, **17** 161, 162, 165;
and nature of God, **11** 738;
need for, in patient, **3** 539, 575;
need of training in, for alienist and neurologist, **3** 470;
needs hypothesis, **11** 460;
needs widening of its horizon, **18** 763;
of neurosis, *see* neurosis *s.v.*;
normal, **18** 889; and pathological inferiority, **1** 3;
not merely subjective, **17** 80;
objective/and objectivity, **3** 406; **6** 8–9, 13; **12** 18, 20; **14** 617–18; **17** 163; **18** 275;
pathological, **18** 832;
of the person, **9i** 91;
personal, **13** 478;
personalist, *see* personalism *s.v.*;
philosophy and/philosophical, *see* philosophy *s.v.*;
and physics, *see* physics *s.v.*;
physiological, **8** 701; **17** 128, 156;
and physiology, **17** 157; of instincts, **9i** 112;
and poetry, *see* poem/poetry *s.v.*;
position of, **17** 165; in universities, **8** 347;
power, *see* Adler, A. *s.v.* power principle;
practical, **6** 85; **8** 678; **17** 172; **18** 34;
practice in, and theory, **10** 1071;
prestige, *see* Adler, A. *s.v.*;
primitive, *see* primitive(s) *s.v.*;
projected, **14** 737;
Protestant attitude to, **11** 76;
and psychic phenomena, **11** 222;
of psychosis, *see* psychosis *s.v.*;
public interest in, **10** 169, 617; **11** 507; **18** 1395;
pure, principle of explanation, **17** 162;

galvanic (galvanophysical) reflex, **2** 1015, 1024, 1036, 1043;
hypothesis, **8** 10, 11;
parallelism, *see* parallelism *s.v.*
psychophysics, **9i** 111; **17** 162
psychophysiology, **7** 407; **17** 162
psychopomp, **9i** 77; **13** 106, 171*n*;
anima as, **9ii** 56; **12** 74; **14** 282, 540;
animals as: dog, **13** 278*n*;
fishes, **9ii** 225; horse, **5** 427;
animus as, **9ii** 33;
Indra as, **5** 659;
Mercurius as, *see* Mercurius *s.v.*;
Proteus as, **9ii** 338;
Virgil (Dante) as, **5** 119*n*
psychosexuality, **3** 436;
term, **5** 193
psychosis(-es), **5** 19*n*, 26*n*; **7** 270, 370; **8** 595, 702; **9i** 82, 259, 494, 519; **11** 489, 781; **12** 188, 324; **13** 428; **14** 184, 494; **16** 37, 474; **17** 209, 260; **18** 832, 909;
TITLE: "The Content of the Psychoses," **3** 317–87;
aetiology of, **18** 905;
affective, **18** 859;
anticipated, **14** 756;
autochthonous descriptions of, **18** 829;
beginning of, **3** 529;
behaviour of unconscious, **3** 442;
borderline cases, **5** 681;
childhood, **17** 139;
chönyid state as, **11** 846;
classification of, **18** 901, 919;
and collective unconscious, **18** 1159;
confusional, **18** 66;
degenerative hysterical, **3** 141;
delusions in, **17** 25;
development of, **7** 254; from neurosis, **3** 517;
dissociation in, **5** 683;
distortions in, **14** 454;
and feeling of isolation, **5** 683;

ideas and images in, **5** 474;
latent, **3** 518, 539, 558–9; **5** 58*n*; **7** 192; **11** 545; **14** 184; **16** 18, 381, 476; compensation in, **8** 547; and manifest, ratio, **3** 558; **16** 381*n*;
mass, **8** 518, 595; **13** 52; **17** 159; in Germany, **10** 465, 466, 472, 476 (*see also* psychology *s.v.* mob/mass);
Miller's, **5** 675;
of mother, animal behaviour in, **5** 504; **17** 107;
motility, *see* catatonia;
mythological fragments in, **18** 594;
outbreak of, **18** 836;
predisposition to, **3** 480;
prevention of, **3** 481;
psychology of, **7** 2; **18** 826, 1478;
psychotherapy of, **3** 482;
and separation from mother, **5** 624*n*;
as state of possession, **16** 196;
totalitarian, **16** 442;
unconscious in, **3** 491;
unconscious manifestations preceding, **5** 684;
unleashed by analysis, **14** 755;
yoga and, **11** 847;
see also catatonia; manic depression; mania; insanity; psychotic; schizophrenia
psychosomatic: disorders, **11** 15;
instincts, **13** 475;
medicine, **16** 232; **18** 834, 839;
phenomena, **8** 440
psychosynthesis, **18** 935
psychotechnics, **15** (*p*84)
psychotherapist, **5** 258; **10** 882; **11** 285, 464, 530, 905; **12** 2, 36;
TITLE: "Psychotherapists or the Clergy," **11** 488–538;
authority of, **16** 2;
and clergyman/theologian, **11** 450, 462, 510;
and enthusiasm, **3** 539; **4** 634;

Q

colours in, **14** 430;
diet/food of, **14** 420–7;
dissolution, in bath, **14** 537;
of heaven/Heaven, **9i** 61, 132,
190, 195; **12** 500;
as Luna, **14** 532;
Mercurius as, **14** 534;
of Motherhood, Mary as, **13**
228*n*;
as mother of God, **14** 350*n*,
429;
psychic pregnancy of, **14** 424;
Sapientia/Wisdom as, **12** 466–7,
473; **16** 496;
self expressed by, **9i** 315;
of Sheba, **12** 443, 518*n*; **14** 329,
533, 535, 543;
and Sol, **14** 534;
of the South/*regina Austri*, **12**
466*n*, 467, 473; **14** 535–6; **16**
496;
with white lily, **12** *fig.* 142a, b
Quercetanus, J., *see* ALCHEMICAL
WRITERS: *Theatr. chem. s.v.*
quest, the, **18** 673, 688;
for the stone, **13** 394
questionnaire, **11** 511
questions: children's, **17** 11*n*, 17*n*,
19–20;
in confession, **11** 542;
and senseless answers, **1** 236
Quetzalcoatl, **5** *fig.* 30; **11** 340;
mother of, **13** 132
Quicherat, J.: *Procès de condamnation
et de réhabilitation de Jeanne d'Arc,
dite la Pucelle,* **1** 101*n*
quicklime, **9ii** 243*n*; **12** 446*n*; **13**
404
quicksilver, **9i** 545, 554; **9ii** 215,
240, 243; **10** 629–30; **11** 160,
276; **12** 172, 365, 401, 406, 409,
445, 469, 484*n*; **13** 95, 103*n*,
105*n*, 119, 142*n*, 265; **14** 140,
142, 317, 337, 636, 715;
as *aqua permanens,* **11** 161*n*; **13**
168*n*;
as arcanum, **13** 97*n*; Paracelsan, **13** 168*n*, 171*n*, 176*n*;

expulsion of, **11** 355; **12** 405;
fixation of, **13** 97*n*;
Luna as, **14** 87;
meaning of, for alchemists, **9i**
554;
Mercurius and, *see* Mercurius
s.v.;
parā-da, Indian system, **9ii** 237;
in patient's pictures, **9i** 554–7,
559, 609; **13** 343;
as *prima materia,* **12** 425;
and Saturn, **9ii** 215; **13** 274;
spirit of, **13** 273;
stone (philosophical) as, **12** 99;
and sulphur, **14** 135&*n*;
as water, *see* water;
see also *argentum vivum; hydrar-
gyrum;* mercury (metal)
Quicumque, *see* creed(s) *s.v.*
Athanasian
quid: of Dorn, **13** 394;
and quis, distinction, **9ii** 252,
261
quietism, Eastern, **10** 190
Quimby, P. P. (Christian Scientist), **4**
748&*n*
quincunx, **8** 559; **10** 737, 749, 752,
755, 774; **18** 1602
quintessence/*quinta essentia,* **8** 388*n*,
931&*n*; **9ii** 245*n*; **10** 628, 738,
741; **11** 104, 160&*n*; **12** 165, 394,
442, 512; **13** 102, 115, 117, 148,
170*n*, 171, 187, 203, 209, 215,
226, 243, 336; **14** 114, 439, 450,
655, 719; **16** 402, 404, 410, 454,
534;
Chinese doctrine of, see *ch'i;*
Christ's blood as, **13** 384;
as *coelum,* **13** 268;
ether as, **12** 371;
four elements and, **12** 310; **13**
207*n*; **16** 402;
"maid" as, **14** 450;
Mercurius as, **13** 268;
of philosophical tree, **13** 287;
production of, **14** 681–5;
sun as, **14** 114
Quisling, V., **18** 1384

Quispel, G., **9ii** 119*n*, 298; **18**
(*p*651&*n*), 1515*n*, (*p*826*n*);
 "Note sur 'Basilide'," **9ii** 298;
 "Philo und die altchristliche
 Häresie," **9ii** 119*n*;
 "Tragic Christianity," J.'s

foreword to, **18** 1478–82
Quito, **9i** 227*n*
quotation(s), **2** 211–12, 217, 273–5,
 290, 314–16, 321, 323–5, 329–30;
 3 244

R

R., Mr., and his brother P. R., in S. W.'s séances, **1** 55–6
Ra, **5** 292*n*, 356, 408*n*; **9i** 661; **9ii** 187; **14** 14, 351*n*, 482*n*;
    death of, **5** 451–5;
    gods identified with, **5** 147;
    Khnum and, *see* Khnum;
    ship of, **5** 367;
    true name of, **5** 274;
    see also Ammon-Ra
Rabanus/Rhabanus Maurus, **11** 358;
    Allegoriae in universam sacram scripturam, **9ii** 157; **12** 466*n*; **13** 389&*n*; **14** 6*n*, 47*n*, 701*n*, 728*n*; **16** 525*n*
rabbi, **10** 27
Rabbi, son of Josephus Carnitolus, **13** 411
Rabbi Eliezer, *see* Eliezer
rabbits, *see* ANIMALS *s.v.*
Rabelais, F., **5** 311*n*
race/racial, **7** 235/455;
    differences of, **7** 240&*n*; **13** 11;
    heredity, **5** 154; **18** 79;
    history, activated residues of, **7** 159;
    memories, **7** 434;
    study of, **18** 94
Rachaidibus/"Rachaidibi . . . fragmentum," *see* ALCHEMICAL COLLECTIONS: *Art. aurif. s.v.*
Rackham, H., *see under* Pliny
radar, **10** 591, 604, 618, 630, 782, 786
Radbertus, Paschasius, **6** 36–9
Radhakrishnan, S.: *Indian Philosophy,* **14** 46*n*;
    The Principal Upanishads, **9ii** 348*n*
radial arrangement, **8** 401
radical moisture, **13** 89, 101, 103*n*, 114, 173, 188
radices, four, *see* roots *s.v.* four
Radin, P., **9i** 470, 477, 480;

The World of Primitive Man, **9i** 480*n*
radioactive decay, **8** 959, 966
radioactivity, **8** 356, 963; **18** 1271
radio weather, **8** 875
radium, **11** 447
radium decay, *see* radioactive decay
radius, see ray
radix ipsius, see root(s) *s.v.* of itself
Raecke, J., **1** 226, 296;
    on hysterical ailments, **1** 349;
    on hysterical twilight state, **1** 279;
    on loss of knowledge, **1** 298;
    on stupor in criminals, **1** 284;
    WORKS:
        "Beitrag zur Kenntnis des hysterischen Dämmerzustandes," **1** 279*n*;
        "Hysterischer Stupor bei Strafgefangenen," **1** 279*n*, 320*n*
rage(s), **17** 133, 213–14, 228;
    as compensatory power manifestations, **17** 213;
    in mental patients, **11** 85
Raguel, **4** 742, 744*n*
Rahab, **9ii** 185;
    meaning of name, **5** 380
Rahner, H., **9i** 413*n*; **14** 28&*n*, 372, 727*n*; **18** 1160;
    "Antennae Crucis II: Das Meer der Welt," **9i** 559*n*; **14** 255&*nn*;
    "Das christliche Mysterium von Sonne und Mond," **14** 173*n*;
    "Earth Spirit and Divine Spirit in Patristic Theology," **9i** 428*n*;
    "Flumina de ventre Christi," **9ii** 336*n*, 373*n*; **14** 372*n*;
    "Die Gottesgeburt," **14** 379*n*;
    Griechische Mythen in christlicher Deutung, **11** 176*n*;
    "Mysterium Lunae," **14** 19*n*, 20*n*, 28&*n*, 154*n*, 155, 630*n*; **16** 355*n*;

Rahner, H. (*cont.*):
"Die seelenheilende Blume . . . ," **9i** 604*n*; **13** 409*n*; **14** 157*n*
railway(s): earliest German, **18** 740&*n*;
    journey, **12** 54;
    "spine," **7** 15*n*;
    station, as dream motif, **8** 535
Raimann, E., **4** 37&*n*;
    Die hysterischen Geistesstörungen, **2** 1068*n*
rain, **13** 270, 341; **14** 727&*n*;
    fertilizing, motif of, **5** 395;
    -god, **13** 341;
    -lake, splitting of, **5** 395, 439*n*;
    and the tree of life, **5** 306*n* (*see also* Vouru-Kasha);
    -maker, **14** 604*n*;
    sign of, **5** 421;
    silver, **12** *fig.* 142 O
rainbow, **12** 148, 263, 287, 321, *fig.* 142YY; **13** *figs.* 26, 29; **14** 142, 389&*n*, 392&*n*;
    bridge, **12** 69–70, 75, 148, 305;
    contract with Yahweh, **11** 577;
    symbol of lapis, **14** 389
Rainbow Goddess (Navaho Indian), **9i** 700, *fig.* 45
Raison, Déesse, *see* Reason, Goddess of
Rakshas, **12** 533
ram, *see* ANIMALS *s.v.*; zodiac, twelve signs of *s.v.*
Rama, **5** 306
Ramakrishna, **11** 952, 958, 962;
    The Gospel of Ramakrishna, **11** 958*n*;
    Worte des Ramakrishna, **11** 958*n*
Ramakrishna mission, **11** 861
Ramana Maharshi, Shri, **11** 950–3, 955–9, 961–3
Ramanuja, **9i** 675; **10** 875; **14** 271*n*;
    The Vedanta-sutras with the Commentary of Ramanuja, **14** 271*n*
Ramayana, tr. Manmatha Nath Dutt, **5** 306, 311; **6** 327&*n*; **12** 534

Rameses II, **9ii** 130
Ramsay, W. M.: "The Cities and Bishoprics of Phrygia," **9ii** 127*n*
randomness, **8** 964
Rangda, Balinese witch, **5** pl. XLVIII
Rank, O., **4** 328, 478; **9i** 259*n*; **15** 155; **18** (*p*446*n*), 1160, (*p*551*n*);
    on hero, **5** 494;
    on myth, **5** 28;
    theory of sexual neuroses, **5** 654;
    WORKS:
        Der Künstler, **5** 28*n*;
        Die Lohengrinsage, **5** 332*n*;
        The Myth of the Birth of the Hero, tr. W. A. White, **5** 2*n*, 28*n*, 34*n*, 306*n*, 494*n*; tr. F. Robbins and S. E. Jelliffe, **9i** 259*n*;
        "Ein Traum, der sich selbst deutet," **4** 328*n*; **5** 3*n*; ed. *Imago*, **18** 1031*n*
Ranschburg, P., **2** 62&*n*, 145&*n*, 392;
    and Balint, E., "Über quantitative und qualitative Veränderungen geistiger Vorgänge in hohen Greisenalter," **2** 20*n*, 577&*n*, 884*n*, (*p*271);
    and Hajós, L., "Beiträge zur Psychologie des hysterischen Geisteszustandes," **2** 116&*n*
ranunculus, **13** 193*n*
rape: in case-histories, **1** 117, 197, 309, 311;
    theme of mythology, **5** 34
Raphael, archangel, **9ii** 174; **11** 681; **14** 575; *see also* Byron
rapidity of speech, **3** 53
rappings, **8** 602
rapport, **6** 618;
    between patient and doctor/therapist, **3** 573; **16** 239, 276, 279, 287, 366; **18** 331, 385, 515, 516;
    disturbance of, **3** 559;
    emotional, lack of, **3** 152, 492;

hypnotists on, **17** 181;
see also transference
rapture, **8** 383
Rascher's Yearbook, **4** 199, 200; **7**
(*p*3), 407*n*
rashes, skin-, **8** 639
Rashi (Solomon ben Isaac), Talmud
commentary, **9ii** 133, 134; **12** 543
Rasis, *see* ALCHEMICAL WRITERS:
Rhazes
Rasmussen, K., **18** 674;
Across Arctic America, **18** 674*n*
Rasmussen, K.: *Die Gabe des Adlers,*
16 519*n*
Ras Shamra, **9i** 673; **9ii** 181
ratiocinative method (Dubois), **4**
527&*n*
rational, **6** 785–8 (Def.);
and irrational, **7** 72, 75, 110,
121;
tied to conscious mind, **7** 110;
types, *see* type(s) *s.v.*
rationalism, **6** 386; **7** 24/436, 150,
257, 483, 493; **9i** 697; **9ii** 141,
235; **11** 465; **12** 59; **13** 66; **15** 45;
18 625, 1588;
analysis and, **11** 904;
and archetypal figures, **5** 388;
and city dwelling, **10** 648;
enlightened, **11** 81;
of feeling, **6** 518;
and Holy Ghost, **11** 222;
"inner" reality, **5** 221;
and James's typology, **6** 507,
518, 522–3, 865;
materialistic, **18** 1689;
modern, **5** 113;
and religious ideas, **5** 339;
scientific, **10** 501; **12** 562;
and superstition, complementary, **18** 759;
and unconscious, **6** 80;
view of gods as artificial, **5** 576;
and Zen, **11** 880
rationalist(s), **10** 653; **12** 38;
doctrinaire, **17** 159;
and neurosis, **10** 355
rationalistic, **9ii** 346;

attitude, *see* attitude *s.v.*;
consciousness, **13** 474;
intellect, **13** 456, 474;
methods, **11** 507;
opinions, and neurotic symptoms, **8** 808;
systems, **12** 7
rationality, **7** 72, (*p*124); **8** 922; **9ii**
390*n*; **13** 24, 59, **18** 759;
of cosmos, **12** 186;
male, **9ii** 100
rationalizations, **7** 320, 347; **8** 272,
656; **11** 274;
of consciousness, **8** 739;
of inner perceptions, **8** 594
Ratna-Sambhava, **11** 852
Ratramnus, **6** 36
rattlesnake, *see* ANIMALS *s.v.*
Rauschenbach, Emma, *see* Jung,
Emma
"Raven, The" (Poe), **5** 81–3
raven, *see* ANIMALS *s.v.*
Ravenna, **18** 1715
ray(s): death-, red, **13** 401;
of God, *see* Schreber *s.v.*;
of light/*radius*, **9ii** 292*n*;
of Surya, **13** 340
ray(fish), *see* ANIMALS: fish *s.v.*
Raymond (in Melusina legend), **13**
217–18
Raymundus, **12** 220
Raziel, **13** 173*n*; **14** 572&*n*
Re, **13** 360
reaction(s): definition of, **2** 730;
delayed, **3** 147;
disturbed by complexes, **8** 199,
592;
-dreams, **8** 499;
indifferent, and complex, **3** 93;
infectiousness of emotional, **17**
83;
meaningless, **1** 312&*n*;
secondary, **17** 237;
slowness of, **1** 309;
-time, *see* reaction-time;
-types, similarity in families, **4**
695;
value-predicate, **4** 700;

reaction(s) (*cont.*):
-words, complex-toned, **5** 219;
see also "all-or-none" reaction
reaction-time, **2** 12, 347, 360, 364,
524, 560–638, 1081; **3** 108, 203;
arithmetical mean, **2** 571;
in association tests, **8** 592;
in constellations, **2** 293, 339,
548*n*, 552, 605, 607, 621, 645,
650, 743;
in criminal investigations, **2**
771–4, 785, 1322, 1360–70;
in epilepsy, **2** 541, 550;
feeling-tone and, *see* feeling-
toned complexes;
in galvanometer experiments,
2 1091–1117, 1127, 1139–49;
grammatical form and, **2** 585;
in hysteria, **2** 798, 813;
measurement technique, **2**
563, 966;
of neurotics, **2** 993;
in pneumograph experiments,
2 1117;
probable mean, **2** 551, 570,
772, 967;
prolonged, **3** 175, 208; **18** 100;
concept, **2** 601, 944, 946, 1081;
in psychoanalysis, **2** 673;
reaction word and, **2** 594–8;
reproduction disturbance and,
2 922–5;
sex and, **2** 577–8;
sexual/erotic complexes and, **2**
196, 295, 297;
stimulus word and, **2** 584–93,
622–32;
in theft case, **2** 771–3, 785
reactivation of parental imagos, **4**
569
reactivity, **4** 411*n*
Read, J.: *Prelude to Chemistry*, **9i**
686*n*; **14** 87*n*
reading, **17** 224, 228;
addiction to, **1** 206;
indiscriminate, by children, **17**
237;
mistakes in, **3** 109;

-tests, **1** 154
real:
TITLE: "The Real and the Sur-
real," **8** 742–8;
and imaginary, as opposites, **7**
121
realia, **7** 506
realism/realist(s), **3** 419; **7** 199; **9ii**
235, 274, 368;
child's outgrowing of, **17** (*p*6);
Eastern, **13** 2, 378;
French, **16** 66;
and introversion, **6** 508;
in medieval philosophy, **6** 40,
44;
Plato's, **6** 43;
"relative," in Abelard, **8** 4*n*;
Schiller on, **6** 220–2;
and symbol, **5** 343;
symbolical truth, **5** 336;
see also nominalism; scho-
lasticism/Schoolmen
reality(-ies), **6** 60–1; **7** 187, 322,
507; **12** 148, 283, 321; **13** 75;
absolute, **7** 354;
adaptation to, *see* adaptation
s.v.;
alienation from, in early Christian era, **5** 107;
of archetypes, **7** 158;
blocking of, and fantasy substitutes, **5** 254;
Chinese view of, **11** 969;
conscious and unconscious, **7**
120, 354, 470;
desire to transcend, **5** 335;
differential, **13** 55;
disappearance of, **4** 274;
dissociation from, **5** 58;
in dreams, **5** 261;
of earth, **13** 81;
escape from, in fantasies, **5**
465;
experiencing of, **11** 766, 850;
and extraversion and introversion, **5** 259;
and fantasy, **7** 351;
fantasy-substitute for, **7** 183;

fear of, **7** 510;
flight from, **4** 411; **7** 288;
function, *see* function(s) *s.v.*;
"geometric" idea, **8** 982;
God as: pure, **11** 289; quintessence of, **8** 677;
Indian view of, **11** 910;
inner, **6** 19, 77; vs. outer, **5** 221; **7** 319;
lack of, **10** 426;
living, **13** 81;
loss of, **1** 319; **5** 192, 200, 621; and multiplicity, **14** 659;
of neurosis, **11** 17;
neurotics and, **4** 428;
not purely material, **8** 743;
opposing, **7** 354;
and persona, **7** 246;
potential, **12** 399, 557;
principle, **4** 772;
of psyche, *see* psyche *s.v.*;
psychic, **5** 222; **7** 151, 158; **8** 681, 683, 743, 748; **9ii** 85; **11** 376, 766, 888; **12** 93; **13** 62; concept of, **13** 76n; and conscious, **16** 111; of man, **13** 293; of Melusina, **13** 216; oneness of, **8** 682;
relative, **13** 55;
replacement by collective unconscious, **8** 598;
representations of, by artists and by schizophrenics, **15** 174;
requires polarity, **9ii** 423;
scientific, **7** 353;
of the self, **7** 267;
soberness of, **4** 634;
spiritual, lack of experience of, **10** 651; and symbolical truth, **5** 336;
subjective, of the world, **5** 344;
subtle, **12** 400;
and super-reality, **8** 742;
-thinking, **5** 11;
thought and, **11** 280;
of unconscious, **7** 292, 354, 469; **13** 62, 249; paradoxical, **13** 250;

withdrawal from, **5** 457, 520, 629;
of the world, **7** 397, 501n
realization, **7** 224; **11** 251, 288; **12** 239, 279, 321, 330, 400; **13** 120; conscious, **7** 393; **9ii** 377n; **13** 293; value of, **16** 315;
imaginative, **13** 216;
incomplete, **16** 490;
of the opposite, **13** 30;
of personality, **7** 186;
process of, **7** 88, 97; **13** 482;
of the self, *see* self (2) *s.v.* *-realization;*
of Tao, **13** 30;
of unconscious contents, **11** 542;
of unconscious fantasy, **7** 358, 464n
realm: of light, **13** 334;
of spirit, **13** 395
reanimation, **14** 742
reason, **7** 110, (*p*124), 237, 370, 483; **9i** 22, 175; **11** 27, 272, 531; **13** 15, 229, 286, 294, 303, 438, 454, 469;
and the archetype, **11** 222;
and catastrophe, **8** 683;
and Christian doctrine, **11** 444;
flimsy barrier against pathological tendencies, **17** 136;
incarnate, **8** 934;
and instinct, **16** 178;
laws of, **13** 294;
limitations of, **11** 83;
and nature, **8** 739;
relativity of, **8** 47;
supremacy of, **11** 735
Reason, Goddess of/Déesse Raison, **6** 116, 119; **9i** 173; **9ii** 155; **10** 544;
in Notre Dame (Paris), **10** 174; **13** 294; **14** 342; **18** 598
re-association, compensating desire for, **5** 58
Rebecca, **14** 556
rebirth, **5** 363; **7** 172; **9i** 248; **9ii** 333; **13** 446; **16** 455;

rebirth (*cont.*):
TITLES: "Concerning Rebirth," 9i 199–258; "Symbols of the Mother and of Rebirth," 5 300–418;
of Adam, *see* Adam *s.v.*;
in alchemy, 13 459; death and, *see* death *s.v.* rebirth; of philosophical tree, 13 376, 459 (*see also* king);
archetype of, 9i 207; 17 6n;
ascent of bird as, 5 538;
of Buddha, *see* Buddha *s.v.*;
burial customs and, 5 349;
ceremonies, 7 314; 13 92;
into childhood (symbolic), 5 335, 351; incest and, 5 332;
concept of, five forms, 9i 199–205;
death and, *see* death *s.v.*;
Faust's, 5 417; 6 317;
fish as symbol of, 5 290;
hero and, *see* hero *s.v.*;
and initiation rites, *see* initiate/initiation;
longing for, 5 617, 626;
of man, 5 335; 13 41;
maternal vessel of, 5 631;
through mother, 5 312, 332, 408, 609, pl. XLII; magic and, 9i 158;
motif of, 6 297, 459; 9i 95;
"narrow passage" of, 5 417; 6 310&n;
perfection through, 5 351;
of phoenix, 5 538;
primitive rituals of, *see* rite/ritual *s.vv.* rebirth, renewal;
psychic reality of, 9i 206–7;
spiritual, 5 332–5, 494, 511, 577, 671; 13 41, 97; into *novam infantiam*, 5 106n; 7 393;
symbol(s), 5 495; 8 809;
as transformation, 9i 258;
through water, 5 319, 609; 13 89n; and spirit, 5 510; and wind, 5 485;
see also regeneration; reincarnation; renewal

Rebis (hermaphrodite), 9i 292; 9ii 245, 426; 11 107; 12 305, 343, 500, 517, *figs.* 125, 199; 13 *fig.* B3; 14 41, 391; 16 398, 468, 520, 522, 533;
alchemical structure of, 14 337;
"made of two," 11 107n, 162n;
synonyms for, 16 526
Récamier, Mme., 1 63
reciprocal action, body-psyche, 8 33
recognition, 8 288, 290, 755;
of unconscious contents, 9i 84
recollection of ancestors and gods, 5 250
reconciliation of opposites, *see* opposites, union of
reconnaissance, aerial, 10 600
reconstruction stage in treatment, 4 595
recovery, motives for, 4 639
recruits, study of, 2 1312–15
rectangle, *see* square *s.v.* oblongs
Recueil stéganographique, *see* ALCHEMICAL WRITERS: Colonna *s.v.* Béroalde de Verville
red/reddening, *see* COLOURS *s.v.*
"redeemed": term, 5 380
redeemer/Redeemer, 6 316, 439; 9i 561n; 11 229; 12 41, 169, 417; 13 404; 16 381;
in alchemy, 13 390; 14 124, 487; and fairytale, 9i 448; king as, *see* king *s.v.*; lowly origin of, 12 33; 13 182n; Mercurius as, *see* Mercurius *s.v.*; *opus* and, 13 393;
archetype of, 9ii 285; 11 202; 12 33; 18 1687;
birth of, 13 393;
Christ as, *see* Christ *s.v.* mediator;
Christian, *see* Christianity *s.v.*;
Gnostic, *see* Gnostic(s)(-ism) *s.v.*;
Marduk as, 11 173;
motif, 18 80;
-personality, 17 303;
symbolism of: animal, 8 229; 10 679; 16 254; fish/serpent, 9ii 285, 291; 16 254;

and unconscious, **9ii** 283; "well-beloved," **5** 175

redemption, **3** 407; **5** 95, 104; **6** 28, 230, 316, 317, 326–7, 329, 330, 348; **9i** 74, 453; **9ii** 66, 299, 403; **11** 516, 518, 658, 841; **12** 493; **13** 80, 168, 181, 183, 196, 228*n*;
  in alchemy (liberation), **12** 26, 414–24, 436*n*, 441, 451, 461, 463, 493, 496, 557; **13** 142, 252; of divine soul/spirit/Anthropos from matter/Physis, **12** 306, 413, 415, 420, 452, 557, 562, *fig.* 178; **14** 353–4; goal of (Paracelsan), **13** 227; of God, **12** 420, 451, 452; by rose-coloured blood, **13** 390;
  Christ's work of, *see* Christ/Jesus Christ *s.v.* mediator;
  of the dead, **9ii** 72;
  doctrine of, **11** (*p*357–8); Christian, **6** 114; **9ii** 125, 272; **11** (*p*358); **12** 36, 415–16, 450, 453; devil's part in, **11** 252;
  drama of, **12** 495; trinitarian, **11** 207, 241;
  Holy Ghost and, *see* Holy Ghost *s.v.*;
  hope of, **5** 119; **11** 203;
  of man, *see* man *s.v.*;
  myths, **11** 814;
  and uniting symbol, **9i** 285;
  see also salvation

red-green blindness, **1** 395, 415

Redlich, J., **1** 118*n*;
  "Ein Beitrag zur Kenntnis der Pseudologia phantastica," **1** 117*n*

Red Riding Hood, *see* fairytales, INSTANCES: German

Red/Erythrean Sea, **9ii** 128;
  in alchemical symbolism, **12** 475; **14** 234, 256–75, 403;
  crossing of, as death and rebirth, **14** 257, 274, 287;
  in Maier's mystic peregrination, **14** 276–86, 287

reductio in primam figuram, **18** 175, 176

reduction, **3** 413; **4** 679; **7** 67–8; **8** 94, 109, 496;
  of dream-content, **8** 452;
  to infantile material, **18** 1060, 1063;
  to instinct, **16** 40;
  of opposites to unity, **13** 358;
  of symbols, alchemical/Freudian, **13** 396;
  and transference, **7** 96, 259

reductive, **6** 788 (Def.);
  analysis, **7** 76; **13** 480; **16** 24, 282, 286;
  analytical-reductive method, **3** 389, 390, 391–2, 423; **6** 427, 788; **7** 113, 471; **16** 9, 25; **17** 194 (*see also* Adler, A. *s.v.* reductive method);
  causalism, **7** 128; in Freud, *see* Freud *s.v.*;
  caused-reductive method, **18** 1147;
  viewpoint, **6** 855; **11** 547; **17** 195

réeducation de la volonté, **4** 414; **10** 333; **11** 539; **16** 1

re-em, *see* ANIMALS *s.v.* unicorn

Rees, J. R., **18** 304

reference, delusions of, **3** 169

refining, **13** 35

reflection, **3** 138; **7** 242/463; **8** 61; **9ii** 33; **11** 235&*n*, 272, 421, 961; **12** 149, 247, 410, 472; **13** 452;
  and action, as opposites, **7** 80;
  God manifest in, **11** 238;
  Holy Ghost a product of, **11** 236, 241;
  as instinct, **8** 242;
  and introversion, **7** 80;
  left and right reversed by, **12** 225;
  rational, **13** 208;
  torment of unlimited, **13** 442;
  twilight of, **13** 334;
  in unconscious, **8** 362;
  and will, **7** 72

reflex(es), **8** 368; **15** 135;
  arcs, **8** 607;
  chains of, **8** 955;

reflex(es) (*cont.*):
emotional, **4** 569;
and instincts, **8** 955;
tests of, **1** 7, 233, 333, 395
reflexio, **8** 241
"reflex machines," **3** 193
Reformation, **4** 748, 750; **6** 96, 400,
433; **8** 649; **9i** 22; **9ii** 149, 159,
277; **10** 326, 434; **11** 470, 742; **12**
9, 489;
Holy Ghost movement and, **9ii**
143
reformation of God-image, **9ii** 73
refrigerium, **10** 745
regatta, as symbol of self, **8** 396
regeneration, **12** 96; **13** 228*n*;
alchemical, **12** 450, 455, 486,
fig. 152;
in mother's body, **5** pl. XLII;
symbolism: Haloa Festival, **5**
pl. LXIIIa; snake, **5** 677;
see also renewal
regenerative function of world-ash,
5 367
regicide, *see* king/Rex *s.v.*
regimina: four, **12** 31;
three, **12** 310
regina, *see* queen
regio: aetherea, **12** 430;
nymphididica, **12** 116
regius filius, *see filius regius*; king *s.v.*
son of
regression, **4** 276*n*, 407–8, 470,
517–18, 565, 693–4; **5** 506–7,
631; **7** 117, 151, 159, 239; **8** 43;
10 340, 475; **12** 239–40, 246; **13**
323–4, 332, 365; **16** 186; **17** 204;
18 1046–7, 1312*n*;
TITLES: "Progression and Regression," **8** 60–76; "Sensitiveness and Regression," **4** 391–5;
"The Teleological Significance
of Regression," **4** 404–6;
alchemical projection as, **16**
440;
to archaic thinking, **11** 159;
to archetypes, **5** 466, 508;
of child, **5** 465;

to childhood, *see* childhood *s.v.*;
and compensation, **5** 587, 660;
13 473;
conditions of, **4** 378, 383;
cultural, **5** 345;
and deviation into sex, **5** 220;
in dream-thinking, **5** 25;
effect of, **4** 401;
and emotional reaction, **18**
1312;
end of, **4** 423;
energic view, **8** 72–3, 75–6;
and fear, **5** 551;
to Helios, **12** 99;
historical, **12** 116;
into history, **18** 1323;
and incest, **5** 313, 332; **12** 171;
infantile, **18** 365;
to infantilism, **5** 278, 345;
and inhibition of sexuality, **5**
226;
introversion and, *see* introversion *s.v.*;
of libido, *see* libido *s.v.*;
to man's prehistory, **16** 18;
to mother, *see* mother *s.v.*;
national, **18** 1322;
and need for new adaptations,
5 450;
to nutritional phase, **5** 206–7,
519, 654;
to paganism/antiquity, **12** 12,
112, 115, 178;
to parents, **6** 201;
to prenatal/pre-infantile phase,
5 264; **7** 120;
prevention of, **5** 379;
to primitive stage, **17** 104;
and rebirth of consciousness, **5**
558;
as *reculer pour mieux sauter*, **16**
19;
and religion, **5** 138, 553;
unconscious, **13** 324;
to unconsciousness, **12** 563
regressive: concretization, **16** 446;
dissolution, **7** 238;
longing, **7** 261/477;

restoration of persona, *see* persona *s.v.*;
tendency, **16** 54–9; of child, **17** 144
regressiveness, conscious, **7** 182; **17** 281
Reguel, **9ii** 362; *see also* Jethro
Regulus (chief star in Leo), **14** 493*n*
regulus (metallurgy), **14** 467
Reibmayer, A.: *Die Entwicklungsgeschichte des Talentes und Genies*, J.'s review, **18** 917
Reich, German: founding of, **10** 433;
"thousand-year," **10** 396, 438
Reichardt, M.: *Leitfaden zur psychiatrischen Klinik*, J.'s review, **18** 896–9
Reichstag fire, **10** 409
Reichstein, T., **12** 347*n*
Reid, T., **8** 265;
Essays on the Active Powers of Man, **8** 265*n*
Reil, J. C., **3** 22
Reinach, S., **16** 146;
Cultes, mythes, et religions, **13** 270*n*
reincarnation(s), **9i** 201, 518; **10** 181; **11** 831;
and anima, **10** 87;
in Jung's case of S. W., **1** 63–4, 120;
and Karma, **11** 845;
theory, **17** 6&*n*, 96;
see also Buddha; rebirth
reinforced object-libido, **2** 953
Reinwald, P.: *Vom Geist der Massen*, **10** 477*n*
Reith, M., **18** (*p*692*n*)
Reitzenstein, R., **9i** 79*n*;
on alchemy, **12** 332; **13** 252;
WORKS:
"Alchemistische Lehreschriften," **12** 386*n*, 404*n*; **13** 278&*n*;
Die hellenistischen Mysterienreligionen, **5** 102*n*; **12** 125*n*, 456*n*; **14** 14*n*, 726*n*;

"Himmelswanderung und Drachenkampf," **14** 300*n*;
Poimandres, **9i** 238*n*; **9ii** 128*n*, 162&*n*; **11** 92*n*, 350*n*; **12** 66*n*, 185*n*, 338*n*, 410*n*, 456*nn*, 457*n*; **13** 97*n*, 236*n*, 276*n*; **14** 14*nn*, 121*n*, 732*n*;
and H. H. Schäder, *Studien zum antiken Syncretismus aus Iran und Griechenland*, **9ii** 389*n*; **13** 119*n*, 269*n*, 446*n*; **14** 21*n*, 68*n*, 587*n*, 595*n*; **16** 416*n*, 531*n*;
Zwei religionsgeschichtliche Fragen, **14** 14*n*
reivas plant, **13** 458*n*
rejection, motif of, **12** 91, 95, 103, 105–6, 112, 160, 201, 255
rejuvenation, **5** 388;
drink of, **5** 634;
Faust's, **12** 558;
magic, **5** 363–4;
motif of, **5** 569
relapse, **4** 169; **7** 208, 501
relatedness, **13** 60;
inferior, **13** 60
relationship: of analyst and patient, *see* analyst *s.v.* patient;
anima and, *see* anima *s.v.*;
animus and, *see* animus *s.v.*;
and choice of mate, **17** 329;
collective biological and spiritual, **17** 342;
compensated, **7** 279;
compensatory, **7** 204/445, 274;
conflict of, **7** 277;
conscious and unconscious, **7** 336;
counter-crossing, **16** 421–6;
of doctor and patient, *see* doctor *s.v.* patient;
extra-familial, **4** 440;
function(s) of, **6** 280; **7** 387; **9ii** 29; **13** 62; and archetypes, **5** 388;
heterosexual, **7** 179; **17** 278–9;
homosexual, *see* homosexuality;
human, **9ii** 34; and imperfec-

relationship (*cont.*):
    tion, **10** 579; and projections, **8**
    507; and transference, **16** 284;
    impersonal, **7** 284;
    inadequate, **9ii** 37;
    infantile, **7** 134; in transfer-
    ence, **16** 357;
    mother-child, *see* mother *s.v.*;
    to object, **7** 223;
    parent-child, *see* parent *s.v.*
    child;
    to partner, **9ii** 42;
    personal, **7** 330, 373;
    psychic, **7** 519;
    psychology of, in marriage, **17**
    324;
    space-time, *see* space-time;
    symbolical, **16** 469;
    transference, *see* transference;
    and unconscious, **17** 326
relative(s): and association reac-
    tions, **4** 696;
    dead, primitives and, **8** 575
relativism, **18** 6;
    philosophical, **10** 188; **16** 146;
    Protestant, **11** 34
relativity: of consciousness, **8** 397;
    of God, *see* God *s.v.*;
    of moral values, **18** 534, 536;
    of space and time, *see* space and
    time *s.v.*;
    theory of, **10** 182; **18** 140;
    of the unconscious, **8** 385
religere, **8** 427
religio, **5** 669; **7** 164; **9i** 271; **11** 74,
    454, 982&*n*; **16** 395&*n*;
    medica, **13** 161; **18** 1465
religion, **4** 761; **6** 326, 422–3; **7** 156,
    219, 302, 305; **8** 95, 683; **11** 51,
    509; **12** 293, 296; **13** 81; **14** 342,
    346, 584; **16** 20, 21, 254; **17** (*p*4),
    271, 343; **18** 378;
    TITLES: "Alchemical Symbolism
    in the History of Religion," **12**
    516–54; "The Function of
    Religious Symbols," **18** 560–77;
    "Psychology and Religion," **11**
    1–168; *Psychology and Religion:*

West and East, **11**; "Religion
and Psychology: A Reply to
Martin Buber," **18** 1499–1513:
as absolute experience, **18** 692;
anaemia of, **18** 598;
and anima, *see* anima *s.v.*;
and archetypes, **8** 405, 426–7;
11 222; **12** 35, 38; **17** 210; **18**
1229;
as attitude, *see* attitude *s.v.*;
authority of, **14** 342;
autonomous psychic contents
and, **8** 712;
changes of, **6** 313;
Christian, *see* Christian/Chris-
tianity; Church;
classical, **12** 41;
cognition and, **11** 768;
collective, **8** 110;
and collective consciousness, **8**
426;
comparative, **4** 745; **9i** 89, 115,
148, 318; **13** 1; **15** (*p*84); **16** 96,
111; **18** 834;
and conflict, solution of, **5** 122;
consciousness and, **11** 555,
557;
contradictions in, **12** 18;
creed and, **16** 20, 392; **18** 1637;
cultural symbols in, **18** 579;
and death, **8** 804;
decline of, and psyche, **10** 160,
168;
and dogma, see dogma *s.v.*;
in dreams, *see* dream(s) *s.v.*;
Eastern/Oriental, **7** 118; **13** 1,
70;
East/West, contrasts in, **11** 911;
12 8; **13** 1, 79, 80;
and education, **12** 7;
Fascism as, **18** 373;
founders of, **14** 782;
Freud and, *see* Freud *s.v.*;
"fulness of life" and, **11** 60;
future, **18** 633;
and future life, **8** 790;
goals of, **10** 513;
history of, **7** 459; **12** 38; **13**

252; comparative, **7** 326; and fantasies, **4** 738*n*; hero-motif and, **10** 101;
individual, **8** 109–10;
infantile constellations and, **4** 729*n*;
instinct and, **14** 603 (*see also* instinct(s) *s.v.* religious);
intellectual approach to, **13** 51;
inter-War development of, **10** 372–3;
and libido, canalization of, **5** 259;
and life, compensatory relation, **6** 229;
and mass-mind, **10** 505–16;
meaning of term, **11** 6–9; *numinosum*, **11** 9, 450–1;
as mental hygiene, **18** 1578;
modern attitude to, **10** 193; **16** 392;
mystery-, *see* mystery *s.v.*;
and myth(s), **5** 30; **14** 474*n*, 751;
and mythologems, **11** 450;
mythological motif(s) in, **5** 42;
and nature, **5** 109–10;
nature of, **8** 805;
need for, **5** 104;
and neurosis, *see* neurosis *s.v.*;
outward form of, **12** 12;
pagan form of, relapse to, **7** 41;
paradoxes of, **12** 18;
and parental imagos, *see* imago;
phenomenology of, **13** 49;
and philosophy, **13** 70; **16** 182–3, 250–1;
pre-Christian, **12** 26;
primitive, **7** 108, 172, 325; **8** 109, 516; **11** 375, 537, 556; Elgonyi and, *see* Elgonyi; "night," **10** 59;
primordial images in, *see* primordial image(s) *s.v.*;
psychic process and, **9i** 11, 261;
of healing, **13** 478; **16** 249; as psychic fact, **10** 1045;

psychoanalysis and, **4** 457;
"psychologizing" of, **18** 1495;
and psychology, **7** 215; **8** 526; **11** 137, 148, 160, 771; **12** 9, 14–17, 20, 35; **13** 447; **14** 455*n*; **15** 98; **16** 389*n*; **18** 1135, 1140; and medical psychology, **11** 1;
psychology of, **8** 405; has two categories, **11** 751;
as psychotherapeutic system, **5** 553; **18** 370, 1231, 1494, 1578;
and psychotherapy, **14** 346, 514; **16** 20, 390;
reasonableness of, **8** 792;
and regression, **5** 134, 553;
rites of, **16** 215; degeneration, **5** 581;
sacrifice in, **4** 350;
and salvation, **11** 293, 539;
and science, *see* science *s.v.*;
and second half of life, *see* life, stages in;
sects/sectarianism in, *see* sects; sectarianism;
and sexuality, *see* sexuality *s.v.*;
spirit in, **9i** 393;
State-, **8** 92; **10** 522;
as substitute, **11** 75;
and symbol(s)/-ism, **4** 350; **5** 332, 336; **7** 156; **8** 111; **11** 293; **16** 351; **18** 481; (*see also* religious symbols);
symbolic contents, **6** 80;
task of, **9i** 393;
and tree, myth/symbol of, **5** 349, 368;
truth of, **12** 565;
and unconscious, *see* unconscious, the *s.v.*;
unconscious fantasies and, **4** 341, 342;
understanding of, difficulty in, **10** 543, 544;
and value, relationship, **11** 137;
world-, **14** 789; **18** 565;
see also *unio mystica*

religious:

    TITLES: "Introduction to the Religious and Psychological Problems of Alchemy," **12** 1–43; "Jung and Religious Belief," **18** 1573–1679; "Religious Ideas in Alchemy," **12** 332–554;

    activity, **10** 330;

    aspects of unconscious, *see* unconscious, the *s.v.*;

    attitude, *see* attitude *s.v.*;

    ceremonies, **13** 31;

    conversion, *see* conversion *s.v.*;

    convictions, **3** 90, 489;

    convulsions, **7** 115;

    development, future, **18** (*p*267);

    devotion, **6** 201;

    education, *see* education *s.v.*;

    enthusiasm, **3** 105;

    experience, *see sep. entry below*;

    faith, *see* faith *s.v.*;

    feeling/mania, **1** 214, 216; and new sects, **1** 34;

    figure, **5** 95, 575;

    function, *see* function *s.v.*;

    idea(s), **13** 396; diversity of, **8** 728; Jung's treatment of, **5** 339;

    instinct, **10** 653, 659; **17** 157;

    language, **13** 77;

    life, decline of, **11** 514;

    man, and God, **17** 296;

    motifs, **7** 250;

    mystery, **13** 194;

    myth, value of, **5** 343;

    observances, **9i** 275;

    phenomenology, *see* phenomenology *s.v.*;

    practice, **13** 70;

    problem, **13** 80 (*see also* Schiller *s.v.*);

    projection, **12** 11;

    rites, *see* rite(s)/ritual *s.v.*;

    spirit, **13** 80;

    statements, **11** 222, 554; **14** 273, 374, 782, 786;

    structures, libido in, **5** 669;

    symbol(s)/symbolism, *see sep. entry below;*

    thought, **13** 68;

    viewpoint, and psychological attitude, **11** 771

religious experience, **7** 400; **10** 566, 655; **11** 106; **12** 9, 13, 16; **14** 514; **17** 157;

    absoluteness of, **11** 167;

    in antiquity, **5** 102;

    creeds and, **11** 10;

    definition of, **11** 106;

    intuitive, **14** 208;

    phenomenology of, **9i** 126;

    reality of, **11** 889;

    subjectivity of, **5** 95; **11** 168;

    of West and East, **13** 79

religious symbols(-ism), **4** 490, 555, 680, 777; **5** 340; **6** 202, 428; **7** 326; **10** 541; **12** 166; **17** 159; **18** 1827;

    TITLE: "The Function of Religious Symbols," **18** 560–77;

    archetypal character of, **10** 550;

    canalization of libido into, **5** 259;

    genesis of, **8** 805; **11** 339;

    psychology and, **14** 457;

    purpose of, **18** 567;

    revelatory, **8** 805;

    of unconscious processes, **11** 3;

    see also religion *s.v.* and symbols

religiousness, and typology, **6** 528–9

Rembrandt, **12** *fig.* 55

remedy(-ies), arcane, **13** 171, 193*n*

reminiscence(s), **4** 29, 37, 304, 365, 376, 569; **7** 5/414;

    and dreams, **4** 326, 337;

    emotional, **8** 510;

    excited by hypnosis, **4** 211;

    infantile, **7** 21/434, 75;

    of patients, **7** 11/420, 45, 75;

    personal, **7** 122;

    transformation into fantasies, **4** 394

remission of sins, **13** 355
remora/sucking fish, *see* ANIMALS *s.v.*
   fish: *echeneis*
remorse, **3** 490;
   as reason for simulation, **1** 391,
   418;
   in *I Ching,* **11** 980
Rempham, **9ii** 128*n*
Remus, *see* Romulus
Remusat, C.F.M. de, **6** 68, 71–2;
   Abélard, **6** 68*n*
Renaissance, **6** 313; **9ii** 78, 149,
   156; **11** 84, 860; **12** 112; **13** 238;
   14 646; **15** 154; **18** 1665;
   and anima motif, **18** 1279;
   feeling for nature, **5** 113;
   and licentiousness, **7** 17/427;
   spirit of, **13** 152; **14** 454
Renan, J. E.: cult of the sun, **5** 138*n*;
   rational image of God, **5** 176;
   Dialogues et fragments philoso-
   phiques, **5** 138*n*
Renaudin, L.F.E., **1** 112
René d'Anjou, **14** 646; **18** 1280,
   1711
renewal, **7** 91; **9i** 208;
   in alchemy: of Ethiopian, **12**
   484; fount of, **13** 446*n*; of king,
   see king *s.v.*; sea of, **12** *fig.* 222;
   tree and, *see* tree *s.v.* transformation; word of, **13** 271;
   of life, *see* life *s.v.*;
   and magic, **5** 404; **9i** 203, 231;
   of personality, **7** 172;
   psychic, and symbols of rebirth, **8** 845;
   rite of, *see* rite/ritual *s.v.*;
   symbolism: cross, **5** 404; fish, **5**
   290;
   see also regeneration; *renovatio*
Reni, Guido, *Crucifixion,* **5** 665; **11**
   342
renovatio, **9ii** 156*n*;
   rebirth/renewal, **9i** 203
renovation of the age, **9ii** 156
reparation of the collective, **18** 1097
repentance, **9ii** 299; **11** 448, 862; **12**
   36

repercussion, alchemical, **13** 173*n*
repetition, **3** 11, 53;
   of actions, significance of, **4**
   106;
   experiment, **8** 199;
   in galvanometer experiments,
   2 1054–6;
   in reactions, **2** 104, 220–1, 223,
   224, 230, 235, 242, 243, 249,
   257, 280, 299, 313, 332, 335,
   343, 349, 351–2, 368, 372, 676,
   954, 955;
   of stimulus-words, **2** 95, 454,
   455, 539, 541&*n*, 542, 543,
   554, 556, 558, 954, 955
representation(s), **8** 352, 354, 364,
   608;
   collective, *see* Lévy-Bruhl *s.v.*;
   Herbart on, **8** 350;
   inheritance of, **8** 269*n*;
   primitive, **8** 127;
   shadowy/dim, **3** 440; **18** 8;
   see also image(s)
représentations collectives, see Lévy-
   Bruhl *s.v.*
repression, **4** 32, 225, 286; **5** 91–5,
   261, 263; **6** 306*n*, 861; **7** 21/434,
   39, 42, 77, 146, 148, 156, 218/
   450, 240, 320, 474; **8** 17, 104,
   270, 321, 492, 588, 702, 706–7,
   709; **9i** 314, 540; **9ii** 357; **10** 3,
   340, 610; **11** 129, 543; **12** 74; **13**
   6, 51, 108, 332, 464; **15** 52; **16** 75,
   125, 176, 452; **17** (*p*6), 13*n*, 154,
   173, 199a–200, 203–6, 218–19;
   18 423;
   TITLE: "The Concept of Repression," **4** 210–14;
   analysis of, **7** 202/443;
   and artistic creation, **15** 156;
   associations and, *see* associa-
   tion(s) *s.v.*;
   of collective psyche, **7** 237/459;
   of complexes, *see* complex(es)
   s.v.;
   conscious, **4** 212;
   contents, **13** 51; of collective
   unconscious, **8** 425;

repression (*cont.*):
 and creativeness, **17** 206;
 definition, **2** 619*n*;
 dissociation and, *see* dissociation
  s.v.;
 and dreams, **4** 73; **8** 703; **18**
  863–4;
 of eroticism, **6** 307;
 forgetting and, **2** 640, 657;
 of former idols, **7** 115;
 Freud on/in Freudian psychology, **2** 619*n*, 639–40, 657, 661,
  920; **4** 210; **6** 90, 92, 839, 861;
  7 29, 202–3, 205/443–6; **8** 19*n*,
  35, 212, 372, 704; **11** 129; **13**
  48, 62, 108; **15** 64, 66, 104–6;
  16 34, 48, 231–2; **18** 423,
  1148–9;
 of functions, **6** 93, 115, 171,
  175; **7** 505;
 and hysteria, *see* hysteria *s.v.*;
 of incest-fantasies, **16** 140;
 of infantile memories and
  wishes, **13** 463;
 of instincts, *see* instincts *s.v.*;
 moral, **7** 319; **9i** 135; **16** 245;
 and neurosis, *see* neurosis *s.v.*;
 in normal persons, **3** 148; **17**
  199a;
 of Oedipus complex, **4** 351;
 of parental imago, **6** 201;
 personal, **7** 247, 250; lifting of,
  7 236;
 release of, **6** 172;
 of religious function, **7** 150;
 of *représentations collectives*, **9i**
  130;
 and reproduction disturbances,
  2 920;
 and schizophrenia, *see* schizophrenia *s.v.*;
 sexual/of sexuality, **4** 440; **6**
  373, 405, 716; **10** 331, 653,
  655; **11** 517; **13** 48; **15** 45, 46,
  100; **17** 79, 200; God and, **4**
  741*n*; **11** 142; religion and, **17**
  157; and spirit, **10** 652;
 and sin, **16** 124;

superego and, **10** 828;
 and the unconscious, *see* unconscious, the *s.v.*;
 and unfulfilled desires, **5** 436,
  438
reproduction, biological: evolutionary change in principles, **4**
  279, 284;
 goal of first half of life, **13** 69
reproduction, verbal: capacity for,
  3 16;
 in cryptomnesia, **1** 182;
 disturbance(s) of, **2** 918–38; **3**
  30;
 method, **2** 641, 664, 745, 992,
  1086, 1352; in criminal investigation, **2** 974, 1322; in galvanometer experiment, **2** 1020
reproductive: instinct, *see* instinct
  s.v.;
 organs, development of, **4** 235
reputation, **11** 12
res, **13** 440;
 quaerenda, **13** 374;
 simplex: in alchemy, **12** 367*n*,
  427*n*; **14** 732, 759–60; **16** 398;
 God as, *see* God *s.v.* alchemy
  and; Platonic "Idea" as, **14**
  493*n*
rescue, of Christ, **11** 229
"rescue circles," English, **13** 76*n*
research: comparative, into symbolism, **13** 352, 463, 473;
 psychological, **5** 3
resentment(s), **9ii** 32;
 of chthonic man, **10** 918;
 early, **10** 352;
 moral, **7** 218/450; **8** 702;
 personal, **13** 472;
 Swiss, **10** 915;
 as theme in work of Joyce, **15**
  169
resignation, **13** 424, 436
resin of the wise, **12** 209
resistance(s), **3** 425–8, 433, 436; **4**
  248, 392, 535, 657; **5** 45; **7** 89,
  129, 224, 290, 509; **9i** 122, 124,
  235; **10** 347; **12** 300; **13** 21, 323;

16 75, (p165n);
  and abreaction method, **16**
  273;
  active, **3** 16, 27; **17** 199a;
  in analysis, **7** 24/436, 27/438,
  182, 470; **10** 889; **16** 381; **17**
  158n, 189, 281; initial, **4** 438,
  626; **17** 184 (*see also*
  psychoanalysis *s.v.*);
  of analyst, **4** 421;
  children's, **17** 15–16, 18, 29,
  222;
  to complex, **4** 43, 80, 349;
  aroused by dreams, **17** 189;
  in dreams, **4** 73, 75, 79;
  and fear, **5** 456;
  forcible breaking down of, **17**
  181;
  Freud on, **2** 859;
  to Freud's theories, **7** 411;
  hypnosis and, **4** 594;
  inner, **13** 155;
  of instinct, **5** 338;
  and lapis, **13** 436;
  to life, **8** 797;
  to mother, **9i** 170–1;
  muscular, negativistic, **3** 193;
  neurotic, **8** 798;
  to object, **7** 58, 82;
  over-compensated, **16** 335;
  to parents, **17** 222, 260;
  in psychoanalysis, *see* psychoanalysis *s.v.*;
  against psychological standpoint, **11** 465;
  in psychotherapy, **7** 61;
  and regression, **5** 253–4;
  secret, **7** 21;
  to self-knowledge, **5** 1;
  to sexual problem, **4** 387;
  and shadow-side, **7** 78; **9ii** 16;
  and tie to mother, **5** 329;
  and transference, **7** 94, 145; **8**
  519; **16** 381n;
  of unconscious, **9i** 543n;
  to unconscious, **5** 587; **8** 230;
  12 60;
  to wish-fulfilment, **4** 179;

  to work, **4** 529;
  to wrong interpretations, **7**
  189; **16** 237;
  see also unconscious (adj.) *s.v.*
  opposition
respect, for facts, **11** 519
respectability, **10** 265; **11** 12, 129;
  18 1539
respiration, **3** 134n;
  curve, **8** 23;
  galvanometer experiments, **2**
  1047, 1060–4, 1197–1229;
  internal, and visions, **13** 41–2;
  pneumograph experiments, **2**
  1037, 1058–65, 1186–90, 1220
responsibility, **7** 221/451, 240, 373,
  375; **13** 391;
  in case of epileptic stupor, **1**
  342;
  child's, **17** 220, 225;
  diminished, **8** 200; **13** 48;
  juridical conception of irresponsibility, **1** 470;
  in jurisprudence, **9ii** 8;
  legal, **1** 336, 426–7, 454–5;
  limited by hysteria, **1** 475–6;
  and moral defect, **1** 430, 433,
  470;
  and pathological self-deception, **1** 439–42;
  of prophet, **7** 263–4;
  social, **7** (p5);
  subjective, **7** 323;
  for unconscious, **7** 221/451
rest cure, **1** 29
restitution, **14** 474;
  ceremonies, **9i** 84
restlessness, **1** 190, 209–10;
  inner, **1** 193, 198, 222, 330,
  414;
  neurotic, **8** 815
restoration of persona, *see* persona
  s.v.
restraint, lack of, American, **10** 957
restriction(s), sexual, **10** 652
result(s): suggestive method and,
  16 3;
  of treatment, **7** 198

Rhabanus Maurus, *see* Rabanus Maurus

Rhazes/Rhasis/Rasis, *see* ALCHEMICAL WRITERS *s.v.*

Rhea/Cybele, **5** 303, 662*n*; **9i** 339; **9ii** 186, 310; **11** 10, 348, 718*n*; **12** 26; **14** 27*n*, 576; **18** 1287;
Attis, son-lover of, **5** 595, 659, *fig.* 20; **9i** 156, 162; **12** 26; **14** 27*n*; in Bithynia, **5** 662*n*; priests of, **5** 662; ritual castration in, **5** 299, 662 (*see also* Attis/Atys)

Rheinau Sanatorium (canton Zurich), **18** 1007

Rhein-Verlag, **15** (*p*132)

Rhenanus, J., *see* ALCHEMICAL WRITERS *s.v.*

Rhine, J. B., **8** 914, 940, 965; **10** 743, 744, 780; **14** 411*n*; **18** 1133, 1185, 1189, 1198;
experiments in ESP, **8** 833–8, 846–7, 848, 855, 856, 857, 905, 911–12, 975–80, 994; **9i** 197; **9ii** 287*n*; **10** 660; **11** 401*n*; **14** 662;
"probability-exceeding" results in, **8** 441, 836;
see also extra-sensory perception;
WORKS:
Extra-Sensory Perception, **8** 833*n*; **16** 254*n*;
New Frontiers of the Mind, **8** 504*n*, 833*n*; **9i** 249*n*; **14** 662*n*; **18** 747*n*;
The Reach of the Mind, **11** 974*n*; **14** 662*n*; **18** 747*n*;
see also Pratt;
and Humphrey, B. M., "A Transoceanic ESP Experiment," **8** 834*n*

Rhineland, **10** 375

rhinoceros, *see* ANIMALS *s.v.*

rhizomata, **13** 242

rhizome, **13** 120

Rhoda (in *Shepherd of Hermas*), **6** 381–2, 385, 388, 407

Rhodesian rock-drawings, *see* rock-drawings

rhyme as response, **2** 79, 80, 181, 306, 419*n*, 611

rhythm(s): of dance, **5** 481; infectiveness of, **10** 965; in riding fantasies, **5** 370; three, **12** 307, 310, 318

rhythmic activity/movement, **4** 291; and discovery of fire, **5** 227; and emotional processes, **5** 219; in infancy and childhood, **5** 206; libidal regression to, **5** 218; and sexuality, **5** 219; transference to "decoy mechanisms," **5** 219

ri and *ki,* **6** 370

Ribot, T. A., **1** 110; **5** 190*n*; **6** 966; **10** 2;
Die Persönlichkeit, **1** 112*n*, 113*n*; **6** 797*n*;
The Psychology of the Emotions, **6** 723*n*

rice, **14** 603

Richard of St. Victor: *Benjamin Minor,* **9i** 403*n*

Richardus Anglicus/Richard of Wendover, *see* ALCHEMICAL COLLECTIONS: *Theatr. chem. s.v.*

Richarz, F.: "Über psychische Untersuchungsmethoden," **1** 339*n*, 346*n*;
see also under Böcker

Richer, P., **1** 110;
Études cliniques sur l'hystéro-epilepsie, **1** 13*n*

Richet, Alfred, **18** 750

Richet, C., **1** 77, 148; **8** 830;
"Relations de diverses expériences sur transmission mentale etc.," **8** 830*n*;
La suggestion mentale et le calcul des probabilités, **1** 77*n*

Rickaby, J., *see under* Ignatius Loyola, St.

Rickert, H., **18** 1732&*n*

rope-dancers, in *Zarathustra,* **7** 36

Roques, Mrs. H. von, **9i** 401*n*; **18** 1134

Roquetaillade, Jean de, *see* ALCHEMICAL WRITERS: Rupescissa

Rorschach, H., **6** 917;
  tests, **10** 748, 753, 754, 770; **16** 202, 245

rosa mystica, **11** 126; **12** 257; **13** 389

Rosario de la gloriosa vergine Maria, **12** *fig.* 87

rosarium (rose-garden), mandala as, **9i** 564*n*

Rosarium philosophorum, see ALCHEMICAL WRITERS *s.v.*

"Rosarius" (rose-gardener)/"Rosarium" (book title), *see* ALCHEMICAL WRITERS *s.v.*

"Rosarius minor," *see* ALCHEMICAL COLLECTIONS: *De alchemia s.v.*

Roscellinus, Johannes, **6** 58

Roscher, W. H., **5** 440;
  Hermes der Windgott, **12** 473*n*;
  Lexikon der griechischen und römischen Mythologie, **5** 183*n*, 184*nn*, 198*n*, 208*nn*, 274*n*, 289*n*, 298*n*, 364*n*, 439*n*, 450*n*, 528*n*, 530*n*, 547*n*, 577*n*, 662*nn*, *figs.* 10, 20; **9i** 604*n*; **9ii** 332*nn*; **11** 173*n*, 176*n*, 350*n*; **12** *fig.* 77; **13** 176*n*, 270*n*; **14** 18*n*, 24*n*, 384*n*, 493*n*, 589*n*

rose(s), **5** 619; **12** 99, 139, 229, 235–7, *figs.* 13, 29, 30, 83, 193; **13** 387–8; **14** 419–22, 619*n*; **16** 454, 469; **17** 41;
  and Christ, **12** 139*n*; **13** 387;
  flowers of Venus, **13** 228*n*;
  garden of philosophers, **12** 155, 235;
  heavenly, **13** 389;
  in mandalas, **9i** 646, 652, 654; **13** 389;
  mystic, **9i** 661; **18** 176;
  mysticism, **13** 390;
  mystique of the, **13** 387;
  noble, **12** 348&*n*;
  sign of the, **13** 390;

symbol: of mother, **9i** 156; of self, **9i** 315;
  window, **9i** 577

rose-chafer, *see* ANIMALS *s.v.*

rose-coloured blood, *see* blood *s.v.*

rosemary/*ros marinus,* **14** 683&*n*, 688, 701

Rosenbach, —, **18** 900–901

Rosenberg, A.: *Zeichen am Himmel: Das Weltbild der Astrologie,* **8** 928*n*

Rosencreutz, C., *see* ALCHEMICAL WRITERS *s.v.*

Rosenthal, H., **18** 1727, 1825*n*;
  "Der Typengegensatz in der jüdischen Religionsgeschichte," **18** 1727*n*

ros Gedeonis, see dew of Gideon

Rosicrucian(s)/Rosicrucianism, **6** 314*n*, 316; **7** 385, 494; **9i** 652; **10** 764; **12** 99, 422*n*, 515; **13** 391; **14** 312; **16** 416, 501&*n*;
  see also Waite, A. E.

"Rosie Crosse," **12** 99

Rosinus, *see* ALCHEMICAL WRITERS: Zosimus *s.v.*

"Rosinus ad Euthiciam," *see* ALCHEMICAL COLLECTIONS: *Art. aurif. s.v.*

"Rosinus ad Sarratantam Episcopum," *see* ALCHEMICAL COLLECTIONS: *Art. aurif. s.v.*

Ross, Mary, and Tongue, Mary C.: *Atlantida* (tr. of *L'Atlantide*), **17** 339*n*

Ross, T. A., **18** 283

Rossellini, N.F.I.B.: *I Monumenti dell'Egitto e della Nubia,* **5** 400*n*

Rossi, G. B. de: *Mosaici cristiani delle chiese di Roma anteriori al secolo XV,* **11** 431*n*

Rostand, E., **5** 48, 72;
  Cyrano de Bergerac, **5** 47–51, 70, 72, 167, 430, (*p*448)

rota nativitatis, **9ii** 211; *see also* wheel

rotatio, circle and, **12** 214; *see also* *circulatio*

rotation, **8** 401; **9ii** 388*n*, 406; **11** 114; **12** 133, 165, 214, 267, 290,

315, 433;
    in mandala, **9i** 646; **18** 1332;
    motif, **12** 283;
    spiral, **13** 349;
    see also circumambulation
Rothe, Frau, **18** 725
Roth-Scholtz, F.: *Deutsches Theatrum
    chemicum,* **13** 194*n*; **14** 31*n*; **16**
    506*n*
rotundum, **9i** 538; **9ii** 376, 377; **10**
    715, 765; **11** 92, 158, 160*n*; **12**
    116,*figs.* 34, 165, 166; **13** 101; **14**
    5*n*, 500;
    as alchemical vessel, see *vas;*
    anima as, **14** 498;
    and Anthropos, **9i** 532; **9ii**
    388, 391; **14** 498, 731; and ar-
    chetype of, **9ii** 406;
    as arcane substance, **11** 152;
    as archetype, **10** 803;
    city as, **12** 166*n;*
    cubile, **9ii** 377*n;*
    head as, *see* head *s.v.;*
    in mandala, **9i** 660;
    Mercurius as,*see* Mercurius *s.v.;*
    as Monad, **8** 929;
    motif in alchemy, **9i** 660;
    as Okeanos, origin/seed, of
    gods, **13** 101;
    prefiguration of gold, **12** *fig.*
    164;
    as symbol: of self, *see* self *s.v.;*
    totality/wholeness, **10** 621, 803,
    808, 814; **16** 454;
    as world-soul, *see* world-soul;
    see also circle; moon; omega;
    round *s.v.* element
Rouma, G.: "Un Cas de
mythomanie; Contribution à
l'étude du mensonge et de la
fabulation chez l'enfant," **18**
(*p*421)
round: body, **13** 173;
    element, **11** 366; **13** 95, 101
    (see also *rotundum*);
    and square, as opposites, **12**
    436;
    substance, **11** 92

"round" motif, examples of: *anima
    mundi,* **12** 109*n*, 116, 433;
    circle, **12** 167;
    croquet ball, **12** 150;
    fish in the sea, **12** 433*n;*
    gold/*aurum aurae,* **12** 109*n*,
    116,*fig.* 209;
    hat, **12** 53;
    head, **12** 116;
    Hermes, **12** 172;
    lapis, **12** 167, 220, 433, 486;
    original man, **12** 109*n;*
    potter's wheel, **12** 281;
    simple body, **12** 220;
    soul, *see* soul *s.v.* as sphere;
    table, **12** 238, 240, 241, 242*n*,
    260;
    temple, **12** *fig.* 26;
    vas/vessel, **12** 116, 167*n*, 338&*n;*
    wholeness/self symbolized by,
    12 150, 281;
    see also *rotundum;* sphere
roundness, **9i** 278; **14** 499;
    and the mother, **14** 500;
    see also *rotundum*
Rousseau, J.-J., **6** 120–3, 133–4, 159;
    and Mme. de Warens, **10** 223;
    and return to nature, **8** 739,
    750; **11** 868;
    Emile, ou l'éducation, **6** 120&*n*,
    121*n*, 122*n*, 134*n;* **7** 455*n*
Rousselle, E.: "Drache und Stute,"
    14 636*n;*
    "Spiritual Guidance in Con-
    temporary Taoism," **9i** 81*n;* **9ii**
    20*n*
royal: art, **13** 252, 355;
    marriage, **12** 496; **13** 358, 435;
    pair, *see* pair *s.v.*
Royal Society of Medicine, **8** 954
Royce, J.: "The Case of John Bun-
    yan," **3** 28*n*
rta, **6** 192, 348, 349&*n*, 350–5, 358
ruach/ruah (Hebrew), **11** 240;
    and ruh, see *ruh*
Ruach Elohim, *see* Elohim *s.v.*
rubbing, and fire-making, **5** 208,
    210, 248

S

Saalburg, **18** 259
Sabaean(s), **9ii** 128, 129*n*, 190, 307*n*; **12** 462*n*; **14** 6*n*, 326, 757; **15** 37*n*; **16** 472*n*;
  alchemy, **14** 731;
  and human sacrifice, **14** 690, 731;
  and Ion, **13** (*p*60*n*);
  "Liber quartorum," *see* AL-CHEMICAL COLLECTIONS: *Theatr. chem. s.v.* "Platonis liber";
  temple of Mercurius, **13** 272
Sabaoth (seventh archon), **9ii** 129
Sabazius mysteries, **5** 530; **12** 184
Sabbath, **9ii** 128; **11** 350; **13** 301; **14** 637;
  defiler of, **10** 676; **11** 394*n*
Sabellius, **9ii** 397*n*
Sabina S., *see* Fürstner
Sabine women, **5** 34
Sacer, G. W., **5** 270
Sachs, H.: ed., *Imago*, **18** 1031*n*
Sachse Codex, *see* CODICES AND MSS
Sachseln parish church, *see* Brother Klaus *s.v.* painting
sacral action, and unconscious contents, **11** 543
Sacrament(s), Christian: alchemical parallel, **13** 193–4, 232, 236;
  Christ, source of grace in, **11** 7&*n*;
  Church and, *see* Church (Catholic) *s.v.*;
  and pagan mysteries, **11** 448; **14** 312; **16** 124;
  see also baptism; Mass
sacred, **11** 451;
  myth/legend, **13** 393;
  precinct, see *temenos*;
  texts, psychology and, **11** 788
Sacred Books of the East, ed. F. Max Müller, **11** 859
  The following works published in this series are listed under their titles in this Index:

(1, 15) *The Upanishads,* tr. Max Müller
(4) *Vendidad,* tr. J. Darmesteter [not in later edns. of vol. 5]
(5) *Bundahish,* in *Pahlavi Texts,* tr. E. W. West
(8) *Bhagavadgītā,* tr. K. T. Telang
(10) *Sutta-Nipata,* tr. V. Fausböll
(12, 26, 41, 43, 44) *Shatapatha-Brāhmana,* tr. J. Eggeling
(16) *The Yi King,* tr. J. Legge [indexed here under *I Ching*]
(23) *Tir Yasht,* in *Zend Avesta,* tr. J. Darmesteter [indexed here under *Song of Tishtriya*]
(25) *Laws of Manu,* tr. G. Bühler
(34, 38, 48) *Vedanta-Sutras*
(42) *Hymns of the Atharva-Veda,* tr. M. Bloomfield
(49) Ashvaghosha: "Buddha-carita" and *Amitāyur-dhyāna Sūtra,* in *Buddhist Mahayana Texts*
sacrifice, **5** 660, 668, 671; **6** 339, 349; **7** 207–8; **11** 7, 303, 389; **13** 95;
  TITLES: "The Psychological Meaning of Sacrifice," **11** 381–413; "The Sacrifice," **5** 613–82;
  Abraham's, of Isaac, *see* Abraham *s.v.*;
  in alchemy, **11** 361–3;
  animal(s), **5** 399*n*, 577, 659, 665, 668*n*, 674; **13** 66, 91, 360; **16** 398; and human, **5** 675 (*see also* ANIMALS: bull, horse, lamb, serpent *s.v.*);
  archetype of, **11** 403–13;
  child-, **9i** 324;
  of Christ, *see* Christ *s.v.*;
  Christian, **6** 24, 28–9; and Mith-

sacrifice (*cont.*):
raic, *see* Christian *s.v.* and
Mithraism;
cosmic, **5** 646;
to the dead, **12** 61*n*;
dismemberment in, **13** 91;
etymology of, **12** 417;
fantasy of, **4** 350;
fertility/fruitfulness through, **5**
354, 526, 671, pl. XXXIII;
gift and, **11** 390;
of god, *see* god(s) *s.v.*;
of hero, *see* hero(es) *s.v.*;
human, **5** 503, 671; **11** 339,
397, 406; **14** 690;
of king, *see* king *s.v.*;
knife as instrument of, **11** 324;
13 110;
of libido, *see* libido *s.v.*;
magical, **11** 362–3;
in the Mass, *see* Mass *s.v.*;
meanings of, **5** 461, 577, 646,
671;
Mithraic, *see* Mithras *s.v.*;
motif of, **14** 525;
of phallus, in ancient cults, **18**
1083;
power from, **5** 657;
priest as, *see* priest *s.v.*;
of primal being/man's unconsciousness, **5** 651–2;
problem of, **5** 654; **18** 1058,
1062;
sacrificer and sacrificed, **5** 246,
668; **11** 346, 397–402; **13** 91,
106, 110; Christ as, **11** 324,
388, 418; **12** 417; unity of, **11**
353, 397*n*;
self-, *see* self *s.v.*;
of son, **11** 328, 406, 661 (*see also*
Abraham; Christ *s.v.*);
sword as instrument of, *see*
sword *s.v.* sacrificial;
symbol(s)/-ism, **4** 342, 348; **5**
645, 671; **11** 339; bread, **11**
310; circumcision, **5** 671; fire, **5**
240; in Negroes' dreams, **18**
1285&*n*;

as transformation of energy, **5**
669;
voluntary, value of, **5** 553
sacrificium: intellectus, **6** 15; **11** 763;
12 59; **18** 1643 (*see also* Tertullian);
phalli, see Origen
Sadger, I.: "Analerotik und Anal-
charakter," **4** (*pp*76, 77);
Konrad Ferdinand Meyer, Eine
pathographisch-psychologische
Studie, J.'s review, **18** 795–6
sage(s): ancient, **13** 29;
in contemplation, **13** 46,
(*pp*30–3);
Oriental, **13** 55
Sagittarius, *see* zodiac, twelve signs of
s.v.
Sahara, **10** 603
sahasrāra, **16** 560
sailor, **9ii** 174
saint(s), **7** 236, 306; **10** 651, 680; **13**
50, 93, 225, 365;
anima and, **16** 504;
as archetype, **7** 377;
body of, becomes stone, **13**
133;
dreams of, **10** 306;
in ecstasy, **7** 108;
fire- and light-symbols of, **5**
163;
hallucinations of, **1** 117;
haloes of, **5** 163; **7** 108;
legends of, **3** 92;
marriage to/living with, **11** 130,
291;
simulation of, **1** 352;
sometimes heretics, **11** 481;
stigmata of, *see* stigmata *s.v.*;
surrounding Christ, **11** 229;
and temptation, **5** 436;
theocentric, **14** 531*n*;
visions of, *see* vision(s) *s.v.*
Saint-Denis, Abbey of, **14** 267
Sainte Bible . . . , *see* BIBLE
Saint-Exupéry, A. de: *The Little*
Prince, **5** 392*n*; **13** *fig.* 2
Saint-Germain, Comte de, **5** 282

sanctions, Christianity and, **10** 438
sanctity: odour of, **14** 421;
    and temptation, **5** 436
Sanctus (in Mass), **11** 321
sand (arena), **14** 263, 319
Sand, G.: "Daily Conversations with
    Dr. Piffoel," **9i** 237&*n*
Sanders, D. H.: *Das Volksleben der
    Neugriechen*, **5** 170*n*
sand painting, *see* American In-
    dians: NORTH: Navajo *s.v.*; Pueblo
    s.v.
sanguine temperament, **1** 187–8; **6**
    546–7, 883, 933, 960;
    and moral insanity, **1** 220&*n*
sanguis, **10** 629;
    spiritualis, **16** 398;
    see also blood
Sanhedrin, *see* Talmud
Sankhya philosophy, **9i** 158; **11** 798
Sanskrit, **18** 139, 172, 409;
    meaning of *tejas* in, **5** 237
Sans Souci, **18** 480
Santa Claus, **9i** 229; **17** 214
san-tsai, **6** 366
Saoshyant, **6** 453; **18** 1528
Sapientia/Wisdom, **9ii** 246; **11** 221,
    240, 358; **12** 443*n*, 478, 487, 500,
    figs. 201, 232, 257; **13** 162, 168,
    321, 448; **14** 443*n*, 729; **16** 484,
    486, 519;
    TITLE: "*Aurora consurgens* and
    the Doctrine of Sapientia," **12**
    464–79; *austri, see* Queen of the
    South/*regina austri*;
    Dei, **9ii** 194; **11** 609; **14** 9*n*,
    124, 150, 170; **16** 389, 413,
    480; in alchemy, **11** 263; **12**
    465, 473; **14** 73*n*, 443, 531;
    Holy Ghost and, **12** 466; **14**
    205, 432;
    Mercurius as, *see* Mercurius *s.v.*;
    sal/salt and, **14** 324–7, 335, 340,
    364, 366 (see also *sal sapientiae*);
    and salt-point, **9ii** 345;
    and Sophia, **9i** 93; **14** 576;
    and tree, **11** 612; **13** 419;
    and Virgin Mary, **16** 361
saponaria, **14** 401*n*

sapo sapientum, see *sal amarum*
sapphire(-irine), *see* COLOURS *s.v.*
Saqqara/Sakkara, **5** pl. XXX*b*; **10**
    158
Sara, in Book of Tobit, **4** 742–3,
    744*n*
Sarah, wife of Abraham, **5** 579*n*; **14**
    556
sarcoma of spinal cord, **3** 468–9; **18**
    114
sarcophagus(-i), **9i** 157; **14** 560; **16**
    496; **17** 208;
    in dream, **9i** 398;
    Roman, **14** 658;
    vision of, **18** 1708
Sardis, **11** 704
Sargon, **7** 284
sarkikos, **9i** 243*n*, 244
Sarpanitu, **11** 176
Sassanids, **5** 131*n*; **9ii** 178
Satan, *see* devil
Satanäel (Gnostic): as demiurge, **9ii**
    229;
    elder son of God, **9ii** 77, 229;
    11 249; **13** 271; **14** 124*n*, 589
sat-chit-ananda, **15** 189
satori, **9ii** 260; **11** 877, 879–81, 883,
    887–8; **14** 771;
    a natural occurrence, **11** 884;
    in the West, **11** 883, 890
Satorneilos, *see* Saturninus
Saturday, *see* Saturn *s.v.* day of
Saturn/Saturnus (♄) (planet/god/in
    astrology/alchemy etc.), **9i** 5*n*; **12**
    figs. 134, 152, 200; **14** 1, 6*n*; **16**
    408, 515;
    abode of the devil, **9ii** 128; **13**
    209, 276;
    animals of, **9ii** 129;
    as arcane substance, **9ii** 215;
    ass of, **9ii** 129;
    as Beelzebub (Cabalistic), **13**
    276;
    child of, **13** 274&*n*;
    darkness of/dark/black star, **9i**
    535*n*; **9ii** 129&*n*, 215, 307; **11**
    350; **13** 161*n*; **14** 306&*n*, 308;
    16 510, 513 (see also below *sol
    niger*);

autism in, **5** 37;
Bleuler on, **3** 505;
brain changes in, **3** 471, 497, 503, 505;
causality of, **3** 498;
and collective contents of the unconscious, **18** 1156;
and complexes, strength/persistence of, **2** 1353–4; **3** 75, 106, 141, 195, 210, 434, 546, 579–81; **18** 150; splinter-complexes, **18** 1155;
and cure, **18** 227;
degenerative traits, **3** 471–2;
delusions, **11** 454; **15** 65;
and demonism, **18** 1474;
diagnosis of, **18** 914, 916;
dissociation in, *see* dissociation(s) *s.v.*;
dissolution of consciousness in, **12** 116; **16** 476;
dreams in, **2** 839;
dulling of affect in, **8** 50;
ego split in, **18** 19;
and external conditions, **3** 472, 476–9;
fear of father in, **17** 52;
and feeling for nature, **5** 624*n*;
and fragmentation/disintegration of personality, **5** 683; **9i** 279; **12** 439; **15** 174; **16** 248, 361; **18** 19;
Freud's importance for, **18** 922;
galvanometer and pneumographic experiments in, **2** 1045, 1066–78, 1157–79, 1247–70;
hallucinations, **3** 150, 299, 471, 498, 574; **15** 65; **18** 922; of solar phallus, *see* solar phallus *s.v.*;
hysteria and, **2** 1067–70; **18** 959;
infantilism in, **4** 276*n*, 294;
intentionality of, **3** 434;
irritability of, **3** 428, 433;
language of, **8** 360; **11** 442;
neologisms, **18** 827;
latent, **3** 539, 559; **9i** 320;

and libido, **4** 271–8, 289; **5** 190–2; regressive introversion of, **6** 860–2;
and loss of reality function, **5** 192, 200; **7** 469;
mythological/archaic images in, **3** 568; **4** 521; **5** 205; **6** 858; **8** 281, 589; **9i** 136; **11** 779, 781; **16** 18; **18** 1082;
nature of, **2** 1066–71;
and neurosis, compared, **3** 506, 559; **17** 207;
and obsessional neurosis, **3** 503, 509;
and organic/toxic factors, **3** 76, 195, 471–2, 493, 533, 537, 581, (*p*272); **13** 48; **18** 794;
origins of, **3** 72, 75;
paintings in, **18** 407;
personality changes in, **18** 19 (*see also above* fragmentation of personality);
predisposition to, **3** 480;
among primitives, **8** 576;
prognosis of, **5** 58*n*;
psychogenesis of, **3** 318–19, 471, 480, 493, 498, 503, 532, 541, (*p*272); objections to, **3** 537–8, 577–8;
psychology of, **3** 498; **18** 832;
psychotherapy/psychoanalysis and, **3** 503, 539–40, 549; **4** 456; **10** 1070;
and regression to presexual stage, **5** 206;
and repression, **3** 61, 64–7, 70–1, 76;
resistance and, **3** 426–8;
symbolism and, **4** 456–7; **13** 141;
terminology, **3** 317, 497, 544; **5** 58*n*, 631; **7** 233;
thought disturbances, **3** 434;
two groups of, **3** 531; **16** 249;
types and, **3** 418–19; **6** 862;
unconscious in, **18** 832;
violence of affects in, **3** 151, 578, 580

Schwartz, C., **14** 100;
   Acta eruditorum, **14** 56*n*, 100*n*
Schwartz, W.: *Indogermanischer Volks-
   glaube,* **5** 421*nn*, 423*n*
Schwartzenburg, Gervasius von, **14**
   610*n*
Schwarzwald,   —:   "Beitrag   zur
   Psychopathologie der hysteris-
   chen Dämmerzustände und Au-
   tomatismen," J.'s abstract, **18**
   1024–5
Schweitzer, Albert, **10** 783, 912; **18**
   1535–7, (*p*697*n*);
   *Geschichte   der   Leben-Jesu-
   Forschung,* **14** 12*n*;
   The Quest of the Historical Jesus, **5**
   42*n*
Schweitzer, Bernard: *Herakles,* **13**
   270*n*, 272*n*
Schweizerischer Beobachter, **18** 782
Schweizer Lexikon, J.'s article in, **18**
   (*p*648*n*)
Schwestrones, **9ii** 139*n*
science(s), **6** 60; **7** 3/411, 302, 330,
   405, 484, 494, 502; **10** 162, 164,
   543; **13** 2, 3, 47, 63, 84, 141, 163,
   293; **15** 176:
   alchemy and, *see* alchemy *s.v.*;
   and archetypes, **8** 342, 794;
   authority of, **18** 1120;
   and causality, **3** 392, 405, 467;
   8 829;
   China and, **11** 967;
   Chinese, **10** 188; **15** 80–1;
   and consciousness, **12** 40;
   and correspondence theory, **8**
   939;
   danger of, **9i** 195;
   and deification of matter, **9i**
   195;
   and directed thinking, **5** 21;
   and dogma, **4** 746;
   European, **15** 90;
   and the exceptional, **10** 701;
   and faith, **9ii** 268–9; **10** 171; **11**
   225; **12** 15;
   and fantasy, **6** 84–9;
   and Freudian theory, **15** 56;

of God, **12** 465, 474; **13** 127;
humane, **17** 165;
and hypotheses, **4** 782;
images in, **8** 278;
and independence, **4** 613;
and the individual, **10** 498;
limitations of, **8** 625;
limits of, **16** 524;
magic and, **8** 90;
modern, **9ii** 144;
modern man's faith in, **11** 81;
mystic, **1** 65–70; derivation of
names in, **1** 144; diagram of
forces, **1** 66, *fig.* 2; groups of
forces, **1** 67–9; as heightened
unconscious   performance,   **1**
148;
and myth, **6** 428; **8** 327;
as myth, **9i** 302;
natural, **9ii** 52; **11** 778, 800; **13**
145, 149, 195, 395; **17** 160–3;
of the psyche, **16** 537; rise of,
9ii 235;
one-sidedness of, **8** 426;
and philosophy, division, **11**
860;
philosophy of, **11** 762;
as power for good or ill, **18**
1373–4;
power of, in Europe, **11** 869;
and primordial images, **6** 512;
psychic   consequences   of,   **18**
1366–7;
psychology as, *see* psychology
s.v.;
and reality, **8** 623;
and religion, **5** 95, 336; **11** 763,
863; **18** 691–2;
and religious experience, **14**
457; **18** 1671;
and the soul, **8** 650, 790;
and subtilization of projections,
11 140;
symptoms of man's psyche, **8**
752;
trinity in, **9ii** 409;
and *Weltanschauung,* **8** 731,
736;

Western, **13** 2;
and wholeness, **8** 864;
see also arts and sciences
Science, Christian, **7** 494
scientia/Scientia, **12** 487; **13** 162; **15** 38;
   Creatoris, **13** 299, 301;
   creaturae, **13** 299;
   hominis, **13** 301
scientific: attitude, **7** 216; contemporary, **6** 516, 529; toward symbol-formation, **5** 338;
   discovery, **15** 154;
   investigation, **7** 407;
   materialism, *see* materialism;
   method, **3** 320, 392; **5** 22; **6** 674; **15** 99;
   mind, **7** 483;
   scepticism, **7** 495;
   superstition, **7** 496
"scientism," **3** 406; **6** 72
scientist(s): asceticism of, **11** 786;
   and religion, **18** 693;
   and *Weltanschauung,* **8** 697
scintilla (-ae), **11** 152&*n*, 759; **14** 42;
   in alchemy, **8** 388–9, 394–5; **9i** 246*n*; **14** 42–50, 416*n*;
   "Animae Mundi," **14** 703;
   as archetype(s), **8** 388; **14** 700;
   as light of nature/*lumen naturae,* **14** 48;
   self as, **8** 388; **18** 1638, 1660;
   "soul-sparks," **8** 430; **9i** 717; **10** 766; **12** 410*n*, 472; **14** 42;
   vitae, **9ii** 344;
   see also soul-spark; spark; spinther
Scites, *see* Socrates, pseudo-
Scorpio, *see* zodiac, twelve signs of
scorpion, *see* ANIMALS *s.v.*
Scott, H. von E., *see* Bland, C.C.S.
Scott, W., see under *Corpus Hermeticum*
Scotus Erigena, abbot of Malmesbury, **6** 36–9
scourging of Jesus, *see* Christ *s.v.*
Scoyaris/Scoyarus, **12** 422*n*
screen: causes, **3** 148;

memories, *see* Freud *s.v.*
"Scriptum Alberti," *see* ALCHEMICAL COLLECTIONS: *Theatr. chem. s.v.* Albertus Magnus
Scripture, E. W., **2** 451, 730; **4** 154&*n*;
   "Über den assoziativen Verlauf der Vorstellungen," **2** 451*n*, 730*n*
Scriptures, Holy, *see* BIBLE
sculpture, **15** 174;
   obscene, **9ii** 339*n*
scurrility: in dreams, **9ii** 315;
   of Gnostic nomenclature, **9ii** 364;
   see also aischrologia; obscene stories; smutty talk
Scylla, **5** 265;
   and Charybdis, **7** 110, 113, 224; **13** 181; **16** 418, 448, 502
scyphomedusa, *see* ANIMALS *s.v.* jelly-fish
Scythia, Upper, **11** 194
Scythian(s), **11** 348; **13** 92;
   juice, **13** 102;
   king, death of, **5** 595
Scythianos, **14** 31&*n*
sea, **12** 56, 57&*n*, 154, 265, 434, 441&*n*, *figs.* 142 G,NN,ZZ, 186; **13** 64, 75, 122, 173, 218, 241, 256*n*, 301, 306, 382, *fig.* 1; **14** 9, 110, 244, 264, 658, 688, 727; **16** 14–15;
   TITLE: "The Regeneration in Seawater," **14** 315–19;
   of the alchemists, *see below* "our";
   -anemone, **10** 748;
   as *aqua permanens,* **14** 157*n*, 244;
   bitterness/*amaritudo* of, **14** 234, 245–6, 255, 339;
   black, **12** 469; immersion in, **16** 454; "Indian Ocean," **14** 7–8;
   -born, **13** 225;
   bottom of, **13** 33;
   circular, **16** 409;
   crossing of, *see* Red Sea;

sea (*cont.*):
　　dead, **14** 260, 262;
　　depths of, **13** 116*n*; **14** 255, 328;
　　desiccation, **14** 45, 260;
　　-dew/*ros marinus,* **14** 688, 701;
　　in dreams/visions, **12** 56, 57&*n,* 154;
　　forbidden, **14** 110;
　　-hawk, **9ii** 292*n,* 296;
　　-horse, **9i** 327;
　　and horse, **5** 426;
　　immersion in, **14** 262; **16** 453–4;
　　imprisonment in, **14** 328;
　　journey, *see sep. entry below;*
　　kingly substance hidden in, **13** 181;
　　mineral of, **14** 245;
　　-monster, *see* ANIMALS *s.v.* monster;
　　and moon, **14** 157, 244;
　　as mother, *see below* symbol;
　　nettle, **9ii** 196*n;*
　　as original chaos, **14** 6;
　　"our"/*mare nostrum,* **9ii** 219; **10** 629; **13** 183; **14** 3; **16** 402;
　　Mercurius as, **10** 629; **13** 284*n;*
　　Paradise in, **13** 406*n;*
　　personified by Leviathan, **5** 383–5;
　　of the philosophers, **12** 475&*n;*
　　as *prima materia,* **12** 336, 425; **14** 7*n,* 246;
　　regeneration in, **14** 315–19;
　　of renewal, **12** *fig.* 222;
　　as seat of hell, **14** 255;
　　-serpents, **8** 335;
　　and serpent, **5** 681*n;*
　　and sun, **5** 306–7, 319; **12** (*p*286);
　　symbol, **5** 319, 416; **9ii** 240; **14** 234; of mother, **5** 319, 373; **9i** 156; of unconscious, **5** 320; **9i** 298, 698; **9ii** 219; **12** 156, 203, 265, 305, 436, *fig.* 222; **13** *fig.* B5; **14** 3*n,* 6, 8, 257, 262, 372; **16** 408; **17** 102; of unconscious,

collective, **12** 57; **16** 15;
　　tear of Kronos, **14** 339;
　　treasure in, **12** 154–5;
　　tree planted in, **13** 406;
　　Typhonian, **14** 110, 246, 338, 366;
　　and the unconscious, *see above s.v.* symbol;
　　-urchin, **9ii** 239*n;*
　　-water, **12** 336; **13** 406, 408; **14** 110, 234, 244, 246, 315–19, 688;
　　weed, **5** 362;
　　Western, **9i** 605;
　　as world, **14** 255;
　　see also Okeanus; Red Sea; salt *s.v.* Tartarus; water
sea journey/voyage: Miss Miller and, **5** 51, (*pp*448, 450);
　　royal marriage and, **14** 658;
　　sun and, **5** 289–90, 306;
　　see also *nekyia;* night sea journey
seals, *see* ANIMALS *s.v.*
seal(s) (impressed wax/lead), **15** 40;
　　seventh, **9ii** 137
séance, spiritualistic, **10** 597;
　　educated people and, **18** 760;
　　and S. W., J.'s case, **1** 45–53; **3** 555;
　　see also spiritualism
searchlight, consciousness as, **8** 610
season(s), **12** 314;
　　four, **10** 775; **11** 90, 109, 120, 229; **12** 172, 282, 283, 469; **14** 1, 5;
　　myth of, **4** 496
seat of heavenly light, **13** 28*n*
Sebastian, St., **5** 445
second: Adam, Christ as, *see* Christ *s.v.;*
　　Coming, Christ's, *see* Christ *s.v.* coming of;
　　half of life, *see* life, stages in *s.v.;*
　　sight, **1** 37;
　　tetrad, *see* tetrad *s.v.*
secrecy, **7** 239;

Selene, **14** 24, 187; **16** 353*n*;
as Helen, **9ii** 41; **14** 160&*n*;
see also Simon Magus *s.v.* Helen
Seler, E., **11** 348*n*
self (1) (expressing reflexive action):
-aggrandizement, **9ii** 44;
-analysis, *see* analysis *s.v.*;
-assertion, *see* Adler, A. *s.v.*
-assertiveness, **11** 773;
-awareness, **8** 516, 523; **13** 120;
-belittlement, **7** 259;
-born, **11** 60 (*see also* Auto-genes);
-brooding, **13** 39;
-collection, **11** 60;
-complacency, **3** 211;
-conceit, **7** 243*n*, 467;
-confidence, **14** 756; exaggerated, **1** 189, 190, 199, 214; **7** 221–2/451–2; **17** 246; loss of, **11** 12; stifling of, **7** 235/457;
-conquest, **4** 443, 444; heroic, **13** 69;
-consciousness, **17** 318;
-containment, **5** 405;
-control, **4** 200; **10** 79; and complex, **3** 93, 521; in hysteria, lack of, **1** 175; in malingering, **1** 303; in schizophrenia, lack of, **3** 151;
-cremation, **12** 416*n*, 469;
-criticism, **3** 456; **4** 380, 590, 774; **7** 41, 262; **8** 165; **9ii** 46; **10** 577–8, 674, 911; **11** 86; **17** 111; of doctor, **16** 173, 236–7, 239; lack of, **1** 173, 175, 219; **10** 843;
-cure, neurosis as, **4** 405, 574;
-deception, **1** 437, 439; **13** 4, 248;
-defence, **3** 487;
-deification, **7** 110;
-depreciation, **7** 467;
-destruction, **13** 105; **16** 361; of Mercurius, **13** 283;
-determination, **6** 33;
-devouring dragon, *see* ANI-MALS: dragon *s.v.*;

-education, *see* education *s.v.*; transformation;
-esteem, exaggerated, **1** 212–13, 218; **3** 211, 214, 276;
-fertilization, **5** 447; **9ii** 322–3; **12** 209, 530; **13** 105; **16** 419;
-generation, **13** 283;
-glorification, of manic patient, **1** 214;
-incubation, **12** 441;
-injury, **7** 194;
-interest, **18** 1355;
-irony, **3** 313;
-laceration, **7** 110;
-magnetization, **1** 49;
-mastery, **7** 380;
-observation, **8** 165;
-possession, **11** 958;
-preservation: of analyst, **7** 461; instinct of, *see* instinct *s.v.* preservation; in schizophrenia, **4** 276*n*;
-reliance, **11** 292; **14** 756;
-reproduction, **5** 496; of Mercurius, **13** 283;
-restraint, **16** 130;
-torture, **1** 353;
-violation, **5** 447
self (2) (archetypal concept), **6** 789–91 (Def.); **9i** 396; **13** 226, 372, 433; **14** 38*n*, 63, 129*n*, 141, 276, 670, 700, 756; **16** 400, 472*n*;
TITLES: "Christ, a Symbol of the Self," **9ii** 68–126; "Gnostic Symbols of the Self," **9ii** 287–346; "The Self," **9ii** 43–67; "The Structure and Dynamics of the Self," **9ii** 347–421; "The Undiscovered Self (Present and Future)," **10** 488–588;
alchemy and/alchemists' concept of, **9ii** 411; **11** 400; **16** 219, 220 (*see also sep. entry below* self-knowledge);
alienation of, **6** 499, 502–3; **7** 267;
androgynous, **9i** 653;
and anima, **14** 129*n*;

animal as symbol carrier of, **14** 283;

animus in place of, **13** 342, 346, 458;

Anthropos as, *see* Anthropos *s.v.*;

Antichrist and, **9ii** 79;

antinomial character of, **9ii** 115, 257, 355; **11** 399*n*; **12** 24 (*see also below* paradoxical);

appearance of, in unconscious products, **9ii** 297;

appears in all shapes, **9ii** 356;

apprehension of, **13** 330;

as archetypal idea, **6** 791;

as archetypal symbols, **9ii** 116, 261;

as archetype, **5** 497, 611; **9i** 306; **9ii** 257; **18** 1158; of order, **10** 805; **18** 1638, 1660; of unity, **12** 30;

archetype(s) of, **5** 576, 612; **8** 599; **9ii** 123, 261, 422; **10** 622, 771; **11** 231, 757; **12** 20, 25, 31; **13** 115; **14** 103, 776; **18** 1567;

arithmetical symbols of, **9ii** 354, 358;

assimilation of, by ego, *see* ego *s.v.* and self;

as atman, *see* atman *s.v.*;

attainment of, **9i** 194;

attitude to, **12** 247;

better, **10** 843;

birth of, **9i** 550; **13** 336;

body and psyche in, **14** 717;

borderline concept, **12** 247, 452*n*;

Brahman as, **6** 330; **9ii** 348;

as centre, *see* centre;

"chariot of Aristotle" as symbol of, **14** 261;

"chariot" in the sky as model of, **14** 265*n*;

chemical symbols of, **11** 276;

child as symbol of, **16** 378;

Christ as, *see* Christ *s.v.*;

Christ-figure as, *see* Christ *s.v.* -figure;

circle as symbol of, *see* circle *s.v.*;

city as synonym for, **18** 269;

as *coincidentia oppositorum*, **5** 576; **12** 259; **14** 129*n*, 176;

collective nature of, **13** 287; **16** 474 (*see also below* and unconscious, collective);

as compensation of conflict, **7** 404; **14** 146;

as *complexio oppositorum*, **6** 790; **9ii** 355, 423; **11** 283, 716; **13** 289;

as conflict, **12** 24, 259;

and consciousness: coming to consciousness, **11** 398, 714; cannot attain complete consciousness, **7** 274; seeks consciousness, **18** 1630;

cosmic, **12** 137;

cross as, **13** 364;

-culture, **7** 327;

deus absconditus as element of, **13** 289;

devaluation of, **12** 9;

-development, **13** 220;

differentiation of, **6** 183;

Ding an sich, **12** 247;

divine dynamism of, **13** 372*n*;

divine nature of, **14** 176;

-division, **7** 18/430, 116;

dragon as forerunner of, **14** 296;

dream-symbols and, **9ii** 203*n*;

Eastern and Western conceptions, **11** 808–9;

ego and, *see* ego *s.v.*;

and ego-consciousness, **14** 129*n*;

identification with, **9i** 254;

as *eidos,* **9ii** 64;

Elijah as, **18** 1526;

embodiments of, **14** 548;

empirical, **6** 789; **9ii** 76; **11** 399*n*; **14** 272, 283;

enlightenment and the, **11** 884;

entelechy of, **12** 248;

exists/does not exist, **11** 399*n*;

experience of, **9ii** 62–3; **16** 219, 221;

self (2) (*cont.*):

Ezekiel's vision as symbol of, **14** 269, 271;
as the father, **11** 398, 400;
filius as, **13** 177;
filius philosophorum as, **9ii** 194;
fish as, **9ii** 219, 223;
fixation of, in the mind, **9ii** 259;
formulation of concept, **6** 183*n*;
in four dimensions, **18** 117, 119;
four functions of, **5** 611;
as garden with fountain, **12** 155;
geometrical symbols of, **9i** 315; **9ii** 354, 358; **11** 276;
Gnostic symbols of, **9ii** 287–346, 358, 428;
as goal of life, **7** 404;
= God, **11** 959;
a God-image, *see* God-image *s.v.*;
"God within us," **7** 399;
as hero, **5** 516; **9i** 256;
higher, **15** 192;
higher spiritual man as, **14** 548;
Hindu definition of, **14** 271;
-hood, coming to, **7** 266; **17** 334;
human figures as symbols of, **9i** 315; **9ii** 354, 358;
identification with, **13** 331, 332;
-immersion, **9i** 710;
immortal, **13** 210;
and immortality, **7** 303;
incorruptible, **16** 220;
indefiniteness of, **12** 20, 22;
in Indian philosophy, **11** 281, 956;
individuality of, **12** 22;
and individuality, **6** 183*n*; **7** 266, 404; apotheosis of, **9ii** 115, 116;
and individuation, *see* indi-

viduation *s.v.*;
instinct as origin of, **12** 157;
and integration, **12** 105; **16** 474;
integration of, **9ii** 312*n*; **11** 400; **12** 296; **16** 474;
intuition of, **13** 36;
as intuitive concept, **14** 129*n*;
Khidr as symbol of, *see* Khidr *s.v.*;
king as symbol of, **9ii** 310;
-knowledge, *see sep. entry below;*
Krishna as, **13** 339, 342;
lapis/stone as, **9ii** 194, 257, 264, 387, 426; **11** 154; **12** 155; **13** 134, 289, 394; **14** 329*n*, 364, 524, 649, 716, 776; *invisibilitatis*, **12** 247;
latent, **12** 105*n*;
laurel as symbol of, **9i** 582;
-liberation, **11** 770, 773, 779, 784, 792, 802, 841, 958; yoga of, **11** 814;
light and darkness in, **5** 576;
light of the, **13** 301;
loss of, **18** 43;
as lotus, **12** *fig.* 75;
luminosity as, **8** 396;
mandala as, *see* mandala *s.v.*;
in matriarchal society, **13** 131;
as mediating symbol, **10** 779;
"Mental Self," **11** 808;
Mercurius as, **13** 284, 289, 296;
as microcosm, **9i** 550;
mind and, **11** 808–11;
and monotheism, **9ii** 427;
Moses' experience of, **9i** 253; **13** 428;
mountain as symbol of, *see* mountain *s.v.*;
as non-ego, **12** 155;
numinosity of, **5** 612; **14** 776;
as object, **9i** 315;
objective and subjective, **16** 474;
as objectivity of psyche, **12** 32;
one's own: becoming, **7** 266; conflict with, **7** 218/450;

and opposites, **14** 129*n*; **16**
536; combination of, **10** 640;
differentiation of, **6** 183&*n*; as
union of, **6** 790; **10** 622, 779;
11 396; **12** 22, 25, 30, 259; **16**
474 (*see also below* union);
as organizer of the personality,
10 694;
"other," **7** 43;
paradoxical, **9ii** 257; **12** 22; **14**
4, 145; **16** 474 (*see also above* antinomial character of);
and persona, **6** 370; **7** 248, 269,
512;
and personality, *see* personality
s.v.;
as phallus, **9ii** 357;
phenomenology of, **12** 22; **14**
145, 329;
plant symbols of, **9i** 315; **9ii**
356;
as Pole, **12** 265;
prefiguration of, **14** 217;
prima materia of, **14** 282;
as process of growth, **13** 304;
a product of cognition, **9ii** 124;
projection of, **5** 576; **16** 454*n*;
as psychic reality, **11** 233;
as quaternion of opposites, **9ii**
115;
quaternity of, *see* quaternity
s.v.;
reality of, **16** 532;
-realization, **7** 218/450, 266–7,
291, 310; **9i** 286; **9ii** 123; **11**
233; **12** 279, 291, 330; **13** 80,
332; **14** 778; **16** 219; **18** 1567,
1573; and tree symbol, **13** 243;
rebirth of, **14** 548;
-recollection, **11** 400&*n*;
-redemption, **12** 252;
-reflection, **7** (*p*4); **11** 401, 617;
reflection of, **11** 230;
-regulating systems, **13** 18;
-regulation, **7** 92, 275, 303,
311; unconscious, **7** 257;
as religious mythologem, **9ii**
57;

-renunciation, **11** 390;
rooted in body, **13** 242;
roots of, **13** 247;
rotundum as symbol of, **10**
621, 805, 808;
roundness of, **12** 150, 281;
-sacrifice, **4** 555; **5** 671, 675; **7**
72, 306, 437; **11** 390, 392, 397,
400; **12** 415; **13** 331, 433; **17**
339; fear of, **11** 849;
and selfish, **7** 267;
shadow of, **9ii** 76; **10** 640; **14**
128*n*, 129*n*;
"smaller than small," **9i** 289;
9ii 223, 257;
as source of energy, **9ii** 203*n*;
as spirit, **12** 327;
as *spiritus rector*, **9ii** 257;
spontaneous manifestations of,
16 531;
stone as, *see above* lapis/stone as;
as stranger's hat, **12** 255;
sun as, **12** 108;
as superego, **11** 396;
as supraordinate quantity, **6**
790; **7** 274; **9i** 315; **9ii** 1, 264;
-surrender, **11** 390;
surrender to, **14** 704;
as a symbol, **11** 810; **16** 474;
symbol(s) of, **5** 569; **9i** 291,
315; **9ii** 411; **10** 621, 806; **11**
232, 278*n*; **12** 20, 121, 323–31;
13 296, 362*n*; **14** 146, 269, 329,
716–17, 719, 776; **16** 474; circular, **14** 523; in dreams, **11**
808; and symbols of God/Deity,
10 644; **14** 269; **18** 1624; uniting, *see below* uniting; IN-
STANCES: *see lists at* **9i** 315; **9ii**
354, 356, 358; **11** 276; *and see
individual subheadings above;*
synthesis of, **9i** 278;
table as symbol of, **16** 378;
as taskmaster, **16** 531;
theological aspect of, **18** 1495;
theriomorphic symbols of, **9i**
315; **9ii** 356;
timeless, **16** 378, 531;

self (2) (*cont.*):

as totality (of man), **5** 460; **6** 790; **7** 274; **8** 430; **9i** 248, 396, 717; **9ii** 426; **10** 621, 693; **11** 140, 230, 419, 716, 755, 808; **12** 137; **13** 134, 173; **14** 4, 63, 129*n*, 145, 181; **16** 531; **18** 1624; of psyche, **12** 44, 247, 310; **14** 133, 498; of religious figures, **12** 20;

totality of, **9i** 542; **11** 232;

as total personality, **9ii** 9; **11** 414;

a transcendental postulate, **7** 405; **9ii** 115, 124, 264;

transcends consciousness, **12** 247, 305; **16** 474;

as treasure hard to attain, **12** 155, 211;

tree as, *see* tree(s) *s.v.*;

true, **7** 373; and false, **6** 370; unconscious, **7** 218/450, 247; **14** 144; collective/impersonal, **9ii** 261; **14** 129*n*, 372 (*see also above* collective nature of); and conscious in, **7** 274; **14** 524; hero as, **5** 516; theriomorphism as visualization of, **9ii** 224;

as union: of conscious and unconscious, **9ii** 115, 426; of good and evil, **12** 24–5; of opposites, *see above* opposites;

union with, **13** 331;

and uniting symbols, **8** 396; **16** 474;

unity of, **16** 532; broken into plurality, **10** 633;

use of term, **11** 400*n*;

visualization of, **14** 763;

as wholeness, **5** 460, 576; **9i** 278; **10** 721, 779; **12** 20, 150, 330, 436*n*; **14** 704, 757; essence of, **11** 959;

wholeness of, **13** 330;

will subordinated to, **8** 430; **9ii** 9;

as world, **9i** 46; **15** 192

self-knowledge, **4** 156, 525, 615; **7** 28, 218, 223, 275, 381; **9ii** 33, 250–6, 347; **10** 321, 490–6, 525–6, 565–81, 674; **11** 390, 794, 1000–1; **14** 674–5; **17** 88, 111; **18** 1356, 1815, 1816;

TITLE: "Depth Psychology and Self-Knowledge," **18** 1803–17;

and alchemy, **9ii** 256; **11** 411; **13** 39, 126&*n*, 301&*n*, 372; **14** 104, 283, 364, 657, 664, 707–19, 736, 739, 741, 760;

ethical consequences of, **14** 778;

increased, **9ii** 39, 43;

meaning of, **10** 582–8;

projection of, **7** 375;

and shadow, **9ii** 14;

in therapist, **10** 350

Seligmann, C. G.: *The Melanesians of British New Guinea*, **8** 123*n*, 129*n*

Sellin, E.: *Introduction to the Old Testament*, **14** 592*n*, 625*n*

"selves," multiplication of, **10** 634

Sem/Shem, **5** 460*n*; **12** 458; **14** 556

semel credidisse, **12** 12

Semele, **9i** 195

semen, **5** 208*n*, 210; **11** 359; **14** 41*n*, 42;

and soma, **5** 200*n*, 246&*n*;

see also sperma

Semenda Bird, *see* ANIMALS *s.v.* phoenix

semiotic, *vs.* symbolic, **6** 93&*n*, 788, 814; **8** 88, 148, 366

Semiramis, **5** 34

Semitic gods and *paredroi*, **5** 294

Semon, R. W., **7** 219;

engram theory, **6** 748; **7** 159&*n*;

on mneme, **6** 624;

The Mneme, **6** 624*n*; **7** 159*n*

Sena/Senae, **13** 218

Senard, M.: *Le Zodiaque*, **9ii** 147*n*

senarius, see NUMBERS *s.v.* six

Senate, Roman, **3** 525, 566

Sendivogius, *see* ALCHEMICAL WRITERS *s.v.*

Seneca, **5** 129;

41st letter to Lucilius, **5** 103, 114*n*;
on religious oneness with nature, **5** 110;
Ad Lucilium epistolae morales, tr. R. M. Gummere, **5** 103*n*
senex/Senex: *draco,* **13** 269*n*;
Israel, **9i** 576*n*;
ithyphallicus, **13** 278;
Mercurius as, **13** 269, 301;
Saturn as, **14** 298
senile: dementia, *see* dementia *s.v.*;
deterioration, *see* deterioration *s.v.*
Senior, Adolphus, *see* ALCHEMICAL WRITERS *s.v.*
Senior, Zadith, *see* ALCHEMICAL WRITERS *s.v.*
Senn, G., **13** (*p*251)
Sennezem, **11** 348*n*
sensation, **6** 792–6 (Def.), 951, 953–4; **8** 349, 669; **13** 43;
of body, *see* body *s.v.*;
extinction of, **18** 873, 876;
and extraverted attitude, **6** 604–5;
feeling-, *see* feeling *s.v.*;
function of, *see* function(s) *s.v.*;
and introverted attitude, **6** 647–9;
and object, **6** 219;
and thinking, **6** 173, 187;
type, *see* type(s) *s.v.*;
use of word, **8** 292
sensationalism, in James's typology, **6** 507, 523
sense(s): and cryptomnesic image, **1** 145;
dulling of, **3** 145;
functions: and consciousness, **8** 367; paralysis of, **1** 21;
hallucinations of the, *see* hallucination(s);
hyperaesthetic unconscious activity of, **1** 148;
-impression: of Communion, **6** 96–8; as psychic images, **8** 680;
strength of, and attention, **1** 73;

mind and, **8** 742;
organs: in hallucinations, *see* hallucination(s); partial paralysis of, **1** 114;
-perceptions, *see* perception(s) *s.v.*;
retention of, in hysterical lethargy, **1** 125;
truth and, **8** 683
senseless answers, *see* answer(s)
sensibility: disturbances of, **1** 281;
and genius, **1** 174–5;
and interpretation of intended tremors, **1** 148;
tests of, **1** 255;
unconscious, of hysterical patient, **1** 138
sensitiveness, **4** 384, 390–1, 395–400, 411&*n*;
congenital, **4** 572;
excessive/abnormal, **3** 480; **4** 396–8;
inborn, **4** 397;
and inferiority, **7** 85;
intensification of, **18** 102;
symptom of disunion, **4** 396
sensualist type, *see* type(s) *s.v.*
sensuality: in Indian art, **11** 908;
and spirituality, **17** 336
sensuous instinct (Schiller), **6** 152, 161, 165, 169–70
sensuousness/sensuous feeling, **6** 145–6, 156, 165–6
sensus naturae, in animals, **8** 393; **13** 148
sentence: as reaction, **2** 346, 519–20, 522–3, 530–2, 539, 885;
as stimulus, **2** 1196, 1210, 1212
sententia communis, **11** 457
sentiment, **8** 292
sentiment(s): d'automatisme, **3** 170;
de domination, **3** 170;
de perception incomplète, **3** 171;
d'incapacité, **3** 170;
d'incomplétude, **3** 170, 172, 174, 207
sentimental poet, *see* Schiller *s.v.* naïve and sentimental poetry

desires, repressed, **7** 128;
development, infantile, of Goethe, **3** 397;
difficulties in marriage, **5** 326;
disturbances/aberrations, **5** 249;
education, **17** 74;
energy, *see* energy *s.v.*;
ethics, **18** 912;
excesses, **1** 193, 451, 460;
excitement, **13** 108; **17** 221;
factor, **7** 43;
fantasies, *see* fantasy(-ies) *s.v.*;
function, *see* function(s) *s.v.*;
goal, **17** (*p*4);
ideas/reminiscences, in patient's psychoanalysis, **2** 707–24;
images, creative aspect of, **5** 180;
instinct, *see* instinct *s.v.*;
latency, **4** 370–2;
libido, *see* libido *s.v.*;
life, denial of, **11** 718, 728;
misdemeanours, **18** 926;
morality, *see* morality *s.v.*;
mysteries, **18** 1081;
objects as first objects, **5** 652;
obsession, transformation of, **5** 562;
perversion, *see* perversion(s);
precocity in children, *see* child(ren) *s.v.*;
problem/question, **7** 17/427, 428, 429, 438; **8** 105, 762; **10** 213–14, 254; in America, *see* America *s.v.*; and separation from family bonds, **5** 644;
psychology, **7** 49; **9i** 61;
restrictions, **10** 652;
rites, **9i** 311;
symbols, *see sep. entry below*;
terminology, **4** 267–70;
theory, **13** 467; Freud's, *see* Freud *s.vv.* sexual trauma theory; sexuality, his concept of; of neurosis, *see* neurosis *s.v.*;
of psychic substance, **9ii** 313;

trauma and hysteria, *see* hysteria *s.v.* trauma;
urge, **16** 241;
zone, and rhythmic activity, **5** 206;
see also erotic(ism)
sexual: symbols/symbolism, **3** 285–6, 291; **5** 7, 297–8; **16** 340;
Christ and, **9ii** 314;
in dreams, *see* dream symbols *s.v.*;
Freud and, **4** 63;
interpretation of, **10** 653;
of the unconscious, **7** 471
sexualism, **8** 51
sexuality/sex [instinct/drive], **2** 198, 612–14, 679, 682, 697–702; **3** 413; **6** 67; **7** 57; **8** 708; **9i** 561; **10** 555; **13** 323;
TITLE: "The Theory of Infantile Sexuality," **4** 230–50;
achievements as substitute for, **5** 219;
in A. Adler's theory, **6** 88;
aggressive, in woman, **10** 246;
alchemists and, **16** 533;
and Amfortas, **6** 372–3;
Anglo-Saxon attitude to, **16** 66;
as appetite, **5** 187;
attitude to, **6** 373;
balancing factor to, **17** 156;
biological conception of, **18** 1039;
Catholic Church and, *see* Church (Catholic) *s.v.*;
as causative factor, **10** 35;
as compensation, **16** 277;
and complexes, **3** 140;
concept of, **4** 234–6, 259, 342;
deviation into, **5** 220;
in dreams, **2** 198, 816, 845, 849–50, 857–62; **4** 548–51;
and ego, **6** 690;
fantasies of, *see* fantasy(-ies) *s.v.*;
fate of, and life's fate, **4** 738*n*;
and forms, **10** 637;
Freud's concept, *see* Freud *s.v.*;

sexuality (*cont.*):

in Gross's theory, **6** 471–2;
horse as symbol of, **5** 421;
and hysteria, formation of, **4** 6–8, 36;
importance of, **4** 779; **8** 107; **10** 5;
individual evaluation of, **4** 666;
infantile, **4** 780; **7** 49, 67, 471; **15** 104; **17** (*pp*4–5, 7); Freud and, *see* Freud *s.v.* infantile sexuality; and infantile fantasy, **4** 227–8, 230, 232, 243; **17** (*p*4); and libido, **4** 290–3; not perverse, **4** 368; repressed, **11** 77; **15** 47; **17** 200; and spiritual functions, **17** (*p*5);
inflated idea of, **5** 193;
inhibition of, **5** 226;
as instinct, *see* instinct(s) *s.v.*;
intellect and, **13** 343;
and libido, *see* libido *s.v.*;
limp, **7** 308;
and love, *see* love *s.v.*;
mature and immature, **4** 268;
in men, **10** 216–17;
and metaphor, **10** 637;
monomorphic, **4** 246;
and morality, *see* morality *s.v.*;
and negativism, **3** 428, 436;
and neurosis, *see* neurosis *s.v.*;
normal, **17** 330; formation of, **4** 293;
and Nous, opposition, **13** 344;
and nutrition, **4** 283, 687; **10** 5;
in older persons, **4** 664;
between parents and children, **4** 730*n*;
pathology of, **18** 904;
permutations of, **4** 250;
and piety, **5** 332*n*;
and pleasure, **4** 241;
as plurality of drives, **4** 244;
polymorphous-perverse, *see* polymorphous-perverse sexuality;
premature enlightenment on, **17** 143;

presexual phase/stage, **4** 263–6; **5** 206;
primitives and, *see* primitive(s) *s.v.*;
and psyche, **17** 156;
psychization of, **8** 239;
and psychoanalysis, *see* psychoanalysis *s.v.*;
at puberty, eruption of, **8** 756; **10** 216;
reduction to, **8** 38*n*; **16** 12;
and relation to object, **6** 24;
in religions/religious cults, **5** 102; **10** 652, 655; **17** 157;
repression of, *see* repression *s.v.*;
sacrifice of, **5** 299;
and the spirit, **8** 107;
and spirituality, **14** 634;
study of, **10** 188;
and symbol-formation, **9ii** 147*n*;
of symbols, **16** 340;
terminology of, **7** 33;
and thinking function, **17** (*p*5), 79;
and three phases of life, **4** 263–6;
and transference, **16** 276–7;
two components of, **4** 248;
Ufos and, **10** 631;
and unconscious, **10** 5;
undervaluation of, **9ii** 357;
in women, **10** 216; as centre of psychic life, **3** 140; and marriage, **10** 255;
young people and, **8** 113; **10** 216–17;
see also bisexuality; erotic(ism)

Sgarra, Chico, **9i** 464
Shaare Kedusha, **9ii** 340*n*; **14** 38*n*
Shabtai, **14** 637
shadow, **7** 47; **9i** 44, 62, 474, 477–8, 560, 634, 705; **9ii** 13–19, 35, 57, 63, 402, 410; **10** 559*n*, 560, 653; **11** 131, 245, 277, 286, 725; **12** 36–8, 43, 121, 297; **13** 70, 293, 342; **14** 125, 175, 330, 332, 602,

646; **16** 134, 145, 254, 399, 470; **18** 638, 1158, 1417;

TITLES: "The Fight with the Shadow," **10** 444–57; "The Shadow," **9ii** 13–19;

acceptance of, **9i** 600; **11** 528;

alchemists on (*umbra*), **12** 192*n*, 220*n* (*see also below* arcane substance; *and see* sun *s.v.* umbra solis*);

St. Ambrose on (*umbra*), **11** 313&*n*;

of American, as Negro or Indian, **5** 267;

and anima, *see* anima *s.v.*;

and animus, *see* animus *s.v.*;

Antichrist as, **9ii** 76;

arcane substance as (*umbra*), **9ii** 292*n*;

as archetype, **5** 611; **7** 152, 185; **9i** 80, 86, 309; **9ii** 13; **14** 128&*n*;

assimilation of, **9ii** 16; **16** 452; **18** (*p*708), 1594;

autonomy of, **9ii** 15, 422;

brother, **5** 393;

at Christ's birth (Gnostic), *see* Gnosticism *s.v.* Christ-figure;

as Christ-symbol, **14** 147;

of Christ/*umbra Jesu*, as shadow-figure, **9ii** 167;

Christianity and, **14** 704;

collective, **9i** 469; **10** 572;

compensatory significance of, **14** 148; **18** 1410;

conflict with, **7** 42;

confrontation with, **10** 872, 885; **13** 335; **14** 514, 673, 706–8, 741; **18** 1830;

consciousness and, *see* consciousness *s.v.*;

of contemporary man, **10** 440;

definition of, **7** 103*n*;

and demon, **7** 154;

destructive, **18** 580;

devil as, *see* devil *s.v.*;

discovery of, **10** 440;

doubling of, **9ii** 185;

ego and, *see* ego *s.v.*;

encounter with, **9i** 61, 485*n*; **12** 37, 41;

fascination of, **14** 343;

of "fatherly" angels, **9i** 552;

fear of, **9ii** 62;

fish as shadow of God, **9ii** 183;

Freudian psychology and, *see* Freud *s.v.* and shadow;

of Gilgamesh, **13** 425;

in Gnosticism, Christ's, *see* Gnosticism *s.v.* Christ-figure;

good qualities of, **9ii** 423;

Hitler as, **10** 454–5;

identification with, **7** 41;

ignorance of, in hysterics, **10** 424;

and imitation of Christ, **11** 717;

individuation and, **11** 292;

inescapable, **10** 362;

infantile, **9i** 396;

and infantile-sexual fantasies, **5** 654;

as inferior/negative side of personality, **5** 267; **7** 78, 103*n*; **9ii** 370, 422; **10** 714*n*; **11** 292;

integration of, **9i** 485*n*; **9ii** 42; **14** 513; **16** 462; **18** 1414;

Irenaeus on (*umbra*), **9i** 469*n*;

and Iron Curtain, **18** 561;

jumping over one's own, **10** 417, 578;

living one's own, **18** 41;

loss of, **10** 559; **18** 40;

of Madonna, **9i** 189;

man and his, **13** 296;

man's, and woman, **10** 236, 261;

man without a, **8** 409;

Mephistopheles as, **10** 439;

of Moses, **9i** 244;

in Moses quaternio, *see* quaternity *s.v.* Moses;

a narrow door, **9i** 45;

need for, **7** 400;

negative feeling-value, **9ii** 53;

shadow (*cont.*):
  and neurosis, **11** 132;
  and opposing will, **11** 290;
  and opposites, **7** 78;
  of Osiris, **5** 566;
  our own, **18** 562;
  portrait of introverted man, **6** 271;
  possession by, **9i** 222;
  prima materia as, **9ii** 240; **12** 425;
  projection of, **9i** 513; **9ii** 16; **10** 418; **11** 140; **12** 36; **14** 203, 513; **18** 367;
  psychological concept of, in alchemy, **14** 148;
  quaternio, *see* quaternity *s.v.*;
  realization of, **8** 409;
  recognition of, **8** 426; **9i** 485*n*; **10** 579; **14** 342, 705, 741; **16** 452;
  as representative of chthonic world, **9ii** 64;
  as repressed tendencies, **11** 134;
  and self, *see* self *s.v.*;
  -side, **7** 27/438, 225; **16** 234; **18** 509; of Abelard's thought, **6** 76; Freud and, *see* Freud *s.v.*; in full control, **18** 43; of patient's father, **7** 248; of psyche, **7** 27, 438;
  snake as, **9i** 567; **9ii** 390*n*;
  and soul, **8** 665;
  spirit as, **9i** 396;
  stepping on, **7** 388; **8** 665;
  of the sun, *see* sun *s.v.* umbra solis;
  suppression of, **11** 133;
  trickster and, **9i** 485;
  in Trinity, **18** 1617, 1683;
  umbra: Jesu, see above Christ; *in lege,* **9ii** 167*n*; *solis, see* sun *s.v.* umbra (*see also above* alchemists on; St. Ambrose; arcane substance; Irenaeus);
  unconscious, **6** 268; **9i** 479; **9ii** 370; **10** 544, 714*n*;

  and unconscious, personal, **5** 267*n*, 393; **7** 103*n*; **9i** 513; **9ii** 261; **12** 38; **13** 481; as personification of, **14** 128, 129*n*, 257;
  union with, **7** 35; **13** 435;
  -world, **14** 235*n*; **18** 38;
  of young persons, **17** 327
Shah Jehan, **10** 990
Shakespeare, W., **10** 332;
  Julius Caesar, **5** 429, 430, 431&*n*, 432, 433, (*p*461);
  Macbeth, **6** 438
Shakti, **5** 405; **9i** 312*n*, 631–2, 653, 677; **11** 113, 152, 486; **12** 125; **13** 126, 223, 278; **14** 235*n*, 534, 580, 673; **15** 195; **16** 380, 410, 504, 562; **18** 263
Shaktideva, legend, **5** 318*n*
Shākyamuni, *see under* Buddha
shaman(-ism/-istic), **9i** 457; **10** 22, 977; **13** 132, 305; **14** 2*n*, 34*n*; **18** 578*n*, 1473;
  amulets, **5** pls. XXII*b*, XXXVIII*b*;
  anima, **13** 399, 460;
  ayami/guardian spirit/familiar in, **13** 460, 462;
  dismemberment motif in, **11** 346*n*, 410; as individuation process, **11** 411, 448, 460;
  heavenly bride/spouse, **9i** 115*n*; **13** 399, 457, 460;
  heavenly journey of, **13** 399, 407;
  and mountain, **13** 407;
  psychology of, **13** 91*n*, 462;
  and spiritualism, **10** 21, 101;
  tree of, **13** 350, 399, 402, 407, 457, 460, 462, *fig.* 2; inverted, **13** 462;
  world-tree of, **13** 402, 404
Shamash, **11** 173
shame, **3** 64; **4** 51, 58, 60, 61
shamming, energy required for, **1** 305
Shankara, **10** 875
Shankaracharya, **9i** 398*n*

shape: changing, **9i** 457;
   sexual significance of, **10** 637;
   and spirit-fire, **13** 54;
   of Ufos, *see* Ufo(s)
shards, **9i** 576&*n*; **11** 595&*n*, 624
shark, *see* ANIMALS *s.v.*
Sharpe, S.: *Egyptian Mythology*, **5**
   401*n*
Shatapatha Brahmana, see Brahmanas
shaving the head, **11** 348
Shaw, G. B.: in dream **11** 40; **12** 176;
   Man and Superman, **4** 658; **18**
   372&*n*;
   St. Joan, **11** 58; **12** 293
She, see under Haggard
Sheba, Queen of, *see* Queen *s.v.*
Sheed, F. J., *see* Augustine: *Confessions*
sheep, *see* ANIMALS *s.v.*
sheikh, **4** 85
Shekinah, **9i** 576*n*; **9ii** 425; **11** 727;
   14 18, 652; **16** 497*n*
sheli (immortal body), **13** 29
shell-shock, **7** 14*n*; **16** 126; **17** 176
Shem, *see* Sem
Shemesh, **5** 460*n*
shen, see China/Chinese: soul, doctrine of *s.v.*
Shêng Chi-t'u: The Life of Confucius,
   12 *figs*. 259, 260
Sheol, **11** 679
Shepard, O.: *The Lore of the Unicorn*,
   12 552*n*
shepherd, **9ii** 162;
   of Aries and Taurus, **12** *fig*. 17;
   Christ as, **11** 229, 691; **12** *fig*.
   18;
   Christian allegory of, **12** 72;
   good, **9ii** 162; **12** 416*n*; **14** 305;
   Hermes Kriophoros (lamb-
   bearer) as, **9ii** 162; **14** 305;
   Orpheus as, **9ii** 162;
   as personification of guiding
   principles, **8** 632;
   and snake, *see* Nietzsche: *Zarathustra s.v.* vision
"Shepherd, The," *see* Hermas

shield, **5** 604&*n*;
   -holders, **9i** 644
shining bodies, *see* body(-ies) *s.v.*
ship, **12** 138, *fig*. 97;
   of death, **5** 368;
   in dreams, **12** 132, 304–5;
   see also steamer
Shiraz, **10** 990
Shiur Koma, **14** 592
Shiva, **5** 306, pl. XXIII; **9i** 631–2,
   653, 661, 677; **10** 989; **11** 113,
   454; **12** 125, 139*n*, 169, *fig*. 75; **13**
   254*n*; **14** 534, 622; **15** 195; **18**
   263, 413;
   Ishvara, **12** 199;
   -Shakti concept, in Tantrism, **9i**
   631; **11** 152, 486; **13** 278; **14**
   235*n*, 580; **16** 380, 410; **18** 263
Shiva-bindu, **9i** 631, 664, 668; **12**
   246
shock, **7** 9/418, 47, 80, 187; **8** 499;
   emotional, **11** 274;
   nervous, **4** 206; English theory
   of, **7** 8/417;
   neurosis, *see* neurosis *s.v.*;
   see also trauma
shoemaker of Alexandria, **11** 953
shoes, movement of sewing, **3** 358
shofar, **10** 27, 28
Shri-Chakra-Sambhara Tantra, **11**
   791*n*; **12** 123&*n*
Shri-Yantra, **12** *fig*. 39
shroud, holy, **14** 526*n*
Shu, **9ii** 322;
   air god, **13** 360;
   four pillars of, **13** 360, 362
Shulamite/Sulamith, **9ii** 329; **14** 44,
   185, 268, 591, 592&*n*, 600, 606–
   11, 639, 644–8; **16** 361;
   Adam and, **14** 592, 598, 600
Shunamite, **18** 1526
Shvetashvatara Upanishad, see
   Upanishads
Siberian shamans, **13** 462
sibyl(s), **14** 300;
   Cumaean, **5** 119;
   Erythraean, **9ii** 127*n*; **14** 277,
   282, 285, 303

165; **18** 242, 1280;
   fire-tree of, **13** 408, 459*n*;
   and flaming sword, **11** 359;
   Helen/Helen of Troy (Selene)
   and, **9i** 372; **9ii** 307*n*; **14** 160,
   161; as anima-figure, **9i** 64; **10**
   75; **14** 181*n*; **16** 361*n*;
   world-tree of, **13** 320
simple, the/simplicity, **12** 165, 220,
   371, 372*n*; **13** 20, 187&*n*; **14**
   493*n*, 759;
   and complexity, **17** 331c, 333;
   see also *res simplex;* soul *s.v.*
   simple
simple-constellation type, *see* constellation *s.v.*
simpleton, devil as, **9i** 456
simplification, Puritan, **11** 543
simulation, **18** 885;
   TITLES: "A Medical Opinion on
   a Case of Simulated Insanity,"
   1 356–429; "On Simulated Insanity," **1** 301–55;
   affects as source of, **1** 423;
   and auto-hypnosis, **1** 422;
   concept of, **1** 352;
   confession of, **1** 306, 391,
   418–19;
   conscious, **1** 419;
   "dans le caractère" (Paulhan),
   6 283;
   diagnosis of: difficulty in, **1**
   351, 356; in doubtful cases, **1**
   302–3, 305–6; mistaken, **1** 353;
   earlier writers on, **1** 339, 351;
   effect on mental state, **1** 339;
   excellence of, **1** 337, 419;
   half-conscious, **1** 357;
   hysterical symptoms and, **1**
   305;
   passage from conscious to subconscious, **1** 320;
   passage into insanity, **1** 419;
   patient's explanation of, **1**
   329–30, 390–3, 418–19;
   physical examination, **1** 327;
   unmasking of, **1** 351
simultaneity, **8** 828, 840, 916;
   of two psychic states, **8** 855

Sin (Babylonian god), **11** 173, 175
sin(s), **3** 486, 489; **10** 676; **11** 698;
   12 24, 192, 475;
   Adam's, *see* Adam *s.v.* fall/sin;
   capacity for, **5** 673;
   Christ and, **5** 95; **11** 229; as expiation for, **11** 698;
   confession of, **5** 95, 97; **10**
   676;
   consciousness of, **5** 105; **11** 86;
   delusion of, **3** 335–6;
   eating of tree of knowledge
   as, **7** 243*n* (*see also below* original);
   forgiveness of, *see* forgiveness
   s.v.;
   Gnostics and, **11** 133;
   God cannot will, **11** 248;
   Mary and, **11** 625–6;
   and mental disease, **3** 321;
   original, **4** 729*n*; **6** 33; **7** 35; **8**
   426; **10** 571; **11** 248, 252, 263,
   619, 625–6, 691, 746, 758; **12**
   24, 36, 453; **13** 244; **14** 86, 774;
   16 186; **17** 87; *peccatum
   originale,* **18** 1551;
   "outside," **12** 9;
   painting of, **5** pl. X;
   of parents, **12** 152;
   problem of, **7** 285; **12** 37;
   Protestantism and, **11** 547;
   "register," **3** 180*n*;
   remission of, **13** 355;
   and repentance, **12** 36;
   and repression, **16** 124;
   "taking a sin," **17** 137;
   unconscious sinners, **11** 130;
   wages of, **13** 276;
Sinai, Mount, **12** 298
Singer, C.: *Studies in the History and
   Method of Science,* **11** 62*n*
singing, *see* song(s)
"sinister" side, as unconscious, **12**
   166, 211; *see also* left
Sinn, **13** 28
sinology(-ists), **13** 1, 9
Sioux, *see under* American Indians
siren(s), **9i** 53; **12** 61; **13** 180&*n*;
   nine, **13** 218

sister, **12** 91, 92, 108;
   as anima, *see* anima *s.vv.* -image, sister as, *and* mother-sister-wife;
   brother and, *see* brother;
   in dream, **12** 151;
   imaginary twin, **17** 225, 227;
   imago, **9ii-1** 24;
   -wives, of Osiris, *see* Osiris *s.v.*
Sisyphus, labour of, **18** 1377
Sita, **5** 306
situation: experimental, **8** 195;
   momentary, **11** 973;
   psychic, and dreams, **8** 536;
   total, **8** 863
Situri-Sabitu, **14** 75*n*
six, *see* NUMBERS *s.v.*
sixty-four, *see* NUMBERS *s.v.*
size, of Ufos, *see* Ufo(s) *s.v.*
skeleton(s): hallucinations of, **1** 7, 26;
   "in the cupboard," **8** 208
skin(s), **13** 87, 122;
   casting of, **5** 569, 580;
   formation of, **9i** 572, 576;
   of head, **13** (*p*60);
   libidinal interest in, **4** 291;
   stuffing of, **13** 92
skinning, **13** 87, 93, 95
skirt, concealment under, **14** 385
Skolts, Lappish (Finland), **18** 1754
skull/*occiput*/cranium, **12** *fig.* 135; **14** 731;
   and head, in dream, **12** 107, 108;
   as *vas*/vessel, **9ii** 377; **12** 116, 376, 517*n*, *fig.* 75; **13** 113; **14** 732;
   worship of, **11** 372
sky: -god, **13** 341*n*;
   the human, **11** 160;
   as mother, **5** 408–9;
   as *prima materia,* **12** 425;
   quintessence and, **11** 160
Sky-Father, **13** 130
Sky-Mother, Egyptian, **9i** *fig.* 47, 702
skyscraper(s), **10** 978;

in dream association, **3** 124–5
sky-woman, **9i** 340–1, 351
slang, American, **10** 955; **11** 339
slaughter, mystical, **11** 324–5; **12** 417
slave(s): fugitive/*servus fugitivus:* lapis as, **14** 188*n*; Mercurius as, **12** 84, 187; **13** 218, 259; **16** 478; red, *see* COLOURS: red and white *s.v.* red man/slave
slavery/enslavement: and rebellion, **10** 500; in Roman empire, **5** 104*n*, 335; **10** 249–50;
   subjective/inward, **6** 108; **10** 249
slave's post, **9ii** 129*n*, 130
Slavonic Book of Enoch, *see* BIBLE: Apocrypha/etc. *s.v.* Enoch
slaying of alchemical authorities, **13** 427; *see also* killing
sleep, **3** 137&*n*, 523–4; **5** 501; **8** 957; **13** 148*n*;
   consciousness in, **8** 296; **11** 53;
   disturbed/sleeplessness, **1** 8, 217; **3** 181, 524; **8** 566;
   dreams as preserving, **8** 485;
   ecstatic, **1** 123;
   enchanted, **5** 567&*n*;
   fantasy in, **16** 125;
   in Homer's *Iliad,* **5** 363, 364*n*, 567*n*;
   of incubation, **13** 139;
   longing for, **5** 501, 503*n*, 553;
   magnetic, **18** 702;
   onset of, and hallucinations, **1** 43, 100;
   partial, and suggestibility, **1** 28;
   prodromal stage, **1** 280;
   seldom dreamless, **8** 580;
   "waking," **18** 702;
   -walking, *see* somnambulism
sleepers, seven, *see* NUMBERS: seven *s.v.*
Sleeping Beauty, *see* fairytales, INSTANCES: German *s.v.*
sleeping state, **3** 579–80;
   following double hypnosis, **1** 294;

S. W.'s, **1** 122
sleeplessness, *see* sleep *s.v.* disturbed
Sleipnir, **5** 423, *fig.* 28; **10** 384
slipping out (of fish/monster's belly), *see* Frobenius *s.v.* night sea journey
slips, *see* memory *s.v.*; tongue *s.v.*
Sloane, W.: *To Walk the Night*, **9i** 356
Slocum, J. J., and H. Cahoon: *A Bibliography of James Joyce*, c.f. **15** 163–203
slogans, **10** 490, 536
"smaller than small:" motif, **9i** 283;
self as, *see* self *s.v.*
smell(s): in alchemy, **14** 432;
of Holy Ghost, **14** 432, 658, 701;
see also odour; olfactory hallucinations
smiling, infective, **10** 965
Smith, Carlton, **10** (*p*245)
Smith, E. M.: *The Zodia*, **9ii** 147*n*, 149*n*
Smith, George, **5** 375
Smith, Hélène, *see* Flournoy *s.v.*
Smith, W., **2** 116*n*, 451;
Zur Frage der mittelbaren Assoziation, **2** 451*n*
smoke, **12** 394*n*, 398, *fig.* 142C;
from the north, **9ii** 158&*n*;
sacrificial, **11** 302; *see also* vapour
smutty talk, **4** 502; **10** 217; *see also* obscene stories; scurrility
Smyrna, **11** 701
snail, *see* ANIMALS *s.v.*
snake, *see* ANIMALS *s.v.* serpent
Snell, L., "Über Simulation von Geistesstörung," **1** 346*n*
snow, **13** 263
Snow White, *see* fairytales: INSTANCES: German *s.v.*
Soal, S. G., **8** 966;
"Science and Telepathy," **8** 966*n*;
and F. Bateman: *Modern Experiments in Telepathy*, **8** 833*n*
Sobk, water-god, **5** 147*n*, 148*n*

social: behaviour in manic mood disorder, **1** 197–9;
changes, and psychology, **8** 594;
democracy, **10** 155;
elevation, delirium of, **3** 154;
factors, **7** 227;
inadequacy, **1** 219;
instinct, **7** 235/455;
order, **7** 242/463; and Trinity, **11** 223;
problems and projections, **11** 140;
relationships, attitude to, **16** 241–2;
security, **16** 502;
sense, in animals and primitives, **4** 641;
service, **10** 929;
status, dissatisfaction with, **3** 154
socialism, **10** 1019; **11** 688; **18** 1320, 1335
sociality, **7** 240
societies, secret, in America, **10** 977
society, **7** (*p*5), 30, 201, 227, 228*n*, 230, 234, 237, 254, 278, 305, 311, 318, 429, 438, 462*n*, 518;
abstract nature of, **10** 504;
and imitation, **7** 242/463;
and the individual, **5** 102–4; **7** 234–5/455, 240, 246; **16** 224–5, 248; **18** 1103;
matriarchal, **13** 131;
moral degeneration of, **7** 240;
natural organization of, **16** 445;
outside the individual, **7** 231;
patriarchal, **11** 223;
and persona, **7** 246, 305, 518;
and personality, as opposites, **12** 557;
primitive, connection between rhythm and work in, **5** 219;
state and, **16** 226;
temptation to unconsciousness, **16** 225;
see also office; organization(s)

Sommer, R. (*cont.*):
 trischen Vorgänge an der menschlichen Haut," **2** (*pp*491, 580)
somnambulism(-ist), **3** 58*n*, 157, 171, 176, 298, 313, 555; **4** 581; **7** 199 (*p*123); **8** 295; **13** 31*n*, 37; **16** 231; **18** 702, 705, 757, 797, 884;
 TITLE: "A Case of Somnambulism in a Girl with Poor Inheritance," **1** 36–71;
 automatisms in, **1** 42;
 course of, **1** 134;
 cryptomnesic reproduction of object, **1** 143;
 dissociation of personality in, **1** 117;
 ego, *see* ego *s.v.*;
 and hallucinations, **1** 26, 33, 98; **3** 161;
 hypnotic, **1** 122&*n*, 256;
 hysterical/in hysteria, **1** 5, 272;
 intentional, **5** 253;
 intuitive knowledge of, **1** 147&*n*;
 nature of attacks, **1** 121–31;
 pallor in, **1** 39, 45–6, 50–3, 125;
 semi-, **1** 44, 58–9, 77–9, 114;
 spontaneous, **1** 5, 110;
 suggestibility of, **1** 148;
 see also Jung: CASES: vol. 1, S. W.
somnambulistic state(s), **1** 39–44; **8** 809; **13** 48;
 behaviour in, **1** 40;
 induced, **1** 124;
 second state, **1** 107–11; and change in character, **1** 107–20, 135–6; with and without amnesic split, **1** 111;
 see also personality, second
"somnia a deo missa," *see* dreams *s.v.* sent by God
son(s): of chaos, **12** 119;
 as consciousness, **5** 393;
 and crown of victory, **16** 496;
 of darkness, **12** 41;
 devil as God's, *see* devil *s.v.* God;

eldest, **17** 214;
 existence of, **13** 76;
 father and, *see* father *s.v.*;
 -gods, **5** 392;
 of the Golden Head, **13** 95;
 of Great World, **12** 390; **13** 127 (see also *filius macrocosmi*);
 as husband substitute, **17** 328;
 kings', *see* king *s.v.*;
 -lover: Adonis, **5** 530*n*; Attis, **5** 595, 659; Iasion, and Demeter, **5** 528*n*; of mother-goddess, **5** 466;
 mother and, *see* mother and son;
 mother-complex of, *see* complex *s.v.* mother-;
 of one day, see *filius unius diei;*
 only begotten, **13** 209*n*;
 of philosophers, see *filius philosophorum;*
 ruler over earth, **16** 495;
 sacrifice of, *see* sacrifice *s.v.*;
 -ship: duality of, *see* devil *s.v.* God; Ebionites *s.v.* Christ and Satan;
 -ship: threefold/third, *see* Basilides *s.v.*;
 "of the sun," **9i** 84;
 as symbol for God, **9ii** 304;
 as symbol of self, **9i** 315;
 of Tiamat, **12** 29;
 upper and lower, **12** 26;
 of the Virgin, **16** 517;
 see also *filius*
Son, The, **9ii** 290–1; **13** 40; **14** 122;
 divine, archetype of, **14** 744;
 Father and, **9ii** 301; **13** 149;
 of Macrocosm, see *filius macrocosmi;*
 of Man, *see sep. entry below*
"so-ness," **8** 871
Son of God/*filius Dei*, **11** 126, 197, 272, 486; **12** 139, 144, 415; **13** 137*n*, 196; **14** 639*n*;
 and Adam, **12** 456(7), 457;
 and Antimimos, **12** 456 (9, 10), 460;

Sophia (*cont.*):
  Isis as, **14** 14;
  Jerusalem/city as, **11** 612, 711,
  727; **14** 574;
  and Lilith, **11** 619;
  and Logos, **11** 193, 240, 610;
  and Mary, **8** 336; **11** 625, 628,
  646, 714, 743; **14** 744; **18** 1552;
  as "master-workman," **11** 609,
  617, 624, 628, 634;
  Maya character of, **11** 613;
  as mother, **11** 714, 721, 739,
  742; **13** 406; **14** 574;
  Prounikos/Prunicus, **9ii** 99,
  307*n*; **14** 576;
  and Ruach, **11** 611, 619;
  -Sapientia, **9i** 93; **14** 576;
  as self, **16** 518;
  as Shekinah, **11** 727;
  as sun-woman, **11** 710–11, 721;
  and Yahweh, *hierosgamos* of, see
  hierosgamos s.v. Yahweh
Sophism, **6** 49; **13** 381, 444
Sophocles: on Chronos, **8** 394;
  dream of Herakles' vessel, **18**
  250;
  Philoctetes, **5** 450*n*;
  Sophoclis Fabulae, ed. A. C.
  Pearson, **18** 250*n*
Sophonias/Zephaniah, Apocalypse
  of, *see* BIBLE: Apocrypha/etc. *s.v.*
Sorbonne, **18** 106
sorcerer(-ess), **6** 46; **7** 154; **12** 276;
  13 154; **18** 360; *see also* magician;
  magus
sorcery, **13** 154, 156; **17** 204; **18** 784
Sorin, **16** 476*n*
Sorokin, P. A., **18** 1461*n*
soror mystica, **13** 96; **14** 161;
  and adept, **9i** 53*n*; **14** 181; **16**
  421–2, 437, 538*n*;
  and artifex, **12** *figs.* 132, 140,
  215, 237, 269;
  of hierophant/philosopher, **9i**
  372
Sosnosky, Th. von: *Die rote Dreifaltigkeit: Jakobiner und Bolscheviken*,
11 252*n*

So-to-shu College, **11** 879
soul(s), **4** 753; **5** 268, 344, 500,
  634*n*; **6** 318; **7** 108; **8** 663; **9i** 56;
  9ii 219; **10** 136; **11** 19; **12** 19,
  126, 243; **13** 93, 182*n*, 198; **14** 93,
  198, 673; **16** 45, 225; **17** 81, 170;
  TITLES: "Crime and the Soul,"
  18 800–21; "Psychoanalysis
  and the Cure of Souls," **11**
  539–52; "The Soul and Death,"
  8 796–815;
  and aer/air, *see* aer *s.v.*;
  in alchemy, *see sep. entry below;*
  ancestral, **7** 233*n*; **9i** 224; **13**
  128 (*see also* Australian
  aborigines *s.v. alchera*);
  androgyny of, **14** 527;
  as angel, **16** 517;
  and anima (J.'s term), *see* anima
  s.v.;
  animal, spinning woman as, **9ii**
  20*n*;
  animal soul in man, *see* ani-
  mal(s) *s.v.*;
  animals as, *see* ANIMALS: birds;
  fish *s.v.* eyes of; peacock;
  of animals, *see* animal(s) *s.v.*;
  and archetype of wise old man,
  9i 74;
  ascent of, **16** 475–82; and descent of, **5** 487*n*; **13** 114*n*, 137;
  14 289; **16** 475, 493 (*see also
  below* descent);
  -atoms, *see* Australian aboriginals *s.v.*;
  belief in, **8** 577–9, 586;
  as bird/-bird, **5** 315*n*, 368*n*,
  547; **8** 845; recall of, **8** 586;
  "twittering," **8** 845*n*; **9ii** 327;
  blood and, *see* blood *s.v.*;
  and body, *see* body *s.v.*;
  breath-, **13** 57, 262;
  and breath-body, **14** 748;
  as bride of Christ, **9ii** 72;
  bush-, *see* primitive(s) *s.v.* soul;
  and centre (Plotinus), **9ii**
  342–3;
  children's, among Australian

aborigines, **13** 128;
in Chinese philosophy, *see* China/Chinese;
Christian idea of, **9i** 119, 229;
and Christianity, **12** 12–13; **16** 223;
as circle, **9ii** 342; **10** 622; **11** 124*n*;
collective, **7** 456&*n*; **13** 287*n*;
and collective function, **18** 1104;
-complex, **7** 295, 298; autonomous, **7** 302–3; **8** 587; feminine quality of, **7** 295, 297–8, 301, 303;
concept of, **7** 295, 371; **10** 84–5; **16** 212; philosophical, **7** 302; primitive, **8** 665; religious, **7** 302, 371; as substance, **8** 649;
conglomerate, self as, **9i** 634;
cortical/medullary, **8** 368;
creative power of, libido as, **5** 176;
crucifixion of, **7** 36;
cure of, *see* cure of souls;
daily need of, **18** 627;
dark night of, **4** 762; **8** 431; **9i** 563*n*; **16** 479;
dark part of, **8** 361; **13** 184;
crocodile as symbol of, **13** 105*n*;
of dead, *see* dead *s.v.*;
definition(s) of, **6** 797–807; **8** 662–4; **9i** 391&*n*; **12** 9&*n*; as *aiolos*, **8** 663;
descent of, planetary, **14** 299, 309;
desiccation of, **5** 553;
devaluation of, *see below* Western;
duality of, **13** 150, 263;
earth-, and *anima telluris*, **8** 935;
ego and, **7** 303; **8** 586–7;
Egyptian, see *ba*;
etymologies of, **8** 663–4;
existence of, after death, *see below* immortality of;
feminine, **10** 79;

feminine element in, **13** 57; **14** 282; and masculine, **13** *fig.* A6 (*see also above* -complex);
and fire-substance, **5** 149*n*;
-flower, **9i** 596, 604;
-force/-stuff, **10** 21;
God and, *see* God;
grain and wine as, **11** 385;
as guide, **12** *fig.* 19;
and Heimarmene, release from, **5** 644; **12** 457;
"herd," **7** 462*n*;
Hermes and, **9ii** 325; **12** 409*n*, *fig.* 139;
hero and, **5** 259;
hymn to, Gnostic, **9i** 37–8;
-images, *see sep. entry below;*
immortality of, **8** 577, 662, 669; **16** 223; **18** 741, 761; as dogma, **12** 11; personal, **7** 302;
"inspired," **7** 113;
intellect and, **13** 7, 286;
lack of, **12** 74;
language of, **18** 671;
Leibniz on, **8** 937;
as *ligamentum spiritus et corporis*, **9ii** 118;
lonely, **18** 632;
loss of, **7** 239; **11** 688; **13** 48; **18** 93, 440, 442, 633 (*see also* primitive(s) *s.v.* soul); as danger in opus, **14** 144*n*;
of mankind, **10** 136;
masters/rulers of, **13** 244;
materialization of, **13** 316;
and matter, **9ii** 307*n*; **13** 76*n*;
as microcosm, **10** 635;
Mistress, **5** 459; **6** 320; **7** 374;
moon and, **5** 487&*n*, *fig.* 31; **14** 155&*n*, 167;
and mother-imago, **5** 406&*n*;
"-murder," **5** 459*n*;
"mutilated," of devil, **9ii** 85;
"My Lady Soul" (Spitteler), **9ii** 25; **13** 460;
and name, **5** 274;
"of the nation," **10** 907;
"nations of the," **10** 175;

soul (*cont.*):

as "nothing but," **13** 75;

Paracelsan concepts of, **13** 150, 171*n*, 175, 201–2, 210, 222; **14** 41;

paradoxical, **18** 1553;

part-, **7** 104, 141, 274; **18** 741;

"passage of" *(animae transitus),* **14** 578;

"perils of," **11** 23; **16** 124, 412 (*see also* primitive(s) *s.v.* soul);

personification of, **3** 321; of unconscious, *see* unconscious *s.v.*;

Pindar on, **11** 373;

plurality of, *see* primitive(s) *s.v.* soul;

pneuma and, **5** 659; **12** 409*n*; fiery, **12** 370*n*; second Eve as, **9ii** 321;

primitive(s) and, *see* primitive(s) *s.v.*;

problem of, **18** 1293;

in projection, **6** 279; **7** 297; **9i** 116; child's, on parents, **17** 97; in matter, **14** 93, 147; of unconscious, **9ii** 219;

Prometheus and, **6** 277–81, 284, 289–92, 296–7, 303, 306;

psychology and, **8** 343, 356–8, 649; **12** 9–10, 15; **13** 286;

and psycho-neuroses, **11** 491;

raising of (Manichean), **12** 469&*n*;

realities of, **5** 615;

reasoning, **13** 301*n*;

recall of, **8** 586;

redemption of, **12** 415;

religion not a substitute, **12** 293, 296;

religious function of, **12** 14;

salvation of, **5** 634*n*; **11** 539;

and shadow, *see* shadow;

of the sick, **13** 132;

skin as, **13** 95;

-sparks/atoms, of Australian aborigines, **8** 278*n*; **9i** 116 (*see also* scintilla; *spinther*);

as sphere, **9ii** 212; **10** 621, 635; **11** 124*n*; **12** 109; **16** 405*n*;

and spirit, *see sep. entry below;*

spiritual development of, **18** 1553;

and spiritual world-system, **8** 677;

square (Pythagorean), **11** 61*n*, 124, 246; **12** 439*n*; **16** 405*n*;

-stones, **13** 129, 132;

as substance, **8** 649;

suffering of, **13** 455; **16** 20;

and sun, wanderings of, **5** 141*n*, 487*n*;

supratemporality of, **11** 837, 845, 855;

symbol/symbolism, **5** 344; **10** 622; **16** 405*n*;

Tertullian on: (anima) "naturaliter Christiana/religiosa," **4** 739; **6** 19, 28; **11** 771; **12** 14*n*, 24; **15** 195; **17** 310; testimony of, **6** 18; **11** 556–7;

transformation and, **9i** 238*n*; **14** 321, 493;

transmigration of, *see* metempsychosis;

tree-, **13** 247, 420;

"twittering," **8** 845*n*; **9ii** 327;

"two," in Goethe, **3** 105;

and the unconscious, *see* unconscious *s.v.*;

unity of, **14** 761;

universal, **5** 296*n* (*see also* world-soul);

vision of, rising from sarcophagus, **18** 1708;

wandering, *see* primitive(s) *s.v.* soul;

Western ideas of, **11** 835; devaluation of, in West, **12** 9, 10, 126; and Eastern, compared, **11** 768; **12** 9;

and wind, **5** 484*n*, 659;

winged, **12** *fig.* 139;

woman and, **13** 60;

of the world, **13** 166;

world-, *see* world-soul;

worship of, **6** 386; and of women (Goethe/Hermas/Spitteler), **6** 375–81
soul(s) in alchemy, **13** 103, 110, 113–14, 126, 176*n*; **16** 454, 468, 494–524;
  "accrescent," **14** 374, 426;
  as active principle of *prima materia*, **13** 157;
  aerial, *see* aer/air;
  affliction of, **14** 674, 687; **12** 386; and *nigredo*, **14** 446, 741; **16** 479;
  and arcane substance, **13** 260;
  spiritual martyrdom of, **13** 442;
  and body, **12** 397–400;
  in "chains"/"fetters"/imprisoned, **9ii** 307*n*, 326*n*; **10** 633; **11** 152*n*; **12** 409*n*; **14** 168*n*, 321, 353;
  concept of, **14** 748;
  dew as symbol of, **13** 114;
  extraction of, **13** 95, 441*n*, 442; through moon, **14** 155;
  fountain of, **14** 191;
  freeing of, **14** 297, 480*n*, 673, 674, 700, 730;
  as homunculus, **16** 481;
  imprisoned, *see above* in "chains;"
  as intermediate nature, **13** 261 (see also *anima media natura*);
  and lapis/stone, extraction from, **13** 89; **14** 372;
  as *lapis pretiosissimus*, **14** 41*n* (*see also below* philosophers' stone);
  liberation of, **12** 306;
  Mercurius as, *see* Mercurius *s.v.* anima;
  as mid-point of heart, **14** 41;
  moist, of *prima materia*, **13** 103*n*, 114&*n*;
  as "monster"/"worm" (Böhme), **12** 215;
  in *opus*, **12** 396, 399–400;
  philosophers' stone and, **9i** 238*n*; **11** 153; **13** 89, 283*n*, 381

(*see also above* lapis);
  as redeemer, **14** 41*n*;
  redemption of divine-, **12** 413–14, 420; **14** 353, 354;
  retort/spherical vessel as, **13** 245;
  return of, **16** 487, 503;
  rooted in aether, **13** 412*n*;
  salt as, **14** 321;
  simple/simplicity of, **12** 372, 427, 517*n*; **13** 117*n*;
  -substance, **7** 151; **12** 109; **13** 433;
  as *vas*/vessel, **13** 114;
  as *vinculum*, **16** 454, 475, 504;
  world soul, *see* world soul *s.v.* in alchemy
soul and spirit, **9i** 391; **13** 76*n*, 260, 276, *fig.* B6; **14** 663;
  animation through, **14** 673;
  and body, *see* body *s.v.* soul/body/spirit;
  as opposites, **14** 3, 35, 41;
  as spiracle/*spiraculum*, **14** 670;
  union of, **14** 707
soul-images, **6** 281, 380–2, 387;
  and anima (J.'s term), *see* anima;
  and animus, *see* animus *s.v.*;
  birds as, **5** 315;
  definition, **6** 808–11; **12** 9*n*;
  flame/light as, **5** 149&*n*;
  and mother-imago, **5** 406;
  Pandora as, **6** 304–6;
  woman and, **7** 297, 314
sound, **8** 608, 680;
  associations/reactions, *see* association(s) *s.v.*;
  creation of, **5** 65;
  -frequencies, **8** 367;
  light and, *see* light *s.v.*;
  as oscillations, **18** 12;
  -shift, centrifugal/centripetal, **2** 85–9;
  see also clang
source of life, **12** 92, 105, 112, 157, 159, 171, 174; **13** 350
South, T., **14** 181*n*; **16** 505
south: the queen of, *see* queen *s.v.*;

sphere(s) (*cont.*):
13 40; 16 535;
anima mundi as, 12 109*n*, 116;
black, 9i 558, (*p*315);
in dreams, 10 683; 12 198–9;
315*n*;
Empedoclean σφαῖρος, 12
112*n*, 433;
heavenly, 9i 679;
as ideal of completeness, 11
246;
movement of, 13 99;
Original Man as, 12 109*n*;
in *Pistis Sophia*, 9ii 148*n*;
seven, 12 315; planetary, 12 66,
410;
somatic, 13 328;
soul as, *see* soul *s.v.*;
vas/vessel as, 12 116, 167*n*,
338&*n*;
of water / aquasphere, 12
433&*n*;
winged, 12 *fig.* 209;
world-soul as, 12 433;
see also globe; rotundum;
"round" motif
sphingidae, see ANIMALS: moth(s) *s.v.*
Sphinx/sphinx: apparition of, 5
261, (*p*458);
as fear animal, 5 264, 265;
genealogy of, 5 265;
masculine and feminine, 5 266;
Oedipus and, 5 261, 264; 10
713, 714;
pleasure emblem, 5 261*n*;
riddle of, 9i 486; 10 714;
as symbol, 5 265, 272, 536;
as Terrible Mother, 5 261, 264;
of Thebes, 5 266
spider, *see* ANIMALS *s.v.*
Spiegel, F.: *Erânische Altertumskunde*,
5 240*n*, 306*n*, 367*n*, 426*n*, 581*n*,
636*n*, 662*n*, 664*n*, 668*n*;
Grammatik der Parsisprache, 5
664*n*
Spiegel, H. W., 2 1357*n*
Spiegelberg, W., 14 352;
"Der Fisch als Symbol der

Seele," 9ii 187*n*;
"Der Gott Baït in dem Trinitäts-
amulett des Britischen Muse-
ums," 14 352*n*
Spielmeyer, W., 4 25;
untitled note in *Zentralblatt für
Nervenheilkunde und Psychiatrie*,
4 25*n*
Spielrein, S., 4 478;
on archaic definitions of words
in paranoia, 5 200, 201;
on death instinct, 5 504*n*;
as J.'s patient, *see* Jung: CASES
vol. 4 case (1);
on symbols, 3 390; 5 201;
CASE: of schizophrenic woman:
and arrow wounds from God,
5 445*n*, 547*n*;
and boring associated with fire
and procreation, 5 217, 439*n*;
and communion wine/water, 5
581*n*, 634*n*;
on the cross, 5 460*n*;
and dismemberment motif, 5
354*n*;
on flesh-eating horses, 5 427*n*;
and God's ray, 5 638;
and snake, 5 459*n*, 677;
WORKS:
"Die Destruktion als Ursache
des Werdens," 7 33*n*;
"Über den psychologischen
Inhalt eines Falles von
Schizophrenie," 3 390*n*; 5
200*n*, 677*n*; 8 589*n*; 11 781*n*;
13 91*n*
Spier, J.: *The Hands of Children*, J.'s
foreword, 18 1818–21
Spiess, K. von: *Marksteine der Volks-
kunst*, 5 pl. VIII
spinal cord: negativism and, 3 27;
and reflex arc, 8 607;
sarcoma of, *see* sarcoma;
snake as personification of, 9i
282, 667; 9ii 291, 369
Spinning Woman, 9ii 20&*n*
Spinoza, B., 6 770; 8 276; 9i 385,
390; 10 27, 199;

vision of, **1** 100*n*;
Ethics, **8** 276*n*

spinther / σπινθήρ (Gnostic), **9ii**
344&*n*; **12** 138-9, 410*n*, 472; **14**
42&*n*; *see also* scintilla

spiraculum (spiracle), **14** 670

spiral, **9i** 648, *fig.* 4;
of inner development, in
dreams, **12** 34, 242, 246, 325;
rotation, **13** 349

spiration, **11** 235&*n*; *see also* Holy
Ghost *s.v.*

spirit (1) (immaterial part of man;
alchemists' conception; as archetypal concept etc.), **7** 369; **9i**
35; **13** 6, 45, 51, (*pp*60-1, 64),
148*n*, 186*n*, 370; **14** 727; **16** 486;
17 207, 315; **18** 750;
TITLES: "The Phenomenology
of the Spirit in Fairytales," **9i**
384-455; *The Spirit in Man, Art,
and Literature,* **15**; "Spirit and
Life," **8** 601-48;
in aether, *see* aether *s.v.*;
air and, see *aer*/air;
alchemical conception of, **9i**
386; **9ii** 141; **11** 160; **12** 351,
456; **13** 103, 136, 137&*n*, 163,
430; **14** 251, 252, 328, 742;
ambivalent/antithetical nature
of, **9i** 433; **13** 288; **14** 170, 728;
and anima, **5** 678;
animus and, **9i** 439; **9ii** 33;
in arcane substance/*prima
materia,* **12** 376, 394, 425, 444,
447, *figs.* 129, 229, 232;
archetype, **15** (*p*v);
and archetype, **5** 337, 641; **8**
405-6, 420; **9i** 413, 682; **9ii**
141; **18** 1475; ambivalence of,
13 288;
as ash of Hermes, **14** 247;
as attitude, *see* attitude *s.v.*;
as autonomous affect, **8** 628;
autonomous reality of, **5** 338; **8**
379, 585&*n*, 587, 628, 643,
660; **9i** 396;
birds as symbols of, **5** 538; **14**

247-8;
black, **13** 439;
blood a synonym of, *see* blood
s.v. synonym;
body and, *see* body *s.v.*;
as boy, **9i** 396;
breath as, **5** 334; **10** 146;
breath of, **9i** 35; **12** (*p*285), *fig.*
115;
and Christianity, *see* Christian/
etc. *s.v.*;
of Christianity, early, *see* Chris-
tian/etc. *s.v.* early;
chthonic, **13** 154; **14** 736; unconscious as, **14** 742;
coagulation of, **14** 734;
"cold breath of," **9i** 387;
collective, **10** 945;
colour blue as, *see* COLOURS:
blue *s.v.*;
as complexes of the collective
unconscious, **8** 597;
corporeal, **14** 293;
creative, **12** 398;
"crime of," **14** 41*n*, 49*n*;
danger of, **10** 917;
darkness of, **11** 232; **15** 141;
diabolical, **13** 174;
Dionysus as, *see* Dionysus *s.v.*;
divine, **11** 160; **13** 40;
double nature of, **9i** 567*n*;
doubling of, **11** 197*n*;
dove as symbol of, **5** 492; **9i** 93;
in dreams, **9i** 396;
East and, **8** 682; **13** 72;
and ego-consciousness, **8** 643-
5;
eternal (Bohme), **12** 214;
etymological derivation, **8** 628;
existence of, **18** 748;
expulsion of, **14** 247;
extraction of, **11** 160; **13** 185,
222*n*;
eyes of, *see* eye(s) *s.v.* mind/
spirit;
fiery, **12** 562; **13** (*p*63); **14** 251
(see also *spiritus igneus*);
fire, *see* fire *s.v.*;

spirit (1) (*cont.*):
    Freud and, **15** 72;
    ghostly (Paracelsus), **13** 174;
    gold and, **14** 353–5, 736;
    of gravity, **12** 79;
    hallmarks, **9i** 393;
    happiness in, **18** 1346;
    as higher consciousness, **8** 643;
    human, **8** 359; **13** 224*n*;
    as ideas, **8** 596, 597;
    iliastric, *see* Paracelsus: ARCANA *s.v.* Iliaster;
    as images, **8** 628;
    imprisoned: in darkness of the world, **12** 557; in matter, *see below*;
    impure, **14** 589;
    innate, life-giving, **13** 148&*n*, 176*n*;
    and instinct(s), *see* instinct *s.v.*;
    intellect and, **9i** 32; **12** 178;
    and invisibility, **5** 291*n*;
    in lapis/stone, **12** 390, 512; and soul and body, **14** 525, 773 (*see also* stone, alchemical *s.v.* "that hath a spirit");
    liberation of psyche from, **14** 775;
    life and/of life, **8** 645–8; **13** 263; **14** 232, 270, 734*n*;
    as *ligamentum animae et corporis*, **9i** 386;
    light of, **14** 742;
    Lilith as "mistress" of, **14** 589;
    living, **9i** 40; **11** 538; being and, **8** 621; and culture-creating, **17** 159;
    Lord of, **13** 294;
    male, **14** 536*n*, 736;
    in/of man, **9i** 386*n*; **13** 59, 171*n*;
    in Mass, ritual of, **11** 317, 319;
    material and spiritual, **13** 175;
    and matter, **8** 420, 748; **9i** 195, 197, 385, 392; **12** 405–13; **13** 261, 263; descent into, **12** 436;
    immateriality of, **9i** 197, 392;
    imprisoned in, **11** 150; **12** 376, 404, 512; rotunda, **10** 766; split between, **18** 1658;
    meaning of term, **8** 102, (*p*300), 602–4, 626–9; **9i** 385–8 (see also *Geist*);
    Mercurius as, *see* Mercurius *s.v.*;
    of metals/metal-, **11** 347; **13** 119, 121, 392;
    metaphysics and, *see* metaphysics *s.v.*;
    and mind, **8** 102, (*p*300), 621;
    ministering, **13** 132, 219;
    natural, **7** 290; **13** 229; **14** 427;
    and nature, *see* nature *s.v.*;
    objective, **9i** 386; **13** 248, 286;
    and subjective, **9i** 392;
    ocean as "spirit of world," **9ii** 219;
    Paracelsus on, *see* Paracelsus *s.v.*;
    paradox of, **8** 427;
    parental, **7** 294, 296;
    passion of, **5** 615;
    as personal being, **8** 643;
    and Physis, descent into, **11** 161; freed from, **12** *fig.* 178;
    pneuma as, **9i** 95; **11** 160;
    poor in, **13** 250;
    postulation of, **8** 661;
    primacy of, **14** 672;
    in *prima materia*, see *prima materia s.v.*;
    primordial experience of, **11** 535;
    as projection of the unconscious, **9ii** 219;
    as psychic phenomenon, **7** 293; **8** 251; **18** 746;
    of quicksilver, *see* quicksilver *s.v.*;
    of quintessence, **11** 160; **12** 165; "fifth essence," **13** 166;
    rebirth through, **4** 783; symbolism of, **5** 334–5;
    red, **13** 103;
    redeeming, **10** 629;
    religio and, **11** 8;

Renaissance, *see* Renaissance *s.v.*;
salt as, **14** 246, 251, 324, 326, 328, 336; *sal spirituale,* **14** 241;
of Saturn, *see* Saturn *s.v.*;
scientific, **12** 168; **13** 121;
self as, **12** 327;
as "senex et iuvenis," **9i** 80;
sexuality and, **8** 107;
shên, see China/Chinese *s.v.* soul;
and soul, *see* soul *s.v.*; and body, *see* body *s.v.* soul/body/spirit;
"spellbound," motif of, **13** 246;
spermatic, **5** 492, pl. VIII;
as spiracle, **14** 670;
as spiritual life, **9i** 572;
of stars, **13** 224*n*;
of stone, *see* stone, alchemical *s.v.*;
subjective, **9i** 392;
-substance, **12** 406;
"subtle," **7** 368;
sufferings of, **13** 7;
sulphur of the king as, **14** 752;
superiority of, **8** 643;
supracelestial, **13** 263; of waters, **13** 102;
symbols as expression of, **8** 643–4; **9i** 50;
symbols of, *see above* birds; breath/wind; dove; salt; *below* unicorn; water;
"teachings of the," **8** 599;
theriomorphic symbolism of, in fairytales, **9i** 419–35;
traditional, **12** 93; father as, **12** 59, 83, 92, 159;
transformation into, **14** 714;
as transforming substance, **12** 31*n*;
and tree, **13** 247–9;
of truth, **13** 166; Mercurius as, **13** 263;
is unconscious, **9ii** 219;
unicorn as symbol of, **5** 492;
and union of sexes, **14** 106;
victory of, over senses, **13** 453;
as volatile body, **13** 76*n*;

water and, **9i** 40; **11** 354–5; **13** 101–3; as death and rebirth, **13** 136; descent into, **11** 161;
water as, **10** 629; **13** 103;
water as materiality of, **9i** 566*n*;
of the waters, **13** 102–4;
and wind, **5** 334; **7** 219; **10** 146;
-world, **7** 293, 322;
world-spirit, **9ii** 219; **12** 512; **13** 261

spirit(s) (2) (incorporeal being(s), not connected with material body):
TITLE: "The Psychological Foundations of Belief in Spirits," **8** 570–600;
ancestor-(ral), *see* ancestor(s) *s.v.*;
belief in, **8** 210, 570–600; mental illness and, **8** 576; as reaction against materialism, **8** 571–2; and in souls, **8** 577–9, 586; sources of, **8** 579;
in bottle, *see* Grimm brothers *s.v.*;
in case of S. W. (Jung's patient), **1** 41–50, 59–60, 99; language of, **1** 59; types of, **1** 126;
communicating with, **18** 697;
communications of, and unconscious psyche, **18** 748;
of the dead, **1** 77; **8** 335, 629; **9i** 388; as personified unconscious content, **18** 751; psychogenesis of, **8** 598;
as devil, **14** 252;
devil as aerial spirit, **12** *fig.* 36;
earth/Earth-, **12** 444; **13** 105*n*, 392; **14** 251; hermaphroditic, **12** 447;
evil, **5** 551, 552; **8** 629; **9i** 394, 446–8, 689; **10** 843; **13** 244–9, 288; exorcizing of, **9i** 47; and mental illness, **3** 321, 528; possession by, **3** 528; **8** 576, 627;
reality of, **13** 249;
familiar, *see* familiar;
God as, *see* God *s.v.*;

spirit(s) (2) (*cont.*):
    of God: four (Böhme), **9i** 535,
    588; seven, **9i** 535*n*; **9ii** 167*n*;
    12 468;
    guardian, see *familiar/paredros;*
    "guiding," **8** 629;
    of heaven/heavenly, **13** 215,
    256;
    Holy, *see* Holy Ghost;
    Land of, **5** 552;
    medicine-man's communion
    with, **7** 154*n*;
    not always dangerous, **8** 596;
    planetary, **13** 273, 275, *fig.* B5
    (*see also* Mercurius *s.v.*
    planetary);
    primitives and, *see* primitive(s)
    s.v.;
    projection and, **8** 585;
    and "telluric powers," *see*
    Keyserling, Count Hermann;
    valley-, **9i** 40
spirit of the age/*Zeitgeist,* **6** 29; **8**
    653, 655, 657; **9i** 386; **10** 545,
    584; **13** 150; **14** 454, 740, 743,
    754; **16** 22;
    Keyserling as mouthpiece of,
    10 945
"Spirit in the Bottle, The," *see*
    Grimm brothers *s.v.*
Spirit and Nature, see Eranos
    Yearbooks, Papers from
spiritism, **18** (*p*293*n*)
spiritual: in alchemy, *see sep. entry
    below:*
    attitude, *see* attitude *s.v.*;
    being, **13** 77;
    and biological, *see* biology *s.v.*;
    development, **7** 172; **13** 70,
    294;
    functions, and infantile sexual-
    ity, **17** (*p*5);
    and material truth, **13** 302;
    parent, Church as, **7** 172;
    and physical, **13** 76*n*;
    power, **13** 46; in hallucinations,
    1 106;
    symbols, **13** 81;
    understanding, **13** 429

spiritual, in alchemy: blood, as
    symbol, **13** 103*n*;
    fire, **13** 187*n*;
    Iliaster, *see* Paracelsus: AR-
    CANA *s.v.*;
    man, *see* man *s.v.*;
    trends of alchemy, **13** 180*n*
Spiritual Disciplines, see Eranos
    Yearbooks, Papers from
Spiritual Exercises, see Ignatius
    Loyola
spiritualism/spiritualist(-ic), **6** 279; **8**
    341, 628; **9i** 457; **10** 169, 172,
    176, 977; **11** 845, 857; **14** 765; **18**
    153, 725, 734, 740, 746, 1473;
    TITLES: "On Spiritualistic Phe-
    nomena," **18** 697–740; "Psy-
    chology and Spiritualism," **18**
    746–56; American, **18** 715,
    750;
    and automatic writing, **7** 312;
    as a collective phenomenon, **8**
    599;
    compensating significance of,
    18 750;
    dual nature of, **18** 697;
    and materialism, *see* mate-
    rialism *s.v.*;
    and mediums, *see below;*
    physical phenomena in, **18** 737,
    739, 761;
    (primitive) projection in, **10**
    137; **18** 756;
    and primitive spirits, **7** 293;
    rappings, **8** 602;
    and religious belief, **18** 697;
    and the unconscious: collective,
    contents of, **8** 599; complex, **8**
    602; personal, **8** 599;
    see also occultism; parapsychol-
    ogy; table-turning
spiritualist mediums, **1** 45, 48, 54,
    58, 82, 85, 94; **3** 174; **5** (*p*462); **11**
    857; **18** 699, 715, 722, 724,
    732–4, 738, 747;
    communications of, **10** 137;
    "controls" of, **5** 276, (*p*460); **13**
    58, 60; **18** 746; Imperator
    group, **13** 60*n*;

Cook, Florence, **1** 63;
hysterical symptoms among, **18** 725;
ionization investigations of, **18** 1498;
Miss S. W. as, **1** 36, 45–8, 54–60, 81–5, 94;
phenomena of, **8** 600; **10** 788; **13** 49;
Schneider brothers, **18** 1326;
see also Davenport brothers; Home; shaman; White, Betty
spirituality, **10** 934; **11** 51; **13** 69, 154, 229, 454;
albedo (alchemical) as, **13** 263;
of Christ, **13** 127, 455;
Eastern, **11** 773; and the West, **11** 778;
Indian, **11** 933; **14** 520;
and sensuality, as opposites, **17** 336
spiritualization, **4** 406;
alchemical, **11** 352; of body, **14** 763, 764, 773;
Christian principle of, **11** 43, 286; permanent, **14** 672;
in Mass, ritual of, **11** 307, 310, 317, 319–20, 338
spiritus, **9i** 387; **9ii** 246, 292; **13** 260; **18** 359;
aquae, **13** 173;
et corporis ligamentum, **9ii** 118;
and *corpus;* duality, **9i** 555;
creator, **12** 398;
familiaris, **14** 707 (*see also* familiar);
humidus et aereus, lapis as, **13** 137*n*;
igneus, **12** 473 (*see also* spirit (1) *s.v.* fiery);
loci, collective national attitude, **10** 972;
mercurialis, see Mercurius *s.v.*;
metallorum, see metals *s.v.* spirits of;
mundi, **8** 931; **12** 512;
niger, Saturn as, **11** 350;
phantasticus/creative fancy, **6** 174;

rector (guiding), **3** 507; **5** 543; **6** 85; **9ii** 257; **10** 556;
Sanctus, see Holy Ghost *s.v.*;
vegetativus, **9i** 386; **13** 287*n*; **14** 322 (*see also* Mercurius *s.v.* spirit);
veritatis (of truth), **11** 354;
vitae (of life), **12** 172, 518, *fig.* 109; **13** 160, 168*n*, 171*n*, 175
Spitteler, C., **6** 375, 426*n*, 448; **7** 311; **13** 209; **15** 151;
as introverted type, **6** 288;
WORKS:
Imago, **3** 355; **5** 62*n*; **7** 507; **9i** 145; **9ii** 424*n*;
"My Lady Soul," **9ii** 25; **13** 460;
Olympian Spring, **6** 325, 811; **7** 507; **14** 424; **15** 142, 147;
Prometheus and Epimetheus, **5** 362*n*; **6** 275–326, 434–7, 448–60, 706; **7** 82*n*, 507; **9i** 145; **12** 103, 160; **13** 460&*n*; **15** 154; divine, wonder-child/Messias, in, **6** 311, 435, 442, 454, 458, 459; and rejected jewel as philosopher's stone, **12** 103, 160, 514; and religious problem, **6** 324; and worship of soul, **6** 375–81; *see also* extraverted type *s.v.* Epimetheus; introverted type *s.v.* Prometheus; Pandora
spittle, **10** 146; **13** 128;
magical effect of, **5** 458; **18** 552
"Splendor solis," *see* ALCHEMICAL COLLECTIONS: *Aureum vellus s.v.* Trismosin
splinter psyches, complexes as, **8** 203–4
split/splitting:
TITLE: "Healing the Split," **18** 578–607;
between conscious and unconcious, **9ii** 390*n*; **13** 298;
of consciousness, *see* consciousness *s.v.*;
the earth, **5** 439*n*, 480, 638;

Unter den Naturvölkern Zentral-Brasiliens, **13** 253*n*
Steiner, R., **10** 170; **11** 859; **14** 124; **18** 1536
Steinerus, Henricus, *see* ALCHEMICAL WRITERS *s.v.*
Steinschneider, M.: *Die europäischen Übersetzungen aus dem arabischen bis Mitte des 17. Jahrhunderts,* **12** 116*n*, 336*n*
Steinthal, H., **4** 63&*n*, 507;
  "Die Sage von Simson," **5** 176*n*, 425*n*, 600*n*;
  "Die ursprüngliche Form der Sage von Prometheus," **5** 208*n*
Steissbart, **9i** 396
Stekel, W., **4** 129, 351*n*, 632, 639; **15** 155; **16** 36; 18 (*p*390*n*);
  on "compulsion of the name," **8** 827*n*;
  WORKS:
  "Ausgänge der psycho-analytischen Kuren," **4** 632;
  Note on Gerhart Hauptmann, **5** 460*n*;
  Nervöse Angstzustände und ihre Behandlung, J.'s review, **18** 923–4;
  Die Sprache des Traumes, **4** 645; **5** 680*n*;
  "Die Verpflichtung des Namens," **8** 827*n*;
  ed. (with A. Adler), *Zentralblatt für Psychoanalyse,* **18** 1031*n*
stella marina, see ANIMALS *s.v.* fish
stella maris, see star *s.v.* of the sea
stella matutina, see star *s.v.* morning
"Stempe," and nightmare, **5** 370&*n*
Stenia festival celebrating return of Demeter, **18** 264*n*
stepdaughter, **9i** 410
Stephanos, **14** 316*n*
Stephanos (Stephen) of Alexandria, **12** 209*n*; **14** 155*n*
Stephen, St., **9ii** 128*n*
Stephen of Canterbury: *Liber allegoricus in Habacuc,* **9ii** 174*n*

Stephens, J. L.: *Travel in Central America,* **5** 400*n*
stepmother, **9i** 140*n*, 156; **10** 70
steps, *see* stair(s)
Sterculus, **5** 547*n*
stereotypy, **3** 11, 17, 30, 32, 41&*n*, 182–93, 202, 204, 206–7, 453, 578;
  motility/motor, **3** 186, 202, 288
sterility: feeling of, **9ii** 17;
  king's, **12** 435, 491, 496;
  mental, **7** 236, 242;
  psychic, **11** 497
Stern, James, *see under* Grimm brothers
Stern, L. William, **2** 728, 759, 761; **4** 125; **8** 26; **18** 739&*n*;
  ed., *Beiträge zur Psychologie der Aussage*/"Contributions to the Psychology of Evidence," **2** 728&*n*;
  "Psychologische Tatbestandsdiagnostik," **2** 759*n*, 761*n*, (*p*491);
  Über Psychologie der individuellen Differenzen, **8** 26*n*;
  see also under F. Kramer
Stern, Ludwig: "Die koptische Apokalypse des Sophonias," **11** 431*n*
Sternberg, F. von, *see* ALCHEMICAL COLLECTIONS: *Mus. herm. s.v.* "Gloria mundi"
Stevenson, James: "Ceremonial of Hasjelti Dailjis," **9i** 240*n*; **12** *fig.* 110; **13** 31*n*
Stevenson, R. L.: Jekyll and Hyde, **14** 229
steward, unjust, **9i** 76; **10** 676; **11** 394, 416, 620*n*, 696; **13** 292
stick, twirling, **5** *fig.* 16
Sticker, G., **2** 1035, 1040, 1181;
  "Über Versuche einer objectiven Darstellung von Sensibilitätsstörungen," **2** 1040*n*, (*pp*490, 580)
stigmata/stigmatization, **12** 7, 452, *fig.* 58; **14** 530;

blood of, **13** 380–1, 390;
body/soul/spirit in, **13** 283*n*, 381;
brain-, **12** 517*n*; **14** 626;
cast on dunghill, **13** 182*n*;
-Christ parallel, *see* Christ/Jesus;
and Christ-image, **9ii** 122;
cinedian, **9ii** 213, 214;
colours of, **14** 245, 496;
cornerstone / rejected by builder, *see* Christ *s.v.*; *lapis angularis;* stone *s.v.*;
dragon's, **9ii** 214;
earthly, and Christ, **13** 384*n*;
element of, **13** 414*n*;
as feminine matter, **14** 409–10, 643;
fire from/as fire, **12** 157*n*, 451; **13** 424;
as God-image, **13** 128; **14** 643;
Heracleian, **9ii** 288&*n*;
as hermaphrodite, *see* hermaphrodite *s.v.*;
Hermetic vessel as mother of, **13** 113;
hostile/enemy, motif of, **13** 425–6;
image in, **12** 406;
incorruptibility of, **13** 94;
inner man as (Naassene), **9ii** 326;
as king's mother, **14** 410;
living, **13** 182*n*; **14** 770, 773;
transformation into, **9ii** 264; **11** 154; **12** 187, 378; **13** 286;
as macrocosm, **13** 162;
making of, **9ii** 256; as "child's play," **16** 512;
and man, *see* man *s.v.*;
as mediator, **11** 150; **13** 131;
Mercurius as, *see* Mercurius *s.v. lapis philosophorum;*
as microcosm, **5** 646*n*; **13** 437;
as monolith, **13** 113;
and mountain, *see* mountain *s.v.* in alchemy;
names of, **11** 806, 828*n*;
Nile-, **10** 629; **12** 405, 447; **13**

133;
and philosophical tree, **13** 321, 414;
physical nature of, **14** 773;
pneuma in, **12** 451;
precious, **12** 259, 284–5, 315, 379, 454, 491; **13** 321; faker of, **13** 252 (*see also* jewel);
quaternary form of, **14** 7; circle and, **9ii** 352;
quest for, **13** 394;
as *quinta essentia,* **10** 738;
red, **13** 392;
rejected, **12** 103, 514;
resurrection and, **11** 154*n*;
round white, **13** 101;
as saviour, **13** 132;
secret of/secret, **13** 90, 131, 381*n*; **14** 212, 570;
as self, *see* self *s.v.* lapis/stone;
and serpent, **9ii** 386–7;
and soul, **9i** 238*n*; **11** 153;
soul of, **14** 773;
spirit in, **12** 390, 512; and soul and body, **14** 525, 773;
"that hath a spirit" (Nile stone), **11** 151, 160*n*, 355; **12** 405, 447; **13** 133, 299*n*; **14** 245, 246*n*, 643, 770;
symbolism, **13** 125–33, 286; **14** 643; antiquity of, **14** 765*n*;
synonyms for, **13** 425;
"that is no stone," λίθος οὐ λίθος, **9i** 555; **11** 707; **12** 517*n*; **13** 381*n*, 382; **14** 626, 643, 765; **16** 492;
as total man, **11** 471;
transformation into, *see above* living;
transformation of, **9i** 238*n*;
tree as, **13** 422–5;
uncomely, **12** 246*n*, 413 (see also *lapis exilis*);
and the unconscious, **13** 289;
unity/oneness of, **9ii** 264; **13** 113, 283*n*; **14** 86, 181*n*, 294;
virgin mother of, **16** 529*n*;
as water, **12** 336&*n*;

and creation of automatism, **1** 304;
in hysterical stupor, **1** 237;
influence of darkness on, **1** 97;
negative, **3** 17–18;
normal and catatonic, **3** 160;
of somnambulists, **1** 148;
in states of partial sleep, **1** 28; **18** 893;
and unconscious orientation, **1** 285

suggestion, **4** 216, 615, 648; **7** 110, 242/463, 270, 496; **10** 141, 333; **12** 32; **13** 36; **16** 95, 231, 270, 290, **18** 702, 1386;
"Phenomena of Transitory Suggestion" (Miss Miller), **5** (*pp*447–9);
and analgesia, **1** 235;
and automatic writing, **1** 96;
and cathartic method, **4** 39;
and consciousness, **3** 59;
and constructive method, **8** 148, 150;
definition of, **18** 893;
dependent on psychological possibility, **1** 93;
and hypnosis, **1** 130, 256, 258, 272; **4** 414, 577; **15** 62; **17** 176; **18** 1579;
and hysteria, **3** 160; **4** 28, 206; **7** 4/413;
involuntary, **4** 645;
mass, *see* mass *s.v.*;
and morals, **4** 619;
and motor phenomena, **1** 82;
proneness to, **9ii** 390*n*;
psychoanalysis/analysis and, **2** 903; **4** 526, 577, 615, 652; **9i** 489; **12** 48; **16** 315–16; **17** 181;
psychotherapy and, **16** 198, 359&*n*;
and semi-somnambulism, **1** 63;
therapy, **4** 526, 577–8; **7** 2; **10** 1040; **16** 1, 3, 9–10, 20, 29–33, 238, 315; **18** 798, 1832;
and thought transference, **1** 94;

whispered, **1** 86*n*, 122;
see also auto-suggestion; counter-suggestion

suicide, **3** 571; **6** 573; **7** 192, 231, 344, 354, 386; **8** 547, 868*n*; **10** 79; **16** 344; **17** 118, 181;
attempted, **1** 32, 324, 335, 362, 403, 412, 417; **3** 306;
by drowning, water associations, **2** 744, 751–2;
during therapeutic treatment, **8** 678; **17** 260;
in fantasy, **7** 386;
as sacrifice, **5** 41*n*;
threat of, **1** 209, 219, 329, 330;
unconscious urge to, **16** 128;
wholesale, **18** 597

Suidas: *Lexicon*, ed. Ada Adler, **14** 31*n*

Sukhāvati, **11** 912

Sulamith, *see* Shulamite

sulcus primigenius, **12** 63; **13** 36; *see also* ploughed furrow

Sully, J., **6** 678;
The Human Mind, **6** 678*n*

sulphur(s), **9ii** 265; **12** 215, 401, 435*n*, 484&*n*; **13** 97, 171*n*, 176*n*, 234*n*, 268, 357; **14** 126, 134–53, 203, 235, 292&*n*, 322, 736;
alchemical symbols of, **14** 147;
as anima/soul, **9ii** 394; **14** 136, 493*n*;
and antimony, **14** 466;
as arcane substance, *see* arcane substance *s.v.*;
and arsenic, **14** 195;
Christ as, *see* Christ *s.v.*;
colours of, **14** 16*n*, 32, 110, 118, 134, 138, 140*n*, 404, 405*n*, 720, 734;
comburens/combustible, **14** 139, 183*n*, 187, 236;
devil as, **13** 276; **14** 139, 147, 153, 187, 235;
double nature/paradox of, **14** 134, 135, 139, 143, 148, 654, 720;
as dragon, **14** 135, 140&*n*;

sulphur(s) (*cont.*):
　　effects of, **14** 138;
　　as evil, **14** 32, 138, 140;
　　fiery nature of, **12** 470; **13**
　　276*n*; **14** 134&*n*, 140, 734;
　　as gold, **12** 470; **14** 467, 720,
　　725, 734, 736;
　　and green bird, **14** 136;
　　as "heart of all things," **14** 140,
　　142;
　　incombustible, **13** 177; **14** 143;
　　as life-spirit, **14** 137, 192;
　　lion and, **14** 404, 405*n*;
　　as masculine principle, **12** 470;
　　13 276;
　　as "medicina" and "medicus,"
　　14 144, 148;
　　Mercurius and, *see* Mercurius
　　s.v.;
　　and mercury, as opposites, **12**
　　436;
　　parable of, **14** 110*n*, 140, 144,
　　148, 188, 339;
　　philosophical, **9i** 537;
　　philosophorum, **12** 336, 511*n*;
　　poisonousness of, **14** 140;
　　prima materia, **12** 425;
　　and rainbow, **14** 142, 143*n*;
　　and salt, *see* salt;
　　significance of, **14** 137–8;
　　and sun/Sol, **12** *fig.* 194; **14**
　　112, 126, 134, 137, 151, 467,
　　720;
　　as transformative substance, **14**
　　143;
　　and Venus, *see* Venus (in al-
　　chemy) *s.v.*;
　　as vessel of nature, **9ii** 377*n*;
　　white, as lapis, **12** 475*n*
sulphur auratum antimonii, **14** 466–7
sulphuric acid, self-inflicted burn
　　with, **1** 305
Sumatra, *see* Bataks
Summa Fratris Reneri, **9ii** 226*n*
"Summa perfectionis," *see* ALCHEMI-
　　CAL COLLECTIONS: *Bibl. chem. cur.*
　　s.v. Geber
summa of secret knowledge, **13** 31

"Summarium philosophicum," *see*
　　ALCHEMICAL COLLECTIONS: *Mus.*
　　herm.: Flamel *s.v.* "Tractatus
　　brevis"
Summis desiderantes: Papal Bull, **18**
　　1389
"summit," *see* association-chain(s)
　　s.v.
Summum Bonum, **6** 370; **9i** 12; **10**
　　846; **11** 685; **18** 1630;
　　as Christ's father, **18** 1619;
　　and dark side, **18** 1660;
　　God as, **9ii** 80, 94; **10** 840; **11**
　　252, 470, 478, 662; **12** 547; **18**
　　1551, 1639–40, 1658, 1667;
　　natural, **13** 149;
　　spirit as, **9i** 394;
　　Three/Trinity as, **18** 1600;
　　unconscious as, **7** 394;
　　victims of, **18** 1637;
　　Yahweh as, **11** 651, 685
sums, simple, tests in, **1** 254, 333,
　　397
sun, **4** 610; **5** 140&*n*; **7** 325; **8** 388;
　　9i 252, 267, 588*n*; **12** 220; **13** 42,
　　87, 176*n*, 198, 215, 309, 317, 318,
　　341, 355, *figs.* 12, 13, 23, 32; **14** 6,
　　20*n*;
　　activation of, **13** 38;
　　in active imagination, **14** 128;
　　as active substance, **14** 110–13;
　　aging of, **5** 452;
　　all-seeing, **10** 807;
　　and anima, distinction, **12** 112;
　　as archetype, **7** 109; **9i** 409; of
　　parent, **5** 576;
　　arrows of, **5** 439;
　　in astrology, see *coniunctio s.v.*
　　Sol/Luna;
　　autumnal, as symbol of senility,
　　5 452;
　　and balsam, comparison, **13**
　　188;
　　-barge, Egyptian, **9i** 239;
　　-beam, **5** 638;
　　-Bearer, **13** 130;
　　bird as symbol of, **5** 538 (*see also*
　　below eagle);

birth of, **5** 306–7, 555, 620, *fig.* 24;

black/*Sol niger,* **9ii** 307; **12** 140, *fig.* 34; **13** 337; **14** 21*n*, 113, 117, 172, 175, 229–30, 330–2, 729; **16** 420, 468;

Brahma and, **6** 331, 332;

as bridegroom, **14** 30, 568&*n*;

Buddha Amitābha and, **11** 915, 926–9;

-bull/bull as symbol of, **5** 163*n*, 283*n*;

carbon-nitrogen cycle in, **9ii** 411;

carbuncle of, **13** 267;

in catacomb pictures, **5** 163*n*;

chariot of, **8** 326; **12** 469, *fig.* 206; **14** 267*n*;

-child(ren), **9i** 573*n*; **10** 822–4;

and Christ, *see* Christ *s.v.*;

as circle, **11** 928;

circle of the, **12** 66*n*;

condition, in alchemical opus, **12** 334;

as consciousness, *see* consciousness *s.v.*;

copper and, **14** 110;

countenance of, **12** 99;

course of, **5** 163*n*, 251, 306, 553, 577; **13** 433; *opus circulatorium* as, **12** 469; serpentine, **8** 394; and stages of life, **7** 114; **8** 326, 778, 780, 795;

crowning/coronation as identification with, **5** 133*n*; **12** 53; **13** 86*n*; **14** 519*n* (see also *solificatio*);

-day, **13** 301;

-disc, **5** 24, 133*n*, 135, 138, 143, 146–9, 159*n*, 634, pls. I*b*, VII, IX*a*; **11** 928; **12** 53; **13** 193*n*, *figs.* 17, 24; winged, **11** 177;

dragon and, **8** 394;

in dreams, **7** 189, 250/467; **10** 683, 730; **11** 90; **12** 270–1;

drowning of: in Mercurial Fountain, **9i** 246*n*; **12** 355; **16** 453; in Mercurius, **12** 436;

eagle as symbol of, **5** 633;

and earth, conjunction, **14** 734;

earthly, **14** 120;

-eating: demon, **5** pl. XXXIV; lion, *see below;*

eclipse of, **4** 255; **12** *fig.* 142V, XX; **14** 21, 23, 657;

ego personified as, **14** 129–30;

Elgonyi and, *see* Elgonyi;

evening, **7** 189;

as eye of God, **8** 394;

in fantasy, **9i** 346;

Father, **5** 135, 176; **7** 427; **18** 567, 688; of Pueblo Indians, **9i** 48, 84; **10** 138; **12** 171; **18** 16, 629, 630;

-fire, **9ii** 393; **13** 187&*n*;

and foot, **5** 486*n*;

God as, *see* God *s.v.*;

-god(s), **8** 845; **9i** 7, 106–7; **12** 66, 469; **13** 107*n*, 339*n*; **18** 266; Adityas (Indian), **13** 339; birth of, **5** 555, 620; daughter-wife of, **5** 496; Egyptian, **8** 845; Eskimo, **5** pl. I*b*; Khnum, **5** 410; sacrifice to, **5** pl. XI*a*; Samson as, **5** 176*n*; soul's return to, **12** 66; suicide of, **5** 600*n* (*see also* Apollo; Helios; Marduk; Mitra);

-goddess, **6** 436;

gold as, *see* gold *s.v.* Sol;

hands of, **5** *fig.* 7;

heavenly, in man, **11** 160;

-hero(es), **5** 158, 164, 251*n*, 282*n*, 299, 311; **7** 109; **8** 326; **9i** 7, 605; **12** 469; **14** 277; **17** 318; arrow-shots of, **5** 547*n*; battles of, **5** 374, 537; longing for, **5** 167; missing limb of, *see* Frobenius; Oleg, **5** 450*n*;

hero and, **7** 160;

hero has attributes of, **5** 283*n*, 297;

identification with, **5** 133*n*, 268, 283*n* (*see also above* crowning);

-idol, **5** *fig.* 4;

as illumination/understanding,

648

symbol(s) (*cont.*):

ism," **9ii** 267–86; "Christ, a Symbol of the Self," **9ii** 68–126; "Conceptions and Symbols of the Goal," **12** 335–41; "Concerning Mandala Symbolism," **9i** 627–712; "Contributions to Symbolism," **18** 1082–3; "Dogma and Natural Symbols," **11** 56–107; "The Function of Religious Symbols," **18** 560–77; "General Remarks on Symbolism," **11** 280–5; "Gnostic Symbols of the Self," **9ii** 287–346; "The History and Psychology of a Natural Symbol," **11** 108–68; "Individual Dream Symbolism in Relation to Alchemy," **12** 44–331; "Individual Representations of the Tree Symbol," **13** 304–49; "On the History and Interpretation of the Tree Symbol," **13** 350–482; "The Relation of the King-Symbol to Consciousness," **14** 498–513; "The Stone Symbolism," **13** 126–33; "The Symbolism of the Mandala," **12** 122–331; "Symbols and the Interpretation of Dreams," **18** 416–607; "Symbols of the Mother and of Rebirth," **5** 300–418; "The Symbols of the Self," **12** 323–31; *Symbols of Transformation,* vol. **5**; "Transformation Symbolism in the Mass," **11** 296–448; "The Water Symbolism," **13** 134–8;

and allegory, distinguished, **3** 136; **5** 114, 329; **8** 644; **9i** 7&*n*; **9ii** 127; **14** 677;

as analogies of sexual instinct, **5** 338;

and analogy, **6** 93*n*; **7** 492–3; **14** 667; **16** 215;

antinomial/paradoxical, **11** 277;

archaic, **7** 241/462;

archetypal, **5** 447; **13** 350, 395, 397&*n*, 481; **14** 669;

archetype and, **13** 395; **16** 342;

assimilation of Christ through, *see* Christ *s.v.* assimilation;

as assimilation phenomena, **9ii** 295;

autochthonous, **6** 193;

autonomy of, **5** 600*n*; **9ii** 59;

belief in, and understanding of, **5** 342;

of beloved, **5** 619;

bisexual, **4** 481;

as bridges and pointers, **5** 510;

-carriers, **6** 305;

cause and, **8** 46;

and centring process, **16** 219;

choice of, **7** 129, 139;

coitus-, **3** 285;

collective, **5** 447; **7** 384; **13** 395; in dreams, *see* dream symbols *s.v.* collective; in schizophrenia, **3** 527;

of collective unconscious, **18** 81;

combination of, **6** 459;

comparative research into, **13** 352–3, 463; **14** 275;

compensating, **13** 397; **16** 252;

of complexes, **3** 101, 117;

as comprehension by analogy, **4** 553;

and consciousness, **6** 204;

contrasexual, **13** 458;

convincingness of, **11** 167;

cosmogonic, **12** 30;

creation of, *see* function *s.v.* symbol-creating;

delusions and, **3** 527;

derived from archaic residues / engrams / functioning, **6** 405–6; **16** 253;

dhvaja as, **11** 930;

dissolution of, **6** 401; **8** 148;

dogmatic, **9i** 18;

dual nature of, **16** 398;

ecclesiastical, **10** 700; **16** 471

(*see also* Christianity; Church;

religious symbols);
effect of, emotional, **4** 490;
elaboration of, **9i** 12;
ethnic, **4** 457;
ethnological, **13** 134;
of everything psychic, **5** 77;
explanation of, **7** 341;
as expression of projections, **14** 678;
fantasy images as, **14** 772;
feminine, **16** 518&*n*;
fixed, **16** 340–1;
-formation, *see sep. entry below;*
functional meaning / importance of, *see* function(s) *s.v.* of symbols;
hermeneutic significance of, **7** 492–3;
Hermetic, **13** 289;
historical, **7** 132; and personal, **5** 2;
history of, **3** 526; **8** 931; **9ii** 278; **13** 470; **17** 198;
as images of unconscious contents, **5** 114;
Indian, **9ii** 271;
interpenetration of, **11** 125–6;
interpretation of, **4** 673, 677; **18** 519; causal *vs.* final, **8** 471;
sexual, **10** 653;
knowledge of, needed, **16** 44;
life-promoting significance of, **6** 202–3;
magic of, **13** 44;
mana, **16** 340;
of manners, **18** 35;
meanings of, **13** 397; for alchemists, **14** 677; diametrically opposed, **9ii** 200; diverse, not uniform/fixed, **8** 471; **16** 341; multiple, **14** 634;
as mediator between opposites, **6** 178, 211, 824 (*see also* opposites, union of);
migration of, **8** 228; **11** 781;
multiplicity of, **16** 398;
mythological, **5** 659*n*; **16** 19; **18** 551;

natural, **11** 435, 824; *vs.* cultural, **18** 578; self as, **16** 474;
as natural products, **18** 480;
nature of, **12** 400;
need for, **5** 342; **16** 345;
neurotic, ambiguity of, **10** 360;
never simple, **11** 385;
in non-objective art, **15** 206–10, 213;
not derived from personal sources, **6** 405;
numinosity of, **11** 337*n*; **14** 514; **18** 579;
objective and subjective aspects, **11** 383*n*;
at onset of transference, **16** 381;
of opposite sex, **9ii** 19;
Oriental, **18** 139;
origin of, **5** 201;
overdetermined, **11** 723;
overlappings in, **14** 454;
parable and, **15** 105;
paradoxical, *see above* antinomial;
and *participation mystique,* **11** 337*n*;
in patients' paintings, **16** 111;
pictorial, and psychology, **9ii** 304;
positive and negative, **16** 496;
poverty/impoverishment of, **9i** 11, 23, 28, 50;
is primitive exponent of unconscious, **13** 44;
production, **13** 395;
prospective meaning, **4** 674;
and psyche, its effect on, **6** 455;
psychological truth of, **5** 343;
psychological understanding of, **14** 667, 680;
quaternary, **13** 457; in dreams, *see* dream symbols *s.v.* quaternary;
rational and irrational contained in, **10** 24;
reality of, **6** 202, 211;
of rebirth, **9i** 235;

symbol(s) (*cont.*):

redeeming, **6** 365, 435–43, 445–7, 453, 458;

relation to, **6** 205;

relativity of, **6** 375–433;

religious, *see* religious symbols;

replacing experience, **11** 75;

representing deified man, **11** 158;

representing the organs, **15** 166*n*;

sacred, **17** 310;

sacrificial, **5** 671; **11** 339;

of saviour, **13** 133;

in schizophrenia, **3** 25, 30, 387, 390; **4** 456–7;

shamanistic, **13** 462;

as shaped energies, **6** 425;

and sign, differentiated, **5** 114, 180, 329; **6** 93*n*, 201, 788, 814; **7** 492; **8** 88, 644; **9ii** 127; **10** 637*n*; **15** 105; **16** 339, 362; **18** 482;

as spirit from above, **9i** 50;

spiritual, **13** 81;

spontaneous and prescribed, **11** 854;

of starry heaven, **13** 114;

study of, **18** 607;

subjectivity of, **5** 13*n*;

and symbolic evaluation, **8** 148;

symbolic substitution, **6** 201;

taking refuge in, **18** 648, 649;

ternary, **11** 284;

tradition and, **11** 165;

as transformers of libido, **5** 344;

triadic/trinitarian, **5** 294*n*; **9ii** 382*n*; **11** 172, 284;

two meanings of, **4** 539, 674–7;

typos as, **12** 20;

unconscious, **6** 182–3, 204;

unconscious archetype and conscious mind in, **5** 344;

unconscious as matrix/producer of, **12** 516–17; **18** 603, 637;

of unconscious processes, **11** 779;

unconscious represented by, **11** 810;

of unity, **9ii** 59; mandala as, **12** 32 (*see also* uniting symbol);

use of, in assimilating unconscious contents, **5** 468;

value and purpose of, **5** 336; **6** 204, 212; **7** 492;

vessel as, in alchemy, **12** 338–9;

in visions of saints, **4** 72;

wide range of meanings, **5** 238;

world itself speaks in, **9i** 291;

see also alchemical symbols; dream symbols; libido-symbols; mother, symbols of; phallic symbolism; sexual symbols; uniting symbols;

see also under animal(s); arcane substance; baptism; blood in alchemy; centre; Christ; Christianity; Church/Ecclesia; Church (Catholic); circle; city; *coniunctio;* cross; death; dogma; energy; father; fertility; function(s); Gnostic(ism); goal; God; god(s); individuation; initiation; instinct; jewel; Joyce; lapis; light; mandala; Mass; Mercurius; Mithras; number(s); opposites, union of; perfection; personality; plants; primitive; Prometheus; psychology; sea; self; semiotic; soul; spirit; stone, alchemical; theriomorphic; totality; transformation; tree; water; wheel; wholeness;

for other INSTANCES *see* altar; ANIMALS: bull, crab, dragon, fish, horse, lion, octopus, serpent, tiger, toad, unicorn, uroboros; arrow; bridge; cathedral; child; earth; fire; flame; foot; ford; geometry; giant; Grail; head; hoard; ivory figure; king; lightning; lingam; log; lozenge; magician; mountain; music; ogdoad; priest; quadrangle; quaternity; ring;

T

Tabarī (Muhammad ibn Jarīr Abu-Jafar al Tabarī): *Chronique,* **9ii** 133*n*, 168*n*; **14** 552;
 commentary on Koran, **5** 282, 285
tabernacles, three, **12** 478
Tabernaemontanus, Jacobus Theodorus: *Kräuterbuch/Herbal,* **13** 171*n*, 190*n*, 193*n*; **14** 157*n*, 158, 683*nn*
Tabit ibn Qurra, **14** 170
table: as dream-symbol, **8** 539–40; **11** 90, 109;
 four footed, see *tetrapeza;*
 round, **11** 109, 418; **12** 238, 241, 242*n*, 260;
 symbol of self, **16** 378
table-turning, **8** 602; **10** 21; **18** 699, 702, 704, 715, 725–7, 730–1;
 automatic movement of, **1** 81–106, 126;
 in semi-somnambulism, **1** 44, 80–95, 126;
 unconscious control of, **1** 82
Tableau des riches inventions, see ALCHEMICAL WRITERS: Colonna *s.v.* Béroalde de Verville
taboo(s), **4** 565; **8** 415; **11** 30; **13** 81, 128; **17** 23*a*;
 area, **12** 63, 105, 295 (see also *temenos*);
 and evolutionary instinct, **5** 653;
 incest-, *see* incest *s.v.*;
 infringement of, **7** 239, 243*n*
Tabor, Mount, **12** 540, 545; **18** 1524
Tabula chymica, see ALCHEMICAL WRITERS: Senior (Zadith) *s.v.*
Tabula smaragdina, see ALCHEMICAL WRITERS: Hermes Trismegistus *s.v.*
Tachenius, Otto, *see* Crasselame
tachypnoea, **1** 40
Tacitus, **9ii** 129;

Germania, **7** 296&*n*;
 Historiae/The Histories, tr. W. H. Fyfe, **5** 622*n*; **9ii** 129*n*; **18** 1521
Tages, the Etruscan, **5** 291*n*, 527
Tagus river, **18** 251
Tahmurath, **5** 421*n*
T'ai I Chin Hua Tsung Chi, see R. Wilhelm *s.v. The Secret of the Golden Flower*
tail: -eater, *see* ANIMALS: uroboros;
 of serpent, *see* ANIMALS: serpent *s.v.*
Taine, H., **6** 966
Taittirīya Āranyaka, see Āranyaka
Taittirīya Brāhmana, see Brāhmanas
Taittirīya Samhita, see Samhita
Taittirīya Upanishad, see Upanishads
T'ai-yüan Sheng-mu (Holy Mother), **14** 573, 576*n*
Taj Mahal, **10** 990, 992
Talbot, P. A., **13** 247;
 In the Shadow of the Bush, **6** 397*n*; **13** 247*n*
talents, parable of the, **9ii** 255
talisman(s), **13** 154;
 magic, **7** 261/477; **9i** 404
talkativeness, **1** 194, 198, 208, 210, 212, 216
talking/talk: Americans and, **10** 954;
 compulsive, **1** 184;
 imprudent, **8** 628;
 irrelevant, **8** 22 (*see also* answer *s.v.* irrelevant)
"talking cure"/"talking it away," **3** 145; **7** 5/414
Talleyrand, C. M. de, **8** 198
Talmud, Babylonian, **9ii** 139; **11** 41, 406*n*; **12** 540–6&*nn*; **14** 338*n*, 552*n*, 592*n*; **18** 172, 569;
 and astrology, **9ii** 135;
 on fishes, **9ii** 133, 178, 180;
 and prophecy of 530 years, **9ii** 133, 168, 232;
 Berakoth/Berachoth, **9ii** 106*n*,

658

Tarot cards, **9i** 81

Tarpeian Rock (Rome), **14** 483; **18** 258

tartar, **9i** 537

tartaric: acid, **9i** 537, 575; water, **14** 691

Tartarus/Tartarum, **5** 265; **9i** 535*n*, 537*n*; **14** 683, 691; underworld (alchemical), **9i** 537, 575; **14** 687, 703, 757; see also *sal*/salt *s.v.* Tartarus; *Sal Saturni*

Tarxien, **9i** *fig.* 4 (*par.* 564)

Tathāgata, *see* Buddha *s.v.*

Tatian, **9ii** 81; *Oratio ad Graecos*, **9ii** 81*n*

tat tvam asi, **6** 189; **15** 188

tau: aleph and, **13** 271; signa Thau, *see* cross *s.v.* sign of

Tauroktonos/tauroctony/Taurophoria, *see* Mithras: bull-sacrifice *s.v.*

Taurus, *see* zodiac, twelve signs of

Tausk, V., **18** (*p*433*n*), 1055–64

Tav, **13** 363*n*

Tavistock Clinic (Institute of Medical Psychology), **18** (*p*566*n*); TITLE: "The Tavistock Lectures," **18** 1–415

Tavistock Institute of Human Relations, **18** (*p*606*n*)

taxi, in dreams, **12** 227, 256

Taylor, F. S., **14** 370*n*; "A Survey of Greek Alchemy," **11** 159*n*; **12** 404*n*

Taylor, H. O., **6** 58; *The Mediaeval Mind*, **6** 58*n*

Taylor, T., *see* Plato: *Timaeus s.v.*; Porphyry: *De antro nympharum;* Proclus: Commentaries

teacher/teaching, **11** 453; **17** 107a–10; and analytical psychology, **17** 108, 142; attitude of, **17** 233; as child's love-object, **4** 462, 468–73, 504, 515–18; as dream-figure, **4** 95–128; **9i**

398; and gifted child, **17** 232–3, 236, 240, 243, 246–7, 249; influence of, **2** 1007; J.'s, **17** 232–3, 246; personality of, **17** 107a, 211, 249; psychological knowledge of, **17** 100, 108, 142, 211, 237; self-education of, *see* education *s.v.* educator; and shadow, **18** 1160

team-spirit, **18** 1350–1, 1353–4

tear-drop, Ufo as, **10** 628*n*

tearing to pieces, **5** 316*n*

tebuna/Tebhunah, understanding/ intelligence, **9i** 576*n*; **9ii** 185

Tecenensis, *see* ALCHEMICAL WRITERS: *Theatr. chem. s.v.* Guilhelmus Tecenensis

technical terms, **3** 208, 223, 303

technics, *see* technology

technique(s): TITLE: "Techniques of Attitude Change Conducive to World Peace," **18** 1388–1402; analysis as, **7** 502; of concentration, **7** 366; differentiation of, **8** 731; of educating anima, **7** 323; Freudian, *see* Freud *s.vv.* psychoanalytic method; transference technique; medical, **16** 3; modern, **11** 778; pedagogic, **17** 284; principles of, **16** 99; psychoanalytic, *see* psychoanalysis *s.v.*; psychotherapy and, *see* psychotherapy *s.v.*; religious, **16** 3; spiritual, Eastern, **11** 773; and treatment, **17** 171–2, 203, 240; *see also* method

technology/technics, **10** 624; **11** 443, 444; **13** 84, 163;

661

tension (*cont.*):
    bodily, **8** 609;
    and circular movement, **12** 131, 188, 273, 286;
    conscious/unconscious, **9ii** 40;
    discharge of, *see* abreaction;
    emotional, **10** 608;
    father-son, **11** 204, 241;
    in *I Ching* hexagrams, **11** 996;
    of opposites, *see* opposites, tension of;
    problems and, **8** 757;
    of psychic energy, *see* energy;
    release of latent, **17** 207;
    signified by Christ's advent, **9ii** 78;
    in uroboros, **9ii** 391
tentacles, **9ii** 196
"ten thousand things," **13** 301
teoqualo, see American Indians: NORTH *s.v.* Aztec(s)
Terah, **5** 515
teraphim, **11** 368
Terebinthos, **14** 31
Terence: *Heauton Timorumenos,* **18** 91*n*
Teresa of Avila, Saint, **10** 883; **14** 421, 565*n*
terminology: arcane, **13** 157, 169, 231;
    avoidance of abstract, **7** 340;
    ecclesiastical, **13** 194;
    sexual, *see* sexual *s.v.*;
    see also language
terminus ani, Mercurius as, **13** 269
ternarius, **12** 165; **13** 187*n*; **14** 41; **16** 525*n*;
    Adam and, **14** 554;
    Mercurius, *see* Mercurius *s.v.* threefold
ternary: symbols, **11** 284;
    systems, **12** 123
terra, **14** 404, 729;
    alba foliata, **12** 334; **13** 255*n*; **14** 154&*n*, 264, 319, 626, 630*n*;
    damnata, **14** 319, 729;
    nigra, **14** 264;
    see also earth

terrena (alchemical), **8** 559
Terrible Mother, *see* Mother, Terrible
terror, **8** 609;
    motif of, **12** 118
Tersteegen, G.: *Geistliches Blumengärtlein inniger Seelen,* **14** 196*n*
tertium, **13** 199;
    comparationis, **5** 329, 422; and archetypes, **8** 964; in dream, **18** 853; Gnosticism as, **18** 1482;
    non datur, **6** 66, 68, 169, 790; **7** 116; **9ii** 280; **11** 738;
    see also NUMBERS: three *s.v.* third
Tertullian, **5** 30, 163, 321; **6** 16–21, 23–9, 33, 75; **9ii** 70, 129; **11** 214*n*, 216, 379&*n*, 550, 771, 779*n*; **12** 18, 19, 24, 520, 524; **13** 81; **14** 423; **15** 195; **17** 310;
    introverted thinking of, **6** 19–20;
    sacrificium intellectus of, **6** 19–20, 24–6;
    on souls, *see* soul(s) *s.v.*;
    symbolism for Mary, mother of God, *see* Mary *s.v.* earth/field;
    WORKS:
        Adversus Judaeos, **6** 395*n*; **11** 107*n*, 727*n*; **12** 192*n*, 520*n*;
        Adversus Marcionem, **9ii** 70*n*, 147*n*;
        Apologeticus adversus gentes pro Christianis/Apologia, **5** 163*n*; **9i** 463*n*; **9ii** 129*n*; **11** 656&*n*; **12** 14*n*;
        De baptismo, **9ii** 175*n*;
        De carne Christi, **6** 17&*n*; **12** 18*n*;
        De praescriptione hereticorum, **18** 1528;
        Treatises on Marriage and Remarriage, tr. W. P. Le Saint, **14** 423*n*;
        The Writings of Tertullian, tr. E. Evans, **6** 18*n*
test(s): arithmetic, in case of simulated insanity, **1** 333–5;

for intelligence, **17** 213, 224; psychological, **9i** 111; for thinking and feeling, **17** 224

"Testament of Adam," **14** 556*n*

"Testamentum," *see* ALCHEMICAL COLLECTIONS: *Mus. herm. s.v.* Cremer

testis, meaning, **5** 583*n*

testudo, **12** 203*n*

teth (Hebrew letter), **14** 637&*n*

Tethys, **9ii** 340*n*; **14** 18*n*, 50

tetrad, **8** 870; **9ii** 298, 307*n*; as archetypal structure, **9i** 436; God/name of God as, **14** 619; **18** 1611; second, Valentinian (Gnostic) and Jesus, **13** 366; and synchronicity factor, **8** 961; system: in astrology, **8** 866; in mandalas, **9i** 644, 646

tetragrammaton (name of God) **8** 931; **9i** 579; **14** 619&*n*; **16** 497*n*; *see also* God *s.v.* name; quaternity; tetrad

tetraktys, **12** 220; **13** *fig.* A7; Christ as, **13** 366; and demiurge, **11** 92; psychic, **11** 95; Pythagorean, **6** 791&*n*; **9i** 641; **10** 805; **11** 61, 90, 246; **12** 189; **13** 31, 367; as dream symbol, **11** 90–1&*n*

tetrameria/quartering/τετραμερεῖν, **9i** 552, 581; **9ii** 410; **12** 210*n*, 333; **13** 89*n*; **14** 1*n*, 552, 619; **16** 404; of circle, **12** 283; opus as, **9i** 564; **14** 261; and pseudo-Clement, **9ii** 401; trimeria and, **14** 619

tetramorph: Anthropos as, **12** *fig.* 65; **14** 573*n*; four evangelists as, **5** pl. LX; **9ii** 69; **11** 62*n*, 126, 690; **13** 365; **14** 285; "riding animal," steed of the Church, **11** 97; **12** 139*n*,*fig.* 53; **13** 366

tetrapeza/τετραπεζα/table/platform on four pillars, **10** 751; **11** 97; **12** 139

Tetrarch of Palestine, **18** 241

tetrasomia, **13** 109*n*, 355*n*, 357, 358–68; in Greek alchemy, **13** 357; **14** 136*n*

Tetzen, Johannes de: *Processus de lapide philosophorum,* **14** 624*n*

Teuton(s)/Teutonic: barbarians, **13** 69; conception of the fates, **5** 371; mythology, **13** 417

Teutschen, **4** 354

Teutschenthal, **10** 382

Tewekkul-Beg, initiation, visions during, **6** 47

text(s), magic, **13** 437

textual criticism, **14** 457

Tezcatlipoca, **13** 107*n*

Thabit ibn Qurrah, **9ii** 193

Thabritius, *see* Gabricus

thalamus, **14** 19

Thales of Miletus, **9ii** 243, 311; **12** 206–8, 527&*n*; **13** 420*n*

thanks, giving, **11** 222

Tharthataoth, **14** 575

Thau, *see* tau

Thauthabaoth, **14** 575

Thayer, E., **18** (*p*654*n*)

theatre, as public solution of private complexes, **5** 48

Theatrum chemicum, see ALCHEMICAL COLLECTIONS *s.v.*

Theatrum chemicum Britannicum, see ALCHEMICAL COLLECTIONS *s.v.*

Thebes, **5** 264, 306, 358*n*; **14** 85; jackal-headed Anubis, **5** pl. XXXIIa; vase-painting, **5** 183*n*, 184,*fig.* 14

theft/thieves, **1** 324, 341, 344; in alchemical text, **14** 187, 194, 202–4; charges of, **1** 211–19, 227; Christ and, *see* Christ *s.v.* crucifixion;

theft (*cont.*):
  conviction for, **1** 342, 362, 364, 366;
  delusions of, **1** 229, 249–50, 252, 283;
  discovery through feeling-toned complex, **1** 478–80, 483–4;
  and lying/shamming, **1** 303, 305;
  nurse suspected of, **2** 957–81, 1332–44;
  young man suspected of, **2** 769–92, 907;
  see also evidence, psychological diagnosis of
thema, **9ii** 212
Themis, **5** 119*n*
Thenaud, Jean: "Traité de la cabale," **12** *figs.* 6, 74
theocracy, **10** 463; **16** 222;
  totalitarian claims of, **11** 83
Theocritus, **5** 438*n*
Theodore Bar-Kuni/Konai, **9ii** 307; **14** 21*n*;
  Inscriptiones mandaites des coupes de Khouabir, **9ii** 307*n*
Theodore of Mopsuestia, **11** 334;
  ed. A. Rücker, *Ritus baptismi et missae . . . ,* **11** 334*n*
Theodore Psalter, **12** *fig.* 206
Theodore the Studite, **13** 407*n*; **14** 181*n*, 701*n*
Theodoret, **12** 470*n*;
  Haereticarum fabularum compendium, **14** 31*n*
Theodosius II, **9i** 242*n*
Theologia, **13** 148*n*
Theologia Germanica, anon., **9ii** 144; **11** 886
theologian(s), **11** 532; **12** 6*n*, 13–14, 19, 33, 247; **13** 356;
  co-operation with, **11** 449, 453–6, 462;
  and the psyche, **14** 273;
  young, dream of, **7** 287; **9i** 70–7; **17** 208–9
theological student, case of, **7** 287

Theologoumenon, **18** 1688
theology, **4** 780; **11** 285; **13** 148*n*, 298; **17** 127; **18** 611;
  development of, **14** 669;
  of lapis, **12** 512;
  philosophy and, **11** 834;
  and primordial images, **18** 1616;
  psychology and, **12** 21; **18** 834, 1616, 1686, 1688;
  psychotherapy and, **11** 450, 512;
  rationalistic, and cult of the hero, **5** 259;
  Theologia, **13** 148*n*
theophany, **13** 98*n*; **14** 648
Theophilus of Antioch: *Ad autolycum/Three Books to Autolycus,* tr. B. P. Pratten *et al.,* **9ii** 81; **14** 568*n*
Theophrastus, **5** 316*n*; **8** 927; **9ii** 218, 347; **11** 400; **13** 154, 165;
  school, **13** 166
theoria/θεωρια, **9i** 297; **12** 403*n*; **16** 218*n*, 245*n*; **17** 162;
  of alchemists, *see* opus, alchemical *s.v.* two parts of
Theorica (Paracelsus), **15** 41
theorizing, **16** 218
theory(-ies), **11** 81;
  aetiological, **13** 464;
  and analysis, **17** 181;
  building of, **7** 340;
  of complexes, *see* complex(es) *s.v.*;
  and dream analysis, **16** 318;
  fixed, **17** 173;
  function of, in psychology, **17** (*p*7);
  incorrect, substituted for correct, **17** 25;
  intellectual, **17** 172;
  lack of, in psychoanalysis, **4** 319;
  lack of psychological value, **11** 81;
  meaning of, **16** 245*n*;
  modifications, needed in therapy, **16** 78;

old, alive in unconscious, **17**
44;
of psychotherapist, **17** 202;
and psychotherapy, **16** 198;
sexual, **13** 467;
statistical, **10** 493
Theosebeia, *see* ALCHEMICAL
WRITERS: Zosimus *s.v.*
theosophy / theosophical(-ists), **4**
749; **6** 279, 594; **7** 118, 339, 385,
494; **8** 92, 110, 737; **9i** 28, 471;
10 21, 169, 172, 176, 181, 187,
190; **11** 859, 863; **12** 126; **13** 3;
18 1287;
Indian, **9i** 572; **13** 342, 345; **15**
90;
primitive projection in, **18** 756;
thinking, **6** 594
Theotokos/Θεοτόκος, **11** 251, 252,
469; **14** 237, 744*n*;
in Egypt, **11** 197;
excluded from patriarchal
formula, **11** 198;
Mary as, *see* Mary *s.v.* Mother of
Christ
Therapeutai, *see* Essenes
therapeutic: effect, **13** 66;
method, **13** (*p*4)
therapist: belief of, **16** 4;
character of, **18** 1071;
need of convictions in, **16** 179;
as partner in development, **16**
7;
see also analyst; doctor
therapy, **7** 19/431; **15** 29, 33, 41;
aims of, **16** 81, 479;
analytical, **7** 236 (*see also*
analysis; analytical psychology;
psychoanalysis);
anima and, **9i** 146;
Freud's, *see* Freud *s.v.*;
of neuroses, *see* neurosis *s.v.*
treatment;
occupational, **3** 540;
principles of, **16** 66;
psychotherapeutic view of, **16**
192, 199;
rational, **16** 21–2;

real beginning of, **7** 88;
see also method(s); psychotherapy; treatment
Thereniabin, *see* Paracelsus: ARCANA
s.v.
Therese of Konnersreuth (Therese
Neumann), **18** 1497&*n*
Theriaca, **14** 21*n*
theriomorphic: constellations, **5**
145;
deity, **5** 144;
elements in religion, **5** 89&*n*;
representations of libido, **5** 24,
261;
symbols, **5** 261, 492, 505; **9i**
315; **9ii** 291; **10** 681; **11** 276;
13 228*n*; **14** 2–4, 175, 178, 205,
269, 408, 427; as unconscious
manifestations of libido, **5** 261
theriomorphism: and unconscious
functions, **14** 269;
and the unconscious self, **9ii**
224
thesaurus thesaurum, **13** 414
Theseus, and Peirithous, **5** 449*n*,
468, 654, 671*n*; **12** 438; **16** 138
Thesmophorion(-ia), **5** 530; **18**
264*n*
Thessalonians, First, Second, Epistles to, *see* BIBLE: N.T. *s.v.*
Theutius, **13** 278; *see also* Thoth
Thibout, G.: *La Cathédrale de Strasbourg*, **5** pl. XXXVII
Thiele, G.: *Antike Himmelsbilder*, **5**
460*n*; **9ii** 147*n*
Thierfelsenburg, Elisabeth von
(somnambulistic personality), **1**
54, 63
thieves, *see* theft/thieves
thing(s): -in-itself, **13** 82;
inner, **13** 63;
magical claim of, **13** 65;
new, **13** 18–19;
simple, **13** 117
thinking, **5** 113; **6** 830–3 (Def.); **7**
156, 373, 473, 482; **9ii** 61; **11**
240, 421–2; **16** 486;
TITLE: "Two Kinds of Think-

866*n*; **9ii** 153*n*, 154*n*, 159*n*; **11**
367*n*; **14** 626*n*
Thorpe, B.: *Analecta Anglo-Saxonica*,
14 552*n*
Thoth, **5** 401*n*; **12** 409;
  and Adam, first man, **11** 94*n*;
  12 456*n*, 458; four elements as,
  13 126;
  and Hermes/Hermes Tris-
  megistus, **9i** 79; **12** 173, 175,
  458, *fig.* 68; **13** 261, 278;
  and Mercurius, identified, **13**
  261, 278; **14** 416
thought(s), **6** 834 (Def.); **7** 507; **8**
  580; **11** 183, 226; **13** 46; **18** 553;
  birds a symbol of, **6** 458; **12**
  305; **13** 321, 338;
  as brain secretions, **8** 658;
  cessation of, **13** 433;
  Chinese, *see* China/Chinese *s.v.*
  thinking;
  -complex, *see* complex(es) *s.v.*;
  creative, **7** 292;
  deprivation, **3** 56, 109, 161,
  175&*n*, 179, 186, 215, 217–18,
  256, 288, 310; **8** 22;
  disturbance, schizophrenic, **3**
  434;
  divine, **5** 67;
  dream-, *see* dream *s.v.*;
  -feelings, **7** 473;
  -figures, **13** 47;
  -forms: in Bardo state, **11** 850;
  universal/archaic, **7** 104; **11**
  782–3;
  identity with, **7** 323; **13** 338;
  Indians and, *see* India(n) *s.v.*;
  and language, **5** 12–16;
  libido and, **6** 183;
  location of, **8** 669–70; in belly,
  6 963; **8** 669; **18** 15;
  as objects of inner perception,
  9i 69; **11** 81;
  -patterns, collective/inherited,
  7 219; **18** 539 (*see also* arche-
  type(s) *s.v.* patterns);
  primordial, **9i** 89;
  -processes: feeling-toned, **1**

  423; in somnambulism, **1** 98;
  -reading and table-turning, **1**
  82, 94, 138, 147;
  reality of, **6** 202; **8** 747; **11** 280,
  768, 850;
  and religion, **9i** 140*n*; **13** 68;
  repressed, **1** 132–3; **17** 185;
  "saving," **7** 254;
  sexualization of, **3** 435;
  subliminal, **7** 520; **17** 199;
  "thing-likeness" of, **6** 62;
  train of: and attention, **1** 119*n*;
  feeling-toned, disappearance
  of from conscious mind, **1** 169;
  transcerebral, **8** 957;
  -transference, **1** 44, 147; **8** 319;
  unknown to ego, **8** 613;
  world of, **13** 338–9;
  see also thinking
Thoyth(os), **12** 456&*n*
Thrace, **11** 194
Thracian riders, **9ii** 127
thread, ball of, **9i** 404*n*
threads, rain of, and Ufos, **10** 667*n*,
  668
three/threefold/threeness/third, *see*
  NUMBERS *s.v.*
365 steps, motif of, **5** 572, 577
threshold: of consciousness, *see* consciousness *s.v.*;
  psychophysical, **8** 354*n*
thriller(s), vogue for, **10** 408
throat: lump in, **8** 303;
  snake stuck in, **5** 585
throne: Christ's, **13** 366;
  crystal, **12** 315, 322
throwing upward, **5** 487
Thucydides, **16** 414*n*
Thumb, A., **2** 564;
  and K. Marbe: *Experimentelle
  Untersuchungen über die
  psychologischen Grundlagen der
  sprachlichen Analogiebildung*, **2**
  564&*n*, (*p*271)
thumb, "no bigger than," **5** 178,
  550; *see also* fairytales, INSTANCES:
  Germany *s.v.* Tom Thumb
thunder: -bolt, **9i** 636; **10** 848; **13**

thunder (*cont.*):
  fig. A2;
    -horse, *see* ANIMALS: horse *s.v.*;
    storm(s), **5** 421; **13** 340*n*; in
    dream, **4** 506–9
Thurneisser zum Thurn, *see* AL-
  CHEMICAL WRITERS *s.v.*
Thury, Professor, *see* Cassini
Thutmosis I, **14** 350*n*
Thutmosis III, **11** 197*n*
Thyatira, **11** 703
Thyestes, **6** 43&*n*
Thymopsyche, **3** 33, 35
thyroid gland, **8** 794
Thysia, **11** 302, 304, 307, 319, 324,
  346, 403
Tiamat (Babylonian mother-
  dragon), **5** 375–8, 380, 383; **9ii**
  185; **11** 173; **12** 26, 29; **14** 482*n*;
  18 234;
    chaos of, **12** 31; **13** 286;
    and Marduk, **5** 646, *fig.* 41;
    maternal world of, **13** 283;
    slaying of, **5** 646
Tibet(an), **5** 354; **7** 326; **9i** 564,
  680*n*; **10** 190, 1002; **11** 484;
    *Book of the Dead, see Bardo
    Thödol;*
    Buddhism, *see* Buddhism *s.v.*;
    legend of hero and arrow-
    shots, **5** 547*n*;
    philosophy, **18** 204;
    world-wheel (*sidpe-korlo*), *see*
    wheel(s) *s.v.* world
Tibetan Book of the Great Liberation,
  J.'s commentary, **11** 759–830
Tibullus, **6** 488&*n*
tics, **3** 187; **10** 965;
    hysterical, **1** 340;
    symbolic, **16** 13;
    see also Meige and Feindel
tie, personal, **7** 216
Tiepolo, Giambattista, **15** 176
Tifereth/Tiphereth, **9ii** 425; **10**
  779; **13** 411; **14** 18, 327, 568, 592,
  604*n*, 634*n*, 635; **16** 497*n*; **18**
  1672
tiger, *see* ANIMALS *s.v.*

Tightrope Walker, *see* Nietzsche:
  Zarathustra s.v. visions
Tigris, **9ii** 311
Tikkanen, J. J.: *Die Psalterillustration
  im Mittelalter,* **12** *figs.* 176, 247
Tikkune Zohar, **14** 158*n*
Tiling, T., **1** 220; **3** 72;
    "Die Moral Insanity beruht auf
    einem excessiv sanguinischen
    Temperament," **1** 220*n*;
    *Individuelle Geistesentartung und
    Geistesstörung,* **3** 72*n*;
    "Zur Aetiologie der Geistes-
    störungen," **3** 72*n*
Till Eulenspiegel, **7** 47
Timaeus, see Plato
time, **8** 958; **9i** 316, 356; **11** 118; **15**
  81–3;
    in association experiments, **8**
    22;
    astronomical determination of,
    13 285;
    consciousness, **1** 24;
    and creation, **8** 967*n*;
    and eternity, **12** 318;
    and fourth dimension, **8** 962;
    machine, **10** 738*n*; **18** 54;
    mind's own, **11** 815;
    multi-dimensionality of, **8**
    962*n*;
    in mythology, **5** 425–6;
    one-dimensionality of, **8** 962;
    our, **13** 51;
    of perfection, **13** 214*n*, 227;
    and place, **12** 283, 285;
    primeval *alcheringa,* **13** 130*n*;
    psychic in origin, **8** 840;
    psychic relativity of, *see* space
    and time *s.v.* relativity;
    -reckoning, unconscious, **16**
    376;
    a relative concept, **11** 629;
    in Rhine's experiments, **8** 836;
    space and, *see* space and time;
    -spirit, **9i** 386;
    statements of, in dream, **8** 561;
    stream of, **13** 18;
    -symbol, **5** 423–5; of lapis, **12**

torch, **13** 418;
    dadophors with, **5** 294, pl.
    XX*b*;
    symbol of Hecate, **5** 577
torment(s), **13** 139;
    alchemical, **13** 86, 106, 442; **16**
    478; of fire, **13** 89, 94, 183; of
    hell, **13** 94, 444; of substances,
    13 444;
    see also torture
Torquemada, Cardinal, **12** 550; **13**
    391
Torres Strait, tribesmen of, **8** 120
tortoise, *see* ANIMALS *s.v.*
torture, **4** 185; **7** 172; **12** 438*n*; **13**
    89, 93, 139*n*;
    TITLE: "The Motif of Torture,"
    13 439–49;
    in alchemy, meaning of, **13** 94;
    of body, alchemical, **13** 439–41;
    initiation rites and, **11** 410; **17**
    271;
    projection of, **13** 439;
    self-inflicted, **11** 7;
    in visions of Zosimos, **11** 345–6;
    blood in, **13** (*pp*60, 62, 63), 93;
    see also Chönyid Bardo; dis-
    memberment; torment
totalitarianism, **9i** 453; **10** 451,
    1019; **11** 83, 141; **14** 448; **16** 222,
    442; **18** 1368, 1495;
    see also Fascism; State, the
totality, **9ii** 64, 221; **13** 207, 272,
    289, 296, 342; **14** 8, 22, 261, 777;
    anima as symbol of, **14** 422;
    becoming conscious, **9ii** 410;
    Christ as, *see* Christ *s.v.*;
    Christian, **10** 741;
    chthonic, **9ii** 351;
    circle as symbol of, *see* circle *s.v.*;
    conscious and unconscious in,
    11 230, 959;
    conscious mind is not, **11** 390;
    consciousness and, **10** 635; **12**
    247;
    cross and, **14** 122;
    Eastern apperception of, **18**
    1485;

    as ego plus non-ego, **12** 137;
    of experience, **11** 68;
    as four, **18** 1610;
    goal of, **6** 85;
    God as, *see* God *s.v.*;
    idea of, **9ii** 115*n*;
    image(s) of, **5** 624*n*; **9ii** 73; **13**
    367, 371; **18** 13;
    of man, *see* man *s.v.* wholeness/
    totality;
    mandala as, *see* mandala *s.v.*;
    modern representations of, **14**
    286*n*;
    of personality, **12** 137, 436;
    psyche as, **12** 9*n*;
    of psyche, *see* psyche *s.v.*;
    and quaternity, **14** 261, 265,
    613, 630;
    and quaternity symbol, **18**
    1133;
    self as, *see* self *s.v.*;
    spiritual, **9ii** 351;
    supraordinate, **11** 276;
    symbols, **6** 790; **9ii** 59, 297; **10**
    767, 771; **11** 667, 690, 742; **13**
    127; **14** 6, 122, 144, 269, 323,
    388, 753; non-human charac-
    ter of, **11** 276;
    by synthesis of male and
    female, **14** 656;
    of thinking, **11** 159*n*;
    as three, **18** 1610;
    transcendent, **13** 134;
    of transforming substance, **12**
    173;
    Trinity and, **11** 290;
    see also wholeness
totem, **8** 92;
    -ancestor, **8** 738; **13** 128;
    animals, *see* animal(s) *s.v.*;
    ceremonies, **6** 231, 431; **7** 237;
    clans, **15** 150;
    meal, **11** 339; **14** 525
totemism, primitive, **16** 146
Totenbaum, *see* tree *s.v.* of death
touch: and hallucinatory process, **1**
    25;
    magic, **8** 86.

touchstone, *lapis Lydius*, **13** 94
tough-minded, *see* James *s.v.* two
 types
tower: at Bollingen (J.'s), **18**
 1782*n*;
 in dream, **7** 189, 281;
 Mary/mother of God as, **6** 406;
 12 *fig.* 26;
 phallic, **6** 406;
 symbolism, **6** 390–2, 402; **12**
 138
town, in America, *see* America
Toxcatl, festival of, **13** 107*n*
toxins/toxic disturbances, **3** 75, 76,
 137*n*, 142, 166, 195, 196, 318,
 496, 548, 549, 552, 570, 581, 583;
 13 48
Toyson d'Or, La, *see* ALCHEMICAL
 COLLECTIONS: *Aureum vellus*
tract(s), **4** 717
tractability, **18** 877, 878
"Tractatulus Aristotelis," *see* AL-
 CHEMICAL COLLECTIONS: *Art. aurif. s.v.*
"Tractatulus Avicennae," *see* AL-
 CHEMICAL COLLECTIONS: *Art. au-
 rif. s.v.*
"Tractatus Aristotelis," *see* ALCHEM-
 ICAL COLLECTIONS: *Theatr. chem.
 s.v.*
"Tractatus aureus," *see* ALCHEMICAL
 COLLECTIONS: *Ars chemica s.v.*
 Hermes Trismegistus; *Art. aurif.
 s.v.* "Rosarium;" *Bibl. chem. cur.
 s.v.* Hermes and *s.v.* "Rosarium";
 De alchimia s.v. "Rosarium"; *Mus.
 herm. s.v.* Hermes Trismegistus;
 Theatr. chem. s.v. Hermes Tris-
 megistus; and see ALCHEMICAL
 WRITERS: Hermes Trismegistus
"Tractatus brevis," *see* ALCHEMICAL
 COLLECTIONS: *Mus. herm. s.v.*
 Flamel
"Tractatus de Sulphure," *see*
 ALCHEMICAL COLLECTIONS: *Mus.
 herm. s.v.* Sendivogius
"Tractatus Micreris," *see* ALCHEMI-
 CAL COLLECTIONS: *Theatr. chem. s.v.*

"Tractatus rhythmicus," *see* ALCHEM-
 ICAL WRITERS: Figulus *s.v.*
tradition(s), **7** 430; **9i** 117; **9ii** 282;
 11 524; **13** 352; **17** 305;
 alchemical and astrological, **13**
 160;
 archetypes and, **11** 88;
 authority of, **13** 149;
 Christian, **13** 360, 417;
 as criterion, **10** 651;
 dangers of breakdown, **16** 216;
 ecclesiastical, **13** 393, 427;
 and faith, **5** 345;
 Haggadic, **13** 417;
 historical, and Catholicism, **11**
 76;
 Iranian, **13** 458*n*;
 Jewish, **11** 350; **13** 460;
 modern man and, **11** 516, 528;
 Persian, **13** 376, 406;
 Sabaean, **13** 86*n*;
 secret, and symbolism, **11**
 165&*n*
train, Dionysian, *see* Dionysus *s.v.*
train(s), dream-motif, **8** 535; **17** 51
train of thought, *see* thought *s.v.*
training, psychiatrist's, **3** 527, 541
tram-car, in dream, **12** 151, 153
tramp(s), **14** 690
trampling, **4** 499–500
trance/trance state(s), **8** 440; **9i** 103;
 11 29, 81; **13** 462;
 in brain injury, **8** 949;
 and demonism, **18** 1473;
 hysterical, **3** 183 (*see also*
 hysteria);
 in séances, **1** 44, 48, 71;
 speaking in, **18** 726, 731;
 three-day, **1** 37;
 witch's, *see* witch *s.v.*
tranquillizers, **13** 66
transcendence, prayer and, **18** 1536
transcendental, **11** 764;
 clock, **12** 135;
 energy, soul as, **12** 9*n*;
 prejudice, **12** 20;
 processes, dogma as symbol of,
 5 674;

transformation (*cont.*):
  prefigurations in, **9ii** 414;
  processes, **13** 458*n*;
  of psyche, unconscious, **7** (*p*123);
  psychic, **7** 176; **12** 80, 187, 406, 470*n*; **13** 180, 193, 196; **14** 188*n*, 252, 321, 504–5, 615, 647, 749; **17** (*p*6), 276; in middle life, **8** 781–3; of physical into, **8** 745;
  and psychotherapy, as aim of, **11** 904–5;
  purpose of, **11** 352;
  rebirth as, **9i** 204, 205;
  religious, **11** 890–3;
  rites of, **9i** 205, 225;
  royal, Egyptian, **14** 356–7;
  of self, **5** 674;
  spiritual, **5** 667; **11** 273; **13** 97;
  processes of, **8** 688;
  stages of, **7** 198;
  subjective, **9i** 212–36;
  symbols, **13** 93;
  technical, **9i** 232–3;
  of unconscious psyche, **7** (*p*123);
  in the unconscious, and sacrifice, **5** 669;
  of values, **5** 553;
  yogic, **12** 441
transformation, alchemical/in alchemy, **8** 558; **9i** 238; **10** 630; **12** 99, 172–3, 187, 333, 420, 511, 559, *figs*. 121, 214; **13** (*p*61), 89, 91, 183, 275, 429; **14** 142, 169, 252, 282, 288, 306, 311, 316, 321, 348, 429–30, 503, 508, 540, 606–25, 645, 647, 685, 712, 727; **16** 402, 514;
  of arcane substance, *see* arcane substance *s.v.*;
  of artifex, **13** 277;
  of body, **13** (*p*60);
  and Christ's death and resurrection, **18** 1360;
  and Christ's passion, parallel, **14** 486, 492; **15** 28;

through death and rebirth, **14** 13, 169;
of God, **13** 450; **14** 374;
Greek, **14** 10*n*;
of man, **12** 366; **13** 280;
of Mercurius, *see* Mercurius *s.v.*;
moral-intellectual, **12** 366;
in opus, *see* opus *s.v.*;
Paracelsus and, *see* Paracelsus *s.vv.* Iliaster, Melusina;
process of, **13** 88*n*, 139, 289, 358; symbolized by ogdoad, **13** 416;
as a psychic process, **13** 117, 196;
of royal pair, **13** 435;
stages of, **12** 333; **14** 168, 731*n*;
four, **12** 333; seven, **12** 99, *figs*. 29, 221;
of substances, **14** 110, 142, 185, 374, 388, 545;
tree and, *see* tree(s) *s.v.*;
vessel of, **12** 376, 408; **14** 12, 142, 369; **16** 402; skull as, **9ii** 377; **12** *fig*. 75
transforming/transformative substance:
  as analogy of macrocosm, **12** 472;
  antimony as, **13** 183;
  body, soul and spirit of, **12** 478;
  and Christ, analogy, **12** 517;
  devilish/divine, **12** 173;
  and dreams, **8** 558;
  flos as, **12** 99*n*;
  four elements of, **12** 173;
  gum arabic/resin of the wise, **12** 209;
  head as, **13** 95;
  magnesia as, **12** 165*n*;
  Mercurius as, **12** 172;
  movements of, **12** 214*n*;
  round and square, **12** 173;
  round element as, **13** 95;
  snake as, **5** 676;
  Sol as, *see* Sol *s.v.*;
  see also arcane substance

674

transgressivity of archetypes, **8** 964
transition between sleeping and waking, **5** (*p*457); **9ii** 53
transitivism, **3** 279
transitus, **5** 526;
of adept, **13** 106;
animae, **14** 578;
in Mithraism, **11** 342;
motif, **13** 133;
opus as, **14** 288
transmigration of souls, *see* metempsychosis
transmission: in ESP, **8** 840;
of force, **8** 979
transmutation, **9i** 202;
alchemical, **12** 332, 489, 490; **13** 121;
of elements, **8** 90, 962;
in Mass, **12** 417 (*see also* transubstantiation);
of metals, **13** 158, 196
transpersonal, **7** 159;
contents, **7** 150, 230;
control-point, **7** 216;
unconscious, *see* unconscious, collective
transpsychic reality underlying psyche, **8** 600*n*
transubstantiation, **6** 35–9; **11** 307, 322, 379, 448; **12** 450; **18** 1360;
alchemical parallels, **12** 420, 486, 489, 517; **14** 22, 435;
dogma of, **6** 36, 58, 96;
efficient cause/*causa efficiens,* **11** 379; **12** 417;
of Eucharistic elements, **12** 417–18; **13** 196
Transvaal, **18** 81
"transvaluation of values," **5** 553
transvestism, **15** 134;
TITLE: "A Case of Transvestism Treated by Castration," **18** 822–5
trapeza, **16** 378*n*
Trarames, *see* Paracelsus: ARCANA *s.v.*
trauma(ta), **7** 13; **8** 204, 499–501; **15** 62; **16** 33–4, 276; **17** 176, 201;

childhood/infantile, **4** 215–17; **17** 200;
and hysteria, **4** 37, 205–9, 559, 582;
intensity unimportant, **4** 219;
measurement of effect of, **4** 403;
past, and neurosis, **4** 210, 214;
predisposition for, **4** 218–23;
real, child's part in producing, **4** 227;
sexual, theory of, *see* Freud *s.v.*
traumatic neurosis, *see* neurosis *s.v.*
Trautscholdt, M., **2** 70, 569, 584;
"Experimentelle Untersuchungen über die Assoziation der Vorstellungen," **2** 21*n*, 70*n*, 569*n*, (*p*271), 730&*n*, 868*n*
Travancore, **13** 278
travel, urge to, **8** 240
treading, **4** 502; **5** 370, 481
treasure, **7** 231, 260*n*/476*n*, 261/477, 264, 374; **9ii** 370; **12** 111, 160, 454; **13** 200, 220, 247, 250, 267, 319–21; **18** 375–7;
in the depths, **18** 260;
in field, **6** 423; **13** 321;
guardians of, **5** 569, 577; **7** 374 (*see also below* snake; tree; *and see* ANIMALS: dragon(s) *s.v.* as guardians
hard to attain, **5** 393, 482, 510, 512, 569, 659; **8** 229, 390; **9i** 270, 311, 417, 668; **11** 230, 931; **12** 155, 205, 222, 438, 442, 448;
hero and, **8** 555;
hidden, **7** 105, 231; **8** 390, 558;
-house (alchemical), **13** 112, 117; **14** 2*n*;
integration of, **18** 352;
kingly, **13** 181;
life as, **5** 580;
motif of, **13** 319;
pearl as, **5** 510; **6** 423; **13** 321;
in sea, **12** 154–5;
secret, **13** *fig.* 14;
self as, **12** 155, 211;

treasure (*cont.*):

singular feeling as, **18** 787;

snake as guardian of, **5** 395, 541, 577; **9i** 668; **9ii** 370;

symbol, **6** 423–4; **7** 260*n*/476*n*;

in transference, **18** 327;

tree as guardian of, **13** 320–1, 349, 414;

in water, **9i** 51;

see also hoard

treatment, **7** 254–5; **11** 463; **16** 541; **17** 170;

aim of, **7** 187–9, 198; **16** 293;

analytical, **12** 3, 36–7;

a dialectical process, **16** 239;

four stages of, **16** 122, 134;

hypnotic, **16** 139;

individual, **4** 617; **16** 3, 36, 42;

individuation and, **7** 187;

initiation of, **17** 273;

irrationalization of, **16** 42;

limits of rational, **16** 84;

method(s) of, **7** 369, 480; **11** 537; determined by case, **17** 203;

as mystical fount of healing, **7** 169;

of neurosis, *see* neurosis *s.v.*;

practical necessities of, **7** 117;

and problem of opposites, **7** 88;

reductive, **18** 514;

as religious act, **17** 268;

results of, **7** 198;

risks of, **7** 194, 241/462;

and technique, **17** 171–2, 203, 240;

of young people, **7** 182;

see also analysis; analytical psychology; method(s); psychotherapy; therapy

tree(s): topics, **5** 515; **7** 295; **9i** 535*n*; **12** 33, 217, 232; **13** 228, 239–43, 249, 415;

TITLE: "The Philosophical Tree," **13** 304–482;

Adam and, *see* Adam *s.v.*;

alchemical opus as, *see* opus *s.v.*

tree;

as arcane substance, **13** 354, 382, 414; **14** 404;

archetype(-al), **13** 379, 460;

image, **13** 304, 350–3;

birds and, **13** 414–17;

birth from, **5** 367–8&*n*, 662, pls. XXXIX, XLV; **6** 298; **13** 327, 336, 404; **16** 379; archetype of, **13** 404; and rebirth, **13** 350, 459;

branches of, *see below* metallic;

budding, as symbol, **5** 368*n*;

in Bundahish, *see* Bundahish *s.v.*;

Cabalistic: of Sefiroth, *see* Sefiroth *s.v.*; Yesod as, **14** 636;

centre of, **13** 243;

Christ and, *see* Christ *s.v.*;

Christmas-, *see* Christmas *s.v.*;

of coral, in sea ("sea-tree,") **12** 449*n*, *fig.* 186; **13** 375, 406; **14** 157;

cosmic, *see below* world-;

and Cross, *see* Cross *s.v.*;

daemon, **13** 247–8;

of death/Totenbaum, **5** 368, 494, pl. XXXV; coffin as, **5** 349, 427; **13** 401&*n*; and life, **13** 349;

in dream/vision, **5** 325; **7** 366; **9i** 570, 576, 582; of Nebuchadnezzar, *see* Nebuchadnezzar *s.v.* dream;

of Enlightenment, **5** pl. LV; **13** 413;

of Eve, **12** *fig.* 135;

of faith, **11** 890;

felling of, as phallic symbol, **5** 659, 662;

feminine, **5** 324, pl. XXXI; **13** 418 (*see also below* numen);

fire, **13** 320, 408, 459*n*; **14** 80*n*;

Gnostic, **13** 408; and solar pillar, **13** 408*n*;

five, Gnostic, **16** 378*n*;

fruit-, **13** 203, 403; bread of life and, **13** 403; in fairytale, **9i**

417 (*see also below* sun-and-moon tree);
genealogical, **5** 321; **8** 559;
as gnosis, **13** 419;
Gokard, **12** 536;
golden, *see below* philosophical;
and gold-making, **13** 414;
hanging on, *see* hanging;
and heavenly bride, **13** 460;
hermaphroditic / bisexual, **5** 324, 325;
as Hermetic philosophy (in alchemy) **12** 34;
of Hesperides, **12** *fig.* 189; **13** 314, 405*n*, 461; **14** 85*n*; apples of, **13** 404;
holy, and snake stones, **13** 461;
immortal, **12** 449*n*, 450;
imprisonment within, **5** 362–3;
inverted (*arbor inversa*), **13** 409–14, 460, 462; **14** 158*n*;
man as, **13** 411&*n*–12, 420;
soul of, rooted in aether, **13** 412*n*;
of knowledge, **5** 403; **7** 243*n*; **8** 754; **9i** 560, 673; **9ii** 372; **10** 289; **13** 288, 419, 460, *fig.* 11; **14** 75&*n*, 607; **18** 1383;
as lapis, **13** 421–8;
leafless (dead), **13** 313, 333, 343, 400;
of life, **5** 306*n*, 318, 349, pls. IX*a*, XXXI; **9i** 673; **9ii** 373; **11** 726; **12** *figs.* 26, 264; **13** 110, 354, 411, 418, 459; **14** 73*n*; **16** 484; **18** 1526; blossoming and withering, **5** 423*n*; in Cabala, **13** 411; Christ as, **13** 243*n*; cross as, **5** 349, 368, 398, 671, pl. XXXVI; and death, **13** 349; and flaming sword, **11** 359; on island, **13** 306, 349, 406, *figs.* 1, 23; and life-giving fruit, **12** 298, 449; and mother-symbol, **5** 321, 398 (*see also* TREES: haoma);
of light, **13** 308; and fire, **14** 80*n*;

magic(al), **13** 399, 462 (*see also* shaman *s.v.* tree symbolism);
as man, **13** 411–12, 458–62;
Mayan ritual, **12** *fig.* 190;
as medium of conjunction, **13** 457;
Mercurius as, *see* Mercurius *s.v.*;
metallic, **13** 375, 408, 409&*n*, 446; branches of, four, **13** 119, 446; —, seven, **13** 409, 414;
and mistletoe, **5** 393;
of Mithras, **5** 349;
modern fantasies of, **13** 462;
and mother, **5** 321, 349; **9i** 156, 589&*n*; **12** 499; **13** 326, 418–19; and child, symbolism of, **5** 624*n*, 659; as symbol of Great Mother, **18** 550;
on mountain, **13** 325, 407, 412;
in myths, **5** 349; **13** 354;
in Nebuchadnezzar's dream, *see* Nebuchadnezzar *s.v.*;
numen, **13** 243, 458; as anima(-us), **13** 458; in fairytale, **9i** 417; feminine, **13** 418–20, 458; **14** 73, 75; king as, **9i** 406; Melusina and, **12** 537*n*, *fig.* 257; **13** 247*n*, 416, 418; Mercurius as, *see* Mercurius *s.v.*; snake as, *see* ANIMALS: serpent / snake *s.v.* tree;
nymph, **13** 324, 328, 335, 460;
oracle-, **11** 612;
of paradise, **5** 349, 368; **8** 754; **9i** 428, 560; **13** 180, 243, 247, 316, 398, 400, 410, 419, 420, 460; apple of, **8** 751; Buddha as, **13** 458*n*; Lilith/Mercurius in, **13** 247*n*, 288, 399, 460; as man, **13** 458&*n*; in sea, **12** 449*n*; **13** 173, 406&*n*, 408; two, sun-and-moon, **13** 403&*n*; and wood of cross, **13** 446;
phallic meaning of, **5** 659, 662 (*see also* Adam *s.v.* tree);
philosophical, **9i** 570; **9ii** 372; **11** 357*n*; **12** 357, 393, 498, *fig.*

677

tree(s) (*cont.*):

188; **13** 278, 304–482; **14** 6*n*, 37, 313, 388, 393, 400; **16** 408; alchemical opus as, *see* opus *s.v.* tree; and aqua permanens, **13** 408; golden, **13** 404, 409, 416–17; Melusina in, *see* Melusina; Mercurius and, *see* Mercurius *s.v.*; parallel with human anatomy, **13** 376; seven-branched, **13** 374&*n*; vision of (*res quaerenda*), **13** 374; Zarathustra's vision of, **13** 119, 446, 458 (see also *arbor philosophica*);

of planets, **13** 407, 409;

primordial, **13** 458*n*;

projection into, **13** 248; of anima-figure, **13** 458;

quaternary nature of, **13** 446;

-riddle, **5** 327;

sacred, **5** 321, 368*n*, 545; **6** 697; of Attis, *see* Attis *s.v.* sacred pine-tree; as mother, **5** 577;

and salt, **13** 374&*n*, 406, 408;

secret of, **13** 241–3;

of *sefiroth*, see *sefiroth s.v.*;

as self, **9ii** 356; **13** 241, 243, 407, 458; in process of growth, **13** 304;

and serpent, *see* ANIMALS: serpent/snake *s.v.*;

with seven branches, **13** 374&*n*, 414;

in shamanism, *see* shaman(ism) *s.v.*;

as son, **5** 659;

-souls, **13** 247, 420;

spirit in, **13** 247–9;

stork and, **13** 415–17, 459;

of sun, **13** 88*n*;

sun-and-moon, **12** *fig.* 116; **13** 398&*n*, 403&*n*, 406–9, 459; **14** 73, 157, 181; **16** 533; fruits of, as Sol/Luna, **13** 409;

sword on, **13** 448;

symbol(ism), **5** 348, 349, 367; **13** 241*n*, 305, 347–8, 350; alchemical, **8** 559; **9i** 198; **13** 373; of gods, goddesses, **11** 612; king as, **13** 350*n*; of personality, **13** 241–2, 247, 350, 407; pillar, **13** 408*n*; sapientia/Sophia/wisdom, **11** 612; **13** 419;

and transformation (renewal), **9ii** 372; **13** 354, 418, 447; **14** 76&*n*;

and treasure, *see* treasure *s.v.*;

voice of, **13** 247;

and water, **5** 330; **13** *fig.* 5;

in Western Land, **12** 298, 537–8; **13** 403, 406, 407; **14** 73, 158;

of wisdom, **13** 321, 403, 419, 459;

world-/cosmic, **9i** 198, 427, 445, 447, 452&*n*; **13** 288, 312, 381*n*, 404–5, 409, 411, 459, *fig.* 30; Mexican, **13** *fig.* 8; shamanistic, *see* shaman(ism) *s.v.*;

Zarathustra/Zoroaster and, *see* Zarathustra *s.v.*;

see also *arbor*; forest

TREES: SEPARATE SPECIES

acacia, **13** 401

almond, Amygdalos, **13** 116*n*

ash: legends of, **5** 395*n*; as mother, **5** 439; world-(Yggdrasil), **5** 349, 370, 371, 427; regenerative function of, **5** 367

ashvatta, aswatha, peepul (*ficus religiosa*), **5** 545

baobab, **13** *fig.* 2

Berissa, *see below* Lunatica

bodhi, **6** 298; **13** 418

in Bundahish, *see* Bundahish *s.v.*

cedar: in Egyptian myth and

Trevisanus, *see* ALCHEMICAL WRITERS: Bernard of Treviso

triad(s), **5** 294, 545; **8** 870; **9i** 679; **11** 283–4; **12** *fig.* 185; **13** 187, 270;
> in alchemy: masculine, **16** 406; Paracelsan, **13** 357; **14** 235;
> as archetypal structures, **9i** 436; **11** 209, 222;
> and archetype, **9ii** 42; **11** 173; Christ and, **11** 232; **16** 403*n*;
> double, **16** 451;
> indivisible, **13** 270*n*;
> and Kepler's astronomy, **18** 1133;
> lower/chthonic, **9i** 439; **9ii** 156, 158*n*; **13** 176*n*, *fig* B2; **18** 1604, 1653; as counterpart of Trinity, **9i** 425, 597*n*; **9ii** 351; **13** 228*n*, 271; **14** 643 (*see also below* and Trinity); of gods of underworld, **9ii** 351; **13** 270; and quaternity, *see* quaternity *s.vv.* marriage; mutilated
> of Mercurius, *see* Mercurius *s.v.*;
> Naassene (Gnostic), **9ii** 328;
> of principles, **8** 966;
> triadic mandala, **9i** 644, 646; **10** 775;
> and Trinity, **9i** 11; **14** 643*n*; ancient/archaic, as prefigurations of, **11** 173, 176, 283; Babylonian, **11** 173–6; Egyptian, **11** 177; Greek, **11** 179–80; Plato's, **11** 196, 237, 247 (*see also above* lower/chthonic);
> two antithetical, **9i** 426, 429, 432; body and spirit, **9ii** 100&*n*; male and female, **9ii** 42;
> upper, **13** 202, 204;
> *see also* function(s)/functional; NUMBERS: three

triadic: character of gods of underworld, **13** 270;
> fantasy formations, **8** 401;

nature of Mercurius, *see* Mercurius *s.v.* threefold;
> principle, in *I Ching*, **8** 866;
> symbols, **5** 294*n*; **9ii** 382*n*;
> view of the world, **8** 962

triangle, **9i** 426; **12** *fig.* 75;
> equilateral, **11** 180;
> in Kant, **6** 64;
> "lower," **9i** 439;
> and quadrangle, **12** 165&*n*, 167, 220;
> and square, **13** 272

tribal lore, sacred, **9i** 10

tribe, **7** 235/456; **8** 725;
> organization of, and incest taboo, **5** 332;
> *see also* primitive(s)

Tricephalus, *see* NUMBERS: three *s.v.*

trichotomy(-ies), **9ii** 118

trickster, **14** 332;
> TITLE: "On the Psychology of the Trickster-Figure," **9i** 456–88;
> archetypal figure, **9i** 465;
> Mercurius as, *see* Mercurius;
> and poltergeists, **9i** 457, 469; Satan as, **11** 619, 620;
> and shadow, **9i** 469, 485

trident, golden, **13** 450

Triga chemica, *see* ALCHEMICAL WRITERS *s.v.* Barnaud

trigrams, **8** 866

Trikaya, **11** 790, 817

trimeria, **14** 619

Trimurti picture, **12** *fig.* 75

Trinity/trinity/triunity, **4** 106; **5** 198; **6** 58; **8** 643, 927; **9i** 30; **9ii** 66, 104, 141, 399, 409, pl. II; **10** 765; **11** 81, 91, 107, 125–6, 177, 246, 469, 656; **12** 192, 220, 287*n*, 319, 320; **13** 137*n*, 187*n*, 204, 357, 450; **14** 122, 145, 237, 269, 630, 745; **16** 409*n*, 533&*n*;
> TITLE: "A Psychological Approach to the Dogma of the Trinity," **11** 169–295;
> in alchemy, **12** 446, *fig.* 179; **13**

aetiology of, **4** 209

Tum/Atum, Egyptian god, **5** 133, 134, 147;
    attributes of, **5** 408–9;
    of On-Heliopolis, **5** 408;
    of Pithum Heroopolis, **5** 410;
    as tom-cat, **5** 425

tumbler, *see* glass

tumours, brain, **3** 193

tune(s), **2** 611;
    and feeling-toned train of thought, **1** 168

Turba philosophorum, see ALCHEMICAL WRITERS *s.v.*

turbine, **8** 82

Turfan Fragment, **12** 458*n*

Turin, **14** 526*n*

Turkey, **10** 908

"Turkey," association-chain, **3** 247–8

Turks, Bosnian, **14** 385

turquoise (gem-stone), **13** 130, 132

Turrius, Joannes, **14** 56*n*, 67, 93–4

Turukalukundram, **9ii** 339*n*

Tut-Ankh-Amon, and winged sun-disc, **5** pl. VII

Tvashtri, **5** 515

twelve, *see* NUMBERS *s.v.*

twenty-four, *see* NUMBERS *s.v.*

twice-born, **13** 96;
    Christ as, **9i** 93

twilight, **13** 199, 299*n*, 302;
    of reflection, **13** 334

twilight state(s), **3** 164*n*; **8** 952, 956; **18** 725;
    in dementia praecox, **3** 346, 352;
    epileptic, **1** 31, 130;
    and feeble-mindedness, **1** 319–20;
    hallucinations/visions in, **1** 100, 126;
    hysterical, **1** 35, 126, 270, 272, 277, 279, 294, 296, 304, 306, 337, 419; **3** 160, 163*n*; **4** 30, 300, 303, 361; **7** 4–6/413–15; **10** 426; **18** 999, 1000

twins, **13** 132; **14** 592*n*;

Gemini, *see* zodiac, twelve signs of

imaginary, *see* sister;

Jesus and Thomas, **5** 318*n*;

in mother's womb, **5** 620;

Saviour of the, **9ii** 133*n*, 187*n*

two, *see* NUMBERS *s.v.*

twofold substance, **13** 267, 384&*n*

"two-horned," **9i** 253;
    Alexander as, *see* Alexander the Great;
    meaning of, **5** 283*n*

Tylor, E. B., **7** 108; **8** 118; **18** 1297; *Primitive Culture*, **8** 118*n*; **14** 502*n*

type(s), **2** 984; **4** 675–6, 778; **6** 835–6 (Def.); **7** 82, 93, 461–2&*n*; **8** 399; **9i** 167*n*; **16** 249–50;
    TITLES: *Psychological Types*, **6**; "The Problem of the Attitude Type," **7** 56–96; "The Problem of Types in Dream Interpretation," **18** 495–559;
    abstracting, **6** 497–501;
    aesthetic, **6** 240, 252&*n*;
    affectivity and, *see* affectivity;
    anima-, *see* anima (J.'s term);
    and archetypes, **3** 413&*n*; **9i** 143, 260; **12** 15–16, 329;
    of association, *see below* definition; objective; predicate; *see also* complex *s.v.* constellation;
    attitude-, **6** 556–8, 835*n*, 903, 957, 972, 985; **7** 61; **8** 224; **12** 295; **16** 236, 245; **18** 1130, 1157 (*see also* attitude, extraverted, introverted);
    and balancing of attitudes, **6** 68;
    classic, romantic, *see* Ostwald, F. W.;
    classification into, **18** 504;
    complex-constellation, *see* complex *s.v.* constellation;
    conflict of, **6** 125, 325, 911; **7** 80; biological foundation of, **6** 558; and Pelagian controversy, **6** 33;

U

Uddushu-namir, **11** 176
νδωρ θειον, **18** 1360
Ueli, **9i** 474*n*
Ufo(s), **10** (*pp*309–10); **18** 1431–51;
    TITLES: "Flying Saucers: a Modern Myth," **10** 589–824; "On Flying Saucers," **18** 1431–51;
    acceleration, **10** 602;
    and American Air Force, **18** 1432, 1434, 1448, 1449;
    appearance and disappearance, **10** 630;
    as archetypal images, **10** 622;
    broadsheets illustrating, **10** 758–60, pls. V, VI;
    bureau for recording, **10** 601; **18** 1432;
    in dreams, **10** 626–723, 770;
    "manning" motif in, **10** 698, 703;
    as drop-shape, **10** 628, 630–1, 637, 641;
    and earth, low opinion of, **10** 796–7;
    and extra-terrestrial invasion, **10** 600;
    and extra-terrestrial origin of, **18** 1437–8, 1448;
    flight, nature of, **10** 602–3, 785;
    as gods, **10** 622;
    heat emitted by, **10** 641;
    in history, **10** 757–80 *passim;* **18** 1442;
    Holy Ghost as nickname for, **10** 618*n*;
    hysteria and, **10** 631;
    landings from, **10** 603, 611; **18** 1433;
    as living myths, **10** 614, 625;
    as mandalas, **10** 731, 803;
    materiality of, **10** 789;
    and "mother-ships," **10** 761, 793;
    "Neptune" as pilot of, **10** 800–1;
    not photogenic, **10** 613;
    occupants of, **10** 603, 611; **18** 1433;
    and parapsychological processes, **18** 1434, 1441;
    photographic failure, **18** 1433;
    pilot's view of Jesus, **10** 797;
    plurality of, **10** 633–5;
    as portents of death, **10** 698–9;
    projections and, **10** 608–10, 614, 706, 789;
    psychic nature of, **10** 785, 787–8; **18** 1431, 1441, 1445;
    psychoanalysis and, **10** 631;
    and radar, **10** 604, 630, 785–6;
    as rumours: symbolical, **10** 731; visionary, **10** 598–9, 607–9;
    sexual aspects, **10** 631, 662–3;
    shapes, **10** 602, 618, 635–7, 750;
    size, **10** 603;
    as souls, **10** 621;
    speed of, **10** 602, 605;
    as symbols, **10** 618; **18** 1431;
    threads, rain of, and, **10** 667*n*, 668;
    weightlessness of, **10** 600, 602, 611, 624, 667, 787;
    Zeppelin as, **10** 618*n*;
    Flying Saucer Review, **18** (*p*626*n*)
Uganda, **10** 185;
    ceremony, **5** 594
Ugarit, **9ii** 181
"ugliest man," *see* Nietzsche: *Zarathustra s.v.*
Ugolino, **6** 321
Uhlhorn, **9ii** 400*n*
Uitzilopochtli, **5** 522, 672*n*; **11** 340; **13** 107*n*
ulcer(s), uterine, **16** 552
Ullikummi, **14** 765*n*.
Ulmannus, **12** 505*n*

Ulrich (Zurich), **2** 511, 514
Ulrich von Gerbenstein, *see* Gerbenstein
ultima materia: lapis as, **13** 421;
Mercurius as, **13** 282
Ulysses, *see* Joyce, James; Odysseus
Umail, M. b. *see under* ALCHEMICAL
WRITERS: Senior
umbra, see shadow *s.v.*
unadaptedness, **13** 24; **17** 172
Unamuno, Miguel de, **18** 1339&*n*
unarius, **11** 104*n*, 122; **14** 554;
as the One/unity, **14** 41, 143,
493; **16** 525
Unas, **9ii** 187; **14** 22
unbalance, spiritual, contemporary,
17 157
uncertainty: factor of, **8** 972;
relationship, between conscious
and unconscious, **9ii** 355;
science and, **4** 746
uncleanness, magical, **10** 405
uncomeliness, outward, **9ii** 216
unconscious: *this has been grouped
under the following main headings:*
unconscious (adjective); unconscious, the; unconscious, collective; unconscious, and conscious;
unconscious, and conscious mind;
unconscious, and consciousness;
unconscious, personal; unconscious contents; unconsciousness; unconscious processes
unconscious *(adjective):* apprehension, **18** 733, 735;
aptitudes, *see* aptitudes *s.v.*;
assumptions, *see* assumptions
s.v.;
attitudes, *see* attitudes *s.v.*;
combination, **18** 732;
conflict, *see* conflict *s.v.*;
contents, *see sep. entry below;*
counteraction, **8** 160–1;
counter-position, **7** 118;
effects, perceived indirectly, **17**
112;
factor, **14** 332;
fantasy, *see* fantasy *s.v.*;

fantasy-systems, **4** 256;
identity, *see* Lévy-Bruhl: *participation mystique s.v.;*
individuation, **11** 756;
infantile attachments, **14** 750;
laws, **13** 30, 286;
material, interpretation of, **11**
541;
motives, and free choice, **16**
365;
opposition, **7** 187;
performance, heightened, **1**
137–48;
problems, exteriorization of, **18**
769;
processes, *see sep. entry below;*
products, **18** 11; interpretation
of, **5** 175*n*; over- and undervaluation of, **8** 176; spontaneous, **13** 352, 393, 460, 477;
proliferation, consequences of,
17 313;
psyche, *see* psyche *s.v.*;
regression, **13** 324;
shadow-side, **16** 173;
symbols, **6** 182–3, 204;
tendencies, **7** 137, 216;
thinking, *see* thinking *s.v.*;
traumatic factor, **15** 63;
urges to power, **7** (*p*5);
view of the world, **7** 507
unconscious, the, **3** 353; **4** 248, 528;
5 438, 554, 576, 681; **6** 180–3,
279, 837–43 (Def.); **8** 62, 544,
640–1, 702; **10** 311, 559, 634;
11 440, 760; **13** 13–16, 36, 70–1,
76, 134, 141, 180, 183, 209, 220,
229, 248, 272, 289, 314, 334,
393, *fig.* B5; **14** 52, 151, 257,
261, 277, 342, 749; **15** 104; **16**
12, 17, 55, 294, 356, 389, 469,
518–19, 529; **17** 181, 191, 217*a*;
18 881;
TITLES: "The Attitude of the
Unconscious," **6** 568–76,
626–7; "The Autonomy of the
Unconscious," **11** 1–55; "The
Fantasies of the Unconscious,"

unconscious, the (*cont.*):

4 314–39; "Foreword to White's *God and the Unconscious*," **11** 449–67; "The Function of the Unconscious," **7** 266–95; "The Functions of the Unconscious," **18** 444–60; "General Remarks on the Therapeutic Approach to the Unconscious," **7** 192–200; "Instinct and the Unconscious," **8** 263–82; "The Interpretation and Integration of the Unconscious," **13** 463–82; "On the Importance of the Unconscious in Psychopathology," **3** 438–65; "On the Psychology of the Unconscious," **7** 1–201; "Phenomena Resulting from the Assimilation of the Unconscious," **7** 221–42, 451–63; "The Rapprochement with the Unconscious," **13** 210–12; "The Relations between the Ego and the Unconscious," **7** 202–406; "The Role of the Unconscious," **10** 1–48; "The Significance of the Unconscious in Individual Education," **17** 253–83; "The Significance of the Unconscious in Psychology," **8** 356–64; "The Structure of the Unconscious," **7** 442–521; "The Technique of Differentiation between the Ego and the Figures of the Unconscious," **7** 341–73; "The Unconscious in Historical Perspective," **8** 343–55; "The Unconscious as the Matrix of Symbols," **12** 516–17;

absolute, **8** 311;

activation of, **6** 400; **12** 57;

activity of, *see* activity *s.v.*;

Adlerian view of, **4** 760; **16** 152;

aetiological/causal significance of, **16** 295;

Africa as, **14** 277;

aims of, **16** 86;

alchemy and, *see* alchemy *s.v.*;

ambivalence/two aspects of, **14** 253; **18** 1537–8;

analysis of, **7** 192–7, 205/446, 342, 387, 420; **12** 60; **17** 180, 184, 193, 261;

ancestral/instinctual, **8** 673; **16** 61;

and anima, *see* anima *s.v.*;

animal impulses of, **12** 186, 203;

animal representing, *see* animals *s.v.*;

animation of, **12** 201;

animus as personification of, *see* animus *s.v.*;

antinomies of, **9i** 419; **17** 203;

and apperceptive disturbance, **3** 56;

approach of, **12** 53, 60;

Aquaster (Paracelsus) as, **13** 175;

archaic vestiges in, **16** 205;

archetypal associations of products of, **5** 683;

archetypal configurations of, **13** 304;

archetypal structures of, **5** 337, 611; **14** 558;

and archetypes, **11** 238;

archetypes of, **12** 20; **14** 517;

autonomous, **5** 467;

and artists, *see* artistic *s.vv.* capacity; creation; experience;

assimilation of, *see* assimilation *s.v.*;

an assumption, **11** 64;

attention to, **14** 180, 193;

attitude of, *see* attitudes *s.v.*;

autonomous activity of, **7** 204/445, 205/446;

autonomy of, **8** 545; **10** 634, 832; **11** 1–55, 141; **12** 51, 65, 118, 249, 437*n*; **13** 438; **14** 343;

as barrier, **7** 140;

barriers against, **5** 553;

"behind" as, **12** 55;
beneficial effects of, **16** 501;
cannot be discriminated, **11** 419;
cannot be "done with," **9ii** 40;
cannot be emptied, **7** 205/446, 258/473;
"can only wish," **4** 318; **7** 212, 216;
capriciousness of, **18** 734;
Caucasus of, **13** 13;
centre in, **7** 509; **9i** 492;
chaos of, **16** 392;
chaotic fragments of, **13** 111;
Christ as personification of, **13** 448;
and Christ-phenomenon, **18** 1828;
chthonic, **12** 26;
collective, *see sep. entry below;*
as collective ideal, **17** 218;
comparative research into, **17** 205;
compensatory function/relation of, **5** 272; **6** 30, 574–5, 843, 904; **7** 279, 282–3; **8** 17*n*, 466, 931; **9ii** 191; **10** 23, 448, 732; **11** 802; **12** 63; **13** 294, 454; **14** 149, 192, 221, 286, 312, 470, 486, 492, 514, 705, 707, 756; **16** 372; cannot be compelled, **11** 797; to the conscious, **3** 448–9; **5** 575; **8** 17, 132; **10** 33; **14** 184; **16** 252, 330, 365; to conscious attitude, **11** 779; **16** 12; **17** 282; **18** 1388; to conscious contents, **10** 21; to conscious mind, **5** 98, 587, 616; **7** 204/445; **12** 26, 51; to consciousness, **5** 611*n*; **6** 568, 904; **8** 17*n*; **12** 26, 48&*n*; **14** 736; **15** 152–3; **18** 1377, 1418, 1484, 1491, 1584; purpose of, **10** 732; realization of, **11** 784 (*see also* unconscious processes *s.v.* compensatory);
complexes and, *see* complex *s.v.*;

as condensation of historical experience, **5** 75;
conflict with, *see* conflict *s.v.*;
confrontation/encounter with, **13** 428, 462, 481;
and conscious, *see sep. entry below*;
and conscious mind, *see sep. entry below;*
and consciousness, *see sep. entry below;*
constellated, *see* constellation *s.v.*;
contamination by/of, *see* contamination *s.v.*;
continuity of, **11** 53; **16** 15, 205; **18** 13;
conveys experience of unity, **11** 440;
cosmic aspect, **12** 226;
counterposition in, **14** 257;
creates new contents, **8** 702;
creativity of, **5** 182, 329; **8** 135, 339; **11** 875; **16** 62; **17** 185;
crossing threshold of, **11** 86;
dangers of, **14** 184;
darkness of, **5** 523, 539; **13** 34;
dawn-state and, **9ii** 230;
deadly grip of, **5** 523, 539;
and death, **8** 809;
deeper unity in, **11** 943;
definition/meaning of term, **1** 166*n*; **3** 438–9, 441; **4** 210; **8** 270; **9i** 1; **18** 11;
deliberations of, **18** 545;
demands of, **5** 458;
denial of, **10** 1;
deposit of all experience, **8** 339;
depotentiation of, **12** 163;
depreciation of, **4** 761–2; **7** 352; **12** 60; **18** 468;
descent into, **12** 436–7;
destructive tendency of, **14** 149, 258;
devaluation of, **6** 82;
devil/Satan as representative of, **18** 1653;

689

464, 245/465, 384 (*see also sep. entry below* unconscious, collective);
as impersonal psyche, **9i** 314;
importance of, **9ii** 7;
increase of potential of, **14** 510;
indistinctness of idea in, **3** 218;
inductive action of, **16** 364;
inertia of, **17** 271;
infantile-perverse-criminal, **16** 327;
and inferior function, **6** 171, 502–3;
influence of, **7** (*p*124), 342;
inherited, **12** 184;
instinctive activity of, **7** 253; **8** 270;
instinctuality of native's wisdom of, **13** 448;
integration of, *see* integration *s.v.*;
intellectual activity of, **1** 148;
interventions of, **18** 571;
intuitions of, *see* intuition *s.v.*;
inundation by, **13** 428;
invasion(s) by, **5** 616–17; **7** 163; **12** 57&*n*; **14** 117*n*; **16** 479;
invasion(s) of, **11** 533; **14** 184, 782;
irrational standpoint of, **7** 350;
irreality of, **7** 351;
irruption/breaking through of, **9i** 268; **11** 665, 698, 708; **14** 144*n*, 272;
Janet and, **17** 128;
as land of dreams, **18** 754;
language of, **7** 21/434; **10** 23; **18** 637, 671, 837;
layers of, **7** 118;
left/sinister, *see* right and left: the left *s.v.*;
libido and, *see* libido *s.v.*;
localization of, **18** 761;
loses ascendancy, **7** 382;
lumber-room of, **11** 899;
luminosity/multiple scintillae of, **14** 50*n*, 270, 700 (*see also above* illumination);

lunar character of, *see* moon *s.v.* as unconscious;
magical rites as defence against, **11** 32;
and mana-personality, **7** 390;
in manic state, **18** 829;
manifestations of, **11** 35, 63, 441;
mankind's unwritten history, **11** 280;
mask of, **12** 29;
maternal character of, *see* mother *s.v.*;
"matriarchal" state of, **9i** 425;
as matrix: of consciousness, *see sep. entry below* unconscious and consciousness *s.v.*; of dreams, **8** 545; of the future, **5** 459; of the human mind, **16** 384; of mythology/philosophy etc., **11** 899; of symbols, **12** 516–17; **18** 603, 637;
meaning of concept, *see above* definition;
Mercurius as, *see* Mercurius *s.v.*;
message of, **18** 471;
mother as, *see* mother *s.v.*;
mythological activity of, **7** 160*n*;
nature of, **7** (*pp*3, 124), 203/444, 288–9; **10** 52;
necessary evil, **12** 247;
negative: attitude to, **7** 195; movement of, **7** 357; role of, **7** 166 (*see also below* positive and negative);
neutrality of, **16** 329; **18** 1586;
never at rest, **17** 102;
never deceives, **5** 95;
as *nigredo*, **14** 646;
not directly observable, **16** 356*n*;
not only evil, **16** 389;
numinosity of, **11** 222; **12** 247;
objectivity of, **10** 562;
old theories alive in, **17** 44;
opening up of, **11** 531;

unconscious, the (*cont.*):
opposites in, *see* opposites *s.v.*;
order in, **12** 189;
organising principle of, **9ii** 318;
"our sea" symbol of, **9ii** 219;
outside nature, **12** 400;
overpowering by, **12** 437;
overrating of, **8** 568;
and paintings by mental patients, **15** 206–11;
paradoxical/contradictory, **12** 517; **13** 250; **14** 88;
parental influence and, **4** 739;
perceptiveness of, **11** 608, 638, 738; **18** 781;
and persona, **7** 308; **18** 1102;
personal, *see sep. entry below;*
personalistic view of, **16** 205;
personification of, **8** 673; **14** 128 (*see also* anima; animus; Mercurius; mother; *and see above* Christ; *below* Proteus; soul);
physiological aspect of, **18** 1389;
physiological and psychological, **3** 438;
positive activity of, **8** 702;
positive and negative aspects of, **5** 580, 609 (*see also above* negative);
possession by, **11** 648; **16** 397;
powers of, **18** 1505;
predominance of, **13** 16;
as *prima materia,* **12** 516;
primitives and, **6** 422; **11** 28;
productivity of, **7** 205/446;
and projection, *see* projection *s.v.*;
and Prometheus-Pandora myth, **6** 294, 300;
prospective role of subliminal combinations, **7** 197;
Proteus personifying, **9ii** 338;
psyche and, *see* psyche *s.v.*;
psychic forces and, **10** 387;
as psychic modality, **8** 249;

psychoanalysis and, **2** 662; **4** 562; **10** 2; **11** 539;
psychoid, **14** 788;
psychology of, *see* psychology *s.v.*;
and psychosis, **3** 491;
as a quality, **17** 199;
rapprochement with, **13** 222;
reality of, *see* reality *s.v.*;
as real psyche, **16** 205;
reasons for controlling, **8** 159;
receptivity of, **1** 138, 147;
reductive function of, **8** 496;
reflected in dogma, **11** 81;
regulating factors of, **8** 165;
regulating images and, **13** 396;
rejection of, **5** 450; **6** 83;
and relationship, **17** 326;
is relative, **8** 385 (*see also below* space-time relativity);
and religion, **10** 26; **14** 193;
religion as escape from, **11** 71;
religious aspect of, **7** 471; **10** 565; **18** 1583;
religious function in, **11** 3;
in religious persons, **10** 563;
repressed material in, **16** 61; **17** 199a;
and repression, **7** 202/443;
repudiation of, **7** 472;
in schizophrenia, is dreamlike, **18** 832;
scientific theories and, **16** 478;
and the sea, *see* sea *s.v.* symbol;
secret of opus in, **12** 361;
seeks to divide and unite, **11** 740;
self and, **9ii** 1;
self in, birth of, **14** 548;
self latent in, **12** 105*n*;
settlement with, **7** 342;
sexuality of, **16** 533–4;
significance of, **8** 491, 494; **16** 325;
as skeleton in cupboard, **12** 207;
as "somatic," **16** 231;
soul as personification of, **6**

281, 294, 421, 424; **12** 397;
soul as projection of, **9ii** 219;
soul's relation to, **6** 278–9, 420;
space-time relativity of, **12** 175, 247;
spatial and temporal relations in, **9i** 408;
spectral world of, **18** 759;
spiral/circular movement of, **12** 34, 129, 325;
splitting off of, **7** 195;
spontaneous: manifestation of, **11** 35; statements of, **13** 241; symbolism of, **13** 364;
statements about it unverifiable, **8** 417;
stone as outcropping of, **13** 289;
as storehouse of relics, **18** 84;
structure of, **13** 51, 90, 253; **18** 4;
subconscious/superconscious, **12** 175, 201, 397;
subject and object merged in, **5** 500;
subject of, **8** 369;
subliminal material in, **7** 203/444;
and subliminal perceptions, **18** 747;
submission to, **11** 273*n*;
suppression of, **6** 82–3;
supra-individual universality of, **5** 258;
suprapersonal, **10** 13;
surrender to, **5** 675;
symbol(s) and, **4** 680; **6** 182–3, 202; as exponent of, **6** 204; spontaneous, **13** 364; symbolic language of, **18** 837;
symbol(s) of, **5** 261; **11** 779;
INSTANCES: black, **4** 737;
    dragon, *see* ANIMALS: dragon *s.v.*;
    mother, **5** 450;
    "our sea," **9ii** 219;
    sea, *see* sea *s.v.* symbol;
    snake, **5** 580; **9i** 651; **13**

349*n*, 448–9;
swarm of people, **5** 300;
water, *see* water *s.v.*;
whale, **12** *fig.* 222;
symbol-producing, **18** 603, 637;
symbols representing, **11** 810;
and sympathetic system, **9i** 41;
synthetic work of, **12** 323;
and telepathy, **8** 813;
tendencies of, **17** 199;
therapeutic approach to, **7** 192–200;
theriomorphism and, *see* theriomorphism *s.v.*;
timelessness of, **16** 529, 531;
as "total vision," **11** 897;
transcendental, **12** 175;
transformation of, **11** 854;
transformation process in, **5** 669;
transpersonal, **7** 103;
a treasure-house of lost memories, **18** 747;
treatment of, **14** 274–5;
turning away from, **16** 149;
two parts of, **8** 588–9; **17** 207;
unconcern of, **7** 346;
underestimation of, **12** 291;
undifferentiated, **6** 180–1;
unfavourable side of, **7** 195;
uniformity of, **5** 258;
uniting symbol in, **10** 784;
is universal, **5** 258;
unknowable, **14** 710;
as unknown in inner world, **9ii** 2;
as unknown psychic, **8** 382;
as whale, **12** *fig.* 222;
without qualities, **9ii** 298;
of woman, *see above* female;
working out solution of conflict, **5** 117;
worldwide human, **6** 193;
Wundt's view of, **8** 351;
yoga and, **11** 871
unconscious, collective, **4** (*p*302); **5** 258*n*, 447; **6** 373, 383, 412, 624,

unconscious, collective (*cont.*):
842, 851; **7** (*pp*v, 7), 103, 110, 113, 123, 150–3, 220, 231, 243, 254, 275, 374, 395, 509, 516, 520; **8** 230–1, 254, 270, 311–12, 589, 720; **9i** 3–5, 262, 543, 552, 634, 711; **10** 13, 285, 447, 714; **12** 31, 38, 40, 42, 57, 68*n*, 81, 265, 329; **13** (*p*3), 44, 46, 218, 253, 287, 337*n*, 450, 481; **14** 88, 93, 101, 107, 124, 128, 145, 257, 349, 372, 374, 410, 744; **15** 126, 152, 174; **16** 15, 111, 218, 254, 470, 476, 502, 504, 530; **17** 207; **18** 84–5, 1156;

TITLES: *The Archetypes and the Collective Unconscious,* **9i**; "The Archetypes of the Collective Unconscious," **7** 141–91; "Archetypes of the Collective Unconscious," **9i** 1–86; "The Concept of the Collective Unconscious," **9i** 87–110; "The Hypothesis of the Collective Unconscious," **18** 1223–5; "The Personal and the Collective (or Transpersonal) Unconscious," **7** 97–120;
activation of, **18** 369, 372;
adaptation to, **7** 252;
in alchemy, **16** 531;
and ancestral life, **7** 118;
anima/animus and, **5** 500; **9i** 439, 518;
archetypes of, **5** 224; **9i** 88–90; **12** 38, 42, 329; **14** 101, 107; **18** 80, 1117;
and astrology, **8** 325, 392;
basis of individual psyche, **8** 321;
brain and, **17** 207–8;
Catholics and, **8** 338;
in children, *see* children *s.v.*;
composition of, **7** 520;
contents of, **5** 259; **6** 625, 655; **7** 153, 220, 233, 387, 513, 515, 518, 520; **8** 325, 589; **18** 79; activated, **18** 92–3; autonomy of,

7 233;
danger of its replacing reality, **8** 595;
definition of, **5** 631; **9i** 88–90; **13** 11;
deposit of ancestral experience, **8** 729;
diagnosis not always easy, **9i** 92;
Dionysian state and, **6** 230;
discovery of, **18** 1131;
dominants of, **7** 377, 388;
in dreams, **7** 248;
Elijah as, **18** 1526;
fantasies of, **7** 372, 387;
in Germans, **18** 1322;
and Gnosticism, **18** 1480, 1501;
historical mirror-image of world, **7** 507;
identical in all men, **9i** 3;
images of, play positive role, **7** 183;
immortality of, **8** 673;
influence on individual psyche, **7** 240, 269;
inherited, **8** 676; **9i** 90;
irrepresentable, **8** 840;
and mana-personality, **7** 377, 388;
Mercurius as, *see* Mercurius *s.v.* unconscious, collective;
as microcosm, **8** 931; **11** 373;
mother as, **5** 393; **12** 92;
and mutation of dominant ideas, **18** 1161;
and nations, **18** 1330;
patient's, onslaught of, **18** 354;
and personal unconscious, *see* unconscious, personal *s.v.* and collective;
poets and, **6** 321–3;
and primitive psychology, **18** 1286, 1288;
processes of, **18** 5; in modern man, **13** (*p*4); and mystics, **18** 218;
projection of, **10** 43; **13** 277;
and psychosis, **18** 1159;

purposiveness of, **8** 675;
reaction from, **9i** 44;
regulating influence of, **18** 1162;
sea as, **12** 57; **16** 15;
and self, as ruler of, **5** 576;
sheer objectivity, **9i** 46;
soul and, **6** 281;
spirit in, **5** 641;
spiritualism and, **8** 599;
Spitteler and, **6** 324;
as sum of instincts and archetypes, **8** 281;
symbolism in, **18** 81;
as totality of archetypes, **18** 1536;
unconscious of own contents, **8** 674;
understanding of, **7** 253;
unity of, **10** 849; **16** 254;
why so called, **9i** 3;
Zarathustra and, **6** 322;
see also unconscious *s.v.* impersonal
unconscious, and conscious, **14** 275; **17** 102;
   TITLES: "Conscious and Unconscious," **8** 381–7; "Conscious, Unconscious, and Individuation," **9i** 489–524;
   ascendancy of ucs. over cs., **5** 681;
   assault of ucs. on cs., **5** 459;
   bringing together, **5** 459;
   collaboration, **6** 204;
   compensatory relationship, *see* unconscious *s.v.* compensatory;
   conflict and synthesis, **14** 523;
   confrontation, **14** 257, 294, 306;
   conscious view of unconscious, **9i** 42;
   contamination of, **14** 367;
   differentiation, **6** 268; **11** 64;
   dissociation between, *see* dissociation *s.v.*;
   equal status, **14** 540;
   gap between, **5** 683;

in human personality, **11** 66;
integration of, **5** 459; **16** 531;
invasion of cs. by ucs., **5** 577, 616–17, 683;
necessity for connection between, **5** 457, 463;
in neurotic, **17** 203;
opposition between, **6** 910;
personality, **14** 705;
separation of, removed, **8** 145;
split between, **9ii** 390n; **13** 48, 298;
ucs. made cs., **14** 258, 446, 498;
union, **4** 761; **5** 614; **6** 187; **11** 285; **13** 223; **14** 364, 541, 593, 706, 770; **16** 474; feminine personification of, **13** 225 (*see also* unconscious, and conscious mind *s.v.*; unconscious, and consciousness *s.v.*)
unconscious, and conscious mind, **12** 23, 137, 166, 192, 436n, 452; **16** 12, 125–6, 522; **17** 195, 227;
   attempts to abolish separation between, **12** 174;
   collision, **16** 533;
   compensatory relation, *see* unconscious *s.v.* compensatory;
   complementary relation between, **14** 124;
   conflict of, *see* conflict *s.v.*;
   conjunction, **5** 672;
   descent of cs. into ucs., **12** 437;
   dialectic, **12** 3;
   energy attracted by ucs. from cs., **5** 671;
   fear of ucs., **9ii** 355;
   forward striving checked by ucs., **5** 458;
   and guidance, **15** 114;
   influence of ucs. on conscious mind, **15** 114, 123;
   invasion of conscious mind, by ucs., **5** 577, 616–17;
   mistrust between, **14** 145;
   modification by ucs., **12** 26;
   products of, **11** 64;
   separation of, **12** 12, 174;

172-9

underworld, **9i** 156; **12** 29, 437, 438, *figs.* 69, 151;
    dragon chained in, **13** 290;
    Egyptian, **5** 566;
    gods of, **9ii** 351;
    imprisonment in, **14** 316;
    journey to, **5** 449, 572, 654;
    life in, **5** 634;
    psychic, **18** 581;
    and upper world, **5** 449n;
    and water, **18** 259, 271;
    see also darkness; Hades

undifferentiated unconscious state, **5** 650

unemployed, in Germany, **10** 373, 420

Unesco (United Nations Educational, Scientific, and Cultural Organization), Second General Conference, **18** (*p*606n);
    J.'s memorandum to, **18** 1388–1402;
    Royaumont Conference, **18** (*p*606n)

unfaithfulness, in marriage, **17** 334

Uniate rites, **11** 311n

unicellular organisms, psychic function and, **8** 233

unicorn, *see* ANIMALS *s.v.*

unification/*henosis*, **13** 357, 358

uniformity, psychic, **8** 228, 436

unifying function, *see* function *s.v.*

unigenitus, **10** 751; **12** 458, 521;
    Mercurius as, **13** 283;
    see also Monogenes

unio: mentalis/mental union, **14** 663–6, 670, 674, 679, 682–7, 690, 694–5, 707, 711, 722, 730, 742, 747, 752, 757–9, 773;
    mystica, **5** 438; **14** 208, 634, 767, 771; **16** 354, 419, 462, 525, 532 (*see also* marriage, divine/mystic);
    naturalis, **14** 696

union, **7** 156; **13** 446;
    alchemical, **16** 509; of elements, **16** 451; of king and son,

12 210n, 446;
    with anima, **13** 435;
    of conscious and unconscious, *see* unconscious, and conscious *s.v.*;
    of consciousness/life, **13** 29, 36;
    of dissimilars, **12** 433;
    with feminine personification of unconscious, **13** 225, 226;
    of God and man, **11** 427; **13** 301n; and matter, **16** 381;
    hermaphroditic, *see* hermaphrodite;
    of irreconcilables, **12** 186, *fig.* 72;
    of like and like, **12** 435, 496;
    with mother, **5** 398, 500, 640;
    mystic, **5** 438;
    of nature and spiritual man, **13** 194;
    of natures, in alchemy, **13** 198; **14** 654;
    of opposites, *see* opposites, union of;
    of persons in Trinity, **13** 357 (*see also* Trinity *s.v.* unity);
    with self, **13** 331;
    of sexes, **12** *fig.* 60;
    with shadow, **13** 435;
    with soul, **13** 193;
    of soul and body, **12** 418, 462, 500;
    symbolism of cross as, *see* cross *s.v.*;
    of tree and snake, **13** *fig.* 12;
    of water and fire, **12** *figs.* 72, 160; **13** 310;
    see also *unio* s.v. *mystica*

uniped(s), **14** pls. 4, 5, 6; *see also* Monocolus

uniqueness, **8** 821;
    individual, not always an asset, **17** 256

United Kingdom, **10** 601; *see also* England

United Nations Educational, Scientific, and Cultural Organization, *see* Unesco

United States, *see* America
uniting symbol, **6** 318–74, 434–60,
828; **8** 396*n*; **9i** 285, 293, 523&*n*;
9ii 304; **10** 734, 774, 784; **11**
396*n*, 712, 727, 738; **12** 404&*n*,
553, 557; **14** 669, 707; **16** 451,
462, 474, 533;
   TITLES: "The Significance of
the Uniting Symbol," **6** 318–74;
"The Uniting Symbol in Spitteler," **6** 434–60;
   in alchemy, **9i** 523;
   Brahmanic conception of, **6**
331–47;
   in Chinese philosophy, **6** 358–
70;
   dragon as, **12** 460;
   in Indian religion, **6** 348–57;
   Mercurius as, *see* Mercurius
s.v.;
   of self, **8** 396;
   self as, **10** 779;
   in the unconscious, **10** 784
unity, **4** 556; **8** 927; **9i** 430; **9ii** 59,
60, 64; **10** 299; **12** 165; **13** 40,
226;
   in alchemy, **11** 353; **12** 31, *fig.*
251; **14** 760; absolute, in
Kircher's system, **9ii** 417; of arcane substance/arcanum, *see*
arcane substance *s.v.*; of Mercurius, *see* Mercurius *s.v.* unity;
transcendent, **16** 454; — stone
as, **9ii** 264;
   archetypes and, *see* archetypes
s.v.;
   circle as symbol of, **12** 165;
   of conscious psyche, **11** 443;
   of consciousness, *see* consciousness *s.v.*;
   of cosmos, **11** 440;
   and diversity, **16** 400;
   divine, **12** 31;
   in God, **13** 209*n*;
   of God and man, **11** 177; and
world, **11** 201;
   of individual, and release of instincts, **10** 661;

inner, **16** 444;
   of life and consciousness, **13**
33, 36, 43;
   longing for, **17** 334;
   mandala as symbol of, **12** 32;
   of mankind, **10** 568;
   mystical, in Mass, **11** 378;
   of nature, **8** 865;
   original/primordial, **11** 445; **13**
334, 456;
   and quaternity, as opposites, **10**
774;
   self as archetype of, **12** 30;
   symbol of, **9ii** 59; mandala as,
12 32 (*see also* uniting symbol);
as symbol of the self, **9ii** 358;
synthesis of four as, **12** 165,
210
universal, **7** 241/462;
   association-chain, *see* associa-
tion-chain(s) *s.v.*;
   being, **13** 59;
   and individual, **16** 2–4;
   man, **16** 2;
   midpoint, **13** 349;
   myth-motifs, *see* myth(s) *s.v.*
motifs
universality of collective psyche, **7**
240
Universal Mind, **11** 759–60, 768,
782–4
universals/*universalia,* **6** 40–1, 68–
72, 473, 508; **7** 506; **8** 4*n*; **9i**
149; **13** 378; **14** 630*n*;
   TITLE: "The Problem of Universals," **6** 40–95;
   and "clash of temperaments" in
philosophy, **6** 508;
   Plato and, **6** 56–9; **11** 770;
   see also Abelard; *flatus vocis*
universe: fantasies of antiquity *re,* **5**
24;
   opus a model of, **12** 214;
   threefold and fourfold, **12** *fig.*
1;
   unobstructed, **18** 753;
   see also world
university(-ies), **9i** 156; **15** 86;

and medical psychology, **16** 49;
teaching of psychotherapy at,
10 1070
unjust steward, parable of, **13** 292
unknowable, the, **11** 417
unknown: ego and, **9ii** 2;
    fear of, **17** 146;
    methods of investigating, **17**
    173–4;
    two groups of objects in, **9ii** 2;
    woman, *see* woman *s.v.*
unpleasant events: amnesia for, **1**
319;
    repressed from consciousness,
    1 293, 298
unstable, *see* instability
Unternährer, A., **5** 582–3;
    Geheimes Reskript, **5** 582*n*
Unum, see NUMBERS: one
unus mundus/unitary world, **10** 778,
780, 852; **13** 149; **14** 660–1,
663–4, 679, 718;
    and third stage in alchemical
    opus, **14** 759–75
Upanishads, **5** 227*n*; **6** 193, 357,
411, 526; **9i** 554; **10** 175, 398; **11**
140, 769, 859, 952; **12** 137, 452,
533; **13** 287; **14** 735; **15** 87; **16**
378;
    on horse sacrifice, **5** 424–5,
    657–9;
    on new state of man, **5** 657;
    paradox of great and small in,
    5 183–4;
    tr. by R. E. Hume, *The Thirteen*
    Principal Upanishads, **5** 176*n*,
    657*n*; **6** 328*n*, 329*nn*, 334*nn*; **9i**
    218*n*; **11** 890*n*; **13** 301*n*;
    tr. by A. H. Anquetil du Perron
    into Latin, *Oupnek'hat,* **6** 193;
    10 175; **11** 859; **14** 735&*n*; **15**
    87;
    tr. by Max Müller, *The Up-*
    anishads, **5** 176*n*; **12** 209*n*; **14**
    159*n*;
    tr. by S. Radhakrishnan, *The*
    Principal Upanishads, **9ii** 348*n*;
    Aitareya, **5** 229;

Brihadāranyaka, **5** 227, 229–30,
    246*n*, 424, 657; **6** 328*n*, 329*nn*,
    334&*n*; **9ii** 349; **12** 209; **13**
    301*n*; **14** 159*n*;
Chhandogya, **6** 334&*n*; **11** 809*n*;
    12 533*n*; **13** 267*n*, 412*n*;
Isha, **6** 329&*n*;
Katha, **5** 179&*n*; **6** 329&*n*; **11**
    890*n*; **14** 158*n*; tr. R. Guénon,
    Man and His Becoming according
    to the Vedanta, **5** 179*n*; tr. P.
    Swami and W. B. Yeats, **5** 179*n*;
Kaushitaki, **6** 328&*n*;
Kena, **9ii** 348;
Maitrayana-Brahmana, **9i** 677,
    690; **13** 287*n*;
Shvetashvatara, **5** 176–8, 182,
    296*n*, 596*n*; **6** 329&*nn*; **9i**
    218&*n*;
Taittiriya, **6** 334&*n*;
Tejobindu, **6** 328&*n*
Upa-Purana, *see* Puranas
upper: and lower/*superius* and *in-*
ferius, **12** 25–6, 163, 167*n*, *fig.* 78;
    as opposites, **8** 401; **14** 7, 8;
    world, *see* world *s.v.*
uprootedness, **8** 815
upwards, displacement, **13** 334
Ur, excavations at, **11** 328*n*
Uraeus/*uraeus,* **5** 146, 149; **13** 399*n*
Urania, **9ii** 145*n*
Uranos, **14** 734;
    the One, **5** 198
urge(s): instinctive, **16** 361;
    to power, *see* Adler, A. *s.v.*
    power principle
urination, need for, dream of, **4** 82,
92
urine, **13** 381;
    as *aqua permanens (urina*
    puerorum), **12** *fig.* 121;
    boy's/dog's, **16** 408;
    and fertilization, **4** 511;
    pressure of, **4** 736;
    as *prima materia,* **12** 336;
    of three-legged ass, **5** 428
urn, cinerary, **5** 604*n*
uroboros, *see* ANIMALS *s.v.*

V

vac (speech) in Brahmanas, **6** 340–4, 347

vacuum, **3** 54, 183n, 186; psychic, **17** 185

vagrancy: case of, **1** 19; *see also* wandering

vagus, **7** 206

Vaidehi, **11** 924–5

Vairochana, **11** 852

Vajasanayi Samhita, *see* Samhitas

Vajramandala, **12** 139n, *fig.* 43

Vajra-Sattva, **11** 852

valencies, four, **12** 327

Valens, Emperor, **18** 703

Valentinians, **5** 563; **6** 254; **9i** 120n; **11** 216; **14** 528n, 576n, 602n; on autopator, **9ii** 298; on demiurge as hermaphrodite, **13** 366; *horos* doctrine, **9ii** 118n; and Ogdoad, **9ii** 307n; Secundus, **9ii** 171n; *see also* monad; syzygy; tetrad, second

Valentino, Rudolph, **10** 976

Valentinus (Gnostic), **9ii** 171&n, 370n, 428; **11** 62n, 422; **12** 436n; **14** 379; **18** 1642; Hymn of, **11** 245n; and shadow of Christ, **9ii** 75n, 171; text, **18** 1827

Valentinus, Basilius (pseudo), *see* ALCHEMICAL WRITERS *s.v.*

Valéry, Paul, **10** 943; *History and Politics,* **10** 943n

Valhalla, **10** 397n; **16** 347

validity: general, of psyche's contents, **7** 511, 516; of hypothesis, **7** 216; relative, **7** 118; universal, **7** 229/447, 240/460; and subjective, **3** 406

Valkyries, **5** 427; **10** 389, 393; **16** 347

valley, **13** 17

"valley spirit," **9i** 40

Valli, L.: "Die Geheimsprache Dantes," **12** 235n

Valours, Berthe de (somnambulistic personality), **1** 54, 63

valuation(s), **11** 245; over-, **7** 206, 212, 216; personal, **7** 216

value(s), **7** 80, 84, 115–16, 320, 394; **9ii** 52–4; **13** 24; **16** 58; absolute, **7** 481; accumulation of, **7** 344; change into opposites, **8** 781; Christian, and Eastern thought, **11** 773; collective, **7** 459, 504; and individual uniqueness, **17** 255; comparison of, **8** 16; conscious, **7** 347; **13** 15; disappearance of, **8** 17; created by subjective reactions, **5** 126; discredited, **7** 325; and display of energy, **7** 71; emotional, **13** 341; ethical, **16** 384; of fantasy, **7** 490; feeling and, **18** 23; feeling as function of, **9ii** 61; general, **7** 515; heuristic, of hypothesis, **7** 216; highest, **7** 394; holiness and, **11** 225; idea of, **18** 1; intensities, **4** 779; introvert and extravert, **11** 770; irrational, of child, **17** 81; -judgements, **2** 51–3, 99, 146, 149, 349, 462, 1006; emotional, **5** 1; loss of, **16** 280; and return of, **11** 149; moral, **13** 230; **17** 80; reversal

value(s) (*cont.*):
 of, **13** 228*n*;
 and myth, **11** 451;
 in neurosis, **7** 93;
 and non-value, as opposites, **7** 115;
 personal, **7** 520; and impersonal, **7** 229/448;
 positive and negative, **7** 71–2;
 psychological, **3** 418; **6** 481;
 in psychology, **14** 613;
 quanta, **9ii** 54;
 reactivation of, **18** 1100;
 reality, **7** 350;
 real personal, **7** 94*n*;
 relativity of, **7** 115;
 relativization of, **16** 502;
 revaluation of, **7** 115;
 reversal of, **6** 449; **9ii** 368;
 spiritual, **17** 81;
 subjective, **8** 14–17;
 transformation of, **5** 553;
 true, **7** 261/477;
 unconscious, **8** 17;
 of woman, **6** 399
Vamana, **9ii** 272
vampire, *see* ANIMALS *s.v.*
Van Beek, see under *Passio Perpetuae*
Vancouver, **9i** 39
van der Hoop, Dr., **10** 1048, 1055
Van der Post, L., **11** 370, 371; **14** 690*n*
Van Deventer, J.: *Ein Fall von sanguinischer Minderwerthigkeit,* **1** 188&*n*, 191
Vanen (Icelandic gods), **5** 214*n*
van Gogh, Vincent, **10** 740*n*
van Houten, D., **10** 764*n*
van Liew, C. G., *see under* Ziehen
Vansteenberghe, Edmond, *see under* Cusanus
vapor terrae, **13** 173
vapour(s), **13** 255;
 of incense, **11** 319;
 two, **16** 403, 459
Varendonck, J.: "Les Idéals des enfants," **18** (*p*421)

variability, **7** 267
variety performance, **12** 102, 105, 118, 127
Varro, **5** 183*n*
Varuna (sky-god), **6** 349; **13** 341&*n*
vas/vessel, **6** 371*n*, 397, 406; **9ii** 352–3; **13** 97, 109, 115–16, *figs.* B4, B6; **14** 14&*n*, 75, 181, 261, 284, 296, 399, 402, 438–41; **18** 265;
 as *aqua permanens, see aqua s.v. permanens, vas* as;
 bene clausum/well sealed, **12** 187, 219, 347;
 cave as, **12** 259;
 ciconia vel storea, **13** 416*n*;
 as container, **18** 407–9;
 cover of, **14** 439; *capitelum,* **14** 81*n*;
 distilling, **13** 117, 214, *fig.* B7;
 egg as, **12** 306, 338, *fig.* 22; **13** 109;
 feminine/maternal aspect of, **13** 113; **14** 14, 534, 535;
 furnace as, **12** 338;
 garden as, **12** 338*n*;
 glass, **13** 139*n*;
 Gnostic, *see* Gnostic *s.v.*;
 Hermetic/Hermeticum/Hermetis, **5** 182; **9i** 686; **9ii** 378; **11** 156; **12** 246*n*, 338, 350, 391, *figs.* 23, 120, 121, 153, 226, 230, 236; **13** 95, 97, 113, 245; **14** 373, 433, 742; **16** 467, 496; Anthropos as, **9ii** 380; *cucurbita,* **5** 245; **14** 409, 410, 412, 434&*n*; feminine, **16** 454, 533; fire, water, as, **12** 338*nn*; **13** 113; *naturale,* **9ii** 380; "philosophical Pelican," **9ii** 377&*n*; **12** 167*n*; **13** 115, 185; **14** 8, 10*n*; —, *circulatorium,* **13** 416, *figs.* B2, B7; *rotundum*/round, **11** 123, 152; **14** 261*n*, 265, 373, 626*n*, 731*n*; —, *cerebri,* **12** 517*n*; **13** 113; of transformation, **14** 12, 142, 369; **16** 402;
 ideas as, **18** 745;

verdigris, *see* COLOURS: *viriditas/greenness s.v.*

Verena, St., **18** 1077

veritas, **9ii** 246, 248, 264, 281; **12** 377;
   -prima, **9ii** 276n

Verlaine, P.: "Mon Rêve familier," in *Poèmes saturniens,* **5** 682&n

Verona: Priapus statue, **5** 680, pl. LXI*b*
   Roman inscription, **5** 297

vertebrates, *see* ANIMALS *s.v.*

Verteuil tapestry, **12** *fig.* 264

vertical/horizontal, *see* horizontal

vertigo, **7** 467;
   psychogenic, **6** 656

Verus Hermes, see ALCHEMICAL WRITERS *s.v.*

Vesalius, Andreas, **15** 34

vesicant, **13** 193n

vesicle, germinal, *see* germinal *s.v.*

Vespasian, **18** 1521

Vespers, **13** 390n

vessel, see *vas*

vestments, ecclesiastical, **11** 75n

Vettius Valens: *Anthologiarum* IX, **13** 412n

vetula, **14** 14

via regia, dream as, *see* Freud: on dreams *s.v.*

"Via veritatis unicae," *see* ALCHEMICAL COLLECTIONS: *Mus. herm s.v.*

Vibhandaka, **12** 534

vibrations, **9i** 550

vice, **7** 236, 307, 400;
   collective, **7** 237/458;
   and virtue, *see* virtue and vice

Victorian era, **15** 45–9

victory: crown of, **16** 496;
   of the spirit, **13** 453

Vidarr, fight with Fenris-Wolf, **5** *fig.* 33

Vienna, **7** 6/415, 410; **10** 471, 908, 1055

Vienna Psychoanalytic Society, **18** 1027&n, 1028, 1030n

Viennese school (of psychoanalysis), **4** 342, 658, 673; **7** 442

view: causal point of, **7** 88, 239;
   day-time and night-time, **8** 426;
   teleological point of, **7** 88, 239

vif-argent, **13** 255

Vigenerus/Vigenère, *see* ALCHEMICAL COLLECTIONS: *Theatr. chem. s.v.*

Vignon, P.: *The Shroud of Christ,* **14** 526n

Vigouroux, A., **2** 1181;
   Étude sur la résistance électrique chez les mélancoliques, **2** (*p*580);
   and P. Juquelier: *La Contagion mentale,* **4** 701n; "Contribution clinique à l'étude des délires du rêve," **18** (*p*421)

Vigouroux, R., **2** 1180;
   "L'Électricité du corps humain," **2** (*p*580);
   "Sur la résistance électrique considérée comme signe clinique," **2** (*p*580)

Vili (winged demons), **9i** 413

Villa dei Misteri, Pompeii, **12** 177n

Villa, G.: *Einleitung in die Psychologie der Gegenwart/Contemporary Psychology,* **6** 723n, 792n; **8** 350n

Villanova, Arnaldus de, *see* ALCHEMICAL WRITERS: Arnaldus

vimana, **10** 1003

vinculum, of soul and body, **16** 504

vindemia, **13** 359n;
   Hermetis, **12** 302; **13** 414n

vine/*vitis, see* TREES *s.v.*

vinegar, **9ii** 377n; **12** 336, 387; **13** 103&n, 445;
   celestial, **12** 337;
   of philosophers, **13** 113;
   as *prima materia,* **12** 425;
   as quicksilver, **13** 103n

vineyard, symbolism of, **11** 612; *see also* TREES: vine

vinum ardens, **10** 741; **12** 94, 338n, *fig.* 152; **16** 408;
   Mercurius as, **10** 629;
   see also wine

Viola petraea lutea (mountain pansy), **13** 171n
violation, motif of, **13** 99
violence, in dream-symbols, **10** 447, 449
violet, see COLOURS s.v.
viper, see ANIMALS s.v. serpent
Viraj, **12** 533
Virchow, Rudolf, **7** 282
Virgil, **8** 930; **12** 353,*fig.* 69; **14** 92;
    Aeneid, **12** (*p*39); **14** 92n;
    Eclogue IV, **5** 119&n; **10** 250;
    Eclogue V, **18** 373n;
    Georgics, **8** 930n
virgin(s), **12** 438, 470, 481; **13** 132, 227;
    "anima," **5** 497;
    birth, **9i** 282; **11** 4; **18** 617, 1360 (*see also* Christ/Jesus Christ s.v. birth);
    bride, **12** 484;
    conception by, **5** 497;
    dream-image, **17** 208;
    of light, **12** 506;
    male, **11** 718; **12** 470n;
    Mary as, *see* Mary s.v.;
    Mercurius as, *see* Mercurius s.v.;
    milk of/*lac virginis,* **9ii** 246; **12** 454, 490, *figs.* 152, 222; **13** 255n, 380; **16** 403;
    mother (of stone), **12** 462; **13** 392; **14** 499;
    mother goddess as, **9ii** 164;
    seven, **12** *fig.* 5;
    sign of, *see* zodiac, twelve signs of s.v. Virgo;
    test of, **5** 572;
    and unicorn, *see* ANIMALS: unicorn s.v.
virginity, **14** 527n;
    secret of, **18** 617
Virgo, *see* zodiac, twelve signs of
virgo/virgines, **13** 218;
    redimita (Crowned Maid), **12** 491, 499;
    terrae, **12** 415;
    velandae, **13** 81
Viridarium chymicum, see ALCHEMICAL

WRITERS s.v. Stolcius de Stolcenberg
viriditas, see COLOURS s.v.
Virolleaud, C., **9ii** 181;
    "La Légende de Baal, dieu des phéniciens," **9ii** 182n;
    "Note complémentaire sur le poème de Mot et Alein," **9ii** 182n
vir rubeus, see COLOURS: red s.v. man
virtue(s), **7** 51, 115, 236, 237/458, 267; **9ii** 46, 47;
    Christian, **16** 385, 522;
    collective, **7** 237/458;
    disadvantages of, **11** 291;
    and vice, *see sep. entry below*
virtue and vice: liberation from vice, **11** 826;
    as opposites, **7** 237/458;
    rooted in vice, **17** 195;
    "vice of the virtuous," **7** 306
virtuousness, **7** 50
Vir Unus, **9ii** 320; **11** 419; **14** 388, 490
virus, **11** 447
"visceral thinking," *see* thinking s.v.
Vischer, F. T. von, **18** 1414;
    Auch Einer, **6** 501n, 627; **8** 202&n
Vishnu, **5** 449, 545; **9ii** 176n, 272; **10** 992; **13** 339;
    boar-headed, shakti of, **5** pl. IV*a*;
    bound about body with a rope, **9i** 554n;
    as fish, **5** pl. XLVII, 449; **9ii** 176; **12** 533,*fig.* 255; **13** 334;
    lotus growing out of navel, **5** pl. XLVI*a*, 449;
    as tortoise, **12** *fig.* 75
vishuddha, **16** 560
Vishvakarman, All-Creator, **5** 647
visible and invisible, as opposites, **12** 398
Visigoths, **18** 253a
"Visio Arislei," *see* ALCHEMICAL WRITERS s.v.
vision(s), **1** 106; **3** 565; **5** 157, 158; **7**

229/448, 254; **8** 581; **9i** 263, 309, 318, 506; **9ii** 351; **10** 663; **11** 81, 110, 137, 665; **13** 215, 220, 245, 374; **18** 710, 711;

of alchemists/alchemical, **12** 350, 356, 404&*n*, 449; **13** 88; **14** 446; of Isis, **13** 107; of Krates, **12** 349*n*, 356, 391*n*; **13** 88*n*, 109*n*; **14** 416;

archetypal figures in (wise old man), **9i** 398, 408;

artists', **7** 289, 342; and artistic creation, **15** 139–46;

of city, **5** 348;

collective, **9i** 408; **10** 597, 608, 610, 616; **18** 1431, 1441;

concretization of, **11** 937–8;

and fantasies, **17** 193;

functional, **3** 582; **5** 302;

of God, *see* God *s.v.*;

and hallucinations, *see* hallucinations;

of heaven, **11** 486;

hypnagogic, **1** 117;

hysteric's, of conflagration, **1** 130;

of light, **1** 101*n* (*see also* Brother Klaus; Maitland *s.v.* vision);

as morbid symptoms, **18** 466;

of oneself, **9i** 274;

primitives and, **3** 453; **6** 46; **7** 229; "big," **7** 276;

and Resurrection, **18** 1562;

of saints, **7** 108; as compensations, **10** 650; female, of heavenly marriage, **18** 713;

syzygies as projections in, **9i** 130&*n*, 131;

unconscious and, **7** 214, 217, 469;

unconscious contents and, **9i** 263&*n*; **12** 57*n*;

warning, **18** 783;

see also hallucinations

INSTANCES:

J. S., when a dying man, of his own sarcophagus, **18** 1708;

J.'s patients', **1** 7–8, 12–14; **7** 366–7; **18** 85; epileptic boy child's, of little bearded man and of nun, **17** 137; **18** 810–15; professor's, repeated in old woodcut, **18** 524, 1268; schizophrenic Swiss clerk's, of solar phallus, **5** 151–2, 223; **6** 746*n*, 851&*n*; **8** 228, 317–20; **9i** 105–9; **18** 85; S. W., a somnambulistic young girl's, **1** 43–4; young man's, of stars in river, **7** 231–2, 252;

see also under the following:
ALCHEMICAL WRITERS: Zosimos; Black Elk; Brother Klaus; Daniel; Eckhart; Enoch; Esdras; Ezekiel; Guillaume de Digulleville; Hermas; Hildegard of Bingen; Hölderlin; Ignatius Loyola; John the Evangelist; Maitland; Mechthild von Magdeburg; Nebuchadnezzar; Nietzsche *s.v.* Zarathustra; Paul; Peter; Pius XII; Spinoza; Swedenborg; Tewekkul-Beg; Zarathustra/Zoroaster; *see also* DREAMS, WAKING/FANTASIES

vision: angle of, in swoon state, **8** 955;

field of, **1** 255, 284; **3** 109&*n*

visionaries, **1** 106; **18** 713

"visionary" mode of artistic creation, **15** 139, 141;

sources of, **15** 144

vis Mercurii, **13** 171*n*

visual images, *see* image(s) *s.v.*

visualization(s), **7** 365; **13** 22;

of "creative point," **13** 37

visual sphere: automatism in, **1** 98;

excitation of, **1** 99;

irruption of hypnosis into, **1** 128

"vita cosmographica" (Paracelsus), **13** 205

W

Wachandi tribe, *see* Australian aborigines

Wachlmayr, A.: *Das Christgeburtsbild*, **5** pl. III

Wachsmuth, K., *see under* Stobaeus

Wackerbarth, Graf August J. L. von: *Merkwürdige Geschichte der Gog und Magog*, **9ii** 133n

wading, **5** 503n

Wagalaweia songs, **10** 389&n

Wagner, R., **6** 401, 408, 426n; **7** 306; **8** 162; **10** 383, 432, 435; **11** 58; **12** 293; **15** 143, 151; **18** 1281; archetypes in music of, **14** 754; Fire Music, **12** 293; Loki motif in, **12** 297; *Flying Dutchman*, **18** 366; *Parsifal*, **6** 114, 324, 371; **14** 375, 753; **15** 142, 151; **17** 207; **18** 261, 263, 1684; Amfortas' wound, **6** 105, 371–3; **13** 70; **14** 339; Klingsor, **6** 371; Kundry, **6** 371, 372; **7** 374; **14** 339; Nietzsche and, **7** 43; **8** 162; **10** 435; *Der Ring des Nibelungen*: Brünhilde in, **5** 555, 559–69, 602–10; Siegfried legend, **5** 555–6, 565–9, 598–600, 602–11, (*p*461); **10** 389n; **15** 134, 142; *see also* Wotan *Tristan und Isolde*, **15** 142;

Wagner (in Faust legend), **6** 345

Waite, A. E., **12** 490; *The Hermetic Museum Restored and Enlarged*, *see* ALCHEMICAL COLLECTIONS: *Mus. herm.*; *The Holy Kabbalah*, **14** 18n; *Lives of Alchemystical Philosophers*, **9ii** 204n; *The Real History of the Rosicrucians*, **14** 312n; **16** 500n; *The Secret Tradition in Alchemy*, **11** 165n; **12** 422n, 453; **16** 417n;

ed., *The Works of Thomas Vaughan*, **9ii** 204n; **14** 27n

Waitz, T.: *Anthropologie der Naturvölker*, **5** 487n

wakan concept (North American Indian), **8** 122

wakefulness, systematic partial, **1** 17&n

waking state: content of subconscious personality carried into, **1** 116; hypnotic experiments in, **1** 86n; and objectivation of dreams, **1** 117&n; partial, and complex hallucinations, **1** 106; relation with semi-somnambulism, **1** 114; tremors of hands and arms, **1** 82n; and visual images, **1** 28

wakonda (Dakota Indian), **8** 115, 116

wak-wak tree, **5** pl. XXXIX

Walch, C.W.F.: *Entwurf einer vollständigen Historie der Ketzereien*, **14** 33n

Walde, A.: *Lateinisches etymologisches Wörterbuch*, **5** 188n, 210n, 669n; **13** 376n

Waldenses, **9ii** 139, 235

Waldkirch, Conrad, **12** 464, 493; **13** 158, 356n

Waldstein, L.: *Das unbewusste Ich und sein Verhältnis zur Gesundheit und Erziehung/The Subconscious Self*, J.'s review, **18** 797–9

walen/wälzen, **8** 86

Waley, Arthur, *see under* Lao-Tzu: *Tao Te Ching*

Walitsky, M.: "Contribution à l'étude des mensurations psychométriques des aliénés," **2** (*p*271)

walk, motif of, **12** 78, 100–1
walking, uncoordinated, **17** 213
wall(s), **9i** 654
Wallace, A. R., **8** 571
wallflower, *see* Paracelsus: ARCANA
s.v. Cheyri/etc.
Walpurgisnacht, *see* Goethe: *Faust:*
Characters/themes *s.v.*
Walser, H. H.: "An Early
Psychoanalytical Tragedy," **18**
1033*n*
Walton, R. C., **18** 1689*n*
wampum belt, *see* Hiawatha
wand(s): as dream symbol, **18** 180,
197, 198;
golden, of Mercurius, **9ii** 326;
in Hecate mysteries, **5** 577;
magic, **4** 512; **8** 966; **9i** 535*n*,
553; as libido-symbol, **5** 638;
see also caduceus
wandering(s), **1** 212–13, 215, 219,
323, 362–4;
symbolism of, **5** 299;
see also journey
Wandering Jew, legend of, **6** 454;
see also Ahasuerus
wandering scholars, **13** 154
Wang Yang-ming, **6** 370;
Instructions for Practical Living, **6**
370*n*
war(s), **7** 429; **12** 194, 274; **13** 52;
civil, **11** 523, 531;
outlawing, **10** 155;
preparation for, **10** 163;
as psychic epidemics, **17** 302–3;
rites, **11** 287;
wish for, **18** 627;
World War I, **7** (*pp*4–6), 72–4,
111*n*, 150, 326; **9i** 454; **10** 154,
162, 269, 371, 426–7, 434, 449,
451–2, 467, 469, 597; **11** 83,
531, 868; **12** 563; **16** 281; **18**
92, 144, 371, 1306, 1309; and
judgment of enemy, **8** 516; and
neurosis, **16** 255, 260–1; **17**
176; psychology of, **8** 517; and
reaction dreams, **8** 499; reason
and, **8** 683; woman and, **10**
240;
World War II, **7** 111*n*, 150*n*;
9ii 68; **10** 452, 479–80, 599; *c.f.*
also **18** (*p*582*n*), 1347, 1358,
1364, 1368;
World War III, **10** 687, 691;
see also atom bomb; Boer War
Warda, W., **2** 662
Warens, Mme de, **10** 223
warm-bloodedness, **13** 291
warmth, primal, *see* Stoics *s.v.*
creative heat
Warneck, J.: *Die Religion der Batak,* **6**
417*n*; **7** 293*n*; **8** 125*n*; **9i** 188*n*
Warren, H. C.: *Buddhism in Transla-*
tions, **6** 494*n*
washing: mania, **4** 596;
see also *ablutio*
wasp(s), *see* ANIMALS *s.v.*
Wasserstein der Weysen, see ALCHEMI-
CAL WRITERS *s.v.*
water, **7** 126, 159, 168, 231, 300; **9i**
45; **11** 276, 929, 935, 1004, 1013;
12 367, 551; **13** 34, 88, 89*n*, 99,
104, 117, 147, 173, 182, 198, 225,
241, 263, 266, 267, 313, 358, 374,
408*n*, 425, 432, 462, *figs.* 10, 32;
14 252, 317; **16** 485;
above and below heavens, **13**
188;
above the firmament/heavenly,
13 102, 109, 188;
abyssal, **14** 317*n*;
Adam as, **14** 545;
and air/earth/fire, **10** 727, 745;
11 354; **12** 310, 333, 336*n*, 367,
425, 475; **13** 98, 255*n*, 310 (*see*
also elements, four);
in Amitabha meditation, **11**
915–19, 929;
as arcane substance, **9ii** 245; **13**
371;
associations, *see* association(s),
examples of;
baptismal, *see* baptism /
christening;
and birth, **5** 334, 349, 359;
black, **16** 472*n*;

philosophy, **11** 860, 863;
dogmatists of, **13** 74*n*;
and East/Eastern, *see* East and West;
extraverted attitude of, *see above* attitude;
fear of the other side, **7** 324;
imitation, **13** 3, 5, 25;
intellect, differentiation of, **13** 8; and will, **13** 71;
and introverted mind, **11** 773–5;
and Iron Curtain, **18** 561;
man, **13** 5; acquisitiveness of, **11** 773; as Christian, **11** 771–2;
psychic situation of, **12** 32; and self-knowledge, **14** 709;
mind, **7** 303, 323, 327; **11** 784; **13** 28; and consciousness, **13** 62, 71; and science, **13** 2; split in, **11** 863, 867;
and nature, **8** 682; **11** 868–70;
outlook, **11** 768;
and psychic reality, **11** 769; **12** 10;
psychologist and his task, **13** 59;
and psychology, *see* psychology *s.v.*;
reaction against intellect in, **13** 7;
shuns the unconscious, **11** 778, 780;
sublimation, **11** 776;
theosophy, **13** 335;
unease of, **18** 581;
and yoga, *see* yoga *s.v.*
and Zen/satori, **11** 877, 881, 890, 893–4, 902–7;
see also European
West, E. W.: *Pahlavi Texts*, **12** 535*n*, 536*n*
West Africa, *see* Africa
Western Land/quarter, **5** 357, 364, 544, 642; **11** 913, 914, 923–4; **12** 457*n*;
tree in the, see tree(s) *s.v.*
Western Seas, **18** 193

west wind, as pneuma, **5** 484&*n*
Westphal, A., **1** 349;
"Über hysterische Dämmerzustände," **1** 320*n*, 349*n*
Westphal, C., **1** 29;
"Die Agoraphobie, eine neuropathische Erscheinung," **1** 29*n*
Weygandt, W., **1** 479; **2** 767, 887; **3** 19, 30, 32, 76, 137*n*;
"Alte Dementia praecox," **3** 19*n*;
"Zur psychologischen Tatbestandsdiagnostik," **1** 479*n*; **2** 767*n*
Weyl, H.: "Wissenschaft als symbolische Konstruktion des Menschen," **8** 943*n*
whale/whale dragon, *see* ANIMALS *s.v.*
wheat, **8** 333;
grain of, **13** 403; **16** 467*n*; in vision, **9i** 321;
Osiris as, **9i** 208, 248;
-sheaf, **9ii** 166
wheatfields, in patient's dream, **7** 211; **18** 634
wheel(s), **11** 90; **12** 220, 404, 469–70, 472, *fig.* 65;
in alchemy, opus as, *see* opus *s.v.*;
in Brother Klaus's vision, **9i** 16; **11** 476–7, 484;
in Böhme, **9i** 578*n*, 580; **12** 214–16;
crucifixion on, **18** 81, 203 (*see also* Ixion);
in Egyptian temples, **9i** 573;
eight-spoked, **12** 200, 211, *fig.* 80;
in Ezekiel's vision, *see* Ezekiel *s.v.* vision;
fiery, **5** 208*n*;
four, **13** 206, 362;
four-spoked, **5** 460*n*;
of heaven, **9ii** 212;
of Ixion, *see* Ixion *s.v.*;
in mandala(s), **9i** 573, 646, 654,

empirical, **9ii** 59;

essence of personality, **9i** 540;

ethical, **12** 6*n*;

experience of, **12** 24;

four aspects of, **9i** 637;

four elements as symbol of, **12** *fig.* 93;

fourness symbol of, **9i** 425; **10** 738;

as goal: of man, **12** 6, 210, 328; **14** 276, 287, 290; of psychotherapy, **12** 32;

of the gospels, **11** 146;

idea of, **16** 475, 537;

image of, **9ii** (*p*x), 45; **13** 369–73;

indescribable, **12** 20;

of individual, **9ii** 304;

individual and group, **17** 302;

and individuation process, **9i** 278, 281;

initial state of, **16** 404;

instinct for, *see* instinct *s.v.*;

knowledge as, **9ii** 347;

of man, **5** 460; **11** 745; **12** 36, 112; **14** 152, 239, 679, 760, 779; must be masculine, **9i** 356;

and mandala, **11** 139; as symbol of, **12** 216, 237;

meaning of, **18** 270;

modern representations of, **14** 286&*n*;

of natural man, **11** 264;

and number three, **12** 31;

original, **13** 372, 456;

paradoxical, **9ii** 224;

and perfection, **14** 616;

of personality, **13** 287;

preconscious, **8** 430;

projection of, **12** 152;

psychic, **8** 366; **14** 716, 759; cosmic affinities, **10** 635; and God-image, **9ii** 308; images of, **8** 870; **10** 635;

quaternity and, *see* quaternity *s.v.*;

religion as, **12** 296;

restoration of, **9ii** 410;

"round," **9i** 248; **13** 112;

round table as symbol of, **12** 242*n*;

royal pair in, **16** 471;

self as, *see* self *s.v.*;

of self, **13** 330;

sexuality and, **10** 653;

snake as symbol of, **9i** 567;

son as germ of, **5** 508;

suffering and, **11** 233;

symbol(s) of, **7** 186; **9ii** 73, 265, 304, 308; **10** 644, 784; **11** 231, 285, 727; **13** 423, 457; **14** 286, 290, 500; *cauda pavonis*, **12** *fig.* 111; croquet ball, **12** 150; and God, **9ii** 305; ring, **12** 302; rose, **12** 237; sun, **12** 112; wheel, **12** 216; **16** 454;

of symbol-producing individual, **18** 574;

syzygy symbolizing, **9i** 326;

as threeness, **9i** 425–6;

and transcendence, **10** 779;

transcendent, **16** 456;

Trinity a formula of, **11** 242;

as unconscious fact, **18** 1546;

unconscious tendency toward, **18** 1485;

in union of conscious and unconscious, **5** 614; **9i** 294, 299;

and "upper" quaternio, **14** 239;

water is, **13** 371;

way of release to, **11** 905;

see also completeness; integration; totality; unity

whore: in alchemy, **11** 312; **14** 15; menstruum of, **12** 403*n*

whore of Babylon/great whore, **11** 721; **14** 414, 416, 422

Whyte, L. L.: *The Unconscious before Freud,* **18** 1143*n*

Wichita Indians, *see under* American Indians: NORTH

Wickes, F. G., **18** 1134; *The Inner World of Childhood/ Analyse der Kinderseele,* **18** 1134*n*, 1402*n*; J.'s introduc-

wine (*cont.*):
fiery, see *vinum ardens;*
-press, **11** 720
wing(s): dream-image, **17** 119;
four, of the cherubim, **13** 363;
in mandala, **9i** 693;
of Mercurius, *see* Mercurius *s.v.*
winged: female genies, **13** 363;
tiger, *see* ANIMALS *s.v.*
Winnebago(s), **9i** 467, 474
Winslow, B. F.: *Obscure Diseases of the Brain and Mind,* **1** 17*n*
Winter, J., and Wünsche, A.: *Die Jüdische Literatur seit Abschluss des Kanons,* **14** 158*n*
winter solstice, **5** 353
Winthuis, J.: *Das Zweigeschlechterwesen bei den Zentralaustraliern und andern Völkern,* **9i** 120*n*; **16** 454*n*
Wirth, A.: *Aus orientalischen Chroniken,* **5** 163*n*, 319*n*; **9ii** 178*n*, 180*n*; **12** 92*n*
Wirth, H. F.: *Der Aufgang der Menschheit,* **5** pl. Ib
Wischnitzer-Bernstein, R.: *Symbole und Gestalten der jüdischen Kunst,* **9ii** 178*n*
wisdom, **5** 375*n*, 640; **7** 379, 412; **9i** 188; **11** 28; **12** 313; **13** 102, 222, 414; **14** 334, 729;
crown of, **14** 6;
and folly, **9i** 65;
Fountain of, **9i** 336;
four aspects of, **11** 850;
higher, Khidr as, **9i** 247;
of Holy Ghost, **12** 466;
natural, **11** 824; **13** 349, 448;
centre of, **13** 187;
salt and, *see* Sapientia;
of the serpent, *see* ANIMALS: serpent *s.v.*;
of Solomon, **12** 466*n*, 467;
sons of, **12** 454, 478;
of the south/*sapientia austri,* see Queen of the South;
tree of, *see* tree(s) *s.v.*;
see also Sapientia; Sophia
Wisdom of Jesus the son of Sirach,

see BIBLE: Apocrypha *s.v.* Ecclesiasticus
Wisdom of Solomon, *see* BIBLE: Apocrypha *s.v.*
wise, stone of the, **13** 423; *see also* lapis
Wise Men from the East, **12** 474
wise old man, **5** 611; **8** 558; **9ii** 42, 237, 329, 362; **12** 121, 278, 349*n*;
and anima, **5** 678;
archetype of, **5** 515; **7** 185; **9i** 398, 408; **12** 159; **13** 218; **15** 159; **18** 1158;
in visions, **9i** 398, 408;
see also man *s.v.* old
wish(es), **17** 38, 312;
-conflicts, **7** 275;
erotic/sexual, **4** 175; **5** 220; **7** 435;
-fantasies, **7** 446; **8** 704; **10** 352, 359, 490; **11** 548; **14** 673; **16** 245, 420*n*; myths as, **5** 28; religion and, **16** 245;
infantile, *see* infantile *s.v.*;
-objects, **8** 966*n*;
original meaning of word, **5** 367*n*; **8** 966&*n*;
repressed, **4** 552; **6** 90; **7** 202/433, 218, 435; **10** 3, 649; **16** 144, 317;
the unconscious and, **4** 318–19; **7** 212, 216, 257;
unsatisfied, compensation for, **3** 61
wish-fulfilment, **1** 172; **3** 299, 347, 381–2; **6** 89; **9i** 314; **10** 538; **11** 52; **17** 29;
TITLE: "Wish-fulfilment," **3** 216–57;
dreams as, **3** 163*n*, 255; **4** 70, 140, 151, 160–91, 539; **7** 21/434; **8** 505–6, 512, 514, 527, 541; **9i** 311*n*; **15** 64; **16** 317; **17** 185, 189, 223*n*, 282; **18** 423, 847, 866–7, 1149;
hallucinatory, **1** 283–4;
in hysteria/hysterical delirium, **3** 164, 194;

woman(-en) (*cont.*):
    biological destiny of, **7** 11/420;
    blue, doglike, **13** 278;
    carrier of wholeness, **14** 500;
    city as symbol of, **5** 303–6;
    closeness to nature, **14** 331;
    clothed with the sun, **9ii** 163;
    consciousness of, *see* conscious-
    ness *s.v.*;
    conservation of, **10** 970;
    and the devil, affinity, **11** 104*n*;
    14 238;
    Dionysus and, **10** 386;
    divine, **9i** 331;
    and dragon, **5** 315&*n*, 574*n*; **14**
    15, 30, 65, 168, 293, 657*n*, 669;
    dreams of, **5** 8; **13** 479;
    dress of, **10** 993–4;
    elderly (dream-figure), **17** 275,
    279;
    Eros of, **5** 458;
    erotic complex in, **3** 140, 213;
    extraverted, **6** 260–4, 597, 613;
    father as danger to, **5** 266;
    feminity/feminine persona of,
    7 337;
    furrow symbol of, **5** 527;
    Germanic, Tacitus on, **7** 296;
    and Great Mother figure, **7**
    379;
    hysterical, **7** 387;
    image of/inward, **7** 301, 309;
    9ii 24; **10** 74–5; **17** 338 (*see also*
    anima);
    imago of, **7** 296–7;
    Indian, **10** 993–4, 997;
    infantile, and animus-hero, **5**
    465;
    inferiority of, in Biblical times,
    11 620;
    instrument of fate, **5** 565;
    intellectual, **7** 247, 335;
    introverted, **6** 256–9, 640–2;
    intuitive capacity of, **7** 296;
    and Luna, *see below* moon;
    man and: conscious and un-
    conscious in, **7** 330–1; her in-
    born image of, **17** 338; as op-

posites, **14** 655; relationship
between, **7** 296, 300–1; **9i** 677;
10 240; **13** 58; secret enslave-
ment of, **5** 458;
and mana-personality, **7** 393;
masculinity/masculine traits of,
5 267, 458–9, 462; **7** 128, 137,
141, 297, 336; **8** 780, 782–3; **9i**
171, 223; **9ii** 41*n*; **10** 221,
242–3, 245–6, 259; **13** 339,
458; **17** 222; **18** 1232;
matriarchal psychology of, **13**
131;
and moon, **5** *fig.* 32; **8** 330; **14**
331;
as mother, **17** 330;
mother-imago in, **5** 468;
neurotic difficulties of, **8** 773;
old/Ecclesia (Hermas), **6** 388,
391, 402;
older, and mother transference, **5** 365;
patients, **13** 32;
and personal relationships, **7**
330;
as a personality, **9i** 355;
in Picasso's pictures, **15** 210;
pregnant, **5** 369, 421, 487;
in Protestantism, **11** 753;
psyche of, **13** 344;
psychology of, **7** 296; **10** 240,
255; **13** 59–60;
and psychology, **10** 258;
of Samaria, **13** 137;
sexuality in, *see* sexuality *s.v.*;
from side of Christ, **9ii** 319;
snake-, **13** 180;
star-crowned, **9ii** 22, 163;
sun-woman in Revelation, *see*
sun *s.v.* -woman;
thinking function in, **6** 591;
tree in form of, **13** 458;
and Trinity, exclusion from, **11**
107;
unconscious of, *see* unconscious
s.v. female;
unknown/veiled, **12** 64–5, 67,
73, 107–8, 110, 121, 128–9,

136–7, 147–8, 150, 162–3, 200, 212, 220, 238, 245, 264, 284, 301–2; **16** 16–17 (*see also* anima *s.v.* unknown woman);
unmarried, **3** 165; **10** 248;
unrequited love and, **3** 104;
white/*candida*/*alba*, *femina*/ *mulier*, **10** 790; **13** 124; **14** 2, 73, 154&*n*, 244, 321, 655*n*;
worship of, **6** 375–6, 381, 401;
young man's attachment to older, **10** 223;
see also *femme;* girl(s); salt, female aspect of; wife
womb, **9i** 652; **12** 171, 192;
baptismal font as, **5** pl. XXVII;
7 171; **8** 336; **14** 75*n*; **17** 270;
of Beya, **12** 437, 439*n*;
Church as, **5** 536;
of Church, **7** 171;
descent into earth, **5** 528;
entry/re-entry into, **5** 408, 425, 481; **17** 330;
fantasies, **5** 655;
green, **12** 199;
and incest, **5** 350;
of Mary, **12** 139*n*;
motif of mating in, **5** 619–20;
regenerating, longing for, **5** 626;
as symbol of creative aspect of the unconscious, **5** 182;
symbols of, **5** 306;
of the World Mother, **5** *fig.* 40;
see also uterus; *vas*/vessel *s.v.* uterus
wonder-child, *see* Spitteler *s.v.*
wonder-working plant, **13** 304
wong, **8** 118
wood: bored by fire-stick, **5** 210;
etymology of, **5** 214*n*, 321;
fantasy of planing, **17** 65;
of life, **13** 459;
as mother-symbol, **5** 211&*n*;
in myth, **5** 367;
nymph, **9i** 53;
symbolism of, **5** 321
woodcutter, **13** 239

"wooden-headedness," Swiss, **10** 1026
woodpecker, *see* ANIMALS *s.v.*
Woodroffe, Sir John: *Shakti and Shakta*, **9i** 142*n*; **12** 184*n*; *see also* Avalon (pseudonym)
Woolley, Sir Leonard: *Abraham: Recent Discoveries and Hebrew Origins*, **11** 328*n*
word(s): -addict, **7** 333;
archaic fusion of meanings, **5** 235;
-associations, *see* association tests;
completion, as response, **2** 77, 89, 180;
compound, as reactions, **2** 73;
dependence on, **11** 442;
doctor's, **11** 494;
double meanings, **4** 46;
fetishism, **5** 12*n*; **6** 50; **18** 1595;
magic/absolute meaning of, **5** 22; **6** 48–9, 65, 73; **10** 311; **11** 442; **13** 155; and opening of rocks/caves, **5** 367*n*;
meaningless, and hypnosis, **1** 87;
numinosity of, **18** 590;
-picture composition, Charcot's scheme, **1** 86*n*;
"power-," *see* power *s.v.*;
power of, **5** 201; **6** 65;
prayer-, **5** 557;
primitive, **5** 14;
primordial, and poetry, **5** 460;
reaction-, *see* association tests;
"salad," **3** 17, 157, 190, 215;
in scholasticism, **5** 22;
significance of choice of, **5** 57*n*;
spellbinding, **8** 360;
stimulus-, *see* association tests;
substitutions, **1** 38, 152–5;
superstitious belief in, **18** 1428, 1595;
supremacy/worship of, **10** 554; **11** 443;
tabooed, **11** 30;
and thing, mystical identity, **6**

of light, **13** 456; and dark, **13**
fig. A5;
logos and, in Mercurius, **13**
271;
lower, **13** 311; and upper, **10**
742;
macrocosmic/microcosmic, **13**
263;
man's relation to, **8** 693;
material and psychic, **8** 747;
real or illusion, **11** 290;
metaphysical, **13** 293;
-mother, *see* mother;
-mountain, *see* mountain;
nature of, speculation on, **5**
669;
navel of, **14** 640*n*;
-"negation," (Schopenhauer), **6**
322;
as object, **11** 849;
of objects, **7** 275;
-order, divine, **13** 163;
-Parents, **5** 358*n*;
physical, **13** 121; and percep-
tual, **14** 781; as picture-book, **7**
228/447; transcendent reality
of, **11** 798;
physicist's model of, **11** 973;
-pictures, **8** 696–700; two, **7**
398;
plan of, **5** *fig.* 38;
potential: "caelum" as, **14** 767,
774; as "mundus archetypus,"
14 761; and *unio mystica,* **14**
767;
primordial, **13** 291;
principles, **13** 103; male or
female, **18** 583; three, **12** 123;
and/of psyche, **8** 747; **13** 391;
psychic: mirror-world, **7** 292;
world-image, **8** 700;
quarters of, *see* quarters *s.v.*;
reality of, **7** 397, 501*n*;
-reformer, **7** 502;
-renunciation, **5** 658; and acceptance, **5** 121;
scientific view of, **8** 821;
situation, present, **9ii** 126;

Son of the Great, **13** 127, 383;
-soul, *see sep. entry below;*
and soul, **14** 261;
spirit of, **13** 261;
of spirits, **7** 293, 322;
as subjective phenomenon, **4**
400;
as symbol, **11** 849;
Teacher, new incarnation of,
18 (*p*267);
of thought, **13** 338, 339;
three or four, **14** 235&*n*;
tree as, *see* tree(s) *s.v.*;
of unconscious, **7** 354, 507;
unitary, see *unus mundus;* upper, **13** 311, 462;
view(s): primitive, *see* primi-
tive(s) *s.v.*; two parallel, **9ii** 267;
and will concept, *see*
Schopenhauer;
-wheel, *see* wheel(s) *s.v.*
world-soul, **8** 393, 931; **11** 759; **14**
700; **18** 1116;
in alchemy, **11** 448; **13** 103,
166; **14** 50, 235*n*; imprisoned
in matter/*prima materia,* **12** 306,
557; Mercurius as, **13** 157;
and *anima catholica,* **8** 388;
Hecate as, **5** 577;
and individual soul, **8** 927; **10**
635;
mother as, **5** 426;
Neoplatonic (Plotinus), **5** 198;
8 927;
Plato on, **5** 404, 649; **9ii** 380;
14 373, 729; **16** 531*n*; as
rotundum/sphere, **9ii** 389; **10**
621; **11** 113; **12** 109*n*; **13** 102;
in *Timaeus,* **5** 227*n*, 404–6&*n*;
11 185–8, 280, 290; **13** 263;
and world-body, **5** 405;
Primordial Man as, **13** 450;
Purusha as, **5** 649–50;
redemption of, **12** 557;
sparks of, **18** 1361;
see also *anima mundi; unus
mundus*
World War, *see* war *s.v.*

X, Y

Xanthos, acropolis, **5** pl. XXXVIII*a*
xanthosis, *see* COLOURS *s.v.*
Xenocrates, **9i** 564*n*
Xenophon, **6** 42
Xyrourgos, **11** 347

Yahweh/YHWH/Jehovah, **4** 742,
781; **5** 380, 560, 671*n*; **6** 456; **9i**
394, 458; **9ii** 80, 362; **10** 398; **11**
270*n*, 276, 408, 454, 634, 659,
669; **12** 313; **14** 253, 575, 576,
619, 778; **18** 1536–7;
   active principle of, **18** 1549;
   ambiguity of, **9i** 458, 602*n*; **9ii**
99, 108, 169; **10** 845; **11** 604;
   antinomies/opposites in, **9i** 18;
11 567, 574, 604, 664, 685; **18**
1555;
   changing concept of, **6** 435; **9i**
189; **9ii** 300;
   consciousness of, **11** 638; **18**
1622;
   dark side of, **11** 650, 686, 732;
   and David, **11** 569, 577, 599;
   demiurge, **9ii** 118, 128; **12**
539;
   double aspect/duality of, **11**
560, 608, 617, 652; **12** 522;
   Elijah and, **18** 1529;
   fear inspired by, **4** 738*n*;
   fire of, **10** 733;
   God-image, **9ii** 105; **10** 845;
   hierosgamos/sacred marriage,
with Sophia, see *hierosgamos*
s.v. Yahweh;
   incarnation/intention/desire, to
become man, **11** 648, 665, 677,
686, 740;
   injustice of, **11** 685;
   and Israel/chosen people, **11**
577, 616; and Noah/Flood, **11**
577, 671; sacred marriage
with, **6** 392; **11** 616, 619, 620,
621;

jealous, **5** 396;
   as Mercurius, **13** 270;
   mercy of, **9ii** 108, 110;
   as monad, **18** 1611;
   monsters of (Behemoth and
Leviathan), **9ii** 178, 181, 188;
12 547;
   moral and immoral, **18** 1593;
   on Mount Sinai, **12** 298;
   opposites unconscious in, **18**
1617;
   paradoxical, **18** 1556;
   and prophets, **4** 738*n*;
   as Saturn, in Gnosticism, **9ii**
307;
   transformation of, **5** 396*n*; **11**
193; **14** 507;
   unconsciousness of, **11** 597,
600, 638;
   unicorn as symbol of, **11** 259,
408; **12** 522;
   wildness of, **10** 741;
   wrath of, **9ii** 106, 167;
   Zebaoth, **9ii** 283*n*;
   see also tetragrammaton
Yajñyavalkya, **9ii** 349; **13** 301
Yajuj/Yajui, *see* Gog and Magog
Yajur-Veda, *see* Vedas
Yakuts, **13** 460
Yale University Library, alchemical
works from Mellon Collection,
13 (*p*vi); **18** 1691*n*
Yama, **5** 421; **9i** 644; **9ii** 339*n*
yang and *yin*, **5** 581*n*; **6** 790; **7** 287; **8**
863, 865–6; **9i** 40, 183, 197, 603,
637; **9ii** 104, 281; **10** 65, 295,
772, 913, 917, 939; **11** 291, 375,
791, 996; **12** 43, 192, 436*n*; **13** 7,
13, 14, 37, 57, 433, 460*n*; **14** 86,
251, 393*n*, 573, 607, 655*n*, 669;
15 94; **16** 344;
   as heaven and earth, **6** 366;
   masculine and feminine, **9i**
120; **14** 164*n*, 403;
   as opposites, **8** 865; **9i** 197; **10**

yoni(s) (*cont.*):
    with lingam, **5** pl. XXV
Yoruba myth, **5** 392*n*
young people, **5** 219, 466; **8** 797;
    analysis of, **7** 113–14, 184;
    and independence from par-
    ents, **5** 553;
    and marriage motives, **17** 327;
    neuroses of, **7** 88–9, 91;
    see also adolescence; puberty
youth, **7** 117; **8** 796; **10** 710;
    and age, as opposites, **5** 184; **7**
    114, 117; **14** 7;
    as animus figure, **9i** 326;
    divine, **11** 715;
    eternal, **5** 637 (see also *puer*
    aeternus);
    illusions of, **7** 90, 113–14;
    nettle as symbol of, **13** 193;

    problems of, **8** 759, 761–2, 764,
    769, 771;
    spirit as, **9i** 396;
    unwillingness to part with, **8**
    774, 776–7;
    winged, **14** 187, 196–8, 200,
    202–3
Youth Movement, German, **10** 373,
    375
Yüan-shi t'ien-tsun, **14** 573&*n*
Yucatan, Mexico: Cross of Palen-
    que, **5** pl. XLI*a*
yucca moth, *see* ANIMALS: moth *s.v.*
yuen (generative power), **9i** 640, *fig.*
    2
yugas, **9i** 551
Yusasit, **14** 25*n*
Yves, bishop of Chartres, **11** 312*n*

Z

THE COLLECTED WORKS OF

C. G. JUNG

T HE PUBLICATION of the first complete edition, in English, of the works of C. G. Jung was undertaken by Routledge and Kegan Paul, Ltd., in England and by Bollingen Foundation in the United States. The American edition is number XX in Bollingen Series, which since 1967 has been published by Princeton University Press. The edition contains revised versions of works previously published, such as *Psychology of the Unconscious*, which is now entitled *Symbols of Transformation*; works originally written in English, such as *Psychology and Religion*; works not previously translated, such as *Aion*; and, in general, new translations of virtually all of Professor Jung's writings. Prior to his death, in 1961, the author supervised the textual revision, which in some cases is extensive. Sir Herbert Read (d. 1968), Dr. Michael Fordham, and Dr. Gerhard Adler compose the Editorial Committee; the translator is R. F. C. Hull (except for Volume 2) and William McGuire is executive editor.

The price of the volumes varies according to size; they are sold separately, and may also be obtained on standing order. Several of the volumes are extensively illustrated. Each volume contains an index and in most a bibliography; the final volumes will contain a complete bibliography of Professor Jung's writings and a general index to the entire edition.

In the following list, dates of original publication are given in parentheses (of original composition, in brackets). Multiple dates indicate revisions.

* Published 1957; 2nd edn., 1970.   † Published 1973.

* Published 1960.   † Published 1961.
‡ Published 1956; 2nd edn., 1967. (65 plates, 43 text figures.)

* Published 1971.   † Published 1953; 2nd edn., 1966.
‡ Published 1960; 2nd edn., 1969.

* Published 1959; 2nd edn., 1968. (Part I: 79 plates, with 29 in colour.)

9. (continued)

The Prophecies of Nostradamus
The Historical Significance of the Fish
The Ambivalence of the Fish Symbol
The Fish in Alchemy
The Alchemical Interpretation of the Fish
Background to the Psychology of Christian Alchemical Symbolism
Gnostic Symbols of the Self
The Structure and Dynamics of the Self
Conclusion

*10. CIVILIZATION IN TRANSITION

The Role of the Unconscious (1918)
Mind and Earth (1927/1931)
Archaic Man (1931)
The Spiritual Problem of Modern Man (1928/1931)
The Love Problem of a Student (1928)
Woman in Europe (1927)
The Meaning of Psychology for Modern Man (1933/1934)
The State of Psychotherapy Today (1934)
Preface and Epilogue to "Essays on Contemporary Events" (1946)
Wotan (1936)
After the Catastrophe (1945)
The Fight with the Shadow (1946)
The Undiscovered Self (Present and Future) (1957)
Flying Saucers: A Modern Myth (1958)
A Psychological View of Conscience (1958)
Good and Evil in Analytical Psychology (1959)
Introduction to Wolff's "Studies in Jungian Psychology" (1959)
The Swiss Line in the European Spectrum (1928)
Reviews of Keyserling's "America Set Free" (1930) and "La Révolution Mondiale" (1934)
The Complications of American Psychology (1930)
The Dreamlike World of India (1939)
What India Can Teach Us (1939)
Appendix: Documents (1933–1938)

†11. PSYCHOLOGY AND RELIGION: WEST AND EAST

WESTERN RELIGION

Psychology and Religion (The Terry Lectures) (1938/1940)

* Published 1964; 2nd edn., 1970. (8 plates.)
† Published 1958; 2nd edn., 1969.

* Published 1953; 2nd edn., completely revised, 1968. (270 illustrations.)
† Published 1968. (50 plates, 4 text figures.)
‡ Published 1963; 2nd edn., 1970. (10 plates.)

* Published 1966.
† Published 1954; 2nd edn., revised and augmented, 1966. (13 illustrations.)
‡ Published 1954.

The Development of Personality (1934)
Marriage as a Psychological Relationship (1925)

*18. THE SYMBOLIC LIFE
Miscellaneous Writings

†19. GENERAL BIBLIOGRAPHY OF C. G. JUNG'S WRITINGS

†20. GENERAL INDEX TO THE COLLECTED WORKS

See also:

C. G. JUNG: LETTERS
Selected and edited by Gerhard Adler, in collaboration with Aniela Jaffé.
Translations from the German by R.F.C. Hull.

VOL. 1: 1906–1950
VOL. 2: 1951–1961

THE FREUD/JUNG LETTERS
Edited by William McGuire, translated by
Ralph Manheim and R.F.C. Hull

C. G. JUNG SPEAKING: Interviews and Encounters
Edited by William McGuire and R.F.C. Hull

* Published 1976.
† Published 1979.

SUMMER 83